KT-418-643

UNDERSTANDING GLOBAL STRATEGY

WITHDRAWN

UNDERSTANDING GLOBAL STRATEGY

Susan Segal-Horn

David Faulkner

CRL
658.4012 SEG

SOUTH-WESTERN
CENGAGE Learning™

Understanding Global Strategy
Susan Segal-Horn and David Faulkner

Publishing Director: Linden Harris

Publisher: Thomas Rennie

Editorial Assistant: Jennifer Seth

Content Project Editor: Leonora
Dawson-Bowling and Oliver Jones

Production Controller: Paul Herbert

Marketing Manager: Amanda Cheung

Cover design: Design Deluxe

Text design: Design Deluxe

Typesetter: KGL

© 2010, Cengage Learning EMEA

ALL RIGHTS RESERVED. No part of this work covered by the copyright herein may be reproduced, transmitted, stored or used in any form or by any means graphic, electronic, or mechanical, including but not limited to photocopying, recording, scanning, digitizing, taping, Web distribution, information networks, or information storage and retrieval systems, except as permitted under Section 107 or 108 of the 1976 United States Copyright Act, or applicable copyright law of another jurisdiction, without the prior written permission of the publisher.

While the publisher has taken all reasonable care in the preparation of this book, the publisher makes no representation, express or implied, with regard to the accuracy of the information contained in this book and cannot accept any legal responsibility or liability for any errors or omissions from the book or the consequences thereof . The Author has asserted the right under the Copyright, Designs and Patents Act 1988 to be identified as Author of this Work.

For product information and technology assistance,
contact emea.info@cengage.com.

For permission to use material from this text or product,
and for permission queries,
email clsuk.permissions@cengage.com.

Products and services that are referred to in this book may be either trademarks and/or registered trademarks of their respective owners. The publishers and author/s make no claim to these trademarks.

British Library Cataloguing-in-Publication Data
A catalogue record for this book is available from the British Library.

ISBN: 978-1-84480-149-7

Cengage Learning EMEA
Cheriton House, North Way, Andover, Hampshire. SP10 5BE.
United Kingdom

Cengage Learning products are represented in Canada by Nelson Education Ltd.

For your lifelong learning solutions, visit
www.cengage.co.uk

Purchase your next print book, e-book or e-chapter at
www.ichapters.co.uk

Printed by Zrinski, Croatia
1 2 3 4 5 6 7 8 9 10 – 12 11 10

BRIEF CONTENTS

CONTENTS

4   Emerging economies 71

5   The information industries 94

6   Small is valuable: BOPs and SMEs 109

PART 2 THE CONTEMPORARY ORGANIZATION OF MNCs 129

PART 4 CASE STUDIES 329

LIST OF FIGURES

Chapter 10

Chapter 11

Chapter 12

Chapter 13

Chapter 14

Chapter 15

Chapter 16

LIST OF TABLES

Case Studies	Page	World trade	Outsourcing	Globalization	Organizational forms	Emerging economies	BRIC (Brazil, Russia, India, China)	Information Economy	Small & Medium-sized enterprises	Cooperative strategy	Culture	Learning	International Services	Mergers & Acquisitions	Ethics	Base of the Pyramid
Comparative cost advantage and the American Outsourcing Backlash	330	XX	XX													
Toyota's globalization strategies	340			XX	X											
LG Electronics: global strategy in emerging markets	360			X		XX	XX									
Information economy strategies in the mobile telecommunications industry	373							XX								
Managing a Dutch-Chinese joint venture: where to start?	385					XX	X		XX	X						
IKEA: culture as competitive advantage	391										XX	X	X			
Knowledge management at Cap Gemini Ernst & Young	422				X							XX	X			
Competing by the book: Destination China	445						X			XX				X		
Lenovo's brand-building	452			X		XX	X			X				XX		
Mexico, Mitsubishi & grey whale	459	X								X					XX	
Bank Rakyat, Indonesia	469					X			X							XX

STRATEGIES IN ACTION

Chapter 9

Chapter 10

Chapter 11

Chapter 12

Chapter 13

Chapter 14

Chapter 15

ABOUT THE AUTHORS

Susan Segal-Horn is Professor of International Strategy at the Open University Business School, where she is also Director of the Marketing & Strategy Research Unit. Susan was previously Professor of International Strategy at the University of Kent. She worked for several years in the Strategy Group at Cranfield School of Management. She has been Visiting Professor in International Business at the Ecole Nationale de Ponts et Chaussees in Paris, and in Corporate Strategy at the Graduate School, University of Notre Dame, US. Susan acts as a consultant and facilitator for strategy workshops in the UK and internationally, with government departments, national and multinational companies and professional service firms.

Her research focus is the globalization of industries and firms. She specializes in global strategies in service industries and within multinational service firms. Industry sectors covered by past and present research include: airlines, hotel chains, retailing, advertising, some financial service sectors and several types of professional services such as accounting, management consulting and, most recently, law firms. Susan is a frequent speaker at international conferences, regularly presenting her research on international growth in services and the issues facing companies as a result of globalization and the development of regional trading blocs. Her current research focus is the globalization of 'super-elite' law firms and how to manage cross-border co-ordination within international firms, especially within knowledge-intensive service firms.

Susan has published four books and more than eighty academic papers and articles. Her research has appeared in such journals as the *Journal of Marketing Management*, the *Journal of World Business*, the *International Journal of Service Industry Management*, the *Service Industries Journal*, the *European Journal of Marketing*, the *Journal of Global Marketing*, the *European Management Journal*, the *European Business Journal* and *Strategy and Leadership*. Her books have been recommended texts at many business schools. Susan has been Editor of the *European Business Journal* from 2002 to 2005. She was Chair of the Global Strategy Group for the Strategic Management Society in the US and served as an elected Council member for the British Academy of Management. She is a Fellow of the Royal Society of Arts.

David Faulkner is an Oxford educated economist by background, who prior to becoming an academic in 1990 spent much of his earlier career as a strategic management consultant with McKinsey and Arthur.D.Little. He is Emeritus Professor of Strategy at Royal Holloway, University of London,and was until recently Visiting Research Professor at The Open University. Until 2003 he was Tutorial Fellow in Management at Christ Church, Oxford and Member of the Governing Body, and an Oxford University Lecturer in Management Studies (Strategic Management) and also Director of Studies in Management at Exeter College, Oxford. He has been in recent years Deputy Director of the Oxford University Said Business School, Director of the MBA programme for the University, Director of Undergraduate Programme, Chief Examiner for the MBA, Chairman of the Graduate Studies committee, Chairman of the Faculty of Management. Prior to that he lectured in Strategy at Cambridge, Warwick and Cranfield. During his academic career, in addition to lecturing, he has focused strongly on research output, and in addition to his doctoral thesis, has published twelve books mainly on co-operative strategy, mergers and acquisitions and international business. He is an Associate Fellow of the Said Business School and Dean of Magna Carta College, Oxford, a private college specialising in international graduate studies.

WALK THROUGH TOUR

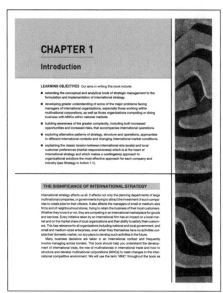

Learning objectives–each chapter starts with a list of objectives to help you monitor your understanding and progress through the chapter.

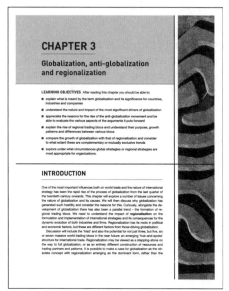

Introduction–appears at the start of each chapter to outline the kinds of principles and issues you will meet in the chapter.

Strategy in Action–in-depth case studies to reinforce principles outlined in each chapter.

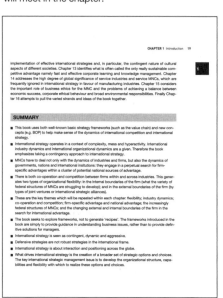

Summary–each chapter ends with a comprehensive summary that provides a thorough recap of the key issues in each chapter, helping you to assess your understanding and revise key content.

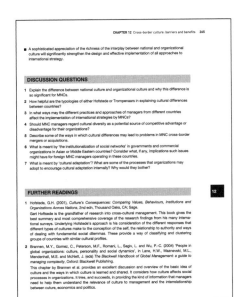

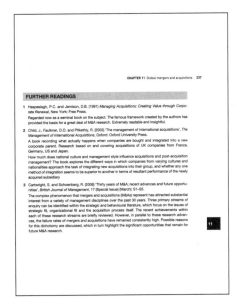

Discussion Questions– provided at the end of each chapter to help reinforce and test your knowledge and understanding, and provide a basis for group discussions and activities.

Further Reading–comprehensive references at the end of each chapter allow you to explore the subject further, and act as a starting point for projects and assignments.

Glossary–key terms are highlighted in the text and explained in full at the end of the books

ABOUT THE WEBSITE

Visit the *Understanding Global Strategy* website at www.cengage.co.uk/segalhorn to find valuable teaching and learning material including:

For Students:
  Case Discussion Questions

For Lecturers:
  Case Analysis Teaching Notes
  Sample Exam Questions and Model Answers
  Downloadable PowerPoint Slides, featuring figures from the book

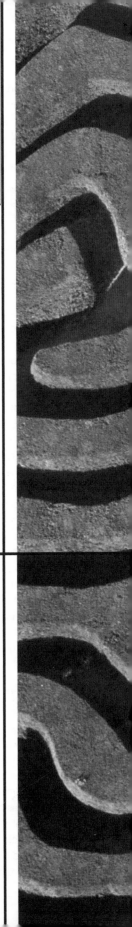

CHAPTER 1

Introductory themes

LEARNING OBJECTIVES Our aims in writing this book include:

■ extending the conceptual and analytical tools of strategic management to the formulation and implementation of global strategy

■ developing greater understanding of some of the major problems facing managers of international organizations, especially those working within multinational corporations, as well as those organizations competing or doing business with MNCs within national markets

■ building awareness of the greater complexity, including both increased opportunities and increased risks, that accompanies international operations

■ exploring alternative patterns of strategy, structure and operations, appropriate to different international contexts and changing international market conditions

■ explaining the classic tension between international size (scale) and local customer preferences (market responsiveness) which is at the heart of global strategy and which makes a **contingency** approach to organizational solutions the most effective approach for each company and industry (see Strategy in Action 1.1).

THE SIGNIFICANCE OF GLOBAL AND INTERNATIONAL STRATEGY

Global strategy affects us all. It affects not only the planning departments of large multi-national companies, or governments trying to attract the investment of such companies to create jobs for their citizens. It also affects the managers of small or medium-size firms and of neighbourhood stores, trying to retain the business of their local customers. Whether they know it or not, they are competing in a global marketplace for goods and services. Every initiative taken by a global firm has an impact on a local market and on the market share of local organizations and their ability to satisfy their customers. This has relevance for all organizations including national and local government, and small and medium-sized enterprises, even when they themselves have no activities outside their domestic market, nor any plans to develop such activities in the future.

Many business decisions are taken in an international context and frequently involve managing across borders. This book should help you understand the development of international trade, the role of multinationals in international trade and how to structure and develop multinational corporations (MNCs) to meet changes in the global competitive environment. We will use the term 'MNC' throughout the book as a generic term covering all forms of international organization, although different authors have used different terminology. We will discuss what drives global strategy and both the advantages and the problems involved in implementing strategy globally. We will explain the strategic alternatives open to an organization when it extends its activities across borders. For both products and services, global strategy may be seen as an outcome of the interrelationship of industry characteristics, strategic flexibility and organizational capability. Your organization may carry out no international activities whatsoever and yet be strongly affected by international trade and the strategies of MNCs. Whether we are aware of it or not, global strategy has an influence on us all.

The terms and conditions of trade for local providers of goods and services in their national/local markets (assuming no protective legislation) are affected by what are perceived by the market to be the most efficient potential providers of each product or service, whatever the sector. Larger providers are likely to have available to them resources and capabilities (financial, human, technical) of greater sophistication and usually (although not always) of greater efficiency. While no such alternative provider exists in a domestic market, local providers can survive and prosper. As soon as national and then global concentration and restructuring begin (whether in aircraft manufacturing, media, steel, energy, utilities, insurance services, health care, children's toys or management consulting) local providers have to be able to provide a similar product or service at similar cost to the other providers or be able to offer additional added-value to justify higher local prices to the consumer. We are all familiar with such examples as local 'mom-and-pop stores' trying to stay in business against the greater product choice and cheaper prices of the local supermarket competitors by staying open for longer and longer hours. It is for this reason that their basis for competing has given rise to the label 'convenience store'. Despite such efforts, and despite campaigns for buying locally grown and sourced food, they fight a steadily losing battle against the prices and choices offered at the large supermarkets.

All types of examples may be cited of industry change wiping out entire national industries or of shifts to niche markets to survive. The world textile and clothing industry has changed dramatically over the last century so that the locus of efficient mass-production has moved away from Europe to Asia as both quality and price of raw materials and labour costs have made broad market competition impossible by the developed economies. European companies are still viable competitors in the higher value-added segments of the market where price competition does not dominate. When the giant US-based retail chain Wal-Mart with around $300 billion in annual sales enters other international markets, it has the effect of transforming the sustainable bases of competition for the incumbent retailers in the marketplace it has just entered. If the market for illegal drugs such as heroine or cocaine is a global one, while the law enforcement agencies trying to combat them are national/local only, the relative scale of resources, and the scope of information and experience brought to bear are incompatible. It is not surprising therefore that pressure builds up for the formation of international cross-border links to manage global drug-fighting or global terrorism more effectively than treating them as purely local issues.

'INTERNATIONAL' STRATEGY IS DIFFERENT

When an organization first decides to expand outside its domestic market, it faces a step change in the complexity attached to every business decision. For all businesses, operating globally is much more challenging than operating solely within their domestic market. In every facet of managerial decision-making it creates greater risks and problems. For example, geographic market selection for international expansion is far more complex than expansion within an organization's domestic market. Although domestic expansion certainly requires careful judgement of relative market attractiveness, potential local competition, adaptation to local market conditions and coping with problems of managing the business over the larger geographic area, wider challenges of a different order arise with selection of markets for international expansion.

International markets often contain barriers to trade, both tariff and non-tariff such as import quotas, or foreign ownership rules. Other obvious but daunting challenges include different laws, different planning regulations, different transportation infrastructure and distribution systems, different languages, different currencies and exchange rates, different consumer preferences and any number of varieties of differences in individual and social behaviour, political systems and religious or ethnic norms. As a result, operating globally involves decisions about how, and to what extent, to adapt products, managers and investment plans to take account of these national and cultural differences. All of this means fine judgements about degrees of political risk, financial risk and commercial risk in every international business decision, which do not arise within the domestic home market.

Although all strategic thinking occurs in a dynamic context, developing robust strategies deliverable across international borders is the most dynamic and complex context of all. In the next section we will introduce a number of key concepts and themes that will be returned to and developed further in later chapters: modern factors of production; the theory of comparative advantage and its interaction with competitive advantage; how the MNC delivers advantage just because of what it is; some different types of international trade and some different types of international strategy; the role of government in international strategy; the place of smaller companies and less wealthy nations and market segments; and the role of risk in global strategy. We hope to convey why local organizations find it difficult to cope with global competition and the repercussions that international trade and MNC activity have in the medium and long term on the opportunities for local organizations in their local markets.

THE MANAGEMENT OF INTERNATIONAL TRADE

Until the last century, international trade was dominated by trading companies or investment houses. Within the last hundred years, international trade has increasingly become dominated by multinational companies. The difference between the former and the latter is that the activities of multinationals are based on foreign direct investment (FDI) locating part of their activities such as design, manufacturing, assembly, sales, distribution or R&D, in other countries. Also, and most importantly, these investments were actively managed in unified corporations as a single operational entity. This has in itself influenced the nature of international trade, since much of it is now internal to these international corporations, and carried out between their own business units and operating divisions, either importing goods produced in their overseas subsidiaries, or exporting products to be sold by these subsidiaries. Multinationals are therefore responsible for overseeing immense resources and many have assets that exceed those of all but the richest nations. This combination of factors means that such firms play an important role not only within their domestic economies, but also in the economies of the many host nations in which they have a presence. It is also the source of their impact on the conditions of local competition for the small and medium-sized firms within these various national markets. The quality of management in multinational corporations is therefore an issue which has implications far beyond the corporations themselves.

Over time, the task of global managers has changed. The early emphasis was on managing large-scale technologies of production and distribution for maximum benefit from scale efficiencies of output. This drove companies to international expansion beyond the domestic market, mainly to develop markets of sufficient size to absorb the new high levels of output and to provide continuity of supply. Chandler (1962) described these developments in detail and we will return to his analysis in Chapter 14. However, gradually overseas subsidiaries became more autonomous, often in response to protectionist barriers erected by national governments against foreign exports. The task of managers became the planning, control and administration of large independent overseas operations.

From the 1960s onwards, another set of trends began a new pattern of convergence. Gradual economic integration via international trade agreements, the development of international communication and transportation systems and technological advances in the miniaturization of products and components, transformed the cost structures of many industries and necessitated a complete rethink of the basic economic assumptions of supply and demand on which they were based. It became possible to deconstruct the whole chain of activities of production and supply (both the value chain of the firm and also the whole value system in which the firm is placed) and redesign them again from first principles. This deconstruction and rebuilding of international business activities usually included much broader options and choices of where to locate business activities worldwide, in order to maximize both efficiency-seeking by the firm and responsiveness to shifting patterns of demand in all its markets. Another phase of this deconstruction and rebuilding of the value chains of MNCs is once again taking place but this time the trigger has been international outsourcing and off-shoring of business activities by firms.

Clearly the management skills required in this latest phase of international business are for high levels of integration and co-ordination across borders. That is the capability being emphasized in much current corporate advertising. The international banking group once called the Hong Kong & Shanghai Bank after its domestic market origins, but now branded internationally as HSBC, has a long-running advertising campaign which features captions such as 'The art of being local worldwide' or 'Never underestimate the importance of local knowledge'. The campaign uses pictures of the same objects with their very different meaning or symbolism in different parts of the world. This is a rhetoric implying local presence, local roots and local services combined with global reach and resources, which can be brought to bear for local customers' benefit. What HSBC is saying in this campaign is that their global reach is enhanced and deepened by their rich and in-depth knowledge of local habits and markets.

International resources do not have to be directly owned by the company but may be available through an alliance or partnership with another firm. The huge growth of co-operative joint ventures and strategic alliances as a common feature of global business means that global managers at most levels must have the ability to adapt and learn from collaboration, as well as from competition, to be effective in the endlessly changing world arena.

TRADITIONAL AND MODERN FACTORS OF PRODUCTION: MOBILE VS. IMMOBILE

In international trade it is important to understand why the greatest economic welfare is not necessarily served by local firms serving their local populations. Adam Smith's (1776) theory of international trade was based upon the simple idea that an overall welfare gain was made if countries produced the goods in which they had an *absolute cost advantage* and traded them with other countries for goods in which those countries had absolute cost advantages.

David Ricardo (1817) increased the sophistication of this theory by developing it into the theory of *comparative advantage*, which is less intuitively obvious. Under this theory a welfare gain is possible so long as the internal cost ratios between the production of two or more goods in one country are different from the internal cost ratios from producing those goods in another country. Thus Country A may produce all its goods at a lower cost than Country B but it will still benefit from trade with Country B so long as its costs are comparatively different in producing one good rather than another from those in Country B. The terms of trade and relative exchange rate will ensure that the goods are traded at prices advantageous to each country. Comparative advantage can be expressed as international differences in the opportunity costs of goods, that is the quantity of other goods sacrificed to make one more unit of that good in one country as compared to another country. Thus if, in a closed economy with finite resources, it is assumed that either cheese or cars can be made, the opportunity cost of cheese is the quantity of car output that has to be sacrificed by using resources to make cheese rather than make cars. Even when Country A produces both goods at a lower cost than does Country B, trade will still be beneficial to both since it is clearly most efficient in terms of resource usage for a country to use as many as possible of its resources in producing the goods it is best endowed to produce in cost terms, rather than those it is less well endowed to produce. Where economies of scale exist, the advantage of specializing in producing goods in which one has comparative advantage is even greater.

This law of comparative costs initially underpinned the development of all international trade, which was mainly in non-branded goods. In the Ricardo model countries develop different costs in producing various goods because they are differentially endowed with the three traditional factors of production: land, labour and capital. Exchange between countries will generally be possible to the advantage of all and will lead to potential welfare gains. From this it follows that impediments to trade like quotas, tariffs and other forms of protectionist policy reduce overall welfare although of course there may be temporary justification for them in specific circumstances, for example to protect infant industries so that they can reach maturity and achieve international competitiveness. This was a strategy used most effectively by the Japanese government in the 1960s and 1970s to protect its infant industries and companies from international competitors until they had grown strong enough to survive full international competition. Firms, governments and international institutions such as the World Trade Organization (WTO) endlessly negotiate and disagree about policy in regard to free trade or tariff barriers in a continuous process of negotiation and renegotiation that affects (and is designed to affect) the workings of comparative advantage in international trade between nations.

This traditional economic theory of international trade based on immobile factors of production and companies without proprietary distinguishing features, culture, management styles or strategies is now too simplistic. Indeed Porter (1990) contended that classical factors no longer generally lead to comparative advantage. He stressed that a modern theory of international strategic management must take account of 'advanced factors' of production, which we will discuss further in Chapter 2. As a brief indication at this point, some typical 'advanced factors' might include *human resources*: in particular managerial and technological skills; *physical resources*: such as the quality and accessibility of a country's climate, natural resources or location; *knowledge resources*: educational and research infrastructure; *capital resources*: financial infrastructure such as the availability of start-up and other risk capital; *infrastructure*: the transportation system, the communication system, the quality of life in the country and its health care facilities may all constitute advanced factors liable to give companies comparative advantage in some countries rather than others. Technological developments may provide the opportunity for rapid shifts in infrastructure advantage. Consider for example the spread of mobile telecommunications (telephones) in emerging economies such as China or Africa which replace the requirement for expensive investment in cable. And although global brand names may often operate against classical trade theory, the position of raw materials and other factors of production still largely obey the traditional rules of comparative advantage.

Almost all economies contain some potential sources of comparative advantage, which may be utilized by industries or organizations within it to generate potential competitive advantage, at least for short periods of time. Any specific comparative advantage is rarely permanent. Consider one of the most commonly cited sources of comparative advantage: labour costs. Low labour costs attract investment from MNCs wishing to sustain low production costs. Gradually, such investment changes the structure of wage levels in the local labour market; they begin to rise. So the standard of living rises and creates increased consumer demand from increased levels of pay in a more competitive labour market. Economic growth therefore drives up labour costs and, over time, will diminish comparative advantage based on low labour costs. Such things are therefore dynamic in nature, not static.

The sources of potential comparative advantage in any given economy are extremely varied. Just to give one or two examples for explanatory purposes, we might think of the advantages of climate in a given country and the specific opportunities to which that gives rise such as the wine industries historically clustered in the warmer southern countries of Europe, and their growth more recently in the equally kind 'new world' climates of Australia, New Zealand, South America and West Coast USA. One may further consider climate and its effect on world leisure industries – whether sun-seeking or snow-seeking for skiing and so on. Strategic assets (Amit and Schoemaker, 1993) such as the pyramids and temples of Egypt or the canals, churches and artworks of Venice may be considered sources of comparative advantage in a similar way, forming the basis for thriving tourist industries or backdrops for film sets and media events.

Where tariff barriers have been largely removed between countries, the gains from trade arise less from the exploitation of different factor endowments than from comparative cost advantages arising through specialization and reduction in comparative unit costs through the economies of scale and scope that a larger international market allows. Indeed the search for scale and (increasingly) scope economies form an important element of global strategy-making. Our definition of economies of scope is:

using a resource acquired for one purpose for additional purposes at little or no extra cost

They can be a powerful tool in global strategy. To define and illustrate the importance of economies of scope for MNCs, some brief examples are given in Strategy in Action 1.1.

Strategy in Action 1.1 *Economies of scope in global strategy*

The US consumer products company Gillette, best known for its razors and shaving products, paid $7 billion in 1996 to acquire Duracell, the world's top alkaline battery maker. Gillette's strategic objective was to achieve bigger sales of Duracell's batteries by selling Duracell batteries through Gillette's huge global distribution network. Seventy per cent of Gillette's sales come from outside the US. The logic of this acquisition should be immediately obvious, since it is based on achieving increased efficiency from scope economies. Gillette intended to sell Duracell's batteries through its existing global distribution network. Batteries and razors are both basic necessary products: small, relatively cheap, impulse purchases. This acquisition perfectly fits the definition of an economy of scope: 'using a resource (Gillette's global distribution network for razors) acquired for one purpose for additional purposes (selling Duracell batteries) at little or no extra cost'.

Other similar examples of such economies of scope in international business include the acquisition by the Japanese consumer electronics company Sony of Universal Film Studios of the US. Once again, the strategic objective was focused on the logic of getting more use value out of the same resource. So Sony was planning to make Universal Film's vast back catalogue of films available as added-value packages for purchasers of Sony televisions and DVD players. The merger failed for other reasons, however, as Sony found themselves having to manage the creative context of film studios, which was a very different business culture from manufacturing the hardware of consumer electronics. The business logic of adding the software (films, music) to the hardware (DVDs, MP3s, etc.) was perfect. However, the different management styles required in the two very different businesses undermined Sony's ability to turn the potential scope economy benefits into reality.

Another quite different example of scope economies occurs when a company expands its operations around the world. For very different firms such as the US fast food chain McDonald's or the Swedish furniture retailer IKEA, opening their outlets in more and more countries gives them the opportunity for scope economies, because they can replicate their business system over and over in the different countries.

As a final point on illustrations of economies of scope, Gillette was in its turn acquired by the even-bigger US consumer products company Procter & Gamble (P&G) in 2005. P&G is a company which lives and dies by the strength of its brands. It has one of the world's most respected marketing management approaches. It therefore made perfect sense for P&G to acquire the ultra-strong brand portfolio of Gillette (including Duracell of course) and apply its marketing strategies to selling it through the same outlets that sell its shampoos, soaps and washing powders.

TYPES OF INTERNATIONAL STRATEGY

The body of knowledge encompassed by the field of international strategy is very wide. It includes a whole range of subject areas such as theories of international trade, exchange rate theory, theory of the multinational enterprise, the structure of international investment, co-operative strategy theory, and a whole set of conceptual approaches governing the evolutionary stages of internationalization (Stopford and Wells, 1972; Melin, 1992). In addition, each separate management function, R&D, production, information systems, finance, marketing and human resource management and strategic management, are all elements which must be made to serve an effective international or global strategy.

It is important to recognize that there are many different ways of being international. Different approaches to international strategy suit different companies in different industries at different times. Indeed, a company may pass through many stages in its own approach to being international. It may simultaneously pursue strategies that are widely different in the different countries in which it has a presence around the world. These differences may weaken the company by loading it with a bloated cost structure, riddled with unnecessary duplication, inconsistent and poorly controlled quality, a confused image to its customers and poor bargaining power with its suppliers worldwide. Or, by contrast, it may be that the duplication of dedicated overhead and the varied positioning in each of the national markets in which it operates, is precisely the reason for the success of the company in those sectors and markets in which it competes. Both these strategies are viable. What is important of course, is that they are each viable in a different context, for specific products, in a specific market, at a specific point in time. Therefore international strategy must, above all, be understood as contingency management.

The four main approaches to being international which firms have most frequently adopted, are summarized in Table 1.1. It distinguishes between *multidomestic* firms who treat each country market as independent and are best serviced by a subsidiary dedicated to meet its local needs and conditions. *Global* firms which emphasize worldwide strategies to benefit from operational scale are heavily centralized, with direction and control emanating mainly from central headquarters. The third type, the *international exporter,* mainly trades internationally via exporting which means it makes virtually no foreign direct investment (FDI) other than for sales and marketing. It may achieve lower levels of efficiency

TABLE 1.1	Four approaches to being international		
Organizational characteristics	*Configuration of assets and capabilities*	*Role of overseas operations*	*Development and diffusion of knowledge*
Multidomestic	Decentralized, self-sufficient and nationally autonomous	Sensing and exploiting local opportunities	Knowledge developed and retained within each unit
Global	Centralized and globally scaled	Implementing parent-company strategies	Knowledge developed at and diffused from centre
International	Core abilities centralized	Purely sales	Knowledge developed and retained at centre
Transnational	Dispersed, specialized interdependencies	Integrated worldwide operations and differentiated country contributions	Shared centre / periphery knowledge development and shared learning worldwide

Source: Adapted from Bartlett and Ghoshal (1989)

1

than the global firm and also lower levels of responsiveness to local conditions than the multidomestic, but since it limits its direct presence in overseas markets to sales and marketing it has lower levels of financial risk, although possibly higher levels of market risk. As indicated in Table 1.1, in our view the *international exporter* type is only a transitional stage in organizational forms. The fourth type, the *transnational* is attempting to build and benefit from interdependent networks worldwide in all the countries in which it has a presence. It both develops and shares the knowledge and expertise held at dispersed international locations (usually subsidiaries). In later chapters each of these four types will be explored in greater detail.

There is a rich and confusing terminology in international strategy. What we prefer to call the 'multidomestic' corporation (Porter, 1986), in Table 1.1, Bartlett and Ghoshal (1989) called the 'multinational'. It means an organization which competes globally by building strong local presence through sensitivity and responsiveness to national differences (usually to take account of specific local trading conditions or differences in consumer preferences from domestic market to domestic market). 'Global' organizations build cost advantage through integration of centralized scale operations, such as super-large design platforms for engines in the car industry worldwide. 'Transnational' organizations exploit parent company knowledge and capabilities through worldwide sharing, diffusion and adaptation. We will be using these terms and discussing the suitability of the global strategies and structures that they represent throughout the rest of this book. The different approaches are discussed in much more detail in Chapter 8. At that point, we then present our views about the alternatives. However, it must be underlined that in the modern globalized world the pure forms defined here are rarely, if ever, encountered in real businesses; they are always adapted in various ways.

All MNCs seek (and hopefully find) their own solutions to the ever-present challenge of providing products that local people in local markets actually want, while at the same time providing them in sufficiently large numbers to achieve the economies of scale needed to be price competitive. All need to pay attention to contingent circumstances in reaching their particular solution to the problem. Before exploring these different approaches in more detail later in the book, Strategy in Action 1.2 illustrates this contingent approach to the global strategy and **organization structure** in relation to recent structural reorganization at the consumer goods giant Procter & Gamble.

Now we need to develop a better perspective on the broader context in which global strategy takes place.

THE ROLE OF GOVERNMENTS AND THE LIMITS TO REGULATION

Global strategy is not a zero-sum game, unlike domestic market strategy. To paraphrase Henderson (1989), enlarging the scope of your global advantage need not 'only happen at someone else's expense'. The mere fact that low labour-cost economies do not remain permanently cheap, makes the point that economic growth through trade creates substantial positive changes over time in the standard of living within those countries.

Japan, Malaysia, Singapore and South Korea in the past are all examples of cheap labour economies, which have rapidly become rich and developed and hence, expensive, as general expectations of standards of living have risen, leading to displacement of labour-intensive jobs elsewhere to countries that are now much cheaper in terms of labour costs such as Vietnam, China and parts of Eastern Europe. Governments have to cope with the internal political tensions that are created as MNCs shift production elsewhere. Only higher-value-added jobs are likely to be retained long-term as economies shift from being 'developing' to 'developed' economies.

In global strategy terms it is cheaper for Germany's BMW and Mercedes-Benz car companies to build new plants in the USA than in Germany or to invest in Poland or the Czech Republic. If they do not do so, the comparative disadvantage of their high-cost German plants will render their necessary

Strategy in Action 1.2 *A contingent approach to MNC organization: integration-responsiveness at P&G*

Procter & Gamble were facing considerable problems at the beginning of the new millennium. They were losing market share and brand recognition globally. Under a new top management team (TMT) they decided on a restructuring programme called 'P&G 2005'. After much discussion and support for alternative radical solutions, the new CEO decided that there was no clean and clear solution. In all their markets there was a pressure to achieve scale economies in order to achieve price competitiveness against their competitors for each brand and in each business category. At the same time, there was also the over-riding need to be sensitive to the market environment and culture and provide products that would be embraced locally. The resulting compromise (based on 'contingency' theory) set up departments based on global products and others based on geographical locations. It was uncertain where profit responsibility would lie but the TMT took the view that this would sort itself out over time as the company embedded the new organization within itself and got used to making it work. Sometimes the geographic chief would become king; in others the global product manager would dominate. Much mutual co-operation and trust would be needed to make such an ambivalent organization work. But P&G's improved performance since this loose reorganization seems to suggest that such a sophisticated and mature approach may be the only way for an MNC to solve the eternal challenge of global scale versus local responsiveness.

price differential unsustainable against (perceived) equally good Japanese models like the Toyota 'Lexus'. Such MNC production-shifting raises ethical issues, which will be returned to later in this chapter. Governments (national or regional) meanwhile must provide public welfare (e.g. through education) and protection (e.g. labour law, consumer protection, pollution policy). However, Grindley (1995) insists that the role of governments in exerting regulatory authority is 'to provide the conditions for the market to work and if necessary correct potential excesses', but not to act as a backdoor way of supporting national industries or firms or of implementing national or international industrial policies. Since these approaches most often result in less robust industries or firms, in the longer term neither industries nor firms nor consumers benefit.

In spite of the short-term nature of comparative advantage, there are examples of the benefits arising in the short to medium term from government intervention in industrial or competition policy. A well-known example is the intervention of Japan's Ministry of International Trade and Investment (MITI) which for decades has acted to provide local Japanese firms and industries with an invaluable period of protection from foreign competitor entry into the Japanese domestic market, until they are strong enough to compete on their own. It must be stressed, however, that the greatest benefit from protection is gained for short-term specific objectives rather than long-term general ones.

MNC STRATEGY AS A WAR GAME

This discussion of MNC strategy as a war game is part of a longer tradition within strategic management that dates back to the Chinese military philosopher and strategist Sun Tzu who wrote his famous book *The Art of War* two and a half thousand years ago. We are going to discuss an approach that links military strategy to global strategy.

Whittington (2001) pointed out that the interaction of oligopolistic global competition may be likened to the Cold War between the USA and the USSR between 1949 and 1989. They followed a doctrine of 'mutually assured destruction' (MAD) which was seen as essential to maintaining peace between these two superpowers. It meant that if either attacked the other, both would be destroyed. However, during the 1970s, the USSR began to question the USA's (and indeed, the West's) will to launch an all-out nuclear war. Since the stability of MAD depended upon the underlying assumption that each superpower was willing to launch its nuclear weapons at the other if necessary, this perception of a possible loss of such will in the USA led to greater instability (e.g. possibly it was the reason Russia invaded Afghanistan for ten years from the late 1970s onwards). It is argued that it was only when the West 'toughened' its stance once more by deploying tactical nuclear weapons that a stable state was restored. Whittington (2001:104) described this situation as follows:

> To preserve stability in the game, therefore, all participants must maintain both sufficient parity to punish potential transgressors, and the reputation for being willing to take the risks of retaliation. Equilibrium would be jeopardized either if any participant became powerful enough and secure enough to launch an all-out war which it could actually win or if one of the participants looked like being soft on aggression.

This military metaphor of MAD may be usefully applied to MNC and global competition. The changes made by OPEC (the Organization of Petroleum Exporting Countries) in oil extraction and production quotas between 1979 and 1986, and again from 2007 onwards provide interesting examples of aggressive action generating instability and destabilizing oligopolistic profits, which had flourished in the previously stable situation. Of course the action is intended to increase profits – which it certainly does for a period of time. Indeed the OPEC cartel enjoys such great market power that they have often been able to raise world crude oil prices to levels many times higher than the historic average. Given that crude oil is a commodity product, this is a significant demonstration of market power by OPEC cartel members restricting and withholding, or just managing to control supply. However, over the time periods in question, OPEC members sometimes broke ranks and began to cheat on their individual agreed production quotas and there was an assumption that Saudi Arabia would always adjust its own production to support the price. In 1986, Saudi Arabia unexpectedly boosted its own production levels with the result that the crude oil price dropped spectacularly from $26 to $8 per barrel in under two weeks, as supply dramatically increased. Similarly 2008 showed huge volatility in the oil price, swinging from between $140 and $40 per barrel. Prices suddenly collapsed partly as a result of a sharp decline in demand and growth within the world's economies, arising from the financial crises of 2008 onwards. Prices may subsequently return to the OPEC highs, but the assumptions underlying its credibility and oligopoly power have to be both sustainable and enforceable. Long-term, the sustainability will be affected by the rush to develop substitute sources of non-oil (and more environmentally friendly) sources of energy such as wind, wave and also of course nuclear power. Also, there is the paradox that the more OPEC succeeds in driving up oil prices, the more economically viable it makes the mining of more expensive alternatives such as oil from the tar sands of Canada.

Another version of this energy war game is being played out in Eastern Europe between Russia and the Ukraine, with major negative impact on many other Eastern European economies including Bulgaria and Slovakia who had their gas supplies completely shut off during cold weather reaching −10°C. What is seemingly a corporate dispute between supplier and customer (i.e. Russia's giant energy company Gazprom and the rather opaque Ukrainian distribution system involving intermediaries) rapidly escalated into a political war game between the respective governments in the late winter of 2008/2009, as the leaders of both countries became directly involved in an erstwhile dispute about payments and pricing levels.

Obviously there are many possible outcomes of an oligopolistic international war game, but they do all assume that the competitors will act rationally and understand the criticality of stability and equilibrium for general profit maximization, except where one competitor (e.g. OPEC or Gazprom) believes that they can win greater market share or greater market power by launching a unilateral offensive. Similarly Hamel and Prahalad (1985) described events that occurred in the US television market in the 1970s. At that time Japanese consumer electronics companies such as Sony and Panasonic (formerly known as Matsushita but it adopted its best-known brand Panasonic as its corporate name in 2008) competed globally, while the US companies (such as GE) remained domestic US competitors only. Thus when companies such as Panasonic began their entry into the US domestic market, the local US producers fought Japanese competitors' penetration of their US domestic market with price cuts in their own domestic market. Since they had no other competitive venue, price reduction at home meant that the US companies put their own margins under pressure on 100 per cent of their (100 per cent US domestic) sales volume. Meanwhile its Japanese attackers were not similarly exposed since their US trade was merely a fraction of their total trade and their Japanese domestic market was unaffected. Therefore we learn that in global competition, the more competitive venues, the better. More locations offer more choices and locations for possible aggressive or defensive strategies. This type of war game theory suggests that competitors should only launch a market share offensive if they are sure they can achieve domination. Otherwise market leaders normally provide a price umbrella from which they and others benefit. This is a view of global strategy based on battles by MNCs for market share of international *cash* flows rather than international *product* flows. Thus cash flows from one market can be used to subsidize market share battles in other markets. This approach to global strategy based on military war games therefore dictates that retaliatory or aggressive action must be taken in those markets where a competitor is most vulnerable to a 'cash flow siege'. This is the basis for effective global strategies being aggressive in style rather than purely defensive.

Much of Hamel and Prahalad's (1985) analysis was derived from the study of the global strategies pursued by many Japanese MNCs in the 1970s and 1980s. This was the period during which major national companies started to build global positions. For example, at this time Toyota was run from Toyota 'city' in Japan, whereas by the 2000s, it had a 'multilocal' set of operating centres around the world. This aggressive/defensive analysis of global strategy and its implications are rarely discussed today in most strategy textbooks but it provides an important insight into many actions that firms take and what target firms need to think about when they respond. Notions of 'aggressive' and 'defensive' moves do capture well the nature of these global strategies and the battles that result from them. Some of these aggressive and defensive strategy objectives, and the choices underpinning them, are captured in the 'map' given in Figure 1.1.

The 'map' in Figure 1.1 suggests that choice of competitive arena (and therefore location of a battleground) is dependent upon: *the defensibility of the home market*, so that the more protected a company feels in its own domestic market, the more it feels safe in attacking competitors' home markets; the *degree of competitive rivalry*, so that the fiercer the competition, the greater the likelihood that a company will carry the battle outside its domestic market and especially into its competitors' domestic markets; the *resource endowment of the firm*, so that the stronger a company's own resource base (financial, physical, human, technological), the more likely it is to exploit those resources in a variety of markets.

Similarly, aggressive or defensive strategy will be dependent upon: *investment timing*, which must take account of managers' judgements about windows of opportunity and the potential benefits of 'first-mover advantage' or 'second strike' strategies; *level of acceptable risk*, since all investment decisions are dependent upon the nature of the company's risk profile and that of its senior management, and aggressive strategies require a higher risk profile than defensive strategies – although in the longer term the aggressive strategy (certainly in the global arena) may be the less risky, since attack may indeed be the best form of defence; *technology/differentiation advantage*, meaning that lack of differentiation and ease of imitability tend to encourage defensive rather than offensive strategies. The reverse is also often the case.

1

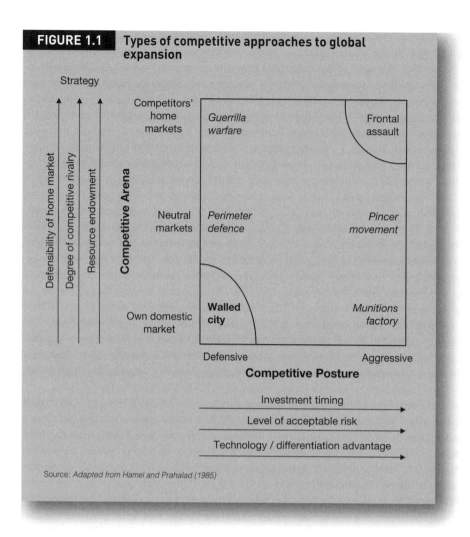

FIGURE 1.1   **Types of competitive approaches to global expansion**

Source: *Adapted from Hamel and Prahalad (1985)*

Figure 1.1 captures a range of different strategic possibilities arising from the variables described. The same company may choose any or several of these strategies at different times and in different markets, according to their perceptions of their own and their competitors' strengths and weaknesses. Some of the characteristics of the potential strategies suggested by the 'map' are as follows:

■ The 'walled city' strategy is about heavily defending a home market. This is rarely successful in the longer term on its own (as described earlier for the US TV firms in their home market). If your domestic market is 100 per cent of your total market, then 100 per cent of your total market is vulnerable to attack, whereas your competitor is only risking a potential new revenue stream. The same point is valid for any company that says they are not interested in global strategy because they only operate in their domestic home market. Our warning to these managers is: just because you are not going to them, does not mean that they will not come to you.

■ 'Frontal assault' strategies are the most risky. They are aggressive strategies and they depend for success on careful timing, together with confidence that the home market can be successfully defended against retaliatory action of the sort that the French food MNC Danone uses against one of its main rivals, Nestlé of Switzerland, in product category after product category such as bottled waters, yoghurts, and so on.

■ 'Pincer' strategies are also aggressive, but more subtle than 'frontal assault'. This is because they take place in a neutral or less important market, in order to attract less attention and less chance of immediate retaliatory action. This gives the intruder time to establish a firm foothold before retaliation is likely to occur. Komatsu, the Japanese earth-moving equipment manufacturer, used this strategy to encroach gradually on the dominant world position of their American rival Caterpillar. It was so successful that gradually Komatsu could shift from 'pincer' movement to direct 'frontal assault' on Caterpillar in their US home market.

FLEXIBILITY, RISK AND ETHICS

It may be appropriate at this point to make some simple statements about global strategy and the role of MNCs. They are complex organizations; difficult to manage; often castigated in the press and public opinion as dinosaurs; and frequently caught out degenerating into bloated and dysfunctional (and also possibly unethical) bureaucracies, inflexible and unresponsive or slow to change. What then is the point of them?

The main strategic benefit in being an MNC is that it gives you flexibility and options and of course financial strength. As with life in general, so with global competition; options allow you to choose between ways of doing things. For domestic firms, their domestic market is 100 per cent of their potential market. Much domestic market strategy is defensive, trying to defend and protect existing positions, whereas more and more volume of world trade is cross-border. MNCs have available to them a wider range of strategies arising simply from the fact of being international and operating across borders.

Governments and supra-national organizations erect regulatory, institutional and tariff barriers to trade, whereas MNCs attempt to configure their global operations to exploit those barriers that are favourable to them (such as international agreements about routes and prices in the airline industry) and avoid those that are not. Such trade barriers include: high tariffs; import quota systems; refusal to sanction licences; nationalistic purchasing and ownership policies; centralized 'command' economies; and excessively chauvinistic domestic demand.

Governments tax immobile assets and national-based consumption and try to set corporation taxes at levels which will provide them with useful sources of tax revenue to spend on services for the public without forcing the corporations to shift their investments in jobs, buildings, research or technology elsewhere. It is for this reason that governments try to attract quality inward investment by MNCs into their countries by offering capital grants, regional grants (especially in employment 'blackspots'), tax-free zones, and so on.

Small is not often beautiful in terms of global competition. Large organizations have available to them an array of advantages. In an important paper, Kogut (1985a) has summarized these as: production shifting; tax minimization; financial markets; information **arbitrage**; global co-ordination; and political risk. These will be explained in turn.

As an example of *production shifting*, the best-known example of production shifting currently is probably the shifting of IT out-sourcing to India. Wipro, the Bangalore-based IT company, has two-thirds of its rapidly growing workforce in 'business process outsourcing' (BPO). BPO is about performing a range of back-office tasks such as data-processing or data analysis for client companies, who are usually based in other (often developed) economies. This is part of what Nandan Nilekani, CEO of Infosys (Wipro's major competitor) calls 'the globalization of white-collar services'. This trend is transforming global supply chains. The range of such work being performed geographically remote from the parent company is constantly expanding. What started as writing software or answering phones in call centres is now moving up the value chain to transcription of medical records, desktop publishing, processing insurance claims or market research. India has attracted a great deal of such production shifting since it is home to large numbers of well-educated, English-speaking, young people, who are currently relatively low paid by world standards.

This example also contains an example of *tax minimization* since MNCs are able to minimize their tax burden by moving their internal and external transactions to the most advantageous national tax location. Although the Indian government historically has not given very favourable tax treatment to MNCs, others do. That is what is meant when certain locations, such as Bermuda or the Cayman Islands, are called 'tax havens'. Also the Indian approach to MNC taxation is gradually easing.

Governments often create *financial markets* and *financial arbitrage* opportunities for MNCs via their policies to attract inward investment (such as export credits, guaranteed loans or corporate tax holidays). MNCs too can create innovative financial products to benefit from financial flexibility. It seems appropriate to comment that some of these financial products (such as derivatives, options and swaps) had perhaps become too complicated for the treasury departments of the companies themselves to understand and control. This has been a main contributing factor to the undermining of the finances and share value of a great many companies, banks and other types of businesses within the so-called 'credit crunch' from 2008 onward. Despite these appallingly negative aspects of financial arbitrage opportunities when they drift out of control, it is nevertheless important to stress that these types of financial management opportunities that arise purely from an organization being able to trade across international borders, are still of great commercial value at reasonable levels of risk. It is perhaps an obvious point to make, but also an important one, that large organizations tend to have better credit ratings than smaller organizations and therefore benefit from cheaper cost of capital. MNCs also organize themselves to benefit from *information arbitrage* including such things as transfer of knowledge about products and markets and the transfer of product or process developments from one location to another (as listed in Table 1.1 under the characteristics of the transnational).

These have so far all represented what Kogut (1985a) calls 'arbitrage opportunities', that is where the MNC seeks to benefit from the exploitation of structural or regulatory differences between markets. These differences may be in the price of an asset, a product or an activity between different marketplaces. These last two he calls 'leverage opportunities', by which he means 'the creation of market or bargaining power because of the global position of the firm'. *Global co-ordination* may cover such possibilities as differential pricing/price co-ordination to consolidate or build market position, or building coalitions for competitive leverage. *Leverage opportunities* capture the bargaining power arising from having globally dispersed operations. They include the power of the threat by an MNC to leave a particular location and withdraw operations. That may be as a result of an increase in perceived *political risk* as discussed earlier or as part of a deliberate strategic choice to move operations to a more financially attractive location.

Judgements about the levels of risk and reward attached to each potential investment opportunity must be evaluated. For example, relatively high political risk of investments in Russia or Nigeria, as compared to a country such as Belgium, which is very politically stable but with much more limited growth opportunities. These contrasting factors must be weighed against the attractions of each of those markets in terms of overall size and long-term development potential. Figure 1.2 shows a matrix of types of exposure to political, regulatory and ethical risk to provide a summary of such contingencies and their potential effects on MNC.

Figure 1.2 refers to 'the actions of legitimate government authorities' and 'events caused by actors outside the control of government'. Despite the fact that individuals and nations differ in the values or beliefs they hold and the experiences that shape those values and beliefs, Hosmer (1994) suggests that there are indeed some fundamental ethical principles that do transcend cultures, time and economic conditions (Campbell, 2007). Whether or not this proposition is tenable, ethical values are an important part of formal corporate policies and therefore of the culture of many organizations. Ethics and values affect both the decisions that companies make, and their ability to implement those decisions in accordance with, or in conflict with, governments or non-governmental forces. Changes in perceived 'ethical' behaviour also affect standards as to what is good or bad in managerial or organizational conduct and hence changes the degrees of risk attached to global decision-making.

Do organizations, which act unethically, achieve some superior advantage? Hosmer (1994:30) encapsulates this position in his discussion of ethics and strategy:

FIGURE 1.2	Exposure to political, regulatory and ethical risk

Source of risk

Types of impact	The actions of legitimate government authorities	Events caused by actors outside the control of government
The voluntary loss of control over specific assets without adequate compensation	■ Total or partial expropriation ■ Forced divestiture ■ Confiscation ■ Cancellation or unfair calling of performance bonds ■ Withdrawal of licences or ownership of property	■ War ■ Revolution ■ Terrorism ■ Strikes ■ Extortion
A reduction in the value of a stream of benefits expected from the foreign controlled affiliate	■ Non-applicability of 'national treatment' ■ Restriction in access to financial, labour or material markets ■ Controls on prices, outputs or activities ■ Currency and remittance restrictions ■ Value-added and export performance requirements ■ Sudden cancellation or charge in agreed terms of a contract ■ Bureaucratic blockages	■ Nationalistic buyers or suppliers ■ Threats and disruption to operations by hostile groups ■ Externally induced financial constraints ■ Externally imposed limits on imports or exports ■ Corruption / nepotism and 'cronyism' ■ Ethical or pressure-group driven investment policies

Source: *Adapted from de la Torre and Neckar (1988)*

I do not claim that all equitable acts lead to strategic and financial success. I do not claim that all inequitable acts lead to strategic and financial disaster. I do however, claim that a pattern of equitable acts over time does indeed lead to trust and that trust to commitment, and that a committed effort, which is both co-operative and innovative on the part of everyone, does eventually lead to success. That success may be slow, but it is certain enough to warrant the attention of management scholars.

Some examples of the conflicts and complexities involved in the interplay between MNC strategic flexibility, business ethics and global strategy are considered in Strategy in Action 1.3.

We have no simple answers to these complex questions. We wish merely to indicate some of the complexity involved. Thus ethical values are in part shaped by culture and are part of culture. They are

1

Strategy in Action 1.3 *MNCs, risk and ethics*

MNCs attract a great many protests against their business activities, particularly those in developing countries. In 2006, the US coffee chain Starbucks was in trouble with consumers for appearing to undermine the establishment of the 'Fairtrade' brand in Ethiopia, a poor country which grows some of the world's finest coffee beans and which is a major supplier to Starbucks. The Fairtrade brand guarantees that farmers growing the coffee are paid a fair market price. It is a hallmark that they are not being exploited. The highly reputable UK voluntary organization Oxfam complained that Starbucks was blocking attempts by the Ethiopian government to establish trademarks for three different types of coffee bean, which was depriving farmers of $90 million per year. Starbucks was sponsoring an alternative scheme which it argued would be simpler and more effective.

Between 2006 and 2008, the German company Siemens, Europe's biggest engineering firm, was involved in a huge bribery scandal. In December 2008, it finally pleaded guilty to charges of bribery and corruption and agreed to pay fines of $800 million in the US and 395 million Euros in Germany, in addition to an earlier 201 million Euros. What had happened was remarkable.

Siemens had, for example, set up 'cash desks' in three of its offices to which employees could bring empty suitcases to be filled with cash. Up to 1 million Euros could be withdrawn at a time. According to the USA Department of Justice, it was to be used to secure contracts for Siemens' telecommunications division. Apparently between 2001 and 2004, about $67 million was carried off in such suitcases. Until 1999, when bribes paid to foreign officials became illegal in Germany, Siemens even claimed deductions for bribes in its annual accounts.

These ethical issues have become high profile and high risk because external stakeholders such as consumer groups or environmental pressure groups have successfully influenced public opinion, affecting both consumer buying patterns (including occasional consumer boycotts) and internal staff morale in the companies concerned. Government sanctions may sometimes also be imposed. For example in the US, the state of Massachusetts has banned contracts with firms doing business in Myanmar.

Some MNCs have been in the forefront of campaigning for higher ethical standards, drawing up ethics statements and appointing ethics officers. To some extent this 'ethical' strategy has paid dividends. Multinationals have shaken off their old sinister image. The United Nations, which used to try to control them, now regards them as agents of modernization and good practice. The developing world, having once feared them, now competes to attract their factories. But they are also now being judged against the high ethical standards which they themselves have helped to promulgate and their fiercest critics, environmental and human-rights lobbyists, have become more organized.

Greenpeace, for example, is no longer an amateurish affair of beards and T-shirts but a professional, global organization which has offices in 33 countries, including Latin America and Eastern Europe, and which is in many ways similar in organizational structure and systems to the multinationals it shadows. In South-East Asia, groups representing local people co-ordinate their campaigns using e-mail, the internet and social networking websites. In Asia and Latin America tribes have put old enmities to one side and joined forces to exert pressure on multinationals and governments; such groups have also formed alliances with the rich world's green campaigners.

SOURCE: COMPILED BY AUTHORS FROM VARIOUS PRESS ARTICLES

The difficulty for companies attempting to avoid trouble is that they may forfeit the best growth opportunities. Much of the world's raw material wealth is located in countries with dubious political regimes and unstable environments. Many MNCs therefore have chosen to combine continued pursuit of their overseas investment strategies with a closer liaison with the campaigners and paying more attention to indigenous groups. Keen to avoid repeating the mistakes it made earlier in Nigeria, Royal Dutch Shell (the Anglo-Dutch oil giant) met members of the local tribes before signing a recent deal to develop a gas field in Peru. The company also holds consultations and workshops with anyone interested in the subject.

Local political or environmental problems, which were once seen solely as the concern of governments, are now seen as the responsibility of the MNC too.

This rising concern of consumers in the richer developed economies with where and how their goods and services are produced often raises complex moral dilemmas which are also about commercial necessities and which have serious unintended as well as intended consequences. Consider the issue of child labour. Even here there are many views and a range of difficult consequences as to the long-term or short-term benefits and trade-offs between the developed and the developing economies. For example, where does 'protection' for children end and 'protectionism' of Western markets and rich economy jobs begin? Consumers in the West are increasingly choosy about the origin of the goods they buy. However, the codes of conduct agreed by companies, such as Nike, which has faced fierce ethical criticism for using 'sweatshop' labour in overseas production plants in the past, cut little ice in the developing world. Faced by

unfulfilled promises regarding overseas aid and the need to export to earn foreign currency and reduce debt, they see their ability to offer cheap and compliant labour as their source of competitive advantage – the bait for footloose global corporations. Their governments, and individual families and households dependent on one child worker as its sole breadwinner, are often reluctant to give it up.

The globalization of the world economy is more than simply a question of cheap imports from the developing world. The Brussels-based International Confederation of Free Trade Unions is at the forefront of a battle raging with the World Trade Organization as to whether countries that fail to abide by five core labour standards should be given unrestricted access to the world's markets. The unions, backed by most of the developed Western nations, say there should be a universal right to organize and to freedom of association. Child and forced labour should be outlawed, as should all forms of discrimination at work. Countries refusing to abide by these standards should face being deprived of access to the West's lucrative markets. Most countries of the developing world argue that this is merely backdoor protectionism, a subtle attempt by the rich countries to respond to growing unemployment in their own countries by pricing low-cost goods out of their markets. Consumer groups also oppose bringing labour standards into the trade arena. They argue that it will inevitably lead to protectionism, raising the cost of goods for consumers, particularly those on low incomes who buy Bangladeshi T-shirts and dresses from Vietnam. These are complex and sensitive issues but are a very real part of global strategy and managerial decision-making.

1

part of the values that we as individuals bring into organizations. In some cases our values might clash with those of the organizations we work for, so that our interests as employees or managers may not be congruent with our preferences as consumers, parents, voters, tourists or environmentally concerned individuals.

OVERVIEW OF THIS BOOK

In reviewing theories of international trade and the changing pattern of global competition, this book draws not only on strategic management research, but also on the fields of organizational behaviour, economics and marketing. Chapter 1 is an extended introduction. It has provided a brief overview of international trade theory in order to explain the theory of comparative advantage and its role in global strategy. This introduction explains the sources of advantage available to multinational corporations (MNC) and the complex relationship between MNCs and governments. Initial definitions of some different types of global strategy have been given. We have stressed that what drives global strategy is strategic flexibility: the creation of a broader set of strategic options and choices that arise simply from being global.

The book commences by setting out the economics, the geography and the structural, cultural and competitive changes over time that are the essential determinants of the context in which managers have to create viable global strategies. Chapter 2 takes an economic perspective on global strategy. It deals with advanced factors of production and comparative advantage within the national 'diamond'. It explains the assumptions of three dominant economic paradigms and their relevance to, and impact on, global strategy. Chapter 3 deals with the formation of regional trading groups, the impact of regionalization and the relationship between regionalization and globalization. It debates the degree of cultural homogeneity that exists across world markets and the current relevance to strategic thinking of issues of standardization and adaptation across and within global markets. It considers in some detail the pros and cons of globalization. Chapter 4 deals with the increasing importance of the emerging economies, especially those now often called the BRIC economies. It discusses the changing balance of power between the developed and the developing economies. It particularly addresses the major importance of institutional context within emerging economies. The significance of business groups, and the existence of many common gaps in infrastructure provision within emerging economies, results in business conglomerates making good business sense in ways that no longer apply in the developed economies. Chapter 5 deals with the implications for global strategies of the newly configured information economy of the high-tech world. It raises the question of whether advanced technology changes the relevance of existing business models. Chapter 6 concerns itself with the newly identified consumers at the 'bottom of the pyramid' (BOP) and to what extent they can be drawn into the global market economy and have specific strategies addressed to their needs. Chapter 6 then identifies the issues facing small and medium enterprises (SME). It discusses to what extent globalization and access to the internet help or hinder the potential international development of SMEs. Chapters 7 and 8, taken together, are devoted to the problems of organizing MNCs. First in the traditional 'four box' way described earlier in this chapter in Table 1.1, and then in the contingent way that actually takes place in reality. We emphasize the importance of a contingent approach to global strategies and structures. Chapters 9 and 10 deal with the important place of co-operative strategies within international strategy, firstly in the looser networked form including virtual corporations (Chapter 9) and then in the form of tighter-knit strategic alliances (Chapter 10). The discussion of strategic alliances focuses very strongly on how to manage them effectively. Chapter 11 discusses the pros and cons, the risks and dangers of embarking on global mergers and acquisitions, risks that are generally ignored by MNCs intent on using mergers and acquisitions to achieve rapid global reach. Chapter 12 addresses the increasingly recognized importance of cultural factors in the design and implementation of effective global strategies and, in particular, the contingent nature of cultural aspects of different societies. Chapter 13 identifies what is often called the only really sustainable competitive advantage namely fast and effective corporate learning and knowledge management. Chapter 14 addresses the high degree of global significance of service industries and service MNCs, which are frequently ignored in global strategy in favour of manufacturing industries. Chapter 15 considers the important role of business ethics for the MNC and the problems of achieving a balance between economic success, corporate ethical behaviour and broad environmental responsibilities. Finally Chapter 16 attempts to pull the varied strands and ideas of the book together.

In the popular press, the terms international strategy and global strategy are often used almost interchangeably. In this book we have attempted to address the problems and opportunities that arise in what is currently known as the 'global marketplace'. Therefore in general discussion, 'international' and 'global' may mean essentially the same thing. However, in Chapters 7 to 8, we use the term 'global' organization to mean the form that is adopted where little, if any, adjustment is made to national differences such as product specifications for different national markets. Elsewhere, global strategy is commonly used as the generic term.

SUMMARY

- This book uses both well-known basic strategy frameworks (such as the value chain) and new concepts (e.g. BOP) to help make sense of the dynamics of global competition and global strategy.
- Global strategy operates in a context of complexity, mess and hyperactivity. Global industry dynamics and global organizational dynamics are a given. Therefore the book emphasizes taking a contingency approach to global strategy.
- MNCs have to deal not only with the dynamics of industries and firms, but also the dynamics of governments, nations and international insitutions: they engage in a perpetual search for firm-specific advantages within a cluster of potential national sources of advantage.
- There is both co-operation and competition between firms within and across industries. This generates two types of organizational flexibility: in the internal boundaries of the firm (what the variety of federal structures of MNCs are struggling to develop); and in the external boundaries of the firm (by types of joint ventures or global strategic alliances).
- These are the key themes which will be repeated within each chapter: flexibility; industry dynamics; co-operation and competition; firm-specific advantage and national advantage; the increasingly federal structures of MNCs; and the changing external and internal boundaries of the firm in the search for global advantage.
- The book seeks to explore frameworks, not to generate 'recipes'. The frameworks introduced in the book are simply to provide guidance in understanding business issues, rather than to provide definitive solutions for managers.
- Global strategy is seen as contingent, dynamic and aggressive.
- Defensive strategies are not robust strategies in the international frame.
- Global strategy is about interaction and positioning across the globe.
- What drives global strategy is the creation of a broader set of strategic options and choices. The key global strategic management issue is to develop the organizational structure, capabilities and flexibility with which to realize these options and choices.
- Global strategy is technically a subset of international strategy but it is currently popularly used as the generic term.

PART 1
THE EXTERNAL WORLD

The five chapters in this first part of the book are about the context in which companies and their managers have to operate and design their global strategies. The chapters are linked by the question: What do managers need to know about broad business, economic and industry contexts to help guide their strategic thinking?

We start with quite a theoretical chapter. Chapter 2 provides a necessary overview of the history and economics of world trade. It is important that managers understand what underpins the things that happen in their industries and also how their industries are likely to be affected by the endless dynamic interplay between comparative advantage: that is the (opportunity) costs of goods made in one country compared to the same goods made in another country; and competitive advantage: the superior performance of one company over another company in the creation of similar products or services. In other words, global strategy can usefully be regarded as a continuous ebb and flow of relative advantages and disadvantages between countries and companies. Global strategies seek to take best advantage of that ebb and flow over time and across borders. Global strategies of firms must take realistic account of the conditions in all other countries and the conditions in their own country. We want to stress that global strategy is based on this interplay between conditions in the 'home base' (i.e. domestic market) country and conditions in every other country in which a company seeks to do business.

Among the key questions that Chapter 2 addresses are: Why do multinational corporations (MNCs) exist? What is the point of them? These questions are fundamental to understanding the basics of international trade and global strategy. MNCs are large companies that produce in countries outside their home country and operate in global markets. In MNCs comparative costs largely determine where in the world specific business activities are carried out, subject to assessment of political, financial and ethical risks. The rise of the MNC has been spectacular in the last 150 years. Many MNCs are now larger and richer than many countries. MNCs are designed to take advantage of their evaluation of comparative and competitive advantage as the basis for their cross-border activities. The discussion in Chapter 2 shows how MNCs may be able to turn comparative advantages into sources of competitive advantage, at least for limited periods of time.

Chapter 2 is where you are introduced to the basic economic theory upon which many global strategy frameworks are built. It particularly emphasizes two influential contributions to global strategy: the national 'diamond' framework; and the concept of national 'clusters' and their importance for understanding the relationship between the individual firm and the global competitiveness of those firms as a result of the national economies in which they are placed. The national 'diamond' framework is used to explain the influence of the 'home base' country on how well or poorly a firm may perform globally, that is outside the home base market. The home base constitutes the cultural, social, economic, political, financial, regulatory and ethical context in which the individual firm develops its identity, its resources and capabilities, and its approach to management. We therefore regard the home base as a significant contributor to the strengths and weaknesses of particular firms in particular industries. The further impact of the home base country is contained within the concept of national 'clusters'. This means that some industries do better in some countries than in other countries. This makes a link between the global competitiveness of firms and the global competitiveness of nations. This is a significant point for developing a global strategy: understand your home base.

In Chapter 3 we become less theoretical and more practical. This chapter is about issues that most people have heard about on the news. It focuses on globalization, which is probably one of the most commonly used concepts in modern politics, trade and business. We explain what globalization means, what happens when industries globalize and what impact the process of globalization has on countries, on companies and on people. Globalization is also a difficult and sensitive political issue and has given rise to what has become known as the anti-globalization movement: we discuss the reasons why that is so. Alongside the well-known issue of globalization there is the less well-known development of regionalization. Regionalization is about the world being gradually carved up into regional trading blocs, each containing a few countries which will then trade with each other on more favourable terms than they trade with others outside the regional bloc. The concept of the 'triad' is explained, that is the three major regional trading blocs in the world's most economically developed regions of Europe, Asia and North America. We explain how these two major world trends of globalization and regionalization are pulling world trade in different directions. The differences between them as approaches to world trade are significant and quite far-reaching. Managers must be clear about the relative impact of each of these trends on their businesses.

Chapter 3 is also where the standardization/adaptation debate is introduced for the first time in the book. It is at the core of global strategy. It asks the question of how far, if at all, it is appropriate to design, market and deliver standard products and services across national market boundaries, or the extent to which adaptation to local market requirements is necessary. The standardization/adaptation debate is part of the global versus regional debate because it raises important assumptions concerning the conditions for successful global or regional strategies: that global market segments exist; that global economies of scale exist; and that a distribution infrastructure is available to realize these potential economies of scale worldwide. The underlying key global strategy question is: Does a global customer really exist for this product or service worldwide? Or is it really a regional customer (pan-European, pan-Asian, pan-African) for this product or service, or perhaps only a local customer?

The discussion about regionalization is carried on into the next chapter when we consider emerging economies. In Chapter 4 we move on to consider the 80 per cent of the world's population who live outside the triad economies. In the last twenty years there has been a massive expansion in the emerging economies. The best known of the emerging economies are China and India, which are also the centres of two of the world's largest populations (1.3 billion and just under 1 billion respectively). Many other emerging economies have had almost as significant percentage economic growth year-on-year (such as Brazil or Russia or many Eastern European economies in the period since their independence from the old USSR), but are less enormous economies. The term BRIC has been developed to capture the idea of the four biggest emerging economies Brazil, Russia, India and China. We therefore discuss the shift in regional power from triad to BRIC. A useful definition of an emerging economy is one that has an average annual per capita income of less than $9,000 and is experiencing rapid growth and economic transformation. Chapter 4 looks in detail at what makes emerging economies different from developed economies, in addition to the obvious outstanding rates of economic growth that they have achieved which outstrip anything seen in the developed economies.

One of the most useful approaches to understanding global strategy in emerging markets is to use an institution-based approach that will help managers understand the rules of doing business in the various emerging economies. The assumption to note is that doing business in emerging economies is a different experience that needs a different approach and a different mindset to doing business in developed economies. The key global strategy question thus becomes: How do we play the game, when the rules of the game are changing and not completely known, especially to managers from outside that emerging economy? For this reason we have chosen to answer this question by discussing the important issue of institutions and institutional context in emerging economies. Institutions (both formal and informal) refer to and govern socio-political transactions such as the role of business groupings in emerging economies; corruption and transparency in business dealings; legal transactions such as regulatory regimes; and social norms such as attitudes towards entrepreneurship and what is regarded as ethical behaviour. Understanding the institutional context of emerging economies helps to answer how to 'play the game' by clarifying at least some of 'the rules'. With the emergence recently of powerful emerging economy MNCs, this has become a part of thinking about global strategy.

Since Part 1 is about the external context in which managers have to think about and plan their global strategies, in Chapters 5 and 6 we look at three more significant background changes that are having a growing impact on global strategy formulation and implementation: the rise of the information industries; the rise of 'base-of-the-pyramid' strategies (BOPs); and the increasing availability of global strategies for small and medium-sized firms (SMEs) often as a result of the internet.

The reason that the rise of the information industries merits a whole chapter (Chapter 5) is that they possess different industry characteristics and different sources of competitive advantage from the traditional industries of the type discussed in Chapter 2. In the information industries, there is a virtuous circle of interaction between knowledge and the application of technology to improve knowledge-generation and information-processing. This represents a new technological paradigm based upon information technology. Just as the industrial economy is organized around the principle of economic growth and towards maximizing output, so the information economy is oriented towards technological development. It is organized around the accumulation of knowledge and towards higher levels of complexity in information processing as the key sources of advantage. These industries are different. They have a different cost structure and they operate under different business models, often with a 'winner-takes-all' outcome. That means that the company which establishes the highest installed base and the most effective network will simply dominate the industry as Microsoft has done in software. In information industries also we see the growing importance of networks, especially virtual networks. The virtual corporation does not need vast capital to successfully exploit new opportunities. Global competition in these industries needs to be understood differently.

Finally we move to our discussion of BOPs and SMEs. We have called Chapter 6 'small is valuable' and BOPs and SMEs represent different aspects of being small and yet being part of changing views of who participates in global strategy. With BOPs it is about a new set of consumers that have largely been ignored by MNCs and by the global strategy textbooks until very recently. MNCs have traditionally focused on consumers who could afford to buy their products and services. This is quite understandable. However, the BOP approach suggests global strategies for MNCs that focus on poorer customers in emerging and developing markets instead of on only richer customers in developed economies. It is estimated that there are 4 billion people in the world out of a total estimated world population of 6.5 billion, who are at the base of the economic pyramid, yet who aspire to join the market economy. BOP global strategy is an approach that could be attractive to social and environmental stakeholders as well as provide some potential growth markets for MNCs.

With SMEs it is not customers but firms that are small and yet becoming an increasing part of international trade and competition, often competing directly with MNCs. For example, the internet has created unprecedented market access opportunities for SMEs similar to those of MNCs, enabling global marketing which otherwise SMEs could not afford. The SME sector is generally characterized as the sector exhibiting the greatest growth in employment and the greatest entrepreneurship, but also as the most vulnerable due to a range of factors, particularly a low level of capital. One major strategic mistake that could be taken in its stride by an MNC could lead an SME to bankruptcy. Nevertheless, all recently grown mega-corporations were SMEs not long ago. Therefore how an SME can globalize should be central to the understanding of managers and has become an unexpected part of the global competitor context for MNCs.

CHAPTER 2

The nature of world trade

LEARNING OBJECTIVES The objectives of this chapter are:

- to describe the rise of the Multinational Corporation using Dunning's eclectic theory which gives an explanation for the development of MNCs

- to explain the reasons for MNCs developing through foreign direct investment (FDI), and how international competitive advantage arises through a combination of comparative and competitive advantage factors

- to discuss Porter's contribution to the field through the analysis of industry structure, advanced factors of production, **industry clusters** and the diamond framework

- to extend Adam Smith's and David Ricardo's comparative cost theory in the light of the growth of branded products and the development of three key types of competition: traditional perfect competition; monopolistic competition; and oligopoly

- to show how this theory needs to be adapted to take note of advanced factors and imperfect competition.

INTRODUCTION

In this chapter we assess the relevance of traditional international trade theory to global strategy. While some traditional economic theory is of limited relevance, other more recent economic thinking gives insight into the appropriateness of different types of international competitive strategies in different contexts. The roots of the structural analysis of industries within strategic management (Porter, 1980, 1985 and 1990), both nationally and internationally, lie within economics. This gives such analysis both its strengths and its weaknesses. Understanding the respective roles of nations and firms within global strategy, and the economic rationale for much international activity, gives meaning to the discussion of particular MNC international strategies and organizational structures in later chapters.

International trade has a history going back at least to the Phoenicians (approximately 500 BC and even earlier). Many of the great expeditions and celebrated explorers in the history books as well as many wars and colonial conquests were about discovering, or taking control of new trading routes or sources of wealth to be traded.

2

The world has generally been dominated by the strongest trading states or nations in each era. Their political power rested largely on their economic power derived from trade, such as that of the Republic of Venice in the late fifteenth and sixteenth centuries in Europe. Throughout the seventeenth, eighteenth and nineteenth centuries, the European powers of France, Britain, Holland, Belgium, Spain and Portugal expanded into Africa and Asia, South and North America. Imperialism and colonial aggrandizement often followed swiftly on the heels of trading exploits or, as in India, political power followed to protect the trading activities of the East India Company. Historically, trade and political power went hand in hand.

Until more recent times, international trade was dominated by large trading companies such as the East India Company (India), Hudson Bay Company (North America) or Inchcape PLC (Asia) who took products manufactured in the home country and traded them for simpler products or raw materials produced abroad.

In the twentieth century, however, international trade increasingly became dominated by multinational corporations (MNCs) who engage in foreign direct investment (FDI) and are organized as unified hierarchical corporations, or more recently, by competition from more loosely organized coalitions of companies and networks led by **flagship firms** (Rugman and D'Cruz, 1997).

This has in itself influenced the nature of international trade, since much international activity is in the nature of transfers within these MNCs, between their business units and operating divisions, either importing goods produced in their overseas subsidiaries or exporting products to be sold by these subsidiaries. The largest MNCs have grown to be more important economically than all but the richest of national economies. Such firms play an important role not only in their domestic economies, but also in the economies of the many overseas territories in which they have a presence. How is that possible if international trade is firmly based on the principle of comparative costs?

THE RISE OF THE MNC

The classical theory of comparative costs would suggest at first sight that local companies would be likely to have inherent advantages in their own countries compared with multinational corporations. Local companies would have lower transport costs, a better understanding of local tastes, better local networks and lower need for the overheads that come with international co-ordination. Yet branded goods sold through MNCs generally dominate most consumer goods markets. By 1970, of the 100 largest economic entities in the world ranked by GDP, 39 were countries but 60 were MNCs. Some of these MNCs have existed longer and are more stable than many countries. Why is this?

MNCs are large companies that produce in countries outside their home country and operate in global markets. In MNCs comparative costs largely determine where a particular activity is carried out, subject to some adjustment for political and other risks. Raw materials may be mined in one country, converted into product in another and marketed and sold in a third. Comparative costs will play a large part in determining which activities are carried out in which countries, but all may then be bundled together and sold through the agency of and under the brand name of a multinational corporation (Inkpen and Ramaswamy, 2006; Peng and Delios, 2006; Krugman, 1995). Dunning's 'eclectic' theory provides a framework for explaining why MNCs exist and are able to achieve competitive advantage in competition both with local firms and firms who restrict their international activities just to exporting. Dunning's (1998) 'eclectic paradigm' consists of three 'OLI' factors:

1 Ownership

2 Localization

3 Internalization.

Ownership (O) factors imply that the company owns certain key resources or capabilities giving advantage in certain markets, for example strong brand names, specific and unique technologies or particular and relevant know-how. These factors give the MNC potential advantage over a local company. Such advantages leading to a high level of sales will contribute to lower unit costs through economies of scale for the MNC.

Localization (L) is about location of activities of the MNC. It means that the multinational finds it an advantage to locate an activity in a particular local market to benefit from some comparative advantage such as low cost or highly experienced labour available there, or to avoid national or regional tariff barriers.

Internalization (I) suggests that there are advantages to carrying out certain activities (such as R&D or marketing) internally within the MNC because not to do so would generate a high risk of losing proprietary knowledge to potential competitors. Outsourcing, quasi-integration with suppliers, or setting up a joint venture or strategic alliance for these critical functions may be ill-advised, since they contain the risk of loss of proprietary information or loss of sources of innovation.

Thus in Dunning's (1998) OLI paradigm for the development of MNC activity, it is the second factor, localization (L), that is critical for international activity.

Consider the four main types of international trade:

■ exporting

■ foreign direct investment (FDI)

■ licensing

■ strategic alliances.

If the conditions governing the ownership (O) or internalization (I) factors are reduced or removed then the opportunity for strategic alliances arises. The theory of foreign direct investment, and of alternative organizational forms to develop business across frontiers, was originally set out clearly by Rugman (1980), who developed a rational decision tree for choosing between the four alternatives. This decision tree is given in Figure 2.1.

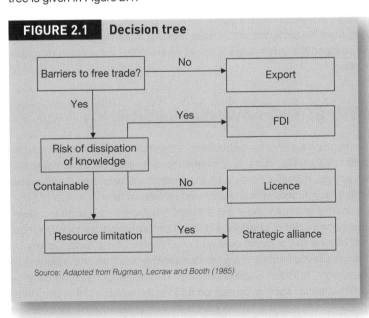

FIGURE 2.1   Decision tree

Source: *Adapted from Rugman, Lecraw and Booth (1985)*

The decision tree in Figure 2.1 shows a decision pathway for deciding which route to global makes best sense under different circumstances for a company. Thus exporting is best in conditions where trade barriers are absent since unit costs can be reduced to a very low level from large-scale production. If trade barriers exist, however, companies will need to set up manufacturing in foreign countries to get underneath those trade barriers, which means they are pursuing FDI and therefore becoming an MNC.

2

They will also do this under tight ownership conditions if they fear losing competitive advantage as a result of the loss of proprietary knowledge. If this is not a major concern, a strategic alliance or joint venture may be the appropriate move.

Dunning's paradigm is called 'eclectic' because the actual circumstances, which make becoming a multinational the appropriate solution, are many, varied and particular to a set of circumstances. However, in Dunning's view the decision about whether the MNC route to golbalization is the appropriate one, or whether another route would be more effective given the conditions, will always need to be made with regard to the three OLI characteristics: ownership, location and internalization. With only ownership (O) factors the company could export to a licensee, and subcontract virtually any of its activities. With only internalization (I) it could operate from a home base and found all its international activities on export trade, as international traders did generally prior to the nineteenth century. With ownership and internalization, it is committed to carrying out certain key activities itself, lest it lose control of those advantages to a competitor. And with all three, ownership, internalization and localization, it is committed to setting up abroad in some form to meet the criteria. In other words it has to become an MNC.

The acronym OLI explains how MNCs prosper through 'Ownership' advantages, for example brand names, 'Locational' advantages where there is for example cheap or skilled labour and 'Internalization' needs which protect their proprietary knowledge and information. The way for a firm with no OLI advantages to succeed in international trade is to configure and co-ordinate a joint value chain with a partner, a possibility that will be returned to later in the book.

Rugman (Rugman, 1996, and Rugman and Verbeke, 2001) developed a similar approach to that of Dunning. Instead of the three OLI factors, he identified two sets called country-specific advantages (CSAs) and firm-specific advantages (FSAs). Rugman's CSAs fit neatly onto 'L' (locational) factors; while Rugman's FSAs fit neatly onto Dunning's 'O' and 'I', since they are firm-specific. Generalizing further, we can argue that multinational firms locate themselves in additional countries to their home base because those countries have advantages for them (such as cost, distribution or market knowledge) which help them to achieve sustainable competitive advantage in global markets.

Multinational corporations are, in Kogut's view (1985b), able to win against most local companies because they have access to the comparative advantage of the nations in which they carry out FDI and can also achieve competitive advantage by designing their value-added chains globally for specific different activities. The value-added chain enables one to identify sources of comparative (country) and competitive (firm) advantage. It is important to understand that **comparative advantage** is about where to carry out each business activity; **competitive advantage** is about where in the value chain to invest. These are now discussed in more detail.

COMPARATIVE AND COMPETITIVE ADVANTAGE FOR MNCs

In Strategy in Action 2.1, the well-known competitive battle between the earth-moving equipment companies Caterpillar (USA) and Komatsu (Japan) illustrates very clearly the difference between comparative advantage and competitive advantage. It shows how companies may be able to turn comparative advantages into sources of competitive advantage, at least for limited periods of time.

It is important to draw lessons from this example about the difference between comparative advantage and potential competitive advantage in global strategy. Komatsu certainly had comparative cost advantages over Caterpillar in terms of steel raw material cost and much lower labour costs. However, these in themselves were not the source of Komatsu's changed competitive position or the source of Caterpillar's difficulties. These arose from Komatsu's determination to turn temporary comparative advantages into longer-term competitive advantages. It formulated and implemented a viable long-term strategy to establish itself in world markets. It was this which enabled existing sources of comparative advantage to support global competitive advantage.

Strategy in Action 2.1 *Caterpillar and Komatsu – comparative advantage and competitive advantage in action*

In strategy terms it must be stressed that although an understanding of comparative advantage is critical to understanding and formulating global strategies, one must never lose sight of the important difference between *comparative* advantage and the potential for *competitive* advantage. A well-known example is that of the battle for global domination of the world earth-moving equipment (EME) industry between Caterpillar (US) and its initially tiny rival Komatsu (Japan). We follow the history over a long time period in order to understand what happened and why.

Throughout the 1950s, 1960s and 1970s Komatsu slowly built up its position against a rather arrogant and therefore unwary Caterpillar which then dominated over 50 per cent of world market share in that industry. By exploiting significantly lower comparative costs in raw materials (steel was 30 per cent cheaper in Japan than US prices) and labour (60 per cent cheaper in Japan than US prices), it was gradually able to undermine the classic differentiation strategy pursued by Caterpillar, which was based on premium pricing for perceived high levels of quality, reliability and service. These latter factors (reliability and service), rather than price, were the critical purchasing criteria for customers for earth-moving equipment. In an industry where one large piece of equipment could cost $1 million, it was the threat of lost 'downtime' and the possible disruption of scheduling on major construction projects that was the cause of overwhelming anxiety for managers. No wonder customers were prepared to pay high prices for reliability and Caterpillar was very successful. Komatsu had a poor reputation for quality and reliability, which was disastrous in this industry.

The situation gradually changed as Komatsu used a time window in the 1960s, provided for it by MITI (the Japanese Ministry for International Trade and Investment) which had refused permission for Caterpillar to begin production in the Japanese domestic market and had instead licensed a Japanese joint venture between Komatsu and a weak US rival International Harvester (IH) for the production of EME in Japan. Komatsu used this opportunity to embark on a series of dramatic quality improvement programmes. It learned rapidly from IH's technology. Eventually it bought out IH's technology licences very cheaply when that company desperately needed money in the early 1970s. However, its greatest success lay in its programme of continuous internal improvement which turned it from a domestic supplier of such poor quality that even Japanese domestic firms would not buy from it, into a rival which could match and occasionally exceed Caterpillar quality, but at much reduced prices. This had the effect of destroying Caterpillar's sources of competitive advantage and the basis of its differentiation strategy. Caterpillar could no longer justify its 20 per cent price premium on the basis of significantly higher quality. As worldwide customers gradually grew to trust Komatsu's quality, Caterpillar was required to reduce prices to match Komatsu. It was unable to do this easily or quickly, since the effortless dominance of its market over thirty years had left the company relatively inefficient in its internal operations. It was also suffering from comparative cost *disadvantage* in labour and raw material costs compared to Komatsu. This had not mattered while Komatsu was a poor supplier of unreliable products, but became very problematic indeed when Komatsu was able to match both Caterpillar's quality and product range.

Another aspect of international competition exemplified in this case was the role of government intervention. Not only did Komatsu benefit from MITI's support in blocking Caterpillar entering Japan at a critical time, but this contrasted with the bad luck experienced by Caterpillar in the 1980s when the then American President Ronald Reagan banned all US firms from involvement in the Alaskan pipeline project – the biggest construction project in the world at that time. That intervention gave Komatsu a golden opportunity for a prestigious shop-window to demonstrate the reliability of its products under difficult geographic conditions, at the end of which all-remaining industry doubts had been removed.

Of course, the situation did not remain static and Caterpillar fought back vigorously. It had received a tremendous cultural shock in experiencing five consecutive years of losses in the late 1980s and early 1990s. It embarked on worldwide plant evaluations resulting in a drastic closure programme. Only those evaluated as most efficient were retained and provided with further investment and upgrading of technology and systems. It also had persistent labour relations problems and difficulties in

implementing flexible working practices against US trade union opposition. This was disastrous for Caterpillar since such practices had already been in place at Komatsu for decades. So the relative labour costs for the two companies was both of absolute levels of wages, but also of working practices that affected the relative productivity of that labour. This was a very significant factor because absolute levels of wages tend to be only a temporary transitional cost advantage and wages will rapidly rise with economic development in any industrializing economy. The same point may be made regarding fluctuations in exchange rate differentials. The current status between these two rival companies sees the two companies still dominating the world market for EME. Caterpillar has regained a proportion of its lost market share and become a much more efficient company as a result of Komatsu's efforts. Komatsu has consolidated its position as the industry's world number two. Caterpillar has never regained its previous level of dominance.

SOURCE: COMPILED BY AUTHORS FROM VARIOUS PRESS ARTICLES

INDUSTRY STRUCTURE

Although the theory of comparative costs still underlies some trade as it did in classical times, a modern theory of global strategic management must account for the changes that have taken place in the pattern of international business since the eighteenth century up to date. Industry structure in most areas bears little resemblance to the perfect competition paradigm implicitly underlying the theory of comparative costs.

The model of industry structure given in Figure 2.2 demonstrates the amount of variation industries face in the forces influencing them. The model (adapted from Porter's 1980 five forces framework) indicates an industry that is attractive to an incumbent firm, since it is one in which the five forces are weak. An unattractive industry is one where they are

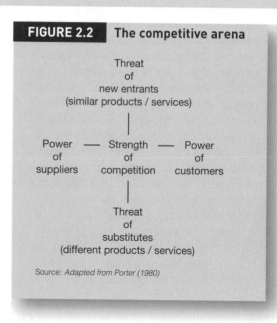

FIGURE 2.2 The competitive arena

Threat
of
new entrants
(similar products / services)

Power — Strength — Power
of   of   of
suppliers competition customers

Threat
of
substitutes
(different products / services)

Source: *Adapted from Porter (1980)*

strong. For example in developed countries, the mini-cab industry is relatively unattractive in most urban areas for the following reasons. Competition is very strong as there are many other mini-cars touring cities only able to charge the going rate and with no ability to differentiate themselves. The existence of substitutes is high in the form of official taxi services (such as Black Cabs in London; Yellow Cabs in New York), trains, bicycles, private cars and walking. There are few barriers to entry so if profits became high, any reasonably enterprising person could enter the market and undercut rates. Only supplier and customer powers are relatively low, which enables the cab drivers to at least make a living.

At the other end of the scale, the pharmaceutical industry is very attractive to a company with a patented cure for cancer, or any other major disease. Substitutes are limited and entry barriers are very high, including high research and development (R&D) costs. Therefore the threat of new entrants is relatively low, although there is increasing competition from generic drugs and the potential for substitutes from the emergent biotechnology sector, and some modest growth in market share for 'alternative' therapies such as acupuncture or herbal medicines. There are strong global competitors and concentration in the industry is continuing, with ever-larger mergers often between firms that were already very large and global, for example Smith Kline Beecham merged with Glaxo Wellcome (already a mega-merger itself) to create GSK. Competition is, however, constrained within particular clusters of diseases such as bronchial or viral and supplier power and customer power are mostly low. Customer power is increasing somewhat as governments in advanced economies struggle to contain spiralling healthcare costs and as hospitals, medical practitioners and insurance companies become gradually more vertically integrated to enlarge their bargaining power, as in the American system of Health Management Organizations (HMOs). Nevertheless, despite such industry developments, pharmaceutical companies can still expect to make extremely good profits in the developed economies.

The attractiveness of an industry to an incumbent will be dependent upon the power of each of the five industry forces in Figure 2.2 and the strength of a company's position in relation to them internationally, just as it is in a national context.

ADVANCED FACTORS OF PRODUCTION

In a global context, in addition to the distortions provided by governments, for example through tariffs and other forms of protection, there are also additional factors of production to complicate the picture still further. These 'advanced factors' are more relevant than the classical basic factors in determining global competitive advantage. Typical advanced factors are human resources, physical resources, knowledge resources, capital resources and infrastructure, as referred to briefly in Chapter 1. We will now discuss these advanced factors in more detail.

In work focusing on sources of national competitiveness, Porter (1990, 1998) outlined those particular 'advanced' factors that are particularly important in the international context. The keys to global competitiveness have become more than the traditional factors of production. As we shall see, these 'advanced factors' have a claim to greater importance in the modern world than the old traditional factors and it is these which are of greater relevance to global strategy. The overall effect of these advanced factors is to explain why the 'perfect market' model of an economy does not work in practice outside the commodities sectors.

Globally mobile factors of production

Land may still be immobile but the ownership of that land may shift from the nation in which it is located to an MNC owned and run offshore. Labour is becoming increasingly mobile in a globalizing world. Well-qualified professionals from South America or Eastern Europe migrate to wealthier countries for employment in pursuit of a higher standard of living or simply a different lifestyle. Similarly, there are frequent periods when what is referred to as a 'brain drain' occurs in which highly qualified people such as doctors, scientists, engineers or academic researchers are attracted away from the home economy in which they trained to acquire their qualifications and move to a better-paying country or one which can provide them with a more exciting or better-resourced work environment. There is something of a scandal developing between developed and developing economies as the richer countries are seen to be poaching from poorer countries their very scarce best resources such as doctors, nurses and IT specialists. Individuals with scarce skills are willing to seek better career opportunities, better working environments or resources, or to escape high taxation areas for lower taxed ones. Also, MNCs themselves are increasingly eager to recruit staff from a wider variety of countries and backgrounds. The immobility of labour, certainly at executive level, is a thing of the past. Declining capital barriers between nations has also led major companies to be able to trawl the world to raise capital at the best rates.

Specific and fast changing technology

In many industries like electronics, telecommunications, software or game designs, no sooner does a technology become widely adopted than another one appears on the horizon to challenge it. It is also impossible to protect technologies despite the use of patents and copyright. These give only temporary protection while imitators catch up and attempt to improve the technology still further or use the information published in the patent registration to create marginally redesigned alternatives. Largely for these reasons, an equilibrium condition is rarely reached in any widely traded industries.

Monopoly power

Monopoly power is the ability to fix prices above marginal costs and to maintain them successfully at that level. The traditional international trade model does not allow for monopoly power in the hands of MNCs. In a market where monopoly power exists, which means all advanced economies to some extent, each product has something of a market of its own and is only imperfectly substitutable for a competitor product. As a result, the producer has some discretion in setting his price and is not in the position of having to accept the externally determined price, as might be the case with commodity products such as coffee, cocoa beans or wheat, which have no distinctive brand characteristics. The consequence of this is a distortion of international trade to the advantage of the monopolist. Of course in global markets, monopoly power is likely to survive for less time than in more restricted markets, due to the larger number of potential suppliers.

Mobility barriers

Mobility barriers may take the form of entry barriers, exit barriers or any factors that inhibit the movement of companies from one strategic group to another within the same industry. A strategic group is defined as a cluster of firms within an industry following similar generic strategies and having similar market positioning (Smith et al., 1997). Such mobility barriers are among the 'five forces' identified by Porter (1980) as determining the intensity of competition in an industry. The most powerful mobility barriers are those that are difficult or impossible to imitate; for example know-how, market leader brand names or strategic assets (Amit and Schoemaker, 1993) such as the art and palaces of Venice or the temples of Petra in Jordan, which are clearly unique. Other barriers that inhibit new entrants, and that exist in most industries, are such factors as access to distribution, learning curve, scale and scope advantages, government regulation, and so on.

Branded products

Classical trade theory does not allow for the effects of brand names. Brands become powerful because customers lack the skills to judge between competing products on the basis of their perceived qualities and because they believe that ownership of these brands may enhance their status. They therefore choose a brand that they know and respect, since they believe that the company owning that brand will stand behind the product in the event of its failure, and furthermore that the company in question is unlikely to field an unreliable product. By definition, customers trust successful brands. This leads to a market distortion as customers develop an over-commitment to a particular branded product or service, rather than to its similar rivals. The effect of this is similar to the creation of monopoly power.

Other advanced factors

Countries benefit from, or are deficient in, many advanced factors of production. These include the level of educated labour, the higher education infrastructure, the communications network in terms of mobile phones, television, internet and broadband availability, road and rail networks and airline routes enabling people in one part of the country to contact those in other parts, and in the rest of the world easily and often relatively cheaply. These 'advanced' factors of production therefore provide sources of comparative advantage in global markets for companies operating in countries which may be deficient in the classical basic factors of production.

NATIONAL OR INTERNATIONAL SOURCES OF COMPETITIVE ADVANTAGE

We will now take this explanation of the relationship between comparative advantage and the potential for competitive advantage one stage further by discussing the work of Michael Porter on national comparative advantage. In 1990, Porter published the results of an extremely detailed study which compared patterns of comparative advantage in thirteen industrialized countries. The book was called *The Competitive Advantage of Nations*. As the title makes clear, Porter is interested in establishing the significance of national conditions (i.e. the overall competitive and socio-economic environment existing within a particular country) for the international competitive advantage of firms within that country. From his analysis arise two influential contributions to global strategy: the national 'diamond' framework; and the concept of national 'clusters' and their importance for the global competitiveness of firms within national economies. We shall discuss each of these in turn.

Comparative advantage revisited: the Porter 'diamond'

Porter (1990) emphasizes the place of comparative advantage in international competitive advantage. His argument is that:

- Although the competitiveness of a country depends upon the firms within it, the national environment exerts a very powerful influence on the performance of these firms. This is often referred to as the influence of the *home base*. The home base constitutes the cultural, social, economic, political, financial, regulatory and ethical context in which the individual firm develops its identity, its resources and capabilities and its approach to management.

In addition to the broad national context, in order for a country to keep its competitive advantage in an industry or sector over time, individual firms must innovate and continuously upgrade the quality of their resources and capabilities. In other words, home base advantage may wither away over time if firms in that sector do not invest in development and innovation. Home base advantage is dynamic, not static. It may atrophy over time. Governments can have a profound influence on creating the conditions that affect innovation by investing (or failing to invest) in the upgrading of resources such as transport infrastructure or education.

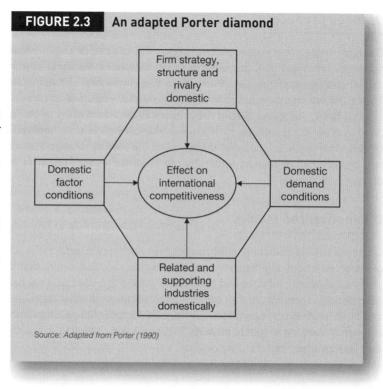

FIGURE 2.3   An adapted Porter diamond

Source: *Adapted from Porter (1990)*

Porter has developed what he calls the national *diamond* framework to show how home base advantage works (see Figure 2.3).

We can develop our understanding of Porter's national 'diamond' in Figure 2.3, and his view of the importance of *clusters* of national resources and capabilities that combine to support certain national industries, by considering the Italian company Benetton (see Strategy in Action 2.2).

Porter is thus convinced that 'home-base' and domestic industry conditions are critical to international success.

National 'clusters' and national competitiveness

We have defined **national industry** 'clusters' as 'critical masses – in one place – of unusual competitive success in particular fields' (Porter, 1998: 78). Therefore clusters can be understood as 'geographic concentrations of interconnected companies and institutions in a particular field' (Porter, 1998). Well-known examples of such strong industry clusters include:

- the motion picture industry clusters of Bollywood (India) and Hollywood (US)

- the computer software industry clusters of Bangalore (India) and California (US)

- the wine industry clusters of Bordeaux, Burgundy or Champagne (France), California (US) and Southern Australia

- the concentration of financial sector expertise in Frankfurt (Germany), Zurich (Switzerland), 'City' of London (UK) or New York ('Wall Street', US).

For each of the examples given, it is a straightforward task to demonstrate a 'strong' national diamond.

Strategy in Action 2.2 *The Benetton diamond*

Benetton's sources of national comparative advantage

Benetton is an Italian global clothing business that designs, manufactures, distributes and retails its ranges of brightly coloured casual clothes around the world. The Benetton business empire began in 1965 in Ponzano, Southern Italy. From the beginning, the business made use of particular resource advantages that were available to them in their local area. There was a long history of local weaving for the textile industry which had existed in Italy for hundreds of years. It was organized on a household ('cottage industry') basis. Labour was therefore not only plentiful and cheap, but highly skilled and could be employed on a contracted-out, part-time basis. Benetton utilized this skilled, flexible, part-time workforce as it grew from a small local firm, to a worldwide multinational company with more than 7,000 retail outlets. Its shops can be found in cities throughout Europe and North America and in large parts of Asia. As a nation, Italians are passionate about fashion. They spend a high proportion of their disposable income on clothing and accessories. Personal appearance is valued highly (*fare una bella figura*) and as consumers they are knowledgeable about style, quality and value. The fashion industry is a major industry in Italy both in design and manufacture. The Italian fashion industry covers not just male and female designer clothing but also top quality leather goods (such as shoes, bags, belts and luggage), furniture and design. Italy is home to some of the most famous global fashion brands such a Prada and Gucci. Milan counts as one of the two most influential fashion capitals of the world, alongside Paris, with Florence usually regarded as the capital of leather.

Factor conditions

The textile industry is a historic industry in Italy with hundreds of years of specialized skill and experience to draw on. Benetton is not just able to use cheap labour in a poor part of Italy, but it is also highly skilled and experienced cheap labour.

Demand conditions

The Italians as a nation are among the most sophisticated customers in the world of fashion. As such they provide a demanding and critical marketplace for Benetton's designs. If you can survive as a fashion retailer in Italy you are likely to have a product that will survive in other international markets.

Related and supporting industries

Italy has a national 'cluster' of very strong industries both in the fashion industry itself, with its numerous designer labels, fashion houses and high priests of the Milan fashion shows, but also in many related industries such as leather goods, shoes, handbags, belts, luggage, and furniture. All these industries share common factors such as high design skills and knowledge of materials. There is also a strong network of largely family-owned intermediate supporting industries to provide an efficient infrastructure for the fashion industry.

Firm strategy, structure and rivalry

Items for consideration in this part of the diamond are the five forces industry analysis issues. Here the point Porter wishes to make is that firms located in very competitive industries with high levels of national rivalry are the ones most likely to do well in international markets. Those with few or no national rivals are unlikely to be as efficient or as responsive to customer requirements. They may nevertheless survive and prosper within a relatively protected domestic marketplace, but are unlikely to perform strongly internationally. Benetton is located in an overcrowded domestic fashion market, from whose competitive rigors it has benefited as an international firm.

2

Porter notes that some industries take successful root in some places and some in others. He sees these productive clusters of excellence in terms of nations. Within a nation, demand conditions are affected by its government's macroeconomic policy; the nature of competition by its antitrust (anti-monopoly) and trade policies; the level and type of skills by the country's education system; and the attitudes of managers, workers and customers by its national culture. Clusters are about linkages and complementarities across industries and institutions that are most important to competition as in the Italian fashion, leather, textile and design cluster already discussed (see Strategy in Action 2.2).

Porter's (1990 and 1998) analysis of national advantage and international competitiveness also suggests that government policies adopted to support local industries (e.g. by means of subsidies, import protection, quotas, local content requirements) are likely to be counter-productive since they will protect national firms from competitive pressure (indeed that is what they are designed to do) and therefore are at risk of discouraging, rather than promoting, efficiency, innovation and upgrading. This is another issue in international trade over which there is disagreement. Does government intervention to protect domestic industries help national industries or hurt them?

We can consider two contrasting examples of government intervention. First, we can return to the example of the Japanese trade and industry ministry MITI intervening to prevent the (then) much larger competitor firm Caterpillar from dominating the Japanese market for earth-moving equipment (EME) when Komatsu was too small to compete with it. That was in the 1960s. It is arguable that if the Japanese government had not intervened at that point, Komatsu would not have survived and the Japanese EME market would have been dominated by Caterpillar. In a much more recent example, there is much concern in the EU at the actions of some European governments in providing a series of financial subsidies to their national airline, for example Air France which, in common with almost all the full-cost European national 'flag-carrier' airlines, has been running substantial losses and Alitalia of Italy which almost managed to be sold but no deal was reached in the end. However, airlines have not earned enough profit to cover the cost of their capital over the last thirty years. For example, in a recent valuation of the large American airlines they had a combined debt of $100 billion on a combined stock market valuation of less than $3 billion. Europe continues with over twenty flag carriers when the market size is better suited to supporting between five and six for Europe and Asia combined. The point here concerning the role of government intervention is that the European (and world) aviation industry has not consolidated and is supported at high levels of inefficiency (in terms of their costs) because they are run more for prestige than for efficiency.

The difference between the MITI intervention and the current European government airline subsidies is one of *timing* and *purpose*. The Japanese intervention was at the start-up phase for an industry, allowing it time to establish itself before full competition occurred. The airline industry is, by contrast, a mature industry, at an advanced stage in its industry lifecycle, whose next stages of industry development are being artificially blocked. There are no national industry clusters in the airline industry.

There is thus a link between the competitive advantage of the firm and its national (country) environment. Furthermore, in the link between national clusters and international competitiveness, the existence and effect of clusters shows that the business context in which the firm is based plays a vital role.

ECONOMIC PARADIGMS

The economic model of international trade developed between the world wars provides a variant of the traditional comparative cost Ricardo model described in Chapter 1. It tells us that trade reflects an interaction between the characteristics of countries and the production technologies of different goods. Countries will therefore export goods whose production is intensive in the factors with which they are abundantly endowed, for example countries with a high capital : labour ratio will export capital-intensive

TABLE 2.1	Reciprocity index of intra-industry trade in the EU
Primary commodities	0.58
All manufactures	0.80
Road vehicles	0.70
Household appliances	0.80
Textiles	0.91
Other consumer goods	0.80

Source: GATT International trade cited in Begg, Fischer and Dornbush (1994)

goods. And those with a superabundance of labour will export labour-intensive goods. Such a theory would suggest that countries with abundant factors relevant to industrial goods would normally export to less developed agriculturally based economies and import food products from them. This seems theoretically plausible.

Despite such theoretical plausibility, this is not how the pattern of international trade has evolved. Table 2.1 shows a reciprocity index for the countries of the EU compiled by Begg, Fischer and Dornbush (1994). It shows that, in general, the main trading partners of industrially developed economies are other rather similar industrially developed countries. Part of the reason for this must be that only developed countries have the wealth to import expensive capital and consumer goods, but that is not the only reason.

The table records an index ranging from 0.00 where one country exports a product and only imports other products, to 1.00 where there is complete two-way trade in the product range. Generally the more products are undifferentiated, the more comparative cost theory operates effectively, so that the country with the resource abundance does the exporting and hence has a low index in the table. For branded products, as we have already explained, comparative advantage may lose some of its importance as customers buy brands for a variety of reasons, not all of which are to do with externally testable value. Thus intra-industry trade becomes more significant.

Often nowadays, tariffs have been largely removed between geographically closely related countries such as the EU. Where this is the case, the gains from trade arise less from the exploitation of different factor endowments, than from the advantages arising from brand name specialization and resultant brand marketing, with the consequent reduction in comparative unit costs through the economies of scale and scope that a larger international market allows.

In international trade in the present day, brand marketing is one of the key factors for success. With the close communication that radio, television, the web and travel provides, a brand developed successfully in one country may instantly have the key to entering a new market and achieving immediate market share in relation to domestic rivals. Some brands such as Coca-Cola or Sony, for example, are known worldwide, and are instantly recognized and powerful brands in any new country they may wish to enter.

Our purpose in this chapter is to explain the relevance of economic theory to global strategy. Economic theory does have within it models which are able to explain modern international trade: however, three models are required rather than one. The characteristics of these three different models are given in Table 2.2. This is important since so much of international trade is based not on the comparative costs of a perfect market, but on the monopolistic competition power of MNCs and the strength of brand marketing to differentiate products that might otherwise be sold purely on the basis of their costs. However, comparative costs come back into their own when we consider the markets for factors of production.

2

TABLE 2.2   Different market structures

	Assumptions	Key characteristicss	Examples
Perfect competition	Complete information Homogeneous products Commodities Constant and rising costs	Price taking Comparative costs key Brands unimportant	Wheat Steel Minerals
Monopolistic competition	Incomplete information Proprietary products Differentiation Scale / Scope economies	Price discretion Advanced factors key Branded goods Limited substitutability	Travel services Electronic goods Consumer goods
Oligopoly	Interdependence Collusion opportunities Differentiation Scale / Scope economies Few large rivals	Price strategy interdependent Advanced factors key Branded goods High advertising Game theory	Aircraft manufacture Major machine tools Defence manufacturers National newspapers

Labour is still bought from countries where it is cheap in order to embed it into products that are then branded and sold internationally as though they have been manufactured in the brand name country not the cheap labour country. This is known as the OEM (own equipment manufacturer) system.

Perfect competition

The classical theory of international trade assumes conditions of **perfect competition**. This abstract and idealized form of economic model assumes perfect rationality, complete information, homogeneous products, profit maximization, and that firms cannot fix prices, but have to accept the 'market price'. Such a model is useful in the analysis of food and other agricultural commodities such as rice, potatoes or wheat, or indeed any other commodity product that does not benefit from branding. These products will still sell on a world market based on their comparative costs so long as governments do not interfere to protect markets or industries. Their price will only be distorted by transport costs and by perhaps the intervention of the EU Commission aiming to prop up prices to support the European farming industry. The Common Agricultural Policy (CAP) of the EU is a current example of the way in which governments can distort agricultural prices that would otherwise be governed by the laws of supply and demand in close to perfectly competitive conditions. In such perfect competition situations Ricardian international trade theory still reigns supreme. Strategy in Action 2.3 gives an unusual example of perfect competition.

Monopolistic competition

A monopoly is a market in which only one company is able to produce and sell its products. This may be because the government gives it and only it a licence to trade in particular goods, for example a

Strategy in Action 2.3 *A case study in perfect competition: the US bicycle industry*

Perfect competition, according to economists, is the most competitive market imaginable. In the real world, it is rare, and there are some economists who feel it may not even exist in its purest form. The example of a market in *perfect competition* that is referenced by those economists who believe it does exist, is agriculture, because it is so competitive that any individual buyer or seller has a negligible impact on the market price. Products are homogeneous, or composed of parts that are all of the same kind. Product and pricing information is also *perfect* in that everyone, including the ultimate purchaser knows everything about the products, including the best prices available in the market.

In a market in *perfect competition* everybody is a price taker, producing and selling essentially identical products and each seller has little or no effect on market price, and is unable to sell any output at a price greater than the market price. Firms earn only normal profit, or the bare minimum profit necessary to keep them in business. If firms do earn more than normal profit (which is called excess profit), the absence of barriers to entry mean that other firms will enter the market and drive the price level down until there are only normal profits to be made. Manufacturing output will be maximized and price minimized.

The best example of perfect competition that I have heard recently is in my own backyard, Madison, Wisconsin, one of the best specialty bicycle retail markets in the country. As most of the industry knows, there are two Trek company stores in Madison, and one of them, located on the East side has been identified as the company's flagship store. Erik's Bike Shop is a successful multi-store retailer headquartered in the Minneapolis–St. Paul Minnesota market. Erik's established a store in Madison several seasons ago, and carries Specialized, as what I understand is its marque brand.

Several weeks ago, according to the buzz among bicycle dealers, Specialized announced to its dealers in Madison that Erik's will open a second store, reportedly directly across the street from the Trek flagship store on the city's East side. By the way, both the Trek flagship and the new Erik's that will carry Specialized are both in direct competition with an established bicycle dealer that has carried both the Trek and Specialized brands for many years – and is just one mile away!

To make this market situation even more 'perfect', the Trek flagship and new Erik's store are located almost within sight of a large new Dick's Sporting Goods that opened last year.

This is a clear example of *perfect competition* at its best, or should I say worst. The most competitive market imaginable, where output will be maximized and price minimized. Consumers, particularly adult enthusiast cyclists have been and will continue to be the clear beneficiaries of this most competitive of markets.

The retailers, including the two backed by deep pocket bicycle brands, will beat on each other and will become more efficient to survive, and as a result prices in the market will be kept very competitive. Keep in mind that in a state of *perfect competition* a firm that earns excess profits will experience other firms entering the market and driving the price level down until there are only normal profits to be made – the bare minimum profit necessary to keep them in business. All of the retailers in this scenario, when it comes to full fruition, including those backed by the big brands, will still only have a negligible impact on the market, including the market pricing.

Most markets exhibit some form of imperfect or monopolistic competition.

2

There are fewer firms in this imperfect competition than in a perfectly competitive market and each can to some degree create barriers to entry. Such barriers would allow the existing firms to earn some degree of excess profits without a new entrant being able to compete to bring prices down.

So far, the consolidation in the US speciality bicycle retail channel of trade hasn't reached a point where there are a small enough number of brands and / or manufacturers with enough product differentiation to allow the creating of barriers to market entry. The number of bike shops has kept falling over the last seven years, but here again, no retail organization has grown to the point that it can create barriers to market entry.

INTERNET BLOG SUBMITTED BY JAY ON SUN, 2006-07-16 22:27

television franchise, or it may be that only one company has access to a particular good, for example state-owned utility companies such as electricity, water or telephone services, which, unless privatized, are mostly monopolists within their geographical areas. In world trade, however, monopolies are difficult to sustain due to the existence of a large number of governments, and a wide variety of at least imperfectly substitutable resources.

In addition, much of international trade takes place in industrial branded goods for which the perfect competition paradigm is not applicable. Such theory cannot therefore be used as a basis for strategy formulation. Internationally traded industrial goods and consumer goods generally take place in conditions of at least **monopolistic competition**. Let us consider the implications of this.

Monopolistic competition is a form of imperfect competition (Chamberlain, 1939). It is the name given to that form of industrial structure that enables competition to take place between branded goods produced by competitive companies supplying similar needs, but which are regarded by consumers as substitutes only to a limited extent. A case in point might be the keen devotee of Coca-Cola who would only reluctantly accept Pepsi as an adequate substitute if very thirsty, despite the obvious similarities between the two products.

Under conditions of monopolistic competition perfect knowledge is not assumed, so advertising can affect the strength of demand. Consumers are still assumed to be rational in their choices, but with the seducing effects of advertising it is possible to act rationally by buying a product in response to its perceived qualities, rather than any actual superior qualities of that good. This gives firms the power to determine the price of their goods within a range limited by the acceptability in the market of their nearest competitive good (e.g. margarine or butter). They have then a market niche in which they have power by virtue of their committed customers. They can then choose prices to some extent, and are not therefore governed by the 'market price'. They are therefore able to develop the size of their production units beyond that possible in a commodity market by developing brands, which gives them a specialized market. It may be said that they control 100 per cent of the market share for their brand and are only vulnerable to the extent that the market is willing to accept other products as substitutes for theirs. Thus they are able to reduce their unit costs through economies of scale, and if they are multiproduct companies often economies of scope as well.

Scale economies arise through a number of technological factors that make it cheaper in unit cost terms to produce a large amount rather than a small amount of a product including the spreading of a fixed level of overheads over a greater level of production. Scope economies come about because once one product has been produced and marketed, some of the factors needed for its production and marketing, such as its brand name, can be used at relatively little additional cost for a second product. A third factor, namely the experience (or learning) curve, aids this cost reduction process even further. Under the influence of these factors, unit costs reduce with cumulative production of a product as manufacturers develop better and better ways of producing a product of a given quality. Table 2.3 illustrates

TABLE 2.3	Sources of scope economies	
	Product range	*Market spread*
Shared physical assets	Factory automation with flexibility to produce multiple products (Toyota, Boeing, Komatsu)	Global brand name (Nike, VISA)
Shared downstream activities	Using common distribution channel for multiple products (Nestle, Gillette, Disney)	Servicing multinational customers worldwide (IBM, Wipro)
Shared learning	Sharing R&D in computer and communications business (Nokia, Sony)	Pooling knowledge developed in different markets (Google, McKinsey, HSBC)

Source: Adapted from Bartlett and Ghoshal (1989)

some of the possible varieties of scope economies and the sources from which they may be derived. We have deliberately used as examples some of the companies that we will be discussing in various chapters of this book. The scope economies arising from the use of common distribution channels by Gillette has been discussed in Chapter 1; and the advantages of flexible production of multiple products in relation to Komatsu in this chapter.

Economies of scale and scope and the experience curve thus enter into the competitive picture and enable unit costs to fall as output increases, either in volume terms or in respect to product range. This may act as a countervailing force to comparative cost theory, if countries less well endowed with economic factors of production are able to achieve sufficiently high levels of sales. It can enable countries like Japan, dominated as it is by rocky island terrain, to match, or even improve upon, unit cost levels of better endowed countries.

We have therefore explained how scale, scope and experience can and do enable large companies to succeed internationally even when they operate within an economy without comparative advantages on a classical comparative cost basis. One of the effects of the increased globalization of world markets is that the bigger the market, the bigger the opportunity for the company. Firms have contributed to this process by seeking increased market size. Under these circumstances, market share opportunities are limited only by market size and not by costs. There is no 'natural' size for a firm in a modern world market. The only limit is the total size of the potential market, as for example when every possible business and home user of a computer has bought Microsoft's Windows Vista or its later versions. Conceptually, there is no definite limit to potential economies of scale for firms, especially in knowledge-based products and services. In the modern world economy, ever faster technological change seems, in some markets, to lead to a situation in which marginal costs continue to decline with increasing output. With ever-declining unit costs there can be no equilibrium, since such a state is only reached when the revenue from selling an extra good is no more than the extra cost of making it, and it is no longer profitable to attempt to sell one more unit. This unusual situation of the information industries (from an economic theory viewpoint) will be discussed in more detail in Chapter 5.

In a dynamic theory of monopolistic competition, continuously changing technology needs to be accepted as a realistic assumption, and therefore the existence of equilibrium in such markets becomes questionable. Turbulence is a more realistic basic assumption, as Strategy in Action 2.4 demonstrates.

Strategy in Action 2.4 *The Curry Wars: competition in the Indian restaurant market – a case of monopolistic competition*

The eating-out sector in the UK

The 'eating-out' sector (i.e. takeaways and restaurants) is a vibrant market in the UK, with sales of some £28 billion per year. The sector exhibits many of the characteristics of a monopolistically competitive market.

Large number of local buyers. Around 86 per cent of UK adults had eaten out over three times within the previous three months.

Large number of firms. In 2005 there were nearly 95,000 hotel, restaurant and pub enterprises in the UK. Other information shows that there were 90 motorway service areas, 8,600 fish and chip shops, over 9,000 Indian restaurants and countless fast food outlets.

Competitive prices. Margins are very tight because firms have to price very competitively to catch local custom. Only around 60 per cent of these businesses survive longer than three years.

Differentiated products. To attract customers, suppliers must each differentiate their product in various ways, such as food type, ambience, comfort, service, quality, advertising and opening hours.

Ethnic foods

Ethnic food forms a substantial part of eating out in the UK. Around 70 per cent of those who had eaten out in 2005 had been to an Indian, Chinese or other ethnic restaurant, according to Mintel market research. With the exception of the medium and premium brand end of the market, there has been limited innovation in the ethnic eating-out sector. Consumers are looking for alternative cuisine when they eat out and have become tired of the traditional format.

Ethnic restaurants are also facing problems on the supply side. Along with the minimum wage legislation, which is affecting the whole sector, a tightening up of the immigration laws is making it difficult to recruit suitably qualified people, and younger members of these largely family-owned businesses are looking to careers outside of the sector because hours are long and rewards low.

The growth in the popularity of Indian food over the past 20 years has led to the proliferation of restaurants and take-away outlets. The traditional Indian curry house accounted for 28 per cent of meals eaten out by UK adults in 2005.

The close geographic proximity of many such businesses on a well-known street in Bristol led in the early 1990s to what became known as the 'Curry War'. The restaurants had appeared to exist alongside one another quite happily, providing a range of Indian food. In line with the assumptions of monopolistic competition, the restaurants competed in terms of non-price factors such as comfort, advertising and opening hours. Business boomed.

Then came a recession in the early 1990s and a price war suddenly erupted. First take-away prices were slashed by 20 and 30 per cent, and eventually by 50 per cent at the peak of the war. Similar price cuts for dining-in meals were soon to follow. As the war grew more intense many restaurants saw their profits fall. This was particularly true for those restaurants which tried to resist cutting their prices.

Due to the geographical proximity and cultural links of these businesses, the cut-throat nature of such competition was eventually averted. The local traders' association formed what amounted to a curry cartel. Minimum prices were fixed for curries and prices rose once again. Increasingly in town after town 'curry cartels' formed as strong cultural ties among the local Asian communities helped to avert such cut-throat competition. It was realized

SOURCE: ADAPTED FROM MINTEL *EATING OUT REVIEW* (2005)

that, as prices in Indian restaurants were considerably less than in Italian and French ones, fixing minimum curry prices would raise incomes. Such activity, however, is illegal in the UK. It is also unlikely to last for long as other segments of the market develop to undercut curry-house prices or attract consumers with a new culinary offering.

Recent developments
In more recent times Indian restaurants have also suffered from changing British preferences and supply-side pressures. They are also facing direct competition from ready-to-eat curries sold in local supermarkets and the sale of curry in local pubs.

The Indian restaurant has had to relaunch its appeal. One reported method of attracting customers to Birmingham's 'Balti Belt' in the early 2000s was for rival Indian restaurants to have the most visible Las Vegas-style neon sign. This, however, has not been a common response and the lower end of the market is still stagnating.

Innovation is starting to develop in the premium end of the market. There has recently been a move towards acquisitions in both the Indian takeaway and restaurant segments of the market. This is small in scale at the moment, but the emphasis is on trying to develop the brand identity. The premium end of the market, with around 17 per cent of sales, is now the most lucrative

Products internationally traded under monopolistic competition conditions currently include automobiles or electronic goods. Indeed monopolistic competition applies in all areas where there are many sellers of branded products with only partially acceptable substitutes, such that each player has some, but only limited, power to set prices. Since advertising is also able to distort demand, it too is therefore a powerful weapon in such competition. Under monopolistic competition, brand name firms compete with substitute brand name firms, for example BMW with Mercedes or Toyota Lexus brand. They fix their prices at their view of what they believe will optimize their position in their markets, but there are sufficient rivals worldwide to mean that the opportunity for price collusion is limited. If such an opportunity is strong then the third category has come about, namely oligopoly.

Oligopoly

Whereas monopolistic competition is limited by the size of the market and the globally large number of competitors, oligopolistic competition is limited by the actions of relevant rival firms. An **oligopoly** is a market with a few, usually large, firms dominating and where this small number of competitors feel their strategies to be constrained more by the actions of their rivals than by those of their customers. It is monopolistic competition with a significantly reduced field of competitors. This third form of competition applies in international trade where there are so few global players that the predominant concern of each are with the possible behaviour of its rivals, with the threat of new entrants and with the risk of substitutes emerging through new technology or changes in consumer taste. In these circumstances game theory comes into its own, where strategies depend on one's estimate of likely competitive reaction to all possible strategic moves (Brandenburger and Nalebuff, 1995).

Under conditions of oligopoly neither the comparative cost requirements of generous factor endowments nor the power of scale, scope or experience curve economies to reduce costs, nor the power of advertising to increase demand, become the primary concern of global strategists. Although these latter two factors clearly will still have a place in these strategic calculations, the primary concern becomes being able to second-guess rivals.

2

Strategy in Action 2.5 *Evidence of oligopolistic collusion? – rip-off Britain*

In recent years there have been repeated allegations that British consumers are paying much higher prices than their European counterparts for their banking services. UK banks are making excessive profits of some £3 billion to £5 billion per year, with bank customers paying up to £400 a year too much in charges and interest rates according to a UK government Treasury report. The report found that current accounts were the least competitive product. They pay little or no interest to customers in credit and charge exorbitant amounts if you go overdrawn. But it was not just current accounts: mortgages, savings accounts, credit cards and personal loans were all identified as often being poor products from the customers' viewpoint.

Banks have tight control over money transmission systems, cheque clearing and cash machines. This makes it difficult for new competitors to enter the market. For example, a new bank without an extensive network of cash machines would find it difficult to attract customers, given the hefty charges for using other banks' machines. In addition, bank customers are often unwilling to consider changing accounts, fearing that this will involve a lot of time and expense.

Small businesses were found to be facing even more excessive charges. The government thus asked the Competition Commission to enquire into this particular aspect of the provision of banking services.

In 2002, the Competition Commission reported that the UK's four largest banks (Barclays, HSBC, Lloyds TSB, RBS) charged excessive prices to small and medium-sized enterprises (SMEs) in England and Wales. This resulted in excessive profits of some £725 million per year. The report found that each of the four banks pursued similar pricing practices. These included no interest on current accounts; free banking offered only to some categories of SMEs, usually start-ups; the use of negotiation to reduce charges for those considering switching to other banks; lower charges or free banking to those switching from other banks. Switching to another bank, however, requires considerable time and effort for most SMEs. They are therefore locked into a particular bank for a long time. The result is very little competition between these four largest banks for the majority of small business customers.

The Competition Commission also found significant barriers to entry to the banking market, and especially to the market for 'liquidity management' services (i.e. the management of current accounts and overdraft facilities) and for general-purpose business loans. It recommended a reduction in barriers to entry to permit more competition within the industry. This could best be achieved by requiring banks to permit fast and error-free switching by SMEs to other banks (to enable SMEs to shop around for the best value in banking services) and either to pay interest on current account holdings or offer free banking services.

In May 2005 the Office of Fair Trading (OFT) referred the supply of current account banking services in Northern Ireland to the Competition Commission. This market is tightly concentrated and the OFT found that the banks impose a number of charges when customers are overdrawn, or in credit, that are not found in the rest of the UK. Furthermore, it found that there is limited switching by customers to other accounts and that firms do not actively compete on price. Indeed, the OFT indicated that there may be price leadership behaviour. However, since the situation was a perfect example of the damaging effects of oligopoly to the consumer if competitor collusion takes place, little could be done without resort to legislation, which the government it appears feared enacting.

SOURCE: JOHN SLOMAN 1995–2006
PEARSON EDUCATION

Postscript
It is interesting to note that the banking sector in the UK has been terribly badly hit by the financial and credit crisis that started in 2007. The profits of one of the largest four, RBS, have collapsed along with its share price. Another (Lloyds TSB) is now 50 per cent owned by the UK government.

2

Aircraft manufacture is a good example of such an oligopoly where Airbus Industrie (Europe) and Boeing (USA) need to keep a keen eye on each other's actions if they are to prosper. An effective understanding of the principles of game theory therefore becomes a critical skill of the strategist under oligopoly. They need to guess correctly what a rival's response to a price change will be, to understand when a new entrant should be accommodated rather than driven out and when a rival should be colluded with, either implicitly or explicitly, rather than fought in cut-throat fashion. Oligopoly is seen to have emerged out of monopolistic competition when competitors in a global market have become so few that their primary concerns become each other's actual and potential actions, rather than solely the changes in the market. In globalized markets oligopoly is less likely to come about than in more regionally or nationally protected markets, since the global market is large and in most industries many competitors emerge.

SUMMARY

- International trade has played a critically important role in the economic development of the world, and in the power relationships between nations.

- MNCs have developed to become larger than many countries in financial value. Dunning's eclectic OLI theory provides a rationale for this growth by explaining why FDI (the basis of MNCs) arises.

- Kogut's contrast of comparative advantage and competitive advantage explains how MNCs can succeed against local competition.

- Porter's industry structure analysis, 'diamond' framework, industry clusters and advanced factors of production, provide important tools to help analysts to assess global business opportunities.

- Much trade is not in conditions of perfect competition nowadays so Ricardo's comparative cost theory does not always apply, although factor costs and perfectly competitive commodities still obey the theory.

- Monopolistic competition theory explains international trade in branded goods where prices are administered and goods only imperfectly substitutable.

- Oligopoly also comes about where companies get so large and so few globally, that they become more concerned with each other's strategic moves than with the customer. Opportunities for price collusion exist in such circumstances.

DISCUSSION QUESTIONS

1 How do you explain the rise of the multinational corporation (MNC)?

2 What is Porter's diamond framework, and what are its implications for a company becoming global?

2

3 How is comparative cost theory to be distinguished from the theory of competitive advantage?

4 How is monopolistic competition different from oligopoly?

5 What is Dunning's eclectic theory and how useful is it?

6 How does Kogut approach the issue of achieving success in global competition?

FURTHER READINGS

1 Dunning, J.H. (2002) *Theories and Paradigms of International Business Activity: The Selected Essays of John H. Dunning.*

The core theory in the area of international business (IB) is the eclectic theory. It was first developed by Dunning. Known as OLI, it deals with the analysis of the multinational corporation (MNC) and provides an explanation for the development of these large global organizations. This book collects together much of his life's work.

2 Tallman, S. (2001) 'Global strategic management', in Hitt, M.A., Freeman, R.E. and Harrison, J.S. (eds) *Handbook of Strategic Management*, Oxford: Blackwell.

Tallman sees two key components at the root of global strategy: first, international expansion ('internationalization') which is about increasing presence in international locations and second, global integration ('globalization') which is about consolidating international markets and operations into a single worldwide strategic entity. He discusses the economic push for companies to move outside their home market and traces the historical development both of types of multinational firms and of multinational capabilities.

3 Chandler, A.D. (1990b) 'The enduring logic of industrial success', *Harvard Business Review*, March–April: 130–140.

Alfred Chandler was the greatest business historian. He died in 2007. This is the shortest, simplest and quickest way to acquire some of his vast knowledge of how industries and firms develop and survive long-term. It is a distillation of his other major theories on international expansion and the role of scale and scope in global competition.

CHAPTER 3

Globalization, anti-globalization and regionalization

LEARNING OBJECTIVES After reading this chapter you should be able to:

■ explain what is meant by the term globalization and its significance for countries, industries and companies

■ understand the nature and impact of the most significant drivers of globalization

■ appreciate the reasons for the rise of the anti-globalization movement and be able to evaluate the various aspects of the arguments it puts forward

■ explain the rise of regional trading blocs and understand their purpose, growth patterns and differences between various blocs

■ compare the growth of globalization with that of regionalization and consider to what extent these are complementary or mutually exclusive trends

■ explore under what circumstances global strategies or regional strategies are most appropriate for organizations.

INTRODUCTION

One of the most important influences both on world trade and the nature of international strategy has been the rapid rise of the process of globalization from the last quarter of the twentieth century onwards. This chapter will explore a number of issues concerning the nature of globalization and its causes. We will then discuss why globalization has generated such hostility and consider the reasons for this. Curiously, alongside the development of globalization there has also been a parallel trend – the formation of regional trading blocs. We need to understand the impact of **regionalization** on the formulation and implementation of international strategies and its consequences for the dynamic evolution of both industries and firms. Regionalization has its roots in political and economic factors, but these are different factors from those driving globalization.

Discussion will include the 'triad' and also the potential for not just three, but five, six or seven massive world trading blocs in the near future: an emerging 'hub-and-spoke' structure for international trade. Regionalization may be viewed as a stepping-stone on the way to full globalization, or as an entirely different construction of resources and trading partners and patterns. It is possible to make a case for globalization as the obsolete concept with regionalization emerging as the dominant form, rather than the other way round. It is equally possible for regional trading blocs to be viewed as problematic barriers to the further evolution of world trade.

WHAT IS GLOBALIZATION?

3

In this section we will be explaining the significance of globalization and its implications for both national and global strategy. The specific design and implementation of global strategies will be discussed in a later chapter.

The starting-point for understanding the much-discussed and overused concept of globalization is that in strategy terms *it is industries and markets that globalize, not countries.* Much of the general public discussion of globalization is based on such unclear assumptions. However, as a result of the global strategies of organizations (both commercial and not-for-profit (NFP)) which operate within global industries, greater linkages, interaction and interdependence build up between nations. When an industry globalizes it undergoes structural shifts, so the organizations within it find that their position in one country is significantly affected by their position in another country. That is part of the definition of a global industry. Similarly, the impact of global industries and global organizations on the countries in which they operate, inevitably creates stronger interconnectedness economically, with some (potential) social and political consequences. These issues will be returned to later.

To start to understand globalization as a concept and as a process, we need to be able to understand why and how it has occurred. We therefore need to begin by looking at what Yip (1996 and 2002) called the 'globalization drivers', that are its causes.

DRIVERS OF GLOBALIZATION

A variety of factors have been driving the spread of globalization across industries (i.e. producers or sellers) and markets (i.e. consumers or buyers). Although their impact and pace has varied according to type of industry, these drivers have been the dominant triggers for change from local to global (or at least regional) industry structures. Although the five drivers discussed here are by no means the only triggers for change, they do represent the most powerful general factors affecting most industries. They are:

- cultural homogenization

- economies of scale and scope

- technological developments

- deregulation and the lowering of trade barriers

- strong international competitors.

These will be discussed in turn.

Cultural homogenization
....

The argument concerning cultural homogenization suggests that national cultures that were very different are becoming less so as a consequence of such developments as increased international travel and global media and communication systems. Influences on consumption patterns include art, films, clothing, television programmes, the internet, ethnic foods and popular music. This has been instrumental in creating some discernible similarities between consumer tastes across geographical boundaries. This has resulted in the national markets that they represent, and hence the customers within those markets, buying similar products and similar services in most parts of the world. The term 'global village' is often used to discuss this phenomenon in which the world's population now shares commonly recognized cultural symbols. Cultural homogenization is seen as providing a global context and marketplace in which global brands such as Nokia mobile phones and Levi jeans become '**aspirational**' lifestyle symbols that are recognized worldwide within very different national cultures. The consequence of this for global strategy is that similar products and similar services can be sold to similar groups of customers in almost any country in the world. Cultural homogenization therefore implies the actual, or at least the potential, for the worldwide *convergence of markets* and the emergence of a global marketplace. One of the most influential early discussions of this trend was by Levitt (1983) who strongly supported this view of a global marketplace. Probably a more accurate approach to the cultural homogenization argument is one that treats the 'global village' view as unrealistic since national cultural diversity clearly continues strongly. Instead, the impact of cultural homogenization on the convergence of markets should be seen as resulting in the emergence of ***global market segments***. These are international groupings of consumers who can be found in all country markets with common needs and preferences, such as the 'business traveller' or the 'youth' market. They have more in common with their counterparts in other countries than they have with other market segments within their own country. The business traveller segment has been the basis of successfully targeted global services by airlines, car hire companies, hotel chains and financial service companies. The global youth segment targets products and services (such as clothing, music, consumer electronic items, TV programmes) at an age segment. Another age-related global market segment is babies since babies are a universally understood customer for universal products (e.g. disposable diapers (nappies)) that have a universal usage pattern. Indeed the global market for disposable diapers is worth about $6 billion, and it certainly fulfils a similar function for its customers in all markets worldwide. These all constitute specific global customer segments towards which companies can direct specific products or services worldwide.

In India for example, the market for consumer durables, once confined to a very small number of wealthy families, has grown at an unprecedented rate, reflecting the rise of a large middle class, now estimated to stand at approximately 20 per cent of a total population of over one billion. This means that a possible market of up to 200 million in India could afford to buy relatively sophisticated and expensive products. Demand for global brands in India now makes it an attractive market for companies which already trade on a global basis.

Strategy in Action 3.1 *A Muslim global market segment?*

An interesting recent emergent potential global market segment may be that for observant Muslims worldwide. There have been a number of start-ups of companies whose global strategies specifically target that customer group on the basis of common consumer preferences across different country markets in the various regions of the world. One obvious example is that of Mecca Cola founded in Paris as a competitor to Coca-Cola and Pepsi Cola for Muslim customers. Mecca Cola's marketing is based on opposition to the commercial dominance of US multinationals and a commitment to give 10 per cent of the price of each bottle or can to support the cause of Palestine. It is now selling in 140 countries.

SOURCE: COMPILED BY AUTHORS FROM PRESS ARTICLES

3

Economies of scale and scope

Economies of scale and economies of scope exist increasingly in more and more industries. The relationship between the availability of **scale** or **scope economies** and the globalization of industries is that in more and more industries, size matters in determining competitive levels of efficiency. A straightforward example of an industry with significant scale and scope economies is the world car industry. Most car companies use similar engines and gearboxes across their entire product range so that the same engines or gearboxes are placed in different models of cars. This generates enormous potential cost savings for such companies as Honda (Japan), Ford (US) or Volkswagen (Germany). It provides for both scale economies (decreased cost per unit of output) from producing a larger absolute volume of engines or gearboxes, and scope economies (re-using a resource from one business in additional businesses) from utilizing the same component over again in more and more models. It is not surprising therefore that the car industry has experienced a wave of merger and acquisition activity largely aimed at creating larger world car companies of sufficient size to benefit from these factors.

Technological developments

Technological development and change operates across international borders and has no geographic boundaries. It is probably one of the strongest drivers of the globalization of industries. Technological development includes the impact of information and communication technologies (ICT), product and process innovations, changes in distribution channels such as web-based selling, internet search and information retrieval and so on. These have had an enormous impact. In some cases entire new industries have been created such as mobile telephony which could not have existed without the development of the ICT which makes it possible. Technological development may also transform traditional industries such as financial services, which have been around for centuries. For example, selling insurance policies or bank loans via the internet is part of the revolution that technological innovation has triggered in the way in which we buy and get information about financial and other services.

Deregulation

What is meant by deregulation is the removal of historic barriers, both tariff (such as import taxes) and non-tariff (such as safety regulations), which have constituted barriers to trade across national boundaries. Deregulation has occurred at all levels: national, regional (within regional trading blocs) and

Strategy in Action 3.2 *The flowering of international logistics*

The restructuring of international supply chains for transportation and distribution has created opportunities for rethinking international logistics operations. Cost reductions, shorter journey times and dramatic technological developments in transportation, have together created new international markets for products which previously had no shelf-life beyond local consumption. Container systems which use computer-controlled temperature, humidity and atmosphere levels have extended the geographic scope for such products as fresh fruit or flowers, just as surely as international information systems have created 24-hour trading on eBay.

international. In Europe, deregulation is most familiar in the context of the European Union (EU). The removal of barriers to the free movement of goods, capital and labour within the EU was embodied in the 1992 Single Market Act. Its purpose was to reduce the barriers to mobility of people, goods, services and finance across member countries of the EU. Similar objectives exist in NAFTA (the North American Free Trade Association between Canada, the United States and Mexico created in 1989). Thus deregulation and the removal of trade barriers encourage globalization since they reduce the time, costs and administrative complexity involved in trading across national borders.

Strong international competitors

Another aspect of a global competitive environment is that it is increasingly difficult to evaluate competition in national terms. 'National champions' may not be significant in international terms. This means that one has to think about global competition quite differently from national competition. It is part of a different industry structure. In a national industry, if all firms are equally inefficient they can nevertheless survive and do reasonably well. However, once that industry has become a **global industry**, if one firm restructures to benefit from potential global economies of scale and scope, the available sources of global competitive advantage makes it very difficult for the others to continue to compete effectively (Kogut, 1985a). Therefore, as soon as one firm globalizes in an industry, the other firms are likely to follow suit or suffer competitive disadvantages. This explains the waves of successive concentration in many industries, such as aircraft manufacturing, energy or pharmaceuticals, as global competition replaces local competition and MNCs need broader resources and markets to continue to compete strongly with fewer, larger competitors worldwide.

Strategy in Action 3.3 'Selling books in China' should provide an illustration of applying the five globalization drivers we have just discussed.

If we consider each of the five globalization drivers in turn, we can understand a little better how they may work in practice in a particular situation, that is book-selling in China.

Cultural homogenization has made both the product (access to a greater range of books and access to foreign books) and the service delivery channel (online) acceptable and of interest to a growing proportion of Chinese customers. There is clearly in general terms a market segment in China for foreign books and online delivery channels.

Economies of scale and scope are obtained for example by having two-thirds of customers concentrated in 12 major cities (distribution scale economies), using the same distribution channel for sale of CDs and DVDs (distribution scope economies), 50 million potential online customers and a database of 210,000 titles (scale), as well as cross-selling additional items to the same customers (scope).

Technological developments: the Dangdang business model would have been impossible in the first place without the development of the internet and of database management software. As online security and payment systems develop further, this too will help Dangdang.

Deregulation and the lowering of trade barriers have occurred gradually in China throughout the 1990s. The terms of trade offered to foreign companies in the China market have been improving although the requirements placed upon foreign firms are still heavy. China's membership of the World Trade Organization (WTO) since 2001 is also helpful in signalling a likely continuous relaxation of barriers to trade. Before the 1990s the availability and importing of foreign books was very difficult and at some periods was banned. Ms Yu herself represents part of a steady return of migrants to China as economic opportunities and conditions for trade have opened up.

Strong international competitors have been allowed to enter the Chinese market as the political and economic climates have changed in the past decade. Although terms of trade are variable by region and have fluctuated as political conditions have fluctuated, the situation that existed before the 1990s was that the only organizations in most industries were the Chinese state-owned enterprises (SOEs).

Edinburgh Napier University Library

3

Strategy in Action 3.3 *Selling books in China*

Peggy Yu and her husband Li Guoqing are the co-founders of China's biggest on-line bookseller Dangdang.com. Ms Yu moved back to Beijing from New York in 1997. While in the US, she had completed an MBA and worked as a management consultant. During this period in the 1990s she saw the rise of Amazon.com and decided to return to China to set up a similar venture back home. Transferring Amazon's business model to China required skill and effort. For example, one of Amazon's key resources is its huge, searchable database of titles. Whereas Amazon licensed this from book wholesalers in the US, China had no such comparable nationwide database. It took Ms Yu and Mr Li two years to build their own, which now covers 210,000 titles compared with the 15,000 available in a typical Chinese bookshop. The Internet was also slower to take off in China. When Ms Yu first had her idea, in 1996, there were only a few hundred thousand online users in China. By the time Dangdang was launched in 1999, this had grown to more than 3 million. It has now grown to over 60 million.

Despite an 86 per cent literacy rate, China has only 77,000 bookshops, with sales in 2002 of 43 billion yuan (approximately $5.2 billion), compared to $40 billion book sales in the US, which has only one-fifth of China's population. There is clearly much potential for growth. Over 7,000 of China's bookshops are part of the state-owned Xinhua news agency. They stock only a limited range of titles, with few foreign books. In more remote parts of rural China there are often no stores at all. Dangdang has experienced enormous demand for Western books, particularly self-improvement books. Two of their best-selling titles have been 'Seven Habits of Highly Effective People' and the autobiography of Jack Welch (retired CEO of GE). By 2003 Dangdang was taking 4,000 orders a day and more than half of these are for CDs and DVDs. Sales are doubling annually.

Ms Yu encourages her 140 employees to order from Amazon's website to get ideas for enhancing her own (e.g. customer wish-lists). She also uses other US firms as role models, in particular Wal-Mart (retailer) for its low costs and UPS (logistics) for its sophisticated supply chain capability.

China had no pre-existing mail order industry, so Dangdang had to build trust for entirely new ways of both distribution and payment. Chinese customers were not accustomed to paying for delivery or to paying in advance. In addition the Chinese credit card market is not yet very developed so that only 10–15 per cent of Dangdang's customers use them. Two-thirds of the business therefore is cash-on-delivery and is concentrated in 12 major cities where the books are delivered by freelance couriers. Ms Yu comments: 'Bicycle boys are the last leg of e-business in China'.

Meanwhile the gradual deregulation of China's book market has encouraged foreign publishers to enter the market. Bertelsmann of Germany already runs a book club in China and its Bol.com subsidiary is number three online after Dangdang and Joyo.com.

SOURCE: ADAPTED FROM *THE ECONOMIST* 23 AUGUST 2003

Now both foreign and domestic competitors co-exist in the Chinese domestic market in most sectors, including book retailing.

As globalization has grown in more and more industries and had a great impact on the structure of local markets around the world, so increasingly criticism and opposition to this process has grown also. We will now discuss this opposition to globalization and its effects.

Globalization or regionalization?
....

Globalization is reversible. The spread of globalization has been driven by technological development and deregulation: it can be blocked in the same ways. As well as the anti-globalization movement, there are two other major factors that are potential strong anti-globalization drivers: regionalism and protectionism. We discuss these next and suggest that in many ways *regionalization* may be the more important international trend.

THE ANTI-GLOBALIZATION MOVEMENT

Anti-globalization pressure groups criticize the impact of globalization on economic growth, on 'free' trade, on trade and wages, on unemployment and the 'exporting' of jobs, on the environment, on the role of multinationals, on intellectual property, on migration and on cultural imperialism.

The most visible part of this widespread critical movement against globalization was born in Seattle, US, in 1999 when street protests, marches and mass demonstrations occurred involving tens of thousands of protestors and massed ranks of police. The events in Seattle seemed to be both the birth of, and the high point of, the mass movement 'against global capitalism and against corporate-led globalization'. The protests in Seattle were directed against the meeting there in November 1999 of the ministers of the WTO and continued against the spring meetings of the World Bank and the International Monetary Fund (IMF) in April 2000. The WTO and IMF are particularly targeted as servants of 'the global capitalist order'. Since 2000, such protests have gradually declined in size and in degrees of violence. Indeed the violence occurring in many such protests, including street battles between protestors and riot police and the smashing of shop windows, may itself have discouraged some of the wide range of interest groups represented, and led them to express their views in other ways.

The anti-capitalist protest movement is made up of an extremely diverse set of groups often with very different, sometimes contradictory, agendas. Nevertheless at its most effective it has been influential in broadening awareness, policy and behaviour in corporate social responsibility (CSR) by MNCs. As a movement it has created a momentum of change in some areas such as anti-'**sweatshop**' campaigns which have united student groups, non-governmental organizations (NGOs) and trade unions to put pressure on clothing importers such as the US global retail group The Gap and US sportswear manufacturer Nike, to improve working conditions in developing economies where many of their production facilities are based. There have been positive (impact on CSR policy and practice) as well as negative (ritual confrontations and some violence) effects arising from this conflict between the conservative economic and political institutions and their radical social and political critics. Recently however, the issue of *accountability* has become part of the debate. This issue of accountability concerns the basis of legitimacy of some NGOs since many NGOs are unelected, self-selecting bodies, exerting pressure on representative, often elected, and certainly accountable, governments, institutions and other public bodies. This is part of the tension between the various groups of worldwide stakeholders involved in how the pressures for, and the institutions of, globalization, are evolving.

We will now discuss a few of the most frequent criticisms of globalization. (For lengthier discussions about globalization see Micklethwait and Wooldridge, 2000; Stiglitz, 2002; Giddens, 2000; Wolf, 2004; Bhagwati, 2004.)

Geography no longer matters
....

Ohmae (1990a) argued that in a global world, that is one without national ties, geography no longer matters because business has become 'borderless'. However, this perspective has severe limitations.

Simply consider transport costs. If transport costs are a high proportion of costs in an industry it is unlikely to become global and more likely to remain a local industry. Equally significant in the continuing relevance of geography to world business are the groupings of 'industry clusters' (Porter, 1998) which were discussed earlier in Chapter 2. Clusters are formed from sets of skills, resources and experience effects which are not be found elsewhere in the world, that cannot easily be recreated or imitated elsewhere and that are location-specific.

Porter's (1998) conviction that domestic industry conditions are critical to international success is in sharp contrast with that of Ohmae (1990a), who believes that national roots must be left behind to be internationally successful. Where Porter talks about understanding the strengths of the national 'diamond' as the springboard for international competitiveness, Ohmae talks about a 'borderless' world in which nations have become less important to companies, whether as home bases or as sources of identity.

Both agree that companies emerge from national origins that establish their competitiveness. The difference lies in global strategy and the characteristics of a successful global firm: Ohmae argues that it should shake off its origins; Porter thinks it must preserve them. Ohmae criticizes MNCs for *'nearsightedness'*, that is being dominated by their parent headquarters, who give too much weight to the views of its domestic customers. Ohmae insists that global managers must act as if equidistant from all customers, wherever they may be. He calls this becoming an *'insider'* in all markets, rather than an outsider; 'true insiders' are honorary citizens perceived as direct investors in each 'home' market in which they operate. With an 'insider' mindset, managers will be free of the standardizing force of headquarters.

Porter argues that global strategy builds on local roots. He sees the continuous enhancements of comparative local factor endowments as the basis of distinctive capabilities and the source of dynamic (i.e. sustainable) long-term advantage. He sees a global strategy as supplementing the competitive advantage created at home base and argues that companies need to retain those elements when they expand abroad. For Porter, global firms like Nestlé, Sony or IBM operate throughout the world, but each firm's character and competitiveness remain Swiss, Japanese and American.

Strategy in Action 3.4 *Becoming 'borderless'*

To establish itself as what Ohmae (1990a) calls a 'truly global' company, HSBC shook off its Asian history and roots as the Hong Kong & Shanghai Banking Corporation and decided to use its HSBC global brand and logo on all its local operations in more than 150 countries around the world. As it acquired local domestic banks, it re-branded them as HSBC. It wanted a truly global identity, not a patchwork of local ones. Furthermore, it created an internal group of highly mobile 'international managers' who lived for two or three years at a time in non-home base countries and continued in this career pattern for most of their career with the bank.

Another useful comparison is between the French hotel and leisure groups Club Med and the Accor Group. Club Med deliberately keeps its French identity (e.g. its 'gentils organisateurs' (GOs) in each holiday camp around the world, who provide leisure activities for guests). By contrast, the Accor Group of France, which is one of the world's biggest hotel groups operating in 140 countries, insists on a '2 by 2 by 2' promotion policy within the group. This insists that in order to be promoted, its managers must speak at least two languages, and have worked in at least two countries and in two different hotel groups within the Accor chain.

SOURCE: AUTHORS

In the earlier discussion of national industry 'clusters' in Chapter 2 it is the concentration of complex expertise in a specific geographic area that is significant. Well-known examples of such strong industry clusters have already been given in Chapter 2 but they include:

- the design, fashion and luxury goods industry cluster around Milan, Italy

- the motor sport cluster (Formula One production teams) (UK M40 corridor)

- the motion picture industry clusters of Bollywood (India) and Hollywood (US)

- the computer software industry clusters of Bangalore (India) and California (US).

In his research on the sources of national and international competitiveness, Porter (1990 and 1998) argues that despite global sourcing, and global transport and communications infrastructures, *location still matters*. If he is right, then in order to establish global competitive advantage, the strategies of firms and the pattern of the country's comparative advantage need to complement each other and will be linked. Therefore firms in particular industries are more likely to be successful in some countries rather than others and therefore *geography matters*.

Another version of this debate that geography no longer matters in a globalized world can be found in comparing the more recent views of Thomas Friedman in his aptly named book *The World is Flat* (2005), with the views of Pankaj Ghemawat as discussed in his HBR article 'Distance still matters' (2001). Their respective views are obvious from the titles. Friedman's argument proposes the death of distance and a 'flattening' of the world resulting from the impact of advanced technologies on the rapid communication of knowledge and ideas all over the world. Such connectivity, he argues, has created a level playing field of much more equal competitors in world trade. This wired world means that everyone and everything is next door even if they are on the other side of the world. (We will return to these ideas in Chapter 5 on the information industries.) For Ghemawat, this argument that 'global communications are shrinking the world, turning it into a small and relatively homogeneous place ... when it comes to business that's not only an incorrect assumption, it's a dangerous one' (2001: 138). He provides detailed evidence of cultural, administrative, geographic and economic differences that impact greatly on industries and countries, and which must be part of our understanding of what the limits of globalization actually are.

Big firms always win

Small and medium enterprises (SMEs) have lower fixed costs and are known for being flexible and having faster response times than large organizations. They can now use the web and internet channels to get a lot of the purchasing economies of scale available to big firms simply by accessing suppliers via the web anywhere in the world. One must also question the assumption that big firms are always efficient. Many big firms become inefficient and inflexible and gradually die. Many MNC mergers and acquisitions fail; many diversification strategies are poorly conceived and poorly implemented. The acquisition by Germany's Daimler Benz of the US car firm Chrysler Motors, although intended to create a new global champion, is widely regarded as a commercial disaster. Instead of one jointly stronger firm, a much-weakened Daimler Benz has been struggling for a solution to the problems of its Chrysler acquisition, which it has taken several years and huge resources to begin to turn around. The bigger firm is also in a much weaker position in facing the very serious problems of the world car industry arising from global recession in the mid-2000s onwards. Big winners can become big losers very quickly.

Globalization is a zero-sum game

This issue summarizes probably the most powerful negative viewpoint of globalization. If globalization is indeed a zero-sum game it would mean that for some people to benefit from globalization, others

3

must lose. By implication it also suggests that there is no such thing as fair trade, only the exploitation of one country or one group of people by another. This viewpoint was summarized in the late 1980s at the time the North American Free Trade Agreement (NAFTA) was being negotiated between the United States, Canada and Mexico, by a presidential candidate in the US. In his election broadcasts, this candidate (Ross Perot) used the phrase 'a great sucking sound' by which he meant to describe the great loss of high-paid American jobs across the US/Mexico border into cheap low-wage Mexico. For that reason, NAFTA sparked massive political opposition, particularly from US trade unions attempting to protect US jobs. In fact, subsequent to the implementation of NAFTA in 1989, Mexican wages have risen by 30 per cent. They are still not the same as American wages, but they have risen and significant job creation has occurred on the Mexico / US border, accompanied by very modest job loss within America, mainly confined to lower-level jobs. It should also be remembered that wages and productivity are different things. Lower labour costs are not the only reason, or even the main reason, why companies decide where to invest. They are much more interested in productivity. The productivity of American workers is much higher than that of Mexican workers because they have much higher rates of investment per job, in education, in infrastructure and in production process. The same contrast can be made between German workers and UK workers in Europe. German productivity has historically been higher than in the UK largely because German companies over the years have invested more heavily than have UK companies. The same debate has occurred around the continuous rise in outsourcing, and particularly in **offshoring** which is defined as outsourcing which takes place in another country. There has been massive growth in off-shoring as IT-related jobs migrated from higher-cost developed economies to lower-cost economies. India, Pakistan (and some Eastern European countries) have become the centre of off-shoring of white-collar technology-related jobs. This has created enormous pressure on developed economy governments to legislate against 'international outsourcing'. Despite this, consumers benefit worldwide from such lowered costs (Farrell, 2006).

Global winners and losers can be created by the policies of national governments. Strategy in Action 3.5 'NAFTA and China' indicates some reasons why growth may be slowing in Mexico, just as it is speeding up in China at least partly as a result of government policy.

Mexico had based its economic growth on two things: cheap labour and location (i.e. next door to the US market). Membership of NAFTA was what allowed Mexico to exploit the location advantage since it created a free trade area with the US and Canada and therefore lowered transaction costs greatly. These were genuine sources of comparative advantage for Mexico. But both advantages have now been eroded by different things. 'Cheap' labour is always *relative* and will inevitably change over time. That is a positive outcome of economic growth, since growth raises national prosperity and standards of living and expectations about rates of pay, which always rise with rising prosperity. The difficulty is that growth therefore requires developed economies to shift continuously into higher value-added sectors and jobs, leaving the lower value-added for developing economies.

In India currently, and more recently in Pakistan, information-technology-based exports are booming. One of the reasons for this is that the technology and software industries in India have a very highly skilled workforce, together with a very high number of graduates in all of the software engineering areas that companies require. However, these skilled graduates cost less than one-tenth of their equivalent from a Californian university in the US. On one level this is exploitation of a much cheaper workforce that is also a very highly skilled workforce. However, such exploitation opportunities will be temporary. Workers' wages in India are rising rapidly to world levels, as has happened rapidly elsewhere as economies have developed. Indeed, in the 1950s and 1960s Japan was a cheap labour economy, as were we all at different times in our histories; but by the 1980s onwards, Japanese labour was among the world's most expensive and with one of the world's highest standards of living. We consider this evidence that globalization is not a zero-sum game.

3

Strategy in Action 3.5 *NAFTA and China*

Since 2001, when China joined the WTO, it has become clear that China is now the favourite destination for the labour-intensive manufacturing that Mexico has specialized in for the past thirty years. Since the mid-1990s, the manufacturing plants of the Northern Mexican states have been an engine of Mexico's rapid economic growth. However, with the downturn of the US economy, to which Mexico is closely linked through NAFTA, Mexico is suffering. Is the Mexican downturn cyclical or structural? If cyclical, it will correct itself when the US eventually moves back into growth. If structural, it will not. Pessimists note that China is about to overtake Mexico as the next largest trading partner with the US, after Canada. The reason is simple. China's labour costs are approximately one-quarter of Mexico's. About 300 manufacturing plants have moved from Mexico to China since 2001. Plants that remain in Mexico have cut wages.

Optimists note that FDI in Mexico is still high and it still ranks second (after India) as an attractive location for back-office outsourcing. Its location (next to the US huge domestic market) is still important. US companies have often found it easier to deal with Mexico's English-speaking, American-educated managers than with managers in China. Some firms have indeed returned to Mexico after unhappy experiences in China.

Pessimists note that Mexico's traditional advantages are disappearing. Not only is Mexican labour being undercut but also, now that China has joined the WTO, it too has direct access to the American market. However, the real problem is that Mexico has done little to counteract the erosion of its sources of comparative advantage by dealing with its growing competitive disadvantages. Its energy and telecommunications costs are artificially high due to state monopolies or semi-monopolies and its transport infrastructure is so bad that it almost cancels out the additional transportation costs from China.

Mexico is sliding steadily down the international league tables of competitiveness. With an income of $6,000 per capita, Mexico is no longer a poor country. Therefore it is not surprising that low-wage jobs should move elsewhere. The more serious problem is that because of the low skills of its workforce, Mexico is not well placed to replace those jobs with better jobs. Mexico is already behind China in its efforts to attract higher-value manufacturing. Mexico produces far fewer graduate engineers than China and has a poor IT training record. Therefore, Mexico now combines relatively high costs with relatively low skills.

SOURCE: VARIOUS PRESS ARTICLES

Mexico's second key source of comparative advantage was location-based. Although that physical location has not changed, its value has been reduced considerably by China's entry into the WTO, since that allows it access to the markets of other WTO members of which the US is obviously one.

It is important to learn that few sources of comparative or competitive advantage are absolute. By now in its development trajectory, Mexico should be much further along the development road than it actually is. Much of the blame for that falls on poor government policy. What has enabled India and Pakistan to develop their higher-level IT-sector jobs, is the quality of their education systems, particularly their higher education. Education and transport infrastructure require direct government investment over the long term, which has not been forthcoming in Mexico.

Sometimes it is national government policy, not global pressures that affect the international context in which organizations have to develop their strategies.

3

Winners and losers
·······························

The zero-sum argument implies winners and losers from globalization. Usually it is assumed that the winners are in the developed economies and the losers in the developing economies. The reality is far less clear-cut. There are also significant numbers of 'losers' from many declining industries in the developed economies such as mining, steel production, agriculture or shipbuilding. It is for this reason that some developed economies (e.g. France within the EU) have continued to fight for agricultural subsidies to protect their own jobs and farming communities. Employment in these industries has been just as affected by globalization as groups in poorer countries. Less well understood, and certainly less well publicized, is the extent to which trading opportunities are denied to third world economies as a result of *not enough globalization* of world trade rather than too much. For example the rich world still keeps many high trade barriers against the poorer world, in which category the EU Common Agricultural Policy (CAP) is still a major problem. Reform of CAP, with its depressing effect on international trade in agriculture, the sector where many developing countries have most of their resources and output, would be of immense assistance to the poor world. There were modest signs of optimism that following the WTO 2001 meeting in Doha which established the 'Doha Round' of world trade negotiations and some positive steps in Geneva WTO negotiations in 2004. However, the possibility of such reform looks no nearer, with vested interests on all sides fighting against it. The last round of Doha negotiations failed in 2008 due to entrenched attitudes within key sets of participants from both the developed and the developing economies.

The 'race to the bottom'
·······························

The strongest criticisms accuse global firms of engineering the exploitation of workers and the environment, of widening inequalities and disparities around the world and of using the developing economies as a dumping ground for products and processes no longer acceptable in the richer world. The popular phrase for this process accuses global firms of creating a 'race to the bottom'. Global MNCs are accused of playing off governments and workforces against each other in a battle for the lowest wages and the lowest costs. That is what strategic management and economic concepts define as the search by MNCs for sources of competitive advantage from national comparative advantage. Much of the argument for and against globalization resolves itself into considering these issues around comparative advantage in economic terms and in social terms: efficiency for global firms translates into exploitation by the critics of those firms.

Global MNCs are responding to the drivers of globalization. Failure to respond is not the answer. Philips, the Dutch consumer electronics MNC, has always strongly pursued a policy of home economy employment to provide high levels of well-paid jobs in its home base in the Netherlands. This policy proved increasingly expensive both in absolute terms and, more importantly, in relative terms compared to the comparable cost structures of their major rivals, the Japanese and Korean consumer electronic giants such as Sony, Panasonic or LG. Eventually Philips had to abandon this policy, not because they were an exploitative firm but for the reverse reason. The home employment policy was putting the future competitiveness of the firm at risk and potentially the remaining jobs at Philips. There are two sides to this issue: producers (seen as exploited) and consumers (happily buying these cheap products). It is therefore also important to recognize the paradox that rich-economy consumers seek high quality at lowest cost in their purchasing behaviour (e.g. T-shirts and shoes made in China and Taiwan, not Europe) which is precisely what makes low-skilled rich-economy jobs unsustainable.

Large national differences in wage rates and living standards exist *within* Europe, as well as between Europe and the developing economies of Asia and Africa. By broadening its membership to twenty-five in 2004 and a future proposed twenty-nine, the EU is responding politically and institutionally to the race to

TABLE 3.1	Time needed for new members to reach the average income per person in old EU15 countries	
Countries	*Average annual GDP growth per person (%)*	*Years to catch up*
Bulgaria	3.8	63
Czech Republic	3.7	39
Estonia	4.8	31
Hungary	4.0	34
Latvia	3.9	58
Lithuania	3.8	53
Poland	3.8	59
Romania	3.8	80
Slovakia	4.0	38
Slovenia	3.2	31
Average years		56

Source: The Economist Survey of EU Enlargement *22 November 2003; Economist Intelligence Unit (EIU)* 'Europe Enlarged; Understanding the Impact'

the bottom. Extending regional boundaries or removing some of the national barriers to migration forms part of redressing the relative inequalities. The US and Mexico in NAFTA, or East and West Germany on reunification, have tried to develop their economies jointly to try to address political, economic and social inequalities and create opportunities for shared standards of living over time. As Table 3.1 shows, this will take time, with an average of 56 years over the ten newer EU members. Shared worldwide political values, shared worldwide standards of living and shared worldwide life expectancy do not exist.

Are such inequalities by definition only part of the globalization process or only exacerbated by globalization? We would argue not, since such inequalities exist at regional levels also. We discuss regional issues next.

THE RISE OF REGIONAL TRADING BLOCS

Regionalization is the grouping of countries into regional clusters based on geographic proximity. These regional clusters have formed regional trading blocs or free trade areas (FTAs), albeit at varying speeds and with varying sophistication of regulatory and institutional structures.

'The Triad'

Regional strategies are of increasing significance for multinational firms planning their international strategies. Thinking about regional strategy has developed from observation of the gradual evolution of trading blocs in the world's most economically developed regions: Europe, Asia and North America. These three

3

regions were labelled '**the Triad**', by Kenichi Ohmae (1985) and are illustrated in Figure 3.1. Most discussions about world trade and regional trade accept the existence of the triad as a fact and many aspects of the internal management practices of MNCs reflect this. For example, many MNCs employ international executives who are expected to relocate between, and feel equally at home operating within, any of the three major regional trading blocs of the triad. Some MNCs such as SKF, the Swedish world leader in bearings manufacture, conducts its internal financial reporting in three world currency zones reflecting the triad trading zones, denominated in dollars, yen and euro.

As far as major FTA groupings are concerned, in addition to the EU and NAFTA, there are also two in Asia, APEC (Asia-Pacific Economic Community) and ASEAN (Association of South-East Asian Nations) and two in South America (Mercosur and the Andean Pact). There is also a proliferation of informal trading agreements and FTAs in many parts of the world including Africa and the Middle East. The US has also actively pursued the creation of an FTAA, a Free Trade Association of all the Americas, and north, south and central and American presidents often attend meetings of APEC and ASEAN – reflecting the Pacific coast border of the USA.

This formation of the majority of the world's economies into trading blocs may represent a significant blockage to globalization since regional trade is often seen as incompatible with global or world trade.

Trade barriers that are removed from individual countries are simply reproduced for a region and a set of countries. Thus all trading blocs create outsiders as well as insiders. This does nothing for the countries that are generally seen as the global losers. Global 'loser' regions like Africa are outside the major blocs and likely to remain so. For this reason globalization is likely to be a more constructive trend for world trade than regionalization, in which protectionism reappears around

FIGURE 3.1   '**The Triad**'

From Global to Regional

"THE TRIAD"

NORTH AMERICA

ASIA PACIFIC   EUROPE

The rise of intra-regional trade

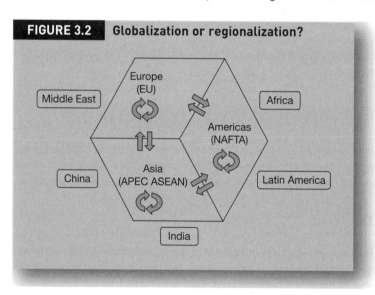

FIGURE 3.2   **Globalization or regionalization?**

Middle East

Europe (EU)

Africa

Americas (NAFTA)

China

Asia (APEC ASEAN)

Latin America

India

regions rather than around individual countries. Figure 3.2 allows regionalism and protectionism to be considered together. It is a diagrammatic representation of regionalization: a parallel trend to that of globalization, but one that is less discussed and whose consequences are less recognized.

Strategy in Action 3.6 describes some of the issues affecting the international trade in agriculture. It should help you think about whether the problems it describes with international trade in agriculture are a global issue or a regional one.

Our view is that the problems are both global and regional. In fact it illustrates the weaknesses in approaching international trade and competition issues from only a global perspective or only a regional one. At the moment, the powerful 'triad' regional blocs are acting in perceived self-interest and in response to pressure from powerful internal pressure groups (e.g. subsidized farmers and cotton growers). Even within these regional groupings their actions and policies (e.g. the CAP) are keeping prices for food artificially higher than they would otherwise be and therefore these policies are not cost-free since their own consumers are paying higher prices. In global trade terms, these policies ignore comparative advantage and also absolute cost advantage. In other words, resources are being wasted. Not only is this inefficient in economic terms, it is also disastrous in world social and political terms.

Strategy in Action 3.6 *International trade in agriculture*

In July 2004, the WTO met in Geneva to discuss potential further liberalization of world trade. Not surprisingly, much time was spent on agriculture. To understand the importance of reaching some agreement on agriculture in world trade, consider the following: the average person in sub-Saharan Africa earns less than $1 per day; the average cow in the EU earned around $2.20 per day in subsidies from Brussels Common Agricultural Policy (CAP). Not surprisingly, European farmers, led by the French farmers lobby, who benefit significantly from the EU's protectionist and subsidized CAP, always bitterly oppose trade talks. Some groups therefore hoped that the current Doha round of talks would fail – as they duly have.

Equally unsurprisingly, developing countries, whose economies are most dependent on agriculture, are desperate to achieve greater access to the developed economies for their farm products. However, developing countries are less enthusiastic about freer trade in manufactured goods. It is the tension between these two issues that has caused the complete collapse of previous major rounds of talks. Unfortunately, such

lack of progress harms the developing economies more than the developed ones.

Pascal Lamy, the then EU trade commissioner, agreed in 2004 to eliminate agricultural export subsidies, providing the US and other countries also eliminate theirs. Altogether, rich countries spend $300 billion on agricultural subsidies every year. That is equivalent to sub-Saharan Africa's entire economic output. According to Oxfam (a UK NGO), the US pays out about $3.9 billion to its 25,000 cotton farmers every year. That drives down prices for such countries as Chad, Benin, Mali and Burkano Faso, whose economies depend on cotton exports.

If all such subsidies were abolished, inefficient US producers would be driven out of business and African countries with a comparative advantage in cotton production could supply consumers instead.

However beneficial such outcomes, the underlying problems are political, rather than economic, with all countries (and governments) perceiving decisions affecting trade barriers as 'concessions'. In 2009, still no agreement on abolition of such subsidies has been achieved.

SOURCE: VARIOUS PRESS ARTICLES

3

GLOBALIZATION OR REGIONALIZATION

The 'triad' (EU, NAFTA, Asia-Pacific) regional trading blocs already exist. However, the potential exists for not three, but five, six or seven massive world trading blocs in the near future, with the giant economies of China and India constituting trading blocs in their own right. China certainly does not fit comfortably into ASEAN or APEC.

Advantages accruing from international trading agreements include overall growth in international trade and political stability, policed by the WTO, the successor to the General Agreement on Tariffs and Trade (GATT). Moves towards the liberalization of international trade have gone hand-in-hand with this formation into larger and larger, and more and more, regional trading blocs. These two issues, growth in international trade and increased political stability, are linked.

The EU has expanded from its original six members after the end of World War Two, to fourteen member countries by 1998 and twenty-five members in 2004. The most recent members joining in 2004 (such as Poland, the Czech Republic, Slovenia) have come mainly from Eastern Europe and included many former Soviet bloc states. Such broadening of EU membership is seen as one way of contributing to the stable adjustment and development of the post-USSR, post-Soviet bloc economies and hence the overall long-term stability of Europe as a whole. Applications for membership still being negotiated include that of Turkey, which would be the first Muslim country to join the EU. There are strong feelings aroused by Turkey's membership negotiations, both for and against. Support for Turkey to join the EU espouses the argument of increased regional political stability through expanded membership provided by shared growth and shared political and economic institutions. Opposition to Turkey's membership expresses concern that it would provide a gateway for cheap labour and even for terrorists via its Middle Eastern borders.

An enlarged NAFTA (currently the US, Mexico and Canada) may well gradually extend to include much of Central and South America. Already many trading agreements are in place in South America, such as the Andean pact between Venezuela, Colombia and Bolivia, or the Mercosur Free Trade Association (FTA) between Brazil, Argentina, Uruguay and Paraguay. Since 1987, the US has signed sixteen 'framework' agreements with Latin American countries. The groundwork exists for a Pan-American trading bloc embracing all the Americas: North America, South America and Central America. A Free Trade Area of the Americas (FTAA) has outline agreement between 34 countries in North and South America. Such a grouping would certainly contribute greatly to political stability across that geographic zone, which in itself would be likely to encourage a follow-on increase in investment and levels of trade. Indeed, by comparison with the 1970s when South America was mainly ruled by military dictatorships and its national economies suffered from hyperinflation, instability and debt, Mercosur is now the world's fourth largest integrated market and a child of the democratic governments now in place in its member countries. In Brazil, it has one of the world's fastest growing economies, as well as oil-rich Venezuela, and it has attracted steady inward investment from corporate and private investors with high but acceptable levels of risk. Mercosur has a (mostly) internal tariff-free zone between members and is some way to creating an integrated external customs union for 'outsiders'.

At least as important as the formation of small or larger groupings is whether such groupings actually implement the trade policy agreements they have signed (see Strategy in Action 3.7).

This discussion of regional trading blocs has focused mainly on the three largest and best-established triad blocs (NAFTA, EU and Asia-Pacific) with some attention to developments in South America. In addition to the three major existing triad regional trading blocs (and as indicated in Figure 3.2 'Globalization or regionalization'). In terms of sheer size and potential, China and India now already constitute regional trading blocs of their own. Each market has the potential to dominate world trade within ten or twenty years. It makes little sense to consider a future China as a member of the Asian regional groupings. There

3

SOURCE: *THE ECONOMIST*, 31 JULY 2004

Strategy in Action 3.7 *Free trade in South-East Asia*

The ASEAN free trade area (AFTA) covers the ten countries of ASEAN. In 2004 it planned to expand from the original six members (Brunei, Indonesia, Malaysia, the Philippines, Singapore and Thailand) to include Cambodia, Laos, Myanmar and Vietnam. The original six have reduced their tariffs on one another's goods to a maximum of 5 per cent and they plan to tackle non-tariff barriers and to expand into new areas such as investment. They also hope to conclude collective bilateral agreements between ASEAN and India, China and Japan. The ASEAN secretariat in Jakarta says trade amongst its members roughly doubled in the decade from 1993 to 2003.

However, ASEAN's trade with the rest of the world has grown just as fast as among its members, while trade with China has grown much faster and more consistently. Within ASEAN, growth has been patchy. Indeed examining internal processes within AFTA shows things are not quite working as planned. Several members failed to lower tariffs on certain critical products. For example, Malaysia has retained protective tariffs in support of its state-owned car

manufacturer Proton, which affects potential markets for Thailand's fast-growing car industry. The Philippines did lower tariffs on petro-chemicals as agreed, but later raised them again. Worst of all, rice, the region's main crop, is excluded from the trade agreements altogether.

The tariff cuts that have already been agreed in the AFTA Common Effective Preferential Tariff (CEPT) are not being implemented. Some estimates put the level of implementation as low as 5 per cent. It is impossible to measure accurately since the member countries have not provided the secretariat with the relevant data. There are many reasons for this. Countries with high tariffs such as Myanmar are often reluctant to cut into existing revenue streams. Furthermore, although at the ASEAN 2003 summit meeting in Bali, ASEAN leaders promised to build an 'economic community' by 2012, ASEAN's members are intolerant of any reduction in national sovereignty in order to promote economic integration (e.g. as has been accepted in the EU). No single authority has been empowered to speak for the group as a whole.

is little to encourage such a development historically and anyway it would totally swamp the combined economies of all the other 'partners'.

The role of emerging non-triad economies (especially China, Russia and Eastern Europe) has grown and changed greatly in the past decade. We discuss these more fully in the next chapter on emerging economies.

Neither have we yet discussed Africa. In that context we may find it useful to reflect on the fact that each of the triad blocs features a 'lead' economy: for NAFTA, the US; for the EU, Germany; for Asia-Pacific, Japan. When Nelson Mandela took over as President of South Africa, managing an unexpectedly peaceful transition from white minority to black majority rule, there was a surge of optimism that Africa may have also found its 'lead' economy. South Africa was home to almost all of Africa's indigenous MNCs and possessed a sophisticated financial infrastructure, despite severe damage inflicted by world economic sanctions during the apartheid era. Several years on, the optimism is a little faded, since much of Africa is once again either embroiled in internal warfare or plagued by political instability, or both. Potential inward investors have once again been scared away by unacceptably high levels of risk in many African nations associated with unreliable government and political instability. Honourable exceptions to this, such as Botswana, can only be

3

welcomed and encouraged. The relationship between political stability and economic growth is once again shown as critical.

Multilateral trade rounds that negotiate to try to achieve agreements on world trade (rather than regional trade deals) are the foundation of the world trading system because they are based on the **'most-favoured-nation'** (MFN) principle. That means that any tariff cuts or agreements offered to one country must be offered to them all. By contrast, regional or bilateral deals are based on discrimination. They lower tariff barriers between those countries in the deal but not for anyone else. This means that although regional deals create new trade among their members, they may also divert it from lower-cost outsiders.

Therefore one further issue regarding regional trading blocs has been raised by Jagdish Bhagwati (2004), a famous economist. He has argued that FTAs are not the same as free trade since free trade areas are, by definition, discriminatory rather than multilateral. The argument is that FTAs deny trading opportunities to 'outsiders' and may cause 'trade diversion'. 'Trade diversion' means that instead of importing goods from countries that can supply most cheaply, members of FTAs are encouraged to buy from fellow members. Thus, rather than creating trade where there was none before, FTAs may divert it from efficient sources to inefficient ones. This distinction between trade creation and trade diversion is at the heart of thinking whether regional trading blocs enhance or reduce economic benefits. Even more important is the question of whether a world with a multitude of FTAs has overall achieved lower trade barriers and hence is moving towards a global freeing of trade. There is no doubt that the growth of regional trading blocs is not the same as unilateral non-discriminatory trade liberalization as achieved initially by GATT rounds of world trade negotiations in the past. It remains to be seen whether its successor the WTO may achieve a broader approach and the necessary agreements about trade-offs between WTO members wearing their 'global' rather than their 'regional' hats.

GLOBAL OR REGIONAL STRATEGIES?

Much recent management practice in international strategy has been aimed at restructuring and rationalization at a regional rather than a global level. Visa International considers global TV advertisements to be inappropriate for their local markets worldwide. It does, however, utilize some 'regional' advertisements in the EMEA (Europe, Middle East and Africa) region. This consists of a basic 25-second commercial to which a Visa member company (such as a local bank) adds on a five-second ending which promotes the individual bank within the overall Visa brand.

Nike is a US sports shoe and clothing manufacturing company which markets its products worldwide. In Europe it had traditionally utilized local national warehousing to supply retailers. In its very competitive industry sector Nike has replaced more than twenty national warehouses with one single European distribution centre located in Belgium. Developing a single European distribution hub follows the company's successful centralization of its American operations at a single hub in Memphis. Such regional concentration of warehousing and distribution is intended to help Nike reduce inventory, avoid duplication, and stock a wider range of its products centrally, so reducing cost whilst improving availability to stores and customers.

The European insurance market has historically been highly fragmented. This has enabled large price differentials to flourish between national markets and has protected national providers. For example, a similar policy could cost three times in Portugal what it cost in France. Since 1994, the European Union has developed a series of 'framework directives' which have gradually opened up the European markets to cross-border competition. These directives have brought about two basic changes: first, they allow companies to sell policies anywhere in Europe based on the regulations in their domestic market; second, they remove the need to submit cross-border policies to local offices for approval. The long-term impact of these changes has been to create increased EU-wide competition undermining the hitherto protected position and profitability of some national champions. However, market differences such as local tax regimes, cultural preferences for different types of insurance products, legal factors and incidence of different types of claims will ensure that cross-border entrants will still have to meet country-specific requirements for some time yet. Nevertheless these remaining differences are not stopping the giants in European financial services, such as Germany's Allianz, from moving into other European markets.

Substantial cost savings may be available from regional-level strategies. In advertising costs, for example, PepsiCo's savings from not producing a separate film for individual national markets has been estimated at $10 million per year. This figure is increased when indirect costs are added, for instance the speed of implementing a campaign, fewer overseas marketing staff, and management time which can be utilized elsewhere.

Global or regional standardization of activities is utilized by practitioners at whatever points in their value chain advantages can be derived, although often falling short of global operations across all functions. Benefits are possible from globalization in any or all of the following: design, purchasing, manufacturing operations, packaging, distribution, marketing, advertising, customer service or software development. Globalization makes possible standardized facilities, methodologies and procedures across locations. Companies may be able to benefit even if they are able to reconfigure in only one or two of these areas. Such a contingent approach has long been recommended for product and market standardization, to allow flexibility between the two extremes of full global standardization and complete local market responsiveness. Indeed both approaches may be used simultaneously to achieve the advantages to be had from global structuring of part of the product / service offering, while adapting or fine-tuning other parts of the same offering to closely match the needs of a particular local market. This process of combining the advantages of both global and local operations is sometimes known as '**glocalization**'.

The experience of KFC, an American global fast food chain, may illustrate the point. After its initial entry into the Japanese market KFC rapidly realized that it was necessary to make three specific changes to its global strategy. First, the product was of the wrong shape and size, since the Japanese prefer bite-sized food. Second, the locations of the outlets had to be moved into crowded city eating areas and away from independent sites. Third, contracts for supply of appropriate quality chickens had to be negotiated locally, although KFC provided all technical advice and standards. After these adaptations to the product and the site, KFC has been successful in Japan. Similarly, Pampers disposable diapers / nappies (made by Procter & Gamble of the US) were only successful in Japan after adapting by sizing downwards to accommodate smaller Japanese baby bottoms. McDonald's restaurants now serve Teriyaki burgers in Tokyo and wine in Lyon. Each of these local market adaptations of the core offering was critical. Yet the global strategy remained unchanged in its essentials. It is debatable therefore to what extent these companies are pursuing 'global' or 'regional' or 'glocal' strategies.

In pursuing a global strategy, managers should not ignore the existence of regional and country-specific differences. Many successful product or service innovations have been a result of ideas observed elsewhere. A presence in international markets creates antennae for gathering market intelligence, mentioned by many global companies as one of the most important benefits of a varied international presence and a factor which is leading to a rethinking of over-centralized global operations into regional groupings to better address the relevant national market characteristics.

THE STANDARDIZATION/ADAPTATION DEBATE

The standardization / adaptation debate is at the core of international strategy. It asks the question of how far, if at all, it is appropriate to design, market and deliver standard products and services across national market boundaries, or the extent to which adaptation to local market requirements is mandatory. The debate raises important assumptions concerning the conditions for successful global or regional strategies: that global market segments exist; that global economies of scale exist; and that a distribution infrastructure is available to realize these potential economies of scale worldwide. We need to know: Is there a global customer or a regional (pan-European, pan-Asian, pan-African) customer for this product or service, or only a local customer?

Douglas and Wind (1987) were early critics of the argument for standardization, calling it 'naive and oversimplistic'. Since then there have been waves of research and practice supporting globalization, 'glocalization' ('think global, act local') and transnational management (Bartlett and Ghoshal, 1989). Indeed this key issue of standardization / adaptation is the basis for one of the most powerful international strategy frameworks: the integration-responsiveness grid (Bartlett and Ghoshal, 1989) which will be extensively discussed in Chapter 7. The arguments in favour of global standardization, as initially stated by Levitt (1983), contained three assumptions:

1 That consumers' needs and interests are becoming increasingly homogeneous worldwide.

2 That people around the world are willing to sacrifice preferences for such things as product features, functions and design, for high quality at low prices.

3 That substantial economies of scale in production and marketing can be achieved through supplying global markets.

These assumptions are now very difficult to support. There is a lack of evidence of homogenization and significant differences still exist between groups of consumers across national market boundaries so that the differences both within and across countries are still far greater than any similarities. In addition, technological developments in production processes allowing flexible, lower-cost, lower-volume, high-variety operations (Sanchez, 1996) have become the norm so that variety at low cost is almost as common as scale economy benefits. Few global strategies are pure standardization strategies. International markets are more complex, requiring global, regional and local adaptations simultaneously. Although globalization offers the advantage of economies of scale for a segmented marketing strategy, this does not necessarily mean providing the same product in all countries, but offering local adaptations around a standardized core (See page 65, KFC and Pampers in Japan).

As Quelch and Hoff (1986) originally argued, the relevant issue 'is not whether to go global but how to tailor the global marketing concept to fit each business'. In its early attempts to sell its Pledge furniture polish in Japan, the American firm Johnson Wax found it to be unpopular with older Japanese consumers. After further market research it was discovered that the lemon scent in the polish reminded them of the smell of the toilet disinfectant which had been widely used in Japan in the 1940s. After the scent was changed, sales rose considerably.

An increasing number of multinationals are standardizing their brands to send a consistent worldwide message and to take greater advantage of media opportunities by promoting one brand, one packaging and uniform positioning across markets. Rather than a patchwork quilt of local brands in local markets, the owners of global brands increasingly want simplified global brand portfolios. Many of these local brands have been nurtured lovingly over the long term by high advertising spend and careful handling and are often held in great affection by their local population. Despite this, they are likely to be swept away. Examples of the successful standardization of global brands and some global products is given in Strategy in Action 3.8, together with an example of regional limitations.

What the three different examples in Strategy in Action 3.8 and all the others discussed in this chapter illustrate is that sensitivity to exact market conditions in each country or region is essential for international, regional and global strategies. Trade-offs are often required between standardization and adaptation to get the fit right for each local or regional or global marketplace for that particular product or service.

Companies increasingly feel that they have to unite behind key brands and rationalize products, brands and the advertising agencies handling their accounts. Focusing on fewer strong brands is seen as the best way of coping with fierce competition from other brands and private-label products, as well as getting the best value from expensive investments in advertising.

SOURCE: COMPILED BY AUTHORS FROM VARIOUS PRESS ARTICLES

Strategy in Action 3.8 *Standardization versus adaptation: free newspapers, TV game shows and Spanish books*

Metro International is a Stockholm-based media group which owns *Metro*, the most successful free newspaper, a fast-growing new segment in the world's newspaper industry. Since its launch in 1995, Metro's daily global readership now has over 100 cities in 19 countries (including Hong Kong, Mexico and France), and 18 languages. However, since its launch in the US in 2001 (in New York, Boston and Philadelphia) it is still not making money. It lost $4.4million in third quarter 2007 alone. Why has the Metro model been successful in so many countries but failed in the USA? Metro emphasizes national and international news. Americans seem to prefer a focus on very local news. They are also up against very strong, popular, paid-for papers with excellent local coverage. Also, many American cities have limited public transport networks – which is where most Metro distribution takes place elsewhere to daily commuters. Delivering free papers to homes is not really affordable.

One media product that does seem to be a pure global product is the TV game show 'Who wants to be a millionaire?' The TV show began in September 1998. Since then it has become a global phenomenon. Its owner, Celador Productions, has currently 67 versions licensed to 105 countries.

The market for books in Spanish is the second-largest in the world and the biggest for books in translation, which currently account for one-fifth of the 120,000 Spanish titles published each year. Growth is strongest in Argentina, Colombia and Mexico. Since many of the world's 400million Spanish speakers live in developing economies, it has great potential. Literacy rates are high and incomes are rising. During the 1970s and 1980s when there was a period of repression and economic crisis in Latin America, most Spanish-language publishing concentrated on Spain, with publishers relatively indifferent to the huge Latin American market. This has now completely changed. Many big international publishers such as Random House Mondadori and Planeta have bought local imprints that let them market books worldwide while selling at local prices. Deals that offer rights across several regions are becoming common. Five Latin American countries now have higher book readership levels than Spain but distribution in Latin America remains a problem. So are counterfeit and pirated copies. Mexico has few bookshops: one for every 82,000 people. Argentina has one bookshop for every 48,000 people and more than 2,000 public libraries. Structurally, cut-price online booksellers have had little impact in Spanish-language markets since many countries such as Spain and Argentina limit discounts on books.

Another aspect of the globalization of brands is in the branding of companies themselves. A trend is observable as companies become established as MNCs rather than just as domestic market champions. Names that are felt to be too nationalistic are made more neutral and therefore more universally acceptable. Examples include previously state-owned enterprises: British Petroleum became BP; and the Korean *chaebol* Lucky Goldstar became the internationally acceptable LG; HSBC replaced the Hong Kong and Shanghai Banking Corporation; and the name AXA was chosen to cloak the French origin of this insurance MNC and thereby make it more regionally and globally acceptable.

Few companies or industries lend themselves to 'naive' global strategies. All require some degree of adaptation to regional and national conditions. Managing successful market entry into the emergent Chinese market has presented a curious set of market research problems. For example, such standard procedures as setting up and tracking panels of shops or consumers, are rendered highly problematic by continuous sample change such as shops closing down and re-opening. In an area like Shanghai they are rebuilding a block a week. Areas are changing physically month by month. In addition to these market structure issues, it difficult to judge the positioning for each product, and packaging and distribution channels are also unique. For example hair shampoos are sold predominantly in sachets rather than in bottles, because people are paid weekly and prefer to make smaller weekly expenditures. Other common problems concern cultural differences, regulatory requirements and human resource issues like recruitment, retention and approach to decision-making. China is an extremely bureaucratic country. If a company wishes to operate in five different provinces, it needs to establish a company in each of the five provinces, each of which will require a great number of permits and approvals to proceed. Income tax returns must be submitted monthly in most provinces and the company's accounts usually must be approved by the government's accountants. Even company computer systems need approval by the authorities. High-quality technical skills are readily available, but financial, business and managerial skills are not.

Similarly, McDonald's took fourteen years to extend its chain to Russia, not only because negotiations with the Soviet authorities at the time were notoriously slow and fundamentals, like legal ownership of outlets, difficult to establish, but also because no supply chain existed for sourcing the raw materials for hamburgers and French fries. The company had to go to extraordinary lengths to create a reliable supply chain of appropriate quality ingredients for its product. These included not only agreements with farm co-operatives to grow the right type of potato needed for McDonald's French fries, but even importing American bull sperm to ensure that Russian beef herds yielded the correct beef quality expected in the hamburgers. Even after opening, aspects of the service were almost incomprehensible to the local customers, such as the menu itself, since the notions of choice and availability were not familiar to the Russian consumer at that time.

The learning to be derived from these company 'war stories' of what standardization or adaptation meant for them in each situation is to understand the relationship between global, regional and local. It is not a matter of trade-offs, but of achieving the balance between interdependencies. Regional trading blocs and regional strategy are part of the current pattern of international trade. As such they are some of the factors driving the emerging 'hub and spoke' structure of MNCs to support their interweaving of global, regional and local into their international strategies.

SUMMARY

- There has undoubtedly been a degree of cultural homogenization in some segments of most world markets.

- This has created opportunities for MNCs to benefit from additional sources of scale economies and scope economies in their global operations.

- The build-up of regional trading blocs has been accompanied by a noticeable increase in intra-regional trade within those regional trading blocs.

- The strength of regionalization may indicate the limits of globalization.

- Regional trading blocs may contribute to the liberalization of world trade (i.e. be trade creating) or act as blockages to global trade with the rest of the world outside their boundaries (i.e. be trade diverting).

- MNCs have learned to adapt their products and services to local, regional or global market requirements.

- This need for adaptation may mean that global standardization is unworkable, or it may refer only to relatively trivial adjustments leaving the core of standardization intact.

- No one right solution exists to the choices open to MNCs between stronger global or cross-border regional integration; it will be contingent upon firm and context.

- How this translates into viable international or global strategies will vary according to industry, product and market segment, and the internal processes of individual firms.

DISCUSSION QUESTIONS

1 Define the term 'globalization'. Does it apply to a firm, an industry, a market or a country?

2 How helpful is the concept of cultural homogenization in making sense of globalization?

3 Is globalization mainly caused by technological change?

4 What does the anti-globalization movement mean when it describes globalization as creating 'a race to the bottom'?

5 What is a regional trading bloc?

6 How far do you think that the trends of globalization and regionalization are in conflict with each other?

7 'Proliferating Free Trade Areas have become a pox on the world trading system' (Jagdish Bhagwati, quoted in *The Economist* 18/10/97). What does Bhagwati mean?

8 Would you argue that regional trading blocs help or hinder globalization?

9 Under what circumstances should a firm pursue a global strategy and under what circumstances should it pursue a regional strategy?

FURTHER READINGS

1 Peng, M.W. and Pleggenkuhle-Miles, E.G. (2009) 'Current debates in global strategy', *International Journal of Management Reviews*, 11(1): 51–68.

   If you are looking for a quick way to understand the current directions for research and debate in global strategy then this article will provide that. It is an extensive literature review of the field of global strategy. It covers four of the central debates concerning: cultural distance; global versus regional strategic direction; issues of corporate governance in global firms; and corporate social responsibility in global firms and global strategy.

2 Ghoshal, S. (1987) 'Global strategy: an organizing framework', *Strategic Management Journal,* 8: 425–440.

   Ghoshal's paper is a classic. He creates a framework that can be used as a 'road map' to guide managers of multinational corporations through their choices for global strategic management. He clarifies what it means to 'manage globally' and sets out options on which decisions about global strategy should be based. Ghoshal reminds us that corporations often 'have globalness thrust upon them' by the initiatives of competitors, and their managers may have little grasp themselves of how to manage under these particular industry conditions. His framework is simple to understand, yet a powerful aid to decision-making.

3 Yip, G.S. (2002) *Total Global Strategy II*, Englewood-Cliffs, NJ: Prentice-Hall.

   Yip's book is where you must go if you want to understand in detail how the drivers of globalization work. He provides guidelines to managers for answering the questions: how global is your industry and how global should your strategy be? It is the handbook for diagnosing and designing global strategies.

4 Ghemawat, P. (2007a) *Redefining Global Strategy: crossing borders in a world where differences still matter*, Boston: Harvard Business School Press.

This is an alternative general strategy book on global strategy written by a very good strategy academic with very interesting ideas about the limits to global convergence of markets. Ghemawat sees cultural and geographic differences as still central, in fact as key, to building and managing effective global strategies.

CHAPTER 4

Emerging economies

LEARNING OBJECTIVES The objectives of this chapter are:

- to define what is meant by 'emerging economies'
- to explain their great and growing significance in world trade
- to explain how and why growth is occurring in a variety of different emerging economies
- to show why institutional context is relevant to understanding different emerging economies
- to emphasize that the world's producers, consumers and markets are changing and affecting the strategies of firms.

INTRODUCTION: BEYOND THE 'TRIAD'

In our discussion of regionalization in Chapter 3, one of the ideas introduced was the 'triad' of three regional trading blocs in the world's most economically developed regions: Europe, Asia and North America. In this chapter we move on to consider the 80 per cent of the world's population who live outside the triad economies. China and India alone contain over two billion people, that is about 40 per cent of the world's population. In 2005 the combined output of emerging economies accounted for more than half of total world GDP, measured at **purchasing-power parity (PPP)**. This means that the rich countries no longer dominate the global economy. Emerging economies are driving global growth and having a big impact on developed countries' inflation, interest rates, wages and profits. As developing countries and the former Soviet bloc have embraced (some) market-friendly economic reforms and opened their borders to trade and investment, more countries are industrializing and participating in the global economy than ever before. Emerging economies' share of world exports has grown from 20 per cent in 1970 to 42 per cent in 2005 and they account for two-thirds of the world's foreign exchange reserves. Since 2000, world GDP per head has grown by an average of 3.2 per cent a year, thanks to the acceleration in emerging economies.

Figures 4.1, 4.2 and 4.3 give useful data related to emerging versus developed economy growth in the past twenty years, as well as possible projections to 2025.

Half of American, Japanese and European exports now go to emerging economies (Enderwick, 2007). This trade between developed and emerging economies is growing

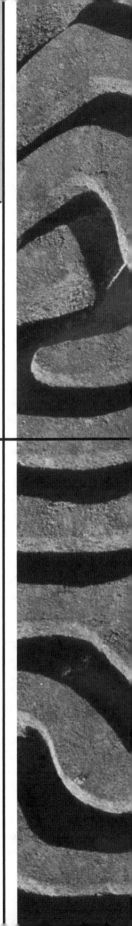

twice as fast as trade between the rich developed economies. While growth in the emerging economies has been surging ahead, economic growth within the developed economies has been much slower, held back by low population growth and an ageing workforce. The force driving the rapid growth rates of the emerging economies has been globalization, which has increased the integration of the emerging economies within the world economy and within the global economic system. At the time of writing this has become something of a mixed blessing with the entire world economy involved in a severe economic downturn and economic recession. The deeper involvement of the emerging economies in the global economy that has been their engine for growth has also meant that they are part of the cycles of growth and recession that recur in the world economy over time. They are no longer excluded from either the opportunities of growth, or the problems of severe economic downturns when these occur, since they are now part of the larger worldwide global trading system, global economic system and global financial markets.

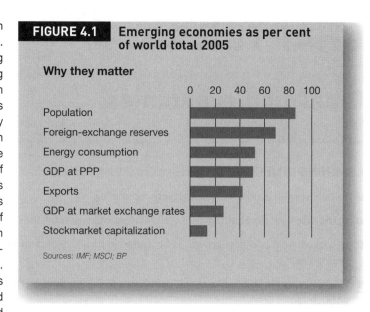

FIGURE 4.1   **Emerging economies as per cent of world total 2005**

The Nobel Prize-winning economist Paul Krugman (2008) argues that financial globalization, that is investors in each country holding large stakes in other countries, has not reduced financial risk as the usual argument about spreading risk across a portfolio would suggest. Instead, for emerging markets there has been a special vulnerability arising from financial globalization. It relates to what Krugman (2008) calls the 'carry trade'. This involved borrowing in countries which had low interest rates (such as Japan) and lending to countries with high interest rates (such as Russia or Brazil). This was a highly profitable global financial trade – until something went wrong. With the crisis in lending (known as the 'credit crunch') from 2007 onwards, funds from low-interest economies such as Japan rapidly dried up, with devastating consequences. As this cheap loan capital disappeared, the value of the Japanese yen soared while the value of emerging market currencies collapsed because there were no longer (cheap) funds

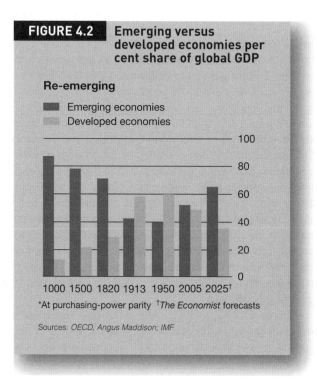

FIGURE 4.2   **Emerging versus developed economies per cent share of global GDP**

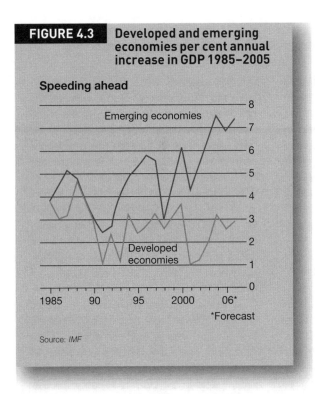

FIGURE 4.3 Developed and emerging economies per cent annual increase in GDP 1985–2005

Speeding ahead

Source: *IMF*

flowing into them. The emerging economy companies, banks or hedge funds which had previously borrowed cheaply from abroad, now faced huge losses. This is the explanation for such bizarre effects as the sudden collapse of the banking system in Iceland or the Dubai property market (see Strategy in Action 4.1) in 2008. Krugman (2008) explains that, for example, in Russia in 2008, banks and companies that had borrowed heavily from abroad because the overseas interest rates were lower than Russian rouble interest rates, suddenly found that their sources of credit were cut off and the rouble value of their debts rose sharply. During the credit bubble years, the Russian government had accumulated $560 billion worth of foreign exchange, while the Russian companies and banks had during the same period accumulated about $460 billion in foreign debt. Even as an oil economy with such a cash mountain from the soaring price of oil in the early 2000s, Russia's government could only support that level of corporate and financial institution debt for a limited period.

WHAT IS AN 'EMERGING ECONOMY'?

The World Bank defines an **emerging economy** as one that has an average annual per capita income of less than $9,000 and is experiencing rapid growth and economic transformation. The term 'emerging market' was originally applied to the former Soviet states and Eastern bloc economies plus China that were *emerging* from a planned, centralized, predominantly state-owned economy into a more market economy. (These were sometimes also called *transition* economies, that is making the transition, from communist to capitalist systems.) Gradually the term 'emerging economy' has become more generally used to replace the previous term 'developing economy' to describe less developed economies which have lower income levels (Cavusgil et al., 2002) than the richer, more industrialized, developed economies.

Characteristics of emerging economies

Emerging economies generally have large agricultural sectors, far larger than those of developed economies. They also have great differences between the urban and rural sectors of society and the economy. Productivity is low compared to developed economies and infrastructure, such as roads, transport systems, communications and education, are very poor. Health, education and life expectancy are all greatly lower, and infant mortality higher, than in developed economies (Enderwick, 2007). However, although all poor countries have these shared characteristics, not all such poor countries can be described as emerging economies. *The Economist* identifies twenty-five countries as emerging economies of which the most-commonly mentioned are Brazil, Russia, India and China (usually referred to jointly as the **BRIC**

4

SOURCE: COMPILED BY AUTHORS FROM VARIOUS NEWSPAPER ARTICLES

Strategy in Action 4.1 *Development in Dubai: truly part of the global economy*

The value of villas in flagship Dubai properties such as the Palm Jumeirah (the man-made island built in the shape of a palm tree) had fallen by 40 per cent in a matter of weeks in late 2008. Instead of deposits of 10 per cent, banks were now demanding deposits of 40 per cent for purchases, which was further fuelling the collapse in prices. Leading Dubai property developers such as Nakheel, Emaar and Damac, were worried that property prices could fall 80 per cent between 2008 and 2009, and were putting further developments on hold. In the Gulf region as a whole, although exposure to US subprime loans was modest, there had been heavy investments by regional banks in local property markets at what were now inflated values. In November 2008, the Chairman of Emaar, the giant state-controlled property development company, took the very unusual step of publicly announcing that government and state-owned enterprises in Dubai owed $80 billion, that is 148 per cent of GDP. The state-owned property companies in particular were very highly leveraged. The stock market slumped by 50 per cent. Revenue from

Dubai's small oil fields has also slumped thanks to the 60 per cent drop in world oil prices in the second half of 2008. At the same time however, Dubai was still growing, albeit by 6 per cent rather than the previous 10 per cent per year. The United Arab Emirates (UAE) has a current account surplus of 22 per cent of GDP. How will the Dubai property slump affect the whole region? Will the Gulf Cooperation Council (GCC) pull together to help the banks of the whole region? Several GCC economies will go into deficit in 2009, including Saudi Arabia, whose budget had been based on an oil price of $50 a barrel, but which still had to continue to make heavy investments in further capacity at the Saudi Aramco oil company. The question was not so much whether Dubai could be supported by the other economies in the Gulf States. Abu Dhabi in particular, the largest state in the UAE, is awash with cash and holds 10 per cent of the world's known oil reserves. It is more a question of what assets (e.g. the Emirates airline; the Jumeirah hotels group; the EmiratesTower business complex) Dubai may lose control of in the process.

economies), plus parts of Eastern Europe, as well as the oil-rich countries of the Middle East and, potentially at least, some of the African economies that are rich in other resources such as minerals.

The types of characteristics most commonly considered to be shared by *The Economist*'s top 25 emerging economies contain economic, socio-cultural, political, technological and what Enderwick (2007) calls 'business systems' characteristics. We will briefly review each of these.

Economic characteristics include very high growth rates; wide, and frequently widening, income polarization between the rural poor and the urban rich; and the important economic contribution made to these economies from income sent to households at home from emigrant workers living and working abroad, often called remittances. World Bank data show that such remittances constituted 3.1 per cent of GDP for India in 2005. In smaller African, Central American or Caribbean economies these remittances can represent a considerably higher percentage of GDP. The high growth rates of emerging economies can be understood by contrasting them to developed economy growth rates. Developed economies such as those of Europe tend to achieve between 2 to 3 per cent per annum at best even in strong growth periods. By comparison, the Chinese economy has enjoyed growth rates exceeding 14 per cent throughout the last decade, although this has now slowed to around 8 per cent due to the world downturn. Indeed there is now genuine concern as to whether growth rates at less than 8 per cent per year will be adequate to absorb the continually growing numbers of new workers entering the labour market year-on-year. At growth rates under 8 per cent there could be social unrest in China.

There is a link between the economic characteristic of income polarization between rich and poor and some socio-cultural characteristics. In the two largest emerging economies of China and India, growth has been largely confined to coastal cities (China) and just four states (out of fourteen in India). One of the contributory causes to this social process is urbanization, that is the drift of rural population to the cities. This endless over-supply of labour to the cities is one result of the fact that the (majority) rural population has benefitted far less from economic growth than has the urban population (Enderwick, 2007; Khanna et al., 2005). Income distribution is therefore skewed not just between socio-economic groups but also geographically. This is definitely a real social and, potentially, also a political problem. Indeed emerging economies have particular and significant political characteristics that generate higher levels of political risk for organizations within them.

In emerging economies, there are often higher levels of political instability and uncertainty than is usually the case in developed economies. Although both China (with the dominant Communist Party) and India (the world's largest democracy) are stable in the styles of their governments, others are less so. Ethnic or religious conflict is more common than in developed economies and many of these conflicts (e.g. Kashmir in India or many continuous conflicts such as those in the Balkans in Eastern Europe or in many African states such as the Congo or Rwanda) are recurrent. Another significant political risk in emerging economies is that the operating conditions for businesses and international investment are subject to sudden change. Degrees of control by the state of either growth industries or strategic industries and shifting policies towards liberalization or privatization of industries can make long-term, or even short-term, planning and investment difficult to predict. Over a short period in Russia from the 1990s to the 2000s, government policies towards business and the role of the state have shifted drastically to such a degree that those who were considered business winners or heroes at one point were imprisoned by the state not many years later. This has had an impact on the flow of foreign investment into Russia and elsewhere as potential investors became less certain about the signals concerning government policy.

The levels of technological development and innovation are growing rapidly but are still much lower than in developed economies. For example the UNCTAD (United Nations Conference on Trade and Development) Innovation Capability Index combines a number of technological and human capital factors to provide rankings of 117 countries in terms of innovation. In 2001, China was ranked at 74 and India at 83 (UNCTAD, 2005). While R&D spending has increased greatly, it is still a fraction of that of the advanced economies. In percentage terms we can compare the two most developed emerging economies China and India, to the US. In 2002 R&D spending as a percentage of GDP was 1.23 per cent in India, 1.29 per cent in China and 2.7 per cent in the US. However, in absolute terms the comparison is more dramatic. These percentages translate into spending as follows: China $60 billion, India $19 billion and the US $252 billion.

The characteristics of business systems (i.e. the ways that business is conducted) in emerging economies is often very different from the business systems in developed economies. This is a very significant aspect of understanding emerging economies and it is often discussed under the heading of 'institutional' context, which will be considered next.

INSTITUTIONAL CONTEXT AND ECONOMIC DEVELOPMENT

One of the most useful approaches to understanding global strategy in emerging markets is to use an institution-based approach (Meyer and Peng, 2005). The reason for this is that emerging economies tend to have more 'fundamental and comprehensive changes introduced to the formal and informal rules of the game that affect firms as players' (Peng, 2003: 275). The key global strategy question thus becomes: how to play the game, when the rules of the game are changing and not completely known? (Peng et al., 2008: 924). This fundamental question applies to both domestic and foreign firms in emerging economies. We therefore choose to begin to answer this question by discussing the important issue of institutions and institutional context in emerging economies. Institutions (both formal and informal) refer to and govern socio-political transactions such as corruption and transparency in business dealings, legal transactions such as regulatory regimes, and social norms such as attitudes towards entrepreneurship and what is regarded as ethical behaviour. Understanding the institutional context of emerging economies helps to answer how to 'play the game' by clarifying at least some of 'the rules'.

As Peng's (2008) fundamental question suggests, most MNCs struggle to develop successful strategies in emerging economies. Khanna et al. (2005) have used the concept of 'institutional voids' to describe the main cause of problems for foreign MNCs in trading within emerging economies. What do they mean? They argue that developed country MNCs take for granted the significant, even critical, role that infrastructure plays in the implementation of their business strategies in their own and in other developed markets. Such infrastructure is often absent ('void') or far less developed in emerging economies. We are familiar with the usual types of 'hard' infrastructure such as roads, railway networks, indeed all aspects of transport systems; general telecommunications infrastructure such as telephone and computer systems networks; education and training; health care, including public hospitals and the training of medical practitioners; financial systems and capital markets for lending and borrowing to grow small and large businesses. Wolf (2004) argues that infrastructure is what economists call a **public good**, that is goods that are consumed collectively and are of benefit to society as a whole, with roads given as an obvious example of what the state is best able to provide for all its citizens. Pure scientific research which a government may finance through grants to its universities is another public good.

Let us consider an example of the importance of public goods and infrastructure in a society. At the time of writing there is a massive cholera epidemic in Zimbabwe. Simultaneously the health care system in Zimbabwe has completely broken down as no medical supplies are available, the supply of power such as electricity is occasional at best and the public water system has collapsed such that very little clean drinking water is generally available (which is likely to be the main cause of the cholera epidemic itself). Despite the statements of its long-serving President Robert Mugabe, Zimbabwe is widely seen as a 'failed' state, that is a country in which the government has ceased to function effectively and can no longer manage to supply necessary public goods such as clean water for its population. These are also countries whose poor government has failed to provide the infrastructure on which economic development depends. Infrastructure therefore means those taken-for-granted structures and institutions that sit behind the day-to-day functioning of a society. An even more extreme example of the result of such institutional 'voids' is the rise of piracy off the coast of Somalia throughout the past decade, in a period where any effective government has been missing and informal ad hoc power structures have emerged.

Governments are also responsible for broad policy levers with powerful economic effects, such as barriers to trade or investment, taxation and public procurement. 'The role of the state in a modern market economy is therefore pervasive.... The first requirement of effective public policy is a range of qualities that come under the headings of *credibility, predictability, transparency and consistency*, both over time and across activities' (Wolf, 2004: 64–65). Strategy in Action 4.2 considers these four headings in relation to Russia, one of the biggest of the emerging economies.

'Soft' infrastructure and institutional 'voids'

To continue this discussion of the role of infrastructure in emerging economy development and also the difficulties faced by foreign firms in operating effectively in emerging economies, we turn now to the concept of 'soft' infrastructure to take the argument one stage further. In addition to 'hard' infrastructure, Khanna et al. (2005) have argued that companies from developed economies depend upon 'soft' infrastructure to implement their strategies. Although this works well in developed economies, most emerging economies either have none at all or very little of such supporting infrastructure. Whereas hard infrastructure usually exists to some degree in almost all emerging economies, 'soft' infrastructure is often totally absent. 'Soft' infrastructure usually refers to specialized intermediary firms, regulatory systems and contract-enforcing mechanisms that ease the flow of business. This might include such intermediary functions as market research firms, recruitment agencies, and business-to-business logistics firms to manage total distribution processes. Khanna et al. (2005) argue that despite the lowering of tariff barriers in increasing numbers of emerging economies, the spread of the internet, satellite and

Strategy in Action 4.2 *Institutional context: doing business in Russia*

By the end of 1999 Russia was growing by 6 per cent a year. In 2000, growth accelerated to 10 per cent and the first IKEA store was opened in Moscow. By 2008, growth had fallen back to 7 per cent per year which is good but does not come near to Russia's potential levels of growth. What has happened in the intervening period?

From 1998 to 2008 Russia had been transformed: its economy was worth $1.3 trillion, it had $480 billion in foreign currency reserves and an additional fund of $144 billion for surplus oil and gas revenues. GDP per head had risen from $2,000 in 1998 to $9,000 in 2008 at current exchange rates. Restaurants, shops and airports were all busy with shoppers and travellers, and foreign cars were everywhere. According to *The Economist* (1 March 2008: 27) three factors supported this rapid growth: a growth in private sector businesses; massively rising oil prices; and macroeconomic stability. By mid-2008, the Russian economy was slowing drastically fuelled by recession, if not depression, in the world economy; a two-thirds fall in oil prices in a matter of months, while the Russian economy remained almost wholly dependent on oil and gas prices.

In its early stages, the Putin government that took power from Boris Yeltsin in 2000 was financially prudent using the oil price windfall to repay debt and build up currency reserves, as well as making many institutional reforms, including legislation to improve the judicial system and to allow a free market in land. However, in mid-2003 began what has become known as 'the Yukos affair'. Yukos was Russia's largest oil company and its boss was Mikhail Khodorkovsky. Initially the attacks by the government on both the company and on Mr Khodorkovsky personally, largely carried out via the tax police, were described as directed against the power of the new Russian business leaders or 'oligarchs'. Yet it was the beginning of a period when the share of oil production in Russia owned by state companies doubled. At the same time growth in oil output in Russia, which before 'the Yukos affair' had been growing by roughly 9 per cent per year, had now fallen back to 1 per cent per year by the end of 2007. The effective takeover of Yukos by the government also put a stop to infant progress on strengthening the rule of law and the legislative systems and process in Russia. Indeed whereas the courts under Mr Yeltsin were independent of the government, that is no longer so. Yukos was dismantled and its assets given to Rosneft, a quasi-state oil company chaired by the Russian President's deputy chief of staff.

It seemed that after 'the Yukos affair', property rights were of no value in Russia. After Yukos, there followed a whole series of similar raids and takeovers of privately oligarch-owned Russian firms by similar means of raids by police and/or tax officials. Another corporate crisis that attracted a great deal of attention was that internally within TNK-BP, a joint venture set up in 2003 between AAR (a Russian consortium owned by four billionaire Russian businessmen) and the UK oil giant BP. By 2007, a disagreement over a dividend payout and general strategy had started extreme internal in-fighting. By March 2008, BP's offices in Russia had been raided twice by the Russian FSB, the state security body (formerly the KGB). The offices of TKN-BP had been inspected four times by the labour ministry and its British Chief Executive Robert Dudley had been interrogated for six hours at the Ministry of Internal Affairs. Mr Dudley's temporary visa was being allowed to expire. Requests for visa renewals for 150 foreign staff at TNK-BP were refused. AAR denied absolutely that it was using the Russian authorities to apply pressure to BP. In 2008 TNK-BP was worth about $50 billion. There was a view that this battle was actually about an ultimate sale of all TNK-BP's assets to Rosneft or Gazprom. TNK-BP was the only big oil group in which the Russian state did not own at least a stake. The ultimate outcome of all the planned international court cases was still likely to be AAR buying out BP's stake in the joint venture at a reduced price and then selling it on to Gazprom for a great deal more.

Business rewards now appear to be in the hands of government and allocated by political criteria rather than commercial criteria. One former government official was quoted as saying: 'it is easier to get a competitor into a jail than to compete with him'. This deterioration of Russian institutions has been commented upon by the World Bank, the World Economic Forum and Transparency International. For 2004, Transparency International ranked Russia the 90th country (out of its list of 145 country rankings) for levels of corruption. Despite this, Russia's economy was still growing, for example the construction sector was growing by 20 per cent per year. Foreign investment is still coming in large amounts too at $27.8 billion in 2007. So maybe these institutional peculiarities do not matter. However, the problem lies in opportunity costs. These are likely to become more evident in a world economy that is declining rather than growing. The Russian economy is overwhelmingly tilted towards a small number of giant oil and gas companies. The share of Russian GDP represented by oil and gas companies has risen from 12.7 per cent in 1999 to 31.6 per cent in 2007. Natural resources account for over 80 per cent of exports. This flow of petrodollars abruptly slowed in 2008. During the boom years the Russian economy did not translate into investment into domestic productivity, which remains far below that of comparable developed economies. Most productivity improvements had been achieved through the absorption of spare capacity from the old Soviet era. The Russian economy, despite its boom years, has been left highly sensitive to the state of the world economy and the level of energy prices. There is a growing gap between the top 10 per cent and the bottom 10 per cent of the population. As *The Economist* argued in 2008: 'Russia will not reach first-world prosperity with third-world institutions'.

Wolf's (2004) headings of *credibility, predictability, transparency and consistency*, may actually be being fulfilled in Russia in its current business, economic, financial and political systems, but in the negative rather than the positive modes.

SOURCE: COMPILED BY AUTHORS FROM VARIOUS NEWSPAPER ARTICLES AND *THE ECONOMIST* 1 MARCH 2008

cable communication links, and improvements in physical infrastructure, developed economy MNCs have adjusted poorly to the different business models and ways of doing business in emerging economies. Their findings conclude that successful developed economy MNCs work around the institutional voids of emerging economies, which may be quite different in each country context. Where advanced economies have large numbers of experienced market intermediaries and effective contract-enforcing mechanisms, emerging economies have unskilled intermediaries and far less effective legal systems.

Innovation is even more risky and time-consuming in emerging economies than in developed economies since some of the infrastructure needed to support a business model (such as established distribution channels) is often absent (Chesbrough et al., 2006). Contracts are seldom a sufficient basis for business activity; courts are slow to act and judgments hard to enforce.

There is also the issue of how companies select new markets in which to invest. McKinsey Global Survey in 2004 carried out a poll of 9,750 senior managers regarding their investment priorities and criteria for emerging economies. Sixty-one per cent gave market size and growth as their main selection criteria for entering new markets; 17 per cent prioritized political risk and stability; only 13 per cent gave structural conditions (i.e. the institutional context) as their main criterion. Although all four BRIC countries (Brazil, Russia, India and China) may be attractive in terms of market size and growth potential, their institutional contexts are quite different. Khanna et al. (2005) suggest that companies should map in detail the institutional context of each country by asking detailed questions about each of five factors: political and social systems; openness; product markets; labour markets; capital markets. Sample questions for each element include:

- To whom are the country's politicians accountable? Are the roles of legislative, executive and judiciary clearly defined? (political and social systems)

- Are the country's government, media and people receptive to foreign investment? How long does it take to start a new venture in the country? (openness)

- Can companies easily obtain reliable data on consumer tastes and buyer behaviour? Can companies access raw materials and components of good quality? (product markets)

- How strong is the country's education infrastructure, especially for technical and management education? Can employees move easily from one company to another? (labour markets)

- How effective are the country's banks, insurance companies and investment companies at the management of savings and investment? Are financial institutions managed well? (capital markets).

They conclude that companies should always consider industry structures only after they have analysed a country's institutional context. As we have already shown in Strategy in Action 4.2, in Russia the Russian government is involved, formally and informally, in several industries. In answer to one of their own questions: Are the roles of legislative, executive and judiciary clearly defined? Khanna et al. (2005: 73) say: 'Government officials at almost any level can exercise near veto power over business deals that involve local or foreign companies and getting permits and approvals is a complicated chore in Russia.'

Similarly with regard to capital markets, in Brazil and India local entrepreneurs use the local capital markets to access sources of finance for investment. By contrast, in China most enterprises (including especially state-owned enterprises) access funds from public sector banks that may be under little pressure to show any profit. Even if profitability is slowly growing in importance for Chinese banks, this remains an important institutional difference in access to capital markets.

The detail in each national context thus varies considerably and understanding each detailed context in its own terms is critical to effective international strategy in emerging economies. This means that contingency theory is the appropriate approach in emerging economies.

FROM 'TRIAD' TO BRIC

In Chapter 3 we discussed the concepts of globalization and regionalization. One of the concepts we used to do that was 'the triad' (Ohmae, 1985) made up of three large regional trading blocs from the world's most economically developed regions: Europe, Asia and North America. This was illustrated in Figure 3.1. However, in Figure 3.2 there is a much broader diagrammatic representation of trading regions of the world including China, India, Africa, the Middle East and Latin America. Over the last twenty-plus years since Ohmae developed his 'triad' concept, the world has moved on greatly. The trading regions of the world outside the triad have been transformed, although not all of them and not at similar rates. All of the countries that we have been discussing as emerging economies exist outside the original triad of developed economies by definition and that is where the most dynamic world growth has been occurring from the 1990s onwards.

The most-discussed emerging economies are those of Brazil, Russia, India and China – the BRIC economies. The term 'BRIC' was invented by the chief economist of the Goldman Sachs investment bank in 2001. It was an acronym to identify the four economies that were expected to become the next world-class developed economies. Probably these BRIC countries (plus probably South Korea and Mexico) should no longer be referred to as 'emerging' economies since clearly they have already emerged and have a major influence on the global world economy. Indeed some 'emerging economy' managers, politicians and businessmen find the term denigrating. Yet there are still ways in which these economies do differ significantly from the developed economies and they are contained in the extensive discussion of institutional contexts in this chapter.

THE BRIC ECONOMIES: APPLYING THE PORTER 'DIAMOND'

In Chapter 2 we introduced the 'diamond' framework (Porter, 1990). One of the important things that the 'diamond' framework does is to bring back the importance of a country's economic, social, financial and political infrastructure, that is its overall institutional context, as a factor in global competitiveness.

Since it is always useful to apply conceptual frameworks to real situations and see whether they provide any insight, we have developed a brief application of the four diamond criteria: firm strategy, structure and rivalry; related and supporting industries; demand conditions; and factor conditions. We have applied these criteria broadly to the four BRIC economies, plus a similar evaluation of a combined generic Eastern Europe. We should stress that this is a very basic analysis using data wholly available in the public domain, mainly from recent detailed country surveys carried out by *The Economist*. We have then tried to produce an investment ranking order for these economies or economic domains, based on the contextual evaluation that the diamond analysis provided. Each of the four criteria is given a score out of five. These four scores are then added up to arrive at an overall ranking score, given in column one under the country name. The results are given in Table 4.1.

This rank order scoring by the authors of the five country 'diamond' results were as follows:

First – China 16
Second – India 15
Third – Brazil 13
Fourth – Russia 11
Fifth – Eastern Europe 10

Outside the developed economies, it is probable that no other region would score as high as 10. Indeed this is a quick but reasonably effective way of explaining the poor growth performance of countries in Africa and the Middle East which often have extremely favourable factor conditions, especially with regard to mineral wealth for both many Middle Eastern economies and many African economies. However these factor endowments are not matched by other elements in the 'diamond'. Demand conditions are most frequently highly skewed towards a wealthy minority and there is little hard or soft infrastructure development or related and supporting industries to help build competitive capabilities. Factors such as the extent of the rule of law and levels of corruption, or whether regulatory conditions are relatively open or closed are far better addressed using the institutional approach rather than the diamond – which is much more effective at capturing hard rather than soft factors.

A small but relevant example of the importance of understanding the relationship between raw materials, factor conditions such as road and transport infrastructure conditions and the availability of related and supporting industries, is provided in Strategy in Action 4.3 by a brief discussion of the poor uptake of the bicycle in African countries.

TABLE 4.1	Applying the theoretical framework of Porter's 'diamond' framework to the realities of international trade and investment			
	Firm strategy Structure and rivalry (5)	*Related & supporting industries (5)*	*Demand conditions*	*Factor conditions (*)*
BRAZIL	Mostly subdivisions of USA MNCs plus smaller local businesses	Moderate to poor	Strong demand conditions but high differential between rich & poor but with growing middle-class	200m workforce; low skill levels; cheap labour; poor education; low investment in infrastructure
13	4	2	4	3
RUSSIA	Small number of very large oligopolies	Weak infrastructure concentrated in few industries esp. oil & gas	Wealthy new oligarchy; overall low living standards but energy-fuelled boom but slowing rapidly	Strong education system & literacy; huge energy resources; poor separation of government and judiciary
11	2	2	3	4
INDIA	Growing number of MNCs plus millions of small businesses	High level of related & supporting in a few key industries such as steel; media; hi-tech business services; generic pharmaceuticals	Strong in the cities; weak in the large rural areas	Good education system, especially higher education but poor overall literacy rate; very poor infrastructure
15	3	4	4	4
CHINA	High presence of Western MNCs; some large Chinese MNCs & number of international brands; OEMs dominate; huge SME sector. State-owned enterprises (SOE) still major part of GDP	Excellent across all sectors	Strong in the cities; weak in the large rural areas	High levels of well-educated labour; huge educational growth; good universities; abundant natural resources; poor communications and transportation outside major cities. Some regulatory and political uncertainty
16	3	5	4	4

4

TABLE 4.1	*(continued)*			
	Firm strategy Structure and rivalry (5)	*Related & supporting industries (5)*	*Demand conditions*	*Factor conditions (*)*
EASTERN EUROPE	Industries catching up with Western companies, often under-capitalized but high levels of recent Western investment	Some strong industry networks but often lacking modern technology & investment	Overall living standards below Western levels; polarization of relatively low living standards with small rich entrepreneurial class	Lack of energy resources; relatively low population; poor communications & transport infrastructures; strong educational systems & cultural depth.
10	2	2	3	3

Source: Compiled by authors from *The Economist* (14 Apr. 2007; 31 May, 29 Nov., 13 Dec. 2008), Khanna et al. (2005)

*Factor conditions commonly include: availability of skilled labour and raw materials such as mineral resources or energy; education system and literacy levels; telecommunications, transport and distribution infrastructure; and so on.

Two contrasting views of China

Having made a very basic overview on five emerging economies in Table 4.1, a more careful look at China, as one of the most discussed of the emerging and BRIC economies, may be helpful. Two contrasting views of China's present and future are presented here. One is the more common hugely positive discussion of China as an economic powerhouse and the economy (and the companies) to target if developed

Strategy in Action 4.3   *Bicycles in Africa*

Even for journeys of short distances, the bicycle has not had very great uptake in most African countries. This may seem odd given that they are a cheap form of transport both to purchase and to maintain. However, many roads in African countries are very poorly maintained with poor road surfaces and many potholes. Frequently there is of course also the extremely hot weather. There are few bike paths or much in the way of road safety provision for bicyclists. Yet bicycles could be a lifeline for rural health workers, villagers and local market traders.

One of the problems is that there is almost no bicycle manufacturing in Africa. One new idea for manufacturing bicycles locally has suggested using a locally available material – bamboo. It is stronger than steel (used as scaffolding for high-rise construction projects in much of Asia), would be light and easy to handle, and certainly strong enough to carry goods. Production is planned to begin in 2009 in Ghana, in Kumasi, a city close to bamboo forests in the Ashanti region. Wheels and parts other than the frame will still have to be imported.

SOURCE: COMPILED BY AUTHORS FROM PRESS ARTICLES

economy MNCs are simply to keep in the competitive global game. The other is a broader overview of the tensions within Chinese society, as well as a less rosy picture of its economic future pathway.

The view of Chinese firms as increasingly competitive powerhouses is strongly argued by Zeng and Williamson (2007). They describe growing firms that have moved very far from the old stereotype of Chinese firms as producers of cheap, low-quality goods for the world's markets. Instead they describe in detail a new approach to global competition that sees Chinese firms targeting high-value goods (although much less so in services) and moving rapidly up the value chain in terms of high value-added activities in engineering, design and R&D. They see Chinese firms developing faster than did the Japanese or South Korean firms that preceded them. Their approach is based on cost innovation, by which Zeng and Williamson (2007) mean using China's sources of cost advantage to bring high technology to mass markets at competitive prices. They are able to offer high customization alongside high variety and low costs, together with massive scale economies. This is a new strategy to address low-volume, high-priced niche market segments and make them accessible to low-cost, high-volume-based global strategies. They suggest that 'retreat to the high end' will lead to defeat for Western firms, since the high end is exactly where Chinese firms with their lower costs are now moving. From detailed studies of well-known successful Chinese companies (and emerging global brands) such as Lenovo, Huawei and Haier, rich with company detail, they develop their argument that there is no longer such a thing as a defensible global niche. Cost innovation is seen as a key source of current and future global competitive advantage and Chinese companies are getting there first.

In great contrast are the data from policy documents issued by bank chairmen, businessmen and state officials, gathered by Huang (2008). He shows that China was in fact more entrepreneurial in the 1980s than in the 2000s, especially in the rural areas where private enterprise was widespread and successful. It is because such enterprises were recorded as 'Township and Village Enterprises' that they have not been recognized as thriving businesses under private ownership at that time. Huang suggests that China is now, in the late 2000s, *less* entrepreneurial than in the 1980s and is more urban and more controlled by the state than before the economic reforms of Jiang Zemin in the 1990s. Rapid urban development was favoured. The countryside suffered, was starved of funds and blocked by red tape. Successful small rural businesses were shut down. All development was focused on investment in the cities, foreign investment was encouraged and GDP soared. However, income differences and social tensions rose. Rural schools and hospitals were closed. Between 2000 and 2005, the number of illiterate adults increased by 30 million. Huang (2008) argues that the weaknesses of China's state-led capitalism are a reliance on inefficient state companies, a weak financial sector, very high pollution and high corruption levels that, together, are increasingly distorting the economy. He also argues that the highly successful Chinese MNCs are almost entirely the result of foreign investment providing venture capital for domestic entrepreneurs and that these successful MNCs, such as Lenovo, are mostly domiciled in Hong Kong or in other ways have major subsidiaries that operate outside the control of mainland China. As described earlier, China's growth has indeed slowed a great deal since 2007. To what extent that is solely due to the global economic slowdown or to deficiencies in China's internal development, as Huang suggests, will no doubt gradually emerge over time.

'Some regions and some people may get rich first in order to bring along other places and other people and to gradually achieve a common prosperity' (Deng Xiaoping, great former leader of China and architect of its economic opening – quoted in Hewitt, 2008). Based on extensive personal interviews, what Hewitt addresses in his study of changes in China over the last twenty years is that the 'get rich first' bit has indeed happened, with little sign of the other part of the prediction of bringing along 'other places and people'. China has become both far wealthier and far more unequal, especially so among the rural poor, among migrant workers, and among city dwellers relocated to make room for new development projects. In terms of the consequences of China's economic policies, Hewitt's (2008) research supports that of Huang (2008). He also provides insight into the position of the teenagers who are the results of China's one-child policy: pampered but also placed under unsustainable expectations and obligations by their families.

This gives a richer and more nuanced picture of what being an emerging global economy, even or especially a very successful one such as China, can mean in terms of the internal tensions of managing growth.

EMERGING MARKET MNCs

A recent stage in globalization has been about developed economy companies outsourcing product development and services to other (often emerging market) countries. However, according to recent research (see Sirkin et al., 2008a and 2008b) from a leading US management consultancy the Boston Consulting Group (BCG), a new stage has now arrived. Sirkin et al. (2008a and 2008b) see the next stage of globalization as emerging economy companies from around the world now competing directly with developed economy MNCs. They compete not just on lower costs but also on greater ingenuity and efficiency. The emerging companies in India, China and Mexico have absorbed and applied lessons from their outsourcing experiences and are now in a position to challenge the companies they first partnered with. The title of their book (2008b) says it all: 'competing with everyone from everywhere for everything'. There are now many emerging economy corporate champions. An increasing number of companies from emerging economies appear in the *Fortune* 500 rankings of the world's biggest companies (see Table 4.2). In 2003, the *Fortune* 500 contained 31 emerging economy companies, mostly from the BRIC economies. By 2008 this had increased to 62.

In 2007, Tata Motors, the car-making division of the Tata Group, India's biggest industrial conglomerate, bought the famous (previously British) Jaguar and Land Rover marques from Ford Motor Company. There

TABLE 4.2	The ten largest *Fortune* Global 500 emerging market companies, 2008		
Company	*Country*	*Global 500 ranking*	*Revenue $bn*
Sinopec	China	16	159.3
State Grid	China	24	132.9
China National Petroleum	China	25	129.8
Pemex	Mexico	42	104.0
Gazprom	Russia	47	98.6
Petrobras	Brazil	63	87.7
Lukoil	Russia	90	67.2
Petronas	Malaysia	95	66.2
Indian Oil	India	116	57.4
Industrial & Commercial Bank of China	China	133	51.5

Source: © 2008 Time Inc. All rights reserved

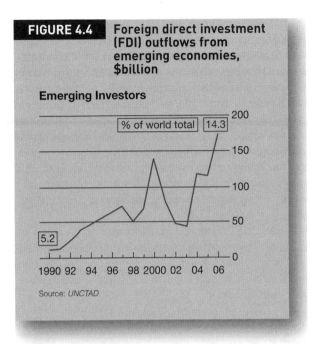

FIGURE 4.4 Foreign direct investment (FDI) outflows from emerging economies, $billion

Emerging Investors

% of world total 14.3

5.2

Source: UNCTAD

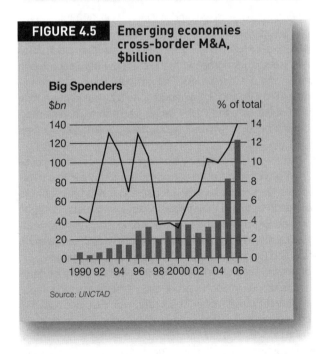

FIGURE 4.5 Emerging economies cross-border M&A, $billion

Big Spenders

$bn   % of total

Source: UNCTAD

was much discussion in the business press that this acquisition was a sign of something new in global business: the arrival in force of emerging market multinationals (see *The Economist*, 10.1.08). Tata Motors followed this rapidly by its announcement of the revolutionary, cheap 'one lakh' car, which will sell in India and South-East Asia for the equivalent of $2,000. The Indian company, which entered saloon car manufacturing only ten years ago, is now beating the industry's established giants into a new growth market segment.

Tata is not the only MNC from an emerging economy. The BCG study research (Sirkin et al., 2008a and 2008b) found 100 companies from emerging markets with total assets in 2006 of $520 billion, more than the world's top 20 car companies. By 2004 the UN Conference on Trade and Development (UNCTAD) listed five companies from emerging Asia in the list of the world's 100 biggest multinationals measured by overseas assets; ten more emerging economy firms made it into the top 200. By 2006 foreign direct investment (including mergers and acquisitions) from developing economies had reached $174 billion, 14 per cent of the world's total stock of global FDI (see Figure 4.4). Also, since 1990, emerging economies' share of global cross-border M&A has been climbing. By 2006 (see Figure 4.5), over $23 billion was spent in 1,000 cross-border deals. This data from UNCTAD reflects a new, fundamental shift in global business: that investment now flows increasingly from south to north and south to south, as emerging economies invest both in the rich world and in other emerging economy countries.

There have been some very large cross-border deals from emerging economy MNCs. In early 2006, Arcelor, Europe's biggest (French) steelmaker faced a bid from Mittal, an international steel group owned by the Mittal family, an expatriate Indian family based in London. The merged company, Arcelor Mittal, became the world's first steel company with an annual output of more than 100m tonnes. The high degree of government regulation in India's markets had led Mittal to look for expansion overseas, first in Indonesia, then Mexico, and then buying Inland Steel and International Steel in America, as US traditional steelmakers declined. Then they moved on to buying old state steel firms in Eastern Europe. Alongside the Mittal/Arcelor acquisition there was also the acquisition by

India's Tata Steel (another division of Tata Group) of the Anglo-Dutch steel giant Corus in 2007. Besides these companies making very big deals, a whole new set of multinationals from developing countries have been growing organically and through smaller deals. The Indian trio of Wipro, Infosys and Tata Consultancy Services (TCS) have built an IT outsourcing industry that has moved upmarket, become global and is competing head-on with established rich-country market leaders such as Accenture and IBM. In China, there is Lenovo which bought IBM's PC business, Haier and Hisense, two business groups expanding globally in domestic appliances and consumer electronics, and BYD, the world's largest maker of nickel-cadmium batteries. Chery Automobile, China's leading car exporter, aims to build plants in eastern Europe, the Middle East and South America. Johnson Electric, of Hong Kong, currently has half the world's market for tiny electric motors. Cemex, a Mexican cement company, has already taken over a big British group, RMC, and started investing in America when its cement exports were hit by anti-dumping suits: it became the market leader. Embraer of Brazil has become the world's third-largest aircraft company, specializing in regional jets. Two Brazilian food companies, Sadia and Perdigão export half their $6 billion sales.

The world's competitive map is changing. According to BCG, thousands of companies like these are expanding sales and production internationally. Costs in their home markets are low. Gradual liberalization in their home markets (as in India since the early 1990s) has exposed them to competition from multinationals in their home markets but also exposed them to best international practice and to entering foreign markets to compensate for lost market share at home.

Emerging economy MNC growth strategies

According to research by the Boston Consulting Group (BCG) (discussed in Sirkin et al., 2008b), emerging economy MNCs are following any of five potential strategies for growth.

The first is taking brands from local to global. China's Hisense is a $3.3 billion consumer-electronics group with over 10 per cent of the market for TV sets in its domestic market. It now manufactures in Algeria, Hungary, Iran, Pakistan and South Africa, with a wider product range that includes air conditioners, PCs and telecoms equipment. It sells over 10m TVs and 3m air conditioners a year in more than 40 countries. Hisense owns the best-selling brand of flat-screen TVs in France. The home Chinese market gives the company a vast, cheap manufacturing base, to which it adds other advantages such as stylish design and a world-class R&D centre.

A second strategy, followed by Brazil's Embraer, is to turn local engineering excellence into innovation on a global scale. Supported by the Brazilian government but now privatized, Embraer has overtaken Canada's Bombardier to become the world's leading maker of regional jets. It has been able to take advantage of a programme by regional airlines to upgrade their fleets to faster small jets. By 2006 over 95 per cent of its $3.8 billion sales were outside Brazil. It is one of Brazil's biggest exporters, combining low-cost manufacturing with advanced R&D. Embraer also has a joint venture with China Aviation Industry Corporation, ahead of their rival major US and European manufacturers Boeing and Airbus.

The third strategy identified by BCG was for growth by global leadership in a narrow product category. BYD, the Chinese battery-maker, uses a more labour-intensive production system than the Japanese firms it competes with to take advantage of low Chinese labour costs. Johnson Electric, based in Hong Kong but manufacturing in mainland China, makes tiny electric motors for products such as cameras or cars. For example, a BMW 5 series car has over 100 tiny motors to move the wing mirrors, adjust the seats, open the sun roof, and so forth; Johnson manufactures 3m a day designed to manufacturers' specifications. This focus has enabled Johnson to achieve 50 per cent of the world market. It now has plants in America and western Europe and R&D centres in Israel, Italy, Japan and America.

The fourth strategy is to take advantage of natural resources at home, and combine them with first-class marketing and distribution. Brazil's Sadia and Perdigão food companies have built sales organizations around the world to make the most of favourable home market resources such as climate and low labour costs, for producing pork, poultry and grain in Brazil.

The fifth strategy is a new or better business model to roll out to many different markets. Mexico's Cemex has become one of the world's biggest suppliers of ready-mixed concrete with annual sales of $18 billion in 2006. Industries such as cement and other building materials are bulky, basic commodities and expensive to transport long distances. They are therefore normally regarded as local-for-local, rather than global, industries. But although it may not be worth shipping cement from Mexico to Europe, Cemex realized that know-how and investment could be easily exported. Even before it bought RMC in 2005, four-fifths of its revenue was already coming from beyond Mexico's borders. It had bought or built businesses in Colombia, Panama, Venezuela, Indonesia, the Philippines, Thailand and the United States before it set its sights on Europe. Its global business model is knowledge-based and had a unique style of managing acquisitions: 'the Cemex way' which used standardized procedures built around highly developed IT systems.

These new emerging economy multinationals have some distinct advantages. They are often family-owned or family-controlled, even when they are public companies. This can help them to make decisions quickly. They also often obtain cheap finance from state banks. These two factors can be very advantageous when organic growth is too slow and companies need to grow overseas very quickly – usually by acquisition. Conglomerates seem still to work well in emerging economies, despite being no longer very acceptable within developed economies where they usually attract a 'conglomerate discount' on their share price since they are viewed as an inefficient corporate structure making poorer use of resources than more focused companies. The fact that a high proportion of conglomerates in emerging economies are family-owned may explain this real difference in corporate strategies and structures between developed and emerging economies. We should also consider the additional explanation that whereas financial and economic capital are prioritized in the developed economies, within emerging economies social capital is at least as important or even outweighs financial and economic capital. Many of these issues are illustrated by the case of India's Tata Group described in Strategy in Action 4.4. Successful Indian, Chinese, Mexican or Brazilian multinationals are beginning to reverse the usual brain-drain of talented locals into the richer economies. Their success is attracting talent back from America and Europe, where they have gained experience that will be useful in their continued expansion abroad.

BUSINESS GROUPS IN EMERGING ECONOMIES

In the discussion of the Tata Group in Strategy in Action 4.4, the concluding point related to the fact that the Tata Group is a conglomerate and it constitutes a large **business group**. Despite both business sentiment and regulation in developed economies being against such large business groups, especially those that form part of a related family-owned group of companies, these business groups nevertheless play a very significant role in most emerging economies. They are called different things in different countries: *grupos* in Latin America; *chaebol* in South Korea; business houses in India. Khanna and Rivkin (2001: 47) define business groups as: 'a set of firms which, though legally independent, are bound together by a constellation of formal and informal ties and are accustomed to taking coordinated action'. Such business groups are ubiquitous in emerging economies and are united in many financial, economic, social and business ties of mutual support. Although such groups vary, most business managers and owners in emerging economies have a clear intuitive understanding of what a business group is. They are seen either as a response to inadequately developed markets or to resource constraints and high transaction costs, or to institutional voids in these markets.

Khanna and Rivkin (2001) carried out a large study of affiliated business groups in fourteen emerging markets across Asia, South America and South Africa to determine how these business groups contribute to economic performance. These included Argentina, Brazil, Chile, India, Indonesia, Israel, Mexico, Peru, the Phillippines, South Africa, South Korea, Taiwan, Thailand and Turkey. They suggested that

Strategy in Action 4.4 *The Tata Group: an emerging multinational giant*

The Tata Group plays a central role in the Indian economy and is among the most international of all Indian companies. It was founded in 1874 by Jamsetji Tata with a single textile mill, and is very strong on corporate social responsibility. The family is still a major influence in running the group. It comprises currently around 100 operating companies and employs some 330,000 people. It is active in seven major areas, information systems and communications, engineering, materials (including steel), services, energy, consumer products and chemicals. It has operations in 54 countries. The Tata organization structure is called the Tata Business Excellence Model (TBEM) and is used as a means of increasing efficiency and tightening business processes. Activities are broken down into market development, planning control and risk management, investment management, operations, supply management, human resource management, and social responsibility and corporate citizenship.

The group is a conglomerate of the type unfashionable in the West. Despite being something of a loose federation of companies, there are a lot of intra-group activities in the form of intra group loans, cross shareholdings and interlocking directorates. There have been periodic attempts to rationalize the businesses, to exit declining areas and

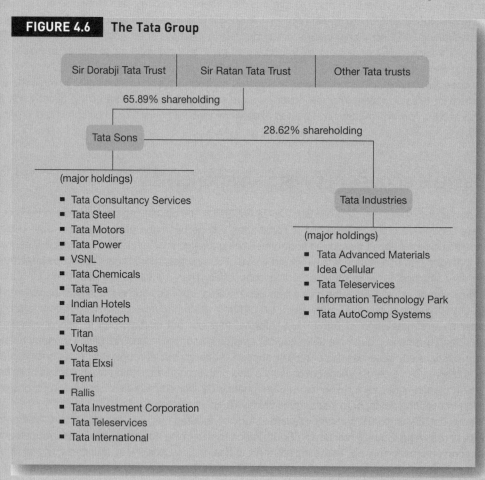

FIGURE 4.6   The Tata Group

Sir Dorabji Tata Trust   Sir Ratan Tata Trust   Other Tata trusts

65.89% shareholding

Tata Sons —————— 28.62% shareholding

(major holdings)

- Tata Consultancy Services
- Tata Steel
- Tata Motors
- Tata Power
- VSNL
- Tata Chemicals
- Tata Tea
- Indian Hotels
- Tata Infotech
- Titan
- Voltas
- Tata Elxsi
- Trent
- Rallis
- Tata Investment Corporation
- Tata Teleservices
- Tata International

Tata Industries

(major holdings)

- Tata Advanced Materials
- Idea Cellular
- Tata Teleservices
- Information Technology Park
- Tata AutoComp Systems

SOURCE: ADAPTED FROM A CASE STUDY BY CASI (CENTER FOR THE ADVANCED STUDY OF INDIA)

to re-focus on growth areas like telecoms, Currently the materials division (including steel), the engineering division (including motors) and the ICT division are the three largest areas accounting for almost 80 per cent of group turnover.

Organization structure

The group has two heads, Tata Sons and Tata Industries (TIL). Tata Sons owns the Tata name and trademark and its chairman has traditionally been chairman of the Tata Group. TIL's mandate is to promote entry into high-tech areas. Thus traditional and hi-tech industries are separated.

The Group Executive Office (GEO) guides the strategy of the group, and identifies where its value added resides. It works closely with the Group Corporate Centre (GCC) to guide the future direction of the group. Through Tata Administrative Services (TAS) the group is coordinated and managers are trained and developed in corporate values.

Internationalization

The Tata Group has been very international since the beginning of the twentieth century. It operates worldwide in both developed and developing economies. However 90 per cent of its sales are still in India. But in 2004 Ratan Tata the Group Chairman preached the need to internationalize in giant strides not token, incremental steps. Having bought Tetley Tea in 2000, acquisitions then speeded up. In 2007 they acquired Corus the Anglo-Dutch steel company for Tata Steel, and in 2008 acquired Jaguar Motors and Land Rover for Tata Motors. Yet at Tata Sons the main Board is still composed of five Indians and one foreigner, so there is a way to go yet before becoming a fully global MNC. However, there is a greater percentage of foreigners further down the management structure.

A large part of growth is through acquisition and this may risk derailing the focus of the core businesses. Problems of integration are generally held responsible for the high failure rate of many international acquisitions. Buying Jaguar and launching the cheap Nano car seem on the face of it conflicting objectives. Also a widely spread conglomerate does not help in the development of coherent and focused strategy. However, it may be a tenable hypothesis that conglomerates still operate effectively in developing countries and with new industrial giants from Russia, India and so forth, whilst they are held to be inappropriate forms for Western MNCs. Clearly the reasons why needs further research.

membership of a business group might either increase or depress the profitability of member firms but that members of a group are likely to earn rates of returns similar to other members of the same group. Some of the reasons for this are indicated by joint approaches within the group to such risky and expensive things as recruitment and training of top management. The leading Korean *chaebol* Samsung pools its international managers. Tata Group of India participates in an internal management labour market which rotates talent to where it is needed in the group. This is likely to be a more efficient practice than external recruitment. Similarly, since product and raw material markets in emerging markets may be highly variable, with few participants and weak contract enforcement, a business group can overcome such problems by trading internally. Khanna and Rivkin's (2001) results are clear. Although data from developed economies strongly supports only related diversification by companies, for emerging economy firms the recommendations are different. Unrelated diversification (which is what business groups do actually provide) works well in emerging economies. Therefore business groups in emerging economies should not narrow the scope of their business operations. One of the strongest explanations for this is that such business groups do help to fill the institutional voids that exist in emerging economies. However, they may act in different ways in different emerging economies since institutional voids will vary according to national context. Group impact is therefore contingent; they will fill different institutional voids in different economies. Therefore we should note that contingency theory applies to emerging economies.

Narayanan and Fahey (2005) cast an interesting light on business groups in emerging economies in their findings concerning the relevance of Porter's well-known 'five-forces' framework to emerging economies. They are looking at how well some strategy frameworks that have originated within developed economies, fit the conditions of emerging economies. As Peng et al. (2008) have already suggested, institutions are about the 'rules of the game' in each context and include both formal rules and informal constraints. As emerging economies evolve, institutional structures gradually move from being based on relationships and networks to 'arms-length transactions' (Peng, 2003). In other words from relationship-based personalized exchanges to exchanges that are based on rules, are impersonal and are enforced by third-parties. Thus 'formal rules replace informal constraints' (Narayanan and Fahey, 2005). However, it remains the case that emerging economies are defined by what North (1990) has called an 'uncertainty discount' arising from additional transaction costs in emerging economies from institutional underdevelopment. The most significant part of the five-forces framework that Narayanan and Fahey (2005) argue is inappropriate in analysing industry contexts within emerging economies is that of competitive rivalry. In developed economies, legally enforced rules do govern competition, anti-trust policy such as unfair trade practices between firms, and protection of intellectual property. In emerging economies such laws may either not exist or not be enforced. Therefore the whole notion of competitive rivalry in emerging economies is very different from that in developed economies. This has great implications for competitive dynamics in emerging economies both for domestic and foreign firms. It also emphasizes the importance of network-based strategies in emerging economies that are relationship-based and that stress co-operation rather than competition between firms.

Many of the uncertainties that comprise the 'uncertainty discount' in emerging economies, and arise from institutional underdevelopment, are external to both the firm and the industry. Since emerging economies rely on informal rules (North, 1990) and personal relationships amongst socio-political networks (Peng, 2003), in the short to medium term, strategies that are directed towards establishing network ties with firms or individuals or to accessing dominant alliances and government networks may be the most effective, indeed the only effective, way of building a market position.

Emerging economies, business groups and corporate governance

Our detailed discussions of aspects of the institutional context, institutional voids, especially relating to soft institutions, and of the role of business groups in emerging economies, lead to consideration of their implications for aspects of corporate governance in emerging economies. In a review paper on corporate governance and the emerging economies, Young et al. (2008) focus particularly on the impact of ownership structures. Concentrated ownership, extensive family ownership and control, business group structures and weak legal protection of minority shareholders all contribute to concerns about potential conflicts between controlling shareholders and minority shareholders, or even between two sets of major shareholders as in Strategy in Action 4.2 for TNK-BP in Russia. Such conflicts alter the dynamics of the corporate governance process. Young et al. (2008: 198) argue that since emerging economies do not have 'an effective and predictable rule of law this, in turn, creates a "weak governance" environment'. That is not to say that emerging economies have no laws dealing with corporate governance. They have often adopted legal frameworks from developed economies either as a result of internally driven reforms (in China and Russia), or as a response to international demands (in South Korea and Thailand). Young et al. (2008: 198) summarize their findings as follows:

> However, formal institutions such as laws and regulations regarding accounting requirements, information disclosure, securities trading, and their enforcement, are either absent, inefficient, or

do not operate as intended. Therefore standard corporate governance mechanisms have relatively little institutional support in emerging economies. This results in informal institutions, such as relational ties, business groups, family connections, and government contacts, all playing a greater role in shaping corporate governance.

Thus, although publicly listed firms in emerging economies have shareholders, boards of directors and managers, ultimately they function rather differently than similar roles and institutions in developed economies because they lack supporting institutions. Assumptions about convergence with developed economy corporate governance practices are premature and misleading. Dominant ownership, continuing control in the hands of a family, make policies designed for developed economies ineffective or even counterproductive in emerging economies.

Corporate governance is embedded in banking, employment, tax and competition laws and involves organizations, markets and political systems. It is therefore a mirror of the broader institutional context.

A similar situation and conclusions to that described in Strategy in Action 4.5 for China is also to be found in India according to Kale and Anand (2006) whose research charts the decline of JVs in India. As in all emerging economies, the regulatory environment plays a very important part in influencing the formation, continuation or termination of JVs in India. Kale and Anand (2006) found that whereas regulatory restrictions encouraged the formation of JVs in India until the mid-1990s, subsequent regulatory liberalization of the business environment in India, especially of regulations affecting foreign entry and foreign investment have had a negative effect on the survival of existing JVs as well as on the formation of new ones. As with the situation of Danone and HSBC in their Chinese JVs, what Kale and Anand (2006: 63) call 'the race to learn' between foreign MNC and local partner, and between MNC increasing pursuit of

---

Strategy in Action 4.5 *Two Western joint ventures in China*

In 1996, Danone, a French food MNC acquired a 51 per cent stake in the Chinese firm Wahaha Beverage. In 2004, HSBC bank acquired a 19.9 per cent stake in the Bank of Communications – the smallest of China's national banks but the only one that allowed the legal possibility of full ownership by a foreign firm. By 2007 however, both these hopeful joint ventures (JVs) were in trouble. The theoretical justification for the JVs was strong. It was a respectable way of entering a new market with relatively poor local knowledge. The foreign partner would provide capital, technical knowledge, access to international markets; the local (Chinese) firm would provide access to cheap labour, local knowledge and contacts and access to the local market. However, the JV arrangements of both Danone and HSBC have collapsed. The allocation of profits and investments was insufficiently clear and led to great disagreement. But perhaps more fundamentally, China's attitude to JVs has changed. Although it had become far more open to JVs in legal terms as part of the commitments made when it joined the World Trade Organization in 2001, its interest in foreign partnerships has declined. Domestic capital is plentiful; availability of cheap labour and land has fallen; and it has come to see its own domestic market as highly attractive. Resentment against foreign ownership (or part-ownership) has increased. Earlier willingness to consider the exercise of any options for full purchase has evaporated. Neither HSBC nor Danone is allowed to buy out its partner and thereby exit from the JV. They are stuck in unsatisfactory partnerships, unable to exit or to buy full ownership.

SOURCE: COMPILED BY AUTHORS FROM PRESS ARTICLES

4

an integrated global value chain via its JVs, have had a similar negative effect. Desai et al. (2004) have shown that as JVs are becoming increasingly risky and costly, globalizing companies have invested more in internal transactions with wholly owned subsidiaries in foreign locations. If the advantages of having globally integrated operations outweigh the benefits (and costs) of having a local partner, MNCs will enter these markets via wholly owned subsidiaries, and integrate these subsidiaries within their global operations (Desai et al., 2004). In effect, regulatory changes, institutional context and fluctuating political climate will affect the viability of JVs as a strategy in emerging economies.

SUMMARY

- Emerging economies have become a major focus for economic growth in the global economy.
- Since they are now part of the global economy, the emerging economies also share in the risks of the global financial system.
- Emerging economies generally have larger agricultural sectors, greater differences between the urban and rural sectors, and poorer infrastructure than those of developed economies.
- Understanding the institutional context (both formal and informal) of emerging economies is central to developing successful strategies in emerging economies.
- The institutional context of emerging economies favours co-operative rather than competitive strategies because of the ubiquity of business groups and networks.
- The existence of 'institutional voids' in emerging economies is a significant factor affecting the ability of developed economy MNCs to compete effectively within them.
- The BRIC economies are the largest emerging economies and are expected to become the next major developed economies.
- Since different international strategies will be suitable for different specific countries within their differing institutional contexts, it means that contingency theory applies to emerging economies.

DISCUSSION QUESTIONS

1 How do you define an emerging economy?

2 What are the major characteristics of emerging economies?

3 Explain why so much attention is now paid by developed economy businesses and governments to the economies of China and India.

4 Discuss some of the difficulties faced by developed economy companies trying to operate in emerging economies.

5 What are 'institutional voids' and how might they affect the growth possibilities of emerging economies?

6 How do business groups affect the way that emerging economy firms operate? Consider this question from the point of view of both local firms and foreign firms.

7 Consider how corporate governance is practised in emerging economies and what factors (e.g. the 'uncertainty discount') impact upon this.

FURTHER READINGS

1 Khanna, T., Palepu, K.G. and Sinha, J. (2005) 'Strategies that fit emerging markets', *Harvard Business Review*, June: 63–76.

This article is full of practical information on how to develop successful strategies in emerging markets. They explain why many MNCs have performed better in their domestic markets and in other developed economy markets than in emerging markets because they have failed to adapt to the different institutional contexts of emerging economies. It argues strongly that 'soft' infrastructure such as contract-enforcing mechanisms, regulatory systems or specialized intermediaries (such as recruitment agencies) are missing in emerging economies. They call these gaps 'institutional voids'. The article gives specific advice for mapping institutional contexts of different emerging economies.

2 Huang, Y. (2008) *Capitalism with Chinese Characteristics: entrepreneurship and the state*, Cambridge: Cambridge University Press.

An unusual and well-argued book in that it provides a detailed analysis of both the Chinese economy and its relationship with the Chinese political system. The conclusions go against the prevailing view of China's future world economic status. Huang argues instead, on the basis of detailed and impressive data, that the Chinese economic miracle is about to go into a steep decline.

3 Peng, M.W., Wang, D.Y.L. and Jiang, Y. (2008) 'An institution-based view of international business strategy: a focus on emerging economies', *Journal of International Business Studies*, 39(5): 920–936.

This is a useful, recent review article which explains clearly why and how the institutional approach in crucial to making sense of international strategy in emerging markets. Peng et al. call institutional conditions 'the third leg in the strategy tripod' alongside industry-level analysis and firm-specific resources and capabilities and then discuss why this is so.

4

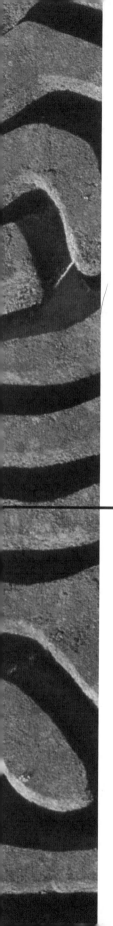

CHAPTER 5

The information industries

LEARNING OBJECTIVES

After reading this chapter you should be able to:

- explain the nature of industry dynamics in the information industries

- illustrate the economic differences between the traditional economy and the information economy

- understand that firms competing in these industries operate to a different business model from traditional industries

- explain the significance of unlimited capacity without rising costs, making diseconomies of scale irrelevant in these industries

- show the importance of installed capacity to the new economy industry and firms

- describe the theory of 'winner takes all' and 'tipping-point' competition and its implications.

INTRODUCTION

Castells (2000: 17) suggests that the operational definition of information is that: 'information is data that have been organized and communicated'. In this chapter we discuss many of the implications of organizing and communicating data for business purposes that have transformed economies, particularly although not solely, the advanced economies, in which such information management is the basis of a large proportion of economic activity. The boom and bust of dot-com companies in the 1990s may have led to over-optimistic forecasts of the degree to which the internet and microchip technology would revolutionize business models, company valuations and asset management techniques, but even a few years after the bursting of the bubble, it is clear in the 2000s that some things in the economic world have changed for ever, and the information economy (as it has come to be known) can be seen to have come into being in a number of industrial sectors.

Although the traditional economy still flourishes in many manufacturing and commodity sectors of industry, the **information economy** has taken in many others, and clear differences in the way economics works can be seen. The traditional world is one of planning and control, scale and scope economies and one in which costs rise after a certain level of output is reached. It is also one where the economists' concept of market equilibrium, strategic optimization, and a tendency to move towards the elimination of excess profits caused by product and company uniqueness, can be frequently seen. In the information economy increasing returns to scale are the norm, and hence equilibrium is rarely found as supply and demand curves do not cross as they do in simple traditional economic textbooks. These high-tech and service economy markets exhibit high uncertainty and very high levels of finance are needed to develop new and improved technology formats. Also, 'winner takes all' is the norm (Eisenmann et al., 2006); it is not good to come second in technology adoption. To have backed the 'wrong' technology means large losses, as both producers and consumers will converge in adopting the successful 'winning' technology of a rival provider if it becomes the new standard.

Organizationally, traditional hierarchies are disappearing in favour of task forces, flatter organization structures and power moving towards those with knowledge rather than seniority. The ability of technology format winners to lock in customers makes traditional movement towards commodities and hence low profit margins unlikely to happen. Instead profits cease to be made only when the existing technology format is replaced by a new one. In the new information industries, economies of scale and diseconomies of scale are irrelevant. Production volume can increase continuously without costs going up: unlimited capacity without rising costs. Technology development is more competence destroying than competence enhancing (Tushman and Anderson, 1986): in other words, existing technological capabilities do not retain their value as they are replaced by the new technology. There are no national boundaries to the information economy, and it constitutes a powerful globalizing force for information transmission and use. *The Economist* (25 Oct. 2008) argued that the latest transformation in the information technology (IT) industries is moving computer power into data centres which are the ultimate form of globalization: vast, virtual computer systems and electronic services that are completely borderless.

The new paradigm of the information industries

Castells (2000) has argued that what is specific to information industries and the information economy is 'the action of knowledge upon knowledge itself as the main source of productivity'. Information processing is focused upon improving the technology of information processing as a source of productivity. It is a virtuous circle of interaction between the knowledge sources of the technology, and the application of technology to improve knowledge generation and information processing. This constitutes the emergence of a new technological paradigm based upon information technology. Each element of technological development contains a performance principle around which technical processes are organized. Just as the industrial economy is organized around the principle of economic growth and towards maximizing output, so the information economy is oriented towards technological development. It is organized around the accumulation of knowledge and towards higher levels of complexity in information processing.

INDUSTRY CHARACTERISTICS

Different industries have different characteristics and competitive advantage within them may be achievable in a variety of ways. Figure 5.1 indicates a classification of the major possible configurations that may lead to competitive advantage for companies that read the situation and the opportunities correctly.

In Figure 5.1, there are two axes: niche players and scale economy companies. They generate four major possibilities for achieving competitive advantage. Firstly there are the small niche companies which are never going to sell large numbers of their product but which have something special about them. The Aston Martin or the Porsche car brands would come into this category. The products are frequently very expensive and have large margins and committed customers who often believe the brand gives them personal status. The Apple Mac personal computer or iBook is often put into this category although it would probably rather not be, as it might appreciate larger sales.

A few large niche operators are found in the industries where oligopoly abounds. In this category it is possible to achieve scale economies without losing the cachet that goes with the concept of providing something special. Companies in these industries have strong brand names that are able to deliver high perceived use value. In the sports footwear industry Reebok or Nike fit easily into this box or Microsoft in computer software.

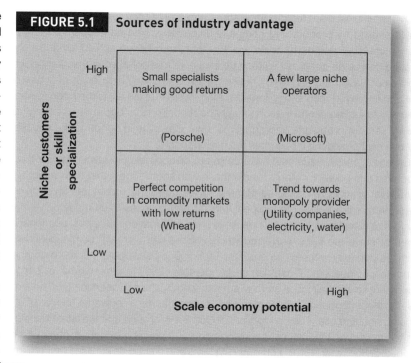

FIGURE 5.1 **Sources of industry advantage**

	Low Scale economy potential → High
High — Niche customers or skill specialization	Small specialists making good returns (Porsche)	A few large niche operators (Microsoft)
Low	Perfect competition in commodity markets with low returns (Wheat)	Trend towards monopoly provider (Utility companies, electricity, water)

The left-hand bottom box contains companies who have little going for them in terms of special properties, and who operate in an industry without obvious scale economies. These include the cardboard box manufacturers or farmers unable to industrialize their farms.

Finally in the bottom right-hand box we have monopolistic or potentially monopolistic industries. Water, power, railways may all be in this category. What they deliver is undifferentiated but benefits from enormous potential scale economies.

Of course the industry dynamics may change. The development of flexible manufacturing systems may erode any specific advantage from scale economies, and industries in the bottom right-hand box may move leftwards. Similarly technological developments may enable scale economies to be achieved in industries where they were not previously thought possible. In service industries moving from bespoke offerings to packaged solutions is an example.

In the top boxes where competitive advantage depends upon specialist skills or perceived unique offerings, positioning is always vulnerable to change in customer tastes which destroy the niches, or the risk that the special skill that protects the niche will become widespread.

THE TRADITIONAL ECONOMY

In the traditional economy all four boxes in the matrix of Figure 5.1 are well populated, and some dynamic movement is always present within and between boxes. It is different for the new economy industries where the top right-hand box is the one that is highly populated, although it may have few, or ultimately even only one company in it, namely the company possessing the dominant technology. The top left-hand box may have smaller technology contributors in it. We need to consider how this has come about.

Going back about a century in time to the historical industrial system, mass production in factories dominated and all services were only bespoke. Products were manufactured in factories by wage-based labour, and costs arrived at by adding overhead costs to unit costs based on the cost of raw materials and of manufacturing processes. Economies of scale and experience curve effects led unit costs to reduce as the level of output increased, spreading unit costs more thinly per unit of output. On the demand side, price was set by the strength of demand in relation to supply; the level of demand generally increases as price declines. Prices were determined at equilibrium, the point at which the supply curve rising, cuts the demand curve declining. Economists believe that output expands to the point at which the marginal supply equals marginal demand. Nonetheless, in the traditional economy, due to diseconomies exceeding economies of scale by the time a certain high level of output is reached, the cost curve eventually turns upwards and equilibrium is believed to occur when the two curves cross. In this traditional economy firms do not become infinitely large, because their cost curves turn upwards and diseconomies of scale occur. Furthermore competitive advantage was generally transient, since in attractive and profitable markets, new entrants come in and compete away excessive margins, and firms and products move towards the status of low-margin commodities. The world was one of large factories, workers travelling to work in them, organizational hierarchies, vertical integration and of planning and control. Of course, as we explained in Chapter 2, not all industries move towards commodity status, since some manage to retain difficult-to-imitate specialist skills that earn extra profit margins over the long-term.

Furthermore market power also prevents high profit margins being competed away as barriers to entry are established, confirming existing companies in their protected market positions. As Saloner et al. say (2001) these entry barriers are of three types.

1 Barriers that come from production and distribution technologies. These are essentially cost barriers, in that a new entrant would be involved in very substantial costs to establish itself in a new industry.

2 Barriers of brand name and reputation. Where these factors are important for success a time element is added as brand names and reputations take time to get established.

3 Legal barriers. These may be absolute barriers. For example under current UK legislation it is not permissible to run a lottery without governmental permission, which is currently granted as a monopoly to a single provider.

Economies of scope provide a means whereby a new entrant to a market may hope to mitigate the costs of the first two of these types of barrier. By introducing products produced in existing factories, distributing them through existing channels and relying on existing brand names and reputation, such available scope economies lower the costs of getting new products onto the market. Despite these market imperfections that lead to the development of imperfect competition, products in the traditional economy are demanded and supplied in a way largely independent of other products. It is this traditional economy and the industry economics that underpin it that is now being steadily undermined by the global technology information industries, with their network economies, and few aspects of competitive dynamics that are recognizable. They have created a new business paradigm.

THE NETWORK ECONOMY

In the network economy, costs continue to decline over any foreseeable product range, and equilibrium is never arrived at and is therefore irrelevant. Furthermore specific proprietary technological recipes come to dominate markets and 'winner-takes-all' situations enable competitive dominance to be maintained over the long-term. In terms of industry dynamics, therefore, the new network economies tend to cluster in the top right-hand box of Figure 5.1. Considerable scale economies prevail and proprietary technology removes the product or service from low margin, commodity status.

The concepts of network can be divided into two parts – real networks and virtual networks (Shapiro and Varian, 1999). Real networks have existed for centuries and include telephony, roads and railways.

Virtual networks are exemplified by computer and software **platforms**. Real networks are generally physical and tangible. They may be one-way (such as broadcasting) or two-way (such as telephone systems). The value of the network to the consumer rises disproportionately higher with the increase in the number of people using the network, since each additional user adds value for all the existing users. This is a simple definition of 'network effects' or 'network externalities'. There is little value in being the only owner of an e-mail address or of a cash card that can only be used in a single remote village. The benefit of the network rises with the number of users and the number of users in turn attracts additional products and services that may be used in relation to that network. The company that is expected to grow the fastest will gain the most market share; the installed base of a technical platform will determine the size of the consumer base. A well-known example of such network effects is that since Apple has only 10 per cent of the market size of the PC network, there have always been fewer software choices for its customers since software designers prefer to work for the computing technology with the larger market share. It is a type of co-evolution.

Virtual networks, although intangible, are similarly liable to the network effects that apply to physical networks. The development of the internet and the web has provided a free means for the rapid exchange of information, and the rapid gathering of knowledge through powerful search engines like Google or Yahoo, that would previously have taken considerable time and money to gather. An important implication of the growing importance of networks is that companies do not have to have vast capital anymore to successfully exploit new opportunities. The virtual corporation can achieve a lot as the business models of Dell, Sun Microsystems and many others have shown.

Sammut-Bonnicci and McGee (2002) identify four levels of infrastructure within network industries: technology standards, the supply chain driven by such standards, the physical platforms that are the output of the supply chains and the consumer networks.

1 *Technology standards* – Automated teller machines (ATMs) must work to the same standard across the world or tourists cannot withdraw their cash when on holiday in foreign parts. The need for global standards is therefore vital. The process to achieve selection of such standards depends on market-based selection and negotiated selection. Market-based selection depends upon the ability of a company to achieve the dominant design paradigm (Teece, 2006). This is a hazardous process and needs substantial finance, strong marketing and a lot of luck. Negotiated selection is less wasteful in competitive terms. An example of this is GSM (Groupe Speciale Mobile) the current standard mobile technology in Europe, which is an association of 600 network operators and suppliers in the mobile phone industry. It has established the industry standard.

2 *Supply chain* – With the growth of telecoms networks, of the internet and of the use of computers in every office on every desk, the construction of supply chains has tended to become unbundled into specialist activities of expert suppliers. The supply chain then tends towards the essence of an ecosystem. Internet service providers (ISPs) supply the chain of information to the internet user. Owners of web pages (companies of varying sizes from one person to major corporations) provide the content. The recently developed 3G telephone system provides an alternative means of both communication and information provision to the computer. Information economy supply chains become complex webs of data and voice transmission with each member having to collaborate with all the other members to be effective. As technology provision becomes more and more standardized, and more 'open' barriers to entry become lower for most providers, the challenge is to achieve some 'killer' applications that cannot easily be copied. However, networks are becoming more important than any one provider, and the more members join a network, the more incentive there is for others to join.

3 *Physical platforms* – These are the technical networks supporting telephones, satellites, TV and local area networks. Wintel is an example of an open platform for PCs. Traditionally many problems exist in connecting physical platforms in one country with those in another, for example historical

variation in national railway gauges from one country to another. The standards that govern how a system and its modules interact are called the network's architecture. The main components of the internet architecture are standard-setting bodies like the worldwide web (www) and the Internet Engineering Task Force (Vercoulen and Wegberg, 1998). The reach of the technical platform determines the possible size of the consumer base. Microsoft, with its open system, has a much larger potential base than Apple with its proprietary architecture. The Ethernet is an early example of an alliance formed to increase the size of a physical platform. Its strength was that it allowed PCs and workstations from different manufacturers to communicate by using an agreed standard. Examples of physical platforms are Wintel, Intel chips, PCs and servers.

4 *Consumer networks* – Products have an intrinsic value in use, and this is the underlying assumption of traditional economic theory. However in a network economy, there is a further value that arises from being able to take part in a network's activities known as its 'synchronization' value. For example, Microsoft and Intel have co-operated to make Windows exclusively compatible with both their architectures; this is known as the Wintel Advantage. If the joint architecture becomes sufficiently popular, it 'tips' the market and achieves lock-in for IT users and owners. Switching costs prevent users moving to another system unless they come to regard it as very superior. The QWERTY keyboard to the traditional typewriter achieves a similar type of lock-in through the switching costs needed to retrain to use a new configuration (Sammut-Bonnicci and McGee, 2002). Examples of consumer networks are PC producers, retailers, offices, educational institutions, government departments and homes.

Cloud computing

It is not only companies that benefit from network effects, but also new geographical 'centres of excellence' in ICT activity that are emerging. Mature industries in developed countries can no longer be guaranteed to dominate. Malaysia is developing two of the world's 'smart cities': Putrajaya and Cyberjaya. Similarly, the small village of Quincy in the middle of Washington State, near the Columbia River is becoming a hub for massive data centres loaded with thousands of computer servers (*The Economist,* 25 Oct. 2008) acting as data farms. The attraction of little Quincy is that its local dams produce cheap, plentiful electric power which is the key resource required by these data server farms, apart from the actual IT equipment itself of course. The reason so much electricity is needed is because these computer server farms use as much power for keeping the machines cool as they do for the computing power itself. Air quality is also important. In fact, Iceland is bidding to become the favourite home of mass computer servers and data farms – what Carr (2008) has called '**cloud computing**'.

'Cloud computing' is the centralization of computer activity away from the IT departments and systems infrastructure of companies (and, of course, of individual home computers), transferring it to massive data centres where it is managed and delivered like a commodity or any other utility. In Iceland, a local company (Data Islandia) is trying to establish the whole country/island of Iceland as a vault for storing the enormous piles of data that all organizations have to store in order to comply with every type of regulatory request. Since Iceland has a cool climate, remoteness for enhanced security and power from geothermal energy sources, it may indeed be the perfect location for the new 'factory' concept in computing of server farms (*The Economist*, 25 Oct. 2008). This is the next stage of the network economy. They will provide computing services on an industrial scale. Operators of computing clouds such as Google and Amazon will replace the inefficient internal IT infrastructure of firms' own computing facilities. They have already developed the sophisticated search algorithms for their core businesses and are extending these to wider business purposes. Currently, most corporate data centres are hugely complex and hugely under-utilized. They need more and more people, space, and power to keep them going. All of this can now be outsourced to a data centre. As Carr (2008) argues, companies will no longer have to house and maintain their own hardware or service their own software. They will just need to connect their offices, via the internet, to the data centre. This will be exactly like plugging a plug into a wall socket to access electricity. The data centre is a new kind of power plant that will turn computing into a cheap universally available commodity. These power plants will power the information economy exactly as the electric power plants powered the industrial economy.

THE INFORMATION ECONOMY

The information economy has characteristics quite different from those of the industrial manufacturing economy. It has the following characteristics:

- High fixed costs but negligible marginal costs (e.g. the costs of an extra pack of Windows software is a few pence). Thus there is a high cost of creating intellectual property, but not of reproducing it.

- Information is an experience good, as economists term it: you have to use (consume) in order to find out if it is any good.

- Information overload becomes the norm, e.g. Google knows everything you need to know, if you can access it with the right keywords. Value resides in the search engines and their manipulation of the vast amount of data that is available.

- An extensive, expensive technology infrastructure is required to produce and distribute information, and this needs to be compatible with other purveyors and receivers of information.

- Pricing is value-based not cost-based. It is determined by what the market will bear, and what the competition cannot compete away.

These characteristics have formed the basis of a systematic shift from the traditional industrial economy to a knowledge-based, information economy.

The creation of the knowledge infrastructure lies in extracting knowledge from the original knowledge providers, encyclopaedia producers, software and telecoms companies, journal article writers and other holders of knowledge. It is then bundled and diffused to a market via the distribution channel of the internet. The implication of this is that much knowledge has become a commodity, available to all, and the tacit knowledge that empowered the vertically integrated firm, becomes converted into explicit knowledge. This leads to the break-up of the extensive proprietary functions of the firm and its replacement by market relationships, out-sourcing, the hollowing out of the traditional corporation and its replacement in many cases by the virtual corporation or at the very least the heavily outsourced and off-shored organization.

Quinn (2001) described the process of the development of the information economy as coming about in six phases.

1 *Economies of scale* are created as large companies capture key knowledge activities, which knocks small firms out of the market

2 *Economies of scope* develop as the same technologies are spread throughout the corporation, embracing new products without an increase in incremental costs.

3 *Disintermediation* then takes place as proprietary links within the firm give way to market links, and the information generation department folds as the internal information management is

replaced by external information management. The visible sign of this shift is access to Google on every desk.

4 *Deconstruction* of the company's vertically integrated systems in the knowledge area then takes place.

5 *Deregulation* of knowledge then happens as new competitors with new knowledge make cross-competition possible.

6 *Redispersion* of knowledge finally takes place as more localized knowledge becomes important for reassertion of competitive advantage. Local brokers and selling agents emerge.

'The open standards and the universal connectivity inherent in information technology enable knowledge modules to be "snapped together" similar to the Lego system, without any expensive customization or reworking' (McGee and Sammut-Bonnicci, 2002).

Table 5.1 summarizes the basic characteristics of each industry type: the traditional and information industries.

TABLE 5.1	Traditional versus information industries	
	Traditional industries	*Information industries*
Source of productivity	Technical productivity	Knowledge
Objective	Maximizing output	Technical development
Sources of success	Economies of scale / scope	Miniaturization; economy packages
Physical characteristics	Large factories; vertical integration	Small factories; virtual organization
Competitive advantage	Transient; move to commodity; costs rise after a point	Locked in consumers; barriers to entry strong; costs decline with output
Co-operative strategy	Not vital	Key in network economy
Cost profiles	Varying fixed costs; substantial marginal costs	High fixed costs; low marginal costs
Market share	Typically spread over several competitors	Tipping point; winner takes all
Pricing	Costs plus; conventional mark-up	Value based
Value chain	Largely integrated	Deconstructed
Information	Proprietary	Commodity; open systems
Feedback	Negative feedback; equilibrium	Positive feedback; no equilibrium

THE NEW BUSINESS MODELS

Evans and Wurster (2000) describe the development of three new business models that have emerged from the restructuring within the information economy: first, the new competitor; second, the deconstructed value chain; and third, the reconstructed value chain. A business model can be defined as a way of organizing business activities in any given industry or firm that results in a profitable business. A business model would include investment decisions and the general design principles of the organization to make it an effective competitor in its industry (Teece, 2007: 1327). Each if these three new business models will be discussed in turn.

The new competitor

This approach involves a brand name company providing product in the traditional way but supplementing it by the provision of information direct to the customer that helps to establish psychological switching costs in the preferences of the customer. Thus customers can order books from Amazon.com and they will experience little difference from buying from an online mail order catalogue. However, once Amazon has got the customer's e-mail address and purchasing history, it can use them at virtually no additional cost (i.e. a classic scope economy) for the creation of preference lists relevant to the known tastes of the customer. This also creates the impression in the mind of the customer that Amazon is in some way its literary adviser, and gives it much greater market attractiveness.

The deconstructed value chain

In this model the service provider focuses on a few, typically knowledge-based, core competences that it believes it provides excellently, and on which its competitive advantage is believed to be based. It has then to ensure that the remaining activities that it is expected to provide can be bought in from quality external suppliers. It attempts to maintain control of its offering by establishing and retaining bargaining with its suppliers and partners. Thus vertical integration gives way to orchestration of a set of suppliers and outsourcing partners. The activities of Nike and Hewlett Packard are examples of such deconstructed value chains. Things can go wrong in this process, as they did for IBM when the outsourced partners Microsoft and Intel became more powerful than IBM. The result can be new powerful oligarchic suppliers, or fragmented specialist activity industries with largely commodity special interest products and minimal economic rents.

The reconstructed value chain

In this model, knowledge-based competences become the controlling element in the supply chains of multiple firms, often in different industries. Thus Apple software is not limited to the computer industry but becomes, through the medium of the iPod and iTunes, critical to competitive advantage in the music industry. A second phase of this reconstruction may lead to the development of corporate level core competences able to manage a whole set of collaborative relationships made up of a web of strategic partners and suppliers. Thus the vertically integrated company is transmuted into a *value web* in which the centre of the web, the knowledge provision competences, are held together by a technological corporate glue and extend across a range of other strategic linkages and traditional value chains. Microsoft is the master of achieving such a position. The points of leverage for this core competence are the specific knowledge-based assets that are applied across different industries. This strategy replaces traditional product-market strategies.

THE IMPORTANCE OF NETWORKS

Just as there is no point in being the only person with an e-mail address, equally it is difficult to be with-out an e-mail address if that has become the dominant form of business communication. Similarly, enjoyment of a sporting event is enhanced by the total size of the crowd. The crowd enhances the excitement level, shared analysis and discussion of the performances, and general memories of the event. This is a very generalized example of a network effect. For products, if consumer commitment is equally strong, there is a tendency towards formation of a single dominant network, platform or stan-dard; hence the power of Microsoft Windows, or the VHS format for video-recording, or iTunes for music downloading.

5

Critical mass
....

Given the situation just described, the battle for critical mass and therefore for the ability to 'tip' the mar-ket in favour of one preferred technology replaces the traditional battle for market share through the sale of branded products. In network economies, the customer will not buy if the installed base of co-users is too small. In the old world economics, value comes in part from *scarcity*. In the new world economy however, value comes from ubiquity, that is having a presence everywhere. In the information indus-tries, the more a product is demanded, and the more it is expected to be demanded, the more valuable it becomes. When the expectations of the market are at such a level that any new buyer considers buy-ing only from the dominant provider because of its dominant installed base (e.g. Microsoft Office), then the market 'tips' into 'winner takes all' mode (Eisenmann et al., 2006). This is often called the '**tipping point**' (Gladwell, 2000), the point at which one more very small shift makes the outcome inevitable. The skill of marketing becomes the management of expectations. For example, in politics many voters might well prefer to vote for a small political party, but in practice they don't, because they know it would be a wasted vote. Most small political parties never reach their tipping point for this reason. In this case, neg-ative expectations are self-fulfilling. In the 1980s there was a saying in corporate life that 'nobody ever got fired for buying IBM'. In other words it was a safe decision. That is what 'winner takes all' has achieved for companies like Microsoft, Google and Amazon. Customers might not love them but they will buy from them.

McGee and Sammut-Bonnicci (2002) agree: 'Traditional economic thinking is based on negative feedback systems in which the strong get weaker at the margin, and the weak get stronger, thus provid-ing a drive towards competitive equilibrium. This is captured in economics by the concept of diminish-ing marginal utility as consumption grows. In the new world of networks, positive feedback rules. In this world the valuation of a product increases the more others consume the product.'

Given these circumstances, firms with a new platform face a difficult business decision: should they adopt open systems and risk other competitors joining a network and managing somehow to appropri-ate the lion's share of the value-added from it; or should they market a proprietary platform, control it and live with the possibility of a lower level of consumers and users. In a well-known disastrous busi-ness decision discussed in every business school class, IBM chose the first route for its PC when it was originally developed in the 1980s. They soon faced a whole army of clones adopting its platform, and competing strongly from a lower cost base. This soon meant a dramatic loss of market share for IBM despite the proprietary technology. Meanwhile Microsoft and Intel, IBM's subcontractors, with less im-mediately appropriable technologies, gained the majority of the value-added available. Apple adopted the other strategy, and remained proprietary. The result was fewer consumers, fewer adopters, higher costs and a market 'tipped' towards the IBM-clones-Intel formula. So both IBM and Apple lost out. Rupert Murdoch with Sky TV seems at present not to have suffered a similar fate as he has built his proprietary network, weathered the storm of possible alternative platforms and seems to be emerging as a winner-takes-all competitor, but only after having to invest heavily in adaptations for each country market.

However, not every competitive situation follows that pattern. In Strategy in Action 5.1 we describe what happened when eBay entered the Chinese consumer-to-consumer (C2C) market.

5

Strategy in Action 5.1 *Alibaba versus eBay in the Chinese C2C market*

This research demonstrates how a local entrepreneurial network (Alibaba) gained competitive advantage over the dominant international market leader (eBay) which had particular advantages in terms of large network size, advanced technologies and a well-established brand. The literature on information industries and the network economy suggests that increasing returns to scale resulting from network effects may result in winner-takes-all outcomes. Global network service firms with large global networks, well-recognized brands, accumulated knowledge and established technology standards are expected to win against local players. In its market, eBay was a first-mover in China, which also should have added to the strength of its position. Looking at both eBay and Alibaba as value networks, they were firms that created value by linking customers who wished to be interdependent. Their purpose was to facilitate exchange relationships between customers who were distributed in time and space. The service was about delivering opportunities to their customers to interact. Therefore their services had strong network effects. With strong network effects it is the size of the network that delivers greatest value to the customer. EBay could provide global network effects; Alibaba could only provide local networks. Local network effects are when customers value relationships to particular other customers. Global or local networks therefore have different composition and value propositions for customers.

In 2003, eBay entered the Chinese C2C market through its purchase of local firm EachNet which had achieved 90 per cent market share at the time it was bought by eBay. As the smaller challenger, Alibaba focused on trade between consumers within China. They were more price-sensitive and keen on strong online and/or offline ties with other users. By contrast, eBay focused on trade between advanced consumers in and out of China. EBay linked Chinese customers to other customers in the West. Only those Chinese customers who could search in English were high users of eBay. They were mostly teenagers. Alibaba linked Chinese customers to other Chinese customers.

From June 2004, eBay started to integrate its eBay China platform into its global platform, thereby leveraging its global C2C network. Gradually, between 2003 and 2006, the market position between Alibaba and eBay in the Chinese C2C market shifted. By 2006 Alibaba's trading revenue in the Chinese C2C market reached about $2.5 billion, with 30 million registered customers. Alibaba launched a successful IPO (initial public offering) on the Hong Kong stock exchange in November 2007. Despite having paid an acquisition price of $100 million in 2003, eBay has now exited from China.

Clearly Alibaba gave more Chinese customers the network service they wanted, whereas eBay's service was limited to a much smaller potential segment of Chinese C2C consumers. What mattered in this contest was not the global network but the local one. It was the local network that gave more customers greater value.

SOURCE: FROM ORIGINAL RESEARCH BY FJELDSTAD, GAO AND BURKAY (2008) AND BASED ON THE CONCEPTUAL FRAMEWORKS DEVELOPED IN STABELL, C.B. AND FJELDSTAD, Ø.D. (1998) 'CONFIGURING VALUE FOR COMPETITIVE ADVANTAGE: ON CHAINS, SHOPS, AND NETWORKS', *STRATEGIC MANAGEMENT JOURNAL*, 19(5): 413–437; WITH PERMISSION

RULES FOR THE NEW ECONOMY

The following rules dominate the information economy as helpfully suggested by McGee and Sammut-Bonnicci (2002).

1 The new information economy depends upon the number of users of an adopted technology. Without the emphasis on users we are back in the old economy of marginal utility diminishing with increased usage. This is the doctrine of the power of *plenty* rather than of *scarcity*.

2 The outcome of competition between rival networks is hard to predict in advance. The management of expectations is critical, and until such expectations point strongly one way or another, anything can happen.

3 The development and marketing costs of establishing a new platform are very high, but the costs of 'rolling it out' are very low. Very high financial resources are therefore necessary in the early phases of taking a market to tipping point. Then the 'winner takes all'.

4 High uncertainty prevails until the market tips, and even then there is no certainty that a new technology may not arise and completely replace the current dominant one. Even now potential cheaper, rival replacements for iTunes are starting to emerge.

5 The law of inverse pricing often applies in order to get **installed capacity**. Thus SKY Broadcasting gave away set-top TV boxes so that the subscriber base for its services could be expanded dramatically. Google is free to users, so that it becomes immensely attractive to advertisers because of its immensely high user base.

6 Open standards are the key to volume, but they bring vulnerability to the appropriation of value-added by others. Protected standards limit one to a niche, and the risk of the market tipping strongly away from you.

7 The successful strategy is, therefore, difficult to determine, and depends absolutely on the difficult first decision of which network to join. If it turns out to be the wrong network, all is lost.

Inevitably such draconian rules lead to waves of dramatic competition and unstable economies. As a result, the new economies are either seeking greater regulation, or the stabilizing forces of collaboration. An example of this is GSM, an association of 600 network operators and suppliers in the mobile phone industry. They have set a common standard for mobile communications in order to create a homogeneous industry where equipment, software, networks (and therefore people/customers) can talk to each other, wherever they are located geographically. Standardization and enforced compatibility to ensure stability, have removed some of the risk from further research and development in the industry.

These conclusions are based on the original work of a maverick economist named Brian Arthur of the Santa Fe Institute in California. He was held in very sceptical regard until recently by his orthodox peers in the world of economics, but has an ever-increasing following, as his unorthodox views proved to have considerable validity under the new industry conditions that we are discussing here. He is most associated with the theory that returns at the margin need *not* decrease with volume, which is exactly what now characterizes the information industries.

The economics of Brian Arthur

Arthur (1990) argued that the assumption of diminishing returns made sense in the bulk processing, smokestack economy of the industrial economy, where the finite size of factories placed limitations on the degree to which scale economies could be achieved. However, developed economies have transformed from bulk material manufacturing to the design and use of technology; from processing resources to processing information. With this transformation has come the movement from diminishing returns to increasing returns, as the limitations of size and scale do not apply in the realm of ideas or information. In the world of information those that get ahead by strategy or luck, tend to move further ahead and those that fall behind get further behind. However, the world of traditional manufacturing (with diminishing returns) still exists alongside that of increasing returns, so both are found co-existing in the modern world.

Limitations in the traditional industrial economies were to be found in the number of consumers who preferred a given brand; in the limitation of national or regional demand; in limited access to raw materials and other resources; in the limitation of the size of existing production resources; and in the bureaucratic inefficiency that tends to come with size and complexity. In the information industries, with their increasing returns, this is not the case. The company that is far ahead can lock-in consumers. DOS was not the best operating system in the view of computer professionals, but it nevertheless succeeded in locking-in the market and from that was built Microsoft's power. That outcome was not predictable before the market tipped.

Developing market dominance in the information industries

Increasing returns, long regarded by orthodox economists as an anomaly, now dominate the technology industries for the following reasons:

1　They have high up-front costs but ever-reducing unit costs as sales increase.

2　Network effects guarantee the establishment of a standard, and this ensures the predominance of the standard bearer.

3　Customers learn to use, and then become accustomed to, specific technologies. From this arises an inertia effect in favour of the incumbent.

Traditional industries typically contained organizations with hierarchies, planning and control, optimization and efficiency. Information industries focus on predicting the 'next big thing'. Thus hierarchies dissolve and companies become task forces, organizationally flat, innovative and with flexible strategies. Optimization is replaced by being smart, guessing well or luckily, and forever changing. It is adaptation not optimization that is the order of the day.

Discounting heavily to establish industry dominance is one possible key to success. Netscape gave away its internet browser free and initially won 70 per cent of the market. Then it profited from spin-off software and applications but it still ended up being bought by Microsoft. So being ahead does not guarantee permanent survival. Since increased usage has become crucial to success, individual companies compete less with individual products than by building webs of alliances of companies organized around a shared mini-ecology of a shared technology.

Psychology is also very important in these markets. Since installed base and market dominance are everything, pre-product announcements, feints, threatened alliances and market posturing can frighten off competitors and also prevent customers making purchases as they wait for your new product launch. Microsoft is notorious for this spoiling tactic. Game theory is used to the full.

SUMMARY

This chapter has discussed the new paradigm of the information industries in the context of the shift from the traditional industrial economy to a knowledge-based, information economy

- The information economy predominantly consists of high technology and information-intensive industry sectors.
- The characteristics of the information economy are spreading into large parts of traditional industries as they in turn become more dependent on computer and knowledge resources.
- Information industries have different industry characteristics from the industrial economy. Information industries have no equilibrium point and no limits on returns to scale. Costs do not increase with the sale of any number of units of Windows by Microsoft.
- 'Winner-takes-all' strategies will occur when one technology (or firm) reaches a 'tipping point' when new customers 'naturally' choose it, since 'everyone else is choosing it'.
- Successful firms in the information economy with a dominant installed base will only fail when a new technology replaces their existing technology.
- Companies operating in the information economy also look and feel different from traditional companies. Their organizational hierarchies are flatter. Power lies in knowledge rather than position in the managerial hierarchy. Many are virtual corporations, and intellectual property rights plus powerful marketing, are the prerequisites for success.
- Even in the event of success, high uncertainty surrounds the sector, and deep financial pockets are needed to continue to stay ahead in the technology game.

DISCUSSION QUESTIONS

1 What are the key characteristics of the 'traditional economy'?
2 How is the information economy different?
3 What are the implications of constantly reducing cost curves?
4 Why is increased usage so important?
5 How far is the information economy likely to spread?
6 What is a 'tipping point', and why is it important?
7 Why does the concept of 'equilibrium' matter to economists?
8 Why are flat hierarchies and subcontracting so common in the information economy?
9 Is the optimum solution always adopted by the market, and if not why not?

FURTHER READINGS

1 Carr, N. (2008) *The Big Switch: rewiring the world from Edison to Google*, New York: Norton Publishing.
This book is really easy to read and yet deals with technically very sophisticated arguments about the direction in which computing is going and its implications for the societies we live in. Carr argues that computing is becoming a utility like electricity. Just like electricity, computing power gets ever cheaper and endlessly more powerful. He argues that 'all technical change is generational

change' and provides fascinating insight into the profound consequences arising from our wired world.

2 Castells, M. (2000) *The Rise of the Network Society*, 2nd edn, Oxford: Blackwell.

This book, is volume 1 in Castells' famous trilogy, 'The Information Age: Economy, Society and Culture'. It is an account of the economic and social dynamics of the new age of information. Based on research in the US, Asia, Latin America, and Europe, it aims to formulate a systematic theory of the information society which takes account of the fundamental effects of information technology on the contemporary world. Manuel Castells describes the accelerating pace of innovation and social transformation. He examines the processes of globalization that threaten to make redundant whole countries and peoples excluded from informational networks.

3 Sammut-Bonnicci, T.A. and McGee, J. (2002) 'Network strategies for the new economy', *European Business Journal*, 14: 174–185.

This article argues that the pace and scale of development in the ICT industries has had major effects on the economics of those industries and on competitive dynamics in general. The authors discuss technology standards, supply chains, physical platforms and consumer networks. They explain the emergence of 'winner-takes-all' strategies in these industries.

CHAPTER 6

Small is valuable: BOPs and SMEs

LEARNING OBJECTIVES After reading this chapter you should be able to:

- appreciate the significance of smaller and non-traditional businesses and markets within the world economy

- define the characteristics of the world's poor as a distinctive market

- explain the reasons for the emergence of BOP global strategies

- describe the differences between BOP and traditional MNC strategies

- identify the particular characteristics of SMEs (small and medium-sized enterprises)

- assess the importance of the internet to SME globalization

- identify the barriers facing SMEs in their quest to become global

- suggest some means whereby these barriers may be overcome.

INTRODUCTION

Most textbooks on global strategy focus on MNCs. This chapter focuses on organizations and environments that do not fit into this category. Instead, we discuss less-developed market segments that are mostly ignored by current global strategy and smaller organizations with the particular issues they face in attempting to globalalize. The first half of the chapter deals with what has become known as the base-of-the-pyramid market which covers a remarkably large percentage of the world's population. The second half of the chapter deals with the type of smaller companies that predominate in emerging and developing economies, but which are still great providers of employment in developed economies, despite developed economies being more dominated by MNCs. Such smaller companies are often highly innovative but suffer from problems related to their size and have further distinctive challenges in their attempts to become global competitors.

BASE-OF-THE-PYRAMID GLOBAL STRATEGY

Traditionally, MNC global strategy has focused on the developed and developing markets of the world and on the consumers within those markets who had levels of discretionary spending at a sufficient level to enable them to purchase consumer durables such as cars and washing machines, or services such as holidays, health care and insurance. In other words, MNCs have traditionally focused their efforts on targeting the needs and habits of consumers who could afford to buy their products and services. This is quite understandable. However, gradually another approach has been emerging.

An early starting point was the vocal criticism from human rights groups of the strategies of the global pharmaceutical companies for focusing their massive research budgets on the diseases and health needs of the richer developed markets of the world. The illnesses of economic growth such as cancer and heart disease absorbed vast research effort; those of the poorer developing world, such as malaria, did not. One of the most successful pressure campaigns of this sort was for drug company help for poorer countries where the AIDS virus was rampant but the price of available AIDS drugs was beyond what either governments or consumers in poor economies could afford. This has led to many agreements between governments and drugs companies to supply drugs at affordable prices to these markets under special arrangements. Although originally seen as part of MNC efforts towards greater corporate social responsibility (CSR), these initiatives have led to the discussion of a different business model – one that regards the poor of the world as potential consumers rather than recipients of charitable giving.

WHAT IS 'BOP'?

In a ground-breaking paper in 2002, Hart and Christensen put forward a new approach in global strategy. They argued that the poor of the world are very badly served by MNCs. They suggested global strategies for MNCs that focus on customers in emerging and developing markets instead of on customers in developed economies. They called these poorer customers the 'base of the pyramid' (**BOP**), that is the estimated four billion people in the world, of a total estimated world population of 6.5 billion, who are at the base of the economic pyramid, yet who aspire to join the market economy for the first time (the 'aspiring poor'). This is partly a response to anti-globalization protests that see corporate expansion as being at the expense of the poor and of the world's environment. MNC pre-occupation with 'top-of-the pyramid' (TOP) markets and consumers has overlooked the four billion BOP people who between them have $9 trillion in hidden assets, for example small parcels of land and other family resources. BOP global strategy is an approach that could be attractive to social and environmental stakeholders as well as provide some potential growth markets for MNCs.

Hart and Christensen (2002) argued that poor BOP customers need separate strategies across world markets different from those that are focused on wealthy or rising middle-class customers. They further argue that 'adaptation' strategies to national market preferences in different national markets is not good enough, since they are often still not the preferences of the BOP market segment, or offerings that are feasible for the BOP. They recommend collaboration with non-traditional local partners with local market knowledge of the BOP. For example, market entry into China or Vietnam for most MNCs has been at the level of TOP. That represents the easy pickings of market convergence and the global market segments that have greatest similarities with existing TOP customers of MNCs in developed economies. They tell MNCs little about the rest of the BOP market in those countries. They see the BOP as 'completely unsaturated' and open to new business models. For example, the Tata Group, an Indian global conglomerate, is producing a 'people's' car called the Nano. This is a small, simple, fuel-efficient $3,000 car aimed at a market segment that could not afford the cars that automobile companies usually produce. Hart and Christensen call this 'creative creation' (as opposed to Schumpeter's (1934) **'creative destruction'**) with disruptive potential for existing MNC products. If successful, it could provide a platform with extraordinary growth potential in all world markets through building a new product for this new BOP market segment.

RETHINKING GLOBAL STRATEGY FOR NON-TRADITIONAL MARKETS

Since the 1990 *World Development Report* from the World Bank, the accepted widespread definition of poverty has been people who live on less than 'one dollar a day'. The United Nations (UN) later adopted this popular definition of poverty as the base line for its policy to cut world poverty in half by 2015. In April 2007 the World Bank announced that 986 million people worldwide suffered from extreme poverty by this definition. This was actually good news since it was the first time that the count of the world's poorest had dropped below 1 billion. However, in August 2008, researchers at the World Bank, using new measures, recalculated the number of poor at 1.4 billion.

This did not mean that poverty had worsened. Instead the bank had made a vast effort to compare the cost of living around the world. Its researchers compared the price of hundreds of products in 146 countries. In many poor countries the cost of living was found to be higher than previously thought, which meant more people fell under the poverty line. The 2008 report from the World Bank also drew a new poverty line more typical of the world's fifteen poorest countries. It defined people as poor if they cannot match the standard of living of someone living on $1.25 a day in America in 2005. Such people would be recognized as poor even in Nepal, Tajikistan and hard-pressed African countries such as the Sudan. But since the 'dollar a day' definition has been so widely accepted, the number of people living on less than that at 2005 prices was also calculated. Table 6.1 gives both the $1 and $1.25 calculations from the World Bank 2008 Report and shows the distribution of these levels of poverty throughout the different regions of the world. Perhaps not surprisingly, the largest concentrations of poverty under either measure were to be found in China and India (both with their huge populations well in excess of 1 billion people) and in many of the stricken or war-torn economies of Sub-Saharan Africa.

People living in deep poverty have different patterns of consumption from that of the general population. They buy in smaller quantities such as a cupful of rice rather than a large bag; a single cigarette rather than a whole packet. As a result of having less to spend, the poor often pay more for their goods. However, in 2008 the Asian Development Bank (ADB) carried out its own study of the prices paid by the poor in sixteen of its member countries (excluding China). It found that in nine of those countries the poor paid less. The reason for that unexpected result was that although the poor buy in smaller quantities, they save money by buying cut-price goods from cheaper outlets: haircuts at the side of the road rather than

TABLE 6.1 Numbers living below the $1 per day world poverty line		
	$1.00	*$1.25*
East Asia and Pacific	179.8	336.9
of which China	*106.1*	*207.7*
Latin America and Caribbean	27.6	45.1
South Asia	350.3	595.5
of which India	*266.5*	*455.8*
Sub-Saharan Africa	299.1	384.2
Other	22.2	37.9
Total	**879.0**	**1399.6**

Source: World Bank Report, 26 August 2008

in hairdressing salons; open-air market stalls rather than supermarkets. The ADB survey found that for example in Indonesia, the poor's cost of living is 21 per cent below the World Bank's estimate and 10 per cent less in countries such as Bangladesh and India. Although the calculations differ, the purpose of this type of poverty count is to estimate how many people fall below an acceptable standard of living in our modern world. Table 6.1 shows the parts of the world in which BOP populations predominate.

So what does this discussion about world poverty have to do with global strategy?

As Prahalad argued in his book *The Fortune at the Bottom of the Pyramid* (2005: 5–6): 'the greatest harm they (MNCs) may have done to the poor is to ignore them altogether... The poor represent a latent market for goods and services. Private sector competition for this market will foster attention to the poor as consumers. It will create choices for them... These markets have remained invisible for too long.' Prahalad also argues that not only do BOP markets provide new growth opportunities for MNCs, but they also provide a genuine forum for innovation since these markets cannot be addressed with existing products, services or solutions.

Strategy in Action 6.1 gives a general summary of the traditional MNC mindset which has formed the basis of traditional global business strategies. It summarizes a business model arising from this mindset which does not see the BOP customer as belonging to a viable market segment worth investing in.

Do those who live at the bottom of the economic pyramid represent a genuine, albeit different, business opportunity that has not so far been addressed by MNCs? What is the business rationale for pursuing this market?

There are two views on this. One view is very positive and is represented by the work of Prahalad (2005); Hart (1997 and 2007); Hart and Christensen (2002); London and Hart (2004); Prahalad and Hart (2002). Theirs is a jointly held view that MNCs and global business growth can and should be part of the solution to the '**triple bottom line**' (Elkington, 1998), that is that global MNCs would seek to create strategies that delivered: first, social benefits; second, environmental benefits; and third, commercial and economic growth. They all argue that MNC strategies need to work positively to meet the needs of the poor. Questions raised include: whether existing products and services can be modified and sustainable technology applied to better meet the needs of poor communities? Are there fundamental market needs that currently remain unmet? Are the poor truly invisible in market terms or do current business assumptions lock MNCs into their existing global strategies as in the attitudes captured in Strategy in Action 6.1? However, there is also a second more critical view that argues the limitations of business solutions to poverty, a misreading of the true (lower) potential of BOP markets and the responsibility of government policy rather than business strategies for the gradual alleviation of the deprivation at the BOP. Strategy in Action 6.2 presents some of the less positive market analysis for BOP opportunities in India.

Strategy in Action 6.1 *Traditional MNC attitudes to BOP markets*

Attitude 1 – that the poor cannot afford our goods and therefore they are not our target customers.

Attitude 2 – our cost structures do not enable us to address the BOP markets.

Attitude 3 – the products and services of developed economies are not suitable or relevant to the needs of BOP populations.

Attitude 4 – only developed economies can afford to pay for innovation and have consumers whose needs provide an incentive for innovation.

Attitude 5 – the BOP provides no long-term growth potential for MNCs. While socially or politically of interest, the BOP markets are of no commercial interest.

Attitude 6 – MNC managers are not interested in BOP markets and are reluctant to work in them.

SOURCE: ADAPTED FROM IDEAS IN PRAHALAD AND HART (2002)

SOURCE: ADAPTED BY AUTHORS FROM VARIOUS PRESS ARTICLES

Strategy in Action 6.2 *The potential of the bottom-of-the-pyramid market in India*

Does catering to the needs of those at the 'bottom of the pyramid' (BOP) offer a business opportunity within the economic reality of the Indian marketplace?

India's estimated discretionary retail consumption in 2009 will be about US$436 billion: 45 per cent urban and 55 per cent rural. By 2013, the total Indian retail market could reach over US$600 billion, with both rural and urban retail markets around US$300 billion each. Food and drink account for almost half of retail consumption both in absolute and percentage terms, although other product and service categories are increasing. Most of this consumption is accounted for by the middle and upper tiers of the economic pyramid. In 2009, of the 222 million households in India, the World Bank estimates that 100 million of these households are below the poverty line, totalling about 456 million individuals. Of the

US$436 billion projected retail consumption in 2009, the bottom BOP (35 million) households will account for only 5 per cent or about US$21.8 billion. Only 9 per cent of this consumption (i.e. about US$2 billion) is spread across the 5,500 towns in urban India, while the balance (91 per cent or about US$20 billion) is spread across the 660,000-plus villages in rural India. Also, consumption by the 200 million individuals in the 35 million BOP households consists of: 72 per cent food; 4 per cent tobacco and alcoholic stimulants; 7 per cent clothing; and 8 per cent basic durables. Since BOP customer purchase frequency is much higher and consists of frequent low value purchases, the transaction costs are greater. BOP success stories may therefore actually start somewhere above these 35 million poorest households rather than in the BOP itself.

The implications of Strategy in Action 6.2 are that the business opportunities represented by the BOP households are likely to prove much more limited than the enthusiastic proposers of BOP business strategies expect. The argument is certainly not all-or-nothing between the two sides. The data about the Indian market given in Strategy in Action 6.2 is more fine-grained than the general figure of 4 billion BOP households worldwide. It emphasizes the gap between urban and rural markets and consumption patterns and also distribution and costs issues. It shows the tiny percentage of BOP household income that could be seen as discretionary, that is available to be spent on things other than essentials such as food, drink and clothing, especially for rural households. Indeed, in rural areas many do not enter into the market economy in any way at all. Many villages in rural areas or in shanty towns in cities in large parts of the world exist within an entirely local barter system. It is therefore probable that although a proportion of BOP is at a standard of living sufficient to benefit from new business approaches to their needs, it is likely that a large number will remain outside these new possibilities.

HOW BOP GLOBAL STRATEGIES MIGHT WORK

In the past twenty years the BOP as an idea and as a new global business strategy has progressed from idealism to practice. Whether the practice has been entirely what the original ideal had in mind may be too soon to tell. Nevertheless there is increasing documentation of examples of new business models in a variety of sectors that are addressing the needs of BOP customers (or perhaps more accurately just above BOP level) and that represent genuine innovation in their industry. Strategy in Action 6.3, 6.4 and 6.5 discuss three different BOP services and products in banking, computers and mobile phones that adopt new approaches.

SOURCE: ADAPTED BY AUTHORS FROM A NUMBER OF ARTICLES FROM *THE ECONOMIST*

Strategy in Action 6.3 *Microfinance: financial services for the poor*

In 2006, Muhammad Yunus and the Grameen Bank of Bangladesh were awarded the Nobel Peace Prize. Mr Yunus and the bank which he founded have pioneered an industry that provides financial services to the poor. In particular he created a means of providing loans to people with no collateral but who could benefit from the availability of small amounts of credit.

The Grameen Bank has 6.7 million customers. Most of them are women and all of them are very poor. It has provided more than $6 million of loans. Most loans are for less than $200. The story is that Grameen Bank emerged out of a loan for $27 that Mr Yunus made in 1974 to a woman furniture-maker. She did have credit but was paying a prohibitive rate of interest for it. Many similar institutions providing financial services to the very poor now exist around the world. Grameen Bank was set up with a set of important operating principles: although loans were made to individuals, small groups had joint liability for them; loans were made for business purposes not for domestic needs; collection of interest was usually weekly; although interest rates were significant often at 20 per cent, they were not extortionate relative to other available sources. By comparison, money-lenders to the poor and non-credit-worthy have been found to charge up to 500 per cent rates of interest. The money was never a charitable gift, always a business investment. Grameen eventually changed its business model when it restructured in 2001. It now places more emphasis on savings rather than credit and uses more individual than group loans. These changes are similar to the approach of other **microfinance** institutions in other countries such as BRI in Indonesia. They are part of a maturing and growing microfinance industry.

Strategy in Action 6.4 *The $100 computer*

In January 2005 at the World Economic Forum, Nicholas Negroponte (American futurist guru and founder of the MIT Media Lab) announced the idea of a personal laptop computer for every schoolchild to be priced at $100 and therefore affordable in the poorest parts of the world. The group developing the project is called 'One Laptop Per Child' (OLPC). OLPC was set up as a not-for-profit (NFP) organization. China, Brazil, Egypt, South Africa and Thailand have committed to buying one million laptops each. To achieve this very low price point, the project combined existing technologies in new ways and its operating system runs on free Linux open-source software. OLPC began selling $200 laptops in October 2007 to governments and institutions to provide further funding for the programme's ultimate objective of the $100 laptop.

Interestingly, this project is not just of interest to the world's poor in the developing world. It also puts pressure on existing computer manufacturers since it would reduce prices and provide a more basic format that might be attractive to many rich-country customers. By 2008, these latent commercial pressures had boiled over. In what was seen as the result of a conflict of interest, the US technology giant Intel pulled out of

SOURCE: ADAPTED BY AUTHORS FROM VARIOUS PRESS ARTICLES

the OLPC consortium and has left the project. Intel's chairman and the OLPC chairman (Negroponte) had been in considerable disagreement. Intel withdrew its funding and its technical help after OLPC insisted that Intel stop supporting other emerging market projects and non-OLPC platforms. Clearly, the success of the low-cost OLPC laptop could create a rival to both Intel and Microsoft in the developing world. The OLPC laptop uses a microprocessor made by Intel's competitor Advanced Micro Devices (AMD).

Strategy in Action 6.5 *Mobile phones – bridging the digital divide*

In the developing economies, traditional communication systems such as roads, postal deliveries and land-line phones are often unreliable or in short supply, since they all depend on underlying infrastructure which may be inadequate or poorly maintained. In bridging the technology gap (the 'digital divide') between rich and poor it is mobile phones that seem to be having the greatest impact. Research has found that a rise of 10 mobile phones per 100 people can boost GDP growth by 0.6 per cent. Nevertheless only about 5 per cent of people in India or Sub-Saharan Africa have a mobile phone. Even with the benefit of pre-paid calling plans, the main problem is the price of handsets. The cheapest handsets cost around $60; they need to be nearer to $30 to significantly boost affordability and uptake. In rich countries average handset prices are nearer to $200, excluding mobile phone operators' packages. Phones for these markets are also complex, with high design values and multi-functionality such as built-in cameras or e-mail as standard. In order to increase adoption in poor countries and boost long-term growth for their products, handset manufacturers have started working with mobile phone operating companies to develop cheap, simple handsets more affordable in poorer markets.

The GSM Association, which promotes the use of GSM to become the dominant world standard for mobile phone technology, invited operators from developing countries to bid for a contract to supply 6 million handsets at less than $40 each. The contract was won by Motorola and the handsets began delivery in 2006. Motorola insisted that this had not been a cross-subsidized internal CSR project but that the company did make a small but genuine margin on each handset produced and sold. This was the first time that emerging market operators had come together. Although each operator is small, the resulting combined market is large enough to encourage manufacturers to design new very cheap phones for the needs of mass consumers in emerging economies. The designs for these phones must be especially robust as they have to cope with particular difficulties in these markets such as unreliable electricity supplies. They must be very reliable and have a great deal of battery storage to allow for the low access to electricity of most of the target customers. The Motorola low-cost handset has a two-week standby time. There are also specific features tailored to local languages and preferences such as featuring a football game in Africa but a cricket game in India. The Dutch consumer electronics company Philips has announced a new range of chips designed to take handset costs below $20. Even so, this much cheaper $40 or even $20 price point still represents a far greater proportion of the customers' income than for customers in rich countries.

A separate problem for cheaper phone availability is government taxes. In Turkey, all new subscribers must pay a tax equivalent to $15 for connection. Uganda has a 10 per cent tax on mobile phones. In Bangladesh, there are taxes on new connections and also an import duty on all imported handsets. For larger markets such as Brazil, manufacturers can build local factories to avoid such import duties. Smaller markets do not justify such investment. Clearly cheaper handsets to achieve greater access to mobile phones require not only industry investment and innovation, but also supportive government policies.

SOURCE: ADAPTED BY AUTHORS FROM ARTICLES IN *THE ECONOMIST*

The services and products discussed in Strategy in Action 6.3, 6.4 and 6.5 represent the realization that MNCs must make products for BOP markets that are useful, cheap and robust, as opposed to those made for the TOP market which are fashionable, sophisticated and expensive. This is an argument about customers who need a $100 computer or a $30 mobile phone, not an iPod or a very beautiful Apple iPhone. While Strategy in Action 6.3, 6.4 and 6.5 represent genuinely new approaches in their industries, nevertheless it is appropriate to ask to what extent are they aimed at the $1 per day poor people of the world or, more accurately are they aimed at the next level up?

THE IMPLICATIONS OF BOP FOR MNC STRATEGIES

We have defined the BOP according to the literature as the estimated four billion people in the world, of a total estimated world population of 6.5 billion, who are at the base of the economic pyramid, yet who aspire to join the market economy for the first time (the 'aspiring poor'). However, there remain questions we need to ask for global strategy. Do all the four billion represent a potential additional market? What proportion of the BOP has the discretionary income to buy these new products? How many in the BOP could be approached as potential customers within a market, as opposed to within the subsistence economy?

Figure 6.1 attempts in very broad terms to demonstrate three levels of world market associated with the varying income levels we have been discussing. Figure 6.1 illustrates the size and nature of the world markets in terms of commercial accessibility for broad groups of consumers with extremely different purchasing power and vastly different locations within the world financial system. We see the BOP as consisting of two different parts. The lowest World Bank $1 a day subsistence poor and the higher level of aspiring poor at the bottom of the market economy (BME).

For business purposes, both MNCs and SMEs must have customers. A target market must contain people companies can sell things to. If they are predominantly at subsistence level of $1 a day or less, this proposition falls. Having hidden assets is not the same as having spending power. At present, research does not show which percentage of BOP are in the realistic market economy at all with any discretionary income. However, clearly where the BOP proposition makes sense is that there is a layer in the BOP that we call the BME that does represent the aspiring poor who can afford to buy the $30 mobile phone or the $3,000 car.

Below what Prahalad regards as the BOP, there is another layer of subsistence populations who are not in the market economy at all: the $1 a day poor. These are to be found in their millions in areas of rural India, China, Africa and parts of Asia and South America. Most of these are simply not part of the market economy at all. The next level up is the BOP BME population. These, though neglected by MNCs, are a ready market for what we might call sub-budget priced goods and services. The third level is what we have termed the TOP layer which has been the traditional market targeted by MNCs.

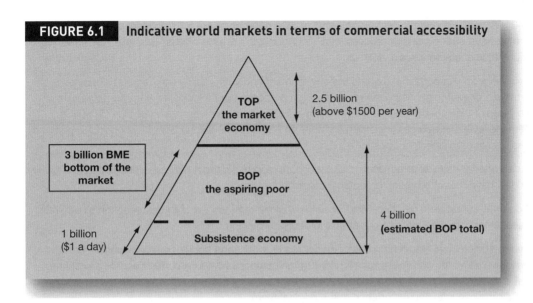

FIGURE 6.1   Indicative world markets in terms of commercial accessibility

We have presented two views (one supporting and one opposing) of BOP strategy as a realistic market opportunity for addressing the needs of the poor. Our own view is that there is a third, more accurate understanding of these developing market segments. The group or market segment that the BOP strategies address in the examples given in this chapter are actually addressing the middle layer (BME) rather than the true bottom of the pyramid.

THE GLOBALIZATION OF SMEs

It is of course one thing to identify the BOP market that is available to MNCs, and it is certainly important to do this if that growing market is to be served. However, there is the equally important issue of how the supply-side is handled. By this we mean how do small and medium-sized companies (SMEs) emerge within both the developing world and the developed world, to compete alongside the MNCs in this increasingly competitive global marketplace. This second part of the chapter addresses the role, significance and growth paths of SMEs in the global arena.

SMEs – WHAT ARE THEY?

SMEs are defined in various ways in the literature and by international bodies. The European Union defines them as organizations with fewer than 500 employees. The Homecomputer website opts for 'an organization of between 30 and 200 employees'. The European Development Fund, on the other hand, has this more complicated definition: 'An organization of less than 250 people with a turnover of less than 50 million Euros, a balance sheet total of less than 43 million Euros and not more than 25% owned by a non-SME.' In the US the definition frequently used is companies with a turnover from $15–50 million.

Whichever definition you choose, the SME sector is generally characterized as on the one hand the sector exhibiting the greatest growth in employment and the greatest entrepreneurship, but on the other hand it is the most vulnerable due to a range of factors, particularly a low level of capital. One major strategic mistake that could be taken in its stride by an MNC without causing a crisis could lead an SME to bankruptcy. Nevertheless, all recently grown mega corporations, such as Microsoft or Google, were SMEs not long ago. An analysis of how an SME can globalize should therefore be central to the understanding of managers.

SMEs, however diverse in technology and market segments, are an important sector for analysis since they have specific characteristics that distinguish them from MNCs. Blili and Raymond (1993) describe these characteristics as follows:

- Environmental – uncertainty towards the environment and vulnerability with regard to business partners. For example, SMEs do lose a very high proportion of their original entrepreneurs within two years of their start date. Decision-making in SMEs is much more restricted than for MNCs. Often the level of resources (including financial and managerial resources) allows only a very limited possible set of business options for survival.

- Organizational – simple structure and lack of spare resources. Most SMEs are under-capitalized and few have thought through an optimal organizational structure.

- Decisional – short term reactive. Most decision-making in SMEs tends to be a reaction to potential crises rather than well-thought-out strategic decision-making.

- Psycho-sociological – dominant role of owner manager. A large body of research shows the dominant role of the entrepreneurial founder of the business which can often become a problem after a certain size is achieved. As a result of growth, other skills are needed which are typically beyond the capacity and experience of the original team.

- Flexibility – proximity to markets, speed of reaction. This is a major advantage of the SME in that it does not have to go through layers of bureaucracy to take decisive action in changing market conditions.

These SME advantages of flexibility, reaction time, and innovation capacity make them central to economic development (Julian et al., 1996). In Raymond's (2003) view 'SMEs are presently at the heart of the growth and renewal of local, regional, and national economies in both developed and developing countries, especially manufacturing and technological SMEs within subcontracting networks.' Many MNCs that are now household names such as the Japanese consumer electronics giant Panasonic, originally Matsushita, best known for its Panasonic global brand, began as small, heavily networked and subcontracted start-ups. Matsushita itself was started in 1918 by the 23-year-old Konosuke Matsushita with $100 to make light bulb sockets in a room in his home. By 1922 the company had 22 employees. By 1985 it ranked 20 in the Fortune 500 list of global corporations.

The United Nations Commission for Europe prepared a substantial memorandum on SMEs in 2002. It noted that 7 million SMEs in the eighteen member states of the Central European Initiative (CEI) such as Albania, Austria, Belarus, Bosnia and Herzegovina, Bulgaria, Croatia, employ over 25 million out of a total SME employed workforce of 80 million employees. The memorandum notes that in 2001 about 25 per cent of manufacturing SMEs in OECD countries were globally competitive and SMEs contributed about 30 per cent of world manufacturing exports. It recommended a more supportive environment be provided for SMEs. The Bologna Charter (2000) also emphasized the significant contribution of a dynamic SME sector and entrepreneurship to restructuring of economies and alleviation of poverty. 'Ministers have also recognized the role of international institutions in fostering the development of SMEs and have therefore recommended further multilateral exchange of experience and good practice in order to strengthen partnerships and co-operation between countries' (Szabo, 2002).

Thus SMEs play a decisive role in emerging economies which have few MNCs. They are significant providers of employment but need high levels of support in accessing capital, skills and ideally also a 'big brother'. SME vulnerability to environmental business conditions makes the growth of emerging economies particularly vulnerable since they are disproportionately dependent upon SME survival and growth. Delphi Genetics (Strategy in Action 6.6) is an SME spin-off which has grown with the strong support of its original university parent. Without this 'big brother' in support it could not have policed its patents.

Strategy in Action 6.6 *Delphi Genetics*

Delphi Genetics of Belgium operates in a global market. It has just nine employees and half a million euros in sales. It makes kits for DNA engineering used by pharmaceutical and university research labs, and has support from its parent university to keep close ties to its global distributors and licensees, and to maintain a strong patent position that supports its core technological invention.

Delphi's story began in 1993, when two university scientists from Brussels came up with a new technology that simplified DNA fragment cloning. The university filed a patent to protect the invention and licensed the technology to a California-based company. In early 1995, this licensee launched a product using the technology. In November 2001 a business was created to manage a growing number of patents and continue research in the field of molecular cloning. With just €80,000 in cash, acquiring the patents wasn't an option, so the founders decided to continue working with the university. The college currently owns nine patents and Delphi holds the exclusive rights to license and sub-license them.

Delphi's customers are distributors who buy and sell its kits (i.e. development tools for DNA engineering) worldwide to large pharmaceutical companies such as GlaxoSmithKline and Sanofi-Aventis, as well as to university laboratories around Europe. In its specialized niche, there are few competitors and most of them are US-based. Seventy per cent of Delphi's sales are European. Another 15 per cent of sales come from Asia, while the remaining 15 per cent are from America.

Managing intellectual property (IP) is Delphi's primary business, and the protection of these assets is vital. Despite the importance of IP, Delphi Genetics is a small player and only limited company resources are devoted to the task. The annual budget for IP is 5 to 10 per cent of the cost of R&D. Fortunately, a strong relationship with the university helps. Not only does R&D take place there, but the university covers patent filing costs.

The task of keeping tabs on new filings and possible infringements is the CEO's job, although it's made somewhat simpler by the fact that Delphi's patents are from the same family, and Delphi scientists are in constant contact with university labs. Working closely with distributors and their customers helps keep the distributors' sales people better informed about the products and gives Delphi's managers new ideas about their products by seeing how they are used.

The CEO learned the hard way about the high costs of fighting infringement. In the late 1990s, a US competitor developed a product that used Delphi's patented technology. He looked to the university for help but the battle was left up to Delphi. Delphi bought the license off the university violating the term of the contract. Perhaps not surprisingly, the company's executives said they didn't see a conflict. The case ended up in arbitration and cost a lot of money. As he says, 'We generally don't have money to fight infringements. . . .If you have good technology you have to think that some day it will be copied. You have to live with that. If it's not a good technology, it won't be copied.'

The experience taught the team some valuable lessons too. The licensing contract had been set for ten years, during which seven years had passed without visits by either company. A little interpersonal contact would have gone a long way.

Delphi prefers to work with American universities which have a process in place for creating agreements. Deals can be made within a few weeks. Delphi is a small fish in a large pond and without a university's support it might never have survived.

SOURCE: ABRIDGED FROM WWW.SME.EUROPEAN-PATENT-OFFICE.ORG WEBSITE

6

SME GLOBALIZATION AND THE INTERNET

In recent years a model for rapid globalization has been popularized and is generally based upon the rapid global growth of internet businesses. This is the framework of the '**Born-Global**' Company (McKinsey, 1993; Rasmussen and Madsen, 2002). In this framework, companies operate globally in less than two years from starting to trade. This can happen particularly due to the abundance of information available through the internet. Products can be advertised and sold globally on the internet, executives recruited, market research carried out, sales agents appointed and joint venture partners found, all with the click of a mouse. This has been an enormous advantage to an SME without strong intelligence back-up capacity. It made possible the choice of non-equity modes of entry to foreign markets that have low resource requirements, and are flexible. These are factors that are important to most SMEs. Hamil and Gregory (1997) describe the way that the internet can provide a low-cost gateway to world markets and help to overcome many of the barriers and obstacles to globalization. Poon and Jevons (1997) note that the internet has created unpredictable and unprecedented opportunities for SMEs to enable access to markets in a similar way to MNCs and thus engage in global marketing which otherwise they could not afford.

Chrysostome and Rosson (2004) identify the advantages and limitations of using the internet approach. They identify the often accidental mode in which an SME may become global. What has happened as a result of the internet is that SMEs may sleepwalk into becoming global. **Strategic markets** (Barwise and Robertson, 1992), that is those markets that will buy your product and provide strong sales, may now be self-selecting without the specific strategic intent of the SME managers. 'The internet does not only help SMEs to begin to internationalize but helps to maintain a strong position in foreign markets through such activities as marketing intelligence, global sales promotion and inter-firm R&D. It is a gateway to foreign markets. It enables SMEs to become international whether it was planned or not' (Lituchy and Rail, 2000). The advantages of the internet that enable an SME to be a Born-Global include: speeding the pace of SME market entry; facilitating multiple foreign market entries; influencing SMEs' choice of market entry mode; and helping SMEs to build inter-firm networks in foreign markets.

However, the internet does have distinct limitations:

1 SMEs using the internet face global competition with transparent pricing from day one, and much of this competition will come from already established MNCs. It does also mean that MNCs have access to much SME business data from their websites.

2 The internet is not a substitute for face-to-face contact when establishing relationships. There are significant trust issues at stake both for the SME in trusting its customers and in the customers trusting the SME, when the only contact is the internet. Also many cultures have extremely strong traditions of building business relationships through personal contacts.

3 Not everything you read on the internet is true and information found there is difficult to evaluate if it is your main source of intelligence.

4 The internet may expose globalizing SMEs to higher operating costs, especially from web-page creation and constant updating and improvement. This point is counter-intuitive, since managers usually expect operating via the internet to be a cheaper method of marketing and expect to save rather than spend additional investment funds.

5 Finally it may well expose unsuspecting SMEs to legal issues in foreign markets of which they are unaware. MNCs have in-house legal departments to check and warn them of all such market specifics, whereas SMEs do not.

Although the internet is available to all and is a mine of useful information, such information is also universally available and the information is difficult to validate. It can help an SME get started internationally, but it cannot make it successful. Creating a webpage may make the smallest company into an international player, but it does not enable it to make a sale. At the outset no one knows the webpage is there, and the exercise in what is called 'driving traffic to your website' is neither cheap nor easy to do. Thus, although the internet undoubtedly aids the SME seeking to globalize by providing low-cost communication, round-the-clock operation and simultaneous exposure to multiple markets both for intelligence gathering and e-commerce, there are also limitations. Relationships established on the internet are shallow without face-to-face reinforcement to build trust and commitment in partners, and competition is stronger and more direct than in pre-internet days.

In Strategy in Action 6.7 the company has managed to create a virtual corporation based upon outworkers with a very small core staff. However, these outworkers are integrated into the company using a number of approaches to motivate the staff. The company therefore avoids the common error of the internet-based start-up of assuming high levels of motivation in employees recruited directly from the web without face-to-face contact.

BARRIERS TO GOING GLOBAL FOR SMEs

Undoubtedly the existence of the internet enables a company with few resources to trade globally for little more than the cost of creating and maintaining a website. 'An SME with a web-site is in effect a global company' (Chrysostome and Rosson, 2004). Indeed many companies with websites and grand sounding names have been found on investigation to consist of no more than a computer literate individual operating from his bedroom. However, this alone is not a sufficient route to global success. It may get you to the starting line, but will not enable you to win the race. Many more traditional resources and capabilities are needed for that. SMEs by their very nature face many disadvantages.

Lack of capital for FDI. SMEs tend to be owned by individual entrepreneurs or small teams of venturers. They are unlikely to have much, if any, free capital and their personal assets are often invested in the company already, and are not liquid. Consequently the idea of setting up a foreign subsidiary is often not financially possible. That requires expending the money necessary to move beyond the internet to achieve real intelligence, that is that which is not already in the public domain, which by definition all internet information already is. Lack of financial resources therefore provides a barrier that does not exist for the established MNC.

Inadequate expenditure on marketing, acquisition of information, salaries or product adaptation. SMEs frequently practise false economies in relation to what they believe to be unnecessary and avoidable costs. They do not spend enough on essentials such as marketing and thus are unable to make their presence felt or even recognized in a market. They do not spend money on market research and other information intelligence support activities. Therefore they frequently make unwise decisions since they lack a realistic picture of the market, and rely on idiosyncratic word of mouth and gossip on the grapevine. They pay their staff badly, and consequently high-quality staff leave to take jobs with larger companies. Sometimes this is overcome by providing equity incentives that would not be available in larger companies, but this can only go so far before the equity required by investors is compromised. Finally they are unable to adapt their products to local conditions perhaps because they do not know how to, but more often because they cannot afford to do so, since such adaptation may be expensive. It may however be necessary if a sale is to be made.

Lack of access to funds or higher costs of capital than for MNCs. Not only are SMEs frequently undercapitalized and short on working capital, they also find it difficult to obtain funds from lending institutions. Banks are frequently unwilling to accept their security. They, in turn, do not trust banks. Venture capital companies are thought to be too greedy by many an entrepreneur and finance, if offered, is far more

Strategy in Action 6.7 *Rauser Advertainment AG: key success factors for SME survival*

Rauser Advertainment operates as a virtual organization worldwide. It has specialized in the development of entertainment and advertising products (e.g. computer games, screen savers). The computer games are used by the customers as advertising tools which are given away as 'freeware' free for duplication. Rauser Advertainment is located in Reutlingen, Germany, the home town of its founder Thorsten Rauser. Since 1989 the company has grown moderately. From the original three full-time staff members it has grown to six. Also the freelance network has grown from less than 10 in the beginning, to around 50 in the mid-1990s and 100 today.

For each new contract a project manager from the group of staff members puts together a team of workers from among the freelancers to develop an advertainment (i.e. combined advertising and entertainment) product on disc or CD-ROM according to customer requirements and specification. The teams are mainly derived from a core group of freelancers of around 30 regulars.

With its organizational and legal construction Rauser Advertainment is a classical example of a virtual organization. The geographical location of the team members and their working times are of no importance; fixed working hours are irrelevant. The company actively searches the web for new talented freelancers for the development of advertainment products. Teleco-operation is the normal way of working and communicating. Personal contacts are the absolute exception. Although communication is carried out via e-mail and file transfer, great emphasis is placed on developing commitment to Rauscher by means of a number of motivational policies. For example share options are available to freelance operators as are company training schemes. With a strict quality orientation Rauser Advertainment has become one of the German market leaders in the advertainment

business and has received a large number of awards for its products.

Operating as a virtual organization of mostly freelancers provides Rauser Advertainment with great flexibility and low fixed costs. For the employees as well as the freelance workers a participation model and associated benefits packages strengthen the ties between them and the company. Workers can stay in the living environment of their choice and do not have to move to the company's location in Reutlingen.

A virtual organization is also an attractive work option for those individuals not interested in working for a sole employer and also seeking high income levels since they can work for a number of different clients at a time.

Barriers to success

High telecommunications costs, low data transfer rates and network bandwidths, loss of data in data transmission, lack of compatibility of systems and data security in data transmission have been the major barriers to success in the past. To some extent these are still in existence and act as constraining factors. Further problems (mostly in terms of product quality and meeting deadlines) sometimes occur when new team members have to be integrated.

Rauser Advertainment plans the continuous expansion and optimization of its pool of freelance workers, The company wants to become the world market leader in the advertainment business. An important prerequisite for this is seen in the best possible networking via telecommunications networks. In addition, the problems in the timing of projects as well as in the development of a team spirit will be worked on and hopefully overcome in the not too distant future. Rauser Advertainment aims at growing in terms of production capacity but also in terms of offerings.

SOURCE: ABRIDGED FROM WWW.FLEXWORK.EU.COM WEBSITE

expensive for SMEs than for their larger MNC competitors. Banks set a higher rate of interest to allow for what they perceive to be greater risk, and venture capital companies demand large amount of equity for their services, which the SMEs are often unwilling to concede lest it weaken their control of their company.

Inadequately developed global networks. SMEs are also generally novices in the global arena and have often not been able to develop an effective global network of potential allies to enhance the inherent skill weaknesses from which all small businesses suffer. They may identify possible partners on the web, but such a method of partner identification is fraught with risk as many websites are not to be trusted. Only time, working together and face-to-face contact can validate the trustworthiness of partners, and SMEs often lack any of these conditions.

Difficulty in recruiting and paying top-quality executives. SMEs cannot easily recruit top internationally experienced managers. Firstly they cannot pay them international level salaries, and secondly the lack of a known brand name makes them unattractive on the job market. They are also frequently deficient in fringe benefits like pensions, life insurance and private medical care that established MNCs can offer as part of a signing on package.

Lack of management with international experience. Not only is it difficult for SMEs to recruit internationally experienced managers, but they are unlikely to have them already in their top management team. Most SMEs are seeking to go global after having established themselves in a niche in their home market. Their managers in all likelihood are not internationally experienced at this point and are likely to be strongly ethnocentric.

Difficulty in establishing a clearly differentiated niche. In order to survive against MNC competition, SMEs need a clear protected market niche or well-understood market segment to address.

Strategy in Action 6.8 *The Faulkner Sports story*

Faulkner Sports was an SME that operated in the UK in the 1980s. It had many of the advantages and vulnerabilities discussed in this chapter. Despite lacking adequate capital, high-quality management, marketing skills and resources or any leverage with the banks, it was successful in marketing the 'Frisbee' (plastic throwing disc) throughout Europe. It did this through its possession (under licence) of the strong 'Frisbee' brand name in a clear niche market. However, to become financially sustainable in the longer term, the SME needed a second product line. It bought a golf ball company only to discover that the advantages that gave it Frisbee success, that is its strong brand name in a well-defined niche leisure market, soon disappeared. The golf ball is not a niche market. Other competitors in the golf ball market are major MNCs with deep pockets for whom this is merely part of their business portfolio. The acquired company, called Penfold, was not an internationally strong brand name in golf balls. Faulkner Sports soon foundered under competition from MNCs with stronger branded products and larger marketing strength and budgets. Despite the continuing success of the Frisbee, the company collapsed due to its failure in the golf ball market. By expanding into the wrong market segment, as an SME it had not sufficient resources to survive its vulnerability in the face of strong MNC competition with their well-established brands. Despite its unique brand name (the 'Frisbee') and its clearly identified niche market in a minor but insufficiently large segment, the SME was successful in the niche market with Frisbee, but ultimately failed in the MNC-dominated golf ball market.

However, it is by no means easy to identify and gain market share when they are unfamiliar with a foreign market.

Weak brand name. To go global it is a great advantage to have an instantly recognizable brand name like McDonald's or IBM. SMEs rarely have high name recognition and find themselves therefore on a par with small local companies in host countries but without the local network or know-how. In Dunning's (1974) terms they lack 'O' (ownership) advantages of which the brand name (e.g. Coca-Cola) is one of the most common ownership advantage possessed by MNCs (see Strategy in Action 6.8).

OVERCOMING THE BARRIERS

Given the barriers listed in the previous section that are problematic for an SME attempting to become global, is it perhaps surprising that SMEs do in fact sometimes go global and succeed. How do they do it?

Firstly some SMEs are just rapidly passing through that status. From foundation to establishment as a full-blown MNC there is obviously a period in which the company is not yet large. However, companies bound for greater things need, even early on, the characteristics that will make them large one day: unique technology and products, a unique business model, industry segments that provide economies of scope and scale, brand names that are establishing themselves globally, and consequent competitive advantage. These may currently be SMEs but they are really evolving MNCs in disguise. Such a description is true of many current world names such as Sony of Japan in consumer electronics in the 1970s and 1980s or the Indian brand Wipro that rapidly established itself in global business systems support services in the early 2000s.

A number of factors can help SMEs overcome barriers to global expansion. The internet itself may be as much a problem as a benefit. Strategy in Action 6.9 describes some ways in which SMEs can overcome barriers to globalization.

With the factors listed in Strategy in Action 6.9 in mind, SMEs can and do operate successfully internationally. Particular attention should also be paid to the majority of the following additional factors.

Find markets in which there are few economies of scale. A market with major economies of scale will inevitably be dominated by large MNCs able to operate on a scale that will lead to the lowest unit costs being achieved. SMEs cannot compete in such markets unless they are fortunate enough to have sufficient capital to grow rapidly to take advantage of the scale economies. Service markets and intermediate industry markets where the need for a globally recognized brand name is not vital may provide the best opportunities for SMEs.

Develop a network of partners in the companies in which the firm wishes to operate. Co-operative strategy can be a very effective way of overcoming SME limitations. Although it is true that the combination of two or more weak unspecialized companies is unlikely to threaten a strong one, alliances and other forms of partnership can be very valuable to SMEs. An SME with a locally well-introduced partner in each country in which it plans to operate has a far better chance of success than one that attempts to go it alone. A well-chosen partner provides not only local market knowledge and networks, but may also help to provide an effective joint value chain delivering into the host country. The SME relying on its own resources would be unable to do this. As well as local market intelligence, networks and a good sales force, a local partner should be sought with complementary assets and a trustworthy record. If such partners can be found the SME's prospects will rise substantially.

SOURCE: ADAPTED FROM SZABO (2002)

Strategy in Action 6.9 *SMEs – overcoming the barriers to globalization*

Company-based activities:

Managerial skills – SMEs wishing to go global need to have a well structured management team, concentrating on core activities, outsourcing less strategically important activities and business support services.

Good planning – entry into global markets needs to be carefully planned, not embarked upon impulsively and opportunistically (as with the golf balls in Strategy in Action 6.8).

Appropriate foreign partner selection – such partners need to know the domestic environment in the proposed new international market, legislative and non-legislative barriers, language, and customer requirements.

Quick adaptability – flexibility and speed of response are advantages that SMEs have over most MNCs. They need therefore to make best use of this advantage.

Government support activities:

Provision of information centres for SMEs – containing databanks of relevant business information at low cost and with easy access.

Training programmes in the field of internationalization – special tailor-made training programmes for SMEs which would help the SME through the complexity of legislation in host countries.

Promotion of foreign direct investment (FDI) – governments should help SMEs to invest abroad, for example by putting SMEs in touch with domestically based MNCs as potential suppliers.

Attract adequate back-up capital. Not all SMEs are undercapitalized. Those with sufficient capital backing have a far better chance of success than those who attempt to go global when underfunded. Almost inevitably there will be mistakes made in developing new territories and in all probability costs will be underestimated. Adequate back-up capital is therefore vital if the SME is to stay the course and become established abroad.

Offer a differentiated niche product difficult to replicate. For an SME to flourish globally it needs to offer a differentiated product that can create a niche. This means a relatively small part of a market with barriers to entry by competitors. It must also be difficult for competitors to replicate the product or to substitute for it with an alternative product. If that can be achieved, the SME has a good chance of success. As White and Campos (1986) put it, SMEs should aim to occupy the interspace in markets not occupied by MNCs.

Develop close relationships with key local government ministers or officials. Though not vital, this may prove extremely useful, particularly in non-democratic countries where personal contacts with the local government officials can make all the difference between success and failure. Where the rule of law is not dominant, licences can be granted or withheld according to the strength of relationships with officials or favoured party members. This can be particularly important for SMEs who lack the power themselves to break into markets unaided.

Strategy in Action 6.10 tells the story of a small business that discovered a unique global niche opportunity almost by accident and was also assisted by some of the other factors just discussed that can help SMEs survive and grow globally.

6

Strategy in Action 6.10 *Drugs for children with rare diseases*

A small UK specialist pharmaceutical company called Special Products reformulates, distributes and exports unlicensed drugs for treating children with rare diseases such as kidney problems. It does not develop any new drugs of its own. It works solely with existing proven products made by the big pharmaceutical companies. However, they are products that the big companies have decided not to sell because the return on investment would be too low since the number of patients is very small. Special Products can supply the necessary specialist drugs in small volumes.

The company was set up in 1997 almost by accident. Its founder was a pharmacist at the Great Ormond Street children's hospital in London, UK. He noticed that children with rare diseases responded better to medicines that he reformulated to taste more pleasant or made easier to swallow, such as preparing a liquid rather than a tablet. He was asked to prepare similar medicines for other hospitals around the world and realized that there was a global market opportunity. The company was set up initially with £6,000 borrowed on the founder's credit card. By 2008 it employed 25 people and sales had reached £7.4 million, mainly from international demand. The company contracts out each formulation to pharmaceutical manufacturers. They specialize in niche medical conditions around the world.

Pharmaceutical companies are banned from advertising unlicensed products. European legislation requires a medical product to demonstrate safety, quality and efficacy to obtain a market licence. However, the EU does allow member states to authorize healthcare professionals to work with unlicensed products. This is common with children's medicines where clinical trials are often difficult to perform.

The company's first venture overseas was to Malaysia. A wealthy Malaysian family brought their child to be treated at Great Ormond Street hospital. Later the father visited the new company at its offices and asked for a large supply of medicines for his child. That was their first experience of exporting. By 2009 sales in Australia were very large where the company had contracts to supply a number of specialist hospitals. They are looking at the US market where, if successful, sales could reach £100 million in a few years. The US market has great government restrictions, however. They would need licensed products and an American partner for manufacturing. The main benefit offered by Special Products is that they can supply specialist drugs relatively cheaply. That makes them attractive to the American healthcare insurance companies who dominate the US healthcare market. To achieve such US sales, however, the company would have to incur the high costs of clinical trials.

There is also a 'cluster' effect helping Special Products. The south-east region of the UK where they are based is home to 30 per cent of the UK's life sciences research and development activity. Major pharmaceutical MNCs such as Pfizer and GlaxoSmithKline have European R&D departments based locally in the region. Smaller, innovative pharmaceutical companies are taking more R&D work on behalf of the major pharmaceutical MNCs who are increasingly looking to outsource activities. The area is also close to the venture capital firms based in London's large financial centre. There is also a regional pharmaceutical alliance: the South East Health Technologies Alliance (SEHTA). SEHTA has identified the Middle East as a major growth area for health products. SEHTA has set up an office in Dubai to help smaller companies find customers and investment financing. Dubai was chosen because it plans to become the centre for healthcare provision in the Middle East.

SOURCE: BASED ON AN ARTICLE FROM *THE SUNDAY TIMES BUSINESS*, 9 JULY 2008

SUMMARY

■ This chapter has discussed non-standard issues within global strategy: the evolution of strategies to address BOP markets and the globalization of SMEs.

■ World poverty is relevant to the design of global strategies. The concept of the 'base of the pyramid' (BOP) has helped to explain the estimated four billion people in the world who aspire to join the market economy for the first time (the 'aspiring poor').

■ MNCs have been preoccupied with 'top-of-the-pyramid' (TOP) markets.

■ BOP markets have been invisible to MNCs, which have exhibited a mindset that does not see the BOP customer as belonging to a viable market segment worth investing in.

■ However, innovatory products and services such as the $100 laptop computer and microfinance are beginning to address the different needs of poorer customers.

■ There are two views as to the existence of the BOP market as a market with genuine commercial potential. One view argues that catering to the needs of those at the BOP offers a business opportunity that has previously been ignored. It also offers opportunity for innovation in products and services that may be attractive in developed markets.

■ The alternative view argues that the disposable income of BOP households is simply insufficient for consumer purchases even at much lower price points than in the developed economies for TOP consumers.

■ A third view has been presented that supports the view that the BOP market is real but argues that only a proportion of it (the BME) is truly being addressed by BOP international products and services. The remaining $1 a day BOP poor remain in the subsistence or barter economy.

■ SMEs are important to employment and innovation within the world economy. However, there are many barriers to initial establishment and subsequent survival of the SME companies, especially when they attempt to globalize.

■ These barriers include inadequate capital or access to it, insufficient marketing expenditures, insufficiently developed global networks, an insufficiently focused niche market, impossibility of recruiting experienced international executives and weak brand names.

■ The internet may help initially but by increasing both transparency and competition it may ultimately damage the prospects of survival for the SME.

■ However if the SME has a clearly differentiated niche product and can establish barriers to competition, makes good use of partnerships, has enough capital and ideally makes good governmental contacts in the host country, the SME can prosper and many do.

DISCUSSION QUESTIONS

1 Explain your understanding of what exactly is meant by 'BOP'.

2 What are the potential business opportunities that BOP markets and consumers represent? How feasible do you think they are?

3 Provide some examples of products or services that may genuinely be considered developed for BOP consumers and markets. In what ways are they different from standard products or services in their sector?

4 Describe some of the ways in which BOP strategies and traditional MNC global strategy might work together.

5 What is an SME?

6 How useful is the internet in the globalization process of SMEs?

7 Name four barriers to globalization of SMEs.

8 How can these barriers to SME globalization be overcome?

FURTHER READINGS

1 Prahalad, C.K. (2005) *The Fortune at the Bottom of the Pyramid: eradicating poverty through profits*, Upper Saddle River, New Jersey: Pearson Education Inc., Wharton School Publishing.

C.K. Prahalad is a famous management academic and also a business guru. This is his manifesto for a win-win relationship between business and the poor such that profitability can go hand-in-hand with the fight against poverty and impoverished lives.

2 Prahalad, C.K. and Hart, S.L. (2002) 'The fortune at the bottom of the pyramid', *Strategy+Business*, 26: 54–67.

This article by C.K. Prahalad and Stuart Hart was responsible for kick-starting the soul-searching and strategy reviews among corporate businessman which launched the corporate movement for serving the poor with relevant strategies to meet their product and service needs.

3 Hart, S.L. (2007) *Capitalism at the Crossroads: aligning business, earth and humanity*, 2nd edn, Upper Saddle River, New Jersey: Pearson Education Inc., Wharton School Publishing.

For the second edition of his best-selling book, there is a Foreword written by Al Gore, the US ex-Presidential candidate who won a Nobel Peace Prize for his environmental campaigning. Hart links global strategy and sustainability with a fascinating range of practical evidence and examples.

4 Audretsch, D.B. (ed.) (2003) *SMEs in the Age of Globalisation*, London: Edward Elgar.

The purpose of this volume is to bring together the leading scholarly papers about how globalization has impacted the role of SMEs. In fact, globalization has affected SMEs in two major ways. The first has been to facilitate the transnational activities of SMEs. Transnational activities, ranging from exports to foreign direct investment to participating in global value chains have become easier as a result of globalization. The second impact of globalization has been to shift the source of competitiveness towards knowledge-based economic activity, which has led to an increased role for SMEs.

PART 2
THE CONTEMPORARY
ORGANIZATION OF MNCs

Part 2 is about strategy and structure: What kinds of organizational structures can deliver what types of global strategies for MNCs? This is the conceptual heart of the book. Part 2 contains an original approach to all the existing organization structure frameworks used in international strategy. The four traditional approaches to the organizational structure of MNCs are summarized in Chapter 7. These traditional forms are then overtaken by the new types of evolving structural forms triggered by the new economy and its roots in technology as discussed in Part 1 (particularly in Chapter 5). These new and evolving structural forms have enormous implications for how we discuss global industries, global firms and current relevant ways of organizing to effectively implement global strategies. The new approaches are discussed in depth in Chapter 8.

The relationship between strategy and organization structure for global firms is one of the biggest debates within the field of global strategy. As we state many times throughout this book, global strategy is dynamic because it takes place within a shifting context with all variables constantly changing. MNCs must continuously strive to align and re-align their organizational structure with the changes they have to make in rethinking their strategies to fit endlessly changing competitive contexts. The organizational structure of an MNC has to be potentially in a state of endless renewal.

MNCs have more organizational choices and options than are available to a national firm. That is one of the benefits of being an MNC. Effective implementation of international strategy choices by an MNC involves the search for potential competitive advantages obtainable from decisions about global **configuration** and **co-ordination** throughout the entire value chain of the firm. Therefore Chapter 7 attempts to provide some answers to the question of how MNCs configure and co-ordinate their international strategies. That is an important part of understanding the link between strategy and structure in MNCs. The configuration / co-ordination matrix is the first of many important concepts introduced in

Chapter 7. Configuration and co-ordination describe two key tasks (and advantages) of the MNC: first, where to locate and carry out the various value chain activities of the firm, that is configuration; and second, how to coordinate between the multiple locations and activities of the firm, that is co-ordination, so that the whole MNC operates smoothly. The second very important conceptual framework introduced in Chapter 7 is the 'global integration / local responsiveness' grid. This grid and the concepts it contains recur over and over in discussing how to think about the firm's international strategy and the most appropriate organization structure for implementing it. All international strategy decisions are made with this trade-off in mind: between the degree of global integration within the MNC and the degree of local responsiveness to specific market conditions. The emphasis is on the optimal functioning of MNCs in the markets in which they operate. The balance of these forces for global integration and **national responsiveness** can vary from one industry to another. This approach is not at all deterministic or prescriptive of organization structure; it is contingent on specific circumstances. We return to the concept of contingency in Chapter 8.

Before concentrating on the specific different organizational types, the process by which the common MNC matrix structure most usually evolves is described. The rest of Chapter 7 takes us in some detail through each of the four traditional forms of international organizational structure: multidomestic; global; international exporter; and transnational. Each of these four represents a set of decisions about the international strategy of the firm and the choice made about the most suitable organizational structure to implement that choice. Many examples are given of the contexts in which each might be the suitable choice. The most sophisticated of the four types is the transnational form of organization, often described as 'being truly multinational'.

As we discuss next in Chapter 8, the evolution of a more global economy in recent years has shown the limitations of these four basic types. MNCs have begun to adopt more contingency-based approaches to how they structure and configure their organizations than the fourfold taxonomy presented in Chapter 7 might suggest. That is why the title of Chapter 8 is: 'How to organize MNCs: what matters now'.

In Chapter 8 we use contingency theory to make sense of the management of international organizations. Contingency theory is about coping with uncertainty and is therefore an appropriate framework for the fundamental dynamic character of the global business context. It states that there is no one best way of organizing and that all ways of organizing are not equally effective. The choice will depend on the situation. We provide frameworks to show how complex such choices are: global or regional or local decisions must be made about every activity and each function an organization carries out, in every market in which it has a presence. Since decisions about structure must be taken at every level from strategic to operational to functional for each division and for each product and market, we argue that no one organizational structure model will work on its own. What actual MNCs do now is to mix and match from all approaches in order to be 'truly multinational'. Managers have the task of determining what works for their organization in order to respond to what we call 'the central dilemma' for MNCs: getting the balance right between global and local; between global integration and local responsiveness. MNCs must find sophisticated ways of coping with this central dilemma for their organization. Most are now using a 'post-transnational' approach which accepts the challenges of combining the strengths of global with the strengths of local at the same time, rather than regarding them as trade-offs as in the four frameworks discussed in Chapter 7.

Modern MNCs must be able to incorporate the management of high degrees of complexity and flexibility, and new ways of integrating activities and resources across borders. Many have found themselves involved in endless series of reorganizations from national to global, and from global back to regional. Effective organizational structures now need to try to do all those things at once and therefore the importance of 'co-ordinating mechanisms' that help to manage across all the different internal organizational arrangements, is critical. We discuss two common sorts of such internal co-ordinating mechanisms in modern MNCs: global account management; and HQ–subsidiary relations.

Chapter 9 takes further the need for a contingent approach to modern international strategy and structure by discussion network organizations and virtual corporations.

A strategic network addresses the issue: What should the organization do internally with its own resources and what is it acceptable or advantageous for the organization to do outside its boundaries (e.g. via outsourcing) either using the resources of other organizations or a number of other organizations? The terms 'strategic network' (Chapter 9) and 'strategic alliance' (Chapter 10) are often used interchangeably. However, there is a clear distinction between the idea of a network with its implication of close but *non-exclusive* relationships, and that of an alliance which, however loosely, implies the creation of a joint enterprise. A virtual corporation generally carries some of the qualities of both.

Networks are not static; entry, exit, and repositioning are constantly occurring. The justification for the cost to a firm of maintaining its position in a network is the belief that such network activity strengthens its competitive position in comparison to operating on its own. Networks depend on the establishment, maintenance, and perhaps strengthening of relationships. It is, therefore, the quality of relationships in networks that govern effectiveness. Networks provide a firm with access to information, resources, markets and technologies but may also, if poorly constructed, lock firms into unproductive relationships. Networks may help members to achieve increased global reach rapidly and at low cost. They enable potential synergies between members to be identified and provide the conditions for the achievement of scale and scope economies through specialization. The growth of networks has been a response to the spiralling costs of doing business as a result of the globalization of technologies and markets. 'Virtual corporations' differ from networks mainly in the fact that they use organizational resources from different companies and synthesize them into a single electronic business entity, using ICT (information and communication technologies). Because they can only exist by means of sophisticated ICT, virtual corporations are very much a feature of the 2000s.

Co-operative strategy is about co-operation rather than competition: working with other firms rather than competing against them, although often firms both co-operate and compete at the same time but in different products or markets. In Chapter 10, we explain the rationale for co-operative strategies and how strategic alliances between firms can work. Most companies reach a stage when they realize they do not have enough resources to achieve their aims alone, particularly when developing global strategies. Co-operative strategy is a relatively cheap and relatively low-risk way for companies to expand quickly, especially globally. Chapter 10 uses resource dependency theory to make sense of alliances and co-operative strategies. It argues that organizational survival is about the ability to acquire and maintain the resources necessary for survival. Often that may mean acquiring them from outside a single firm. The establishment of a strategic alliance can thus be regarded as an attempt by a firm or firms to overcome resource constraints and hence to reduce strategic vulnerability. We are familiar with such well-known types of strategic alliances and networks as the Japanese *keiretsu* groups or the Korean *chaebols*. Chapter 10 discusses in some detail not only the rationale for strategic alliances but also how to manage them successfully.

A merger is a collaborative agreement by two companies to combine their interests, ownership and company structures into one company. Chapter 11 discusses the reasons for mergers and acquisitions remaining such a significant part of global strategy despite their poor performance record and the high proportion of failures. Mergers and acquisitions (M&A) are justified by the extent to which they add value. Cross-border M&As with the highest potential for success tend to be between firms that share similar or complementary operations in key areas. Even when the strategic logic behind the merger is impeccable, the main problem associated with M&A strategy lies in the ability to integrate the two companies. This problem often centres upon lack of cultural fit between the two. However, with the demand for resources within international business endlessly rising, the place of M&A within the global strategies of firms will continue.

CHAPTER 7

Traditional MNC structure frameworks

LEARNING OBJECTIVES The objectives of this chapter are to:

■ show the relationship between the dynamic global context in which strategy is made and the type of strategy that is effective in that context

■ demonstrate how the international strategies of firms evolve in relation to the dynamics of the global context

■ explain why MNCs come about and why they are so frequently successful against local opposition

■ describe a simple form of globalization in stages

■ identify the factors that companies need to take into account in organizing MNCs

■ to explain the multidomestic form

■ to explain the global form

■ to explain the international exporter form

■ to explain the transnational form.

INTRODUCTION

All global competitors have to be perceived to be at least as good as any local firm providing a product or a service in the local market. Poorly organized global competitors may bear higher costs than local competitors, given their more complex structures and systems. Initially also local companies are likely to be equipped with better knowledge of the local market. Therefore one of the key issues in operating globally is how to organize one's enterprise so that it is possible to compete successfully with local companies.

MNCs have more organizational choices and options than are available to a national firm. Global strategy choices by an MNC are complex and involve the search for competitive advantage from global configuration / co-ordination choices throughout the entire value chain of the firm. This chapter attempts to provide some answers to the question of how MNCs configure and co-ordinate their international strategies. We examine various approaches to MNC internationalization. These will include internationalization as a strategy process; stages models of internationalization; studies of the link between strategy and structure in MNCs; and more recent organizational frameworks for MNCs. Finally we will discuss the four basic MNC forms traditionally described in the textbooks. As we discuss next in Chapter 8, the evolution of a more global economy in recent years has shown the limitations of these four basic types. MNCs have begun to adopt more contingency-based approaches to how they structure and configure their organizations than the fourfold taxonomy presented in this chapter might suggest.

We begin by providing necessary understanding of the dynamic context in which MNCs must make their decisions about organizational structure.

THE DYNAMIC CONTEXT OF GLOBAL STRATEGY: NATIONS AND FIRMS

Understanding how industries and firms change over time is much more difficult than understanding the structure of an industry or the strategy of a firm at a specific point in time. Chapter 3 discussed the evolution of industry structure arising from the globalization and regionalization of markets, the development of regional trading blocs and technological development. Despite the social, cultural and technological changes behind the development of global market segments discussed in Chapter 3, there are additional economic and political pressures on governments to create barriers to this increasing transnational flow of goods and services. Fierce global competition and the changed economic structures of many industries may devastate many firms, or indeed entire sectors, in their home markets leading to political pressure for protection. Protectionist policies such as quotas or tariff barriers create constraints on global competition. They are intended to do just that. Deregulation is a deliberate attempt to do the opposite: to improve the efficiency of markets by opening them up to increased competition. It has been most visible in the world financial markets, where the removal by governments of fixed commissions and ceilings on foreign ownership has shifted competition from service to price and triggered a massive shakeout in the industry through either mergers or business failures – at least partly responsible for the disastrous world recession of the mid-2000s. This massive recession then triggered pressure for greater regulation of markets once again, especially in financial services. The two policies (deregulation and protectionism) exist in relation to each other.

> Global strategies rest on the interplay of the competitive advantage of firms and the comparative advantage of countries.
>
> (Kogut, 1989)

GLOBAL INDUSTRY DYNAMICS IN CONSUMER ELECTRONICS

What follows is a brief description on the global competitive position of two rival MNCs in consumer electronics: the Philips Group of Holland and Japan's Panasonic. Did Philips' difficulties at different points in time arise from political or economic pressures, or as a result of the strategy of the firm itself? Philips did not fit the profile of MNCs carrying out global strategies which involve producing standard products with minor variations and marketing them in a similar fashion around the world, sourcing assets and activities on an optimal cost basis and adapting where necessary to local cultures and tastes. Panasonic, by contrast, did fit this profile of the global MNC very closely. We have explained the rise of the MNC in Chapter 2 – single corporate entities selling on a global scale and with activities in many parts of the world. However, by the late 1980s, that type of global strategy and organizational structure no longer met its requirements for further development. It needed to move away from its centralized structure and give more autonomy to its national divisions. External market conditions and internal new product development needs exerted pressure to develop a relatively decentralized network, which is what Panasonic started to build. In many ways Philips already possessed the decentralized structure that Panasonic was trying to create. Yet Philips' strategy and multidomestic organizational structure was unsustainable: inappropriate and too expensive in a global industry. Panasonic on the other hand, has been a global competitor and is becoming a transnational. The reasons are explained in Strategy in Action 7.1.

By applying Porter's 'diamond' framework (from Chapter 2) it is possible to make a further comparison between the two global consumer electronics rivals. Philips and Panasonic are both global competitors in the consumer electronics industry. Each faced entirely different conditions in their 'home-base' country (domestic market). On balance, Panasonic's national 'cluster' was far more advantageous than Philips'. Panasonic has a huge domestic market of sophisticated, discerning consumers; demand conditions are excellent. Factor conditions are fairly neutral, although there has been a recent shortage of software engineers. This may be contrasted with Philips' negative factor conditions (expensive local labour) and tiny domestic market. Local competitive rivalry and supporting industry clusters once again favoured the Japanese corporation rather than the Dutch one. Panasonic is surrounded by equally powerful rivals and therefore faced stiff competition in its domestic market in all the sectors in which it competed, whereas Philips dominated its domestic economy and carried a high degree of social cost within it.

We will now look more broadly at some of the approaches to organization structure that can help MNCs think through the kinds of problems faced by Philips and Panasonic.

CONFIGURATION AND CO-ORDINATION

The multinational corporation (MNC) has dominated the global business environment at least since post-1945. Porter (1986) identified the two key tasks of the MNC: first, where to locate the firm's value chain activities to achieve the optimal form of *configuration*; and second, how to set up the appropriate organizational structure and systems to support the actual choice of configuration of the MNC the (i.e. type and degree of *co-ordination*).

In Figure 7.1 *dispersed configuration* means having value chain activities in many countries; while *concentrated configuration* means having value chain activities mostly in the home country. Obviously an array of possibilities exists along that continuum. On the other axis, we use *high co-ordination* to mean mainly centralized decision-making and *low co-ordination* to mean mainly decentralized decision-making. The company examples used on the matrix in Figure 7.1 are all MNCs which feature in various chapters of this book. Thus in Figure 7.1 Gillette has a globally dispersed

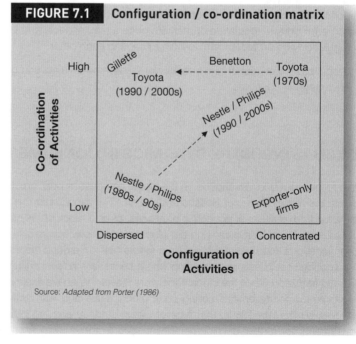

FIGURE 7.1   Configuration / co-ordination matrix

Source: *Adapted from Porter (1986)*

Strategy in Action 7.1 *The dynamics of global competition (1): the Philips Group of Holland*

Philips is Holland's premier industrial company and the last significant European competitor in an industry which has relentlessly been overwhelmed and dominated by large Japanese MNCs such as Sony and Panasonic (formerly known as Matsushita Electric (MEI)). Philips was struggling.

Problems at Philips
In 1990, Philips faced a crisis unprecedented for a major industrial company with some of the best known and most widely used brands in the world. The company was one of the bastions of European business with annual sales of almost £19 billion. However, by the end of 1990 (including heavy restructuring charges) Philips had a net loss of Fl 4.53 billion. It was the biggest loss in Dutch corporate history.

Causes of Philips' decline
From the late 1980s onwards, Philips was under fierce assault from Japanese and Korean competitors and was struggling to restructure itself. Philips was trying to move from being a dispersed international corporation to a centralized global one. Its main problem was high costs, poor central financial and managerial control. It had tremendous strengths as a company. Philips' strengths in R&D and new product development were respected worldwide. Unfortunately, it was far less effective at ensuring it achieved the market share and financial return from its innovative product stream.

Philips had two main problems: its extraordinarily high domestic market labour costs, relative to those of its Japanese competitors; and an unwieldy decentralized, international corporate organization structure, based on a matrix system with nine product groups and 60 countries ('national organizations') with national managerial autonomy. Friction between the centre (Eindhoven) and

periphery (the autonomous national subsidiaries) was frequent. It helped to explain the unfortunate gap between Philips' superb product innovation and poor marketing.

By 1990 Philips still had only 10 per cent of its production in the Far East and 65 per cent in Europe; the single world concept seemed no nearer. Efforts had been made to streamline the organization by reorganizing into four global product divisions with a new central management committee. The reorganization was intended to shift from a focus on national geographic markets towards international product divisions. But Philips never really got to grips with: first, its heavy commitment to 'home-base' jobs and payroll in Holland; and second, the decentralized decision-making procedures which gave country subsidiaries and country general managers local autonomy. Philips' payroll was a political issue in Holland which was a very high labour-cost country. In 1990 Philips was still Holland's largest single employer employing 65,000 people there.

The changing competitive map
When Japanese competitors entered the European market with a much tighter cost-base and centralized control systems, R&D, marketing and distribution and very high quality products, the decentralized multidomestic approach fell apart. Philips had a high local cost-base which only made sense if those costs were the necessary costs of local adaptation of products (televisions and stereos) to suit the needs of different local marketplaces. They were not. Consumer electronics had become a global industry with highly standardized products and components across world markets. Japanese competitors developed broadly homogeneous products for a world market. Philips was bearing local costs in a global market. Despite closing 75 of its 346 plants in

50 countries and shedding 38,000 employees worldwide, half of Philips' factories were still in Europe where labour costs were too high compared to the lower production and labour costs of its main (Asian) rivals.

The dynamics of global competition (2): Panasonic of Japan

Panasonic's global strategy

Panasonic was founded with $100 in a workshop in his own home in 1918 by a young entrepreneur (Konosuke Matsushita). By the 1980s its overseas sales revenues were $1,575 billion. It was run as a highly centralized company with no local autonomy. Its strategy was low-cost, but with a steady stream of new products to attract and keep market share. It regarded itself as a technology 'follower' rather than a technology leader or innovator (like Philips). Its powerful brands include Panasonic and JVC. Panasonic operated a policy of 'hungry divisions'; one product / one division. This was a deliberate approach aimed at avoiding complacency. It set tight financial targets monitored from the centre. In its global expansion, key positions were always given to internal Japanese expatriates who were regarded as custodians of Panasonic's strong culture and 'spiritual precepts'. Its founder had declared himself as setting the terms of a strategy for 250 years, for which each managerial generation would be responsible for 25 years, starting with himself.

Panasonic's problems

The problems Panasonic faced in the late 1980s were different from those of Philips. They were: first, that the company needed a replacement product for the VCR, which was entering its mature phase; and second, there were problems arising from successful centralization. The VCR provided the bulk of Panasonic's revenues. Over the seven-year period from 1977 to 1984, in response to rapid increases in demand, Panasonic had famously multiplied production of the successful VCR product line by 33 times capacity, showing it had excellent responsive capabilities in manufacturing and marketing. This enabled it to drop the price by one-third over the same period. By 1984 the VCR was generating 45 per cent of all its worldwide revenues. It was not obvious where a replacement product of similar magnitude could come from. By late 1980s all the signs were that the next generation of consumer electronics products were likely to spring from technology convergence, perhaps in multimedia. Such a development would require a different organizational structure from the centralized global hub suitable for controlling standardized global production and distribution. Therefore Panasonic wanted to become less of a centralized hub controlled from Japan and more 'truly international'.

Panasonic's localization ('glocal') strategy

Panasonic also faced macroeconomic pressures including: rising protectionist sentiment in some of its main markets; a high yen making its products more expensive; a lack of qualified software engineers in its domestic market; a need to understand technical capabilities abroad and share learning back home internally. So, just at the time that Philips was struggling to exert stronger central control, Panasonic was seeking to show more sensitivity to local markets. By the late 1980s it had granted greater local autonomy to national subsidiaries in: hiring and promoting more local personnel; local sourcing and purchasing; modifying designs for local markets; adapting corporate processes and technologies; incorporating local components; becoming altogether more 'local'. The risks it faced in so doing were of diluting its strong internal culture and values; reduced manufacturing economies of scale; and dilution of internal consistency of quality, product and process.

SOURCE: COMPILED BY AUTHORS FROM VARIOUS PRESS ARTICLES

7

configuration with high centralization of decision-making at MNC headquarters. Nestlé and Philips are shown with a dispersed configuration and low co-ordination in the 1980s, a way of capturing in the matrix their traditional multidomestic MNC structure at that time. Then it should be noted that both Nestlé and Philips had moved away from the multidomestic form so there is a shift up to top right on the matrix. By the 1990s and 2000s, Nestlé has a more complex, responsive, eclectic structure which we discuss later in Chapter 8 (Strategy in Action 8.7). We have also shown Toyota of Japan twice: first (top right) as it was structured in the 1970s, with a concentrated configuration and high co-ordination, which means that it was very globally centralized in its decision-making and resource-allocation processes at that time just like Panasonic; indeed Toyota was one of the world's first pure global firms. Secondly, by the early 1990s and 2000s, Toyota (and Panasonic) had moved towards top left, with a more dispersed configuration and more decentralization of decision-making. The reasons for this shift from global to transnational international strategy are contained in the story told in Strategy in Action 7.1.

Such organizational transitions are part of a long-term international development process which we will now discuss.

THE 'STAGES' MODELS OF INTERNATIONALIZATION

Vernon's (1966) product life-cycle model of the internationalization of a firm suggested that the process should take place in stages. Stage one, a product is developed and sold domestically. In stage two it is exported. In stage three, as scale develops, exporting will be replaced by FDI so that the product will start being produced in the countries in which demand is large. This stage three is thus the growth stage of the life cycle. In stage four, the maturity stage, production moves to lower wage cost developing economies. The final stage is decline, when the product is imported into the country from which it originally emerged. This is a very stylized model, which assumes that the firm with the new product is starting out from scratch with no existing international organization, but its simplicity is helpful and the points it makes are easy to follow. It demonstrates how internationalization can cause production to gradually move away from the home country.

Another 'stages' model developed by Johanson and Vahlne (1977) saw the firm gradually internationalizing through increased commitment to, and knowledge of, foreign markets. The firm is therefore most likely to enter markets with successively greater psychic distance, that is less and less similar to the home base (Perlmutter, 1969). Thus at the outset it sells to countries culturally similar to itself. The model depends on the notion that uncertainty, and hence risk, increases with increasing psychic distance and unfamiliarity. The problem with this model is that there are many examples of internationalizing companies who have merely gone for large rather than familiar markets and also, for many markets at the same time such as Sony Walkman, Wal-Mart, Tata and Levis. The contrast is between the so-called 'waterfall' model of global expansion (one country at a time) and the contrasting 'sprinkler' model (many countries at a time). In current markets with ever-shortening product life cycles, and the strategic importance of 'time-to-market', there is often insufficient time to adopt the waterfall approach. Both of the popular stages models are highly sequential in the stages they describe and are both very deterministic.

In the current global economy the more recent model of 'born global' internationalization (Knight et al., 2004) is becoming increasingly common. '**Born globals**' are companies that internationalize at or near their founding. This clearly involves no stages at all since they are launched as global firms from birth.

STRATEGY AND STRUCTURE IN MNCs

Stopford and Wells (1972) developed a different descriptive model to illustrate the typical progression for companies moving towards a global organization structure. They saw this as a process driven by two dimensions: the number of products sold internationally (foreign product diversity), and the importance of international sales to the company (foreign sales as a percentage of total sales).

They suggested that international divisions were set up at an early stage of internationalization when product diversity and percentage of foreign sales were both low (bottom left). When international expansion led to substantial foreign product diversity companies tended to adopt a worldwide product division structure (pathway (a) in Figure 7.2). Or, if companies expanded overseas without increasing product diversity, they tended to adopt a

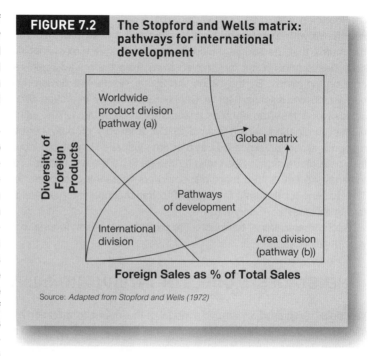

FIGURE 7.2 **The Stopford and Wells matrix: pathways for international development**

Source: *Adapted from Stopford and Wells (1972)*

geographical divisional structure (pathway (b) in Figure 7.2). Finally when both foreign sales and the diversity of products were high, a global matrix emerged. This is the basis of the common MNC matrix structure. Bjorkman (1990), however, concluded that the adoption of new structures was more a matter of fashion than anything else and resulted from firms copying current organizational trends at any specific time.

TRADITIONAL ORGANIZATIONAL MODELS OF MNCs

A different process approach was taken in the 1980s by Prahalad and Doz (1987) and Bartlett and Ghoshal (1989) to MNC management. They emphasized control through information networks and corporate cultures that transcend national boundaries. The key framework that emerged from the process school emphasized *global integration* combined with *local responsiveness*. Both sets of authors have used variations of a global integration / local responsiveness framework in their work. All international strategy decisions are made with this trade-off in mind. This approach is not at all deterministic or prescriptive of organizational structure; it is contingent on specific circumstances. The emphasis is on the optimal functioning of MNCs in the markets in which they operate. Figure 7.3 illustrates how the balance of these forces for global integration and national responsiveness can vary from one industry to another.

Figure 7.3 shows how these different industry forces influence the strategic tasks and hence the appropriate organization structure of the firm. For example, there is little incentive to build a global scale plant for the manufacture of corrugated cardboard or the export of a commodity such as wheat (bottom left in grid) and little basis for differentiating basic commodities by national market. By contrast, consumer electronics (top left in grid – together with batteries and razor blades) offers high R&D and manufacturing scale economies, together with standard design opportunities and has little need for differentiation by national market. Food products, soaps, detergents, together with some services such as insurance (bottom right in grid), all needed to be adapted to meet local consumer preferences and differences in distribution channels per market, as well as various regulatory requirements.

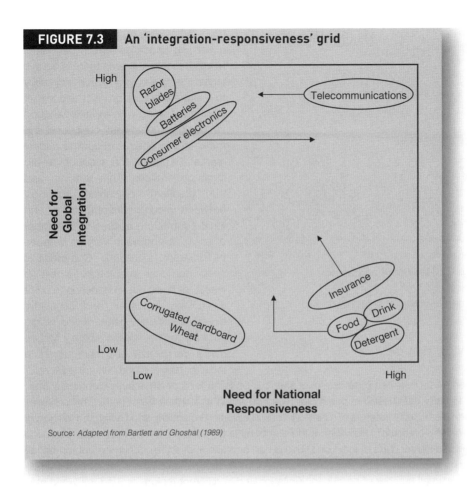

FIGURE 7.3 An 'integration-responsiveness' grid

Source: *Adapted from Bartlett and Ghoshal (1989)*

Telecommunications (top right in grid) requires high capital investment and massive R&D costs, but still must meet the variation in technical standards and service levels required by the different national and regional markets. The direction of the arrows attached to consumer electronics, telecommunications, food and insurance each indicate directions of movement over time for the different industries illustrated, as the forces shaping the industry dynamics shift and change. Each movement around the grid denotes the need for a review of the existing configuration of the MNC, and a corresponding change in its levels of global or regional co-ordination and integration. For example food is becoming less local, with many products (e.g. pastas, yoghurts) acceptable at a regional level.

Each of the four extreme corners of Figure 7.3 corresponds to one of the four approaches to being international described in Chapter 1 (Table 1.1). Working clockwise around the integration-responsiveness grid from bottom left, these are: international exporter, global, transnational and multidomestic. We discuss each in turn.

THE INTERNATIONAL CORPORATE STRUCTURE MODEL

The four possible configurations described above are illustrated in the matrix shown in Figure 7.4. The matrix in Figure 7.4 follows a tradition in international business research used and developed by Bartlett, Ghoshal, Doz and Prahalad, among others, and already cited in this book. Although most authors vary

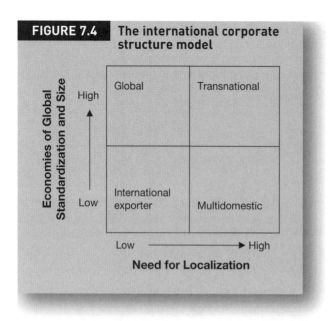

FIGURE 7.4 The international corporate structure model

their definitions to some extent, the underlying principles remain the same. In international business there is always tension between production efficiency to make a standard product and ship it around the world with as little variation as possible at lowest cost, and the marketing to offer a product to a local market that takes into account varying local preferences. This tension, and the resultant perceived trade-off between global standardization and local adaptation, applies in a number of areas. It applies in varying degrees to different industries. Commodities need no local adaptation: wheat is wheat, oil is oil; but a car needs to be fit for driving conditions and consumer tastes in different parts of the world. Similarly for individual countries: McDonald's do not sell beef hamburgers in India for religious and cultural reasons.

A similar tension exists between business functions. It is possible for a pharmaceutical company marketing worldwide to carry out all R&D in one major research site in its home base country. This achieves the greatest economies of scale in terms of running teams of research scientists, and having the resources for them to carry out their research. However, if the company is big enough, it may need more than one R&D establishment in different parts of the world. This is not for reasons of scale economies but for market intelligence-gathering and to give it the necessary flexibility when the market environment changes unexpectedly. Similarly, a small number of production units located in different regions around the world may achieve adequate minimum economic size for scale economies in production, but also be more flexible than one huge plant. And so on for each function of the MNC.

Thus such tensions exist for industries, for markets and for functions. Relevant trade-offs will have different solutions for each contingent set of circumstances; international strategy to be effective must respond to contingency. How then should a multi-product, multi-market global company be organized? There is not one response, but a number of responses to this issue and as environmental circumstances change so will the organizational pressures, and the optimal solutions. Figure 7.4 shows the four most common organizational forms in response to each set of global / local contingencies.

STRATEGIC ISSUES AFFECTING THE FOUR APPROACHES

How then is a market defined as national or global? Not all products are global or even international. The market for corrugated cardboard is said to have a radius of about 50 miles. It is a low-value commodity in which little differentiation is possible and with high transportation and distribution costs relative to value. The same applies to building aggregates. This explains the position of corrugated cardboard in Figure 7.3. A *strategic market* (Barwise and Robertson, 1992) is defined by the relative homogeneity of consumer tastes, and the possible cost structure of the company that enables it to be a credible competitor over varying distances. Global competition means similar products and services are acceptable to customers across borders, often helped by reductions in transportation costs.

Strategic issues affecting the four approaches to international strategy fit into three categories:

1 where to compete

2 resourcing and delivering the product or service at a competitive price in different parts of the world (configuration issues)

3 how the company should organize itself to control its international activities (co-ordination issues).

We will deal with each of these in turn.

Selecting where to compete

A useful and classic framework to help managers decide how to approach the selection, and eventually, the configuration task in their international strategy was provided by Ghoshal (1987). He gives three strategic objectives for any global strategy and three sources of potential competitive advantage derivable from a global strategy. The resulting framework is given in Figure 7.5.

In Figure 7.5 the three basic strategic objectives of a global strategy are:

1 Efficiency, that is carrying out all value chain activities to a required quality at lowest cost. This is the most frequently emphasized objective in the literature. Indeed, it is often the only objective mentioned. Each of the OLI (or FSA/CSA) factors needs to be considered when reaching decisions about the optimal efficiency of any specific activity.

2 Risk management, that is managing and balancing the risks inherent in operating in a number of diverse countries, for example exchange rate risks, political risks, or raw material sourcing risks. This is very strongly concerned with L (location) or CSA factors.

3 Innovation, learning and adaptation, that is the opportunity to learn from the different societies, cultures and markets in which one operates. In this sense having a presence in many markets around the world is a very helpful market-sensing mechanism.

FIGURE 7.5   Global strategy: an organizing framework

Sources of Competitive Advantage

Strategic objectives		*Country differences*	*Scale economies*	*Scope economies*
	Efficiency in current operations	Factor cost differences e.g. wages and cost of capital	Potential scale economies in each value chain activity	Sharing of resources and capabilities across products, markets and businesses
	Risk management	Assessment of risk by country	Balancing scale with strategic and operational flexibility	Portfolio diversification
	Innovation and learning	Learning from cultural variety in process and practice	Opportunities for technology-based cost reduction	Shared organizational learning

Source: *Adapted from Ghoshal (1987)*

Arising from the three types of strategic objective are three key sources of potential competitive advantage:

1 National differences, that is competitive advantage can come from exploiting differences in input and output markets in different countries. Although low-wage countries are perhaps the most commonly cited examples of such factors, that is not the most significant national difference. For many MNCs it is the tax regime or relative cost of capital that are the main 'national differences' that attract them to a particular country.

2 Scale economies provide a source of configuration advantage if one firm is able to operate at the optimal economic scale, especially if competitors fail to match them. Of course, achieving optimal scale economies globally may sometimes lead to dangerous inflexibility. This creates higher rather than lower risk if fluctuating exchange rates alter or destroy these potential economies after plant has been brought on line to take advantage of them. Also manufacturing scale economies are only one type of scale economy; in modern competition it is frequently purchasing economies of scale that are critical, especially for service businesses.

3 Scope economies are the third source of global competitive advantage. These have been more fully discussed in Chapter 1. Simple illustrations of economies of scope are found in the use of global brand names across a variety of products or services. In addition to global branding, IT, any learning or skills are further examples of areas of huge potential scope economies.

Ghoshal's organizing framework enables the manager to identify the potential sources of global competitive advantage available to the firm. If no such benefits exist in relation to any of the three potential sources of advantage or the strategic objectives, then the firm should not be developing a global strategy.

Resourcing global production

International configuration decisions are concerned with what parts of the value chain for a product or service should be produced within the company and where, including what might be outsourced. Although different products and services to satisfy consumers in diverse cultures with diverse living standards are still required in many markets, as we discussed in the standardization / adaptation debate in Chapter 3, increasing proportions of products and services may require little adaptation to suit them for world markets. It is true that more soft drinks are sold in the US per head than in any other country in the world; more tea per head in the UK than elsewhere; the Far East consumes more rice than the West; and the West more potatoes than the Far East. Yet such variations exist alongside other products and services (such as telecommunications) that are sold largely in the same ways. Many of the drivers of regionalization and globalization of markets have brought about the substantial reduction of many of the traditional barriers to trade as discussed in Chapter 3. Significant barriers that remain include transport costs and exchange rates. Transport costs are relative to volume and value of the product or service. They are irrelevant to international trade in diamonds, but of considerable importance in limiting such trade in corrugated cardboard or cement. Exchange rates will continue to be of considerable importance, although any MNC trading across different currencies will have a treasury department whose job it is to hedge the currency risks of the firm.

CO-ORDINATING THE GLOBAL CORPORATION

The rise of outsourcing, virtual corporations and networks as dominant organizational forms, has meant that the MNC's global co-ordination and control capabilities may well be the key to its international effectiveness. The four traditional organizational structure types given in Figure 7.4 represent different

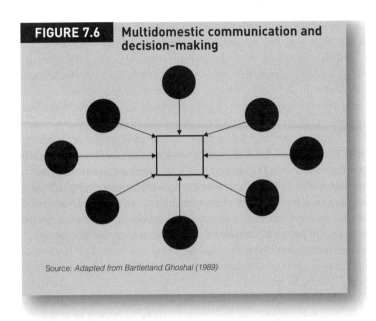

FIGURE 7.6   **Multidomestic communication and decision-making**

Source: *Adapted from Bartlettand Ghoshal (1989)*

approaches to this problem. (As illustrated in Figures 7.1 and 7.3, as particular industries evolve they may well move from one type to another.)

The multidomestic

The **multidomestic** in its pure form is a federation of subsidiary companies each operating in separate countries. The role of the centre is that of a holding company with the limited purpose of monitoring financial performance in its subsidiaries around the world, deciding when and where to increase or decrease its portfolio of companies. It is in effect a series of national companies, each suited to the specific domestic market in which it operates. Its pattern of communication and decision-making is captured in Figure 7.6.

Each of the black circles in Figure 7.6 represents a country subsidiary. Each of them is therefore a repository of a set of resources and functions fit for its unique competitive marketplace. Decision-making and resource-allocation reside with the country subsidiary. The most significant element of the communication and decision-making pathway represented by Figure 7.6 is that in a pure multidomestic MNC organization, the dominant direction of movement is from the subsidiary to MNC headquarters ('bottom-up') rather than top-down from headquarters to subsidiary. The reason for this is that if each national subsidiary in, say, France, Italy, Greece, Turkey, Philippines, South Korea, Indonesia, Canada, US, Mexico, Brazil, Argentina, and so on, faces a unique marketplace, the relevance of information, skills and experience acquired in one marketplace, to any of the others, is minimal. Little lateral communication is either relevant or necessary; equally, the centre has little to offer the domestic subsidiaries, except occasional financial or technical support for specific projects.

Thus the pure multidomestic corporation is responsive purely on a country-by-country basis through the dispersal of resources, initiatives and authority to each country subsidiary. It exhibits few extranational scale economies or experience curve effects, or locational economies. Minimum economic size of production plants will also be relatively small, as each will serve only its local market. For the MNC as a whole, market shares in one location are independent of those in another. In industries for which this MNC form is suitable, such as consumer branded goods, food, beverages, household appliances (Ghoshal and Nohria, 1993), duplication of facilities in each country is necessary. Levels of both product and process standardization are likely to be low as each country centre will have high autonomy and little co-ordination with the other country subsidiaries in the group. Since their markets are different, there is no need for it.

If we think of international strategy as being on a continuum with pure differentiation per country market at one end, and pure global standardization strategy at the other end, the multidomestic corporation will be at the extreme differentiation end of the continuum. This means that for MNC competitor firms in that particular industry, each country will receive a different product specific to its needs, even if the brand name is the same. A strategy may be 'differentiated' in each of its elements: in market and market positioning within that market (e.g. Benetton sweatshirts may be middle-market priced in Italy or France but high-price in the US, whereas The Gap merchandise may be low-price in the US but high-price in the UK); in the characteristics of the product itself (e.g. low-temperature detergents for the US market, but high-temperature detergents for Italy, Germany or Spain); in its marketing in terms of packaging, advertising and distribution channels. For example washing-machines may be sold mainly through department stores in one country, through discount stores in another or through specialist chains or by mail order in another. Similarly, insurance may be sold through agents in one country but by online websites in another according to both what the customers prefer and what the regulatory regime of that country allows.

The multidomestic corporate form is good at 'sensing' future possible trends in global products by identifying them at an early stage in their local market. Multidomestics were very appropriate when each country market had high levels of trade barriers and high transport costs as a percentage of total costs. Hence it was very popular until approximately the 1970s. More recently, however, lower market barriers, regional rather than national market boundaries, the needs of scale economies, technology sharing and emerging greater similarities in market tastes have combined to make it relatively obsolete as a typical MNC organizational form. It is unable to exploit competitive interdependencies and global efficiencies. It sometimes needlessly duplicates facilities when one larger regional or global one would be preferable on a cost basis, and it is not well suited to new product diffusion on account of the independence of the subsidiaries. Indeed, historically Philips' failure to establish its V2000 VCR format as the dominant design paradigm in the video industry in the late 1970s, in opposition to Panasonic's VHS design, is laid at the door of the power, independence and intransigence of its own subsidiary managers at that time. Country subsidiary general managers in multidomestic MNCs have great power and high independence from the centre; country managers are kings, or at least princes. Since country general managers were judged on performance in their own country market and not on performance measures for the MNC worldwide, not surprisingly they acted to defend their own turf and their own domestic market profits, putting the long-term profitability of the firm second. As we saw in the account of the Philips/Panasonic battle in Strategy in Action 7.1, the transition from multidomestic to global is not an easy one.

These issues operate not only in one direction. We have described the multidomestic / global battle in the consumer electronics industry, which is a global industry. If we looked instead at a very different industry, such as cosmetics, we would find almost the opposite story. Many of the products in cosmetics are still heavily differentiated, if not still by country, then certainly still by region. What sells in Asia is different from what sells in Europe, Middle East or Africa, partly because of differences in hair colouring, skin types, and so on, which require different colour palettes and treatments. In the cosmetics, beauty and personal care industry it was the Japanese companies such as Kao, Shiseido and Kanebo which made the initial mistakes with trying to sell standard Japanese beauty products in the European and other world markets. Their initial attempts to enter the lucrative European and American cosmetics markets at first failed when they tried to sell undifferentiated products in a highly differentiated marketplace. Adaptation is mandatory in cosmetics.

In terms of the role of the centre, the modern multidomestic takes more power to the centre where this will enhance competitive strength. So the white box at the centre of Figure 7.6 is likely to play a stronger role than traditionally in resource allocation and the selection of markets. It is certainly likely to have a strong say in anything requiring significant investment such as IT and R&D and in anything concerning strategic alliances and mergers and acquisitions. It will not only receive financial reports but allocate to itself the power to take action if the information in them is a cause for concern. The modern multidomestic is therefore a tighter confederation than its traditional predecessor. It is becoming a more centralized corporation, albeit one with a strong culture of operational decentralization and product differentiation. However if this is the case, it is difficult to call it a multidomestic at all.

The global corporation
······································

The **global corporation** sits in the top left-hand box of the global integration / local responsiveness matrix (Figure 7.3). Some research (Birkinshaw et al., 1995) considers many industries to be

SOURCE: AUTHORS' SUMMARY FROM VARIOUS PRESS ARTICLES

Strategy in Action 7.2   *Gillette – a global corporation*

Gillette refuses to acknowledge cultural differences. Gillette claims it is a 'global' company in the way few corporations are. 'We know Argentina and France are different, but we treat them the same. We sell them the same products, we use the same production methods, and we have the same corporate policies. We even use the same advertising, in a different language, of course.' The company's one-size-fits-all strategy has been effective. The group makes items almost everyone in the world buys at one time or another, including razors, shavers, batteries and pens. It aims to dominate the markets it operates in: its share of the worldwide shaving market, for example, is 70 per cent,

which the company hopes to increase by the launch of a new razor for men. Scale and flexibility are the main advantages of a pure global strategy; also R&D costs less when spread across a world market. Global companies derive high scope economies from intellectual capital as well. Good ideas are worth more when applied to global operations. Globalization makes the company very responsive. It moves its managers from country to country and division to division. However, the company's commitment to standardization inevitably costs it customers in niche markets within countries, but Gillette believes this to be a price worth paying for the cost benefits of standardization.

under-globalized in their global integration. The global products most commonly quoted come from industries such as consumer electronics (DVDs, televisions, digital cameras, MP3 systems), clothing (Levi jeans or Gucci bags), sportswear (trainers), leisure (international hotel and leisure chains, e.g. Accor) and drinks (Coca-Cola or Heineken lager or Guinness) industries. We return to Gillette (the US MNC first discussed in Chapter 1, Strategy in Action 1.1) to illustrate Gillette's approach to global strategy in Strategy in Action 7.2.

In the global form of MNC, the corporate headquarters plays a very hands-on role. It is instrumental in selecting the businesses and markets to be in and those it wishes to stay out of. The centre decides where the various functions are carried out, for example the global configuration for the firm, its locations for production, R&D and the other activities of the value-added chain. In short it determines the configuration and the methods of co-ordination of all activities and corporate assets and resources. It also decides on how resources and activities are to be acquired and maintained, whether through internal development, alliances or acquisitions. Thus in the global MNC, headquarters exercises control not just in a financial way, but also through a centrally determined and administered human resources policy. Strategic and major operational decisions all emanate from the centre.

To be a leader in an industry with a global strategy for global products, a firm must develop and implement a strategy that integrates its activities across countries. Such cross-border integration is the key to a global strategy, although some activities, usually sales and perhaps some marketing activities, must still have a presence in each individual country. Generally in global industries, competition in one country will be strongly influenced by competition in others. This contrasts with the multidomestic with its decentralized federation of semi-autonomous units. The global company can instead be thought of as a centralized hub organization with spokes radiating from the centre, building and exploiting global efficiencies through the centralization of resource allocation, strategic objectives and decision-making. This type of global MNC is depicted in Figure 7.7.

In this figure the white circles each represent a division or a subsidiary and the black square in the centre is corporate headquarters. Communication and decision-making flow outwards from the centre. The conditions most appropriate for a global configuration are those in which a standard product is acceptable in most markets worldwide, and in which there are substantial cost economies to be achieved from large-scale production, purchasing, marketing or distribution. The packaging is now often standard too; indeed consumers are now so accustomed to multilingual packing on everything from food items to cosmetics to electrical goods, that even the need for different languages in different country markets is no longer a barrier to globalization.

Both product and process standardization is likely to be high and activities are directed and co-ordinated strongly from

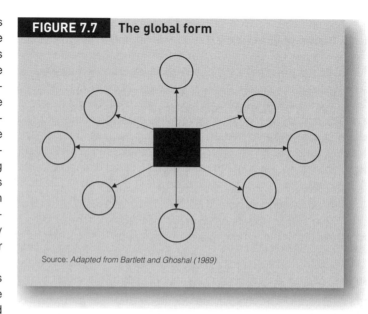

FIGURE 7.7   **The global form**

Source: *Adapted from Bartlett and Ghoshal (1989)*

the centre, that is the company's 'home' country. Birkinshaw (2000) describes how globalization has led MNCs to integrate their globally dispersed activities. Thus where foreign subsidiaries had been set up as miniature replicas of the parent as in the multidomestic form, under the new global philosophy they have taken on specialized roles reflecting their competences and sometimes including a global product mandate. Thus over time, an MNC reconfigures itself from a multidomestic to a global form (as has Nestlé) to secure benefits from scale economies and standardization of product offering.

Yip (1996) identified four categories of benefits that come from global product standardization:

1 *Cost reduction*: these include development, purchasing, production and inventory costs. The greater the development costs, for example ethical pharmaceuticals, the greater the driver to market the product worldwide. Considerable economies can also be achieved by standardizing and hence reducing product lines, gaining large purchasing discounts for volume items, and minimizing inventory through standardized product ranges.

2 *Improved quality*: the fewer the lines in which quality needs to be achieved and maintained, the greater the focus that can be applied to each line. Multiple product lines incur quality risks.

3 *Enhanced customer preference*: where customers prefer to find the same product when travelling as they find at home, their preference is enhanced by access to standardized global products, for example McDonald's fast food, or the use of Visa card services.

4 *Competitive leverage*: the possession of global low-cost products helps companies increase their global reach to achieve market entry to new countries easily. Their brand names are already recognized.

The classical global form was found earliest in the Japanese corporations of the 1970s which caused so much anxiety for their European and North American competitors. These early Japanese global MNCs developed not only production scale economies but also innovative production processes such as lean production and just-in-time inventory methods. In the archetypal Japanese global corporation, strategy and control were strongly centralized. Overseas units were sales outlets used to build global scale. The culture of the corporation tended to be clearly identified, usually set from the centre. Many of the Japanese global MNCs had very strong central cultures. For example, as we mentioned in our earlier discussion of Panasonic (in Strategy in Action 7.1) its founder created a set of 'spiritual precepts' for the management of the corporation. Panasonic placed great emphasis on these precepts as part of the additional training it gave any of its executives who were to work outside Japan in any of its overseas subsidiaries. Until the late 1980s, key positions were always held by Japanese expatriate senior managers. In the traditional global corporation R&D, new product development and production were concentrated principally in the home country for ease of control and quality assurance. This is the simple global strategy, exemplified by global MNCs such as Toyota in the 1960s and 1970s. In that period Toyota capitalized in particular on the automobile industry's (then) huge potential for manufacturing scale economies, leading it to develop a tightly co-ordinated, centrally controlled operation for worldwide export of fairly standardized models from global-scale plants in Toyota City, Japan.

Limitations of global firms were the great distance from point of sale to decision-takers which made it difficult to reflect local tastes. However to have a global strategy now it is no longer necessary to have vast scale factories located in an equivalent of Toyota City, and a tightly controlled corporate. Information and communications technology (ICT), and flexible manufacturing systems have transformed the ways of being global. A presence in other countries means that global MNCs can often benefit from the strong national 'diamond' of that other country. That is part of making configuration / co-ordination decisions work effectively. Therefore succeeding internationally comes from locating functional activities in countries with comparative advantage in order to achieve a value-added chain able to give global competitive advantage (Kogut, 1989).

Global corporations have changed. Until the 1980s they were founded on the operational integration of four things:

1 A strong and low-cost sourcing platform

2 Efficient factor costs

3 Global scale

4 Product standardization.

Since then they have become more sophisticated, focusing on strategic co-ordination and integration as the key factors for global success. Scale and home country control are less critical considerations. Not all functions or business activities need be centralized. A global corporation may appear as shown as shown in Figure 7.8.

Figure 7.8 suggests that some activities may be centralized globally (R&D, product design), others regionally (manufacturing, distribution, some marketing) and still others locally (sales). The value chain configuration will depend on the benefits to be gained from each particular set of variations for that industry. Not only may it be appropriate to locate a particular function in a country or countries other than the 'home' country, but some activities, for example sales may need for greatest effect to be duplicated country by country

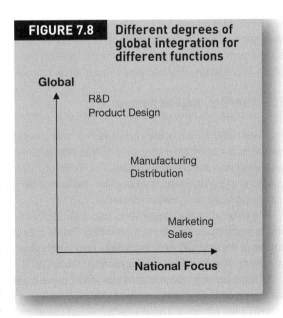

FIGURE 7.8 Different degrees of global integration for different functions

Global

R&D
Product Design

Manufacturing
Distribution

Marketing
Sales

National Focus

even in so-called 'global' corporations. Modern global corporations involve extensive coordination processes, global sharing of technology, global strategic information systems and global strategic planning, budgets, and performance review and compensation systems. Its employees have multi-country careers. Foreign nationals operate both in home and third countries and are involved in extensive travel. The culture is one involving a global identity and strong interdependence of units; this is far removed from the single-country culture of the traditional global corporation.

This concept reveals a distinct change from the origins of the traditional global corporation where the activities and power of the home country were dominant. The growing volatility of world markets has led to global corporations needing to disperse production around the globe. This gave flexibility in the face of changing exchange rates, varying factor costs for labour and raw materials and the inevitable political risks inherent in global operations. If Ford encounters high labour and social costs in Germany, it can switch production to Portugal, Spain or the Czech Republic or Poland, or at least threaten to do so. Locating plants in the US or the EU has the advantage of enabling Japanese or Indian MNCs to duck under US or EU import tariff barriers. These are precisely the points raised by Ghoshal in his organizing framework in Figure 7.5.

For service businesses these issues may affect less the location of a production plant or R&D grouping, and more the infrastructure to deliver the service worldwide and the development of a global mindset for servicing the global customer. For example, the rapid and continuing globalization of the international airlines has provoked competitive moves to control access to routes, airport hubs in good locations to get high international passenger throughput, and control of the best times of take-off and landing slots. In a geographic sense, obviously airlines are international businesses, but they have had nationally based structures controlling national routes for most of their history until deregulation of the skies took off. All national 'flag-carriers' like Lufthansa of Germany or Singapore Airlines are all strongly identified with their national home-base cultures. Their management structures have been wholly national and their current involvement in massive global alliances has created tremendous pressures for change from local to global.

A modern global MNC will take into account the perceived nature of FSAs and CSAs (firm-specific and country / location-specific advantages) in identifying the best way to achieve global competitive advantage, and this will be considered individually by function. Systems remain strongly tied to the centre, since the central headquarters regards itself as responsible for global positioning of the firm. Headquarters' strategic objective is to develop an identity, a mission and key products that are recognizable in all markets, as the Gillette illustration in Strategy in Action 7.2 demonstrates. That means central strategic planning, backed up by monitoring of performance, and executive career development and compensation run from the centre. It also means the ability to disseminate around the worldwide corporation, information skills and new methods developed in specific areas, but with general applicability.

The international exporter

The **international exporter** company has only a well-developed domestic infrastructure but possesses resources for sales, marketing and distribution. It is placed in the bottom left box of the global integration / local responsiveness matrix (Figure 7.3). That box is also, of course, home to the local-for-local company operating in the domestic market only, with low-scale economies, but a sufficiently specific or niche product to survive in its domestic market.

The international exporter form had a strong domestic base, but developed small, mainly sales outfits, in many countries around the world. These subsidiaries depended heavily on their parent for products and the transfer of knowledge, and were generally heavily patronized by the parent, which was dominant. The organization is shown in Figure 7.9.

In this form the corporate centre and power-base is in the 'home' country. There are no country-based national subsidiaries, only sales and marketing affiliates. The dominant decision flow is from the centre to the affiliates. The characteristic of the international exporter is to enable a domestic company to become an international one without the need to change its culture or organization. It is strongly

FIGURE 7.9   **The international exporter form**

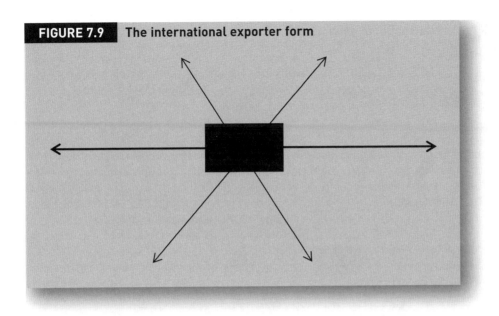

7

ethnocentric in Perlmutter's (1969) terms, not because a product has global homogeneous demand as in the case of modern global companies, but because the home country saw international exporting as the only sensible way to expand, given its lack of international market knowledge and its modest resource base. The international exporter form is a first step in becoming international. If it expands further then this will be a transitory stage of organizational development and it will then have to choose one of the other three organizational forms for the next stage of its international expansion.

The transnational form

Developed first in the work of Bartlett and Ghoshal (1989) and Prahalad and Doz (1987), it is best to think of a '**transnational**' as an idea or a philosophy rather than an organizational structure. The transnational is probably best understood as a state of mind. It is a state of mind which is adaptable and which sees efficiency across international boundaries, as something that companies achieve through responsiveness, flexibility and the ability to learn. Thus decision-making is approached at whatever level, and in whatever geographic context, in a way that is most appropriate for the international objectives of the firm. Achievement of goals, rather than protection of turf, country managers' pet assumptions, or the historical traditions of the firm ('administrative heritage'), is what should influence decisions. The transnational is an attempt to develop a new managerial theory of the firm able to incorporate the management of high degrees of complexity and flexibility, and new ways of integrating activities and resources across borders.

Figure 7.10 illustrates the differences between the two earlier dominant organizational structural types in international strategy: the centralized hubs of the global form (top left); the decentralized portfolios of national subsidiary businesses of the multidomestic form (bottom right); and the transnational organization – defined here as an integrated network (the N-form). The diagrammatic representation in Figure 7.10 is intended to highlight two particular differences in the new transnational form compared to the earlier two. These are: first, multilateral communications between all levels and layers, replacing top-down or bottom-up communication; and second, the idea that resources, responsibilities and decision-making are dispersed across all types of units, not just concentrated either at the centre or at the periphery. Each separate circle, triangle or box shape, large or small, in the main diagram might represent an entirely different type and size of resource unit. One may be a global distribution hub based in

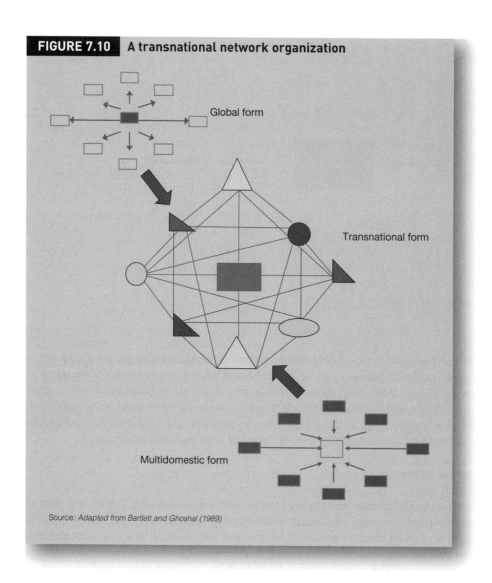

FIGURE 7.10   **A transnational network organization**

Global form

Transnational form

Multidomestic form

Source: *Adapted from Bartlett and Ghoshal (1989)*

Europe, while another may be a small project team working on the design of a new product or service, staffed by employees from a mix of international locations. The project team may be disbanded after six months and a different unit formed, for a different purpose, somewhere else in the organization. These resource units are thus *asymmetrical* in both size and duration, that is they are often temporary. This is what is meant by an N-form (network) organization. Particularly noteworthy are: first, the importance of 'co-ordinating mechanisms' in the N-form; and second, the changed role of senior management.

There are many diverse examples of N-form 'coordinating mechanisms'. Many firms are, for example, redesigning incentive systems to reward employees who help sister companies. IBM has introduced performance measures which reward managers for co-operating with colleagues around the world. Procedures for global account management are a sophisticated illustration of one type of 'co-ordinating mechanism' (discussed further in Chapter 8). They illustrate the internal consequences of network management and the capabilities required by managers in terms of systems and processes for dealing with it. These must ensure alignment of both the internal and the customer-facing processes. Strategy in Action 7.3 discusses efforts involved in creating such a system at Citibank.

Strategy in Action 7.3 *Continuous change at Citibank: building a network-based structure*

In the 1990s the large US banking group Citibank introduced specialized resources and organizational linkages different from its existing traditional decentralized organization.

'The Unique European Bank' Strategy (1988–1989)

Following the 1988 appointment of new executives to head European Institutional and Investment Bank operations, regional management created a common vision for all corporate banking activities in Europe in the form of 'The Unique European Bank'. The vision described the need for a three-dimensional internal partnership, focusing on geography, products, and customer units, an approach very different from the bank's traditional geographic-based structure. Structurally, affiliate staff now reported jointly to local and pan-European unit management. These regional units led to adjustments in grouping resources, including the centralization of administrative and product resources. A European Policy Committee was formed to promote the behavioural changes within each unit required to build teamwork within the region. However in 1990, the changes in Europe were interrupted by two global reorganizations.

Global activity centers' (1990–1991)

In January 1990, Citibank underwent a global reorganization merging the Institutional and Investment Banks and dividing worldwide corporate banking activities into developed JENA (Japan, Europe, North America) and developing markets (referred to as IBF). In August 1990, JENA underwent a further reorganization. It installed a single sector executive, eight senior co-ordinators, and fifty-three 'activity centers'. These were of four types: trading units, customer-contact units, sales units, and product units. Senior bank management described the JENA territory as a 'seamless market with no organizational separation acknowledging geography'. Activity centres were well-defined, stand-alone entities, but required extensive collaboration with other units.

Process focus: pursuing cross-border market opportunities

The transition formalized a cross-border strategy and organization representing an important strategic shift from local *independence*, to emphasizing cross-border *interdependence*. It involved a significant shift in terms of defining target markets. Rather than focusing on competing within geographic markets, this phase witnessed a shift towards competition based on product and customer markets that extended across borders. Although the firm now defined its strategy as competing within specialized markets extending across national borders, its ability to implement the changes was still limited by its traditional organization. Rather than immediately replacing its geographic-based structure, the firm sought to compete in cross-border markets by enhancing linkages across existing affiliates. These linkages introduced *shared* management of local activities, through the formalization of specialized product- and customer-focused units. Whereas previously these specialized units had limited authority over local activities, they began to assume joint responsibility for locally based activities. Adjustments in resources emphasized both the standardization and upgrading of duplicated resources within affiliates and the expansion of specialized resources within centralized regional units.

Installing a European strategy and organization (1992–1994)

The 1990 global reorganization temporarily eliminated any formal European structure.

7

However in early 1992, new executives were appointed in charge of JENA and Europe. The move reestablished Europe as a formal regional organization, although it remained comprised of interdependent activity centres. Initially, the European executive formalized monthly meetings bringing together activity centre heads, which created a management council to devise regional strategies and assist in managing regional operations. The strategy that emerged over the following two years was to be the premier provider of cross-border financial services, moving from being a large *foreign* bank in several markets to an *international* bank providing value-added cross-border financial services. The bank concentrated product unit staff and resources and operational supporting units in London and Frankfurt. Country managers became responsible for customer relationship management, marketing products developed in the centralized units, drawing on support services also from centralized facilities. Regional product units were critical in building sophisticated expertise required to compete with investment banks, while strong local relationship management within each geographic market was essential for competing with local banks. The financial impact of these changes was dramatic. Between 1990 and 1993, regional employment went from 5,500 to 3,500, operating expenses dropped by more than $150 million, and revenues grew by 25 per cent.

Further adjustments to support these changes included altering the way the bank planned, measured and evaluated performance. Whereas its traditional systems were based on an income statement for each geographic unit, a new system collected information and measured results based on a 'grid', with each country reporting financial results by both customer and product dimensions. This enabled more detailed analysis and measurement of regional activities in line with specific targets. The approach was in line with the bank's emphasis on a 'teamwork' culture across borders.

However, a number of threats also challenged the bank. Some European competitors were building regional organizations focusing on similar products and services to Citibank. For Citibank to remain successful, management emphasized the importance of leading product innovations and continuing to strengthen local relationships.

Process focus: integrating regional strategy and organization

The transition during this period involved the implementation of an integrated strategy and organization based on interdependent specialized and distributed resources. In terms of resource configuration, resources were reallocated across specialized units. Activities benefiting from specialized resources and scale were centralized; other resources continued to be decentralized within local markets. In terms of organization, this phase involved moving beyond layering organizational structures on top of the traditional geographic structure. Responsibilities were reallocated across the region based on the interdependent roles to be played by each unit within the strategy. Changes in roles were supported by the formation of cross-functional senior management committees and adjustments in management systems and cultures. Many of these adjustments to management systems took substantial time to define and implement. However, Citibank's European corporate banking structure in 1994 closely resembled network-based MNC models described in the literature.

SOURCE: ADAPTED FROM MALNIGHT (1996)

TABLE 7.1	Roles and tasks of management: the transnational	
Top management	*Middle management*	*Front-line management*
Then Resource allocator **Now** Creator of purpose and challenger of status quo	**Then** Administrative controller **Now** Horizontal information broker and capability integrator	**Then** Operational implementor **Now** Entrepreneur and performance driver

Source: Adapted from Bartlett and Ghoshal (1993)

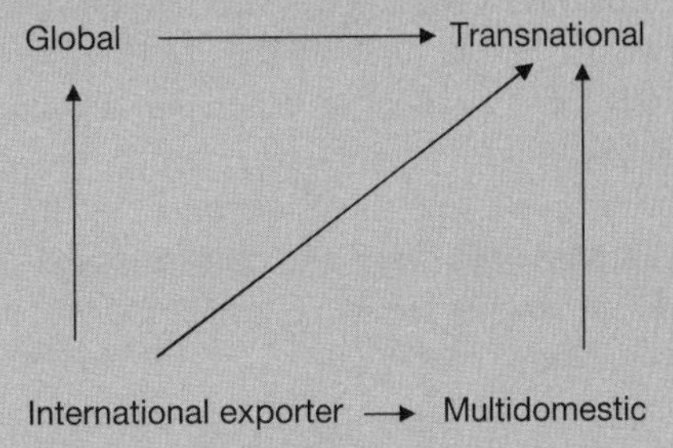

In addition to the emphasis on co-ordinating mechanisms, the N-form also promotes a second requirement: a changed role for senior management to provide shared corporate purpose. This echoes Senge (1992) in his views concerning the change in the role of the corporate leader to become designer, teacher and steward, surfacing, designing, challenging and building new mental models and complex systems. Figure 7.11 summarizes this view of the 'new model' of the roles of management appropriate to N-form network organizations ('now'), contrasting it to requirements in earlier organizational forms ('then').

There is consistency in this approach to managerial tasks and responsibilities in transnational MNCs in Figure 7.11 and that of Senge. They are searching after simple ways of capturing the behavioural complexity, structural complexity and organizational complexity that are essential in a transnational MNC. Now that centralized headquarter bureaucracies have fallen into disfavour,

FIGURE 7.11 Common form transitions

> the favoured form of the firm has become a federal structure of operating divisions drawing on a common source of internal expertise, but where each division belonging to the federation is free to outsource expertise if it so desires.
>
> (Buckley and Casson, 1998: 28)

This is fine in theory, but in practice it has its problems, and some retention of hierarchy seems to be necessary for efficiency and focused direction. Furthermore greater transparency of information has created an increasing requirement for consistency in quality, delivery and marketing of products and services across borders. Not all companies will be able to allocate the resources or develop the capabilities for such management of quality and responsiveness across geographic boundaries. Integration and co-ordination bring great benefits, but many companies are not sufficiently skilled to implement them effectively.

Strategy in Action 7.4 walks us through all four international organizational forms as a pathway over time of the changes in business practices, requirements and ways of working at the US consulting company McKinsey between 1960 and 2000.

Strategy in Action 7.4 *McKinsey as an illustration of the four organizational forms*

Let us suppose that a financial services company in the City of London approaches the McKinsey London office with a 'request for proposal' mandate for a reorganization study. If this were to have happened in the early 1960s, it may have reached the firm when it was basically an 'international' company. The request would have been transmitted to the New York head office. If the proposal were successful, the project would then have been staffed from New York and led by a New York consultant. US analytical models would have been used, largely unadjusted for local conditions, and London people would have been used to provide the necessary local intelligence.

If McKinsey were a 'global' firm, the UK office manager would negotiate the job and global models would be used, not purely US ones but certainly standardized ones. A New York engagement manager would probably come over with his team to run the study. UK consultants would be invited to New York for training and socialization in the ways and products of the firm. This was largely the situation when one of the authors was a member of the firm in the early 1970s.

If the firm were a largely multidomestic company, the McKinsey name would be used to get the study, but it would then be staffed and run from London, developing a

specifically British solution without necessarily any contact with the US. The performance of the London office would be judged by its sales and profits record. Firm-wide training programmes would rarely be held.

By the 2000s however, McKinsey came to fit fairly closely with the criteria for a transnational firm. There is complex multipath information flow globally. Projects are staffed from wherever the expertise exists worldwide within the firm. Centres of excellence in particular specialist areas have been developed around the world, led by expert individuals and teams. Technological and marketing centres of gravity move, often as a result of forces external to the corporation, in search of any better fit (even if only short-term) with particular markets.

In our imaginary illustration the City assignment would be negotiated from London with an international expert on hand. It would then be internationally staffed with the 'best' resources available who would be personally 'bonded' by their identification with the firm culture as developed in particular through international training meetings and working together on international project teams. The recommendations would be sensitively tailored to the specific situation but based on firm-wide expertise and experience.

TRANSITIONAL PATHWAYS OF DEVELOPMENT

As can be seen from the illustration in Strategy in Action 7.4, for any MNC the development from one international organizational form to another is path dependent; most forms can be transitional. The arrows on the matrix in Figure 7.11 illustrate the most common directions of transition.

The transition from international exporter to global, and then on to transnational, is perfectly possible as the need for local adjustments becomes apparent for it to continue to grow a global business. Similarly, a multidomestic can become a transnational as the country units develop a recognition of, and uses for, each other's skills and abilities, and as shifts in various markets create a need for greater scale economies in certain areas. Global to transnational is also feasible and quite common. This shift is about moving from simple global to complex global responses to greater complexity across markets, and less tolerance for simple standardized global products and services. It is also a more efficient use of scarce resources if the organization has the internal capabilities to manage this complex process effectively.

These transitions will be looked at more closely in the next chapter where we focus on a more contingency view of the relationship between global strategy and global organization structures.

SUMMARY

- We have suggested that a firm will adopt an international strategy if it believes that it can achieve a competitive position with any of its businesses in any of the countries it decides to target.

- Often a company has little choice but to begin to trade internationally because its strategic market has become international or global and its competitors are therefore already international or global firms.

- The sources of competitive advantage for an MNC arise from country differences, scale economies and scope economies. These should provide the basis for higher levels of efficiency, risk management and innovation than in national-only firms.

- The key issues in internationalizing are configuration and co-ordination. This means getting the design of the firm's value chain right and also the organizational form within which it will be managed.

- Many traditional international firms adopted the multidomestic solution to the configuration problem, that is an independent subsidiary in every country. This is only an effective international strategy under specific limited market conditions.

- Global firms maximize scale economies but still usually need to take note of local tastes in order to optimize performance.

- International exporters are a primitive, limited and transitory form of internationalization.

- Transnationals, although very flexible and highly responsive, lack central control in a crisis and are very difficult to manage.

- Few actual MNCs fit neatly into these frameworks. Specific local contingencies actually dominate choice of organizational form in practice.

DISCUSSION QUESTIONS

1 What is the rationale for the MNC?

2 What is OLI?

3 How does Vernon describe the stages of internationalization?

4 What is a multidomestic?

5 What is an international exporter?

6 What is a transnational?

7 What is a global corporation?

8 Why are global integration and local responsiveness so important?

9 Is there a best way to organize internationally?

FURTHER READINGS

1 Roberts, J. (2004) *The Modern Firm*, Oxford: Oxford University Press.

The subtitle of this book is 'organizational design for performance and growth'. It provides a comprehensive discussion of how firms should operate and covers all the aspects of the relationship between strategy and organization. It is comprehensive, clever and a brilliant analysis.

2 Bartlett, C.A. and Ghoshal, S. (1989) *Managing across Borders*, London: Hutchinson.

If you are going to read one basic text on the subject of transnationals then this has to be it. This is the original seminal work on the concept of the transnational by the original researchers. It explains how the research was done. It is full of lots of information about the companies involved in the study and is a surprisingly easy read.

3 Ricart, J.E., Enright, M.J., Ghemawat, P., Hart, S.L. and Khanna, T. (2004) 'New frontiers in international strategy', *Journal of International Business Studies*, 35(3): 175–200.

This review article may be useful for those interested in understanding the background to the debates contained in this chapter which is basically about the direction in which international organizations should go. It gives a real sense of many of the most important current debates and what current research is saying about them. They include: 'semi-globalization' or how global is global?; with whom do multinationals compete?; and levels of analysis of international activities, resources and knowledge.

7

CHAPTER 8

How to organize MNCs: what matters now

LEARNING OBJECTIVES The objectives of this chapter are:

- to identify the major influences behind international organizational structures in the current environment

- to explain more fully the network form of organization and reveal its strengths and limitations

- to show why in a crisis networked organizations are ineffective

- to explain how many modern MNCs use a contingency approach to developing their organizations

- to emphasize that local circumstances and traditions influence MNC organization even in the face of globalization

INTRODUCTION

To be effective, MNC **organizational structures** must be compatible with three key things: the tasks the organization exists to carry out; the technologies the organization uses; and the relevant conditions of its external environment. In MNCs, the conditions of the external environment are particularly variable since MNCs, by definition, operate in many countries, which mostly have different external conditions. There is a need therefore for structure to be adaptable to meeting the varying external circumstances the organization encounters. Simply put, MNCs must be organized in such a way that they can cope with uncertainty, indeed with the certainty that there will be uncertainty. Such uncertainty may be about the availability of resources to produce and distribute their product or service; about possible environmental events such as floods, hurricanes or financial market crises; uncertain availability of business or market information; massive price fluctuations in commodity prices of oil or gas; shifting tastes of consumers in various markets or unexpected shifts in their attitudes to risk, as happened suddenly in 2008 and 2009 when the world's financial markets and banking systems were collapsing and consumer behaviour suddenly changed greatly in response.

CONTINGENCY THEORY

We address these complex issues by using **contingency theory** (Burns and Stalker, 1961; Lawrence and Lorsch, 1967; Child, 1972). Since contingency theory is about coping with uncertainty it is an appropriate framework for making sense of the management of global organizations. Contingency theory has a deep appeal given the permanent fluidity and changeability, and the fundamental dynamic character of the global business context. However, it is an approach which rejects certainties and pre-scriptions, and thereby places great strains on the managers of international businesses. It is natural to seek certainty as the reassuring basis for action, and deeply disconcerting to find only continuous uncertainty. But to seek to impose certainties where few exist is a recipe for failure in any business context. It remains more helpful therefore to accept the discomfort, and try to find more and better ways of interpreting and acting within it. It is in response to these uncertainties that the modern eclectic, pick-and-mix approach to international organization has come about.

Contingency theory states that there is no one best way of organizing and that all ways of organizing are not equally effective. In other words the choice of organizational form or structure makes a difference to economic performance (Galbraith and Nathanson, 1978). The choice, however, will depend on the situation. There have been many studies (mainly sociological) that attempted to identify exactly which situational factors made the most significant impact. For example, early work by Burns and Stalker (1961) suggested that it was the rate of environmental change in markets or technology that determined organizational structure. They discussed two contrasting organizational types, the 'mecha-nistic' and the 'organic'. In industries characterized by high rates of change, successful firms would have an 'organic' form. An 'organic' organizational structure was decentralized with ambiguous roles and a great deal of lateral communication. In industries with stable products and markets, successful firms would be 'mechanistic' organizations characterized by centralization and well-defined roles, with communication following the chain of command. This is not so different from Chandler's (1962) discus-sion of strategy and structure, where structure follows strategy. In this case, type of organization struc-ture is contingent upon the rate of change in the environment (which determines strategy).

What fully established the rationale for contingency theory was the work of Lawrence and Lorsch (1967). Their research examined ten firms in three industries and showed that high-performing firms in uncertain environments were more decentralized than poor-performing firms. Similarly, in more predict-able environments, the high performers were more centralized. Adding the element of firm performance to the strategy / structure issue is critical since this line of research showed that *structure had an impact on performance*. All high-performing firms had achieved a 'fit' with their environment. This concept of fit between the organization and its environment is central to contingency theory and central to under-standing the relationship between strategy and effective organizational structure. One last strand of his-toric research is relevant here. Child (1972) argued that strategic choice by top managers directly influenced the organization through their choice of environments (i.e. product / market choices) for the firm and the competitive actions that followed from these choices. Strategic choices by managers are therefore themselves a contingency factor. Choice of strategy must be matched with an appropriate organizational form. Early moves towards a strategy–structure fit by the firm may result in a type of first-mover advantage. However, the real skill lies in endlessly adjusting this strategy–structure relationship as environmental changes occur ceaselessly over time. Many firms start off well but remained locked into a structure that had been effective in the past but was now ineffective under changed conditions.

One important difference exists now that was not so at the time of the research we have been discussing from the 1970s. All environments are now unstable; all firms must now operate in these unstable environ-ments. We argue that there are no longer any stable business environments; all industries are turbulent, just with some moving at even more rapid rates than others. This has been called 'hypercompetition' (D'Aveni and Gunther, 1994). It is now hard to see industries of any type in which 'mechanistic' forms of organization would be effective. All organizations have moved towards the 'organic' in response to the complexity and fluidity of modern economic and business life. So in our consideration of contemporary structures for modern MNCs, it is degrees of flexibility and responsiveness delivered by their organizational form that matter.

Current practical attempts at constructing these new contingency-based forms have emerged in response to the increasing popularity of the **resource-based view** (Grant, 1991a; Teece, Pisano and Shuen, 1997) within international strategy. This view sees competitive advantage generally arising from the unique qualities, resources and capabilities of the organization rather than the structural characteristics of the industry in which it operates. It therefore organizes to direct or fit these capabilities to perceived market needs. Therefore organization structure needs to reflect not just market needs but also the key competences of the organization. A firm that is very strong in advertising and sees that as a distinctive capability will inevitably develop an organizational structure in which these skills have prominence and power. By contrast, firms that have claims to unique technology competences will accord prominence to this function in their organization.

A simple way of illustrating this continuous dynamic of uncertainty, and therefore of the need for an organizational model that can transform itself as the requirements of its context change, is to state how much the idea of globalization itself has changed. The issues that are debated with regard to global strategies have moved on. As discussed earlier, the meaning of 'global' has changed from an emphasis on *operational integration* to its current emphasis on *strategic co-ordination and local responsiveness*. In the earlier simple globalization phase, the focus was on globalization affecting products and components. The dominant concepts in this phase were global operational scale advantages, factor costs, product standardization and global sourcing platforms. In its later character, the focus has turned to globalization of skills, capabilities and knowledge. The dominant concepts in this later phase were: flexible systems to give variety at low cost; regional autonomy; risk avoidance; and deep understanding of customer needs. This shift in emphasis as globalization became more complex meant that in the place of the centralized hubs of the early simple global organizational structures, more complex decentralized structures emerged to meet the need to operate locally, regionally and globally *simultaneously*, for different sets of market and industry conditions. The transnational (as described in Chapter 7) was found to be difficult to operate in crisis situations and transnationals tended to revert to traditional chains of command when in difficulty. For example ABB, the Swedish / Swiss engineering conglomerate which for several years was much-quoted as an exemplar of the transnational organization in its purest and most successful form, subsequently became an example of how difficult it is to make the transnational work in practice. Since the 1990s, organizations have looked at each function and product group individually and applied the global / local criteria to each of them separately in order to determine how to run the organization.

Making contingency work at the level of the organization: a contingent organizational form

In Chapter 7 we described the traditional fourfold approaches to MNC organizational structures. Figure 7.4 illustrated these four traditional forms. In brief, the global form deals with fundamentally large value products in standardized forms; the multidomestic form provides local products to local specifications, usually forgoing scale economies; the international exporter form is generally a transitional form in which a large domestic company exports some of its production abroad; the fourth form, the transnational, attempts to achieve both local adaptation and scale economies but at the cost frequently of some confusion in relation to organizational hierarchy and control.

These forms are valuable as an aid for an MNC to think through its organizational options. However, in most cases the simple pure forms described earlier do not meet the needs of the specific or contingent situation. MNCs find it necessary therefore to achieve some sort of compromise between the extremes of global and local tensions both at a product and a functional level.

8

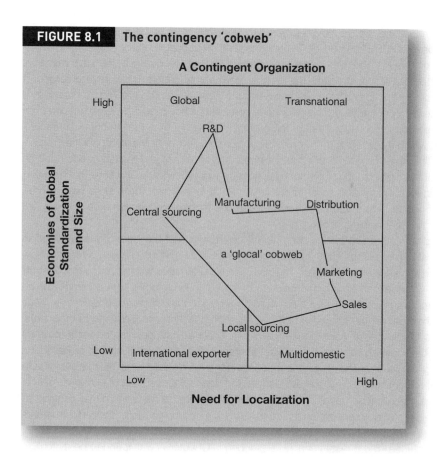

FIGURE 8.1   **The contingency 'cobweb'**

The multinational form that emerges from these internal discussions varies therefore very considerably from MNC to MNC as they compete in different industries and face different specific circumstances. What emerges from such organizational discussions is generally therefore something of a hybrid organization influenced by the need to vary products locally and to decentralize functions. Figure 8.1 illustrates the organizational 'cobweb' that shows (somewhat figuratively) what an actual MNC organization might look like having dealt with its own version of the global / local dilemma. As can be seen, for example, R&D may be organized centrally, whereas the sales function is very likely to be locally based. Manufacturing for an international company may be concentrated in three or four large factories around the world. There are many possible variations of this glocal (both global and local) cobweb – probably as many variations as there are MNCs. Each organization must make the decisions best suited to its products, markets and resources in creating the 'cobweb' that best suits it.

The way in which this actual hybrid organization can be arrived at can be helpfully illustrated by the 'telescope' diagram of the Philips organization developed by Bartlett and Ghoshal, shown here as Figure 8.2. At the time that Figure 8.2 was drawn it illustrated Philips in its multidivisional form with considerable local responsiveness (bottom right of left-hand box).

Figure 8.2 is an elaboration of the 'integration-responsiveness' grid from Chapter 7 (Figure 7.3). Using the same approach, what the 'telescope' in Figure 8.2 is doing is drilling down box by box in the diagram to illustrate that although at that time Philips was in its multidomestic, country-responsive, that is high national responsiveness and low global integration, phase as a company (Figure 8.2, box 1 'Company'), nevertheless, as you look in more detail it is apparent that there are internal organizational variations even then. Figure 8.2, box 2 'Division' shows Philips' five different divisions at that time: medical, audio, telecommunications, video and lighting. Each has a different position on the 'integration-responsiveness'

FIGURE 8.2 Contingency 'telescope' grid

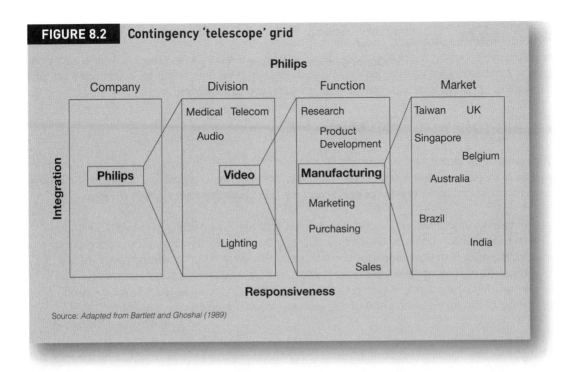

Philips

Company

Division

Function

Market

Integration

Philips

Medical Telecom

Audio

Video

Lighting

Research

Product
Development

Manufacturing

Marketing

Purchasing

Sales

Taiwan   UK

Singapore

Belgium

Australia

Brazil

India

Responsiveness

Source: *Adapted from Bartlett and Ghoshal (1989)*

8

grid. The medical division is the most purely global (top left) and the lighting division the most purely local (bottom right). The video division is regional (centre grid). The next thing shown in Figure 8.2 box 3 'Function' is the 'break-out' of the video division itself into its various functions and shows where each of these functions is located on the grid. Research is most purely centralized global (top left), with sales the most purely local (bottom right). The final box 4 'Market' drills down into just one function: manufacturing – which is regional (centre grid). It shows the geographic distribution of the manufacturing plants of Philips' lighting division. India is placed bottom right which means it is purely national responsiveness. India is a huge market which has distinct local characteristics which need to be supplied by its own manufacturing plant to meet its own consumer preferences. You can continue round the grid of box 4 working out why each manufacturing plant is located where in the world and why. It will always be to serve the needs of a particular local or regional market. Some of these manufacturing plants are making 'local-for-local'. Some are making 'local-for-regional' and some are making 'global-for-global' (Taiwan).

What does Figure 8.2 tell us? That even in its multidomestic phase, there were huge practical differences in how each of Philips' independent business divisions operated because of market conditions. It also tells us why Philips' products were so slow to market and its costs so high, as discussed in Chapter 7 (Strategy in Action 7.1). It had a multidomestic structure when many of its products and markets, even at that time, were regional or global. It also tells us that applying any generic label to an organization, such as centralized–decentralized or local–global, would be confusing and actually misleading. All MNC organizations are messy and they need to be.

Figure 8.2 thus gives a fundamental illustration of the 'contingency' approach in international strategy within the same organization. No longer are we using different approaches, global, regional or local, or multidomestic, global or transnational according to the industry or the firm. Instead, all of them co-exist in the same organization: standardization and adaptation capabilities in the same organization structure. The 'telescope' in Figure 8.2 indicates that not only is there a balance for an industry on the global / local spectrum, but decisions on this spectrum have also to be taken on a functional level. For example, an FMCG MNC might decide that it requires a high level of local responsiveness while keeping its scale as high as possible. However, its R&D may be carried out at one global centre (high global integration) and its sales organization might be much more effectively carried out totally locally (local responsiveness). Its purchasing / sourcing may be done partly at a corporate level for maximum discounts (scale economy) but partly locally for culturally sensitive purchases. There is therefore a further global / local contingent decision concerning each function in each organization. In fact you must take it down to a functional level to determine what works for your organization.

BEING TRULY MULTINATIONAL

The phrase 'truly global' was popularized by Kenichi Ohmae (1989) in developing his view of what he saw as an increasingly 'borderless world'. Since the 1990s onwards, global and globalizing firms have become more significant than ever before. In part this is because there are so many of them.

> From a mere three thousand in 1990 the number of multinationals has grown to over 63,000 today. Along with their 821,000 subsidiaries spread all over the world, these multinational corporations directly employ 90 million people (of whom some 20 million are in the developing countries) and produce 25 per cent of the world's gross product. The top 1,000 multinationals account for 80 percent of the world's industrial output. With its $210 billion in revenues, ExxonMobil is ranked number 21 among the world's 100 largest economies, just behind Sweden and above Turkey.
>
> (Gabel and Bruner, 2007).

Many MNCs are therefore larger and more powerful than many countries. That is why the way that modern MNCs see themselves as organizations and how they are attempting to organize themselves are so important.

Modern MNCs need to fully utilize any resource, wherever it is located, against its competitors and for its customers. That means not only moving production facilities around to benefit from the best expertise or the most productive labour anywhere in the world (what Ghoshal's framework, Figure 7.4 in Chapter 7 would have called 'benefiting from local differences'), but it also means breaking down internal barriers to the free movement of people and, also, particularly of ideas (e.g. to benefit from economies of scope in learning). For example, the Japanese consumer electronics giants Panasonic and Sony announced publicly that to become 'truly global' they must have cultural diversity in their top management. Sony was the first Japanese MNC to appoint a non-Japanese director to its board in 1989 and now aims to give the top job in each of its **subsidiaries** to a manager from that country. This approach to being multinational is based upon two significant assumptions about modern business life. First, that continuous innovation is the key to long-term success. Therefore, it matters how an organization treats its foreign subsidiaries. If the organization relies on just one culture for its ideas and treats its foreign subsidiaries just as output locations, then it gets no greater benefit from its subsidiaries than from outsourcing to subcontractors. Subsidiary–HQ relations have therefore become very important in international strategy (Birkinshaw, 1997, 2000, 2001). Second, that technology is making geographic space and physical distance irrelevant. Software writers in Bangalore, India and Palo Alto, West Coast, US, work together on programmes in different time zones, and these programmes are then specially tailored for local markets.

These factors have had huge implications for company management and organizational structures. Gillette (US consumer-goods firm) has developed a 'federalized' global management system which the company thinks of as operating in 'over 500 states'. The US automobile company Ford spent most of the 1990s and billions of dollars on a massive worldwide restructuring to turn itself into a borderless firm, but with little apparent benefit in terms of its worldwide trading position and profitability. Most MNCs are undergoing major reorganization programmes (often several in rapid succession) to incorporate these changed objectives for the organization and to establish different internal ways of operating. Strategy in Action 8.1 describes some of the efforts and errors that the US motor company Ford has made in trying to develop a global strategy and a global organizational structure to support that strategy.

Strategy in Action 8.1 *Ford motor company: endless reorganization*

Ford was always an international, rather than a purely US, company. Ford of Europe was set up in the 1960s to add regional strength to its European operations. It was ahead of its time in this. Also Ford's top management has often included executives from Britain, Argentina and Germany. Its Chairman and Chief Executive from 1993 to 1998 was an Englishman, Alex Trotman. When Trotman arrived in 1993, Ford had just made a record loss of $7 billion. When he left five years later Ford was making nearly $7 billion annual profit and was the most profitable car company in the world. However, by the mid-2000s its American market share was down at a historic low of 18 per cent. This was a roller-coaster of fantastically successful turnaround, followed by massive failure of its core car business within ten years.

Trotman was totally focused on the challenge of globalization for the world car industry. But despite his many trips to China to build future alliances, it was not Ford but GM and Volkswagen that China chose to partner its local producers. Soon after being appointed CEO, Trotman set up a sweeping reorganization to transform Ford from several regional groups (North America, Latin America, Europe, Asia Pacific) into one seamless global operation with factories and sales companies reporting instantly by means of broadband links. The project was called Ford 2000 and constituted one of the most fundamental MNC global restructurings in the 1990s. It failed. A similar overhaul at GM had also failed a decade earlier.

Ford 2000 drained power from the regions back to Ford HQ in Detroit, US, which was disastrous. In market terms, Detroit HQ could not even keep in touch with consumer demand in other parts of the US market, and

even less so for Frankfurt or São Paulo. In manufacturing terms Ford 2000 resulted in a factory manager in Cologne reporting to a global head of manufacturing 3,000 miles away in Detroit. Many experienced managers were deeply sceptical and the first thing Jacques Nasser (Trotman's Australian successor as chief executive) did when he was appointed in 2000 was to reverse large parts of Ford 2000: South America and Europe regained regional power.

Further damage was caused by the restructuring upheaval of Ford 2000 since it caused the firm to take its eye off its competitors (while focusing on an internal restructuring) just as Japanese and European competitors stepped up competition. They opened factories in America, even challenging Ford in the markets for large sport-utility and other light trucks, where it made most of its profits in the 1990s. The Ford Mondeo, which was supposed to be a 'world car', was only a hit in Europe but flopped elsewhere. However, what did work in the global restructuring effort was linking engineering throughout Ford's empire, enabling car parts to be shared among different models. This brought to Ford some of the techniques that made Toyota great, and lopped $5 billion a year off costs.

Trotman's vision ultimately failed because of extreme over-centralization which was unable to respond flexibly to complex global markets. Today even Toyota, the industry's star producer, recognizes the same dangers as it conquers the world's car markets: it is desperately training foreign managers and supervisors in Japan, and transferring engineering work to Detroit and design to California or the south of France, to avoid being too centralized and too Japanese.

SOURCE: ADAPTED FROM *THE ECONOMIST* 28 APRIL 2005

8

Since few MNCs produce more than 20 per cent of their goods and services outside their immediate or wider home market (Rugman, 2005) and most boards of directors still come predominantly from the company's 'home' culture, the pathway to being 'truly multinational' is still only poorly trod.

THE CENTRAL DILEMMA

All MNCs are struggling with the global / local dilemma. Global firms can shift huge volumes of goods at high speed, while standardization offers huge advantages of scale, speed and lower unit costs. Standardized products require fewer plants, buy from fewer suppliers and reduce duplication. This can cut unit costs by 20–30 per cent. However, local knowledge is also essential, as we have already seen in earlier examples of the size of Procter & Gamble's baby diapers for the Japanese market or Johnson Wax's wrong-smelling cleaning polish. As a result of its international experiences, Procter & Gamble no longer imposes managers from headquarters on overseas subsidiaries. Local knowledge is essential not only to tailor products and services to local market preferences and conditions, but also to get access to local expertise.

Since this global / local dilemma will not disappear. MNCs must find sophisticated ways of surmounting it or, preferably, harnessing it to their advantage. This is where the search for a workable organizational approach based on complexity and flexibility now rests: a 'post-transnational' approach which accepts, and attempts to face head on, the challenges of combining the strengths of global with the strengths of local at the same time, rather than regarding them as trade-offs. This was what the transnational was thought to do but which was so very difficult to deliver in practice. Newer approaches to the management of MNCs must encompass the concept of contingency in their heart. A classic approach to the management of contingency has been various types of matrix structures. We will first discuss the history of matrix structures and then provide examples of newer types of organizational innovations which are now attempting to harness the strengths of the matrix, avoid its pathologies and provide structural flexibility where most needed within modern MNCs.

MATRIX STRUCTURES: ITS HISTORY AND PATHOLOGIES

Almost all multinationals have adopted matrix structures to some degree. At the very least local managers have to face a product boss and a geographic boss. It is a structure designed to avoid the dangers and organizational pathologies of parochialism or NIH ('not invented here') and the 'stickiness' of organizational knowledge that usually occur in MNCs. 'Sticky' knowledge can take many forms but it is basically a way of describing what Szulanski (2003) calls 'the barriers to knowing in a firm' that prevent obvious benefits, such as the sharing of best practice across an organization, from occurring. In multidomestic organizational structures powerful country general managers frequently protected vested interests and provided minimal co-operation to other national subsidiaries. Similar barriers occur between departments in most companies. Professional service firm partnership structures often exhibit similar symptoms, as when one national practice refuses to make a star consultant with a valuable specialist expertise available to another national practice to assist on a particular client project. The reason for this non-co-operation was usually to be found in the two separate profit pools of the two separate national practices. These separate profit pools constituted a disincentive to lending a high-yield senior consultant to improve their national profit pool rather than yours. Under these systems, there is an inevitable tension between the need to increase staff numbers to meet client expectations of service levels to international clients, and the optimal organizational structure of the national practices. Following these experiences, many professional service firm (PSF) MNCs have abandoned their cherished partnership structures to transform themselves into corporations or limited liability partnerships (LLPs). These have very different requirements for corporate governance and often include the creation of a global profit pool, rather than national. Although this doesn't necessarily completely solve the NIH problem, it at least creates a structure in which some of the worst examples of non-co-operation between division, national practices or subsidiaries can be addressed. They can also begin to create rewards for co-operation.

As described by Stopford and Wells (1972) (discussed in Chapter 2), matrix structures emerged at the point in global expansion of the firm when it had both high presence in a range of international markets and extensive spread of an international product range, as a means of simultaneously managing the demands of both. As an organizational structure, the matrix is an arrangement that combines two (or sometimes three) types of responsibility: geographic regions and product groups, or product groupings and functional responsibilities. Table 8.1 illustrates a straightforward, very basic, geographic matrix structure.

This is a structure that relies on a dual command system which is intended to facilitate the development of a more globally or regionally oriented management mindset than the national domestic market mindset often fostered by the (largely now superceded) purely multidomestic or simple global multinational. Since regional managers have responsibility for total levels of business within their region covering all of the MNCs products or services, and product managers have responsibility for the profitability of a particular product line or group of products, their responsibilities are different but require co-ordination if each is to achieve their objectives. *It is this requirement to co-operate which is intended to help bring about organizational co-ordination.* Most operational managers within such a system therefore report to two bosses. That illustration describes only the simplest of matrices. Often they may be three-dimensional covering lines of responsibility for products, regions and functions. One of the major potential benefits of such a multidimensional matrix structure is that it forces the company to face up to the balancing acts often required to deal with complex business issues such as a decision concerning location of a global production function, while simultaneously trying to appreciate the effect this will have on a regional market and the company's ability to resource particular product lines for its individual business units. The matrix structure was seen as the solution to the MNCs central integration / responsiveness dilemma: the need for efficient global integration of functions and processes, combined with the need for flexible responsiveness to national needs (Prahalad and Doz, 1987).

In the 1990s matrix organizations were extremely popular. However, many problems with their implementation and management emerged. These problems with the matrix structure in MNCs lay mainly in its complexity. In particular, the dual reporting structure, rather than facilitating, frequently leads to confusion over responsibilities and decision-making. To avoid such confusion requires a very high number of meetings between the groups and individuals involved in each decision. Bartlett and Ghoshal (1990) suggested that three things were needed for good matrix management: clarity of the firm's basic objectives; continuity in the company's commitment to those objectives over time; and consistency in how the various divisions of the organization work together. If these three 'C's (i.e.

TABLE 8.1	A simple geographic matrix structure		
Product/group	*Country A*	*Country or region* *Country B*	*Country C*
Product group 1			
Product group 2			
Product group 3			

clarity, continuity, consistency) are present, then the matrix structure can be very effective. However, there are many classic historic examples of MNCs having problems with making their expensive and complex matrix structures work effectively. There is a well-known story of Philips' problems with lack of corporate consistency, already cited in Chapter 7, the rejection (in the 1970s) by its own North American subsidiary of Philips videocassette format, in favour of the rival VHS format from Philips' Japanese rival Panasonic. The subsidiary (geographic region) simply refused to support the parent company's global VCR (product) strategy. That destroyed any chance of establishing Philips' video format in the huge American market. Panasonic's VHS format became the industry standard. The German publishing and media group Bertelsmann faced a similar situation in 1998 concerning book retailing on the internet. Although the whole company was aware that the internet was growing *across* all its product lines, the independent divisional heads on Bertelsmann's management board debated book retailing on the internet for two years without taking any decisions. The powerful heads of Bertelsmann's divisions were all present on the management board but did not consent to any dilution in their own independence. Meanwhile Amazon established itself as the world's leading online book retailer, leaving Bertelsmann with a tough task of catching-up. It then bought 50 per cent of the Barnes & Noble (US) website business for $200 million in 1998 to begin the fight back. The failure of Bertelsmann's divisions to co-operate resulted in missing a major market opportunity. Although the need to work together was recognized, the structure to enable that co-operation was missing, and clearly also the will to create such a structure at that time.

Not surprisingly, another problem with the matrix structure is the amount of management time taken by meetings and the elapsed time managers need to understand how the structure works in order to contribute to it effectively. If there is a high degree of staff turnover, such difficulties can be exacerbated. Some MNCs, despite having invested years of management time and billions of dollars in building their matrix, have abandoned the matrix structure and gone back to more simple reporting lines, with clear responsibility being given to geographic or product group managers. Instead of a flexible structure, containing multiple perspectives and able to shift the balance of power between products, markets and functions as commercial need required, the matrix has often amplified any differences in perspective. The dual reporting structure of the matrix often prevented resolution of differences between managers of different views but overlapping responsibilities.

A matrix may sometimes be a route through which the MNC can move to a different form of hybrid organization which it may find more effective in managing across borders. Some organizations have constructed networks of different clusters of specialist local firms in order to benefit from local variations (Ghoshal's 'benefitting from local differences' again). One example is Nike (US sportswear manufacturer), which subcontracts the manufacture of its athletic shoes and clothing to 40 separate locations, mostly in Asia, using a technology-mediated network. Designs are sent to a plant in Taiwan; a prototype is then built; the final plans are faxed to subcontractors throughout Asia. Rather than attempting to meet all global / local requirements internally, some MNCs have opted to build external networks of strategic alliances. However, like all other complex organizational forms, these too are very difficult to manage on a global scale and require their own knowledge and experience to make them work effectively. Running a 'borderless corporation' in a borderless world is about endlessly struggling to resolve the paradox of our central dilemma: balancing product *and* geographic / market focus, thus mirroring the integration / responsiveness central dilemma once again.

MANAGING COMPLEXITY IN SERVICE MNCs: PROCESS AND STRUCTURE TOGETHER

Service firms are characterized by particular combinations of resources and capabilities different from those of manufacturing firms. For example, in service MNCs, there is a particular focus on building an organizational structure capable of supporting positive customer experience of the service in whatever country the customer happens to be. Good experiences arise mainly from customer interaction with the front-line staff, such as reception staff at a hotel check-in. (We return to these issues concerning international services in greater detail in Chapter 14.) Such positive experiences depend heavily upon knowledge-based resources in both the design and delivery of the service, and especially on the tacit knowledge underpinning the routines of the staff, whether hotel receptionists (in Novotel in Strategy in Action 8.2) or global supply chain integrators (in Li and Fung in Strategy in Action 8.3). The combination of structure and process is at the heart of delivery of their global strategies. In Strategy in Actions 8.2 and 8.3 the importance of the creation and sharing of knowledge-based resources are vital. Knowledge-sharing and organizational learning are regarded increasingly as two of the most critical capabilities for all MNCs. This means not just generating knowledge, but even more important, spreading it through the organization (as an economy of scope).

Strategy in Action 8.2 presents the process of structural change in order to achieve long-term capability-building within a multinational hotel chain, Novotel. It looks at the accumulation of skills and learning mechanisms within the firm. The analysis provides an illustration of the organizational structures, processes and routines which attempted to create Bartlett and Ghoshal's (1990) three 'C's across the company's international operations to meet customer expectations in all its hotels worldwide. It needed consistency plus responsiveness, that is enabling all front-line and managerial staff to deal sensitively and helpfully with divergent customer needs worldwide.

What difference did these changes make to the Novotel hotels? The change process described in Strategy in Action 8.2 affected structure and operations of Novotel's corporate headquarters, as well as operations and routines in every hotel in the chain. They tell us something about the new roles and tasks of management in complex international organizational structures. The global strategy benefits arising from these changes included flexibility, responsiveness and the management of organizational learning:

- Information flows throughout the company were changed. Flattening the hierarchy enabled more relevant information to be conveyed faster.

- The role of headquarters was changed. Instead of top-down demands, it now acted more as an information channel filtering useful information to all hotels as 'best practice'.

- Lateral communication (i.e. collaboration across and between levels) increased. GMs organized self-help clusters; training sessions were shared across the group; informal groupings of staff met to discuss innovations; 'clubs de reflexion' were created in some hotels. These 'clubs' contained staff from across all service areas in the hotels and discussion was allowed to touch on any aspect of the hotel.

- The role and style of the GM changed towards that of a team 'coach' responsible for developing the competences of the team with less focus on top-down reporting and decision-making.

- Ways of working have changed for all staff to try to give greater awareness of the business as a whole, to encourage multi-tasking, to push down more responsibility to lower levels.

Novotel management see their concept of 'hospitality' as their competitive advantage. The company's global strategy dilemma is making that happen across all their locations worldwide through the uncertain channel of their internationally recruited clusters of hotel staff. It has to be achieved through clarity of positioning, clear understanding by all staff of corporate objectives and values, and consistent reinforcement of these objectives and values through the human resource management systems of the group: training, learning, sharing, discussing, transferring ideas, knowledge and practice. This closely mirrors Bartlett and Ghoshal's (1990) three 'C's mentioned earlier: clarity, continuity and consistency. Organization structures that can support flexible processes and capabilities provide newer potential sources of advantage in intense global competition.

8

Strategy in Action 8.2 *The history of Novotel: a multinational hotel chain as a learning network*

The first Novotel hotel was opened by two entrepreneurs in France in 1967. By 1995 the chain had grown to 280 hotels in 46 countries around the world, providing 43,000 rooms and employing 33,000 people. Novotel is one of the hotel chains belonging to the Accor Group of France, which operates more than 2,000 hotels worldwide offering more than two million rooms at different ratings and service levels. Other hotel chains in the group include Sofitel, Mercure, Ibis, Formule 1. These range from 4-star (Sofitel) to 1-star (Formule 1). The Novotel hotel concept was based on international standardization as a 3-star chain worldwide. Standardization means achieving consistency in all locations worldwide. It required a system that could guarantee consistent service standards to satisfy customer expectations, irrespective of local conditions or infrastructure. Some of the physical elements of standardization are simple. The design, style and layouts of the hotels are reproduced to precise specifications. For example, bedroom size was standard throughout Europe at 24 square metres. Bedroom furniture, bathrooms, hotel layout, outside amenities such as swimming pools and amounts of free car parking space, were standard.

However, the more interesting elements of Novotel's attempts to implement its global strategy were the management processes which enabled standard service levels to be delivered at all locations worldwide. Since hotel design and guest bedrooms were standardized, basic housekeeping and maintenance functions could in turn be standardized. That meant that training of staff in all basic functions could be simplified and training procedures themselves standardized. Indeed, one of the features of Novotel's parent company the Accor Group, is the

'Académie Accor', set up in 1985 as the centre for all staff training within the group. Its 'campus' is located on the site of group corporate headquarters just outside Paris. From there, all training is still designed and delivered. Standardized procedures and centrally designed training programmes were one of the core mechanisms for achieving consistency. However, maintaining universal quality standards as the chain grew rapidly over a 25-year period became difficult, especially when many new staff were recruited from other hotel groups with different working practices. A system to monitor standard procedures was introduced in 1987. It regulated the thirteen main points of staff / customer interaction. These were: reservation, arrival / access, parking, check-in, hall, bedroom, bathroom / WC, evening meal, breakfast, shops, bar, outdoor games / swimming-pool and check-out. Each of these key interaction points was divided into a series of compulsory directives for staff, for example how to set out a bedroom, lay a place-setting in the restaurant or welcome a guest. A booklet containing all 95 of these compulsory directives was issued to all staff. The booklet became known as the '95 bolts'. Internal inspectors visited each hotel twice each year to monitor standards. They functioned as 'mystery shoppers': they made reservations, arrived, stayed and departed incognito. On completion of their stay they made themselves known to the General Manager (GM) for review and discussion. Percentage grades were awarded and recommendations made. This system, while helping Novotel to control and consolidate after a period of rapid growth, gradually became extremely rigid.

At a meeting in 1992 for Novotel managers, the '95 bolts' was thrown out. Instead new decentralized processes were introduced. The focus shifted from controlling

SOURCE: ADAPTED FROM SEGAL-HORN, 2000; UPDATED MATERIAL FROM VARIOUS ARTICLES IN THE BUSINESS PRESS

staff to enabling them to use their discretion. Horizontal communication channels were established to share knowledge across hotels and countries such as GM groups which clustered together to share ideas, innovations or best practice. These GM interest groups represented different hotel types within the Novotel chain, for example all GMs of motorway locations, or airport locations, or city centre locations. Only three simplified general measures of performance were now used – clients, management and people. One-and-a-half layers of management were eliminated, leaving only one direct reporting layer between GMs and the (then) two co-presidents of Novotel. The role of the GM was redefined as 'maitre de maison', much closer to the social role of a ship's captain. This led to a need for redevelopment of all GMs, who were required to go through an assessment activity incorporating role-play in such situations as conflict resolution with subordinates or guests. Not all GM's were re-appointed.

A very different type of international service is provided by Li and Fung in Strategy in Action 8.3. The globalization of supply chains has created an opportunity to offer an integrated supply chain service to large US and European retailers. To do this, Li and Fung need an organizational structure and internal systems able to manage the detailed co-ordination of local, regional and global complexity needed to deliver their service.

What Li and Fung are selling is knowledge: detailed, in-depth knowledge of the Asian business region to mainly Western (European and American) corporate customers. They are part of the huge shift to outsourcing significant parts of organizational value chains, from the more expensive to the less expensive economies around the world. However, they are not just selling local knowledge; they are also selling a distinctive capability. Their capability is complex regional and global supply chain management, a capability that is not easily imitable. It is offering a complex service (global supply chain management), not just local information. Li and Fung's business model has great further growth potential within current patterns of global competition. Its sources of competitive advantage arise from the business decisions taken about transaction costs and the boundaries of the firm on the part of their MNC customers. They arise from Li and Fung's customers asking themselves what activities should be carried out within the scope of the firm, and which activities it makes sense to buy in from other organizations (such as Li and Fung) outside the firm. These are classic make-or-buy decisions which are the basis of the explosion in outsourcing and off-shoring of large parts of MNC's value chain activities from which Li and Fung are benefitting. As an illustration of the contingency approach to strategy and structure, Li and Fung's particular capabilities are reflected in its organization in that it is the central purchasing function within this organization that is key to its business model.

Global and local: the central dilemma again
....

Strategy in Action 8.3 on Li and Fung illustrates the paradoxical relationship between globalization and localization. There is a continuous tension between the contradictory forces of globalization and localization and how organizations have to constantly manage this tension between the two. For Li and Fung, the opportunity for their new international strategy arose from the interplay between the forces of globalization and the forces of localization. Both are very strong trends and they co-exist. That is what the integration / responsiveness grid helps us to understand. Globalization and localization are not polarized opposites. Li and Fung shows how they need to be understood as complementary, since globalization was both a threat and an opportunity for the company. Their customers were all multinational corporations based in Europe and North America.

8

Strategy in Action 8.3 *Li and Fung's global supply chain management*

Victor and William Fung are two brothers who today run the family business of Li and Fung. It used to be a small company based in Hong Kong that introduced Western retailers of products like toys and clothes, to cheap local manufacturing workshops in China. With the **disintermediation** arising from the spread of the internet at the end of the 20th century and beginning of the 21st, it looked as if there would be little need for their services in the future. So Victor and William were under immense pressure to consider the future of the business. Their analysis focused on the spread of globalization, as one of the factors having the greatest impact on businesses in Asia. Globalization has meant both specialization and greater complexity. Companies whose supply chains used to have five or six links in the chain, now had dozens, and sometimes hundreds of links. How are all these pieces to be fitted together? The solution to this problem has now become Li and Fung's new business strategy.

This is how it works. If a European clothing retailer wants to order several thousand garments, there may be an optimal division of labour as follows: South Korea should make the thread; Taiwan should weave and dye it; a Japanese-owned factory in Guangdong Province (China) should make the zippers; and so on. Since China's textiles quota may already have been used up under some country's import rules, the best place to do the manufacturing may be Thailand. However since this is a very large order, more than one factory is needed to handle it, so five separate suppliers divide the order up between them. The quality of the product, the shipping transportation and the financial lines of credit must also be guaranteed. This is what globalization in practice means for most firms. How to manage and co-ordinate this complex chain of supply requires detailed and in-depth local knowledge.

Finding the best local suppliers at any given time takes enormous research. Many large companies have decided that it no longer makes sense to do this themselves. Instead this knowledge-gathering is outsourced to Li and Fung. They have an army of 3,600 staff travelling constantly around 37 countries, continually intelligence-gathering. Victor Fung describes his staff travelling with 'a machete in one hand and a laptop in the other'. Li and Fung therefore is itself a product of specialization. It has become a company that focuses entirely on optimizing supply chains for other companies. The European clothing retailer described here used to both design its own clothing ranges and plan and manage its own production. Now, it specializes in the design only and pays Li and Fung to manage the logistics of its supply chain.

Maybe then the internet is less of a threat than it originally seemed. Although there are certainly companies that have based their business model entirely on introducing buyers and suppliers via the web (e.g. Global Sources in Hong Kong; Alibaba in China) these have grown much more slowly than Li and Fung. Li and Fung does of course use the internet; however, it is used to make their supply chains more transparent. It does not confuse the internet with local knowledge. The real value of Li and Fung lies in its ability to influence factory owners to reserve capacity for their clients; in monitoring quality; in co-ordinating schedules; and so on. The growth of Li and Fung has been rapid and they recently bought their largest competitor, another Hong Kong firm.

So what could go wrong? Since Li and Fung manages, but does not own factories, potential capacity constraints are not a problem. As it acquires new customers, it looks further and deeper into Asia to find more suppliers. Downturns in the business

SOURCE: ADAPTED FROM *THE ECONOMIST* 2 JUNE 2001

cycle affecting their large European and American retail clients may also simply increase demand for their services, as Western retailers seek to outsource ever more of their value chain to save costs. What Li and Fung are offering is the knowledge to enable their clients to continue to do that effectively.

They had significant parts of their value chain located in Asia but lacked the detailed local knowledge to manage them properly. This created an opportunity for Li and Fung to build a global business based on local knowledge.

COMPARING THE M-FORM AND THE N-FORM

The N-form logic is one of multiplication and combination rather than of division. It also implies role assignments differing from those inherent in the M-form, at all levels of the firm.

(Hedlund, 1994: 74)

Both the multidivisional (M-form) (Chandler, 1977) and the network (N-form) models are ways of managing large, diverse organizations, such as MNCs. In earlier work (Hedlund, 1986) coined the term '**heterarchy**' to describe what he saw as a new organizational paradigm emerging for MNCs. Heterarchies are heterodox, heterogeneous, non-uniform and uncomfortable. They operate in non-hierarchical ways because they have different organizational objectives and are trying to achieve different things. In our consideration of what matters now in the organization of MNCs, Hedlund's (1994) six contrasting themes for hierarchies and heterarchies are useful. He notes that differences between the two organizational forms may be reconciled by considering the following attributes:

1 Whether the organization focuses on *combining* things or *dividing* things in how it puts things together

2 Whether the organization puts people together in *temporary* groupings (teams) or *permanent* structures (departments)

3 Whether the organization makes use of people at *lower levels* within the organization or always handles co-ordination through *'managers'*

4 Whether the organization has more *lateral* dialogue or only *vertical* communication

5 Whether the organization uses senior managers as technical, human and knowledge *catalysts* or as *monitors and resource allocators*

6 Whether the organization *focuses* its development on combining rich areas of knowledge rather than *diversifying* into separate organizational units.

(Hedlund, 1994: 82)

If we apply Hedlund's attributes to the two organizations we have just considered in Strategy in Actions 8.2 and 8.3 we get interesting results that illustrate their structural strengths and innovations. Novotel puts together teams; tries not always to handle things through managers or only through the centre; uses senior managers as knowledge catalysts; and provides structural mechanisms for lateral dialogue. Li and Fung base their business model on combining things (for clients); using the lowest levels of the organization for information gathering; and focuses on combining rich areas of knowledge.

A more recent study of organizational design (Roberts, 2004) has come to very similar conclusions. Roberts (2004) states that the changes found in what he calls 'loosely coupled disaggregated organizations share many of the same features' (2004: 231–232). These are the main features he identifies:

■ Establishing clarity about strategy and about corporate policies

■ Creating discrete organizational units that are smaller than previously preferred

■ Giving the leaders of these units increased operational and strategic authority and holding them strictly accountable for results

■ Reducing the number of layers in the hierarchy in a process of delayering

■ Reducing the number of central staff positions

■ Increasing incentives for performance at the unit and individual levels, perhaps accompanied by increased rewards tied to overall performance

■ Increasing the resources devoted to management training and development

■ Promoting horizontal linkages and communication among managers and staff, rather than requiring all communication to move up and down through the hierarchy

■ Improving information systems that facilitate both the measurement of performance and communication across units and up and down the hierarchy.

These points should be sounding rather familiar by now. They certainly echo those of Bartlet and Ghoshal's (1990) three 'C's' and Hedlund's (1994) 'heterarchy'. Roberts sees this list as being linked by a rich web of complementary relationships, so the impact of adopting any one is increased by doing the others as well. Indeed he found that firms that only did one or two of the list failed to achieve performance improvements, whereas firms that adopted all of them (and therefore their 'complementary relationships') experienced improved performance.

Whether a conventional and traditional M-form or a modern N-form is the more appropriate philosophy depends upon how Hedlund's questions or Roberts' list are answered. In this sense, the soul of the now largely discredited transnational framework lives on in the many varieties of contingency-based organizational structures to be found within modern industries. Hierarchies are flatter; they are based on centres of excellence, knowledge and capabilties; departments are more fluid with frequent use of teams and project groups; and styles of management tend towards the facilitative rather than the autocratic. Even then, the actual organizational form chosen must be contingent on the specific situation of the company and its external environmental context. To make better sense of the context for which modern organizational structures must be contingent, we need to revisit our understanding of 'context'.

LOW CONTEXT VERSUS HIGH CONTEXT

Philosophies of the organizational structures of MNCs fit into two fundamental categories, what Child (2000) describes as **low context** and **high context**. Low-context philosophies concentrate on globalized organizational forms that converge as a result of the pressures from an increasingly homogeneous global environment. Low-context theory would therefore suggest that organizational forms would become increasingly similar as pressures forced the organization in the direction of what came to be considered best practice. The four frameworks discussed in Chapter 7 are generic and as such do not adequately represent specific contexts. Chapter 7 therefore concentrates on the low-context approach to organizational structures. It discusses only three contexts (global, transnational and multidomestic) and one transitional state (international exporter) and all situations are deemed to fit one of these generic structures. Clearly the world is more complicated than this allows. The low-context approach therefore gives little value to specific, as opposed to generic, context. High-context recognizes specific situations in their messy detail.

The low-context approach is epitomized by Friedman (2005) in his book *The World is Flat*. The title summarizes Friedman's argument that globalization is 'flattening' the world. This is definitely a low-context argument. It is suggesting that context is gradually becoming less and less relevant because it is more and more the same. The world is seen as becoming a level playing field as a result of information and communication technologies revolutionizing the available shared knowledge base and creating instant connectivity. It is the argument for the 'death of distance', that is that geography has been neutralized by technology. In a wired world, all firms in all parts of this world, small or large, can potentially compete directly even if they have very different resource bases. The argument is that not only has the world become 'flat', it has also become small with the convergence of what Friedman (2005: 176) calls 'web-enabled multiple forms of collaboration'. These arise from the complementary, self-reinforcing impact of open source software, outsourcing, off-shoring, complex supply chain disaggregation and re-aggregation, and real-time sharing of knowledge and work 'without regard to geography, distance or language'. If the 'death of distance' has happened, then surely context too is dead. Therefore environmental factors become neutralized and meaningless. In reality this will vary by industry. It is most true in electronics and less true elsewhere.

High-context philosophies argue the opposite. They emphasize the importance of specific circumstances. They claim that the local external environment, the national cultural tradition and the institutional background all have a continuing impact on the way local subsidiaries are organized, even in strongly globalized MNCs. High context therefore implies the continuing strength and influence of environmental factors of all types. Ghemawat (2001) clustered such environmental factors into four groupings: cultural (C), administrative (A), geographical (G) and economic (E). He used the acronym 'CAGE' for this framework. Ghemawat's research (2001, 2007a and 2007b) is in complete opposition to that of Friedman. He argues (2001 and 2007a) that 'distance still matters'. He regards the four CAGE factors as the four dimensions measuring the continuing importance of distance.

Interestingly, the CAGE factors bear a strong relationship with factors determining levels of business risk. They may therefore go a long way towards explaining the failures of many global strategies, since such failures often arise from a poor appreciation of differences between markets and consumers and a too enthusiastic embracing of the flat world argument, with its implication that adaptation for specific markets is no longer necessary. Ghemawat (2007a) discusses the well-known example of Star TV launched by media baron Rupert Murdoch to target the Asian elite in Strategy in Action 8.4. It became an embarrassing failure in its Asian target market. It provides a powerful illustration that distance and context do matter.

A more detailed illustration of issues of distance is provided by Geppert, Matten and Williams (2002). They contrast low context and high context using three illustrative case studies in three different countries. They concentrated on the legal framework, ownership structures, educational system and industrial relations of the country of origin of the MNC to determine how much these factors have influenced the organizational system of the whole MNC in its worldwide operations. Their research provided findings of high context, with strong national differences both in market characteristics and in organizational forms. From the low-context perspective they looked at how global forces limit national forces and concluded that in addition to the forces for high national context, there were balancing low-context forces pushing towards globalization of organizational forms as seen in the common global organization of technology, and modern manufacturing methods. However, their comparison of German and British subsidiaries suggested that global MNCs pursuing the development of global products or global manufacturing strategies and the shared implementation of 'best practices' or global accounting systems did not necessarily lead to convergence in management processes at the subsidiary level. In fact

---

Strategy in Action 8.4 *The disastrous launch of Star TV in Asia*

In 1991 when Star TV was launched, it had a simple strategy that seemed destined to be enormously successful. It aimed to deliver television programmes to the top 5 per cent of Asia's newly rich elite who could afford to pay for quality programmes and were also an attractive target market for generating advertising revenues. This was a group with English as its second language, therefore Star planned to use existing available English-language programmes, thus avoiding having to invest in creating costly new programming specially for the Asian market. Programmes would be delivered via satellite network. This looked like a very attractive business model. Indeed the media tycoon Rupert Murdoch found it so compelling that News Corporation (Murdoch's media conglomerate) bought Star from its founders for $825 million in 1995.

However, the strategy was spectacularly unsuccessful. Star lost $500 million between 1996 and 1999. The costs and risks of doing business in Asia were underestimated. The attractiveness of the market was overesti-mated. The level of potential sales was hugely overestimated. These are common difficulties and mistakes in international new market entry. A turnaround was only achieved after Star (and its parent News Corporation) realized that they must invest in specific programming developed by and for the variety of Asian markets. Standardized off-the-shelf programming was simply unac-ceptable and would not sell. After continuing heavy losses, the original strategy was aban-doned in favour of supplying programmes broadcast in the local languages. Its original global segmentation strategy was based on the assumption that a homogeneous televi-sion product could be sold across Asia both to advertisers and to an elite end-consumer. However it quickly became evident that advertising depends on ratings and ratings depend on providing programmes that peo-ple in Asia want to watch. This commercial logic has driven Star's transformation to local programming, in local languages and with a regional management structure.

SOURCE: ADAPTED FROM GHEMAWAT, 2001 AND 2007A

their conclusions state quite the opposite and strongly support the continuing influence of high context:

> We did not find much evidence that national business system patterns lost significance in the change of work systems. ... (in) the case of the global company we would expect a significant amount of convergent and homogeneous business practices. However, looking at the work systems and the change processes on this level in its German subsidiary, we find a nearly text-book-like 'German' company. The stunning contradictory finding in our research seems to be that the more globalized the strategies and structures of a MNC are, the more it allows for and relies on national specifics to play a key role in its global portfolio of national subsidiaries.
>
> (Geppert et al., 2002)

This conclusion fits well with Ghemawat's (2007a) development of the administrative (A) aspects of distance.

Why the world is not flat or borderless

People do things in different ways and want different things (Ghemawat's C factor). The Chinese norm is for hot drinks compared to a Western norm for cold drinks. In a restaurant in China customers will request hot water, whereas Western customers always request cold water. They also like hot milk on breakfast cereals whereas Western preferences are for cold milk. Differences persist.

German corporations emphasize financial control systems; Japanese corporations emphasize technology and tight corporate networks; US corporations emphasize short time horizons. These national preferences continue to dominate the organizational structures of MNCs from those three countries (Pauly and Reich, 1997), at least as much as do the globalizing forces pushing convergence of organizational forms and towards **isomorphism**, that is greater similarity of organizations (DiMaggio and Powell, 1983). This increased similarity between competing companies in the same sectors partly arises from increased standardization of systems and processes used by all of them. For example, standard technologies are used to design similar products to similar standards, while internal operations often use the same systems such as similar resource planning models or investment in the same or similar customer relationship management (CRM) systems.

At its simplest, the high context / low context debate is about similarities and differences. It is also about the tensions arising from such differences and whether these are indeed diminishing as is often claimed. Low context means that context does not matter very much. High context says that context matters a great deal. Both are right up to a point. The remaining differences are huge. It is not a 'borderless' world. In other words specific contingencies, cultural traditions, institutional differences and administrative heritage continue to play a large part in the way in which MNCs approach the task of organizing themselves to serve specific markets.

HOW ORGANIZATIONS MANAGE NOW: DEVELOPMENTS AND ADAPTATIONS

Modern MNCs must be able to incorporate the management of high degrees of complexity and flexibility, and new ways of integrating activities and resources across borders. In a complex MNC, resources, responsibilities and decision-making are dispersed across all types of units, not just concentrated either at the centre (central headquarters) or at the periphery (autonomous national subsidiaries). In the discussion of the transnational in Chapter 7, each black box in the centre 'network' diagram (Figure 7.10) might represent an entirely different type and size of resource unit. One may be a global distribution hub based in Europe, while another may be a small project team working on the design of a new product or service, staffed by employees from a mix of international locations. The project team may be disbanded after six months and a different unit formed, for a different purpose, somewhere else in the organization. These resource units are often therefore *asymmetrical* in both size and duration. Modern MNCs exist somewhere between the M-form and the N-form, partly asymmetrical and partly non-hierarchical. For them the importance of 'co-ordinating mechanisms' is critical.

There are many diverse examples of co-ordinating mechanisms. Many firms are, for example, redesigning incentive systems to reward employees who help sister companies. IBM, the US computer services firm, has introduced performance measures which reward managers for co-operating with colleagues around the world: an attempt to counteract sticky knowledge and NIH. We shall now discuss two important but different arenas for co-ordinating mechanisms in modern MNCs: global account management and HQ–subsidiary relations.

Global account management: organizing for the needs of the global customer

Procedures for global account management are a sophisticated illustration of one type of co-ordinating mechanism. It has become a common part of MNC organization structures, particularly in those MNCs that deal with significant numbers of global customers who wish to have one point of contact with the organization for all their transactions. The concept was first developed n the 1980s as a way of managing the increasingly complex relationship with global customers within professional service firms (PSFs). However, it is now widely used in many sectors. Although an apparently simple idea, making global account management work in practice presents the organization with enormous challenges.

Not all global customers need to be managed as a global account. Birkinshaw and DiStefano (2004) argue that the key factor that drives whether a global account is created for a specific MNC customer depends upon the extent of the demands that a customer places upon that vendor organization. In particular they stress that the most important demand made by a customer that would result in creation for them of a global account, with a global account manager, is the management of consistency in service quality and performance by the vendor. The second most important factor in deciding on providing global account management for a customer is the strategic importance of that customer to the firm. Organizations also have to consider carefully and realistically how many global accounts to create. How many can they manage effectively? Birkinshaw and DiStefano (2004) suggest that companies with large global account management programmes will have conducted a rigorous analysis of their customers to determine which 20 per cent of their customers generate the greatest revenue and that will determine the number of global accounts that will deserve and get special attention.

Although each company will have its own structure for global account management, there tend to be three broad approaches. All three approaches are based around the balance of power between the global account manager (GAM) and the country sales manager. This is the key issue. Since what is best for the local country and what is best for the global customer may frequently conflict, it is this balance of power between the GAM and the country sales manager that will decide what happens. The three approaches are: first, the balance of power lies with the country sales manager (with the GAM acting as co-ordinator across countries); second, there is a matrix organization in which GAMs report to both their local sales manager and to a corporate executive responsible for global accounts; third, the balance of power lies with the GAMs (which means that the company is structured around key accounts with countries secondary). The third approach is the most radical and still the least common, but it is growing. It means that the organization regards the global customer as more important than local sales, so that the company is organized around the key accounts for those global customers. Hewlett Packard was one of the first companies to begin to move its organization towards such a 'third way' system in which power lay with the GAMs. Of course there will always be a very strong administrative heritage of how the organization has historically been run which will need to be overcome before the GAM decision-making power will work as intended.

Based on research by Yip and Madsen (1996) and Yip and Bink (2008), we follow the development of Hewlett Packard's (HP) GAM structure. Strategy in Action 8.5 discusses the triggers for creating such a system at HP and how it gradually developed internal systems to ensure alignment of both the internal and the customer-facing processes.

The key process change that HP made in order for its global account management system to become successful when it had not been before, was to begin evaluating country managers on the *worldwide* performance of the global accounts based in *their* country. Before that, country managers had no incentive to co-operate with GAMs, since country managers had been rewarded purely on their country performance.

Headquarter–subsidiary relations in MNCs

Each type of organizational structure resolves some problems but causes others. Battles may emerge between the different countries, divisions or regions as they fight for organizational resources, possibly exacerbated by cultural differences. Many MNCs may choose to organize themselves along matrix lines: a three-dimensional structure in which product divisions, geographic regions and functional areas

SOURCE: ADAPTED FROM YIP AND BINK, 2008; YIP AND MADSEN, 1996

Strategy in Action 8.5 *Hewlett Packard – global account management system*

As one of the world's largest computer products and systems suppliers, the US-based firm had more than 600 sales and service offices in 110 countries. The challenge for Hewlett Packard (HP) was to get national sales managers in its different national subsidiaries to co-operate in managing the accounts of its multinational customers. To make the proposed system work, apart from the national sales managers, buy-in was also needed from HP's country general managers. Until 1990, the nationally based sales and account management programme blocked co-ordination across geographic lines.

Global customers were increasingly expecting not merely product standardization, but also service standardization to give them greater consistency of customer support worldwide. HP's MNC customers wanted vendor support for their complex, networked global systems. Internally HP needed to speed up its own development as a global organization: it needed co-ordination across its worldwide business operations. HP's internal performance measurement system was based on product quotas per region. This meant that there were no incentives for managers to co-ordinate or to pursue joint initiatives for global business opportunities outside their region.

The proposal for Global Account Management Systems emerged in outline in the 1990s to address the demand for more consistent worldwide support and service. The objective was to co-ordinate on global lines, balancing geographic, product and customer focus. A new role of Global Account Manager was established (GAMs) to be located near the customer's headquarters and to be directly responsible for managing HP's relationship with the global account. GAM's responsibilities were as follows:

■ Worldwide customer sales, support and satisfaction

■ Assuring that HP is perceived as one company at all customer locations

■ Working with HP's senior management to ensure that HP is organized and resourced to service opportunities identified in the global account

■ Establishing close working rapport with the senior managers assigned to support the account.

GAM's are evaluated on the worldwide performance of the global account, while country managers are evaluated on the worldwide performance of global accounts headquartered in their country and on overall country performance. This approach to evaluation provides necessary incentives to country managers to co-operate with the GAMs.

share power and responsibility. However, as Bartlett and Ghoshal (1990) note, in practice, the matrix organization can prove to be almost unmanageable with dual reporting leading to conflict and confusion. Radebaugh and Gray (1997) comment that in a matrix organization, the relationship between the parent and subsidiaries needs informal mechanisms of control and a subtle mindset in their top management (Bartlett, Ghoshal and Birkinshaw, 2004).

Birkinshaw (1997) defines a **subsidiary** as any operational unit controlled by the MNC and situated outside the home country. No single basis of performance measurement will be equally applicable to all units in any MNC. Production-based units might use performance measures of efficiency such as cost reduction, quality control, meeting shipment targets. For sales subsidiaries, primary performance measures would be measures of effectiveness including market share and number of new customers. Problems of control and performance measurement between HQ and subsidiaries are further complicated by issues of interdependencies. For example, a car manufacturer might produce its steel in Japan and have various component parts manufactured in a variety of countries, before assembly takes place in Spain. Problems in one area will therefore have a knock-on effect on the rest of the company so that this will complicate control in terms of determining those elements of performance controllable by local managers in different parts of the company.

As well as these issues of structure and management control, other issues of statutory financial reporting arise. Overseas divisions are likely to have to comply with local reporting rules which may differ from HQ requirements, leading to local–HQ confusion as to which sets of financial figures reflect the 'true' business situation. Sometimes national pride may lead to local reporting requirements of the subsidiary taking precedence over HQ requests. Expatriate managers have many stories of such 'turf battles' that resulted in delays, resentment and political games, with the local managers insisting that their version of the quarterly financial results were the 'correct' ones and refusing to be accountable for what they saw as imposition by HQ management of a different set of results. The same is true of tax since each subsidiary will wish to show an optimal level of profits given the local tax situation.

According to Gupta and Govinderajan (1994), subsidiaries may fulfil quite different roles in MNCs. They may be global innovators, integrated players, implementers or local innovators. The first two types will tend to be high transferers of knowledge to other units and so need relatively flexible management control systems compared with the other two groups. Accordingly, global innovators and integrated players will tend to rely more on behavioural controls and less on more traditional output controls.

Why is the relationship between HQ and subsidiaries so important? One answer can be given in relation to the contribution of subsidiaries to MNC innovation. The proportion of patents granted to Asian, US or European MNCs for work done by overseas operations, gives an indicator of how well, or how poorly, MNCs are utilizing the knowledge resource opportunity that overseas subsidiaries present to the parent company. Structure affects this. For example, in 2006 rounded figures for patents quoted by UNCTAD were 50,000 for the USA per 260 million population; 26,000 for Japan with around 100 million population; and 3,900 for China with a population of 1.4 billion (although up from 1,700 two years earlier).

Birkinshaw (2001 and 1997) feels strongly that many MNCs appear to neglect the creative potential of their subsidiaries. As sources of organizational vitality and renewal, of scarce ideas and knowledge, of potential market intelligence about new products and services, pro-active HQ–subsidiary relationships can foster all these and draw from them to the benefit of the MNC as a whole. For Birkinshaw (1997), the reality is that subsidiaries have many links with other organizations worldwide from which the parent could benefit. His research finds that initiatives by subsidiaries have the potential to enhance local responsiveness, worldwide learning and global integration. The MNC–subsidiary relationship is therefore the perfect example of a complex 'co-ordinating mechanism' that needs to be understood clearly in order to work to improve the performance of the whole organization.

THE MODERN PRAGMATIC APPROACH

The concepts of M-form (multi-divisional) and the N-form (networked) structures are useful concepts to apply to the modern MNC. Modern structures are flatter but still hierarchical; they are also networked. However, now the extremes of each approach are usually avoided and MNCs are built to individual organizational specifications, rather than to simple models. Strategy in Action 8.6 discusses the changes made by Nestlé from a simple to a much more messy but hopefully an effective organization.

A similar contingency matrix-based organization has also evolved at Procter & Gamble. They have adopted an organization structure as shown in Figure 8.4.

Just like Nestlé, P & G have both a regional and a product group matrix. However, there the similarity ends. In P & G the product groups are known as Global Business Units (GBUs) and are responsible for

Strategy in Action 8.6 *Nestlé's changes*

Nestlé, the Swiss food conglomerate with very large chocolate, confectionary and bottled waters divisions, has traditionally been cited as an example of a multidomestic organization since it has always operated in a very large number of countries and the country managers have held the balance of power. However, recently, and certainly since the purchase of the UK chocolate manufacturer Rowntrees, it has transformed itself into a much more eclectic organizational structure. Its products are sold in nearly 200 countries, and the company has offices and factories throughout the world representing Nestlé values, but now with decentralization as their basic operating principle.

Nestlé operates differently in different parts of the world. In the developed world it increasingly markets global brands; in the developing world it still adopts the policy of optimizing ingredients and processing technology to local conditions and uses a brand name that resonates locally. Local subsidiaries still enjoy considerable autonomy with regard to pricing, distribution, marketing and human resources. At the same time the company is organized into seven global product group (SBUs) responsible for higher-level strategy and business development including acquisitions and market entry strategy. Parallel to this is a regional organization with five major geographical zones, responsible for developing regional strategies. The whole organization is integrated through worldwide training programmes, and an expatriate core of nearly about 700 managers who are rotated around the world during their career as international managers.

The R&D process has eighteen different groups operating in eleven countries throughout the world. 3,000 R&D employees

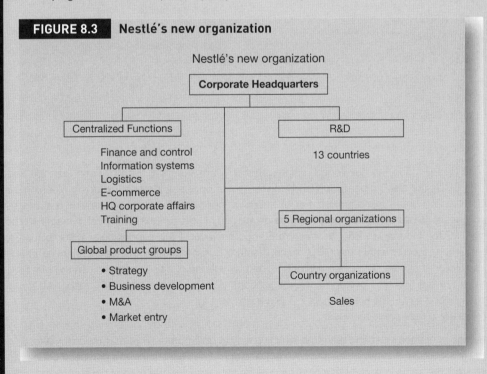

FIGURE 8.3   **Nestlé's new organization**

focus on developing products to fulfill market needs identified by the product group SBUs, in concert with regional and local managers. The Pharma/Cosmetics Division is run centrally, as is Nutrition. There are major central staff functions in finance and control, information systems, logistics and e-commerce support, HRM and corporate affairs.

Overall then the corporation has transformed itself over the last decade from a multidomestic into a complicated matrix organization with facets of global, transnational and multidomestic characteristics.

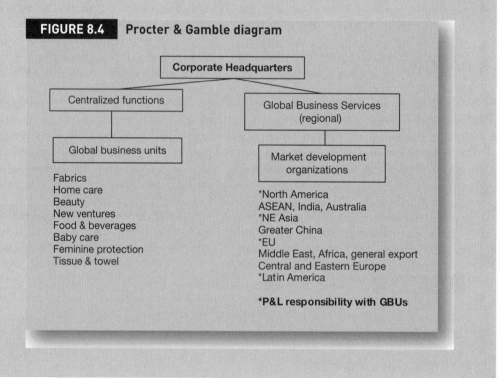

FIGURE 8.4   Procter & Gamble diagram

profit and loss (P&L) in the developed regions, that is North America, the EU, Latin America and NE Asia. The GBUs are also responsible worldwide for global business strategy including planning, brand development and brand management. For example, in Indonesia the GBU will provide a strategy and make suggestions on how the brands could be developed in that context. The local manager will be responsible for the Indonesian P&L. In Western Europe however, P&L responsibility shifts to the Global Product Group director within the GBU, since Western Europe accounts for a substantial amount of P & G's sales in that area. The system is determined by volume of sales revenues. On the other side of the matrix are the Market Development Organizations (MDUs). These have P&L responsibility in the developing world and in the areas where P & G are less strong.

P & G state in their press releases:

> The various entities must find the most effective way to collaborate. That may mean it makes sense for a Global Business Unit and Market Development Organization in a particular country to agree that the same important business unit will be supported by the market development team – or vice versa. Corporate functional experts may be brought in to help with a product launch.

Someone for Global Business Services may be tapped to help a function push towards a new capability or innovation. The principle is 'flow to the work'.

Thus the clarity of the old organizational types is no more. Organizations are now tailor-made, not 'one size fits all': therefore contingencies rule the mindsets of all modern organizational decision-makers. All MNCs use a matrix of some sort, with the particular profile depending upon judgements about balancing the needs of scale economies, local responsiveness and flexibility. It may be that the specific shape of the Bartlett and Ghoshal (1990) transnational is not being formally rolled out in all its specifics, but the mindset of the endlessly flexible, highly collaborative, professionally run, highly networked modern MNC organization is certainly a recognizable development from it.

SUMMARY

- No organizational form is ever the last word in organization structure and new forms emerge as needs and requirements change.

- National and local traditional forces, that is local context, still influences the way in which modern subsidiaries are organized.

- Contingency theory can be usefully applied to MNC organizations nowadays. Different organizations are designed to fit different specific circumstances.

- The four generic organizational forms described in Chapter 7 are rarely found without contingent variations.

- Flatter hierarchical organizational forms which are also strongly networked are popular today.

- This had led to recognition that MNCs have to search for better ways of accessing and utilizing all their scarce resources within the firm.

- Modern MNC organizational structures now must enable optimization of co-ordination mechanisms in order to operate effectively.

DISCUSSION QUESTIONS

1 What are the major characteristics of N-form organizations?

2 What are their strengths and weaknesses?

3 What problems typically emerge in matrix organizations? How can they best be overcome?

4 Is there a best way to organize globally?

5 What problems are likely to emerge from organizing different functions on a different basis?

6 How do we solve the central dilemma between global integration and local responsiveness?

7 Why is the relationship between HQ and subsidiaries so important?

8 What do you think is meant by a 'post-transnational' approach to managing MNCs?

FURTHER READINGS

1 Ghemawat, P. (2007) 'Managing differences: the central challenge of global strategy', *Harvard Business Review*, 85 (March): 59–68.

This article makes the powerful argument for high context in global strategy. It provides rich and fascinating detail about why, in global strategy and global management, distance still matters and geography is not dead. Ghemawat explains that multinationals routinely exaggerate the attractiveness of foreign markets because they are unsophisticated in evaluating global market opportunities. They end up seriously underestimating the risks and overestimating the potential rewards.

2 Yip, G.S. and Bink, A.J.M. (2008) *Managing Global Customers*, Oxford: Oxford University Press.

This is one of the very few strategy books that is also a really practical management guide on how to do something. It deals with the need for MNCs to manage their relationships with multinational customers in a globally integrated way. It draws on research from twenty well-known MNCs from around the world. It helps guide managers how to think about managing global customers as part of their overall global strategy; to overcome barriers to implementation; and to get the whole company to engage with the process.

3 Birkinshaw, J. (2000) *Entrepreneurship in the Global Firm*, London: Sage.

This book looks inside MNCs to contribute to key debates about the transfer of knowledge in firms and network forms of organization. The book focuses on the behaviour of the managers of MNC subsidiaries. It uses new case evidence to discuss the ways in which subsidiary companies evolve over time and how they are able to drive change in the organization as a whole.

8

CHAPTER 9

Strategic networks and the virtual corporation

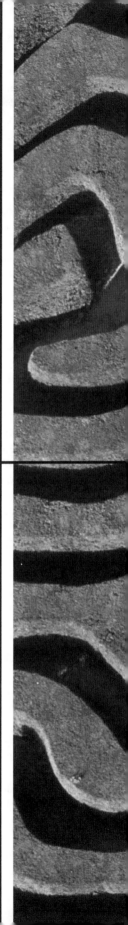

LEARNING OBJECTIVES The objectives of this chapter are to:

- introduce the subject of strategic networks
- illustrate the difference between dominated networks and equal partner networks
- discuss the limitations and strengths of networks
- define the virtual corporation and identify its key characteristics
- distinguish the virtual corporation from the integrated corporation
- assess the strengths and weaknesses of the virtual corporation.

INTRODUCTION

A strategic network is different from both a market and a hierarchy (Williamson, 1975) but addresses the same strategic issue as both of them: what should the organization do internally with its own resources and what is it acceptable or advantageous for the organization to do outside its boundaries either using the resources of other organizations or a number of other organizations? This is an extension of the old 'make-or-buy' decision of every firm. Do we make it ourselves or do we buy it in from another organization or organizations? Table 9.1 lists the main reasons why traditional organizations might choose a 'hierarchy' decision, that is to keep the transaction or resource within the firm; or why it might chose a 'market' decision, that is to buy or acquire the transaction or resource in the wider marketplace from a source outside the firm, for example via outsourcing or an alliance. Let us consider one of the reasons listed in Table 9.1 in favour of a 'hierarchy' decision to keep the transaction or resource inside the firm. One of the reasons listed in the left-hand column of Table 9.1 is 'risk of information leakage'. This would be a strong argument for keeping the transaction or resource in-house since it is made clear that the information is of potential value to competitor firms. Similarly, the point below in the list 'strategic capabilities' implies that the resource in question is of strategic importance to the firm, for example some proprietary technology or a powerful consumer database that should not be widely shared for commercial reasons.

TABLE 9.1	Hierarchies or markets?	
For hierarchies if:	*For markets if:*
Economies of scale, scope or learning	Commodity products
Fewer opportunistic actions	Where market mechanism needed
In thin markets (with few choices)	Profit maximization and motivation important
In complex, uncertain, asset-specific situations	Entrepreneurship necessary
Where information is uneven	Bureaucratic difficulties and / or high governance costs
Risk of information leakage	Routine situations
Strategic capabilities	Commodity manufacturing

The argument is a simple one. Transaction cost economics suggests that the most efficient way to carry out a transaction is whichever way will minimize the costs of that transaction to the organization. Such costs may include the setting up and running of a contract, internal costs of management time and resource, costs of operating at less than optimal scale efficiency, and so on. The idea is that the level of the costs of the transaction will determine whether it is most appropriately carried out internally within the organization itself (within the organizational hierarchy) or in markets (buy the product, component or service in from outside). When making these calculations it is the total cost over the lifetime of the transaction which is the relevant comparison to make with the cost of keeping the transaction in-house. The whole issue of markets or hierarchies concerns choices organizations make about how and where to do things (Table 9.1); understanding some of the reasoning behind the different ways that organizations construct their value chains; and understanding the scope and boundaries of the organization.

What this means is that these kinds of decisions have business consequences for every firm. This chapter discusses how these issues about who controls the resources to perform a particular business activity are played out within the context of network organizations and virtual corporations.

STRATEGIC NETWORKS

The terms 'strategic network' and 'strategic alliance' are often used interchangeably, and indeed there are situations in which they do overlap, for example in the Japanese *keiretsu* form. However, there is a clear distinction between the idea of a network with its implication of close but *non-exclusive* relationships, and that of an alliance which, however loosely, implies the creation of a joint enterprise over a (possibly limited) domain. A **virtual corporation** generally carries some of the qualities of both.

The term 'network' is in fact often very loosely used to describe any relationship, from an executive's private list of useful contacts, to an **integrated company** organized on internal market lines (Snow et al., 1992). However, Powell (1990) created a framework to distinguish between a network, markets and hierarchies. In Table 9.2 these definitions and differences are set out and the table also includes the characteristics of the virtual corporation for comparison. As the last row in Table 9.2 suggests, however, many markets have some of the aspects of networks, and indeed networks may have some characteristics of hierarchies.

TABLE 9.2	Characteristics of hierarchies, markets, networks and virtual corporations			
Key features	Hierarchy	Virtual corp.	Network	Market
Normative basis	Employment relationship	Complementary strengths	Complementary strengths	Contract property rights
Means of communication	Routines	Electronic	Relational	Prices
Conflict resolution	Flat; supervision	Leadership of brand	Reciprocity and reputation	Haggling Resort to law
Flexibility	Low	High	Medium	High
Commitment	High	Medium	Medium	Nil
Tone	Formal Bureaucratic	High-tech Modern	Open-ended Mutual benefit	Precision Suspicion
Actor preference	Dependent	Independent	Interdependent	Independent
Mixing of forms	Informal organization Profit centres Transfer pricing	Equality Subjugation Market relation	Status Hierarchy Multiple partners Formal rules	Repeat transactions Contracts

Source: Adapted from Powell (1990)

Johanson and Mattsson (1991) make a useful additional distinction between network theory and the form of strategic-alliance theory that is based upon transaction-cost analysis. Alliances may be set up for transaction-cost reasons, but networks never are. Networks generally exist for reasons arising from resource-dependency theory, that is that each network member provides one resource contribution which is complementary to, and synergistic, with the differing contribution of other members of the network. Although costs enter into the calculations of whom to admit into the network and continue with as network members, the existence of the network, and the loose bonding implied by it, emphasizes autonomy and choice. This contrasts with the more rigid governance structures applied to alliances and the calculations of transaction costs on which many such alliance decisions are made.

The relationships among firms in networks are generally stable and can basically play the same co-ordinating and development function as intra-organizational relations. Through relations with customers, distributors, and suppliers, a firm can reach out to quite an extensive network. Such indirect relationships may be very important. They are more manageable within networks than in alliances based on the transaction cost approach (Johanson and Mattsson 1991: 264).

NETWORK RATIONALES

Networks of whatever type arise for a number of distinct reasons:

1 *To reduce uncertainty.* Indeed this motive has been suggested as the prime reason for the development of all institutions (North, 1996). Impersonal relationships in markets are fraught with

uncertainty, in that a transaction once made can never be assumed to be repeatable, since it implies no more in relationship terms than is contained in the exchange. By contrast, networks imply developing relationships and thus promise more in terms of mutual solidarity in the face of the dynamics of industries and markets.

2 *To provide flexibility*. This quality is offered in contrast to hierarchies rather than to markets. Vertically integrated companies establish overheads and production capacity, and in doing so forsake the flexibility of immediate resource reallocation that networks provide. Networks can be changed by a phone call or one email.

3 *To provide capacity*. A firm has certain performance capacities as a result of its configuration. If it is part of a network, however, such capacity can be considerably extended by involving other network members to address areas of capacity constraint.

4 *To provide speed.* Speed may be needed to take advantage of opportunities that might not exist for long, and may require a fast response: the classic 'window of opportunity' which is open only for a short period. An existing network can put together a package of resources and capacity to meet such challenges in a customized response which, in its flexibility and scope, lies beyond that of a non-networked vertically integrated firm.

5 *To provide access to resources and skills* not owned by the company itself. In a network such as those found in the clothing industry of northern Italy (Lorenzoni, 1982) the strength of one company is a reflection of the strength of its position in its network, and the ease with which it can call on abilities and skills it does not possess itself, to carry out tasks necessary to complete a project.

6 *To provide information*. Network members gain access to industrial intelligence, and information of a diverse nature with far greater ease than executives within a vertically integrated company. In such firms the 'need-to-know' principle is far more likely to operate than in networks where all members regard information-gathering as one of the principal reasons for establishing themselves in networks. Even in companies that recognize the importance of making their knowledge and experience available to all their members, often by appointing a Chief Knowledge Officer, as does the global accounting firm PwC (formerly known as Price Waterhouse Coopers), the breadth of knowledge may still be more limited than that embedded in a wide network.

Networks are vital to the newly recognized increasing-returns knowledge-based industries (Arthur, 1996) as described in Chapter 5. They tend to operate in dense networks which provide advantages under all six factors listed above. Microsoft could not have achieved its dominance of the word-processing software market without its intense involvement in networks with Intel and others. It has become powerful, not because it has the best system, but because it has the largest installed base of customers. To survive in such industries involves a mindset that emphasizes strategic flexibility and co-operation simultaneously with competition – what Brandenburger and Nalebuff (1998) call 'co-opetition', that is co-operating with your potential competitors. Networks provide the appropriate ecology for companies operating in such fast-changing markets.

Power and trust

If price is the key regulator and dominant factor in markets, then, in Thorelli's view (1986), power and trust are the factors that dominate network relationships. They are the dominant factors in any political economy, and networks have many of the qualities of such institutional forms: 'The inter-organizational network may be conceived as a political economy concerned with the distribution of two scarce resources, money and authority' (Benson, 1975: 229, cited in Thorelli, 1986: 39).

To create a network, firms whose domains overlap need to contact each other and perceive the benefit of working together. Until a certain critical mass has been achieved in the level of co-operation and exchange transactions, the network does not merit the name. Thorelli (1986) identifies five sources of network power for a member:

1 its economic base

2 technologies

3 range of expertise

4 level of trust

5 legitimacy (that it evokes from its fellow members).

It needs to be stronger than its partners in at least one of these areas. All network members, although formally regarded as equals by virtue of their membership, will not have the same degree of power, and it is the linkages between the members and their respective power over each other in causing outcomes that determine the culture of the network.

Although networks accord membership to firms, they are not static closed bodies. Entry, exit, and repositioning are constantly going on in networks occasioned by a particular firm member's success, or failure, and the strength of demand or otherwise for the contribution other member firms believe it can make to their proposed projects. The ultimate justification for the cost to a firm of maintaining its position in a network is the belief that such network activity strengthens its competitive position in comparison to operating on a purely market-based philosophy.

Even networks themselves, however, rise and fall in power. As Thorelli (1986: 43) put it: 'In the absence of conscious co-ordinative management – i.e. network management – networks would tend to disintegrate under the impact of entropy.' Networks depend on the establishment, maintenance, and perhaps strengthening of relationships in the hope of profits in the future. In this sense they are different from markets, which exist to establish profit today. It is, therefore, the perceived quality of relationships in networks that matters, since quantitative measures cannot easily be applied to them.

Parts of networks are often appropriable by individuals in a way that technologies and production capacity are not. To that extent, although a firm may join a network to reduce its vulnerability, it may end up replacing one form of vulnerability with another. The successful corporate finance directors of large corporations or financial institutions depend almost entirely on their networks, and their current companies are eternally at risk of their being bid away to other institutions through a large enough financial offer. In a turbulent and uncertain world, however, few managers can risk being entirely without networks, or conversely, being entirely dependent upon them.

Although trust and reputation are necessary in all exchange relationships, they are at their most vital in network forms. It is true that you need to trust your colleagues in a hierarchy, and you need to trust the trader who sells you a product in a market, at least to the extent of believing that the good is of the declared quality. In such circumstances, tacit behavioural caution and legal remedies can to some degree compensate for doubtful trust in hierarchies and markets respectively. However, without trust, and a member's reputation on admission to a network, such a mode of co-operation would soon wither, probably back into a market form.

A network might be seen as a randomly determined set of business relationships created because its members felt uncertain of the future, believing that knowing particular trading partners well would provided a stronger capability than having only market relationships, or that the costs involved would be lower than the costs of vertical integration. Jarillo (1993) looked at a network as something more. In Jarillo's view what he calls strategic networks are merely another, and often better, way of running the 'business system' necessary for the production and sale of a chosen set of products. By business system he means the stages and activities necessary for designing, sourcing, producing, marketing, distributing, and servicing a product – a concept similar to Porter's (1985) value chain.

Snow et al. (1992) identified three distinct types of network:

1 *The internal network*. This is a curious identification as a network, since it is described as the introduction of the market into the internal organization of the firm. Thus activities are carried out within the firm and then 'sold' to the next stage of the value chain at market prices, with the purchaser having the right to buy externally, if he can get a better deal. The activity may also in turn develop third-party clients external to the firm. This is also sometimes referred to as an internal market.

2 *The stable network*. This is the firm employing partial outsourcing to increase flexibility and improve performance, with a smaller base of permanent employees. It may be similar to the Japanese *keiretsu* in Western form.

3 *Dynamic networks*. These are composed of lead firms who identify new opportunities and then assemble a network of complementary firms with the assets and capabilities to provide the business system to meet the identified market need. Dynamic networks have been called 'hollow corporations' (*Business Week*, 3 March 1986), since the entrepreneur lacks the capacity to carry out the range of necessary activities from its own resources.

Snow et al. (1992) take the network concept further by observing that the change in organizational form leads inevitably to a change in the required qualities of executives. In markets, traders need above all to be quick-witted, streetwise, and able to negotiate effectively. In hierarchies, executives need a range of personal attributes including leadership qualities, administrative abilities and diplomatic capacity. An autocratic style, although not fashionable, is not necessarily an inhibitor to success in many company cultures. In setting up and running networks, however, such a style would almost inevitably lead to the failure of the network or at least to the executive's replacement.

Snow et al. (1992) identify the broker as the ideal network executive, and they specify three distinct broker roles:

1 *The architect*. He is the creator of the network or at least creator of the project in which appropriate firms in an existing network are to be asked to play a part. The architect is the entrepreneur, and, dependent upon his creativity and motivational abilities, he may be instrumental in providing the inspirational vision that brings a network into being, in introducing new members to it, or merely in resourcing a project from existing network members.

2 *The lead operator*. This broker role is often carried out by a member of a downstream firm in the network. He is the manager rather than the entrepreneur, and provides the brain and central nervous system that the network needs, if it is to function effectively on a defined mission. As the name suggests, he needs to provide leadership, but in a more democratic style than would be the case in a hierarchy, as the members of the team in which he operates are not his employees.

3 *The caretaker*. The caretaker will need to monitor a large number of relationships. He will need to nurture, to enhance, and even to discipline network members if they fail to deliver their required contribution. In Axelrod's (1984) 'tit-for-tat' strategy it will probably be the caretaker who applies the network discipline if one member defects or threatens to defect. This role prevents Thorelli's (1986) risk of 'entropy'.

NETWORK RELATIONSHIPS

It is difficult to position networks on the co-operative strategy spectrum of ascending interdependence, since some networks exhibit firm-like qualities (e.g. the Japanese *keiretsu*), while others are little more than a medium for the fast transmission of informal industry information. A simple way of setting out these rising levels of interdependence is given in Figure 9.1.

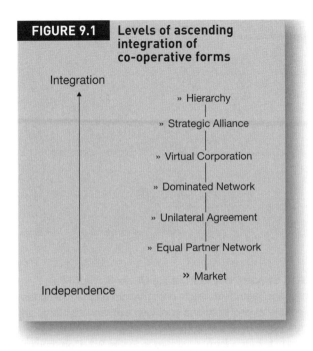

FIGURE 9.1 Levels of ascending integration of co-operative forms

Integration

» Hierarchy

» Strategic Alliance

» Virtual Corporation

» Dominated Network

» Unilateral Agreement

» Equal Partner Network

» Market

Independence

However, the problem becomes easier to solve, if networks are classified into two distinct categories as suggested above: first, the *dominated network*, where one firm maintains bilateral relations with a number of normally smaller companies; and second, the *equal-partner network*, in which a number of firms develop close relationships with each other, and work together in variable configurations on a variety of projects. These forms are similar to Snow et al.'s (1992) stable and dynamic networks. Their third category, the internal network, is regarded as outside the brief of co-operative strategy as it operates purely internally in an organization.

The focus of this chapter now moves to consider three inter-organizational forms: the equal-partner network, the dominated network and the virtual corporation. Because of its greater stability and simplicity as an organizational form, we will begin with the dominated network.

THE DOMINATED NETWORK

This network form owes its growth in the West to two major unconnected factors: the global success of Japanese MNCs and the subsequent interest in their management systems; and the fall in popularity of the large vertically integrated multi-divisional industrial corporation. This latter has been replaced in many companies by the downsized, delayered, capability-based organization, relying on outsourcing for its production in all functions except those deemed to be strategically vital and close to its core business and strategic interests.

The Japanese industrial *keiretsu* represents the archetype of the dominated network.

The vertical keiretsu are tight hierarchical associations centred on a single large parent and containing multiple smaller satellite companies within related industries. While focused in their business activities, they span the status breadth of the business community, with the parent firm part of Japan's large-firm economic core and its satellites, particularly at lower levels, small operations that are often family-run. . . . The vertical keiretsu can be divided into three main categories. The first are the *sangyo keiretsu* or production keiretsu, which are elaborate hierarchies of primary, secondary, and tertiary-level subcontractors that supply, through a series of stages, to parent firms. The second are the *ryutsu keiretsu* or distribution keiretsu. These are linear systems of distributors that operate under the name of a large-scale manufacturer, or sometimes a wholesaler. They have much in common with the vertical marketing systems that some large US manufacturers have introduced to organize their inter-firm distribution channels. A third, the *shihon keiretsu* or capital keiretsu, are groupings based not on the flow of production materials and goods but on the flow of capital from a parent firm.

(Gerlach, 1992: 68)

Although Gerlach's description of the different types of *keiretsu* in Japanese industry is clear and categorical, in the complex world of reality the webs of the *keiretsu* do frequently overlap, and it is possible to have *keiretsu* with dual centres, the one a manufacturing or trading centre and the other a bank. It is also not unusual for the outer members of *keiretsu* to deal preferentially with each other as well as with the core company. Such dominated networks are not unique to Japan, although they are a strong feature of the Japanese industrial system of production and distribution. Many of the large retail chains of the world such as IKEA of Sweden, Wal-Mart of the US, or Zara of Spain have exactly such a tight relationship with their supplier and distribution networks that are characteristic features of the dominated network. These include control over quality and supply in exchange for large annual order commitments. The Korean *chaebols* are also similar in nature.

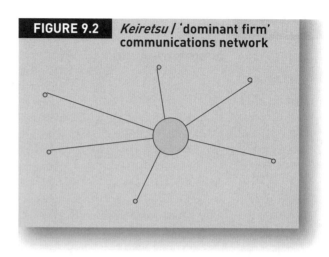

FIGURE 9.2   *Keiretsu* / 'dominant firm' communications network

Relationships within dominated networks typically take the form illustrated in Figure 9.2. Communication is directed outward to satellites from the lead (dominant) firm. There is often only limited networking between satellite companies, except in relation to the business of the dominant company. The dominant company may establish formal links with the satellite through a minority shareholding and / or board membership. But this is not always or even generally the case. The advantage of such networks from the viewpoint of the dominant company is that it can rely on regular-quality supplies at a pre-agreed price without the need to put up the capital and management resources to create them directly. From the satellite's viewpoint, it can economize on sales and marketing expenditure and have the security of reliable orders and cash flow for its planning purposes, which removes many of the risks from its business. Of course at the same time it also removes some of the autonomy, and if the satellite allows too great a percentage of its business to be with the dominant company it is at great risk of giving up to the central company all independent bargaining power over such matters as price changes or product development.

THE EQUAL-PARTNER NETWORK

Equal-partner networks are so named because, unlike in a dominated network, there is no single partner which sets up and controls the network's activities. However, this does not necessarily imply that all partners do in fact have equal power. In all equal-partner networks power relationships are varied and constantly shifting with the fortunes of members. The equal-partner network differs from the dominated network also in that it is not a substitute organizational form for the integrated firm. Rather it is the expression of a set of developed relationships between firms that form a substructure from which competitive organizational entities may emerge.

Figure 9.3 illustrates in a stylized fashion the nature of relationships and contacts between members in equal-partner networks in contrast to those in dominated networks as illustrated in Figure 9.2.

Equal-partner networks can be configured and reconfigured to meet changing market opportunities, often with a different partner in the lead. This is both their strength and their weakness. Although it implies great flexibility, and an ability to respond to changing and uncertain environments, an equal-partner network lacks the permanent brain and central nervous system that will ensure it remains

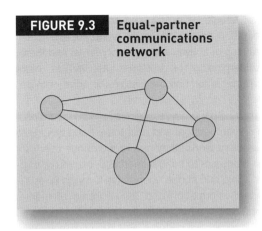

FIGURE 9.3 **Equal-partner communications network**

combative against an integrated organization. Any organization hoping to compete with vertically integrated companies, which possess production and sales capacity and strong brand names, needs to convince the public of its enduring existence. It also requires a leadership capacity to plan and execute strategy, information systems sensitive enough to convey what needs to be done, and performance management systems to ensure that it is done. This cannot easily be achieved via the loose linkages of an equal-partner network, despite its other advantageous qualities. For this reason an equal-partner network is more like a dense set of mutually aware capabilities than an actual organization form. Such networks may therefore often be temporary. They may in due course develop into dominated networks, virtual corporations, or even integrated companies. In economies where networks traditionally flourish, as in information industry hubs in California or in Bangalore, the emergence of new firms out of a deeply embedded network substructure does not disturb the basic network characteristics of the economy. In fact, they reflect it.

BENEFITS AND COSTS OF BELONGING TO A NETWORK

Arguing in favour of networks, Kogut (2000) stressed that firm performance can benefit from membership of a particular network, in proportion to the range and quality of the information it provides, and also from the impetus to development created through being part of an evolving network full of dynamic activity. Afuah (2000), looking on the other side of the coin, finds that performance is lowered if the capabilities in a network are poor as a result of technological change with which the network has not kept pace. Gulati, Nohria and Zaheer (2000) support this view, stating that although networks provide a firm with access to information, resources, markets and technologies, they may also, if poorly constructed, lock firms into unproductive relationships. They conclude therefore that 'networks really do matter in terms of firm performance', either positively or negatively.

Thus we may conclude that being part of a high-performing team raises your game, but being part of a loser network drags you down with it. Therefore the moral is to choose your network partners very carefully. Indeed this is emphasized by Baum, Calabrese and Silverman (2000), whose research shows that the performance of start-ups can be substantially affected by the nature of the networks within which they choose to work. Their research on Canadian biotechnology start-ups confirms their hypotheses that early performance can be enhanced by (1) establishing alliances, (2) configuring them into an efficient network that provides access to diverse information and capabilities with minimum costs of redundancy, conflict and complexity, and (3) judiciously allying with potential rivals that provide a good chance of enhancing learning and low risk of intra-alliance rivalry.

Network theory has long been seen as the basis for new organizational forms (Nohria and Eccles, 1992; Castells, 2000) and for the growth of co-operative strategy as a counterbalance to competitive strategy theories. The MNC transnational form in particular has many network characteristics. At one level, however, networks have always been with us. Shortly after any business start-up, or any further expansion, entrepreneurs (founders) will begin to build up a network out of the associates with whom they interact. In the business world they will be suppliers, distributors, and perhaps to a lesser extent, competitors and customers. Entrepreneurs and managers always consider such key business decisions as the degree to which some potential activities could or should be outsourced and whether to deal directly with the customer or develop sales through a network. In some parts of the world, for example in northern Italy, this has traditionally led to strong specializations of activity among family firms, and therefore the network has become the fundamental underpinning of business activity. In more market-dominated areas, notably much of the US, vertical integration has been more the norm, with co-operative networked activity building up more slowly.

An attractive characteristic of many networks is that they help members to achieve increased global reach rapidly and at low cost. They are flexible within their membership, and able to respond quickly to changing environmental situations. In an increasingly turbulent world, they can reduce uncertainty for their members. They enable potential synergies between members to be identified and, hopefully, captured, and provide the conditions for the achievement of scale and scope economies through specialization. They are also good vehicles for the spreading of information and for all forms of market intelligence. Under conditions of trust between members, they may also reduce transaction costs, in contrast to vertically integrated companies with internally competitive cultures. But such costs are very difficult to assess in advance of membership.

However, networks, if they are to be contrasted with vertically integrated companies and with the arm's-length nature of the pure-market form, also have their downsides. In **dominated networks**, the risks for the dominant partner are of unlicensed technology leakage, poor quality assurance, and a possible diffusion of internal feelings of identity and motivation in the outlying companies. There are also the difficulties of communicating tacit knowledge, and of achieving a sufficient level of co-ordination between members in different companies to compete successfully with the more controlled systems of integrated companies. For the smaller companies in the dominated network there are many different types of problems: feeling too dominated; being unable to influence strategies or decision outcomes; loss of autonomy and motivation; lack of promotion opportunities; insecurity; and the difficulty in recruiting high-quality personnel to small companies with limited prospects.

In equal-partner networks the primary problems relate to the lack of a brain and a central nervous system. By their nature they are loosely organized coalitions without a permanent acknowledged leader. Major investment in such networks is difficult to organize, and there is the perpetual tension between trust and the potential risk of creating a set of future knowledgeable competitors as a result of too much misplaced trust. There is also the difficulty for a network in managing to drive consistently towards a vision of the future, in the way a successful vertically integrated company can.

Nevertheless, there will undoubtedly be a growth of networks in the search for reduced uncertainty resulting from the globalization of technologies and markets and spiralling costs of doing business, such as continuous requirements for ICT upgrades. Co-operative strategy will become more prominent. But it will also compete with, rather than replace, competitive behaviour, if pressures for efficiencies are to be maintained.

THE VIRTUAL CORPORATION

Just as network theory and strategic alliance have become the popular phrases to describe the growing intra-organizational forms of the 1990s, the 'virtual corporation' in its varied forms makes claims to fill that role in the first decade of the 2000s. The virtual corporation differs from the strategic alliance in that it places its emphasis not primarily on how two or more firms can work together to their mutual advantage, but on how one firm can be created with flexible boundaries and ownership, supported by electronic data exchange and ICT (information and communication technologies). As Nagel and Dove (1991) put it: 'A virtual company is created by selecting organizational resources from different companies and synthesizing them into a single electronic business entity.'

However, as with many new concepts, differing understandings develop of what the concepts actually entail, and the distinction between the heavily outsourced company, the strategic alliance, and the virtual corporation is sometimes difficult to define. There is, however, one crucial difference between the strategic alliances and the virtual corporation beyond the key electronic aspect of the virtual corporation. The strategic alliance is generally created to bring about organizational learning. Many commentators highlight the point that successful alliances are not composed of partners involved in skill substitution, that is that one partner produces and leaves the selling to the other. Alliance partners are concerned to learn from each other and thus strengthen the areas in which they are weak. This does not apply to the virtual corporation. In this intra-organizational form, companies each provide different functions, and are linked electronically. Organizational learning is not a basic objective of the exercise, but rather the creation of a flexible organization of companies, each carrying out one or more functions excellently to deliver a competitive product to the customer.

CHARACTERISTICS OF THE VIRTUAL CORPORATION

The concept of the virtual corporation is based on three premises:

1 Few companies are excellent at all functions. Greater value can, therefore, be created if each company concentrates on performing only the functions which it does best, and relies on co-operating partners to carry out the other functions, rather than by attempting to do all things internally within a fully integrated company.

2 World trade and global markets are increasingly volatile and turbulent. In order to survive, companies need to link together flexibly, and be ready to use IT-based architectural transformations to meet changing conditions.

3 Points 1 and 2 are made feasible by: co-operative attitudes, even between competitors; and the existence of increasingly sophisticated ICT.

This definition of what makes a virtual corporation possible includes many assumptions about co-operative behavioural contributions from staff in order to make this type of organization work. Such human aspects forming part of the creation of a potential virtual corporation are dramatically absent from Mowshowitz (1994) who depicts the virtual corporation as a dehumanized electronic entity. *Fortune Magazine* (1994) endorsed this characterization, seeing the virtual corporation as being dependent upon six prime characteristics:

1 A repertoire of variably connectable modules built around an electronic information network.

2 Flexible workforces able to expand or contract to meet changing needs: a small central core and several groups of self-employed freelance workers selling their time as required.

3 Outsourcing, but only to known co-operating firms with strong and regular relationships with the corporation, as in the Japanese *keiretsu*.

4 A web of strategic partnerships.

5 A clear understanding among all participating units of the current central objectives of the virtual corporation. In the absence of such an understanding there is a high risk that the corporation will lack the will and purpose to compete successfully with more integrated corporations.

6 An enabling environment in which employees are expected to work out for themselves the best way of operating, and then to get things done. This is in contrast to the traditional system of working according to orders conveyed with the aid of operations manuals and job descriptions.

Such a virtual corporation could not work effectively in a pre-electronic age, or a non-ICT age. Even with advanced ICT, technology failures are prohibitive within the virtual network.

The virtual corporation is not so much a new concept, as one that has become more fully developed as the information age increasingly influences the design of business strategies and their implementation. Subcontracting and multi-firm projects have existed as long as business itself. Entrepreneurial start-ups have always had to rely on subcontractors, generally due to lack of adequate capital, resources and capabilities to carry out all functions internally (i.e. 'hollow corporations'). Major construction projects have also been organized in a virtual fashion for decades, with a lead contractor and an appropriate number of subcontractors to carry out specialist functions, as is the norm in giant construction projects like building new dams in China. Some companies have always adopted a philosophy of carrying out directly only the functions in which they claim special expertise and subcontracting the others. Even a major IT corporation like Apple began as a 'hollow corporation', carrying out only a limited number of activities directly, but doing them extraordinarily well. Furthermore, many large management consultancies operate with a relatively small number of salaried employees, and a large network of self-employed contractors.

However, since the resource-based view of the firm (Wernerfelt, 1984) has come to dominate management thinking, there has been an increased emphasis on concentrating on the core business, and particularly on developing the core competences and distinctive capabilities, while 'downsizing' its overall employee numbers by subcontracting other functions considered to be less 'core'. However, virtual corporations are far more 'virtual' than this, mainly because they operate through wired connectivity.

Many companies now have some virtual characteristics, although few have all those listed above. For example, many large pharmaceutical MNCs now carry out R&D through virtual research teams working in different parts of the world but connected by e-mail, video conferencing and general web-based connectivity. Virtual companies are unsurprisingly common in the computer industry, with Dell and Sun Microsystems both being well-known for their virtual configurations.

A COMPARISON BETWEEN VIRTUAL CORPORATIONS AND INTEGRATED COMPANIES

To appreciate the difference between the integrated hierarchical company and the virtual corporation, it may be useful to look at both organizational forms and contrast them on a number of criteria. Table 9.3 attempts such a comparison on six basic dimensions.

TABLE 9.3	Comparison of integrated and virtual corporations	
Organizational dimensions	*Integrated corporation*	*Virtual corporation*
1 Organization structure	Formal and flexible	Flat, flexible network
2 Decisions	Ultimately by fiat	By discussion and consensus
3 Culture	Recognizable, encouraging employees to identify	Pluralist, linked by overlapping agendas
4 Boundaries	Clear 'us and them'	Variable
5 Management	High overheads	Minimal overheads
6 Power	From the board ex-officio	Through possession of competences in demand, being the brand company

The basic differences are those of an autocracy and a democracy, if one takes a political analogy. In the autocratic hierarchically organized company, employees are paid salaries, and therefore are contractually bound to accept the orders of those in authority over them. Considerable resources are expended in constructing a governance framework based on motivational mechanisms, sanctions, communications systems, job descriptions and layers of middle management. All employees are encouraged to endorse a common corporate culture and identify with the corporation in all possible ways. Virtual corporations are quite different. Their culture is pluralist and task-orientated. Decisions

---

Strategy in Action 9.1 *Virtual organization in the small business sector: the case of Cavendish Management Resources (CMR)*

CMR connects more than 150 freelance workers with an investment base of £200 million. The company has been operating for over six years and provides a wide range of consultancy and management support services as well as investment funds for SMEs. All members of CMR are former senior executives offering their professional skills within CMR's broad virtual network. However, none is a CMR employee. Each runs their own limited company so CMR is a network of sole traders and small firm owner managers.

CMR members pay a monthly fee in return for attachment to the CMR parent organization. In its brochures, however, CMR is presented as a unified organization, so enabling sole traders to present a scale of operations they could not achieve in isolation and to gain access to the expertise of other members. A skills database is maintained for this purpose.

CMR's operating framework is organized into six geographical regions grouped around a London core which provides coordination and promotion. In addition each region is intent on developing its own collective identity and its own marketing strategy. Dinners are organized monthly in each region to allow members to get to know each other and extend their contact base and help to overcome the loneliness of sole trader life.

Advanced computing and communications systems are employed by most members to maintain their presence in the organization and common software packages are used for ease of swapping material. Although CMR thrives by using ICT, the new technologies were not the driver behind its strategies and organization. Face-to-face meetings are still valued more than virtual ones.

CMR also operates in association with Harvard Interim Management (HIM) in order to offer companies the opportunity of recruiting interim or sometimes permanent managers. CMR also provides the services of a company broker enabling members to sell their businesses when they wish to retire.

From the perspective of the centre, the key challenge in managing CMR is to maintain the interest and loyalty of members in periods when they are not being allocated any work. Some members look to CMR for work; others provide it with work from their more extensive portfolio of activities. CMR has therefore become something of a 'club' in which members engage in some self-promotion to get work from each other.

Problems within such virtual organizations often stem from the difficulty of ensuring consistent quality and internal market controls (so that the best members get the most work). The monthly membership fee helps to ensure commitment and effort from freelance network members. Such virtual service organizations are growing rapidly. They provide a useful combination of skills, flexibility, information and work provision for members and services for clients.

SOURCE: HEAVILY ABRIDGED FROM CASE STUDY BY CHRISTOPHER BARNATT, *INTERNATIONAL SMALL BUSINESS JOURNAL* (1997)

9

are necessarily consensual, and overheads are minimal. Furthermore the boundaries of the corporation are as narrow or as wide as the personal networks of each member. The capability base is flexible, since new members can always be brought on board without difficulty. This flexible boundary issue in fact provides perhaps the most attractive feature of the virtual corporation. Strategy in Action 9.1 provides an example of a medium-sized virtual consulting firm in operation.

However, it is important to emphasize that the difference between co-operation and competition is not, as is sometimes suggested, necessarily highly correlated with ownership and

FIGURE 9.4	**Competition and co-operation do not depend on ownership patterns**	
Common ownership	Vertically integrated company	Bureaucracy Frequently adversarial relationship
No common ownership	Virtual corporation Belief in strength together	Market Arm's length relationship
	Co-operative approach	Non-co-operative approach

Source: *Adapted from Jarillo (1993)*

the boundaries of the firm. As Jarillo (1993) suggests, there may be competition inside a firm and co-operation outside it, as illustrated in Figure 9.4. Thus, under common ownership (the firm), there may be co-operation (e.g. the vertically integrated company united by a common vision and culture), or competition (e.g. many functionally hostile bureaucracies). Similarly, in conditions without common ownership there may be co-operation (e.g. the virtual corporation), or competition (e.g. the market).

There are, of course, limitations and disadvantages too with the virtual corporation: difficulties in achieving scale or scope economies, absence of tacit knowledge, problems with proprietary information leakage, difficulty in financing large-scale R&D, difficulties in maintaining commitment, and so on. When should activities be organized into virtual corporations and when into hierarchies? We have already addressed the underlying issue in the introduction to this chapter and in Table 9.1 which illustrated the markets versus hierarchies analysis. However, this analysis primarily addresses cost-efficiency issues, and says nothing about matters of strategic vulnerability or competitive advantage.

The quest for an optimal governance form in a given set of circumstances is not of course always the way in which virtual corporations are formed. Industries are populated by firms that have existing networks of relationships. These undergo frequent change in response to changing strategic imperatives and technological or market conditions. Virtual corporations may often come about in a largely incremental way. A firm may start out by performing some activities itself and subcontracting others. As it grows and establishes trust and commitment relationships with its subcontractors, it may establish single-source relationships not unlike those of the Japanese *keiretsu*, where a high degree of operational interdependence is developed between firms at different stages of the value chain of activities, but with little if any common ownership. The next stage might be the development of a strategic network between the operators, and then ultimately the establishment of a corporate identity through some form of joint ownership of profit streams. The virtual corporation has arrived, and may be followed as required by lesser or greater levels of integration, and by the development of a variable repertoire of configurations to meet changing market needs.

Rayport and Sviokla (1996) extend the concept of virtuality from the corporation to the **value chain**, that is the linkages in the totality of the business activities carried out by the organization (Porter, 1985). Rayport and Sviokla (1996) identify what they call the physical value chain (PVC) as having typical primary activities of inbound logistics, operations, outbound logistics, marketing and sales, and after-sales service. These activities are supported by activities such as technology development, human-resource functions, the firm's infrastructure and procurement. The PVC incurs costs, sometimes very high costs, as activities move from one linkage in the chain to another, and the most efficiently configured PVC takes advantage of what economies of scale and scope exist in the technologies and processes of the firm. By contrast, they depict a virtual value chain (VVC) as existing alongside the PVC. It needs to be managed separately from the PVC, but in concert with it. It does not require the realization of scale and scope economies to achieve cost-efficiency. Often an activity may be moved from the PVC to the VVC with advantage; thus Ford used to conduct product design by gathering an engineering team in a specific location and charging it with the job of designing a car. This is now done by a virtual team in different parts of the world operating through shared design software, e-mail and teleconferencing. Creating value in the VVC involves five sequential activities: *gathering*, *organizing*, *selecting*, *synthesizing*, and *distributing information*. If these five activities are applied to each part of the PVC, then a value matrix is created that can transform the operations of the company, and sometimes even the economics of the business and the competitive 'rules of the game' of the industry. Boeing, for example, has been able to develop a peardrop-shaped aero engine in virtual form, test it 'virtually' in a wind tunnel, and select the best design at almost zero cost. Activities are thus being shifted from the marketplace to the 'market space': 'Managers must therefore consciously focus on the principles that guide value creation and extraction across two value chains (PVC and VVC) separately and in combination' (Rayport and Sviokla, 1996: 34).

Therefore the benefits of virtuality within the information economies have enabled information to be transformed from a support activity in IT departments into a value-creating activity capable of totally changing the way companies compete in an industry. We return briefly to Benetton in Strategy in Action 9.2 to illustrate this process.

9

Strategy in Action 9.2 *Benetton*

Benetton is sometimes described as the original virtual corporation, set up in the 1970s when the term had not even been coined. It lacks an essential part of the modern concept, it is only partly dependent upon electronic linking, and is also not a virtual integration of equals, each contributing what they are good at. However, it uses electronic communication extensively, and has many of the other key features of the virtual corporation including particularly a disaggregated value chain, with its value-chain activities diffused among many different suppliers, manufacturers and distributors. It also has as its emphasis the linking of subcontractors external to the firm carrying out those activities. As a result of its particular value chain (or the particular way in which it has designed its business), Benetton secures specific advantages such as 20 per cent lower production costs than the industry average, and fast response times to actual customer preferences for types of fashion items in their shops. (This business model has more recently been matched and even improved upon by a competitor, Zara, the Spanish fashion retailer, with its rapid time-to-market for new designs.)

Benetton carries out very few activities directly: choice of designs, technical advice to manufacturers, the dyeing function (strategically critical and needing very specific and expensive assets), and overall management of the sales team, who are individually all self-employed, both sales agents and retailers. Thus the internally employed part of the Benetton team is the visible part of the iceberg, with seven-eighths of the virtual corporation residing below the surface, using the Benetton brand name but running their own operations autonomously and under different ownership and owning their own businesses.

Benetton (as discussed in Strategy in Action 9.2) is frequently cited as a virtual corporation and certainly as a network. In Japan, Toyota is also often cited as little different from a virtual corporation, since its production output is almost the same as General Motors of the USA, while it employs a workforce only 10 per cent the size of that of General Motors. Unlike General Motors, Toyota of course subcontracts most of its activities except final assembly and marketing. Indeed the Toyota involvement in the manufacturing process does not start before the assembly stage, as the components are subcontracted very widely. Of course Toyota again is not a real virtual corporation, as the electronic links are not key, and there is no equality between Toyota itself and the component manufacturers. However, it, like Benetton, illustrates an early and very successful form of organization in which many companies join together under a common banner but retain separate ownership and independence.

APPRAISAL OF THE VIRTUAL CORPORATION

To be a successful virtual corporation it is not sufficient to be able to put together a competent set of value-chain-activity performers, able to deliver the required output on time and to specification. More than this is required for an opportunistic linking to be converted into a virtual corporation. First, it is necessary to have a brand name under which to trade, that comes to be accepted as a mark of quality. Speed and flexibility are the next essential elements that the virtual corporation needs to pitch against the integrated corporation's established physical presence and proven capabilities. It also needs a brain and a central nervous system. By this is meant a centre from which direction comes, and which is able to make difficult choices according to a consistent vision. Such a 'nervous system' must also provide a communication system able to convey information and requirements rapidly and accurately, through which key aspects of quality control systems can be performed. It is, therefore, difficult to conceive of a successful competitive virtual corporation that is not dominated by one brand-name company at its centre.

THE 'FLAGSHIP FIRM'

It is exactly this organization structure with its lead branded corporation providing the brains and nervous system that Rugman and D'Cruz (2000) call the **'Flagship Firm'**. The information architecture of the flagship firm normally includes a data highway to link partners, private access for partners to access key data and applications software, the ability to monitor integrity and security, and an appropriate set of communication tools. Given these characteristics, the virtual corporation should be able to compete successfully against integrated corporations in many industry segments.

Rugman and D'Cruz's (2000) concept of 'the flagship firm' provides a lot of illustration as to how international collaborative networks and virtual organizations work in practice. It is also an iteration of the theme of flexibility in MNC management. A 'flagship firm' provides direction and strategic leadership to a network consisting of four other sets of partners: key suppliers; key customers; selected competitors; and the non-business infrastructure (educational and training institutions, trade associations, government bodies, trade unions, and so on). Successful flagship firms develop trust and deep collaborative relationships with these partners which can become a shared source of long-term competitiveness. Such a system has two key features: the presence of a flagship firm that pulls the network together and provides strategic leadership for the network as a whole; and the existence of firms that have established key relationships with that flagship. The flagship firm is always an MNC and it provides direction for a vertically integrated chain of businesses that operate as a co-ordinated, and often virtual, network. They are often in competition with other similar networks addressing the same end consumer. The flagship sets the strategy; the partners are intimately involved in implementing and achieving the strategy without having any control over it. This process will include certain limited co-operation with direct competitors, for example where a new plant is built and shared jointly because the cost would be too great for either to sustain independently and because the minimum efficient scale in the industry is greater than either could utilize independently. Similar reasons may justify co-operation with a competitor on joint research and development projects. The whole chain is managed as a single system. The direction and control comes from the flagship which co-ordinates all activities from which all benefit. However, the network partners are expected to invest heavily in the success of the network, for example in new equipment and training.

This approach to global competition has developed because the huge levels of investment and the short available time-to-market require a different sort of leadership and resource management to compete in the global marketplace for many global industries. Only the flagship firms have a global perspective and level of resource adequate to the task. What this represents is an integration of parts of the value chain between firms to reflect the complexity of competition in today's global industries.

THE FUTURE FOR VIRTUAL CORPORATIONS

Why has the movement to virtuality proved so slow in coming when the technology necessary for virtuality has been in existence for at least a decade? The strongest factor inhibiting the movement has probably been the rigid mindsets within more traditional companies. There has also been a reluctance to source within a network in the belief that this gives away bargaining power (as in Table 9.1). Partly this is also because if too many resources and capabilities are outsourced or derived from partner organizations, loyalty and commitment may be reduced. There has often been a similar reluctance to share information perceived as 'strategic' (Table 9.1 again) with suppliers and distributors, regarding them more as arm's-length relationships than as business partners, part of the same team. However, major user-friendly improvements in software availability for multiple uses is now causing the virtual corporation to flourish as an organizational form in many areas. It is now relatively easy to set up a virtual corporation by identifying a strategically vital centre, outsourcing everything else, and linking the whole with ICT, with the central core representing the brain, owning the brand name, and maintaining the motivation among the outlier partners by sophisticated relationship development.

Such a development is not, however, without its risks for major corporations. The virtual solution is not a solution to all situations. It has certain inherent weaknesses that are more important in some situations than in others. For example, if an industry is dominated by virtual corporations, it is unlikely to achieve major systemic innovation. This probably requires an integrated firm to take a risk and commit large R&D funds to developing a new technology. It will then need a degree of market power to change the bases of competition in its industry. This is very difficult for a virtual corporation to do, as it can lack sufficient legitimacy or reputation. Chesbrough and Teece (2002) differentiated between autonomous innovations and more systemic ones. They suggested that for systemic innovations (e.g. DVDs replacing CDs), integrated companies are generally the more appropriate forms. However, they also suggested that, with autonomous innovations within a technological paradigm, virtual corporations are much more successful. Systemic change costs more in resources up-front, and needs the driving force of an existing major player to see it through. A loosely knit coalition with resources belonging to the different partners would find this major activity difficult to achieve.

Thus, integrated corporations are likely to remain the dominant form of organization where internal co-ordination is key, where innovation is systemic, where there is a need to establish an industry standard, where tacit knowledge needs to be communicated, and where the major growth opportunities lie in extending existing activities into neighbouring markets. Elsewhere, however, virtual corporations are likely to outperform integrated corporations: in markets where considerable turbulence leads to the need for speed of response, robustness, and flexibility; where resources are needed beyond that available in even a very large MNC. In these circumstances the virtual corporation is likely to exist alongside the integrated corporation over the coming decades as the naturally selected winner in certain markets, and not in others. For many of the reasons outlined above, it may never entirely replace the integrated form, and indeed may often exist on the interface between a number of integrated corporations involving parts of them in variable configurations. Also there is the possibility that the successful but somewhat unstable virtual corporations may over time transform themselves into an integrated corporation as the Dell computer company has largely been doing over the last decade.

SUMMARY

- Networking is the great organizational transformation of the end of the twentieth century and beyond. Its has emerged relatively recently as an organizational form.

- Networks can be 'dominated networks' in which one brand name firm (e.g. a flagship firm) sails ahead with a flotilla of smaller accessory-providing firms following behind.

- Networks can also be 'equal partner networks' which, as the name suggests, have more than market linkages but no permanent leader, although any member may lead on a given project.

- The network form of governance is most appropriate in conditions where partners provide specific assets, where demand is uncertain, where there are expected to be frequent exchanges between the parties, and where complex tasks have to be undertaken under conditions of considerable time pressure.

- The virtual corporation is an electronically co-ordinated heavily outsourced organization controlled by a flagship firm with a strong brand name.

- This differs from a strategic alliance in that the virtual corporation does not have inter-company organizational learning as its prime objective, as does strategic alliance theory. Virtual corporations are indeed all about putting together a variable configuration company made up of existing companies with excellent specific skills. No inter-company learning is necessarily involved.

- Virtual corporations are successful where high flexibility is required.

- However, they are less successful where strong central direction is needed or large amounts of capital are needed to achieve systemic technological change.

- It is uncertain if the virtual corporation is a permanent organizational form, as companies like Dell, which began as a virtual corporation, have tended to move to the traditional integrated form over time and as they have grown more successful.

DISCUSSION QUESTIONS

1 What is the rationale for the development of networks?

2 Explain what is meant by a dominated network.

3 Explain what is meant by equal partner networks.

4 What are the strengths and weaknesses of networks?

5 What is a virtual corporation?

6 How is a virtual corporation different from an outsourced corporation?

7 How is a virtual corporation contrasted with an integrated corporation?

8 What are the strengths and limitations of a virtual corporation?

9 To what extent is the formation and management of a virtual corporation dependent upon ICT?

FURTHER READINGS

1 Chesbrough, H. and Teece, D.J. (2002) 'Organizing for innovation: When is virtual virtuous?', *HBR Classic Article*, August.

   This article outlines the strengths and weaknesses of the virtual corporation. It also provides clear guidance and suggests contexts for when the virtual corporation is, and also, when it is not, the organizational form that makes will be most effective.

2 Gulati, R., Nohria, N. and Zaheer, A. (2000) 'Strategic networks', *Strategic Management Journal*, 21(3): 203–215.

   These authors are strong on contributions to network theory and well worth reading. The paper introduces the important role of networks of inter-firm ties within strategy. They argue that the networks of relationships within which firms are embedded profoundly influence their conduct and performance. They also discuss the constraints and benefits of dynamic networks.

3 Rugman, A. and D'Cruz, J.R. (2000) *Multinationals as Flagship Firms*, New York: Oxford University Press.

   These were the originators of the concept of the flagship firm. This book is their seminal contribution to network theory and the fuller discussion of how the networks surrounding flagship firms are set up and how they actually work in practice. It contains many detailed case studies. The concept of the flagship firm brings the network organizational form to life.

CHAPTER 10

Co-operative strategies

LEARNING OBJECTIVES This chapter deals with co-operative strategies between companies. It aims to:

- show why some forms of inter-firm alliance are considered 'strategic'
- provide a typology of strategic alliances
- discuss alliance strategy in the context of the value chain
- establish why firms choose to co-operate
- consider the pros and cons of co-operative strategy.

INTRODUCTION

Corporate success is built upon sound company competences, skills and capabilities. Competitive advantage can come from the optimal utilization of internal resources and the resultant market position adopted. Most companies reach a stage, however, when they realize they do not have enough competences and resources to achieve their aims alone, particularly when they are contemplating developing global strategies, or when their strategic market forces this strategy upon them. External options involve greater risk than internally generated choices. Such a situation usually arises when a company embarks upon a rapid growth trajectory – often beyond its national market. It may also arise when a company is attempting to block gaps or deficiencies in its resource base or competences. Co-operative strategy in this situation is the only relatively inexpensive and low-risk strategy available that can be put into operation on a short timescale.

THE RATIONALE FOR CO-OPERATION

Co-operative activity between firms has become increasingly necessary due to the limitations and inadequacies of individual firms in coping successfully with a world where markets are becoming increasingly global in scope, technologies are changing rapidly, vast investment funds are regularly demanded to supply new products with ever-shortening life-cycles and the economic scene is becoming characterized by high uncertainty and turbulence. Strategic alliances, joint ventures, dynamic networks, virtual corporations, constellations, co-operative agreements, collective strategies and strategic networks all make an appearance and develop significance. In tune with the growth of co-operative managerial forms, the reputation of co-operation seems to have enjoyed a notable revival, to set against the hitherto dominant strength of the integrated competitive model as a template for resource allocation efficiency.

Why has this revival of the popularity of co-operation come about, since the obvious problem with co-operating with your competitor is that he may steal your secrets? If this is the case, then how can co-operation be justified? A look at the situation found in the Prisoners' Dilemma situation described below shows how co-operation can be the best policy for both partners (Child, Faulkner and Tallman, 2005).

In 1951 Merrill Flood of the Rand Corporation developed a model later termed the Prisoners' Dilemma by Albert Tucker. It addresses the issue of how we individually balance our innate inclination to act selfishly against the collective rationality of individual sacrifice for the sake of the common good including ourselves. John Casti in his book *Paradigms Lost* (1989) illustrates the difficulty effectively:

> In Puccini's opera *Tosca*, Tosca's lover has been condemned to death, and the police chief Scarpia offers Tosca a deal. If Tosca will bestow her sexual favours on him, Scarpia will spare her lover's life by instructing the firing squad to load their rifles with blanks. Here both Tosca and Scarpia face the choice of either keeping their part of the bargain or double-crossing the other. Acting on the basis of what is best for them as individuals both Tosca and Scarpia try a double-cross. Tosca stabs Scarpia as he is about to embrace her, while it turns out that Scarpia has not given the order to the firing squad to use blanks. The dilemma is that this outcome, undesirable for both parties, could have been avoided if they had trusted each other and acted not as selfish individuals, but rather in their mutual interest.

Analytically as shown in Figure 10.1, there are two parties and both have the options of co-operating or defecting.

If the maximum value to each of them is 5 (a positive benefit with no compromise involved) and the minimum value 0, then the possible outcomes and values for the two parties are as shown below:

- Tosca defects and Scarpia co-operates: Tosca scores 5 and Scarpia scores 0; Total 5. Tosca gets all she wants without making any sacrifices. This would have happened if Tosca had killed Scarpia, and Scarpia had loaded the rifles with blanks thus enabling Tosca's lover to escape.

FIGURE 10.1 **The Prisoners' Dilemma**

		Scarpia	
		Co-operate	**Defect**
Tosca	**Co-operate**	R=3, R=3 Reward for mutual co-operation	R=0, R=5 Sucker's payoff and successful defection
	Defect	R=5, R=0 Successful defection and sucker's payoff	R=1, R=1 Punishment for mutual defection

NOTE: The payoffs to Tosca are listed first

- Tosca co-operates and Scarpia co-operates: Tosca scores 3 and Scarpia scores 3: Total 6. Tosca, although saving her lover's life, has to submit sexually to Scarpia in order to do so, which it is presumed represents a sacrifice for her. Similarly Scarpia's compromise involves not killing Tosca's lover.

- Tosca defects and Scarpia defects: Tosca scores 1 and Scarpia scores 1: Total 2. This is what happened. At least

Tosca has killed the evil Scarpia, but he in turn has killed her lover. Not a successful outcome for Tosca or Scarpia, however, but marginally better for her than the fourth possibility.

■ Tosca co-operates and Scarpia defects: Tosca scores 0 and Scarpia scores 5: Total 5. This is the worst outcome from Tosca's viewpoint. She has surrendered herself to Scarpia, but he has still executed her lover. This is the 'sucker's payoff', and to be avoided if possible at all costs.

The dilemma is that, since Tosca does not know what Scarpia will do, she is likely rationally to defect in order to avoid the sucker's payoff. Thus she may score 5 if Scarpia is as good as his word and she can make him the sucker. She will at least score 1. However, if both co-operate they will each score 3 which is the best joint score available. Yet in the absence of trust it is unlikely to be achieved.

In the situation of a co-operative agreement then, the optimal joint score can only be achieved through genuine trusting co-operation; yet this may be difficult to achieve if both parties in the alliance are overly concerned not to be the sucker, and are thus reluctant to release their commercial secrets, for fear that their partner will defect with them. One prisoner defects because he fears that the other one will, and he will end up as the 'sucker'.

However, the payoffs listed above only apply to a single shot game. In a situation where the partners intend to work with each other over an indeterminately long period, the situation changes. In this case trust can be built and the potential synergies from co-operation can be realized. Furthermore, reputation comes into the equation. If one partner is seen to defect he may find it difficult to attract further partners in the future. And if both partners are still reluctant to co-operate in a genuine fashion, the risk–reward ratio can be changed deliberately. If, in the Tosca defection situation, the defector or defector's lover immediately forfeits his or her life, the incentive to defect is radically reduced. In the more prosaic world of business, this might mean that a potential defector automatically forfeits a large sum of money or shares in the event of defection. Thus the situation can be constructed in such a way that the dominant strategy is one of co-operation. A co-operative strategy can then become a stable way of combining the competences of multiple partners to achieve a competitive strategy with competitive advantage.

In sum:

1 The rational strategy of defection (competition) applies on the assumption of a **zero-sum game**, and a non-repeatable experience, that is if you are only in business for a single trade (e.g. buying a holiday souvenir in a market in Morocco), defection is a rational strategy for you.

2 As soon as the game becomes non-zero-sum, for example through scale economies, and/or it is known that the game will be played over an extended time period, or defection is costly, the strategy of defection is likely to become sub-optimal, that is to co-operate and keep your bargain is a better strategy for both players. At the very least if you defect, it will harm your reputation. You will become known as a player not to be trusted.

3 In these circumstances, then, forgiving co-operative strategies are likely to prove the most effective for both partners

Corporate organizational form has also been dramatically influenced by the globalization of markets and technologies, through a decline in the automatic choice of the integrated multinational corporation as the only instrument appropriate for international business development. The movement away from the traditional concept of the firm is accentuated by the growth of what Handy (1992) describes as 'the federated enterprise' (illustrated in Figure 10.2) seen both in the form of newly created joint ventures between existing companies and in the development of so-called virtual corporations where a number of companies co-operate in producing a single product offering generally under a distinct brand-name.

The recent growth of alliances and networks approaches the flexible transnational structure from the other end, that is the amalgamation of previously independent resources and competences in contrast to the unbundling into a **federal structure** of previously hierarchically controlled resources and

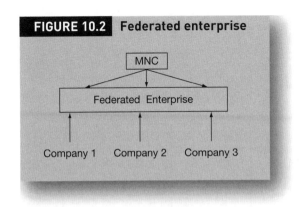

FIGURE 10.2   Federated enterprise

competences. Where the traditional concepts of firm, industry and national economy start to become concepts of declining clarity, and thus to lose their exclusive usefulness as tools for strategic analysis, the need for an adequate theory of strategic alliances and other co-operative network strategies becomes increasingly important.

The search for sustainable competitive advantage is of course the essence of competitive strategy. Yet this is a factor that often cannot be measured directly. Its extent can only be inferred from the measurement of other factors like profit, market share and sales turnover. It is nonetheless what all firms seek to find and to maintain. Coyne (1986) identifies it as stemming from:

1 Customers' perception of a consistent superiority of the attributes of one firm's products to its competitors.

2 This being due to a capability gap.

3 The capability gap being durable over time.

4 The superiority being difficult to imitate.

It is this configuration of knowledge, skills, core competences and superior products that strategic alliances and networks seek to achieve, where the partners believe that they cannot achieve it alone.

Co-operative activity is frequently implicitly founded on the resource-based theory of competitive advantage. This theory (Grant, 1991b) holds that competitive advantage is most productively sought by an examination of a firm's existing resources and core competences, an assessment of their profit potential, and the selection of strategies based upon the possibilities these reveal.

The task is then to assess the current core competences the firm has, and fill whatever resource or competence gap is revealed by the inventory taking of existing resources and competencies, in relation to the perceived potential profit opportunities. This is where strategic alliances and networks come in. The matrix in Figure 10.3 suggests how the make / buy / or ally decision should be influenced both by the strategic importance of the activity in question and by the firm's competence at carrying it out. Under this schema alliances should be formed if the activity is at least moderately strategically important, and the firm is only fairly good at carrying it out.

The resource-based theory of competitive advantage suggests that a firm should not invest in an enterprise not strongly related to its own core competences. Only strategies based upon existing core competences could, it would hold, lead to the acquisition and maintenance of sustainable competitive advantage. The resource-based approach emphasizes that firms do not always tend towards similarity, and markets towards commodity status, in a situation of stable equilibrium. If the opportunity requires certain competences in addition to those already present within the firm, a strategic alliance with a partner with complementary skills and resources or a network of complementary companies may represent a low-risk way of overcoming that deficiency.

The resource dependency perspective (RDP) theory (similar to but different from the RBV) (Pfeffer and Salancik, 1978) proposes that the key to organizational survival is the ability to acquire and maintain resources necessary for survival. Thus in the last resort it is organizational power, and the capacity of the organization to preserve itself, that determines competitive survival, not merely organizational efficiency. The unit of analysis for the RDP is the organization–environment relationship not the individual transaction. To deal with this uncertainty, firms attempt to manage their environment by co-operating with key parts of it, for example by co-operating with other companies owning key resources for them. An RDP approach treats the environment as a source of scarce resources, and therefore views the firm as dependent on other firms also in the environment.

Resource dependency theory stems from the much earlier theory of social exchange which holds that where organizations have similar objectives, but different kinds of resources at their disposal, it will often be mutually beneficial to the organizations in the

| FIGURE 10.3 | The make / buy / ally matrix |

Strategic Importance of Activity

	Low	Med	High
High	Alliance	Invest & Make	Make
Med	Alliance	Alliance	Make
Low	Buy	Buy	Buy

Competence Compared with the Best in the Industry

pursuit of their goals to exchange resources. Classical international trade theory is based on similar foundations. Organizations have as their rationale to seek to reduce uncertainty, and enter into exchange relationships to achieve a negotiated and more predictable environment. Sources of uncertainty are scarcity of resources, lack of knowledge of how the environment will fluctuate, of the available exchange partners, and of the costs of transacting with them. These are all factors very common in the modern business world.

The degree of a firm's dependence on a particular resource is a function of the critical nature of the resources in the exchange to the parties involved, and of the number of and ease of access to alternative sources of supply. Where few alternatives exist, and the resources are essential, a state of dependency exists. This creates a power differential between trading partners, and the dependant firm faces the problem of how to manage its resources with the resultant loss of independence, since unchecked resource dependence leads to a state of strategic vulnerability. Such strategic vulnerability can be tackled in a number of ways. Western firms may do it by multiple sourcing of materials and components, internal restructuring, merger or acquisition; Japanese ones by the establishment of semi-captive suppliers within *keiretsu* groups; Korean ones by operating within a *chaebol*. The establishment of a strategic alliance can thus be regarded as an attempt by a firm or firms to reduce strategic vulnerability, and hence to overcome perceived constraints on their autonomy in choosing their strategic direction. Strategic alliances and networks can be seen as attempts by firms to establish a negotiated environment, and thus to reduce uncertainty. On the basis of this argument, alliances and networks will occur most when the level of competitive uncertainty is greatest.

In RDP-motivated alliances and networks, all parties typically strive to form relationships with partners with whom balance can be achieved at minimum cost, and with a desirable level of satisfaction and determinacy. Thus wherever possible they will link up with firms of a similar size and power. Otherwise they only increase their vulnerability.

Strategic alliances are frequently formed from resource dependency motives, and the ability of the partners to achieve and sustain competitive advantage in their chosen market is strongly influenced by the degree to which they place corporate learning as a high priority on their alliance agenda, and

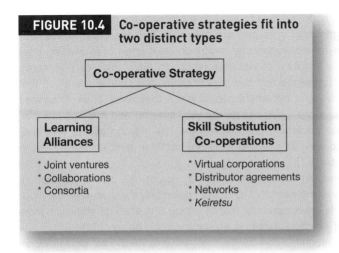

FIGURE 10.4 Co-operative strategies fit into two distinct types

Co-operative Strategy

Learning Alliances
* Joint ventures
* Collaborations
* Consortia

Skill Substitution Co-operations
* Virtual corporations
* Distributor agreements
* Networks
* *Keiretsu*

seek to cause the alliance to evolve in a direction based on that learning. In a sense, corporate learning can be seen as the dynamic counterpart to the resource dependency theory of the firm. Thus a firm will diagnose its resource and skill deficiencies in relation to a particular external challenge, and through the process of deliberate and planned corporate learning set about remedying its weaknesses. Truly strategic alliances are generally competence-driven, that is explicitly adding to either the task or the knowledge system or to the organizational memory of each partner. The idea of the organization as a place for learning is a popular one. Decision theory emphasizes the importance of the search for information to enable organizations to make informed choices. Prahalad and Hamel (1990) stressed the role of learning as a source of competitive advantage, through the development of unique competences.

Strategic networks on the other hand are more likely to be formed for skill substitution reasons, for example company A forms a network with companies B and C who carry out specific functions such as R&D or sales and marketing, while A does the production. Figure 10.4 illustrates the differing situations of networks and alliances.

Even faced with success stories of the evolution of an alliance through mutual learning leading to competitive advantage, nagging doubts may well remain about the role of value appropriation in the form of learning by the partners, and about the consequent stability of the alliance. It is often suggested in fact that the alliance is an inherently unstable and transitory arrangement, and undoubtedly, given opportunistic attitudes by the partners, it can be, particularly in alliances between competitors.

The often-cited comparison of an alliance with a marriage is pertinent here. Marriages could be regarded as unstable as they currently have a high failure rate. In fact they have many of the qualities of strategic alliances. The partners retain separate identities but collaborate over a whole range of activities. Stability is threatened if one partner becomes excessively dependent on the other, or if the benefits are perceived to be all one way, But none the less, successful marriages are stable, and for the same reason as successful alliances. They depend upon trust, commitment, mutual learning, flexibility and a feeling by both partners that they are stronger together than apart. Many businesses point to the need to negotiate decisions in alliances as a weakness, in contrast to companies, where **hierarchies** make decisions. This is to confuse stability with clarity of decision-making, and would lead to the suggestion that dictatorships are more stable then democracies.

In this analogy, commitment to the belief that the alliance represents the best available arrangement is the foundation of its stability. The need for resolution of the inevitable tensions in such an arrangement can as easily be presented as a strength, rather than as an inherent problem. It leads to the need to debate, see and evaluate contrasting viewpoints. Similar points arise in relation to strategic networks, although to a lesser degree since the closeness and interdependence of a network is typically lower than that of an alliance.

The movement of enterprises away from a simple wholly owned corporate structure to more federated forms is accentuated by the growth of alliances, and strategic networks, which aid the development of global loyalties and co-operative endeavours, quite distinct from those encouraged by the traditional national and firm boundaries.

10

Transaction costs is another body of theory applied to provide a rationale for the development of co-operative relationships, or hybrid organizations as they are called by TCA theorists. In **transaction cost analysis**, organizational forms are conventionally described on a scale of increasing integration with markets at one end as the absolute of non-integration, to hierarchies or completely integrated companies at the other. It is suggested that the organizations that survive are those that involve the lowest costs to run in the particular circumstances in which they exist. Thus, integrated companies will be the lowest cost in situations when assets are very specific and markets are thin. Where conditions are highly complex and uncertain, opportunism may be rife and assets very specific. In these circumstances, it would be very difficult and therefore costly to handle transactions in a fragmented, market-place way (see Table 9.1).

At the other extreme, transactions are best carried out in markets where no one deal implies commitment to another, and relationships are completely at arm's length. This is most commonly the case when the product is a frequently traded commodity, assets are not specific, market pricing is needed for efficiency, there are many alternative sources of supply, and the costs of running a company would be very high.

Between the extremes of markets and integrated companies, there are a range of inter-organizational forms of increasing levels of integration, which have evolved to deal with varying circumstances, and where they survive, may be assumed to do so as a result of their varying appropriateness to the situation. All forms between the extremes of markets and hierarchies exhibit some degree of co-operation in their activities. It is even likely that most hierarchies include internal markets within them in order to create situations where market pricing will improve efficiency, for example an SBU may be empowered to use third-party marketing advice if it is not satisfied with that available internally. Figure 10.5 illustrates forms of ascending interdependency, all of which are co-operative except the markets at the base of the triangle.

Hence, arm's-length market relationships may develop into those with established suppliers and distributors, and then may integrate further into co-operative networks. Further up the triangle of integration come the hub-subcontractor networks like Benetton's close interrelationships with its suppliers. Licensing agreements come next, in which the relationship between the licensor and the licensee is integrated from the viewpoint of activities in a defined area, but both retain their separate ownership and identities.

Between licensing agreements and completely integrated companies, where rule by price (markets) is replaced by rule by fiat (companies), comes the most integrated form of rule by co-operation, namely that found in strategic alliances. Alliances may be preferred organizational forms where sensitive market awareness is required, the price mechanism remains important, risks of information leakage are not considered to be high, scale economies and finance risks are high, there is resource limitation and flexibility is important.

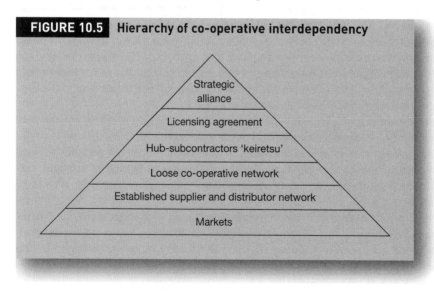

FIGURE 10.5   **Hierarchy of co-operative interdependency**

Strategic alliance

Licensing agreement

Hub-subcontractors 'keiretsu'

Loose co-operative network

Established supplier and distributor network

Markets

THE MOTIVATION FOR CO-OPERATION

The most common motivations behind the development of co-operation between companies as suggested by Porter and Fuller (1986) are:

1 To achieve with one's partner, economies of scale and of learning.

2 To get access to the benefits of the other firm's assets, be they technology, market access, capital, production capacity, products, or manpower.

3 To reduce risk by sharing it, notably in terms of capital requirements, but also often R&D.

4 To help shape the market, for example to withdraw capacity in a mature market.

Another motive behind co-operative strategies is the need for speed in reaching the market. In the current global marketplace, first-mover advantages are becoming increasingly important, and often the conclusion of an alliance between a technologically strong company with new products and a company with strong market access is the only way to take advantage of an opportunity. There may also be opportunities through the medium of co-operation for the achievement of value-chain synergies (Porter and Fuller, 1986) which extend beyond the mere pooling of assets, and include such matters as process rationalization, and even systems improvement.

External challenges

For co-operation to come about there needs to be at least one external force in play that challenges would-be players in the marketplace, and at least one internal perception of vulnerability or need in responding to that force. Such a response may well be to form a strategic alliance or network.

A number of external forces have stimulated the growth of strategic alliances and networks in recent years. Among the most important are the globalization of tastes and markets, the rapid spread and shortening life cycle of new technology and its products, the development of opportunities for achieving major economies of scale, scope and learning, increasing turbulence in global economies, a heightened level of uncertainty in all aspects of life and declining international trade barriers.

Levitt (1960) was credited over forty years ago with first having drawn attention to the increasing convergence of tastes, leading to the development of the 'global village'. Since that time the globalization movement has spread to an increasing number of industries, and as Ohmae pointed out (1989b) it is now possible to travel from New York to Paris, to Riyadh and on to Tokyo, and to see very similar articles on display in department stores in all four cities.

After the Second World War, trade barriers between nations placed a limit to the development of a world economy. With economic recovery, the move towards increasing international trade was stimulated by international agreements to reduce trade barriers, and thus increase overall economic welfare by allowing greater specialization on the basis of comparative costs and the development of global brand names as easily recognizable in Istanbul as in New York or London.

The WTO, the EU and other institutional structures and trading blocs' markets enabled national firms to develop opportunities internationally, and to grow into multinational corporations. Over the past twenty years, the reunification of Germany, the establishment of NAFTA (North American Free Trade Association), the break-up of the communist bloc and movement of some of its members into the EU, have accelerated this movement, and in so doing stimulated the growth of strategic alliances between firms in different nations.

However, not only have markets become global, but the most modern technologies, namely microelectronics, genetic engineering and advanced material sciences, are by now, all subject to truly global competition. The global technologies involved in the communications revolution have also succeeded in effectively shrinking the world (Friedman, 2005), and led to the design and manufacture of products with global appeal, due to their pricing, reliability and technical qualities. But, not only has technology become global in nature, it is also changing faster than previously, which means a single firm needs correspondingly greater resources to be capable of replacing the old technology with the new on a regular basis.

The globalization of markets and technologies leads to the need to be able to produce at a sufficiently large volume to realize the maximum economies of scale and scope, and thus compete globally on a unit cost basis. Although one effect of the new technologies is, through flexible manufacturing systems, to be able to produce small lots economically, the importance of scale and scope economies is still critical to global economic competitiveness in a wide range of industries. Alliances are often the only way to achieve such a large scale of operation to generate these economies. The advantages of alliances and networks over integrated firms are in the areas of specialization, entrepreneurship and flexibility of arrangements, and these characteristics are particularly appropriate to meet the needs of today's turbulent and changing environment.

Oil crises, wars, the subsequent aggravated economic cycles of boom and recession, and the current so-called 'credit crunch' developed as a result of excessive sub-prime mortgage lending, have made economic forecasting as hazardous as long-term weather forecasting. Strategic vulnerability due to environmental uncertainty has become a fact of life in most industries. Co-operative strategy helps to reduce that vulnerability, by enabling 'co-operative enterprises' to grow or decline flexibly, to match the increasing variability of the market situation.

10

Strategy in Action 10.1 *Ragn-Sells in Estonia*

Ragn-Sells is a wholly owned Swedish waste-treatment company which started to operate in 1966. There was no plan to invest in Estonia, and it happened largely by chance. By the end of the 1980s, Ragn-Sells received visitors from local governments of Estonia as a part of the Helsinki agreement. They visited one sewage-treatment plant and were impressed. The Estonian authority asked Ragn-Sells in 1991 for help with refuse collection and street sweeping. Ragn-Sells accepted the offer. A joint venture agreement was signed with the Estonian government on a 50/50 ownership basis during 1991/92.

Ragn-sells hired an Estonian graduate from the Swedish Royal Institute of Technology to serve as the chief executive in the joint venture. He was very competent and spoke both Swedish and Estonian. Initially there were 45 employees in the company but the number gradually decreased due to the introduction of better-equipped vehicles and increased efficiency in the company.

Ragn-Sells invested capital in the beginning and the local partner made investments in kind. All technological support came from Sweden, as the concept of waste management and services related to it were largely unknown to the Estonians. Ragn-Sells offered active support over the years to the alliance to sell the service concept and to make the local people aware of the need for waste management and energy extraction from the waste material. They stressed the quality of the services to make the offerings visible and locally acceptable. This attempt proved to be successful as the market for waste treatment rapidly expanded and

SOURCE: ABRIDGED FROM *COMPETITIVENESS REVIEW*, 16(3), HYDER AND ABRADA, 2006.

Ragn-Sells established a wholly owned subsidiary in Tallin in 1994. Continuous support and Ragn-Sells' closeness to the market was necessary for selling such service-dominated products. The contribution of the local partner was limited in the development and operation of the joint venture. But its presence gave the alliance legitimacy and also helped a lot to build up necessary contacts with local customers which were mainly local municipalities and government institutions.

The board of directors met four times a year. The joint venture developed valuable personal contacts with government authorities, which helped it to expand business in Estonia. Its contact with the government gave the joint venture a special status in the community and it was awarded a prize by the country's president for its outstanding contribution to the environment.

The growth of alliance activity was positive and steady over the years. At the initial stage, it was important to share risk and also to get access to local competence and resources. The local chief executive was an important asset for the company as he was mentally motivated to work there and develop the company. His presence made the adaptation process easier and helped to make the alliance profitable within a short time.

Ragn-Sells was very active in the operation while the local partner's help was confined to moral and political support. Ragn-Sells came to know what the local people wanted concerning the environment and how to do business in a country with a communist past. The people had little idea about the environmental aspects and how the service offering would be developed and marketed. They also learnt the necessity of environmental protection and its commercial aspect. The general environment was quite favourable for the alliance operation.

There were some minor cultural differences. Early entrance in the country was advantageous for Ragn-Sells in getting acquainted with the local environment and earning goodwill. When the country badly needed foreign support, Ragn-Sells was there. This early presence gave it respect and trustworthiness. It succeeded in selecting efficient and well-connected people for the board of directors.

Ragn-Sells made a survey of the waste collection and disposal in Estonia and suggested some solutions. This report was helpful for the local government in understanding the problem and in taking measures to comply with the European Union's regulations. Initially no service was offered for waste collection and disposal in the country but gradually the market for such activities became more developed.

Internal conditions

A range of external conditions and challenging situations may stimulate the creation of strategic alliances and networks. However, firms will enter into such arrangements only when their internal circumstances make this seem to be the right move. These internal circumstances have most commonly included a feeling of resource and competence inadequacy, in that co-operative activity would give a firm access to valuable markets, technologies, special skills or raw materials in which it feels itself to be deficient, and which it could not easily get in any other way.

In conditions of economic turbulence and high uncertainty, access to the necessary resources for many firms becomes a risk, which raises the spectre of potential strategic vulnerability for even the most efficient firm. This leads to the need to reduce that uncertainty, and secure a more reliable access to the necessary resources, whether they be supplies, skills or markets. Strategic alliances or a developed network with firms able to supply the resources may then develop where previously market relationships may have dominated.

For co-operation to be appropriate, both partners must be able to provide some resource or competence the other needs, or reach a critical mass together that they each do not reach alone. If the needs are not reciprocal, then the best course of action is for the partner in need to buy the competence or resource, or, if appropriate, to buy the company possessing it. Co-operative arrangements require the satisfaction of complementary needs on the part of both partners.

There are many forms of resource dependency that provide the internal motivation for co-operation:

1 Access to markets.

2 New technology.

3 Access to special skills is a similar form of resource need to access technology. The special skills or competences may be of many types, and include the know-how associated with experience in a particular product area.

4 Access to raw materials.

Other internal circumstances that have stimulated the search for alliances have included the belief that running an alliance would be less costly than running and financing an integrated company, or the belief that an alliance, or a series of alliances, would provide strong protection against take-over predators. Others may be that firms believe it is the best way to limit risk, or to achieve a desired market position faster than by any other way. Transaction cost theory encompasses these motivations within its orbit. However, accurate calculation of the costs involved in various organizational forms is very difficult to calculate, since it involves assigning costs to some unquantifiable factors, for example opportunism or information asymmetry. The lowest-cost concept is still valuable in determining whether a particular activity is best carried out by internal means, by purchasing it in the market or by **collaboration** with a partner. Where the transactions cost perspective is taken as the justification for the development of the alliance, this suggests the priority is to improve the firm's cost and efficiency rather than quality position.

Alliances are also frequently formed as a result of the need to limit risk. The nature of the risk may be its sheer size in terms of financial resources. Thus, a £100 million project shared between three alliance partners is a much lower risk for each partner than the same project shouldered alone. The risk may also be a portfolio risk. Thus £100 million invested in alliances in four countries probably represents a lower risk than the same figure invested alone in one project. The trade-off is between higher control and lower risk. An acquisition represents a high level of control but is expensive, and however well the acquirer may have researched the target company before purchase, it may still receive some unexpected surprises after the conclusion of the deal. A strategic alliance involves shared risk, is probably easier to unravel if it proves disappointing, and enables the partners to get to know each other slowly as their relationship develops.

The need to achieve speed is a further internal reason for alliance formation. Many business objectives can only be achieved if the firm acts quickly. In many industries there is a need for almost simultaneous product launches in retail markets worldwide if opportunities which may not last for ever are not to be missed. This suggests the need for alliances, which can be activated rapidly to take advantage of such opportunities.

Alliances and networks are not all formed with expansionary aims in mind, however. Many are the result of fear of being taken over. Thus, in the European insurance world, AXA and Groupe Midi of France formed an alliance and eventually merged to avoid being taken over by Generali of Italy. General Electric of the UK formed an alliance with its namesake in the US for similar defensive reasons.

STRATEGIC ALLIANCE FORMS

A **strategic alliance** has been defined as:

> a particular mode of inter-organizational relationship in which the partners make substantial investments in developing a long-term collaborative effort, and common orientation.
>
> (Mattson, 1988)

This definition excludes projects between companies that have a beginning and pre-ordained end, and loose co-operative arrangements without long-term commitment. In establishing the 'collaborative effort and common orientation' the alliance partners forsake a competitive strategy in relation to each other in agreed areas of activity, and embark on a co-operative one.

Alliances can be classified along three dimensions that define their nature, form and membership:

1	Nature	Focused	Complex
2	Form	Joint venture	Collaboration
3	Membership	Two partners only	Consortium

Figure 10.6 illustrates the options available from which a choice may be made.

Focused alliances
....

The focused alliance is an arrangement between two or more companies, set up to meet a clearly defined set of circumstances in a particular way. It normally involves only one major activity or function for each partner, or at least is clearly defined and limited in its objectives. Thus, for example, a US company seeking to enter the EU market with a given set of products may form an alliance with a European distribution company as its means of market entry. The US company provides the product, and probably some market and sales literature, and the European company provides the sales force and local market knowledge. The precise form of arrangement may vary widely, but the nature of the alliance is a focused one with clear remits, and understandings of respective contributions and rewards.

10

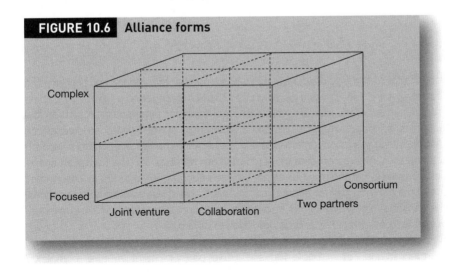

FIGURE 10.6 Alliance forms

Complex alliances

Complex alliances may involve the complete activity cost chains of the partners. The companies recognize that together they are capable of forming a far more powerful competitive enterprise than they do apart. Yet they wish to retain their separate identities and overall aspirations, while being willing to co-operate with each other over a wide range of activities. It is a question of their joint value chains possibly leading to competitive advantage, whereas individually their value chains may not be strong enough to do so.

Joint ventures

A joint venture involves the creation of a legally separate company from that of the partners. The new company normally starts life with the partners as its shareholders, and with an agreed set of objectives in a specific area of activity. Thus, a US company may set up a joint venture with a UK company to market in the EU. The partners provide finance and other support competences and resources for the joint venture in agreed amounts. The aim of the joint venture is normally that the new company should ultimately become a self-standing entity with its own employees, and strategic aims quite distinct from those of its parent shareholders. Unilever is a good example of a joint venture set up by a Dutch and an English company in the 1920s, and which has grown into a major multinational enterprise. Joint ventures usually involve non-core activities of the partners, and are characterized by having clear boundaries, specific assets, personnel, and managerial responsibilities. They are not generally set up in such a way that their products compete directly with those of the founding partners. Ultimately, they are divestible by the partners in a way that the non-joint venture form is not. They are the most popular form of alliance, being responsible for about half of all alliances reviewed in the samples of several alliance researchers.

10

Collaborations

The collaborative alliance form is employed when partners do not wish to set up a separate joint venture company to provide boundaries to their relationship. This might be because they do not know at the outset where such boundaries should lie. Hence the more flexible collaborative form meets their needs better. Collaborative alliances are also preferred when the partners' core business is the area of the alliances, and therefore assets cannot be separated from the core business and allocated to a dedicated joint venture. The collaborative form can be expanded or contracted to meet the partners' needs far more easily than can a joint venture.

The consortium

The consortium is a distinct form of strategic alliance, in that it has a number of partners, and is normally a very large-scale activity set up for a very specific purpose, and usually managed in a hands-off fashion from the contributing shareholders. Consortia are particularly common for large-scale projects in the defence or aerospace industries where massive funds and a wide range of specialist competences are required for success. Airbus Industrie is a consortium where a number of European shareholders have set up an aircraft manufacturing company to compete on world markets with Boeing. The European shareholders, although large themselves, felt the need to create a large enough pool of funds to ensure they reached critical mass in terms of resources for aircraft development, and chose to form an international consortium to do this. A consortium may or may not have a legally distinct corporate form. Airbus Industrie originally did not have one, but has recently restructured itself to have one.

There are then eight possible basic configurations of alliance covering the alliance's nature, its form and the number of partners it has, for example focused / two partner / joint venture, complex /

consortium / collaboration and so forth. The alliance type that involves setting up a joint venture company is currently by far the most popular method. There are also well-trodden paths by which alliances evolve. For example, focused alliances that are successful frequently develop into complex alliances, as the partners find other areas for mutual co-operation. Two partner alliances often recruit further partners, and develop into consortia, as the scale and complexity of opportunities become apparent. Alliances, initially without joint venture companies, frequently form them subsequently, as they experience difficulty in operating in a partially merged fashion, but without clear boundaries between the co-operative and the independent parts. It is also quite common for one partner in a joint venture to buy out the other. This need not mean the alliance was a failure. It may have been a considerable success, but the strategic objectives of the two companies may have moved onto different paths.

Other paths of evolution, however, are probably less likely to be followed. Consortia are unlikely to reduce to two partner alliances. Alliances with joint venture companies are unlikely to revert to a non-joint-venture situation, but to keep the alliance in being. Thirdly, complex alliances are unlikely to revert to a simple focused relationship between the partners.

It is not possible to predict definitively which form of alliance will be adopted in which specific set of circumstances, since certain companies show policy preferences for certain forms rather than others, irrespective of their appropriateness. However, most alliances fit into three types:

1 two-partner joint ventures

2 two-partner collaborations

3 consortium joint ventures.

Firms seeking strategic alliances generally choose between these three forms, before moving on to define their relationships in a more specific way.

SELECTING A PARTNER

The creation of a strategic alliance does not of course guarantee its long-term survival. Research by the consultancy firms McKinsey, and Price Waterhouse Coopers (PwC) has shown that there is no better than a 50 per cent survival probability for alliances over a five-year term. Porter's (1987) research into the success of acquisitions concluded that the success rate of acquisitions was even lower. Undoubtedly the 50 per cent failure rate of alliances could be considerably reduced if firms learned the managerial skills necessary to develop and maintain successful co-operative relationships, an aspect of management theory given only limited emphasis at business schools.

One of the keys to a successful alliance must be to choose the right partner. This requires the consideration of three basic factors:

1 The synergy or strategic fit between the partners.

2 The cultural fit between them.

3 The existence of only limited competition between the partners.

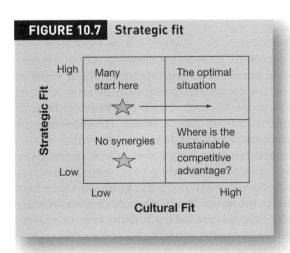

FIGURE 10.7   Strategic fit

	Low	High
High	Many start here	The optimal situation
Low	No synergies	Where is the sustainable competitive advantage?

Strategic Fit (vertical axis) — Cultural Fit (horizontal axis)

The importance of strategic fit and cultural fit can be illustrated in Figure 10.7.

A high degree of strategic fit is essential to justify the alliance in the first place. Strategic fit implies that the core competences of the two companies are highly complementary. Whatever partner is sought, it must be one with complementary assets, that is to supply some of the resources or competences needed to achieve the alliance objectives. These complementary needs may come about in a number of circumstances:

1 *Reciprocity* – where the assets of the two partners have a reciprocal strength, that is there are synergies such that a newly configured joint value chain leads to greater power than the two companies could hope to exercise separately.

2 *Efficiency* – where an alliance leads to lower joint costs over an important range of areas: scale, scope, transaction, procurement and so forth, then, this provides a powerful stimulus to alliance formation.

3 *Reputation* – alliances are set up to create a more prestigious enterprise with a higher profile in the marketplace, enhanced image, prestige and reputation.

4 *Legal requirements* – in many developing countries it is legally required that international companies take a local partner before being granted permission to trade.

Strategic fit, of some form or another, is normally the fundamental reason why the alliance has been set up in the first place. It is important both that it is clearly there at the outset, and that it continues to exist for the lifetime of the alliance. Strategic fit implies that the alliance has or is capable of developing a clearly identifiable source of sustainable competitive advantage. Garrette and Dussauge (1995) classify strategic fit into two forms of alliance: *scale* (where two competitors come together to achieve scale economies) and *link* (where two companies at different points in the value chain link up to reduce transaction costs). Clearly the tensions and risks of co-operation alliances will generally be greater in scale than in link alliances. Whatever partner is sought, it must be one with complementary assets, that is to supply some of the resources or competences needed to achieve the alliance objectives. Co-operative arrangements require the satisfaction of complementary needs on the part of both partners in order to work successfully together.

Cultural fit

However, for the alliance to endure, cultural adaptation must take place, leading the most successful alliances to graduate to the top right-hand box of Figure 10.7. Cultural fit is an expression more difficult to define than strategic fit. In the sense used here, it covers the following factors: the partners have cultural sensitivities sufficiently acute and flexible to be able to work effectively together, and to learn from each other's cultural differences. The partners are balanced in the sense of being of roughly equivalent size, strength and consciousness of need. One is not therefore likely to attempt to dominate the other. Also, their attitudes to risk and to ethical considerations are compatible. Strategy in Action 10.2 describes a successful strategic and cultural fit.

Cultural difficulties are very frequently cited as the reason for the failure of an alliance, but the question of compatible cultures is rarely explicitly addressed when an alliance is being set up. Additionally clearly different cultures (e.g. UK / Japan) often make for better alliances than superficially similar ones (e.g. UK / US). Indeed in support of this point, research has shown that an ethnically Chinese American national has a far more difficult task running a US / Chinese joint venture in China than an explicitly Caucasian American. Less tolerance is accorded to the ethnically Chinese American for cultural lapses in China although he may never in fact have visited China previously.

Strategy in Action 10.2 *Accel in Lithuania*

Accel produces and sells climate system components and electronic equipment for the car industry. The aim of Accel in the alliance was to have access to well-educated and low-paid manpower in Lithuania to manufacture competitive products for export. The other motive was to find a local partner with the capacity for product development. The MD of Accel visited Lithuania in 1993 and identified a local partner who had gained competence in the field through a previous collaboration with a military institute during the Soviet period. An alliance was therefore formed in Lithuania in 1994 and production started in 1995. The local partner acquired 51 per cent of the ownership, and Accel 49 per cent.

Accel was in charge of sales, customer relationships, and purchasing. The Lithuanian partner was responsible for operations and product development. Accel was also partly involved in product development as it had direct contact with the customers. The local partner possessed general technical knowledge but lacked information about the actual requirements of the car industry customers. The foreign partner collaborated with customers in preparing product specifications, which were sent to the alliance. The products were less complicated and did not require after-sales services. All the products were sold to the foreign buyers.

The local partner contributed to its share of the capital with factory buildings and machinery, while Accel's contribution was mainly cash. Accel could expand its local network through its contacts with the local partner. One of such contacts concerned a local firm which produced electronic micro-sockets. Accel co-operated with this firm to develop solar sensors for the car industry. It also developed contact with another local firm which supplied several parts to the Lithuanian operation. However, Accel could not develop useful contacts with government authorities because all official matters had been carried out by the local partner.

The result exceeded the partners' expectation from the alliance. In a relatively short time the partners succeeded in building a company which could manufacture the required products and as sales grew steadily, both firms earned a good return from the investment. The success was achieved due to low price and high quality of products. Both partners had a strong interest to continue with the relationship and also sought other joint projects together.

Accel learned a lot from the co-operation. It was impressed by the local partner's technical competence and capability to swiftly adjust to customers' needs. It also learned important technological know-how. The Lithuanian partner learned substantially about the car industry. The mutual learning had a positive impact on the co-operation. It became easier to agree and also to draw up long-term plans. Initially, Accel advised the local partner as to how people think in the car industry. But after developing a good number of projects together, the local partner gradually learned to identify and satisfy customers' needs itself.

The impact of the general environment was quite substantial. The working speed of the local people was slow. Trust was very important in the beginning of the relationship. Long-term planning was absent and therefore Accel had to work hard to establish this practice in the alliance. Negotiations with the customs authorities were difficult and time-consuming. The authorities could delay customs clearance without any proper reason. The local partner handled such problems and succeeded most of the time. Overall the alliance was successful both from the learning and performance viewpoints.

SOURCE: ABRIDGED FROM *COMPETITIVENESS REVIEW,* 16(3), HYDER AND ABRADA (2006)

10

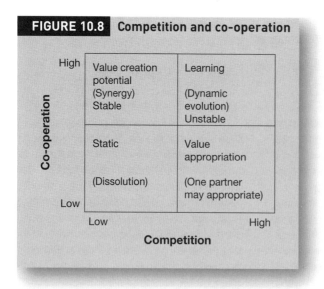

FIGURE 10.8 Competition and co-operation

	Low — Competition — High	
High Co-operation	Value creation potential (Synergy) Stable	Learning (Dynamic evolution) Unstable
Low	Static (Dissolution)	Value appropriation (One partner may appropriate)

Limited competition

It is also important that the partners are not too competitive see Figure 10.8.

Alliances in the top left-hand box should be relatively stable since their areas of co-operation are far stronger than those of competition. Alliances in the bottom left do not have strategic fit and are likely to dissolve over time. The top right-hand box alliances may be very dynamic, and significant mutual learning may take place. However, the high level of potential competition between the partners renders them ultimately unstable, and they are likely to have a future of either complete merger or break-up to reduce this competitive tension. Partners in the bottom right-hand box have strong competitive characteristics and only weak co-operative ones. Such a situation is likely to lead to the appropriation of key skills by one partner or the other. It is generally fairly simple to analyse the situation at the outset of an alliance, and avoid the dangerous bottom right-hand box. However situations change with time and alliances can slip unnoticed into this box after starting out in the more healthy top-level boxes. Such changes need to be guarded against by constant monitoring of the situation.

THE MANAGEMENT OF ALLIANCES

The management of an alliance consists of two primary factors:

1 The systems, mechanisms and organization structure chosen to operate the alliance.

2 The attitudes of the partners towards each other.

Much the same concerns apply to a network but in a rather looser way. Although the mechanisms chosen will obviously vary widely according to the co-operative form chosen, the attitudes necessary for success are similar in all forms. The relationship of the partners is a key to the success of the arrangement as in Strategy in Action 10.2. It may not be a sufficient factor by itself, since the successful alliance needs positive quantifiable results, but it is certainly a necessary condition. An appropriate attitude has two major components: commitment and trust.

Lack of commitment can kill an alliance in a very short time. Alliances have failed because the partners have not allocated their best people to the project, have placed it low on the priority agenda, or have set up too many relationships, in the hope that at least some would succeed. These attitudes have the seeds of failure within them.

Trust is the second key factor for survival. Unless this develops early on in the partnership the alliance soon ceases to be the best organizational arrangement for the partners, as they spend an increasing amount of time and resources monitoring each other's activities as a result of their mutual lack of trust. Trust may be classified in three forms.

1 *Calculative trust* which exists at the outset of a relationship because the partners perceive that it is in their self-interest to set up the relationship, and to do so they must accord their partner some measure of trust.

2 *Predictive trust* develops as the partners discover by working together that each is as good as his word, and his actions may therefore be accurately predicted to be as he commits to them.

3 *Bonding trust* or a warm human relationship may then develop over time, but does not necessarily do so in all business relationships. If it does, however, it is the best guarantor of a successful relationship.

Trust does not imply naive revelation of company secrets not covered by the alliance agreement. It implies the belief that the partner will act with integrity, and will carry out its commitments. The appropriate attitude must be set from the start. During the negotiation stage, friendliness should be exhibited, and a deal struck that is clearly good for both partners, qualities quite different from those that often characterize take-over negotiations.

Goal compatibility is vital to the long-term success of a partnership. Of course, the specific goals of the alliance will evolve over time. However, if the goals of the partners at a basic level fundamentally clash, the alliance cannot be anything more than a short-term opportunistic affair. Compatibility does not necessarily mean the partners' goals must be identical. There is no fundamental incompatibility in having different sets of goals so long as they do not conflict.

The mechanisms for running a joint venture are quite distinct from those of a collaboration. A joint venture, whether two-partner or consortium, involves the creation of a separate company from those of the partners. There are therefore two types of relationship to cope with, that is the relationship between the partners, and the relationship between each partner and the joint venture company. The most appropriate systems for running a joint venture are also the simplest. The venture should be set up with sufficient resources, guaranteed assistance by the partners while it is young, and be allowed to get on with the job of realizing its objectives and targets. Involvement by the partners should be limited to board level, except at the request of the venture company. A chief executive should be appointed and given sufficient autonomy to build the joint venture company. Although this seems common sense, it is surprising how many joint ventures falter or fail through the unwillingness of the partners to give them sufficient autonomy and assets, and to realize that the venture inevitably will not have fully congruent objectives with those of the partners. Joint venture companies inevitably develop cultures, lives and objectives of their own, and owner partners frequently find this fact difficult to adjust to. The now-retired managing Director of the EVC joint venture between ICI and Enichem is on record as claiming that both partners expected him to pursue their interests rather than those of the joint venture company he was employed to run, and both accused him of being biased in favour of the interests of their partner.

The relationship between the partners is different in nature between partners in collaborations. Here the 'boundary spanning' mechanism is the area crucial for success. The interface between the companies is the area where culture clashes, or conflict of objectives will probably show themselves first. The establishment of a 'gatekeeper' executive or office, as a channel for all contacts between the partners at least during the settling down period of the alliance, is a good way to avoid unnecessary misunderstandings.

In all circumstances, a good dispute resolution mechanism should be established before the alliance begins to operate. If this is left to be worked out as necessary, there is a high risk that its absence will lead to a souring of the relationship between the partners at the ultra-sensitive early stage of the partnership.

An effective system for disseminating alliance information widely within the partner companies is a further important factor for ensuring that both, or all, partners gain in learning to the greatest degree possible from the co-operative arrangement.

A procedure for divorce should be considered at the outset of an alliance in the event of a wish by either party to end the alliance, since this will increase the feeling of security by both parties that an end to the alliance does not represent a potential catastrophe.

ALLIANCE EVOLUTION

Bleeke and Ernst in a 1995 article in the *Harvard Business Review* claim that there are six possible outcomes to alliances including the dissolution of the alliances and the swallowing of one partner by the other. Only one solution was that the alliance continue successfully largely unchanged over an indefinite time period, and it is certainly true to say that two firms running an enterprise may well lead to an ultimate outcome of the simpler 'one firm running it' type. However, this is not necessarily the case.

One key factor in the life of an alliance seems to be that, if it ceases to evolve, it starts to decay. The reality of a successful alliance is that it not only trades competences but also demonstrates synergies. Whereas the resource dependency perspective identifies a key part of a company's motivation for forming an alliance, the successful evolution of that alliance depends upon the realization of synergies between the companies, and the establishment of a level of competitive advantage for the partners that each could not as easily realize alone.

Important conditions for evolution include (Child, Faulkner and Tallman 2005):

1 Perception of balanced benefits from the alliance by both partners.

2 The development of strong bonding factors.

3 The regular development of new projects between the partners.

4 The adoption of a philosophy of constant learning by the partners.

It is commitment to the belief that the alliance represents the best available arrangement that is the foundation of its stability. The need for resolution of the inevitable tensions in such an arrangement can as easily be presented as a strength, rather than as an inherent problem. It leads to the need to debate, to see and evaluate and to reconcile contrasting viewpoints.

SUMMARY

- Co-operative strategy, whether in the close form of strategic alliances or the more loosely coupled form of networks, requires attitudes and approaches to management quite distinct from those found in hierarchies.

- It generally emerges when one company finds itself unable to cope with a global or other challenge because of limitations in its resources and competences and it seeks an ally to make good its weaknesses.

- Where this new mode of organizing its business is approached flexibly and sensitively by the partners, enduring, successful and mutually beneficial relationships can be created and maintained.

- Indeed there are grounds for believing that the future of these more flexible organizational forms as exemplified in alliances and networks is likely to be bright.

- Such arrangements will not survive, however, if partners play power politics with each other, show lack of commitment, distrust and lack of integrity and do not make very positive steps to deal with the cultural differences between the partners that will almost inevitably exist.

- It is these mishandled situations that have led to the reported 50 per cent failure rate of recent alliances.

- The need is to understand the key factors for success in managing alliances as competently as the lessons from management theory in handling integrated hierarchical corporations.

- They are as different as the contrast between giving orders from a position of authority compared with developing a consensus for action in a community of equals.

- Only when this difference is appreciated and translated into changed behaviour, will the failure rate of co-operative arrangements begin to decline.

DISCUSSION QUESTIONS

1 What are the two main types of strategic alliance in terms of motivating factors?

2 How is value added in a strategic alliance?

3 When should joint ventures / collaborations / consortia be adopted?

4 Why do firms co-operate?

5 What are the two main qualities required of a partner when entering into a strategic alliance?

6 How do you best manage a strategic alliance?

7 Why is evolution important in the life of an alliance?

FURTHER READINGS

1 Child, J. Faulkner, D.O. and Tallman, S. (2005) *Cooperative Strategies*, Oxford: Oxford University Press.

   This widely adopted co-operative strategy book is now in its second edition with the addition of Steve Tallman as third author to add a US perspective. It has extensive breadth of coverage of the practical and theoretical literature on co-operative strategy. All topics of relevance to alliances are covered.

2 Lorange, P. and Roos, J. (1992) *Strategic Alliances: Formation, Implementation and Evolution*, Oxford University Press.

   This book was one of the seminal works in the period in which strategic alliances were first analysed as a popular area for academic research. It contains one of the first comprehensive analyses of strategic alliances and co-operative strategies. It remains amongst the best of the field. It is easy to read and provides very valuable frameworks and compelling insights into alliances and joint ventures.

3 Bleeke, J. and Ernst, D. (eds) (1993) *Collaborating to Compete*, New York: Wiley.

   This book, produced by two management consultants from McKinsey, provides a very valuable practitioners' perspective on alliances. It is particularly valuable in its conclusions that most alliances end up in acquisitions of some sort or in dissolution.

4 Y. Doz and Hamel, G. (1998) *Alliance Advantage: The Art of Creating Value by Partnering*, Harvard Business School Press

   After years spent re-eningeering and downsizing, many companies are leaner, more efficient, and acutely focused on their core business. Yet today's growth opportunities in global markets and new technologies demand a wider range of skills than even very large companies possess. More and more, firms must turn to alliances (often with competitor firms) to find the right resources for pursuing new opportunities. However, few managers are accustomed to working with undefined boundaries. Doz and Hamel have put together an insightful blueprint for making alliances work successfully.

10

CHAPTER 11

Global mergers and acquisitions

LEARNING OBJECTIVES The objectives of this chapter are to:

■ identify the strategic, financial and managerial motives for acquisitions

■ assess the overall performance of acquisitions

■ discuss how global mergers and acquisitions can add value

■ explain how post-acquisition integration can be achieved.

INTRODUCTION

Although **mergers** and **acquisitions** are often treated together in the literature, legally they are transactions of a different kind. An acquisition is an outright purchase of one company by another. It occurs when one company acquires enough of another company's shares to gain control or ownership. A merger is in theory a collaborative agreement by two companies to combine their interests, ownership and company structures into one company. However, mergers are not normally a marriage of equals. A joining in one company of two significant brand name companies is often presented to the world as a merger largely to save the face of the company being acquired. For example Chrysler (US) and Daimler-Benz (Germany) was announced as a merger of two world-famous car companies. However, it soon became apparent that it was in fact an acquisition by Daimler-Benz of Chrysler. The composition of the new board and the background of the new CEO generally show which company is actually the acquirer. In this chapter therefore the terms merger and acquisition are used interchangeably, and frequently referred to as M&A activity.

Mergers and acquisitions are generally presented to shareholders as highly rational strategies with clearly defined goals and objectives. Typically these are of a financial and / or strategic nature. Financial goals include increasing shareholder wealth and financial synergy through economies of scale, the transfer of knowledge and increased control. Strategic reasons include increasing market share, the reduction of uncertainty and the restoration of market confidence. Mergers and acquisitions can also be sought by companies seeking to ward off hostile take-over bids.

MERGER TRENDS

Rapid globalization has encouraged a high degree of cross-border merger and acquisition activity. It emerged as the business growth area of the mid- to late 1990s. By

1996, M&A activities were worth more than $250 billion per annum. Some of the largest mergers and acquisitions during this period occurred in the finance sector. For example, in late 1998, Deutsche Bank launched a £6 billion takeover of Banker's Trust of the US. This had been preceded by the £3.1 billion acquisition of Mercury Asset Management Group by Merrill Lynch & Co. in 1997, and the 1996 union of Invesco plc and AIM Management Group Inc., valued at £977 million sterling. Other influential business sectors, such as the oil industry, witnessed a major period of consolidation in the late 1990s. For instance, the 1998 acquisition of PetroFina by Total created a combined market capitalization of almost $40 billion. The $75 billion Exxon and Mobil merger, which occurred in the same year, became the largest merger on record at the close of the twentieth century.

The trend towards merger in the US banking sector was further consolidated when, in 1997, Morgan Stanley, the investment bank, merged with Dean Witter. In April 1998, Citicorp and Travelers Group announced a $160 billion merger, to create a worldwide financial services giant with operations ranging from credit cards and banking (retail, investment, private) to fund management and insurance. The new company was named 'Citigroup'. The market responded by adding $30 billion to the value of the two firms' shares in a single day.

More recently 2007 was a boom year for mergers and acquisitions around the world. In the US alone, it was the single biggest year since 1999. The majority of mergers took place in the sectors of finance, healthcare, technology and energy, with the latter two attracting higher average selling prices for individual businesses. Mergers and acquisitions also took place in the utilities, capital goods, consumer staples, basic materials and consumer cyclicals sectors but the levels of the final buyout prices were nowhere near the level of those in the former sectors. However, in terms of the number of mergers and acquisitions, it was the consumer sector that saw the majority of the deals. The top ten deals in 2007 were:

1 $85.6 billion – The acquisition of BellSouth by AT&T in the technological sector.

2 $35 billion – The acquisition of Burlington Resources by Concoco Phillips in the energy sector.

3 $25.1 billion – The acquisition of Guidant by Boston Scientific in the healthcare sector.

4 $24.2 billion – The acquisition of Golden West Financial by Wachovia in the financial sector.

5 $21.3 billion – The acquisition of HCA by private equity buyers from Bain Capital, Merrill Lynch, KKR, Global Private Equity and the founder of HCA, Thomas F. Frist, Jr. in the healthcare sector.

6 $16.2 billion – The acquisition of Freescale Semiconductor by private equity buyers from the Blackstone Group, Carlyle Group, Texas Pacific Group and Permira Advisers LLC in the technological sector.

7 $16 billion – The acquisition of Kerr-McGee by Anadarko Petroleum in the energy sector.

8 $13.6 billion – The acquisition of North Fork Bancorp by Capital One in the financial sector.

9 $11.7 billion – The acquisition of Lucent Technologies by Alcatel in the technological sector.

10 $10.5 billion – The acquisition of AmSouth Bancorp by Region Financial in the financial sector.

MERGER LOGIC

Mergers and acquisitions are justified by the extent to which they add value. Value is added if distinctive capabilities or strategic assets are exploited effectively. Adding value requires some synergy, which may be obtained from matching distinctive capabilities or strategic assets, winning access to complementary assets, or deriving economies of scale and scope related to the core business. Cross-border

M&As with the highest potential for success tend to be between firms that share similar or complementary operations in such key areas as production and marketing. When two companies share similar core businesses, there can be opportunities for economies of scale at various stages in the value chain (e.g. R&D, sales and marketing, distribution). Complementary operations + competencies = value added. The main problem associated with merger and acquisition strategy lies in the ability to integrate the new company into the activities of the old. This problem often centres upon problems of *cultural fit*.

The strategic logic behind M&A is generally impeccable, particularly in terms of cost-reduction, especially of labour costs. For example the Exxon / Mobil merger was estimated to realize cost savings of $4 billion per annum. Yet many fail to produce the value added predicted, for example Sony's 1989 acquisition of Columbia Pictures resulted in Sony being forced to accept a $3.2 billion write-down in 1994. As Strategy in Action 11.1 illustrates, a failure to look for / develop / foster synergies between companies prior to a take-over, can often lead to real operational problems afterwards.

MOTIVES BEHIND ACQUISITIONS

A PwC (Price Waterhouse Coopers) investment management survey found that the primary rationale for most acquisitions is that they provide the fastest route to growing revenues. This can be achieved in a number of ways:

1 Helping to reach critical mass or otherwise increase penetration in existing markets

2 Bringing together complementary assets, for example product and distribution

3 Providing an immediate track record in a new market.

This is especially true when setting out to develop new business in other countries, where local knowledge and expertise are required or regulations demand a local presence (PwC, 1998). Acquisition also allows quick access to new product and/or market areas. A company may lack the internal resources or competences to develop a particular strategy and may, therefore, acquire a company for its R&D expertise. Furthermore, acquisition may be used as a means of avoiding the danger of excess capacity in static markets, that is excess capacity can be retired in a planned manner. Other financial motives include the fact that a firm with a low share value may be a tempting target. This may result in short-term gain through 'asset stripping'. Finally, as already mentioned, acquisition strategy can benefit a company through increased economies of scale. This emerges not only through lower unit costs but also increased capital for investment in service.

Acquisition strategy often proves problematic, particularly when there is insufficient cultural fit between the acquirer and the acquired. Indeed Porter (1987) found that they are more often than not failures in terms of meeting the expectations of the buyer.

M&A is an alternative growth strategy to internal development and strategic alliances. Depending upon the specific circumstances, each of these three means of development may be preferred, but each has distinctive characteristics and drawbacks. In short, internal development preserves control and proprietary information in the company, but limits the strategic assets to those already possessed and also tends to be slow to show results. Alliances are relatively low-risk and inexpensive but involve dilution of control and the high possibility of culture clash. M&A can be very expensive (35 per cent average share premiums on purchase), may lead to hostility in the acquired company workforce and / or the loss of the best staff, and frequently involves integration problems. However M&A remains the most popular means of growth and extension of global reach. It has been estimated that there are ten examples of M&A annually for every one strategic alliance. The year 2006 recorded acquisitions worldwide to a total value of $3.7 trillion, 40 per cent of which were in the United States (Thomson Financial securities data).

Strategy in Action 11.1 *One big unhappy family at Mellon Bank*

SOURCE: ADAPTED FROM HILL AND JONES (1998) *STRATEGIC MANAGEMENT: AN INTEGRATED APPROACH*, P. 329

In the early 1990s Mellon Bank conceived of a corporate strategy that would reduce the vulnerability of Mellon's earnings to changes in interest rates. Its solution was to diversify into financial services to gain access to a steady flow of fee-based income from money management operations. As part of this strategy, in 1993 Mellon acquired The Boston Company for $1.45 billion. Boston was a high-profile money management company that manages investments for major institutional clients such as state and corporate pension funds. In 1994 Mellon also acquired Dreyfus, a mutual fund provider. As a result, by 1995 almost half of Mellon's income was generated from fee-based financial services.

Problems at Boston began to surface, though, soon after its acquisition by Mellon. From the start there was a clear clash of cultures. At Mellon, many managers arrive at their offices by 7 a.m. and put in twelve-hour days for pay that is modest by banking industry standards. They are also accustomed to a firm management hierarchy that is carefully controlled, where the management style emphasizes cost containment and frugality. Boston managers also put in twelve-hour days but they expect considerable autonomy, flexible work schedules, high pay, ample perks, and large performance bonuses. Mellon executives who visited The Boston Company unit were dumbstruck by the country club atmosphere and opulence which they saw. In its move to streamline Boston, Mellon insisted that Boston cut expenses and introduced new regulations for restricting travel, entertainment, and perks.

Things started to go wrong in October 1993 when the Wisconsin state pension fund complained to Mellon of lower returns on a portfolio run by Boston. In November Mellon liquidated the portfolio, taking a $130 million charge against earnings. Mellon also fired the portfolio manager, who it claimed was making 'unauthorized trades'. At Boston, however, many managers saw Mellon's actions as violating guarantees of operating autonomy that Mellon had given Boston at the time of the acquisition. They blamed Mellon for prematurely liquidating a portfolio whose strategy, they claimed, Mellon executives had approved and that moreover, could still prove a winner if interest rates fell (which they subsequently did).

Infuriated by Mellon's interference in the running of Boston, in March seven managers at Boston's Asset Management unit proposed a management buyout to Mellon. Mellon rejected the proposal and the Boston CEO promptly left to start up his own investment management company. A few days later Mellon asked its employees at Boston to sign employment contracts that limited their ability to leave and work for this competing business. Another thirteen senior managers refused to sign. These thirteen all quit and went to work for the rival money management operation. These defections were followed by a series of high-profile client defections. The Arizona state retirement system, for example, pulled $1 billion out of Mellon and transferred it to the new firm.

Reflecting on the episode, the Mellon CEO noted that 'we've been clearly hurt ... but this episode is very manageable. We are not going to lose our momentum.' Others were not so sure. In this incident they saw yet another example of how difficult it can be to merge two divergent corporate cultures and how the management turnovers that result can deal a serious blow to any attempt to create value from an acquisition.

11

TYPES OF ACQUISITION

Cartwright and Cooper (1992) describe three different types of acquisition:

1 *Friendly*: When the first take-over bid is accepted, it is classified as friendly.

2 *Contested*: When there are specific issues which need to be debated and resolved, the take-over is classified as contested.

3 *Hostile*: This is the type that attracts the most attention in the media. When a company realizes that a take-over bid is inevitable, it can deploy tactics to ward it off. One such tactic is to make a bid for another company in order to force up the price of its shares. Another is to seek a more attractive bid from another interested company, often called a white knight.

Mergers may be classified in a very similar fashion:

1 *Rescue*: This occurs when one company is rescued from liquidation or insolvency by merger with another.

2 *Collaborative*: Mergers can be friendly, mutually satisfactory or beneficial arrangements.

3 *Contested*: As in the case of an acquisition, a contested merger is one in which specific issues need to be discussed.

4 *Raid*: This type of merger may be considered to be analogous to the case of a hostile take-over.

However, note that the frequently dubious distinction between what the press and the actors describe as a merger, or alternatively an acquisition, limits the value of the above classification.

Motives for making an acquisition are many and varied, and not always those that are declared to the press when the bid is announced. They can be classified into three categories: *strategic motives*, *financial motives* and *managerial motives* (Schoenberg, 2003).

Strategic motives
....

An acquisition may be carried out to increase a firm's overall strength and presence in world markets. More specifically it can establish it overnight in new segments of a market or in new geographical markets, and give it the vehicle to extend its brands into areas in which it was previously not represented. By giving it access to new strategic assets, core competences and capabilities, it can strengthen its portfolio of product value chains, and facilitate the successful development of new products. It can give it a stronger presence in its existing markets and dramatically change the pecking order for market share and hence buying power and customer power. If two companies each have 20 per cent of a market and a third company has 30 per cent, the acquisition of one of the 20 per cent companies by the other will immediately catapult the acquiring company into the position of market leader with all the cost and reputational advantages that go with it. Similarly a company may acquire another in order to retire its capacity from the market, and thereby remove surplus capacity and enable improved margins to be achieved from an improvement in the supply–demand balance. An acquisition policy may also be adopted in order to achieve a better balance of sales over the year through increased diversification. In such a way a company focusing on Christmas sales may attempt to iron out sales peaks and troughs by acquiring a company focusing on summer sales. In terms of acquiring strategic assets, a company, particularly in the service sectors, may make an acquisition in order to attract a particularly talented marketing or research and development team, for example an investment bank or a bio-tech company. In such circumstances, however, they would need to ensure the watertight nature of the talented team's contracts.

Other strategic motives for acquisitions may involve asset stripping, that is buying undervalued assets in order to dress them up more attractively and sell them off at a profit. In the 1980s, Hanson Trust (UK) and GE (US) were famous for famous for making large-scale acquisitions and then selling off the unwanted parts in order to pay for a large part of the whole. With the rise of MNC ethics (see chapter 15), this strategy has fallen into disfavour. This is sometimes called 'unbundling', as a company buys a job lot of assets held by an unfashionable and hence lowly rated investment trust or latter-day conglomerate, and frees the constituent business units up either to float independently as PLCs, or to find new parents in related and hence more rationally relevant sectors. When Philip Green acquired Sears in 1999 it included six retail businesses in distinctly different sectors of the market. The acquisition cost him £540 million. The businesses were sold off over the next six months for approximately the same value, but leaving him with a property portfolio estimated at £200 million (*Financial Times*, 9 July 1999). An example of a strategic acquisition in the global drinks industry is given in Strategy in Action 11.2.

Financial Motives

The unbundling or asset-stripping motive can be classed as strategic from the viewpoint of the entrepreneur carrying it out. It also falls very clearly within the category of financial motives. Other financial motives include cost reduction. Acquiring a company in the same market sector improves a company's strategic position in that market, but it also generally provides the opportunity for considerable organizational rationalization involving substantial workforce reductions and hence cost savings. Two sales forces are not necessarily required. Nor are two R&D departments necessary, particularly if their activities overlap to a large extent. The same level of overhead staff will often be able to monitor and support the activities of two companies as easily as one. Economies of scale and hence unit cost reduction will therefore result from the spreading of the overheads over a larger sales turnover. A collaborative merger in the US banking industry intended to achieve greater economies of scale is detailed in Strategy in Action 11.3.

It may well be also that the predator has observed that the target company displays considerable cost inefficiencies in its business, and many of these can be eradicated immediately by the elimination or shrinking of unwanted and under-performing staff departments such as corporate planning, human resources or management services departments. Some acquirers buying companies with large staff departments (i.e. departments that have no direct line management responsibilities) do immediately close them down, since such departments represent high overhead costs with no direct contribution to revenues. Therefore such departments needed to be strongly justified if they were to survive under the new ownership.

There are also more direct financial motives for acquisitions, targeted at financial manipulation rather than direct business activities. Companies can be acquired to take advantage of their tax losses or their high balance sheet liquidity, thereby saving on corporation tax in the subsequent year and improving the acquirer's cash ratios. Similarly acquirers with a strong set of financials can substantially enhance the prospects of an acquiree previously undercapitalized and consequently overgeared, and unable to carry out the necessary marketing expenditure to develop its otherwise strong product portfolio.

Managerial motives

Companies wishing to make a bid to acquire always justify this to their shareholders and the financial public by pointing to the strength of the financial and strategic arguments for the acquisitions. The word 'synergy' does overtime in such bid documents. For example, when BAE bought Rover car company (UK)

11

Strategy in Action 11.2 *M&A in the global drinks industry*

As an example of a strategic acquisition, the acquisition of the UK Allied Domecq drinks group by Pernod Ricard of France gave it access to new strategic assets (well-established drinks brands in parts of its portfolio where it was currently weak) and strengthened its product portfolio. It also gave Pernod a huge one-off jump in market share.

From small beginnings in 1932 as a local firm in the south of France making pastis, an aniseed-flavoured aperitif, Pernod merged with Ricard, another pastis-maker, in 1975. In 1978, Paul Ricard, the son of the Ricard founder, became chairman of the joint Pernod Ricard company. He immediately started a series of international acquisitions: Wild Turkey brand whiskey from the US; Irish Distillers; and Jacobs Creek, an Australian wine company. Finally, in 2001, he acquired 38 per cent of Seagram, a Canadian conglomerate with a large spirits portfolio. Despite this M&A spending spree, the acquisition in 2005 of Allied Domecq of the UK at a cost of Euros 11.4 billion was a transforming deal for Pernod Ricard. With that acquisition it almost doubled in size overnight, with turnover 2005 to 2006 increasing from Euros 3.5 billion to Euros 5.8 billion. The acquisition (for an acquisition it clearly was) turned Pernod into the second-largest drinks company in the world, second only to the giant Diageo. Pernod is seen as a quintessentially French company, as symbolized by the famous drink of pastis which bears the Pernod company name. The product ranges of the two companies are quite complementary, with the UK company Allied Domecq strong on whisky and gin brands. However, there was a view that Pernod had bought a set of rather tired brands and a large amount of Allied tax liabilities.

Diageo and Pernod, despite being number one and number two in the same industry, are run entirely differently. Diageo believes in centralization and standardization, whereas Pernod has always given local operations and local brands plenty of autonomy. Pernod has extended this principle of local autonomy to the Allied Domecq brands such Beafeater gin and Malibu rum. In an industry in which branding is everything, the contrast between Pernod and Diageo is most noticeable in their approaches to marketing. Pernod focuses on catering for local demand. It adapts its advertising campaigns to each country and employs a large number of local advertising firms. By contrast, Diageo uses far fewer agencies and runs big global advertising campaigns for its top brands. As an example of one of Diageo's global campaigns, the publicity for its Johnnie Walker whisky is the same everywhere, whereas adverts for Pernod Ricard's Chivas Regal brand are adjusted to local audiences.

So far Pernod Ricard has managed to balance global scale with local appeal, but this will get harder and harder with a much bigger group. With its previous acquisitions Pernod has built up an excellent record of turning around dying brands. It has revived both the Chivas Regal brand (run down by Seagram) and also the Martell cognac brand. However, its localization strategy gives it a higher cost base than Diageo's global standardization strategy and it has less control over its brands.

SOURCE: COMPILED BY AUTHORS FROM PRESS ARTICLES

in the early 1980s much was made of the supposed technological synergy between the fibre optics avionics in its aircraft, and the modern dashboard of up-market cars. When the acquisition was completed, however, the car division was run as a completely separate business to the aircraft business and no more was heard of these supposed synergies. This is more the norm than the exception. Where managerial

SOURCE: THIS CASE IS REPRODUCED FROM HILL AND JONES (1998) STRATEGIC MANAGEMENT: AN INTEGRATED APPROACH, P. 146

Strategy in Action 11.3 *The Chemical and Chase Banks merger*

In August 1995, two of the world's largest banks, Chemical Bank and Chase Manhattan Bank, both of New York, announced their intention to merge. The merger was officially completed on 31 March 1996. The combined bank, which adopted the Chase name, had more than $300 billion in assets, making it the largest bank in the United States and the fourth-largest in the world. The new Chase was capitalized at $20 billion and was number one or two in the United States in numerous segments of the banking business, including loan syndication, trading of derivatives, currency and securities trading, global custody services, New York City retail banking, and mortgaging services.

The prime reason given for the merger was anticipated cost savings of more than $1.7 billion per year, primarily through the realization of economies of scale. The newly merged bank had good reason for thinking that these kinds of cost savings were possible. In a 1991 merger between Chemical and Manufacturers Hanover, another New York-based bank, cost savings of $750 million per year were realized from the elimination of duplicated assets, including physical facilities, information systems and personnel. The cost savings in the Chase–Chemical combination had several sources. First, significant economies of scale were possible from combining the 600 retail branches of the original banks. Closing down excess branches and consolidating its retail business into a smaller number of branches allowed the new bank to significantly increase the capacity utilization of its retail branching network. The combined bank would be able to generate the same volume of retail business from fewer branches. The fixed costs associated with retail branches – including rents, personnel, equipment, and utility costs – would drop, which translates into a substantial reduction in the unit cost required to serve the average customer.

A second source of scale-based cost savings arose from the combination of a whole array of 'back office' functions. For example, the entire bank now only had to operate one computer network, instead of two. By getting greater utilization out of a fixed computer infrastructure – including mainframe computers, servers and the associated software – the combined bank should be able to drive down its fixed cost structure even further. Substantial savings would also arise from the combination of management functions. For example, the new Chase bank had doubled the number of auto loans and mortgage originations it issues but, because of office automation, it could manage the increased volume with less than twice the management staff. This saving implied a big reduction in fixed costs and a corresponding fall in the unit costs of servicing the average auto loan or mortgage customer.

motives actually dominate financial or strategic ones, the shareholders should beware the probable impact on their earnings per share.

Where M&A is motivated by the self-interest of the top management team or the CEO, managerial hubris as it is often called, the results are unlikely to lead to a value improvement for the shareholders. It has been suggested that in too many acquisitions the winners are the management team of the acquirer with enhanced salaries and share options, and the previous shareholders of the acquiree, who walk away with perhaps a 35 per cent premium on the earlier value of their shares before the bid. The losers are the acquirer's shareholders with a substantially reduced earning per share, as they have to face an extra 35 per cent of 'goodwill' on their balance sheet resulting from the high costs of acquisitions rarely balanced by achieved synergies. Other losers of course are the management team of the acquiree, as many lose their jobs, and even the survivors lose their independence. Research shows that a strong board of directors with independent analytical skills and the willingness to use them can limit the ability of CEOs to indulge their managerial hubris and allow ambition for size to cloud their judgement (Hayward and Hambrick, 1997).

ACQUISITION PERFORMANCE

Acquisition performance at its most charitable interpretation tends to disappoint its advocates as a vehicle for corporate strategic development and as a means of replacing poor corporate governance with an improved variety. Bleeke and Ernst (1993) reveal that in their research 43 per cent of international acquisitions fail to produce a financial return that met the acquirer's cost of capital, in other words they destroy shareholder value.

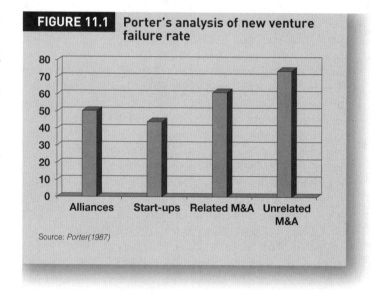

FIGURE 11.1 Porter's analysis of new venture failure rate

Source: Porter(1987)

This statistic is similar to Porter's (1987) article demonstrating the limited success from all types of new activity as shown in Figure 11.1.

This suggests that according to Porter's assumption that an acquisition sold within five years of its purchase can be regarded as a failure, over 70 per cent of acquisitions in unrelated sectors in his sample are failures, and over 60 per cent even in a closely related sector.

Schoenberg (2003) suggests that:

> recent research along these lines indicates that 45–55% of acquirers are neutral to highly dissatisfied with the overall performance of their acquisitions. Interestingly the failure rates are similar for domestic and cross-border acquisitions and show no improvement over figures reported in 1974 from the first such study.

The high divestiture rate is not, however, all bad. As Kaplan and Weisbach (1992) show, 40 per cent of divestitures are sold on at a price in excess of their acquisition cost. Clearly the unbundling strategy and asset-stripping can pay.

Financial economists have attempted to estimate the wealth generation of M&A activity by calculating the change in share price of bidder and target at the time of the acquisition announcement. A study of UK acquisitions between 1980 and 1990 found that target companies gained about 30 per cent in share value and bidders lost about 5 per cent. The results suggest that overall wealth creation is nil to negligible, and that the gains, as suggested above, generally go to the shareholders of the target company. This of course does not answer the question of whether the M&A activity was a 'good thing', since any synergies realized would take some time to come about. Furthermore on the bright side, most studies do show that up to 50 per cent of acquirers do make good returns. It may be concluded, then, that at most one in two acquisitions can be classed as successful for the acquiring company. The question is therefore raised as to how an acquirer can ensure that he is in the positive 50 per cent.

Larsson and Finkelstein (1999) suggest that good results depend on three factors:

1 The acquisition's potential for value creation is high

2 The post-acquisition integration of the acquired company is purposeful and rapid

3 The level of employee resistance to the acquisition in the acquiree is low.

A study by the management consultants Braxton Associates (1988) provides some general insight into why acquirers believed their acquisitions had failed to lead to the gains they expected. They identified three factors:

1 Poor industry selection

2 Poor company selection and negotiation

3 Poor implementation.

Going into more detail, they stated that poor industry selection had come about through insufficient attention being paid to the closeness of the relationship of the target's industry to their own, and hence to their existing competences, to an overestimation of the target industry's growth potential and to an unexpected and dramatic change in the industry's environment since the acquisition.

Expanding on the issues of poor company selection and negotiation, they claimed that inadequate due diligence had been carried out into the existing condition of the target company; that the wrong company had been chosen based on a range of factors; and that there had been a distinct cultural clash or at least a mismatch between their culture and that of the new acquisition.

As regards the third factor, that is that of poor implementation, they stated that there had been inadequate implementation planning and execution, that too many of the target's key personnel had left shortly after the acquisition had been completed, and that the new company had failed to generate a sufficiently strong stream of new products. All of these factors might seem to be intuitively fairly obvious, but this does not detract from their importance and impact. It does, however, pose the question of how a larger percentage of acquisitions can be made to be successful, and how value can be created and realized.

ACHIEVING AND REALIZING VALUE

Porter (1987) identified three tests that in his view a potential acquisition must pass before the acquisition proposal should be validated by the shareholders. These have proved to be very influential guidelines.

1 *The attractiveness test* – The target must be in an industry that is deemed attractive after a Porter five forces' analysis. However it should be noted here that some very powerful industrial conglomerates have been built by buying in unattractive industries, since prices were lower and competition less severe, so this test is clearly not a 'must'.

2 *The cost-benefit test* – The cost of acquisition including the premium paid must be less than the clearly realizable benefits in financial terms that can be achieved from the deal.

3 *The 'better-off' test* – Synergies must be achievable such that the target company must bring something of value to the parent or vice versa.

Again these criteria are intuitively apparent, but in the heat of a take-over battle they are often not heeded by the would-be acquirer, as the price premium is bid up beyond levels that would pass the Porter tests.

Price Waterhouse Coopers have identified several actions that need to be carried out if M&A success is to be achieved. These are:

■ *Clarify the deal objectives and business case*: The proposed deal price, expected implementation costs, value of inevitable losses as a result of the combination (e.g. staff), and the value of synergies, should all be made clear at the outset.

■ *Monitor implementation against contribution to shareholder value*: Effective progress in mergers requires an understanding of not just what tasks have been completed but also what benefits have been realized. Flexibility is also required, to accommodate change along the way.

■ *Integrate quickly*: A major contributor to risk in merger situations is uncertainty and the impact it can have on motivation and staff performance. This means that merging entities should quickly identify those activities and functions which are essential to the immediate bringing together of the companies and other improvement projects which can be undertaken subsequently.

■ *Focus on maintaining the performance of the existing business*: A merger can cause a shift in focus from external to internal at the very time when the merging enterprises are under greatest scrutiny from both clients and investment consultants. As a result, opportunities to win new business are limited and the importance of retaining existing business is emphasized. It is therefore important that sufficient resources are devoted to maintaining 'business as usual', protected from the distractions of the merger process.

■ *Focus on retaining key people*: During a merger, senior management must also focus on retaining key staff, especially in sectors such as investment banking where the value of the business is so heavily linked to key people. A significant proportion of the value of the deal could be lost if key individuals are lost early in the merger process.

These factors are derived from cross-sectoral surveys as well as hands-on experience, given the merger of Price Waterhouse and Coopers & Lybrand to create PWC in 1997.

Many of the recommendations of the consultancies as listed in Figure 11.2 are of course self-evident truths, yet the results do not bear out the hope that these lessons are learnt by over-optimistic acquirers.

Schoenberg (1999) argued that value creation in acquisitions depends a lot on successful knowledge transfer. Acquirers therefore need to identify in advance which knowledge needs to be transferred, determine mechanisms for its transfer and engender an atmosphere conducive to its successful transfer post-acquisition. This is rarely explicitly done.

In a very influential article, Haspeslagh and Jemison (1991) identified four generic value-creation mechanisms that apply in all acquisition situations. They are:

1 *Resource sharing* – This applies principally in acquisition of similar companies. In such cases R&D departments may be combined. Factories can be rationalized, as can sales forces. Substantial costs can be saved and economies of scale achieved through such rationalization. Schoenberg (2003) cites the Glaxo Wellcome / Smith Kline Beecham (afterwards known as GlaxoSmithKline and now known as GSK) merger as identifying potential annual savings of £1 billion.

2 *Knowledge and skills transfer* – Superior knowledge and skills in all areas of activity may be transferred from the parent company or from the acquired one to enhance the competences of the other. This may be in technology, marketing, R&D administration, production or financial control. Knowledge transfer is particularly important in cross-border M&A where geographical distance makes the sharing of resources difficult.

FIGURE 11.2   Improve shareholder value through M&A

❏ Improve breadth and depth of product range

❏ Leverage innovation and technology investment

❏ Exploit economies of scale

❏ Spread development risk

❏ Overcome regulatory barriers

❏ Alter competitive landscape

❏ Enable entry into new markets

❏ Improve supply and distribution

❏ Increase market share

Source: *Price Waterhouse Coopers (1998) Pursuing profitability variations on a theme, p.9*

---

3 *Combination benefits* – Major M&A activity can transform industry structure and catapult a new combine into market leadership overnight. The new market leader will then enjoy the benefits that such a position brings in enhanced market power, better supply terms, improved profit margins and reduction of competitive intensity in the industry through the taking out of an erstwhile rival.

4 *Restructuring opportunities* – In this way surplus assets can be sold off, organisations can be streamlined and rationalized, and substantial cost savings can be achieved. The skill comes from the acquirer's ability to identify the real value of the target's assets, which may have been concealed due to a low price–earnings ratio resulting from poor overall economic performance.

The frequent failure of acquirers to achieve the anticipated synergies from M&A arises from their inability to activate these four generic value-creation mechanisms. This is particularly the case with knowledge transfer in hostile take-overs. Much knowledge is tacit and its transfer requires the active willingness of both parties to teach and to learn. This is difficult to achieve if the take-over has been hostile, and may even be lost altogether if the knowledge holders leave the company as a result of the take-over.

POST-ACQUISITION INTEGRATION

When the deal is done and the investment banking advisers have been sent home, the excitement rapidly fades and the hard work of integrating the acquisition and creating value from it begins. It is at this point that the all too frequent lack of post-acquisition planning becomes apparent. Appointments are made to key posts and the new executives are left to get on with the job. There are, however, many different ways of integrating an acquisition in addition to the non-way of just taking it as it comes and reacting to events – a sure recipe for failure.

Haspeslagh and Jemison (1991) developed a popular four-box framework for post-acquisition integration positioning which depends on the trade-off between the degree of strategic interdependence

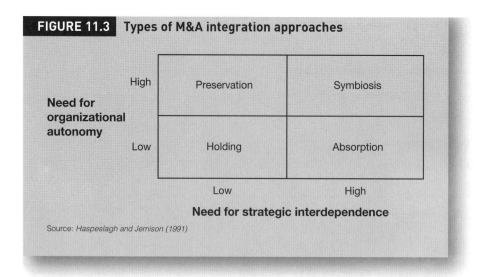

FIGURE 11.3 Types of M&A integration approaches

	Low	**High**
High	Preservation	Symbiosis
Low	Holding	Absorption

Need for organizational autonomy

Need for strategic interdependence

Source: *Haspeslagh and Jemison (1991)*

between parent and new acquisition and the extent of organisational autonomy needed to maintain its distinctive capabilities (see Figure 11.3).

1 *Absorption integration* involves the acquirer consolidating the new acquisition into its organisation root and branch. This may even involve the discarding of existing brand names, and generally does involve the change of name of the company to that of the parent and its physical integration into the parent group. As a result little continues to exist of its former identity, and staff members are encouraged to identify closely with the history, culture and operational methods of the acquiring company. As Child, Faulkner and Pitkethly (2000) found, this is most commonly the preferred integration method of US acquirers. Angwin (2000) found that 15 per cent of UK acquirers in the 1990s employed this method of integration. It often leads to substantial executive departures from staff unhappy with the new imposed culture, but can lead to considerable cost saving from resource sharing, knowledge transfer, combination benefits and sometimes restructuring.

2 *Symbiotic integration* – This method of integration attempts to achieve a balance between preserving the operational independence of the acquired firm while transferring capabilities between the two firms to enhance the strength of both value chains. The CEO of the acquired firm is often retained and great care must be taken to preserve much of the subsidiary's existing culture. This form of integration is often used where the acquirer buys a firm that is making good profits and has clear skills and competences valuable to the acquirer. Such integration requires exceptional judgement from the acquirer in striking a balance between absorption and autonomy in its integration activities. Child, Faulkner and Pitkethly (2000) found it to be the favoured integration form of Japanese acquirers in particular.

3 *Preservation* – This form of deliberate non-integration is adopted particularly when the acquired company is a successful one but may be undercapitalized, thus making it a take-over target. Despite the fact that preserving the autonomy of the new subsidiary makes it very difficult to activate many of the generic value-creating mechanisms, particularly combination benefits, it is the most common way of treating a new acquisition in the UK. Angwin (2000) found that 49 per cent of all UK acquisitions were treated in this way over the period of his study.

4 *Holding* – This form is adopted where a turnaround is required. Low levels of strategic interdependence are required, but the new subsidiary is granted low levels of autonomy. Frequently the acquirer

puts in a project team of turnaround executives who proceed to tighten financial controls, probably bring about a wholesale change in company culture and attempt to bring a failing firm back into profit. Angwin (2000) found that this form of post-acquisition plan was adopted by 27 per cent of acquirers in his sample.

These four forms of integration are of course archetypes, and are rarely found in their pure form as described. Actual situations may well require a combination of forms. Furthermore different nationalities have been found to favour different approaches. Child, Faulkner and Pitkethly (2000) found for example that UK acquirers typically attempted to achieve performance improvements in their acquisitions through product differentiation, strengthened marketing and granting a relatively high level of operational autonomy. Japanese acquirers favoured the adoption of priced-based competitive strategies. The French introduced tight cost control, allowed considerable operational autonomy, but retained strategic control firmly in the parent company. They found little if any difference in overall effectiveness on a national basis of the differing integration styles.

Other post-acquisition problems

Although a firm achieving acquisition success in a hostile take-over may be initially energized by its victory against opposition, such a take-over situation does not bode well for the future. It is likely to lead to substantial employee resistance to the new owners, and where employees are unable to get another job, they are likely to show passive resistance in carrying out their current one, making knowledge and skill transfer difficult if not outright impossible. Other more marketable executives are likely to leave the firm, thus reducing the attractiveness of the acquisition, where they have rare and valuable skills. Cannella and Hambrick (1993) found that high rates of management turnover are associated with poor acquisition performance.

Issues of culture clash may also cause problems for the new parent, particularly in cross-border acquisitions where national culture differences are imposed on corporate culture problems. The individualistic, performance-orientated US corporate culture is always likely to meet problems when it acquires a company used to a more collectivist culture, say from Germany or Japan, and if it is to be successful may need to take account of this in its integration planning.

A decision to wade in with a thoroughgoing absorption approach and just accept the inevitable staff resistance and management exit may lead to the loss of substantial skills and experience from the acquired firm not easily recovered. Many Japanese acquisitions in the West have avoided this problem by careful analysis of the contrasting cultures, and the adoption of a hybrid culture based partly on the Japanese philosophy, but also retaining important aspects of the human resource practices that the acquired company are more familiar with and attached to. This can help overcome some of the culture shock that inevitably follows from a cross-border acquisition (Child, Faulkner and Pitkethly, 2000). Also not all introduction of a new culture has detrimental effects. The adoption of enlightened human resource policies from an acquirer of an old-fashioned and poorly performing company can lead to effective reenergizing of the management team of the new subsidiary.

FINAL THOUGHTS

M&A activity is still by far the greatest and most popular approach to corporate growth particularly when a company is involved in extending its global reach. Cross-border M&A seems to be the easy answer to a company rapidly establishing itself in a new part of the world. For every strategic alliance concluded, there are an estimated ten examples of M&A activity. Yet all the academic evidence suggests that at best one in every two acquisitions fails. One must conclude either that this message is not reaching corporate executives, or alternatively that widespread managerial overconfidence makes many CEOs mistakenly believe that their acquisition will be one of the ones that succeeds. A third possibility of course takes us back to agency theory which suggests that the interests of the shareholders and the top management team are not always aligned. Although many acquisitions do not prove to add value to the shareholders' portfolio, almost all enhance the positions, power and personal financial situation of the top management team of the acquiring company. Thus, acting in their own personal interests, if not in the interests of their shareholders, they are motivated to continue to pursue M&A policies. Current corporate governance systems give a fragmented ownership structure in most MNCs little power to prevent an ambitious CEO from pursuing an active M&A strategy even if the shareholders fear it will reduce their earnings per share as a result of having to pay a large bid-premium. Their only resort is to sell their shares, which if they do in sufficient numbers will bring about the result they fear by deflating the share price. Given these circumstances, a reduction in the popularity of M&A is very unlikely to come about in the foreseeable future.

SUMMARY

- This chapter has discussed merger and acquisition activity as a possible growth strategy for a company, particularly one with global ambitions.
- It has analysed the key motivations for a company pursuing such a strategy and categorized them under the headings of strategic, financial and managerial motivations, noting that the managerial motivations are the ones least likely to lead to value-added for the shareholders of the acquiring company.
- It has noted the prevalence of managerial hubris in acquisitions that fail to realize their value-creating potential.
- It has discussed Porter's three tests of (1) industry attractiveness, (2) cost-benefit and (3) the 'better-off' test, which he claims must be met in all acquisitions if they are to go ahead.
- It has described Haspeslagh and Jemison's four types of integration strategy namely, absorption, symbiosis, preservation and a holding strategy.
- It has discussed the various types of post-acquisition integration, and given illustrations of circumstances in which each is most appropriate.
- It has noted that at best only one in every two acquisitions succeeds, and it has attempted to identify reasons why this is so, blaming managerial over-confidence, poor target selection and employee resistance as key factors behind this disappointing record.
- Finally it has noted that despite this, M&A is unlikely to decline as a growth strategy, since even if it is so frequently unsuccessful in increasing value per share for the shareholders of the acquirers, its ability to improve the fortunes of the acquirer's top management team keeps it popular.

DISCUSSION QUESTIONS

1   What is the difference between a merger and an acquisition?

2   What are the principal motives for acquisitions?

3   Why is hubris so dangerous?

4 Why is the performance of acquisitions historically so poor?

5 What can be done to avoid poor performance of acquisitions?

6 What are the most common post-acquisition problems encountered?

7 What are Haspeslagh and Jemison's four forms of acquisition integration?

FURTHER READINGS

1 Haspeslagh, P.C. and Jemison, D.B. (1991) *Managing Acquisitions: Creating Value through Corporate Renewal*, New York: Free Press.

Regarded now as a seminal book on the subject. The famous framework created by the authors has provided the basis for a great deal of M&A research. Extremely readable and insightful.

2 Child, J., Faulkner, D.O. and Pitkethly, R. (2003) *The Management of International Acquisitions*, Oxford: Oxford University Press.

A book recording what actually happens when companies are bought and integrated into a new corporate parent. Research based on and covering acquisitions of UK companies from France, Germany, US and Japan. How much does national culture and management style influence acquisitions and post-acquisition management? The book explores the different ways in which companies from varying cultures and nationalities approach the task of integrating new acquisitions into their group, and whether any one method of integration seems to be superior to another in terms of resultant performance of the newly acquired subsidiary

3 Cartwright, S. and Schoenberg, R. (2006) 'Thirty years of M&A; recent advances and future opportunities', *British Journal of Management*, 17 (Special Issue) (March): S1–S5.

The complex phenomenon that mergers and acquisitions (M&As) represent has attracted substantial interest from a variety of management disciplines over the past 30 years. Three primary streams of enquiry can be identified within the strategic and behavioural literature, which focus on the issues of strategic fit, organizational fit and the acquisition process itself. The recent achievements within each of these research streams are briefly reviewed. However, in parallel to these research advances, the failure rates of mergers and acquisitions have remained consistently high. Possible reasons for this dichotomy are discussed, which in turn highlight the significant opportunities that remain for future M&A research.

11

PART 3
THE MODERN WORLD

Of the five chapters in Part 3, four chapters cover significant areas of growing importance to MNCs and within global strategy: culture; learning; services and ethics. The fifth and final chapter in this section gives an overview of the major themes from the whole book that we would like to return to and emphasize. Although culture, learning, services and ethics are of relevance to all companies and to all national strategies too, they are each particularly problematic for organizations to get right when they move across borders.

Cross-border culture is a very well-researched topic within international management. Chapter 12 discusses culture as referring to the values, customs, behaviour and symbols that represent more than just their face value to members of societies and organizations. Most people experience two major groups in their daily lives: the organizations in which they work and the society in which they live. These have given rise, respectively, to the concepts of 'organizational culture' and 'national culture'. Organizational culture consists of the shared values, beliefs and ways of behaving and thinking that are unique to a particular organization. It may therefore be a positive means of integrating people around common purposes or a source of conflict which threatens the success of international activities such as a change of ownership in a cross-border merger. National cultures are acquired during childhood and reinforced simply by living one's life in a particular society. A very large part of the intricacies of implementing an international strategy of whatever type is the integration of the practices, mindsets and behaviours of many differing national and organizational cultures and melding them into one organization.

National cultures are a highly significant element in global strategy. They affect not only obvious things such as the meanings of brand names in different languages which can sometimes cause unintentional amusement or embarrassment. They are also part of the mindset which both the corporate headquarters and the national subsidiaries bring to their dealings with staff, suppliers, customers or local government agencies in another country, and also with each other. Many different definitions of the key attributes and dimensions of national culture exist. Chapter 12 discusses several approaches to modelling the effect of national culture on the behaviour of individuals in organizations, including Hofstede's five-dimensional model and Trompenaars's seven-dimensional model, as well as the more recent findings of the far-reaching GLOBE research project.

MNC strategies bring together people from different national cultures into organizations within which they are expected to develop a working relationship. The MNC may hope to benefit from such cultural diversity among its staff, especially from their national marketplace knowledge. Chapter 12 discusses the benefits of cross-cultural inputs within MNCs, but also the barriers and difficulties which often prevent such potential benefits being realized. The goal for global strategy is to achieve cultural fit within and between its various parts.

Chapter 13 discusses 'organizational learning'. The term has come to be used to emphasize that organizations, just as individuals, can acquire new knowledge and skills with the intention of improving their future performance. Indeed it has been argued that the only sustainable competitive advantage for the company of the future will be the ability of its managers to learn faster than its rivals. This is an especially relevant issue in modern knowledge economies and information industries. In the framework that we use in Chapter 13, we include the additional elements of wisdom and judgement which we regard as constituting the key foundations of strategic decision-making. They are in addition to the more usual elements of organizational learning: data, information, learning and knowledge.

Organizational learning is complex because an organization does not necessarily benefit from the acquisition of knowledge and understanding unless and until these are applied to improving organizational actions. Learning outcomes therefore include not just the potential for, but the actual realization of, improvements and changes. The central problem in organizational learning is that knowledge is created only by individuals. Therefore organizations learn only through the experiences and actions of individuals. So the most important element of organizational learning is how to transfer such learning from the individual to the organization. The transfer of knowledge and learning within organizations is often blocked by organizational barriers arising from existing organizational routines. That is why knowledge is often referred to as 'sticky', that is it gets stuck where it is in the organization and is very difficult to shift around. When a company is global, such barriers to organizational learning are almost inevitably increased by the variety of different national identities in the employee group. Such barriers may reduce the willingness to transfer knowledge between different parts of an organization, or between different national partners in a cross-border alliance. Obstacles to the necessary transference of knowledge within MNCs also include cognitive barriers and emotional barriers that arise because of divergent approaches to sense-making associated with the social identities of the different participants and stakeholders that make up an MNC.

As we move on to discuss the difficulties specific to managing global strategies in service MNCs in Chapter 14, all of the factors related to international culture and learning become yet more difficult. Service industries and service firms have distinct characteristics which add risk and delivery problems to the design and implementation of global service strategies. Service industries are those whose output is not a physical good or product but an intangible 'experience'. Therefore the globalization of services is mostly about the management of intangibles across borders. This underpins an essential difference in the significance of globalization or globalization in services as opposed to manufacturing. Global service delivery is about controlling the quality of the offering at the point of sale to the customer. The expectation of the customer is for consistency and predictability in the delivery of the service in any location worldwide.

Most advanced economies are dominated by services rather by manufacturing businesses. Therefore managing service MNCs effectively matters greatly. The most important focus for service firms, and where a major proportion of resources are allocated, is at the point of contact between the firm and its customers. With manufacturing organizations their major activity occurs away from the eyes and ears of customers. With service firms, their major activity occurs in combination with customers and that is part of the definition of what we mean by a service. This has serious implications for the design of service MNCs. In Chapter 14 we discuss how many major strategy frameworks such as the value chain, or scale and scope economies, need to be understood and applied differently in service organizations. However, the rapid development and application of ICT to services has changed many of the parameters for the design of global service organizations. There are now potential new global value chains in services that allow many of the customer-facing 'front-office' activities in services to be decoupled from the customer and performed as 'back-office' operational activities. There has been an explosion in services outsourcing and off-shoring. This is extremely significant for global strategy in services. If the global value chain for a service MNC can be reconfigured to increase the proportion of back-office activities, then both risks and costs of global strategies for services are greatly lowered. These ICT developments enable the reconfiguration of services value chains which can be disaggregated and activities located geographically for optimum scale, scope or cost advantage just as for product MNCs.

Chapter 15 discusses a set of related issues that are growing in importance and have acquired a central place in global strategy. How can an MNC that, by definition, operates in a huge variety of cultural and legal contexts, be ethical? One of the most difficult problems facing organizations that operate across borders is to decide which ethical standards to adopt: those of the home base country or those of the new country markets. Either choice carries costs and creates problems. Obvious examples of the relative differences in international law and ethics must include attitudes to bribery and corruption; to relative pay and working conditions in home or local markets; to copyrights, patents and intellectual property rights. These are familiar and difficult areas. They are also areas filled with risk for MNCs in managing their global networks, since mistakes or wrong-doing in one national office may discredit or even cause the collapse of the whole global corporation. Chapter 15 analyses many examples of different types of fraud and corruption in which MNCs and governments have become involved. A significant conclusion is that MNCs must ensure robust internal mechanisms to ensure that similar standards operate, and are enforced, at all their global offices.

Another central part of the ethical MNC is growth in concern for sustainability in the behaviour of companies, governments and societies. Sustainability is enacted through three areas: environmental, economic and social sustainability. These are often now known as the 'triple bottom line'. Previously, companies were only expected to report on their economic bottom line, mainly in regard to the relative profitability of their business activities. Now however, as a result of a shift in the profile of CSR and the influence of wider stakeholders, rather than just the shareholders of the organization, companies often report on all three. In other words they should seek to record, and be accountable for, the social and environmental costs of their business in addition to the economic costs and financial performance. Indeed it has been argued that adopting CSR measures, despite the costs involved, may be to the firm's advantage in the longer term. For example, environmental legislation could trigger innovations that may lower the total cost of a product or service or improve productivity. Since there is now evidence of deep public interest and concern in ethical business issues, governance and CSR, Chapter 15 also discusses whether CSR is only what companies have to do to preserve their business reputation and survive in a world where more and more of their behaviour is under a microscope, or perhaps, more positively whether there is virtue in being a virtuous, that is ethical, organization. In other words, it is possible to argue that MNCs benefit commercially from being perceived by consumers as an ethical firm. It is also noteworthy that there is now evidence of CSR spreading as an issue into emerging economy companies as well as developed economy companies.

The final chapter of the book is not intended to be a summary of everything that has gone before but instead to highlight key themes that the authors particularly value. So Chapter 16 emphasizes once again that global strategy occurs within the most sensitive mix of dynamic factors in relation to which no permanent, or even stable, solution is possible. That is why we have argued strongly for a contingency approach to global strategy for international managers. It is the approach that is most likely to succeed in managing MNCs within complex shifting contexts. We emphasize once again that many types of (national) comparative advantage may be relatively short-lived and that therefore governments have a responsibility to invest in and nurture their 'home-base' resources and any strong national industry 'clusters' a country may possess. We revisit the concept of 'institutional voids' in helping MNC managers to understand the additional attention that must be paid to differences in doing business in developed and emerging economies. We also ask to what extent global ethical standards may, or may not, be converging between countries in different parts of the world. Lastly we reflect once again on the significance of knowledge competition, not just in the information industries but as a feature of all industries and organizations. However, although competition to acquire resources such as specialist knowledge and to use them most effectively, is at the heart of global strategy, it is nevertheless right to end by saying that over the longer term, and sometimes in the short term, most sources of advantage fade away.

CHAPTER 12

Cross-border culture: barriers and benefits

LEARNING OBJECTIVES After reading this chapter you should be able to:

■ appreciate the impact of culture upon the design and implementation of global strategies

■ explain how culture can provide a valuable input into the design of a global strategy

■ understand how culture can create barriers to global strategies

■ understand the difference between organizational culture and national culture

■ describe some approaches to managing culture within global strategies

■ explain the relevance of culture in global strategy

■ appreciate that cultural diversity creates both problems and opportunities in global strategy.

INTRODUCTION

Culture is a much used anthropological and sociological concept attempting to capture the intangible, but universal, aspects of human social life. Such aspects of culture usually include: knowledge, values, preferences, habits, customs, practices and behaviour, as well as more tangible things like artistic and architectural artefacts (Keesing, 1974). The ancient temples of Angkor Wat in Cambodia or Kyoto in Japan, the Arc de Triomphe in Paris, the Lincoln Memorial in Washington, US, are all well-known examples of such architectural artefacts. They are not just buildings; they have significant emotional symbolism for the members of their respective societies. Similarly, the values, customs, behaviour and artefacts of modern work organizations represent more than just their face value to organizational members. They have the power to shape attitudes and behaviour within those organizations, both between organizational members and in the organization's relationships with its external stakeholders such as its suppliers, customers, investors, host governments and the general public.

NATIONAL CULTURE AND ORGANIZATIONAL CULTURE

Within the management field, the seminal work which triggered immense interest in the relevance of culture to management practice was that of Hofstede (1980, 1991) arising from his original research across different national divisions of IBM. Hofstede defined culture as 'the collective programming of the mind which distinguishes the members of one group or category of people from another' (1991: 5). This definition focuses on the intangible aspects of culture and stresses that culture is learned and shared within social groups. Most people experience two major groups in their daily lives: the organizations in which they work and the society in which they live. These have given rise, respectively, to the concepts of 'organizational culture' and 'national culture'.

Organizational culture is usually taken to comprise shared values, beliefs and ways of behaving and thinking that are unique to a particular organization. Brown (1995) concluded that 'an organization's culture has a direct and significant impact on performance. Organizational strategies and structures and their implementation are shaped by the assumptions, beliefs and values which we have defined as a culture' (p. 198).

Schein (1985) distinguishes between the assumptions, values and artefacts which together make up an organizational culture. Assumptions are those factors that the members of an organization take for granted and what they believe to be reality. Assumptions therefore influence what members of the organization think and how they behave. Organization members also have values, which are the internal beliefs which they share and to which they attribute intrinsic worth. Artefacts are the tangible, external manifestations of a culture, such as an organization's physical style and dress code, its ceremonies, its stories and myths, its traditions, rewards and punishments. For example, most new technology companies encourage very informal dress codes and patterns of working such as wearing jeans and trainers to work and working totally flexible hours, which contrasts dramatically with most traditional MNCs with more formal dress codes and specific expectations about the structure of the working day.

Organizations may also contain more than one culture. The dominant organizational culture may be shared by all the members of an organization and may act as an integrating mechanism for a diverse set of organization members. However, often there are also organizational subcultures representing different groups within an organization such as the 'techies' versus the accountants; production versus sales; or headquarters versus the business units. Most common in global strategy are the differing organizational subcultures of groups of managers and staff from different geographic locations who either do not wish to work together, or perhaps do not understand each other well enough to do so effectively. Such common circumstances as a merger between MNCs of different parent nationalities, such as the acquisition of Jaguar and Land Rover cars (UK) by Tata Motors, the carmaking division of Tata Group, India's biggest industrial conglomerate in 2008, require procedures for international team-building, and time for such processes as the building of trust to develop. That is made even more complicated in that particular example since these UK car companies had already previously been (unsuccessfully) acquired by Ford Motor Company (US) in 1989 and 2000 respectively. Another change in ownership and nationality will inevitably trigger another set of major cultural and organizational adaptations. Other types of acquisitions such as that by Sony, the Japanese consumer electronics giant, of the Universal Film Studios (US) combine even more complex layers of risk. It involved not only the cultural differences between a Japanese and an American company, but also the very different industry knowledge and traditions of Japanese electronics and American creative 'movie' content, with their very different management styles, attitudes to risk and financial investment models.

Organizational culture may therefore be a positive means of integrating people around common purposes or a source of conflict which threatens the success of international activities when a particular organizational culture is so deeply embedded that it persists beyond a significant structural change, such as a change of ownership. The Sony / Universal merger has been generally regarded as a failure.

12

SOURCE: ADAPTED BY AUTHORS FROM *THE ECONOMIST*, 15 SEPTEMBER 2007

Strategy in Action 12.1 *Cultural compatibility*

Web 2.0 internet sites which let people share information or link up with friends for social networking or video-sharing are booming in China. They are not run by the companies that originated these concepts such as Facebook for social networking and YouTube (now owned by the US search engine company Google) for video-sharing. These companies do not have official Chinese versions. Instead many Chinese web entrepreneurs have created start-ups that imitate the ideas and the graphics used by their originators. YouTube alone has more than 200 copycats in China. Internet investment is booming with the websites localized to suit Chinese tastes. Social networking sites are so popular in China that there is not enough bandwidth to keep up with demand. As a result many of these websites are extremely slow to use. However, one thing that is not a problem is cultural compatibility. Chinese society is built to a very high degree upon personal connections (*guanxi*). Online social networking is a development globally that imitates such relationships on a superficial level and which is therefore attractive to young users, although it lacks the benefit of *guanxi*'s deep family ties. Online social networking may perhaps be seen as a more 'Western' approach to *guanxi* because it is not based on deep personal contact, although it does imitate it.

National cultures are acquired during childhood and reinforced simply by living one's life in a particular society. The strength of national cultures can be illustrated by reflecting on how different they can become in only one or two generations, as in East and West Germany during the period of their separation by the Berlin Wall from 1945 to 1989. Similarly, national cultures may change equally rapidly in one or two generations. Recent research in China (Hewitt, 2008) found that the younger generation which has grown up during the age of economic and social change of the past twenty years, displays more individualistic and materialistic attitudes than the older generation. In global strategy terms this has made the younger generation of Chinese extremely open to new products and services, as discussed in Strategy in Action 12.1.

National cultures are a highly significant element in global strategy. They affect not only obvious things such as the variable meaning of particular brand names or corporate logos in different languages which can sometimes cause unintentional amusement or embarrassment through insufficient understanding of local translations or idiom. National cultures are also part of the mindset which the corporate headquarters brings to its dealings with staff, suppliers, customers or local government agencies in another country. To use Ohmae's (1989a) concept, MNCs may be perceived as either 'insiders' or 'outsiders' by their local employees, their customers and the host government of the country in which they are located (Stopford and Strange, 1991). However, unsurprisingly, different definitions of the key attributes and dimensions of national culture exist. The two best-known typologies for modelling the effect of national culture on the behaviour of individuals in organizations (the aspect which affects strategic thinking) are those of Hofstede's (1980, 1988 and 1991) five-dimensional model and Trompenaars's (1993) seven-dimensional model.

Hofstede's well-known typology of national culture is divided into five dimensions, as summarized in Strategy in Action 12.2. First, *individualism versus collectivism*: individualism describes societies in which the ties between individuals are loose. Each individual is expected to look after himself or herself and his or her immediate family, rather than to belong to strong, cohesive groups such as clans, tribes or extended networks. Second, *power distance*: this captures the extent to which the less powerful members of institutions and organizations within a country expect and accept that power is distributed

12

12

Strategy in Action 12.2 *Hofstede's five core cultural dimensions*

Power distance: The extent to which members of a society accept that power in institutions and organizations is distributed unequally. It identifies some societies as more, and others as less, unequal. Countries with democratic political systems are seen as low power distance cultures.

Uncertainty avoidance: The level of anxiety within members of a society in the face of unstructured or ambiguous situations. Such anxiety tends to be expressed as follows: in aggression and emotion; in institutions promoting conformity; and in beliefs promoting certainty. It describes a society's intolerance for ambiguity: from one extreme of trying to control it at all costs; to the other extreme of accepting and living with it. It identifies some societies as rigid and others as flexible. This often also implies quite different levels of tolerance of differences, e.g. religious, lifestyle, sexual and so on.

Individualism versus collectivism: Individualist societies expect people to take care of themselves and their immediate families only. In collectivist societies, individuals throughout their lives remain emotionally integrated into in-groups, which protect them in exchange for unquestioning loyalty.

Masculinity or femininity: Masculinity-based societies have strongly differentiated sex roles: the masculine role implies achievement, assertiveness, sympathy for the strong and material success. Femininity-based societies have overlapping sex roles characterized by warm relationships, care for the weak, and quality of life. This pair places tough, competitive societies in opposition to tender, supportive societies.

Time orientation: an emphasis on either the long-term or the short-term gratification of needs. The former is more orientated towards future (deferred) gratification of needs. It gives high value to perseverance and thrift, together with ordered relationships and having a sense of shame or honour. Short-term time orientation is much closer to a consumerist culture based on instant gratification of needs.

unequally. Third, *uncertainty avoidance*: this dimension describes the extent to which the members of a culture feel threatened by uncertain, ambiguous or unknown situations. Fourth, *masculinity versus femininity*: the dominance in any given society of a set of values and attitudes usually associated with men (e.g. aggression or competitiveness) in contrast to those usually associated with women (e.g. concern for people and relationships). Fifth, *time-orientation*: an emphasis on either the long-term or the short-term gratification of needs. The former is more oriented towards the future. It gives high value to perseverance and thrift, together with ordered relationships and having a sense of shame or honour. This dimension emerged from research among Chinese populations (Hofstede and Bond, 1988).

Trompenaars's typology of national culture has seven dimensions. First, *universalism versus particularism*: which means always applying a standard rule as opposed to deciding on the basis of the specific case. Second, *individualism versus collectivism*: whether people regard themselves primarily as individuals or primarily as part of a group or community. Third, *neutral versus emotional*: the importance attached to being objective and detached as opposed to allowing emotions to affect one's judgement and decisions. Fourth, *specific versus diffuse*: confining business to the contractual as opposed to allowing personal involvements also. Fifth, *achievement versus ascription*: evaluating people on merit and achievement as opposed to evaluating them according to background and connections. Sixth, *attitudes towards time*: having an orientation towards the future as opposed to an orientation to the past; and how the relationship between past, present and future is viewed. Seventh, *attitudes towards the environment*: the view that individuals can shape the environment and other people ('inner-directed'), as opposed to the view that we have to live in harmony with the environment and with other people and should therefore behave in accordance with these considerations ('outer-directed').

While there are some obvious similarities between Hofstede's and Trompenaars's two well-known typologies, such as time-orientation and individualism / collectivism, our concern in international strategy is to understand the effects such national cultural differences may have on organizational behaviour and strategic thinking, rather than conduct a detailed comparison of the typologies themselves. What these typologies do is to provide us with a rationale for understanding different behaviours, thought processes and responses. These may be either among colleagues of different backgrounds working for the same companies or consumer behaviour within different markets for our products and services. Global managers should never assume common meaning or understanding. They should always start from the assumption that basic differences in perception and understanding exist that need to be explored and shared. Hofstede's or Trompenaars's typologies give managers a way of framing such differences. Trompenaars's fourth and fifth dimensions may be helpful in understanding the unfortunate set of business decisions described in Strategy in Action 12.3. The significance of these dimensions may also shift and change over time as the societies themselves shift and change economically, socially and politically.

Strategy in Action 12.3 *Problems of trust*

Trust is important in all business relationships. However, the bases of trust vary in different cultures. In Japan, reputation and long-term relationships are more important than legal arrangements. This is almost the opposite to the situation in Anglo-Saxon companies where the culture is closer to mistrust, with all transactions being very tightly legally monitored and controlled. The number of corporate lawyers in Japan is very low compared with other major world financial centres and the number of business frauds is also low.

Given these characteristics, it makes a recent case of fraud involving the American bank Lehman Brothers and a highly respected large Japanese trading house Marubeni all the more noteworthy. Teams from both parties met several times at Marubeni's prestigious headquarters to arrange terms for a bridging loan. A complex agreement was reached whereby Lehman provided over $350 million in financing to a small firm with ties to Marubeni. Marubeni agreed to guarantee repayment.

However, when Lehman contacted Marubeni after a payment was missed, Marubeni found all contracts supposedly signed by a Marubeni director to be forgeries and the manager who had met with Lehman to be an imposter. Two Marubeni employees involved in negotiating the deal have been fired but otherwise Marubeni has refused to repay Lehman the $350 million and Lehman is suing Marubeni for that amount.

Who is at fault? Undoubtedly the due diligence checks that the Lehman executives performed regarding this deal were far more lenient than they would have been for an equivalent American deal of this type. How far was this because Lehman accepted different standards of trust and behaviour from a Japanese company?

Indeed Japan's high-trust business culture provides many benefits to all parties. However, global standards and practices are much more formal. The more Japan's financial deals are increasingly occurring within the global finance domain, the more its informal ties of trust are likely to be replaced by more formal legal and administrative ones.

SOURCE: ADAPTED BY AUTHORS FROM *THE ECONOMIST*, 26 APRIL 2008

12

WHY CULTURE IS RELEVANT TO GLOBAL STRATEGY

MNC strategies bring together people from different national cultures into organizations within which they are expected to develop a working relationship. These MNC staff may themselves have been recruited from national organizations or overseas subsidiaries which have their own distinctive organizational cultures. Thus Forsgren et al., (1995) describe the impact of geographic location of a subsidiary on its power relations with corporate headquarters. They stress that the decisions of overseas subsidiary managers must be understood to be based 'on local or contextual rationality' (Forsgren et al. 1995: 488).

The MNC may hope to benefit from such cultural diversity among its staff, especially from their national marketplace knowledge. In all global strategy decisions such as new product development for overseas markets, many aspects of market entry strategy, the ability to carry out processes of negotiation and contracting, managing relationships with customers, suppliers, distributors, even whether to grow by acquisition or organically, and so on, the MNC needs to understand the people and the market and the institutions that it is dealing with. The MNC organizational culture will hope to gather some of that understanding from the distinct national cultures of its individual staff. However, sharing of knowledge and subsequent learning within the organization cannot take place until national cultural differences are understood, and any possible barriers to adaptation or integration have been removed or at least reduced.

The GLOBE Study

Some major recent research into aspects of organizational and national culture and the relationship between them has come out of the GLOBE research project. Its findings can add to our understanding of cultural integration problems arising from diversity within MNCs.

GLOBE stands for 'the Global Leadership and Organizational Effectiveness' research programme. GLOBE is a long-term research programme designed to develop and test the relationship between culture and social, organizational and leadership effectiveness. It has been a huge undertaking. A team of 160 scholars have worked together since 1994 studying societal culture and organizational culture in 62 countries. House et al. (2004) reported the findings of the first two phases of the GLOBE project. Their book is based on the results of surveys of over 17,000 middle managers in three industries: banking; food processing and telecommunications. GLOBE is a truly cross-cultural research programme. Some of the articles published from this research (e.g. Waldman et al., 2006) list 36 authors from the cross-country research teams. It has been a remarkable effort. In Waldman et al. (2006), data from 561 companies located in 15 countries were reported. Compared to Hofstede's original research which took place on only one company (IBM), although in a great many of its locations and offices worldwide, the sheer scale and diversity of the GLOBE data are noteworthy.

As a flavour of the types of conclusions arising from the GLOBE research is their discussion of the relationship between national (societal) culture and managers' attitudes to CSR (corporate social responsibility), which GLOBE defined as including: shareholders / owners; stakeholders; and the wider community. They found that in high power distance cultures (see Strategy in Action 12.2 for definitions) managers tended to devalue all aspects of CSR. The GLOBE discussion suggests that: 'When there is a strong belief in society that there should be distance among people in terms of power, relatively high-level managers who have the power, may be more self-centred or lacking in concern for shareholders / owners, broader stakeholder groups and the community / society as a whole as they make decisions' (Waldman et al., 2006: 834). They further comment that these findings may raise concerns for proponents of CSR in a global context, since they point towards power distance variables as a strong cultural predictor of managerial decision-making in regard to stakeholder CSR.

The findings suggest that cultures with stronger power distance values may lead managers to show little concern for such stakeholders as employees, environmentalists and customers. Their results also show that managers in wealthier countries are clearly less inclined to think about the welfare of the wider community or society in their decision-making. A key implication for MNCs from these results is that while stakeholder-based CSR values and policies of the MNC at the firm level might be strong, and this might reflect the home country's high institutional collectivism and low power distance (see Strategy in Action 12.2), managers in a subsidiary country might have weaker stakeholder CSR values in line with that country's weak institutional collectivism and high power distance. In other words, the MNC corporate values and the subsidiary manager's values will diverge. That is likely to mean that implementation of the parent MNC's CSR policy will also be weak.

The GLOBE versus Hofstede debate

One of the extraordinary things that has come out of the GLOBE project has been a big fight (in academic terms at least) between the GLOBE team and Geert Hofstede himself. It is to be found in a Special Issue of the *Journal of International Business Studies*, Vol. 37 No. 6 in 2006 (see Javidan et al., 2006 and other articles in the same issue of the journal). Hofstede is very critical of GLOBE. The criticisms focus on research methodology and definitions and the general approach to the research. It is worth just giving a small flavour of this debate here. We quote part of Javidan et al.'s (2006: 910) response to Hofstede's criticisms:

> To his well-deserved credit, Geert Hofstede is among the pioneers of research in cross-cultural psychology and international management. However, the overwhelming influence of his 1980 book, based on his IBM consulting project, has perhaps made it too easy for other researchers to use his culture dimensions and associated scores in an uncritical manner. This . . . perpetuates a prevalent and false sense of confidence that all dimensions of national culture have been discovered. GLOBE has proved otherwise . . . Researchers tend to assume that . . . the country characteristics obtained by Hofstede some 35 years ago . . . and the prevalent use of his constructs . . . seems to be a tradition that can only be called *Hofstedian hegemony*. No single researcher or research team should own the cross-cultural research field!

As academic fights go, that is pretty strong language. It has all been most enjoyable.

CULTURAL BARRIERS IN GLOBAL STRATEGY

Finding ways of bridging distinctive organizational and national cultures which individuals and groups bring to MNCs is essential to the effective functioning of the MNC. National cultural differences can display themselves either as simple misunderstandings or at the more fundamental level of conflicts in values (Child et al., 2000). Misunderstandings about language and about the interpretation of behaviour are common. What is understood as humorous or ironic in one language, may be taken literally in another. Although in a fast-changing world some of these stereotypes may no longer be so typical, behaviour is still likely to be interpreted in contrasting ways by people from different national cultures. These may lead to misunderstandings or give great offence. Eye contact can signify respect in one culture but a lack of it in another. Physical touching may denote warmth in one culture and an unacceptable invasion of personal privacy in another. In Scandinavian culture it is polite to wait until another person has finished speaking before speaking oneself. In East Asian societies it is a mark of respect to pause before replying, thus indicating that what the other person has said is deserving of careful consideration.

Such external cultural differences, once they are appreciated, may be dealt with by MNCs briefing staff properly and encouraging a healthy attitude of mutual respect. However, beyond such surface behavioural factors, deeper cultural values may generate far more serious differences. Let us consider the implications of the first two of Trompenaars' (1993) dimensions of national culture: universalism versus particularism and individualism versus collectivism. As stated earlier, the definitions for these two dimensions are:

■ *Universalism versus particularism* – always applying a standard rule as opposed to deciding on the basis of the specific case.

■ *Individualism versus collectivism* – whether people regard themselves primarily as individuals or primarily as part of a group or community.

Decision-making on the basis of personal relationships is acceptable in *particularistic* societies but not acceptable in *universalistic* ones. So, in a particularistic culture, people will tend to support friends and relatives rather than an abstract universalist principle such as 'the rule of law'. Trompenaars questioned around 15,000 employees in many different countries (75 per cent managers) about types of personal decisions likely to be made in different circumstances. He found the 'Anglo-Saxon' and 'northern' (Australia, Canada, Denmark, Finland, (West) Germany, Ireland, Japan, Norway, Sweden, Switzerland, UK, US) countries to be the most universalistic; while China, South Korea, Indonesia, Russia, Venezuela and the former Yugoslavia, were the most particularistic countries. How then would this affect the managerial relationships or customer relations between a German and a Chinese company, or between the joint German and Chinese partners in a German joint venture in China, or indeed between the German managers of their own Chinese subsidiary? The two groups are likely to be suspicious of each other. The (German / Canadian / Danish / etc.) universalists would regard the other group as untrustworthy 'because they always help their friends first' and the (Chinese / Korean / Venezuelan / etc.) particularists would regard the universalists as untrustworthy because 'they would not even help a friend'. The consequences of these types of universalist / particularist differences are discussed in the research on strategic alliances cited in Chapter 10. It shows the differences in criteria used in selection of an alliance partner by Chinese compared to their foreign partners. Most foreign companies selected on the (universalist) basis of the best available partner, according to their requirements, regardless of any personal connections they might have with existing managers or staff. Indeed, such personal connections were frowned upon as being potentially unethical, unfair or even corrupt. In contrast, Chinese companies tended to favour the recruitment of family members, since it is a (particularist) Chinese social norm that members of an extended family should help each other, and managers also believe that recruitment on the basis of personal connections will encourage the employees concerned to be loyal members of the organization.

As far as *individualism* and *collectivism* are concerned, it is the highly industrialized countries which have high degrees of individualism, that is the 'Anglo-Saxon' nations; the Netherlands; some of Eastern Europe; although Austria and Germany have less individualistic attitudes than other West European countries. Individualistic cultures' prime orientation is towards the self rather than the group or the community. Collectivism is stronger in the developing economies and in those sharing a Chinese cultural heritage, as discussed in Strategy in Action 12.4. Interestingly, Hampden-Turner and Trompenaars (1993) found Japan to be the most collectivist among the highly industrialized countries.

Individualism and *collectivism* generate different management styles. Individualistic cultures value quick decisions, individual responsibility, expression of individual views and goals, competition between people for recognition and advancement, and individual incentives. Collectivist cultures have other decision-making processes. They value consultation to gain consent before decisions are made, group responsibility, sharing common organizational objectives, high levels of personal and departmental co-operation, and a system of rewards that does not single out individuals. The history of MNC–subsidiary relationships is littered with examples of misunderstandings arising from such differences. The contrast between Japanese, Middle Eastern and Anglo-Saxon styles of negotiation and even what each regards as a 'successful' outcome, differ widely. It is perhaps not surprising that process

Strategy in Action 12.4 *Contrasting assumptions: Western and Asian versions of capitalism and competition – individualism versus collectivism*

It is important to understand the effect of cultural, institutional and regulatory contexts on strategic decision-making and managerial mindsets. Genuine differences in context and culture do have a profound influence on Asian and Western mindsets. They are in many ways direct opposites in assumptions and practice. There are differences in the underlying assumptions between Asian and Western notions of industries and markets and therefore in the contrasting organizations, values, social relations and ultimately, strategies, that each generates (Woolsey Biggart and Hamilton, 1992). The assumptions of Western economic individualism and its resultant social, legal and institutional structures are that social relations or personal networks in a market lead only to such uncompetitive practices as price-fixing and various other forms of collusion. In other words, the Western view is that social relations and economic relations must be kept strictly separate. Individual competence is seen as the just way of selecting and rewarding people and organizations. Personal relations in the workplace or between organizational members are seen as collusion and favouritism.

By contrast, Asian economies are organized through social networks. Western economies have legal and regulatory frameworks for ensuring autonomy and separateness.

Asian economies have institutions that encourage and maintain ties and links between people and groups. In other words, Asian nations have built economic policies around the existence of social relations among market actors. What many Western governments, organizations or managers regard as impediments to free trade, is an ethnocentric view of the economic institutions of capitalism. Asian history and experience has led to the institutionalization of social networks in governments and organizations. The beliefs and institutions of individual autonomy are deeply Western in origin and history. The pervasiveness of networks (social, economic, family, organizational and institutional) is equally deeply Asian. The implications for managerial practice and strategic thinking and decision-making (and misunderstanding) are profound.

Nevertheless, it is only fair to add that there is sometimes a difference between what actually happens and what is supposed to happen. For example, such things as 'cronyism' and 'old boy' networks do exist in Western countries. However, probably the most significant point of contrast is that such networks are frowned upon and are censured and possibly illegal in Western societies, whereas they are regarded as normal and desirable in Asian ones.

12

innovations such as total quality management (TQM) or just-in-time (JIT) production and distribution systems were created in an individualist culture (US), but adopted first and made to work effectively in a collectivist culture (Japan). Even in cross-cultural strategic alliances these individualist / collectivist cultural differences make themselves felt. As we have discussed in Chapter 10, some Japanese / US alliances came under strain because the Japanese learned more from them than did their American partners. Casson's (1995) explanation of this outcome is subtle. He suggests that the difference in learning benefit is due, at least in part, to cultural differences. The individualism and competitiveness of the Americans generated a sense of mistrust which prevented them from learning within the alliance, while the high-trust Japanese were more open to learning from their alliance partners, and did so notably more successfully.

Given the national cultural differences already discussed, we might expect there to be significant differences in management practices in different countries. Strategy in Action 12.5 lists the dominant management characteristics of the main industrialized nations. We may particularly note the extreme contrast between US and Japanese practice.

It may be helpful to illustrate Hofstede's (1980 and 1991) and Hampden-Turner and Trompenaars (1993) cultural dimensions by applying them to the interpretation of one or two of the cultural comparisons in management practices outlined in Strategy in Action 12.5. For example, the strong technical emphasis within German management results in a generally high level of technical training for both managers and employees. More German managers have an engineering background than in the other countries, and a graduate degree is very important for advancement. This production orientation within the German system certainly contrasts strongly with the finance-dominated British and American approaches to management and managerial training and development.

Culturally, the Germans emerge from surveys as tending to have high levels of uncertainty avoidance and they also tend to score highly on Hofstede's measure of 'power distance' (Hofstede, 1991).

Strategy in Action 12.5 *Characteristics of different national management practices*

Japanese management practice
Policies and practices associated with Japanese companies are:

■ Long-term orientation
- strategic rather than financial
- emphasis on growth
- long-term employment commitment

■ Rewards based primarily on seniority and superior's evaluation

■ Internal training and seniority system; heavy investment in training

■ Collective orientation
- collective participation in, and responsibility for, decision-making and knowledge creation

■ Flexible tasks with low specialization

■ Emphasis on lean production and continuous improvement.

Management practice in the US
Policies and practices associated with US companies are:

■ Short-term financial orientation

■ Rewards related to specific performance indicators

■ High rate of job change and inter-company mobility

■ Rationalist approach: emphasis on analysis and planning

■ Reliance on formalization and systems

■ Delegation down extended hierarchies.

German management practice
While the picture of German management policies and practices is not so clear-cut as that portrayed for American and Japanese management (for example there are differences in sampling large versus Mittelstand, that is medium-sized, firms), its main characteristics are the following:

■ Long-term business orientation
- towards production improvement rather than short-term profit distribution
- but orientation towards employment is not necessarily long-term

■ Strong technical and production emphasis, including a substantial investment in training

SOURCE: CHILD, FAULKNER AND PITKETHLY (2000)

- Managers and staff tend to remain within one functional area during their career

- Emphasis on planning, procedures and rules

- Preference for participation and collective action.

French management practice

France is also a difficult country to categorize, and the same applies to its management practice. Hampden-Turner and Trompenaars' (1993: 333) comment that 'France defies easy categorization. It requires a sense of irony, for which the French are famous, to make sense of seemingly contradictory results.' Bearing this caution in mind, the policies and practices which have been described of French companies are:

- Strategic rather than financial orientation

- Tall organizational hierarchies, with a large proportion of managerial personnel

- High degree of specialization

- Widespread use of written media

- Individual rather than collective working and decision-making

- Centralization of decision-making.

UK management practice

Policies and practices associated with British companies have some similarity with those associated with US companies, but with far less emphasis on formal systems and records:

- Short-term financial orientation

- Large general management superstructures

- Low level of functional specialization

- High mobility of managers between functions

- Use of formal meetings, especially committees

- Interactive informality – limited formal and paper-based reporting

- Limited importance attached to standard operating systems.

This is associated with attaching a high value to stability and has been interpreted as a main reason why in German organizations there tends to be a strong orientation to the use and adherence to rules, and a heavy stress on control procedures (Hampden-Turner and Trompenaars, 1993). There are many checks and balances within the German corporate system against managerial freedom of action. For example, there are two boards of directors, an executive board and a supervisory board which contains a significant representation from trade unions. As with the Japanese, loyalty is stressed, and in-house training emphasized. Germans are said to prefer group participation and collective action, in contrast to Anglo-Saxon individualism (Hampden-Turner and Trompenaars, 1993). These factors point to quite a strong collective orientation which has more in common with Japanese management practice than that of France, the US or the UK. Indeed a key characteristic of the French management system lies in the elite Grandes Ecoles system in which the top tier of French managers has generally been educated. This leads to strong networks connecting the top tiers of French companies and government departments. French companies often combine a paradoxical mixture of feudal-paternal and rational-legal-bureaucratic approach to management. French managers and employees score fairly high on Hofstede's scale of power distance (Hofstede, 1991), with decision-making rather concentrated towards the top of company hierarchies. This may be one of the reasons for the conservatism of many French MNCs within the global economy, although with pressure from high levels of global competition this may be slowly beginning to change.

UK management practice has tended to reflect the fact that industry in general, and technical qualifications such as engineering in particular, have historically been of relatively low status in Britain. Indeed there has been a lower level of education among British managers generally when compared to other industrial countries. In contrast to the US, the MBA qualification is still regarded less favourably in the UK than accounting and finance qualifications as a route to senior management roles. It is not surprising then that an emphasis on short-term financial targets has dominated the UK managerial mindset.

PROBLEMS WITH CULTURE IN GLOBAL STRATEGY

Cultural differences increase the chances of mutual misunderstanding and even personal offence. They therefore have to be transcended before a basis for trust can be established. That is usually a time-consuming process. Cultural distance may be associated with a preference for particular types of overseas market entry, that is those that offer MNCs higher control. For example, US manufacturing MNCs often prefer FDI to licensing as their preferred mode of new foreign market entry, because FDI allows for higher levels of monitoring and higher levels of interaction with overseas staff than does licensing. The issue at stake here is one of trust. Hofstede (1980) found that the dimension of power distance (i.e. the extent to which the less powerful members of institutions and organizations within a country expect and accept that power is distributed unequally) is also about societal trust. He found that power-distant societies exhibited low interpersonal trust and a high need for controls on the behaviour of individuals, especially hierarchical organizational controls.

Acceptance of such hierarchical monitoring varies across cultures. Such cultural differences may also lead to operational problems. Such problems are common, particularly in sensitive situations such as MNC mergers or cross-border acquisitions. The $13 billion merger in 2006 between two large telecommunications equipment companies Alcatel of France and Lucent of the US had been discussed on and off since 2001. Although the merger made sense strategically, technologically and financially, there had been long-standing awareness of the difficulties that would be faced in merging the two cultures. The financial press at the time, such as the *International Herald Tribune* (April 2006), openly discussed the fact that it would be the 'melding of cultures' which would be key to the success of the merger. The CEO of Lucent, Patricia Russo was to become chief executive of the combined company and to be based in France, but she did not speak French. Also, the financial case for the merger included $1.7 billion per year of cost savings to be achieved by 8,800 job cuts worldwide. These would be both very politically sensitive in France and also bitterly resented. Fear and mistrust are frequently generated in such situations as to what the future may hold for the staff of the acquired company and are exacerbated by the misinterpretation of signals between acquirers and acquired. Cultural differences will reinforce this unless considerable effort is made to overcome them.

Other common everyday areas of MNC life that require intensive effort at cultural accommodation are the relationships between parent and wholly owned overseas subsidiaries. Such cultural accomodation may require acceptance of what appear to be inefficiencies in the managerial practices of their subsidiaries. At a very general level, whereas a Western company is likely to operate individualistic, universalistic and short-term performance norms, an East Asian company is likely to operate collectivist, particularist and longer-term performance norms. The Western parent may view the East Asian subsidiary as inefficient because it sees what appear to be protracted decision-making processes and a lack of individual accountability and performance measurement. East Asian managers will take into account the employee's commitment and loyalty to the company, as evaluated by their manager, rather than apparently more objective information. Western managers are expected to take little account of personal circumstances, but to evaluate and reward in terms of purely task-specific criteria. These are common areas of misunderstanding. Some of the genuine complexity of the cultural issues faced in cross-border operations is captured in the description of the Castech Mexican joint venture in Strategy in Action 12.6.

Strategy in Action 12.6 *Cultural accommodation at Castech, Mexico*

Established in 1999, Castech was formed as a Mexican / German Joint Venture (JV) to design and manufacture aluminium engine blocks and cylinder heads, primarily for the US market. The partners were Grupo Industrial Saltillo (GIS), a large engineering company located in Saltillo in northern Mexico and VAW, a subsidiary of the German utility and engineering company VIAG, which had expertise in aluminium casting for the motor industry. The Mexican parent, GIS, was founded in 1928 and floated on the Mexican stock market in 1976. The company today operates in four business areas: aluminium blocks and heads; metal and automotive parts; building products; and home products. In 2002 the German parent VAW was purchased by Norsk Hydo, the part state-owned Norwegian oil, aluminium and fertilizer company. It is now a Mexican / Norwegian / German JV.

Despite successful production and expansion, Castech has faced a range of management challenges. It operates in a highly competitive sector (automobile parts) dominated by a small number of large customers. It is answerable to two parents with overlapping, but not identical, strategic objectives. It integrates a range of national cultures in its staffing and direction. And it is dependent on NAFTA.

The Castech JV
Castech started construction in 1999 and began production in 2000. Initial contracts were for the production of aluminium cylinder heads for General Motors (GM) of the US. Sales in 2002 were US$709 million, of which US$406 million was within Mexico and US$303 million exported within NAFTA. Of the exports, 79 per cent came from automotive products. Earnings before interest, tax, depreciation and amortization (EBITDA) were US$140 million. From 2003, production was diversified into the manufacture of aluminium engine blocks, which have higher margins than cylinder heads.

The motor industry is rapidly replacing iron with aluminium in engine manufacture, to reduce weight. The new material brings with it new challenges: while the engine design is becoming more sophisticated, the physical structure of the engine parts is increasingly complex. Demands for improved fuel efficiency and reduced pollution must be achieved against shorter time scales, with increasing standards of safety and environmental performance, and in competition with well-established in-house and independent suppliers.

Norsk Hydro (Annual Report 2002)
Owned 43 per cent by the Norwegian government, Norsk Hydro (NH) describes its business purpose as follows: 'We deliver oil and energy, aluminium and plant nutrients. We supply natural gas and electricity to drive industry and heat and light homes, aluminium to build structures, petroleum to fuel and lubricate cars, and fertilizers to cultivate food.'

It is therefore a business focused on extractive industries. It has shown little growth in revenues over the past three years, with declining profitability. It is sensitive to movement in raw material prices, and appears to have generated little organic growth. However, NH actively uses acquisition for growth and to move into higher value-added businesses. The acquisition of VAW from its German parent VIAG, in 2002, brought its share in Castech.

The joint venture (JV)
VAW had a leading position in the European market but this was mature and offered little prospect of growth; so they needed to enter the US market. Having explored opportunities in the US, they decided to invest in Mexico and chose GIS as their potential partner. GIS had a strong US market presence in iron casting, but this market was declining. GIS needed to get access to aluminium technology to sustain and grow their

12

automotive market. VAW was an obvious suitable partner. There was little trust between the JV partners initially, and every issue was interpreted as an attempt by one partner to gain advantage over the other. Insistence that employees were employed by Castech (rather than by the JV parents) helped resolve this.

The JV was established on the basis of a contract to develop and manufacture V8 heads for GM. This rapidly fell behind schedule, and then GM brought the delivery date forward by three months. Failure to meet this contract would have meant the end of the JV. But Castech delivered, met the quality and quantity targets and was awarded GM supplier of year prize in 2000. Thus began a virtuous circle: the JV became source of pride for both partners, GM placed orders for new products, the partners were willing to make capital investments, staff were motivated and good staff retained.

VAW was part of the German conglomerate VIAG and was not a core business. The acquisition of VAW by NH allowed them to become no 3 in the world and no 2 in Europe in aluminium; it also gave them entry to the US market.

The JV needs to broaden the customer base, but this has to be part of a controlled expansion within available resources and capabilities. A presence in S or SE Asia or China will be necessary to compete in Japan. But the JV parents are not willing to undertake this risk of new market entry yet.

JV learning and knowledge transfer

GIS is learning aluminium casting technology from Europe and is developing considerable expertise in implementation. NH has six foundries and carries out comparative benchmarking: Castech came first in seven out of ten measures, and second in the other three.

While VAW only saw Mexico as a passive recipient of German technology, there have been positive changes since NH took over. The JV CEO is now invited to join in regular discussions with other foundries in Europe. The Norwegian manager responsible for continuous improvement spends time in Mexico to identify good practice. Technical staff from the JV are now invited to attend meetings in Europe (Germany).

Cultural issues

Strong differences exist between NH and VAW. For NH safety is the first priority and is the principal KPI for Marco Barraza (the Castech CEO). The JV has a worse safety record not only than Hydro but also than GIS. Castech currently employs 8 expatriates: 3 UK (two of whom are now on local terms), 2 French, 1 German, 1 Canadian (in Canada) and 1 Australian (in Australia). They are used to fill specific functions, provide skills and expertise, and develop cultural links. Mexican staff visit Europe at present only for training. Mexican managers could be asked to work in Europe at some point, although they are too important in Mexico to be released yet. Although NH strategy implementation is top down, it involves discussion at several stages. Since Mexican culture is to work in teams, this consultative approach and sits more easily with the participative Norwegian management style than the top-down German style.

NAFTA issues

Castech's reliance on the US market may not be politically sustainable in the long term. Hence it is important to begin to think about diversifying outside the NAFTA market. Benefits from NAFTA include Castech having to operate to US environmental standards, which will require considerable investment. Already compliance with ISO 14,000 is required in order to be able to supply US customers. Castech is planning to work to European standards, which are higher than those of the US.

SOURCE: GIS (WEBSITE PRESENTATION TO SANTANDER INVESTMENT; NOTIGIS EDICION ESPECIAL MAY 2003)

12

In terms of the integration process Norsk Hydro's (NH) Norwegian management style has worked well with local Mexican teams and as part of NH's benchmarking process, the Norwegian manager responsible for continuous improvement spends time in Mexico to identify good practice. In Castech one of the reasons that the JV was a success was that the JV partners learned to work well together after a difficult start. However, it became easier once the German partner (VAW) was taken over by a Norwegian company, with whose consultative managerial style and values the Mexican company was more comfortable.

Organizational interactions, especially cross-cultural ones, can result in misunderstandings and conflict. This conflict is often made worse not only by differences in cultural styles, but also by people's ignorance of such differences. People tend to react negatively to behaviour that deviates from their own norms and standards, and accurate perception is often reduced because people tend to interpret the behaviour of others from their own perspective. In moving across borders, MNC managers can only operate effectively if they learn to understand and work within their host environment.

MNCs are communication-intensive and relationship-dependent, and they therefore cannot function well if they are internally divided by substantial cultural barriers. If cultural distance is not reduced, or at least channelled into a form that avoids conflict, it is likely to give rise to serious breakdowns in communication of information and integration. This may have mattered less in the multidomestic and international exporter types of MNC, where little cross-border integration was being attempted. It was, however, critical in global and transnational MNCs, where cross-border integration of processes, operations and information are mandatory. In the current complex, networked and integrated forms of MNC, these processes for blending understanding within the various parts of the organization are critical and unavoidable.

BENEFITTING FROM CULTURAL DIFFERENCES

Although these international differences in management practice can create many difficulties in the management of MNCs, cultural diversity also creates opportunities to use the competences and knowledge contained in different cultures for the benefit of the MNC as a whole. Recognition by some Western MNCs of the value attached to collectivism in the host society can, for example, result in a modification of human resource management (HRM) policies in ways that might increase the commitment of local employees (e.g. from individual to group assessment and reward). Indeed these modifications may, in time, be extended to the 'home' staff.

MNCs seek to benefit from having a diversity of cultures among its organizational members. At best this should provide a stimulus to learning and sensitivity to local markets. This does not happen by accident. Organizational cultures need to be managed so that they become forces for integration rather than division. There is a parallel here with effective organizational learning (discussed further in Chapter 13). Learning arises from synthesis: selecting strands from the diversity present within the organization and integrating them to create shared understandings and eventually a shared commitment. Both the management of culture and of learning within MNCs require a reconciliation and integration of differences.

Corporate cultures can be an important resource available to the leaders of organizations (Hampden-Turner, 1990; Brown, 1995). They can promote social cohesion and act as the 'glue' that bonds an organization together. Because a shared culture encourages people to accept common goals and to identify with each other, it can also facilitate the processes of co-ordination and control within a complex organization. MNCs are by nature very complex organizations. By giving the members of such organizations some common reference points and shared ways of interpreting their working reality, a common organizational culture can reduce uncertainty and promote cross-border consistency of best practice, both internally (across departments or country groupings) and externally (to customers and other stakeholders). In providing meaning to their work and to their membership of an organization, an appropriate and cohesive culture can also be an important source of motivation for employees.

MANAGING CULTURAL DIVERSITY WITHIN GLOBAL STRATEGY

Cultural diversity is becoming commonplace with regionalization, globalization and the continually increasing levels of international trade. How MNCs manage to achieve integration between their various national and global divisions, or successfully integrate a cross-border acquisition, or even get an internal multicultural team to work together effectively, depends on their ability to achieve a 'fit' between these various cultures. 'Fit' refers to the extent to which different cultures are brought into a workable relationship that permits them to operate without undue misunderstanding and tension between their divisions, their alliance partners, their businesses or their staff teams.

The active management of cultural diversity is aimed at the achievement of a 'cultural fit' between groups, divisions or teams. Cultural fit means that cultures are combined in a mutually acceptable manner. 'Fit' does not necessarily mean integration of the cultures; there may be other ways in which they can be accommodated. There are a number of broad options for the management of cultural diversity. Some will provide a better cultural fit than others.

The two basic choices in the management of MNC cultural diversity are:

1 whether headquarters MNC culture should *dominate* or whether to strive for a balance of contributions from the subsidiaries' cultures;

2 whether to attempt an *integration* of headquarters' / subsidiaries' cultures (with the aim of deriving synergy from them) or to segregate the various subsidiary cultures (with the aim of avoiding possible conflict and reducing the effort devoted toward cultural management).

These two dimensions of choice give rise to the four broad possibilities shown in Figure 12.1. Following Perlmutter (1969) we have drawn on his well-known cultural typology which offers the following MNC organizational types:

> *Ethnocentric* – all key positions filled by parent company nationals.
> *Polycentric* – host country managers in domestic subsidiaries while parent company nationals dominate HQ.
> *Geocentric* – best people for jobs regardless of nationality.

Perlmutter has thus provided the vocabulary for describing our four MNC options given in Figure 12.1. The first three are all options offering a basis for cultural fit, though not generating the same level of benefit from the different cultures. The fourth possibility is one of failure, likely to lead to parent–subsidiary conflict and, at best, sub-optimal performance.

1 *Geocentric* – a policy aimed at cultural integration of both or all headquarter / subsidiary cultures.

2 *Ethnocentric* – a policy aimed at cultural integration on the basis of dominance by the headquarters' culture.

FIGURE 12.1 Management of cultural diversity in MNCs: four options

Domination by headquarters		Integration	
		Yes	**No**
	No	Geocentric	Polycentric
	Yes	Ethnocentric	Culture clash

Source: *Adapted from Tung (1993), Figure 1*

3 *Polycentric* – a policy aimed at an acceptable balance between the influence within the MNC of various subsidiary / divisional cultures, but not striving for integration between them.

4 *Culture clash* – which may occur when headquarters seeks domination but fails to secure integration or acceptance.

Geocentric aims at achieving the fullest possible fit between cultures. It is the policy best suited to optimizing and promoting learning between the different constituent parts of the MNC. With synergy, elements from each participant culture are combined to bring about an effective management system and deployment of resources. The idea of synergy is that the whole is greater than the sum of its parts. The key idea is that the 'positive aspects of the various cultures are preserved, combined, and expanded upon to create a new whole' (Tung, 1993: 465). The achievement of synergy does not ignore or suppress cultural differences, but requires that time and effort be devoted to discussing them openly.

An *ethnocentric* policy is one that aims at integration on the basis of dominance by the headquarters' culture. In some circumstances that may be the sensible thing to do. For example, an MNC may be recognized as having a general superiority in technical and managerial know-how from which the whole company and all its subsidiaries could benefit. In these circumstances, an ethnocentric policy may make the best sense.

Polycentric is a policy which aims at an acceptable balance between the cultural inputs of subsidiaries, teams, alliance partners or divisions, but does not attempt any integration or synthesis between them. In an international joint venture, say, one partner may introduce its own systems for production and quality control, while the other partner continues to manage external transactions in the field of supply, distribution and government relations as before. This form of accommodation, though acceptable, clearly can be a sub-optimal solution in other respects. Cultural segregation between subsidiaries means a separation of tasks which each business unit will manage itself. Such an approach obviously reduces the opportunities for mutual learning to a very low level. This was the situation in the earlier stages for Castech when it was poorly managed and poorly integrated within VAW. It may also lead to a poorly integrated and inefficient management system for the MNC as a whole, with unnecesary duplication of effort and with continuing problems due to limited communications, and a sense of rivalry, between different functions within the organization.

Polycentrism may also give rise to personal problems for individual managers who are sent to work in the overseas subsidiary, especially if they are expatriates. It can create difficulties for an expatriate to acquire the local language or understand the behavioural norms of the country where the subsidiary is located. The expatriate and his or her family will tend to be isolated, possibly in their own foreign 'ghetto', with a high chance of family stress and personal failure in the role.

The fourth possibility is *culture clash*. This situation can arise if headquarters attempts to pursue a policy of domination without securing adequate levels of operational co-operation and co-ordination. Tension and conflict will result, with performance adversely affected. Such clashes can develop out of the MNC headquarters (perhaps after an overseas acquisition) unilaterally introducing its own norms and practices, derived from its own culture. If this situation is handled badly, then culture clash, and eventual possible breakdown, is the more likely outcome. This is a surprisingly common situation of either very poorly managed companies or even a complete lack of integration strategies. Divestment is likely to occur in due course after this type of disastrous post-acquisition management process.

ACHIEVING CULTURAL FIT

Much of the responsibility for improving cultural fit within an MNC lies with its chief executive and other senior managers. The senior management team is responsible for generating a sense of common purpose within the organization. The idea of cultural fit only makes sense if some genuine understanding exists among the MNC's managerial groups as to the style and content of the various cultures co-existing within it. Therefore the content of cultures within an MNC need to be assessed, so that actual degrees of difference between them may be appreciated. Only in this way can the MNC harness the resources offered by each culture and attempt to develop realistic policies for constructive integration.

Some cultural attributes are more deeply rooted than others, and although all organizational cultures are supported by 'cultural webs' (Johnson, 1990), these will differ considerably in their responsiveness to change. Johnson (1990) described the cultural web of an organization as consisting of the structures of power and authority, control systems, routines and rituals, symbols, stories and myths which represent the reality to which the members of that organization have become accustomed, and which in turn act to maintain and reinforce its dominant cultural paradigm. Just as the elements of the cultural web for a steel manufacturer or an oil exploration company are likely to be different from those of a law firm or a fashion designer, so will cultural web characteristics vary by nation. For example, within an individualist culture, common organizational stories might include those about organization 'mavericks', that is those individuals who do not conform and who often acquire heroic stature as a result of their non-conformist exploits. Although such mavericks would be more likely to be acceptable in a fashion house than in a bank, unfortunately there have been a large number of cases of such individuals operating outside organizational procedures in the investment arms of large banks or even being encouraged in their risky trading strategies in pursuit of higher revenues for the bank. The resulting appallingly poor risk management has been asserted as one of the reasons for the so-called 'credit crisis' badly affecting the global financial system in 2007 to 2009. In a collectivist culture such stories would make little sense and may be virtually incomprehensible. If they existed at all, they would be more likely described as bad role models rather than organizational heroes.

Such an analysis may be similarly applied to the web of a national culture: its political structures, institutional bodies, rituals, symbols, historical stories, and so on. The general principle here is that the more deeply entrenched the web reinforcing a culture, the greater will be the resistance of its constituent individuals and groups (such as shareholders, financial institutional stakeholders, professional associations, labour representatives, the separate nationalities, government agencies) to cultural change. The more a given culture is perceived by stakeholders to serve their personal interests, the more entrenched it is likely to be. Consider for example the high levels of resistance to changes in employment law affecting job security in France. Unemployment amongst French under-25-year-olds remains at about 25 per cent and is a contributory factor to the numbers of young French people leaving France to look for work elsewhere. Despite this labour market inflexibility in France being considered to be at least partly responsible for the very high levels of unemployment, it remains nevertheless an area that French governments are unable to reform.

The constituent parts of a cultural web will indicate which elements need to be addressed as part of the process of bringing the divergent cultures closer, as in the context of a cross-border acquisition discussed earlier, or in MNC headquarters' managers gradually learning how to help make an overseas subsidiary work effectively. This process of mutual (although asymmetrical) acculturation process has been common for Japanese parent company managers learning how to manage local European or American subsidiaries throughout the 1970s and 1980s. Pure Japanese management systems and practices did not take take root: they were adapted to absorb some of elements of local working practices. Sony was the first Japanese MNC to appoint non-Japanese executives to its board in the 1980s as a major shift in its cultural adaptation processes. This process of cultural adaptation is of course also occurring for European and US firms operating in Japan, East Asia, the Middle East and Africa. The current extensive global expansion amongst Indian, Chinese and Middle Eastern companies will in turn require the same attention to cultural adaptation and learning in order to try to avoid the 'culture clash' outcome.

One interesting area that is often particularly poorly understood in terms of cultural adaptation is that of management control systems. Hofstede (1980) saw accounting as a field in which the technical elements are weak and he therefore argued that we should expect accounting systems to vary along cultural lines. He argued that the less an activity is technically defined, the more it is ruled by values and thus influenced by cultural differences. For example in strong 'uncertainty avoidance' countries (e.g. many Asian and Middle Eastern countries), accounting systems will be more detailed and theoretically based, whereas in weak uncertainty avoidance countries, systems will be more pragmatic. Furthermore, in high 'power distance' countries, accounting and management control systems will tend to be used more frequently to justify the decisions of top management. Hofstede therefore has argued that MNC top-down imposition of HQ accounting and control practices on foreign subsidiaries is likely to lead to problems since they will be interpreted differently according to national values and different cultural characteristics. Furthermore, members of different cultural groups may react differently to the *same* control mechanisms or conversely, may require different control mechanisms to achieve the same behaviour.

Control issues do not come down to simple questions of organizational design. Instead, considerable subtlety is required of MNC senior management in terms of their mindset in deciding on the use of 'soft' informal controls as well as on the implementation of 'hard' control and performance measurement systems. They must also consider cultural and ethnic problems in exerting management control. Hopper et al. (2003) argue that the effects of culture on management accounting must recognize the interaction between subcultures and family sub-units, ethnic groups and traditional status systems. They cite the example, in a gold mine in Ghana, of the miners and the office workers belonging to different ethnic groups, which resulted in conflicts over rewards and supervision. It was difficult for accountants to get their budgets accepted by workers from the other ethnic group.

Expatriate MNC managers often assume that 'Western' norms of legal rationality will prevail, that decisions are based on collective not personal goals, that appointments are made on merit and that employees generally accept the hierarchies of authority. However, in many developing economies, employees' loyalty may lie primarily with their family, village, ethnic or religious group, rather than with their employer. Hopper et al. (2003) argue that this behaviour follows norms based on personal and traditional obligations rather than impersonal market contracts.

These issues present serious problems for MNC managers because it means that the design of management accounting and control systems is inconsistent with employee values. Hopper et al. (2003) argue for better understanding of conflicting cultural expectations concerning the nature of 'rational' management and what loyalty to the organization means to local employees and managers. Such apparently basic assumptions can differ widely across cultures, regions and parts of the same MNC organization.

Achieving personal cultural fit

The cross-cultural adjustment of individual managers is a huge problem for MNCs. Black and Mendenhall (1990) found that between 16 and 40 per cent of all expatriate managers given foreign assignments, ended them early either because of their poor performance or their inability to adjust to the foreign environment. They also found up to 50 per cent of those who stayed were functioning poorly. They estimated the direct costs of failed expatriate assignments to US MNCs at over $2 billion a year. This estimate did not include intangible costs such as reputation effects or loss of potential business. Their data is now approximately twenty years old and in the intervening period, both the volume of international trade and the frequency of such international assignments and their associated costs have only risen.

Two policies frequently adopted to reduce such adjustment problems are: selecting people for such assignments who have previous international experience and anticipatory training. Neither policy has been shown to be universally effective. For example, for executives with experience of previous international roles, the nature of that previous experience is relevant. Many expatriate managers and their families simply withdraw into an expatriate community, thus avoiding much real cross-cultural contact.

12

Such expatriate ghettos not only prevent any real adjustment, they also may encourage the wholesale application of 'home' practices (i.e. doing things according to the expatriate's own national or organizational norms). MNCs need to choose staff for such roles who have have demonstrated a positive approach during their previous experience.

Anticipatory training must offer language proficiency to an appropriate standard, since a high standard of communication skills is necessary to avoid misunderstandings, as well as to enhance relationships. Any general and specific cultural information must be well-informed, realistic and up-to-date. Although these points may be obvious, many such training programmes convey inaccurate knowledge. The trainer should therefore be someone who is from the relevant country and who has maintained regular contact with it. Such training is costly and time-consuming. Increasingly, where possible, MNCs try to draw on their existing staff who themselves come from mixed cultural backgrounds and who may therefore already be bilingual, such as Chinese-Americans. Longer-term anticipatory socialization (rather than just short-term training) is intended when entrepreneurs or executives send their children to study abroad or encourage overseas periods of secondment as part of the development of future international management skills for the firm.

In practical terms, cultural integration often consists of getting multicultural teams to operate effectively. Such teams arise in meetings between managers and staff within and between MNC subsidiaries, as well as internal groups that are specially constructed project teams or task forces that may work together for specific periods of time on dedicated projects. Such ad hoc groups are an increasingly important part of flexible global management processes and they almost always incorporate staff from a variety of national cultures drawn from many parts of the MNC.

Achieving inter-cultural communication

An obvious element in achieving inter-cultural communication is the issue of languages. Language is not just a potential source of competitive advantage for companies, as discussed in Strategy in Action 12.7. It is also increasingly important for individual managers in their international careers. Managers who are only monolingual, that is speak only one language, will be increasingly less successful within MNCs than colleagues who are multilingual. Monolinguals will be less able to move around the divisions and headquarters of MNCs and pick up the kind of experience on their CVs that will get them into senior managerial positions in the future.

Strategy in Action 12.7 *Language as a source of competitive advantage*

Britain rates 27th out of 28 European countries in foreign language skills and four out of five British export managers cannot negotiate in a foreign language. However, Eversheds, a large British law firm, has used language and cultural training to achieve a major expansion in its international business. Between 2001 and 2006 it has grown from a mainly British operation to having offices in fifteen countries, with a 4,500 professional workforce. It has doubled its inter-national business within the past three years. The chairman speaks French, German and Spanish in addition to his native English. He has invested heavily in training 500 partners and other employees in language and cultural skills. Eversheds is now able to use its competence in languages and cultural awareness to offer clients an understanding not only of the legal system in different countries but also of their business and social preferences.

SOURCE: ADAPTED BY AUTHORS FROM *THE SUNDAY TIMES*, 16 APRIL 2006

12

MNC communication takes place between the divisions and subsidiaries, between the staff working within these business units and between all levels of business units and the parent headquarters. Each of these lines of communication may cross boundaries both of organizational and national cultures. Many MNCs have begun to develop roles which are conceived as 'boundary spanners' (Newman, 1992a and 1992b). Newman defines this role as follows:

> The process of boundary spanning builds a bridge between two different organizations or between two or more people coming from different cultures. Boundary spanners – the persons who perform the bridging activity – need several talents: 1) An empathetic understanding of the customs, values, beliefs, resources, and commitments of people and organizations on each side of the boundary; 2) understanding of the technical issues involved in the relationship; and 3) ability to explain and interpret both 1) and 2) to people on both sides of the boundary.
>
> (Newman, 1992a: 149)

The key role played by boundary spanners in contributing to the requirements of global integration in MNCs is described in the example of the Global Account Manager's (GAM's) role as developed within Hewlett Packard (described in Strategy in Action 8.5). A different type of boundary spanning role may be that of the chief executive of a cross-border joint venture, whose political and communication skills are often key in smoothing the difficulties that arise. In the initial phase establishing the cross-border strategic alliance between the Royal Bank of Scotland and the Banco Santander of Spain, the role of the (then) boundary-spanners CEO's Walter Stewart (Royal Bank of Scotland) and Jose Saavedra (Banco Santander) was key. Their joint ability to identify cultural differences between the partners and deal with them sensitively has been a major factor in the success of that alliance between the two banks. We have already mentioned the problem represented by the American CEO of Lucent who does not speak French despite taking over as joint CEO for the merger with Alcatel. The availability of boundary spanners, together with relevant anticipatory training and people with relevant experience, are all management practices which can enhance opportunities for positive cultural fit and cultural learning.

WHAT SHOULD GLOBAL MANAGERS DO?

A very interesting piece of cross-cultural research carried out by Fu et al. (2004) reports a study carried out over twelve countries including Thailand, Hong Kong, Singapore, the US, Taiwan, India, the Netherlands, Turkey, France and Japan. It was designed to look at the relationship between cultural values, individual beliefs and the effectiveness of different types of managerial influence strategies. What that means is that the effectiveness of global managers depends upon their ability to exercise influence in culturally mixed organizational networks – which is what all MNCs are. What are the most common approaches that managers use in dealing with their staff and how effective are they?

They looked at three broad types of influence strategies: persuasive, assertive and relationship-based. 'Persuasive' strategies use rational persuasion, logical arguments, consultation or appeals to the values and ideals of the individual or even to the greater good of the firm or society. 'Assertive' strategies consist of persistent pleading, pressure using threats or persistent reminders or upward appeals to higher managerial authority. This approach is about coercion. 'Relationship-based' strategies include giving gifts, informal invitations to non-work environments (the researchers call this 'informal engagement'), personal appeals asking the individual to carry out requests as a personal favour, socializing and exchanging, that is offering something in exchange for agreement to the request. With this strategy the manager tries to use a social relationship or to establish a social relationship to influence individuals that they are managing to do what they want.

One of the findings is that these three types of influence strategies appear to be recognizably similar (although not identical) in all cultures. The persuasive strategy received the highest rating for effectiveness in absolute terms for all countries and cultures. The relationship-based strategy was (perhaps surprisingly) consistently rated the lowest, that is least effective across cultures. There were cross-cultural variations but although, as would be expected, managers from high uncertainty avoidance cultures gave lower ratings to persuasive strategies than managers from low uncertainty avoidance cultures, they still perceived the persuasive influence strategy to be more effective than the relationship-based strategy.

What does this tell us? It is important for managers to have knowledge of the influence strategies that are effective across cultures as well as to understand the strategies that are relevant to specific cultures. Leadership programmes for managers on overseas assignments could ensure that managers are knowledgable about, and skilled in the use of, multiple influence strategies. Managers who are knowledgeable about the relationship between different social beliefs and influence strategies can be more effective. Lastly, a clear understanding of *their own* social beliefs could help managers understand the reasons why they are more comfortable using particular influence strategies as their preferred way of managing their international staff.

SUMMARY

- All MNCs contain a complex mix of organizational cultures and national cultures that they have to manage.

- The differences between national cultures may strongly affect the ability of different parts of the MNC to work together effectively and to avoid misunderstanding, both internally within the MNC and with all its external stakeholders.

- Cultures give rise to differences in typical management practices and policy orientations. All these differences have to be accommodated within the various subsidiaries, divisions and teams that make up an MNC.

- Cultural diversity reveals itself in many ways, from variations in what constitutes forms of polite address to fundamental values.

- Although people rarely change their underlying values, possibilities do exist for achieving cultural adaptation and accommodation between individuals and groups who come from very different cultural backgrounds. Organizational cultures may, and do, adapt to different national cultures.

- A mixture of national and organizational cultures is not always a problem for MNCs. It may also bring positive benefits to the organization, since cultural diversity creates opportunities for adaptation and learning.

- There are many ways of accommodating cultural differences and differences in managerial practices within organizations: MNC parent culture may be adopted as the dominant mode; the subsidiary cultures and practices may co-exist and operate effectively in different parts of the MNCs operations; or differing practices may be integrated for the benefit of the MNC as a whole.

- Managerial efforts to improve cultural fit within the MNC can: assist individuals to adjust to different cultures; promote better communication between staff from different cultures; and improve the effectiveness of cross-cultural teams.

- Managerial practices throughout the MNC may benefit from the organization's absorption of different cultural practices. These may become competences from which the organization as a whole may learn.

■ A sophisticated appreciation of the richness of the interplay between national and organizational culture will significantly strengthen the design and effective implementation of all approaches to global strategy.

DISCUSSION QUESTIONS

1 Explain the difference between national culture and organizational culture and why this difference is so significant for MNCs.

2 How helpful are the typologies of either Hofstede or Trompenaars in explaining cultural differences between countries?

3 In what ways may the different practices and approaches of managers from different countries affect the implementation of global strategies by MNCs?

4 Should MNC managers regard cultural diversity as a potential source of competitive advantage or disadvantage for their organizations?

5 Describe some of the ways in which cultural differences may lead to problems in MNC cross-border mergers or acquisitions.

6 What is meant by 'the institutionalization of social networks' in governments and commercial organizations in Asian or Middle Eastern countries? Consider what, if any, implications such issues might have for foreign MNC managers operating in these countries.

7 What is meant by 'cultural adaptation'? What are some of the processes that organizations may adopt to encourage cultural adaptation internally? Why would they bother?

FURTHER READINGS

1 Hofstede, G.H. (2001) *Culture's Consequences: Comparing Values, Behaviours, Institutions and Organizations Across Nations*, 2nd edn, Thousand Oaks, CA: Sage.

Gert Hoftsede is the grandfather of research into cross-cultural management. This book gives the best summary and most comprehensive coverage of the research findings from his many international surveys. Underlying Hofstede's approach is his consideration of the different responses that different types of cultures make to the conception of the self, the relationship to authority and ways of dealing with fundamental social dilemmas. These provide a way of classifying and clustering groups of countries with similar cultural profiles.

2 Brannen, M.Y., Gomez, C., Peterson, M.F., Romani, L., Sagiv, L. and Wu, P.-C. (2004) 'People in global organizations: culture, personality and social dynamics', in Lane, H.W., Maznevski, M.L., Mendenhall, M.E. and McNett, J. (eds) *The Blackwell Handbook of Global Management: a guide to managing complexity*, Oxford: Blackwell Publishing.

This chapter by Brannen et al. provides an excellent discussion and overview of the basic idea of culture and the ways in which culture is learned and shared. It considers how culture affects social processes in organizations. It tries, and succeeds, in providing the kind of information that managers need to help them understand the relevance of culture to management and the interrelationship between cuture, economics and politics.

12

3 Clissold, T. (2005) *Mr. China: a Memoir*, New York: Harper Collins.

This may not be to everyone's taste but some may enjoy it very much. Clissold worked for the accounting firm Arthur Anderson in Hong Kong, where he became fascinated with China. He landed in 1990 in Beijing, where eventually he helped to start, raise money for, and manage a $400 million fund that invested in Chinese business enterprises. This is very far removed from an academic book. It is a personal account of social and business experiences in China. It is not an objective book. Instead it is a vivid description of one man's disastrous attempt to build and manage his businesses in a totally different cultural context.

CHAPTER 13

Learning within MNCs

LEARNING OBJECTIVES After reading this chapter you should be able to:

■ explain common theories on how we learn as individuals

■ distinguish between different tools for evaluating knowledge

■ explain the nature of systems thinking

■ explain the relevance of learning to global strategic management

■ explain the different types of learning

■ identify the barriers to corporate learning

■ perceive how to overcome some of these barriers.

INTRODUCTION

Successful strategies are those which develop a fit between the competences of organizations and the opportunities presented by their environments. This applies to both global and domestic strategy and generally involves 'organizational learning'. The term has come to be used to emphasize that organizations, just as individuals, can acquire new knowledge and skills with the intention of improving their future performance. Indeed it has been argued that the only sustainable competitive advantage the company of the future will have, is the ability of its managers to learn faster than its rivals (De Geus, 1988: 740). We apply these ideas to developing and implementing global strategies.

To begin our discussion of learning within global strategy it may be helpful to start with a very simple outline of the component parts of this complex subject. There are many models and frameworks that deal with the relationship between the different elements of organizational learning: data, information, learning and knowledge. However, since existing frameworks do not address the additional elements of wisdom and judgement that we regard as constituting the key foundations of strategic decision-making, we provide an alternative framework. Figure 13.1 illustrates our understanding of this set of relationships.

The first level in Figure 13.1 is *data*. An illustration of data might be 1 billion. *Information* provides a context such as: 'India has approximately 1 billion population.' This information can be used for a variety of purposes. If we were in a geography class such information could lead to learning. For example, the lecturer might teach us that the US has about 250 million inhabitants, India approximately 1 billion and China 1.3 billion. This can lead to us *learning* something about the population size of different

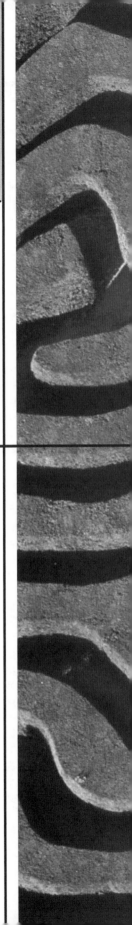

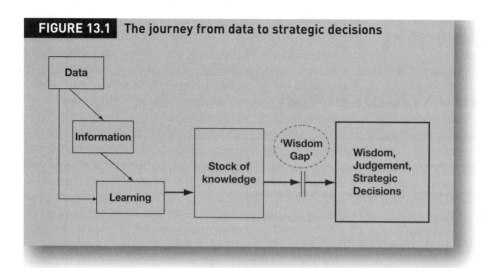

FIGURE 13.1 The journey from data to strategic decisions

countries. Therefore learning depends upon data and information. Learning in turn adds to our *stock of knowledge*, that is that which we already know. Strategy in Action 13.1 illustrates the nature of stocks of knowledge and their historical accumulation.

Additional, new information is more important and meaningful to someone with a larger existing stock of knowledge than to someone without one. This point is important in organizational learning. Software companies can deal with new learning about new software better than can old technology

Strategy in Action 13.1 *The beginning of collected knowledge*

Knowledge has been accumulated in societies for a very long time. The first evidence of preserving knowledge through writing dates back to 3000 BC when the Sumerians developed cuneiform writing with styluses on clay tablets. Scribes were trained as apprentices to a master or *ummia*, and ranked just below the high priest in their society in social status. The topics covered on these tablets included administrative records, the Code of Hammurabi (which was the first known codification of law), marriage contracts, legends and mythology. These tablets were collected and catalogued. A room full of clay tablets was found by archeologists at the ancient royal palace of Ebola in Syria dating back to 2300 BC. The palace library provided a training ground for scribes and promoted the preservation of knowledge similar to that in our modern universities.

In Ancient Egypt the papyrus was the medium for the storage, sharing and transmission of knowledge. Papyrus was much lighter than tablets and easier to transport. It was used for more informal records. Formal inscribed knowledge was stored in stone buildings, for example in the sacred library built by Rameses the Second which contained texts on poetry, astronomy, history, engineering, agriculture and fiction.

In Ancient Greece, knowledge collection and exchange became more widespread and books came into existence written on papyrus or parchment. Such books included Homer's *Iliad* and *Odyssey* and Plato and Aristotle's works. In 323 BC Ptolemy I, one of Alexander the Great's generals, became king of Egypt and commissioned the greatest library of antiquity in Alexandria.

SOURCE: SELECTED AND ADAPTED FROM JASHHAPARA (2004)

13

engineering companies. This point will recur when we discuss capacity to learn, often called **absorptive capacity** (Cohen and Levinthal, 1990). Cohen and Levinthal (1990) defined absorptive capacity as a firm's general ability to add value, assimilate and commercialize new, external knowledge. They suggested that an organization's absorptive capacity tends to develop cumulatively, to be path dependent, and to build on earlier investments made in its individual members' absorptive capacity.

In Figure 13.1 there is a break point between knowledge and *wisdom, judgement and strategic decisions. Wisdom* and *judgement* are qualitative, subjective, rather than quantitative, objective attributes. They are derived from *values, norms, culture and experience* but found in individuals rather than organizations. Indeed it is obviously individuals who take decisions in organizations. *Wisdom* and *judgement* are not discussed very often within strategy, although they are implicit in almost all frameworks about strategic analysis and strategic decision-making. One of the most interesting of the relatively few attempts to analyse the role of judgement in strategy is Mosakowski (1994). She asks whether the insight of managers can generate long-term economic rents (revenues) for the organization. Her discussion centres on whether there can be a general 'rule for riches' (Rumelt, Schendel and Teece, 1991), that is general rules or knowledge for taking decisions that will generate wealth. Teece (2007) discusses the ability of individual managers to recognize (business) opportunities as depending jointly on the individual's capabilities and also those of the firm in which the individual has to exercise judgement. He says (2007: 1323) that exercising judgement: 'requires specific knowledge, creative activity, and the ability to understand user / customer decision-making, and practical wisdom (Nonaka and Toyama, 2007). It involves interpreting available information in whatever form it appears.' The concept of 'practical wisdom' developed by Nonaka and Toyama (2007) is a truly helpful way of labelling what we generally mean by exercising judgement.

THE NATURE OF ORGANIZATIONAL LEARNING

Organizational learning has both cognitive and behavioural aspects. While learning is clearly a process, the concept of learning also incorporates the outcomes from such learning processes. Thus an organization does not necessarily benefit from the acquisition of knowledge and understanding unless and until these are applied to improving organizational actions. Learning outcomes therefore include not just the potential for, but the actual realization of, improvements and changes.

There is a paradox at the heart of the idea of organizational learning which Argyris and Schon (1978: 9) describe as follows: 'Organizational learning is not merely individual learning, yet organizations learn only through the experience and actions of individuals'. As Nonaka and Takeuchi (1995) recognized, in a strict sense knowledge is created only by individuals. Therefore the role of an organization can only be to support creative individuals or to provide suitable contexts for them in which to create knowledge. Nonaka and Takeuchi's description of 'organizational knowledge creation' provides an indication of how this individual learning can become available, and be retained, within the organization as a whole. In so far as this increased knowledge can be incorporated into improved systems and routines, the learning can be captured by the collectivity, and extended beyond the individual.

This touches on the very practical question of how learning by individuals, or groups of individuals, can become transformed into a property of the organization. The challenge here is partly one of how to make explicit, codify, disseminate and store the knowledge possessed by the members of an organization in ways that convert it into a collective resource. This is a particular challenge for MNCs, which may encompass individuals of widely varying national cultures and experience. It is also partly a problem of how to reduce the barriers which organizational structures, cultures and interests can place in the way of knowledge-sharing and learning. Of course the nature of learning achieved in an organization will vary according to its organizational form and culture. Organizational learning in a transnational, for example, is likely, to exceed that in a global company since it will draw on knowledge from all subsidiaries in the organization rather than just from the centre.

13

The nature of the knowledge contributed by members of an organization is of considerable significance for the process of learning. An important requirement for converting knowledge into an organizational property is to make it sufficiently explicit to be able to flow around the knowledge network. Polanyi (1966) distinguished between **tacit knowledge** and **explicit knowledge**. The former is usually regarded as personal, intuitive and context-specific. It is therefore difficult to verbalize, formalize and communicate to others. Explicit knowledge, by contrast, is specified and codified. It can therefore be transmitted in the formal systems and language of the organization. To make tacit knowledge available to the organization as a whole, in a form which permits its retention for future use, it has to be converted into a codified or programmable form. By definition, tacit knowledge is not amenable to such codification. Furthermore, where an organization makes efforts to better capture and codify the knowledge which exists within it, it may be extremely difficult to accomplish this, either for technical reasons or because the people with tacit knowledge do not wish to lose their control over it, or more frequently neither they nor the organization recognize either the existence of such tacit knowledge or their possession of it. If this is the case, then the only way to put tacit knowledge to organizational use may be to delegate responsibility for action to the persons concerned and / or to persuade them to share their knowledge with others on an informal basis.

CATEGORIES OF LEARNING

A distinction which has important implications for practice is that between the different categories of organizational learning. This distinguishes between *technical*, *systemic* and *strategic* types of organizational learning (Child, Faulkner and Tallman, 2005). The technical level includes the acquisition of new, specific techniques, such as techniques for quality measurement or for undertaking systematic market research, or blueprints for the application of new technologies. This type of learning may be thought of as routine learning. The systemic level refers to learning to introduce and work with new organizational systems and procedures. The focus here is on the restructuring of relationships and the creation of new roles and ways of doing things. The strategic level is the highest form of learning and involves changes in the mindsets of senior managers, especially in their criteria for organizational success and their mental maps of the factors significant for achieving that success. The emphasis here is on vision, which is somewhat different from 'learning how to learn', but there is a parallel in the cognitive processes involved with a view to generating new insights and being proactive.

Learning is required at all three levels – technical, systemic and strategic. Technical learning is the easiest type to achieve. Given the complex nature of many modern technologies, and the necessity of deploying these technologies by harnessing human skills and the motivation of employees, a multidisciplinary technical competence is required. The absence of certain technical skills can cause problems in global companies. An example of such an obvious and basic technical skill is that needed in languages. Hamel (1991) noted that employees of Western firms lacked Japanese language skills and cultural experience in Japan and how this limited their access to Japanese know-how. Their Japanese partners did not suffer from a lack of language competence to the same degree, being generally competent in English, and they benefited from the additional insight this gave them into the knowledge-base of Western partner firms and into their ways of doing and thinking about things. Sadly, not so much has changed in regard to language since this research was originally carried out in 1991.

There is a conceptual difference between what we learn, and how we learn. Therefore in addition to these different categories of learning, Andreu and Ciborra (1996) pointed to the different dynamic processes of learning which link these three categories of learning together. They describe these different learning processes by means of three 'loops': the *routinization* learning loop; the *capability* learning loop; and the *strategic* loop. At the technical learning level is the routinization learning loop. This level of learning is aimed at mastering the use of standard resources and gives rise to efficient work practices.

Andreu and Ciborra (1996) cite as an example 'mastering the usage of a spreadsheet by an individual or a team in a specific department, to solve a concrete problem'.

The category of systemic learning is required in order to make the most innovative use of new knowledge or technology which is acquired. For example, the introduction of mill-wide computerization in the paper and pulp industry in the 1980s opened up radical possibilities for the constructive redesign of mill organization and the combined empowerment and enrichment of mill workers' jobs (Child and David, 1987). This technological development came about through close co-operation between paper manufacturers and system suppliers. The ability of UK paper manufacturers to take full advantage of the potential offered by the new systems depended on their organizational vision and competence, in terms of being able to envisage and accept radically changed roles and relationships. Such new working practices can be internalized by the firm in the form of routines, and in this way they become part of its capabilities. This gives rise to Andreu and Ciborra's second type of learning process, the *capability* learning loop, in which new work practices are combined with organizational routines. The learning process is systemic in character, because it involves generalizing working practices and techniques, and placing them into a wider context. This defines not just what the practices do and how they work, but also the circumstances under which it becomes appropriate to use them, and who has the authority or competence to apply them.

In the *strategic* learning category, the ability of a senior executive to derive broad strategic lessons from a business experience ('practical wisdom' again) rather than the more restricted perspective only of narrower issues, is a common problem. It often displays itself in international strategies in clinging to strategies based on historic industry 'recipes', rather than on new insights into the actual industry dynamics. General Motors (US), for example, approached its NUMMI joint venture with Toyota (Japan) with the expectation that what it could learn from Toyota would be confined to production skills in the manufacturing of small cars. As a consequence, although the lessons to be learned were actually of general relevance, they were unfortunately not applied to General Motors as a whole (Inkpen, 1995). Sadly the consequences of GM's limited 'absorptive capacity' are now part of the reason for the collapse of the firm.

In Andreu and Ciborra's third type of learning process, the strategic loop, capabilities evolve into core capabilities that differentiate a firm strategically, and potentially provide it with a competitive advantage. Capabilities may be identified as 'core' (i.e. central to the firm's activities), or as 'key' (i.e. having strategic potential) by reference to the firm's mission regarding what will give it a distinctive edge in its competitive environment (Bowman and Faulkner, 1997). MNCs and global alliances offer the potential for learning in all three categories and by all three processes. MNCs may provide direct and fast access to improved techniques and specific technologies. They can facilitate the transfer and internalization of new systems, such as lean production or Six Sigma quality, and both can be utilized to develop new strategic insights for the realization of new strategic opportunities.

FORMS OF ORGANIZATIONAL LEARNING

Learning also takes different forms. Some forms of learning become far more embedded within the firm's evolving culture than others (Child, Faulkner and Tallman 2005). We discuss six different forms of learning.

The first form is *forced* learning. Here there is no change of cognition, and hence understanding, but new behaviour is acquired under some managerial pressure perhaps. A common example of forced learning might arise when MNC headquarters insists on the unilateral introduction of new organizational routines or systems without other parts of the firm either understanding the rationale for them, or indeed being offered adequate training in how to implement them. Although the term 'forced' refers here to how the acquisition of new behavioural practices is brought about, and not necessarily to how the process is perceived by those on the receiving end, it is likely to meet with some reluctance on their part. Forced learning can readily arise in a situation where there is strong centralization of power in the firm and a low motivation to learn by members outside head office. We discussed an example of this process in Chapter 7 Strategy in Action 7.3 which described the attempts to build a network-based structure at Citibank.

A second possibility also results in the adoption of new practices (behavioural change) but without any appreciable learning about the rationale behind them (cognitive change). This is *imitative* learning. There is probably at least a moderate level of motivation to learn in this situation, but the fact that the learning takes the form of imitation might indicate some limitation in the quality of training offered to support the learning process. Markoczy and Child (1995) provide an anecdote of an occasion in China when Child had to go in and out of one hotel in China several times in succession with various packages. He was greeted on each entry by the same commissionaire with 'Welcome to our hotel' and on each exit with 'Have a nice day, sir'. The two situations mentioned so far are ones in which behaviour and practices have changed, but without any significant increase in know-how or understanding. However, the opposite can also occur, when the members of an organization undergo changes in cognition that are not reflected in their behaviour. This could be due to inadequacies of resourcing which prevents implementation, an over-general or theoretical formulation of the new knowledge (as with the endless 'have a good days' which was true to the letter but not the intention of the greeting), or existing strongly held beliefs displacing the new knowledge.

These factors cause the translation of new understanding into revised behaviour to be blocked. *Blocked* learning can arise when staff receive training, on a management development course perhaps, but are not accorded the resources or opportunities to put what they have acquired at the cognitive level into practice when they return to their department, or they find that their boss has not had that specific training and is sceptical of their newly acquired ideas. Their motivation to learn may well be high, but the additional training may not be matched to that of the responsibilities and resources allocated to that individual or to the group in which they work. This may be one reason for a marked preference by MNCs that executive training and development programmes should more frequently involve groups of internal MNC staff undergoing the development programme together, rather than sending an individual manager on an outside programme, where no other representatives of the MNC would be present.

Another aspect of learning is that individuals learn both cognitively and behaviourally. This might take the form of a unilateral process of *received* learning when one executive willingly receives new insights from another. It is also the purpose of telling 'war stories', recounting to others particular situations that individuals have found themselves in and what they or others did.

If both parties endeavour to express and share their knowledge and practices, a level of *integrative* learning may be attained. Integrative learning has the potential for organizational learning in its most advanced form, that in which innovative synergy is attained between the different contributions and approaches which the participants in an MNC bring to their interactions. Integrative learning involves a joint search for technical, system-building and strategic solutions for the needs of the MNC. It means that people are receptive to the concepts and practices brought in by others, and are willing to modify their own ways of thinking and behaviour in light of these.

Two further forms exist. The first is *segmented* learning (Child, Faulkner and Tallman, 2005). This is a situation in which, at best, very restricted learning can take place because the firm is organized such that separate responsibilities are allocated very clearly. That would be typical of the multi-domestic MNC organizational form but also generally in any large organization where there are 'silos', that is poor lateral integration or relatedness between departments.

The final possibility is that no learning takes place at all. This is likely to arise when the motivation to learn is low and / or because there is low transparency of knowledge between the parts of the firm. For example in the case of a Chinese–European joint venture, reported by Child and Markoczy (1993), a negative learning priority was illustrated. The Chinese partner attempted to resist the reconfiguration of production and support functions along more effective lines because it saw this as reinforcing the power of the European management over the running of the venture's facilities and over their labour force.

REQUIREMENTS FOR LEARNING

Even when a corporation undertakes to adopt a learning philosophy, there are certain requirements for learning to take place. The first is that the intent to promote learning is high on the personal and corporate agendas of senior executives, so that learning objectives are automatically included in the formulation of objectives and outcomes at all levels in the organization. As part of this philosophy, managers must also be able to identify and attach value to those learning opportunities which do arise. Second, the corporation must have the necessary capacity to learn. Most importantly, it needs to be able to convert the knowledge into a collective property so it that can be disseminated to the appropriate persons or units within its organization, understood by them, and retained for future use. These factors are not easy to achieve in practice.

Learning intent

In a detailed study of nine Western–Asian MNC international strategic alliances, Hamel (1991) found that the partners varied considerably in how far they viewed the collaboration as a learning opportunity, and that this attitude in itself was an important determinant of the learning which they actually achieved. For instance, several of the Western firms had not intended to absorb knowledge and skills from their Japanese partners when they first entered alliances with them. They appeared, initially, to be satisfied with substituting their partner's competitive superiority in a particular area for their own lack of it. In every case where this skill substitution intent was maintained, the partners failed to learn much from their collaboration. Whereas other companies, especially the Japanese partners in the same alliances, entered into the alliance regarding it as a transitional device in which their primary objective was a learning objective. They therefore had an explicit strategic intent to understand, capture and transfer their partner's skills. In several cases, partners undertook co-operative strategies specifically for the purpose of learning the business, especially to meet international requirements, master a technology and establish a presence in new markets. These are illustrations of a company's intention to use the learning opportunities provided by collaboration to enhance its competitive position and internalize its partners' skills, as opposed to collaborating over the long term and being content merely to gain access to a particular partner skill, without attempting to acquire such skills itself. Where one partner has a learning objective and the other merely a skill substitution objective, the threat posed to an unwitting partner is obvious. Such an imbalance does not provide the basis for an enduring long-term co-operative relationship. In fact, when learning from a partner is the sole aim, the termination of a co-operative agreement cannot necessarily be seen as a failure, nor can its stability and longevity be seen as evidence of success.

Hamel also noted that one partner's ability to outstrip the learning of the other alliance partner contributes to an enhancement of that partner's bargaining power within the co-operative relationship, reducing its dependence on the other partner, and hence providing a gateway to the next stage of internalizing those partners' knowledge and skills. For these reasons, in order to realize the learning opportunities offered by an alliance, a partner must both give priority to learning and consciously consider how to go about it. This conclusion applies not just to international alliances but just as powerfully to internal attitudes and processes for facilitating intra-unit, cross-border learning in MNCs.

13

Learning capacity

A company's capacity to learn will be determined by a combination of factors: the transferability of the knowledge, the receptivity of its members to new knowledge, whether they have the necessary competencies to understand and absorb the knowledge, and the extent to which the company incorporates the lessons of experience into the way it approaches the process of learning. *Transferability* indicates the ease with which the type of knowledge can be transferred from one party to another. Explicit knowledge, such as technical product specifications, is relatively easy to transfer and to be absorbed. Tacit knowledge is, by definition, far more difficult.

The more receptive people are to new knowledge, the more likely they are to learn. When the members of an organization in different parts of the world adopt the attitude of students towards their teachers, they are being more receptive to insights than if they assume that they already possess superior techniques, organizing abilities and strategic judgement. For example, some Chinese partners in joint ventures with foreign companies make the mistake of assuming that they could learn useful motivational practices from their foreign collaborators, because they already had a superior specific 'home' knowledge of Chinese workers (Child and Markoczy, 1993; Child, Faulkner and Tallman, 2005). Equally, some foreign partners unwisely overlooked or ignored advice from their Chinese collaborators on the best ways to relate to external governmental authorities, which in China wield an unusual degree of influence over the conditions for doing business.

Hamel (1991) found several influences on a partner organization's receptivity to learning new knowledge within international alliances. Firms which had entered an alliance as competitive 'laggards' in their sector, in order to provide an easy way out of a deteriorating competitive situation, tended to possess both little enthusiasm for learning from the other partner and little confidence that they could achieve such learning. They tended to be trapped within deeply embedded organizational cultures and behaviours which made the task of opening up to new knowledge all the more difficult. In clinging to the past in such a way, they were not capable of the 'unlearning' which is a necessary prerequisite to receptivity to learning (Hedberg, 1981). Receptivity also depended on the availability of some time and resource to engage in the processes of gathering knowledge, and embedding it within its own routines through staff training and investment in new facilities.

The organizational learning paradox thus emerges for poorly performing organizations. Deteriorating competitiveness creates great pressure to learn and need to learn for the poorly performing organization; yet this pressure itself constitutes the largest constraint on being able to achieve learning and move forward. Sometimes this may be resolved by additional cash and other resource forthcoming from MNC headquarters, or injected by the other partner in an alliance. If an organization has slipped far in the skills and competences necessary for it to absorb new knowledge in its sector, or a collaborator has slipped too far behind its partner in an alliance, it may find it extremely difficult to close the gap. Similarly a low-technology company may not be sufficiently receptive to new knowledge for it to be able to transform itself into a high-technology company even when such an opportunity arises, simply due to the limited educational level of its key employees (Faulkner, 1995b)

Cohen and Levinthal (1990) argue that a firm's 'absorptive capacity' is a crucial competence for its learning and innovative capabilities. As defined and explained earlier in this chapter, absorptive capacity is largely a function of the firm's level of prior, related knowledge. Hence existing competence favours the acquisition of new competence. That implies that a partner entering an alliance with learning objectives should ensure that it does so not only with a positive attitude towards learning but also with at least some appropriate level of skills. If those skills are not available, the training of staff to acquire them should be an immediate priority.

Experience can be both an enabler and an inhibitor. Previous experience of the learning process will normally enhance one's capacity to learn because it leads to greater knowledge of how to learn: how to manage, monitor and extract value from new information. However, prior knowledge which has been converted into existing organizational routines can become a barrier to further learning, especially that of a discontinuous rather than merely incremental nature. Being good at single-loop learning may therefore become a handicap for double-loop learning (Argyris and Schon, 1978). This is also what Szulanski (2003) was referring to when he called knowledge 'sticky,' that is it is not absorbed easily but is often blocked by organizational barriers arising from existing organizational routines.

MAKING KNOWLEDGE COLLECTIVE

Drawing largely upon cases of successful Japanese innovation, Nonaka and Takeuchi stressed that the creation of knowledge for organizational use is a 'continuous and dynamic interaction between tacit and explicit knowledge'. For this process to succeed, in their view, the possibility must exist for four different modes of knowledge conversion:

1 *Socialization (tacit knowledge / tacit knowledge):* 'A process of sharing experiences and thereby creating tacit knowledge such as shared mental models and technical skills' (p. 65).

2 *Externalization (tacit knowledge / explicit knowledge):* 'A process of articulating tacit knowledge into explicit concepts'. This form of knowledge conversion is typically seen in the creation of concepts which offer wider access to the knowledge and also links it directly to applications.

3 *Combination (explicit knowledge / explicit knowledge):* 'A process of systematizing concepts into a knowledge system. This mode of knowledge conversion involves combining different bodies of explicit knowledge ... through media such as documents, meetings, telephone conversations, or computerized communication networks'. Typical examples are: training manuals, for example how to submit a proposal, for new management consultants; or how to lay out a slide to improve presentation skills; or how to answer the telephone and take messages properly.

4 *Internalization (explicit knowledge / tacit knowledge):* This process is closely related to 'learning by doing'; knowledge acquired by practice. It involves the embodiment of explicit knowledge into individuals' tacit knowledge bases in the form of shared mental models of personal technical know-how, for example putting a student teacher into a classroom with a more experienced teacher to see how the more experienced professional handles given situations.

Nonaka and Takeuchi (1995) emphasized that organizational learning depends upon the tacit knowledge of individuals, and upon the ability first to combine tacit knowledge sources constructively, and then to convert these into more explicit forms which are subsequently combined. Tacit knowledge itself is enhanced by explicit knowledge, taking the form, for example, of training inputs. This continuous evolution of knowledge Nonaka and Takeuchi (1995) call the 'knowledge spiral' indicating a virtuous cyclical process. Theirs is an insightful framework for understanding the processes which must be in place for new knowledge to become a property available to the whole organization, and hence to constitute organizational learning.

13

BARRIERS TO ORGANIZATIONAL LEARNING

There are often obstacles to the smooth operation of organizational learning which derive from the nature of an organization and its culture. When a company is global, such barriers are almost inevitably increased by the variety of different national identities in the employee group. Such barriers reduce transparency and openness of one person to another, and the willingness to transfer knowledge between different parts of an organization, or between different national partners in a cross-border alliance. In international alliances in particular, managers were often concerned about unintended and unanticipated transfers of knowledge – transparency by default rather than by design. Obstacles to the necessary transference of knowledge identified by Nonaka and Takeuchi (1995) are liable to arise because of divergent approaches to sense-making and are associated with the social identities of the different participants and stakeholders that make up an MNC.

When MNC organization members come together to collaborate, of course they will also bring their own social identities with them. These social identities are sets of substantive meanings which arise from a person's interaction with different reference groups during his or her life and career. They derive therefore from belonging to particular families, communities and work groups within the context of given nationalities and organizations (Tajfel, 1982). The receptivity of the members to knowledge transfer from other parts of the MNC or from their alliance partners, and their ability to learn collaboratively from their knowledge resources, are bound up with their social identities. Social identities are likely to create the greatest difficulties for learning in relationships between MNC firm members who are distinct culturally, nationally and in terms of the economic development level of the society from which they come. Learning is not a socially neutral process. All forms of knowledge and practice transferred from one MNC member impinge on the other members' mental constructs and norms of conduct. Their social identity derives from a sense both of sharing such ways of thinking and behaving, and of how these contrast with those of other groups with whom they are brought into contact within the MNC, such as on internal training courses. The process of transferring practical knowledge between different managerial groups will be interdependent with the degree of social distance that is perceived between the parties involved. So, if initially this distance is high, the transfer is likely to be difficult. If the transfer is conducted in a hostile manner or in threatening circumstances, then the receiving group is likely to distance itself from those initiating the transfer. There is a clear possibility of virtuous and vicious circles emerging in this interaction, and thus contributing to positive and negative learning outcomes.

MNCs present a particular challenge for organizational learning, since MNC learning is intended to draw upon knowledge transferred between the firm members and to build upon the potential synergies between their complementary competencies (Child and Rodrigues, 1996). In other words, MNCs are expected to be able to generate and capture economies of scope from learning. However, while global organizational networks are an extremely important means for international knowledge transfer, they introduce special sensitivities into the process which can mean that potential synergies (such as economies of scope from learning) are not captured. It is often difficult to accommodate the interests of their various constituent groups and to manage the cultural contrasts between them. These differences can contribute to a sense of separate social identity, rather than social cohesion, between staff.

Some types of internationally transferred knowledge have an impact on group social identity more than others. This is particularly true of knowledge relating to new systems and strategic understanding. Resistance to the transfer of such knowledge is likely to heighten the separate identities of groups, including those doing the knowledge transfer for whom persuading their recalcitrant colleagues may take on the nature of a crusade. The relationship between social and cultural identity and international knowledge transfer is a dynamic one, in which contextual factors such as performance also play a part. By contrast, the sharing and transfer of technical knowledge is normally less socially sensitive. Indeed technical knowledge transfer is likely to benefit from the common engineering or other common technical, professional or managerial occupational identity shared by the staff directly involved.

Members of an organization will be reluctant to give up the beliefs and myths which constitute important supports for their social identity. Jonsson and Lundin (1977) write of the 'prevailing myth' as one which guides the behaviour of individuals in organizations, at the same time as it justifies their behaviour to themselves and hence sustains their identity. Beliefs and myths also form an important conceptual part of the 'cultural web' (Johnson, 1990) by sustaining an existing organizational paradigm or mindset (such as 'we are the biggest firm in our market', irrespective of continuously declining profitability), and a set of practices, and retaining them unrealistically. Thus the social identities of MNC members are likely to be affected by their distinctive and separate beliefs and a rigid adherence to the existing organizational paradigm.

There are many common barriers to organizational learning that need to be recognized and managed.

Cognitive barriers

A lack of intent to learn can be an important cognitive barrier in the way of realizing the learning potential within, or between, organizations. This can arise because an MNC is focusing on objectives other than learning, such as spreading the costs and risks of R&D across its different businesses, or achieving production economies of scale. Often in global alliances, one partner may not even appreciate that it has something valuable to learn from its alliance partner, not simply because it has other primary objectives for the alliance than learning, but because it takes time to become more familiar with that partner's capabilities and the possibilities for learning and knowledge transfer that they offer. Inkpen (1995) found several examples of American firms which did not have a learning intent when entering into a collaboration with a Japanese partner, and only developed this when they became aware of their inferior levels of skill. Ways of reducing inadequate prior knowledge include programmes of visits and secondments to prospective partner organizations, and close examination of their products and services. Strategy in Action 13.2 gives an example of approaches to reducing cognitive barriers to learning and promoting trust in a global law firm.

Emotional barriers

Emotional barriers to learning often boil down to a problem of mistrust. Trust cannot be instantly established. It is, nevertheless, possible to identify conditions which promote trust and therefore to derive practical guidelines to further the building of trust within the MNC across its various divisions and businesses or between alliance partners, as is illustrated in Strategy in Action 13.2. Commitment to the relationship, and a degree of direct personal involvement by senior managers, are again important here. Personal contact enhances and reinforces trust-building. If the time and trouble is taken to establish a close personal relationship, this builds both confidence and trust, as explained in Strategy in Action 13.2 by the UK lawyer who had spent time on secondment to one of the firm's offices in Italy. The opposite is also the case, as when inter-departmental or inter-divisional rivalry generates a deterioration of trust and increasing suspicion and lack of co-operation or effective integration. The conditions for reducing emotional barriers to learning within MNCs and alliances require a long-term view and sufficient visible managerial commitment, especially from the top (Faulkner, 1995a). These points apply particularly in the integration of cross-border MNC acquisitions.

Organizational barriers

Serious organizational barriers are created if the senior managers do not know how to benefit from the opportunity to learn. Inkpen (1995) found that a major problem arose where American and Japanese managers and staff had to work together, because of the arrogance of the American staff as to the superiority of their knowledge, systems and procedures. Clearly under such circumstances, both the recognition of potential learning opportunities and the potential exploitation of such opportunities will be

---

Strategy in Action 13.2 *Building a learning organization in a global law firm*

Global law firms now reflect many of the most commonly mentioned features of global strategies. For the implementation of global integration within legal professional service firms (PSFs) and to provide consistency in service delivery, they are finding ways of overcoming the limitations and barriers presented by local / national firm cultures and processes. They are building the capabilities to respond to the global customer within multi-local markets. The building of professional trust and strong intra-firm working relationships between offices and professional staff in different countries is critical. Staff frequently will have to work together on complex international projects for clients at very short notice. Professional staff on such international project teams need to trust each other, to be able begin working together immediately, and be able to learn from each other and share best practice. This is of ever-increasing importance within PSFs as firms become larger and client projects more complex. This is operationalized through common training programmes, partner retreats, social events and secondments.

Secondments have become a common practice in PSFs such as law firms or consulting firms. These can be secondments to another country within the firm's own international network of offices or another common practice is the secondment of professional staff to client offices usually for a six-month period.

I spent a little while in Italy and not necessarily that there was much UK work for me to do in Italy when I was there but I met all the tax people, I could put names to faces, and if you had a transaction with Italian tax advice, and you've got a face in your head, it's so much easier to pick up the phone and it's so much easier if you think they're not quite doing what they should be doing to say it to someone if you've met them rather than someone you don't know.

The creation of intra-firm networks (e.g. working groups across practice areas) at both practice and interpersonal levels is essential for maintaining service levels, for professional development and for retention of the best professional staff.

SOURCE: ADAPTED FROM SEGAL-HORN AND DEAN (2007)

13

---

missing. No organizational mechanisms were established to assist potential exploitation. In some cases they resisted even the idea that there was something to learn from the Japanese. In US–Japanese alliances this attitude often contributed to a situation of blocked learning where joint venture managers could not get their improved understanding carried over into practical actions (Inkpen and Crossan, 1995).

Managers and staff will take their cue from senior levels. Senior management is in a position to establish organizational procedures and provisions which foster the learning process. Inkpen and Crossan (1995) identified ways in which such provisions can be designed, or practices encouraged, by senior managers which facilitate links across boundaries within the organization and which promote the learning process. These included (p. 609):

1 The rotation of managers from the businesses or the divisions back to the parent headquarters; regular meetings between divisional and headquarters management, or for joint ventures, between JV and parent management.

2 Plant visits and tours by groups of managers from different parts of the organization or different international partners.

3 Senior management involvement in cross-border divisional or JV activities.

4 The sharing of information between the businesses or international divisions and the MNC headquarters.

A further organizational feature which can facilitate learning is control. There are two main aspects to this:

1 Establishing limits to the actions of participants in the learning process.

2 Assessing outcomes.

Control is not usually regarded as a facilitator of learning. Indeed, learning is normally associated with autonomy and creativity which are considered almost the opposite to control. However, control seems to be a very important condition for a learning intention to be given clear direction. Also, the systematic assessment of outcomes should ensure that these are recorded and so entered into the organization's memory. In addition, systematic assessment provides feedback on the effectiveness of the learning process and therefore should enable MNC or global alliance members to improve their capacity to promote learning.

This focus on the facilitation of learning by senior and middle managers derives from their pivotal position in the middle of the vertical communication and decision-making hierarchy of most organizations (although not of the transnational form). It echoes the conclusion reached by Nonaka and Takeuchi (1995) that what they term the 'middle-up-down' style of management can make a crucial contribution to fostering knowledge creation. Middle managers can reduce the gap that often exists between the broad strategic vision coming down from top management, and the hard operational reality experienced by employees in their day-to-day functioning. The manager in the middle has the additional responsibility for articulating the objectives for learning and providing the practical means to facilitate it.

The organizational aim is to promote the conditions for integrated learning. Therefore breaking down the hostile stereotypes which may exist within a firm is important. If these are allowed to persist, little trust or bonding will occur. Organizations must remain sensitive to the cultural mix when deciding on specific methods to use for this purpose. The 'confrontation meeting' approach which often works well with North American staff could cause grave offence if tried with staff from East Asia. Once the problems inherent within such stereotypes are recognized, various techniques for team-building are available to promote a collaborative approach to learning between members of the firm.

ACHIEVING OPEN COMMUNICATION AND INFORMATION CIRCULATION

A climate of openness can facilitate organizational learning. It involves the accessibility of information, the sharing of errors and problems, and acceptance of conflicting views. The idea of 'information redundancy' expresses an approach to information availability which is positive for organizational learning. Redundancy is

> the existence of information that goes beyond the immediate operational requirements of organizational members. In business organizations, redundancy refers to intentional overlapping of information about business activities, management responsibilities and the company as a whole.

> (Nonaka and Takeuchi, 1995: 80)

This may also be known as organizational slack. This adds flexibility to the organization, as in a changing environment it ensures a pool of knowledge available to draw on to implement new strategies.

For learning to take place, information, data, ideas, or concepts available to one person or group need to be shared by others as suggested by sharing best practice. Redundancy helps to build extensive communication channels, often combining both horizontal and vertical channels for reporting information – as recommended in Hedlund's heterarchy (1986). Non-hierarchical interchange, including Nonaka and Takeuchi's 'middle-up-down' process, helps to promote learning on the basis of procedures which are different from those already formally specified by the organization. Existing procedures and communication are usually better at providing existing solutions to old problems, rather than new solutions to new problems (Nonaka and Takeuchi, 1995).

ICT makes a very significant contribution to the promotion of information redundancy, through its capacity for information storage, and more importantly, through its ability to transmit that information to virtually all points within an organization. E-mail in particular offers access to information and the facility to communicate in ways which are not constrained by boundaries of time, geography or formality. Strategy in Action 13.3 discusses how PepsiCo makes use of information redundancy and ICT to promote internal cross-border learning.

Strategy in Action 13.3 *PepsiCo's approach to creating information redundancy*

PepsiCo is one of the world's largest global food and beverage corporations. It operates through many local alliances, and stresses the value of open communication both within its corporate systems, and with its partners. An illustration of open communication with its partners is the fact that, in PepsiCo's joint ventures in China, all the general managers speak Mandarin Chinese, and its Asia-Pacific budget meetings are conducted entirely in Mandarin.

Despite its size and scope, PepsiCo does not operate with organization charts or many formal procedures, but instead prefers to encourage informal communication flows and to promote the empowerment of its constituent units. As one corporate officer said, 'at the end of the day, the most relevant information for me and the job I have to do, is going to come from the people who are closest to the project ... so the lines of communication are open at all levels'. Senior officers of the corporation stress the benefits of this approach for encouraging learning.

PepsiCo circulates information within its corporate network to the point of redundancy. Its internal e-mail system is an important vehicle for this information circulation. It overcomes international time differences, permits simultaneous communication with several people, is very fast, and encourages an open, informal expression of views. Consolidated reports for different countries and regions are also widely circulated. If, as a result, managers wish to learn more about developments elsewhere in PepsiCo's worldwide operations, they have access to all the company's telephone numbers and are encouraged to make direct contacts and to decide whether to travel to the location, subject only to their travel and entertainment budgets. Many examples are told of how this rich circulation of information, and the ability to act upon it, have promoted learning and the transfer of beneficial practices throughout the corporation. For instance, it facilitated the transfer from their Hungarian operation to their JVs in China, of knowledge about ways of curbing theft on distribution runs.

SOURCE: PERSONAL INTERVIEWS BY JOHN CHILD, CITED IN CHILD, FAULKNER, AND TALLMAN (2005)

13

SUMMARY

- In this chapter, organizational learning has been defined in three basic categories: *technical*, *systemic* and *strategic*. These categories each need to be managed by the organization.
- There are six basic forms of learning: forced, imitative, blocked, receptive, integrative, segmented.
- For learning to take place in an MNC or in a global alliance, there are several requirements. There must be an *intention* to learn; there must be the necessary *capacity* to learn.
- There must also be the *competence* and *absorptive capacity* within the organization to transform individual knowledge into a usable organizational resource.
- Each of these is associated with different degrees of organizational and interpersonal change in understanding and in behaviour.
- Organizational learning is more or less likely within the different MNC organizational forms we have discussed in earlier chapters.
- The successful promotion of organizational learning within an MNC, and within global alliances, requires a number of important organizational and interpersonal conditions. These include the surmounting of cognitive and emotional barriers to learning and the reduction of organizational barriers to learning.
- Finally, organizational learning needs openness of communication and effectiveness in dissemination of information throughout the organization so that actual, rather than just potential, learning outcomes may be realized.

DISCUSSION QUESTIONS

1 What is the relationship between data, information, knowledge, judgement and wisdom?
2 What are the major forms of learning?
3 What are the major barriers to learning?
4 How can barriers to learning be overcome?
5 How can organizational knowledge become a source of competitive advantage?
6 How does tacit knowledge differ from explicit knowledge?
7 What are the basic requirements for learning to take place?

13

FURTHER READINGS

1 Jashapara, A. (2004) *Knowledge Management*, Financial Times Prentice Hall.
   A good introductory volume covering information and knowledge management and giving many fascinating historical insights.

2 Kogut, B. (2008) *Knowledge, Options and Institutions*, Oxford: Oxford University Press.
   A collection of published papers by the outstanding strategic thinker Bruce Kogut and colleagues linking knowledge management, philosophy, sociology and economics in a fashion rarely attempted.

3 Bromiley, P. (2005) *The Behavioural Foundations of Strategic Management*, Oxford: Blackwell Publishing.

This is a seminal book of extremely high quality. It is a tough but brilliant analysis of all the underlying assumptions within strategic management that managers use, usually implicitly rather than explicitly (i.e. consciously) to underpin their decisions.

13

CHAPTER 14

Global strategy in services

LEARNING OBJECTIVES After reading this chapter you should be able to:

- appreciate the significance of service industries within the world economy
- define the characteristics that distinguish services from products
- explain the reasons for the globalization of service industries and service firms
- describe the sources of additional risk faced by service firms when globalizing
- define the role of economies of scale and economies of scope in the globalization of services
- understand the management issues involved in the management of intangibles across borders
- explain the role of outsourcing in the growth of global services.

INTRODUCTION

While service MNCs may follow any of the strategies or structures discussed in the preceding chapters, service industries and service firms have distinct characteristics which may add risk and delivery problems to the design and implementation of global service strategies. This chapter will present research into service developments and approaches to managing 'intangibles' across borders. It will cover potential sources of economies of scale and scope in services, and internal management processes for the effective implementation of global strategies in service firms.

Service industries are those whose output is not a physical good or product but an intangible 'experience'. This underpins an essential difference in the significance of internationalization or globalization in services as opposed to manufacturing. Global service delivery is about controlling the quality of the offering at the point of sale to the customer. The expectation of the customer is for consistency and predictability in the delivery of the service in any location worldwide.

As part of appreciating the changes that have occurred in service industries, it is helpful to understand what Levitt (1986) called the '**industrialization of service**'. Services can be industrialized in a variety of ways. First, by automation that substitutes machines for labour, for example automatic car-wash, automatic toll collection, ATM cash machines, and so on. Second, by systems planning, substituting organization or methodologies for labour, for example self-service shops, fast food restaurants, packaged holidays, unit trust investment schemes. Third, by a combination of the two (e.g. extending the shelf-life of food or flowers in global retailing via centralized warehousing and distribution networks for chilled, fresh or frozen foods in technically advanced temperature- and humidity-controlled trucks). Such industrialization of service is based on large-scale substitution of capital for labour in services, together with a redefinition of the technology-intensiveness and sophistication of service businesses. It also assumes a market size sufficient to sustain the push for volume. This is the point at which a firm is likely to shift to international operations since the domestic market provides insufficient volume to support minimum efficient scale. This may come earlier for service firms than for manufacturing firms since for many types of services the option of exporting is not available.

GROWTH IN INTERNATIONAL SERVICES

Historically, the literature on global strategy (Porter, 1986; Ghoshal, 1987; Prahalad and Doz, 1987; Yip, 1996; Bartlett et al., 2004) has taken its evidence overwhelmingly from manufacturing industry, despite the extensive data which has existed for some time (Riddle, 1986; Enderwick, 1989) concerning the importance of service industries in terms of output, jobs and trade balances. Indeed, services now account for some two-thirds of GDP in developed economies (see OECD World Economic Outlook Annual reports). Agreement on freeing trade in telecommunications was finally reached by the World Trade Organization (WTO) in 1997 and the highly controversial General Agreement on Trade in Services (GATS) has been signed by all 148 member countries of the WTO, although many countries retain limitations on their areas of compliance. Under GATS, any funding available to domestic suppliers of a service must also be made available to foreign suppliers. Many problems still remain about the treatment of such services as health and education under GATS since these services are often regarded as public goods which should not be traded for profit. However, both health and education services contain large numbers of commercial companies trading across borders (e.g. AMI health care group, EF language schools). This also includes many of the world's most prestigious universities starting to trade on the strength of their global brand names to open overseas campuses in attractive growth markets such as China.

Despite the difficulties, such deregulation allowing freer international trade in services will help to clarify comparative advantage in services. For many years, consumers have been used to airlines and insurance firms outsourcing such activities as ticketing or claims processing to systems and software engineers in developing countries. Any value chain activity that can be conducted online or down a wire can now be carried out anywhere in the world and linked to other offices or corporate centres anywhere in the world. This should both drive down prices to customers and create additional employment, sometimes in unexpected ways.

Consider (in Strategy in Action 14.1) a small business idea that has used the same technology developments as the large airline and financial service companies to build an international person-to-person service business.

A prolonged process of concentration and cross-border restructuring has been occurring for the past twenty years in most service industries. Mergers and acquisitions have been commonplace. In many service industries over this period of time, industry leaders with well-known brand names have emerged from a series of mergers, for example in the advertising industry worldwide firms such as WPP or Interpublic are the result of large mergers between previously independent agencies such as J. Walter Thomson. In banking (the Hong Kong & Shanghai Bank acquiring Midland Bank then rebranded globally as HSBC); in global retailing (Wal-Mart of the US acquiring Asda of the UK); in

SOURCE: ADAPTED BY AUTHORS FROM *THE ECONOMIST*, 23 JUNE 2007

Strategy in Action 14.1 *Off-shoring extra school lessons*

The Indian company TutorVista was set up in 2005 when its founder Krishnan Ganesh, a serial entrepreneur, realized that most American parents could not afford extra tuition for their children. His original business idea was to deliver this service via the internet using tutors based in India. The tutors were experienced teachers, often retired, who worked from home. India's comparative advantages of lower wage costs for skilled staff and high levels of English language usage was the basis for very aggressive pricing. Unlimited tuition in a wide range of subjects is offered for a fixed fee per month. This was $100 in the USA and £50 in the UK when TutorVista launched in the UK in 2007.

Further expansions into Australia and Canada are planned. Building trust for an unknown Indian brand has been taken very seriously as critical to the success of the business. Local managers are used in the US and UK markets. Quality control of sessions is assured by a policy of recording all sessions and providing a shared monthly call between student, parents and teacher to check progress. Since much teacher–student communication is carried out by means of a shared virtual whiteboard, the potential pitfall of difficulties with regional accents is largely avoided.

Annual revenues from 'person-to-person off-shoring' by individuals and small businesses are estimated to increase from $250 million in 2007 to $2 billion by 2015 (research by Evalueserve). Other similar services well suited to this business model might include tax planning or interior design.

professional services such as accounting, management consulting and now also some corporate law firms following the same path of international merger and consolidation.

Many services (e.g. credit cards, automated teller machines, airline seats, software, automatic carwash) have emerged relatively recently in human society. Therefore, in global terms, they have the advantage of no prior patterns of usage or acculturation, thereby making them more easily acceptable across national boundaries. However, alongside social, cultural and technological changes affecting demand for services, there are additional economic and political pressures on governments to create, or remove, regulatory barriers as the WTO has been attempting. Current difficulties affecting international trade in services still include immense difficulties in the protection of intellectual property rights (IPR). The TRIPS (Trade-Related Aspects of Intellectual Property Rights) agreed by the WTO in 1994 has gone at least some way to addressing this, although it remains very difficult to enforce in many parts of the world, especially in developing economies.

In service industries it is often the customer who globalizes first, with the service company following to meet the needs of important clients that have themselves globalized their strategy and operations. Omnicom needed to build global networks of agencies to service MNC clients, particularly those requiring the delivery of global advertising campaigns.

Service growth has also partly come as a consequence of organizational trends towards **outsourcing** and **offshoring**. Specialist service suppliers are replacing service provision previously carried out in-house. Firms like EDS, the US technology and facilities management company, or more recently, Wipro, the Indian IT outsourcing giant, grew rapidly, nationally and internationally, as the outsourcing of information technology (IT) services and IT management for client companies became an important aspect of business restructuring and the rethinking of cost structures in most industries. Large service firms can standardize and replicate facilities, methodologies and procedures across locations. Specialization and standardization are leading to high-quality provision at

14

lower cost to the client company or customer, whether in such different service businesses as car repair (e.g. exhaust, brake and tyre centres) or management consultancy. Building global brands for services has become an important guarantee of quality and consistency around the world.

THE PARTICULAR CHARACTERISTICS OF SERVICES

Services do differ from products. The IMF defines international transactions in services as 'the economic output of intangible commodities that may be produced, transferred and consumed at the same time' (IMF, 1993). This definition suggests a set of specific differences between products and services. Service firms are 'upside-down' firms. They can best be understood as inverted pyramids. The most important focus for service firms, and where a major proportion of resources are allocated, is at the borderline of contact between the firm and its customers. Although all organizations state as a matter of course that they are customer-focused, with manufacturing organizations their major activity occurs away from the eyes and ears of customers. With service firms, their major activity occurs in combination with customers and that is part of the definition of what we mean by a service.

There are four distinct characteristics that define the most important differences between products and services: *intangibility*, *heterogeneity*, *simultaneous production and consumption*, and *perishability*. Table 14.1 provides a summary of each of these characteristics, then contrasts them with the comparable characteristic for a product and explores some of the consequences of each difference. Each will then be more fully discussed.

TABLE 14.1	Services are different	
Products	*Services*	*Implications*
Tangible	Intangible	Services are difficult to describe, exhibit or communicate.
Easy to standardize	Heterogeneous; difficult to standardize	Guaranteeing a standard experience to the customer is problematic. Final implementation of the strategy is dependent on employees. Quality of service delivery is always partly personality-dependent.
Production and consumption occur separately	Simultaneous production and consumption	Customers cannot 'test drive' a service. Services are higher-risk purchases for customers. Both customers and employees participate in and affect the service outcome. Some parts of a service always need to be decentralized close to the customer.
Durable	Perishable	Services cannot be kept in stock, returned or re-sold. Capacity utilization is problematic but critical.

Source: Segal-Horn, S. (2003) 'Strategy in service organizations', in Faulkner, D. and Campbell, A. (eds) *The Oxford Handbook of Strategy*, Vol. 1

Intangibility

Intangibility is probably one of the most influential factors in relation to services. As a result of intangibility, many services have no second-hand or part-exchange value since there is nothing tangible to sell. The nature of a service therefore may be best understood as an 'experience', or 'outcome' of an interaction, rather than a thing. For this reason one of the most effective ways of selling a service is through word-of-mouth recommendation. Since a service cannot be inspected before purchase, the most reliable way of making the purchasing decision is on the recommendation of someone who has already experienced it.

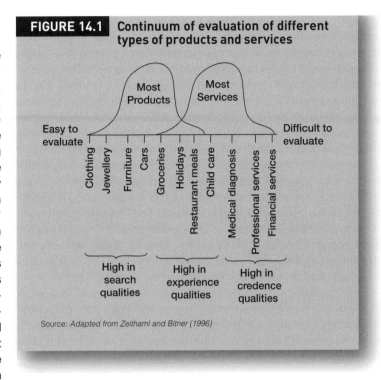

FIGURE 14.1 Continuum of evaluation of different types of products and services

Source: *Adapted from Zeithaml and Bitner (1996)*

However, 'intangibility' in services is only accurate up to a point. In fact services may be tangible or intangible or a combination of both. Figure 14.1 illustrates degrees of intangibility for different types of products and services. It represents intangibility by means of how easy or how difficult it is for consumers to evaluate the product or service that they think they have purchased. To do this Figure 14.1 draws on the economic concepts of *search, experience* and *credence* goods. A search good is one which can be researched or tested by the potential consumer *before* deciding whether to buy it or not (e.g. going for test drive in a car or sitting in an armchair before you buy). An experience good is one that you need to have *already experienced* or consumed before you can judge whether it was satisfactory or not (e.g. a meal in a restaurant). For credence goods, even *after* you have bought them *and* consumed them you are unsure as to whether they are satisfactory or not (e.g. insurance policies or pensions or hiring a lawyer). These are called credence goods because you have to believe that they are fit for the purpose for which you bought them.

The implication of Figure 14.1 is that services are mostly either experience goods or credence goods. This creates a particular relationship between the service provider and the customer that the strategies of service firms must embrace. In particular it means that establishing and retaining trust between the service provider and the customer has great strategic significance in service organizations. This point also explains the important role of branding in services because brands are implicitly about positive reputation that the consumer can trust.

Heterogeneity

Services are 'personality-intensive' because they often rely on people to deliver them by means of a face-to-face (or telephone) interaction with the customer or client. In the services literature this is known as 'the service encounter' or 'the moment of truth' (Normann, 1991; Bowen, Chase and Cummings, 1990). It is by the quality of outcome for the customer of this service encounter that a service strategy is judged. Service encounters may be notoriously *heterogeneous,* that is they are difficult to standardize and guarantee because the encounter relies on the personality or mood of the individual responsible for that service encounter, in that organization, at that point in time, on that day. Whether a particular service business is capital-intensive or labour-intensive (and services may be either or both) is not the significant factor. What matters in services is how to manage the quality of service delivery to the customer at *the moment of truth* that occurs for each organization thousands of times each day. That is why so many service firms (including the public sector) have training based around what are often ironically called 'smile' programmes: intensive customer care programmes which try to teach staff the importance of their manner and personal behaviour in relating to customers.

Strategically what is interesting about **heterogeneity** is that service strategies depend least on the quality of the analysis going into the design of the strategy in the first place, and most on the implementation of that strategy by the front-line staff of the organization. That is what is meant by calling service organizations 'upside-down' organizations. They have to find ways to allow front-line staff, those in direct contact with customers, to drive the organization, with everything else in support. Paradoxically, such front-line service staff are usually relatively junior within the structure of the organization, at a modest level in the reward structure and with relatively little influence on strategic decision-making. Yet they are critical to the strategy implementation and hence, to the service experience for customers.

The significance of heterogeneity for global strategies in service industries is very great. Successful implementation of a global strategy in a service business means being able to control and guarantee the quality of the service encounter at the transaction point with the customer in whatever country, culture, time zone or language that it takes place. Thus heterogeneity is a major challenge to the globalization of services.

Simultaneous production and consumption

With a product, production of the product and then consumption of that product by a customer occur at different times. They follow the sequence of production, distribution, and then consumption. With many services it works rather differently. The sequence is more likely to be distribution, followed by production and consumption occurring simultaneously. For example, a hotel is built first then the customers and staff stay in it together, co-producing the service experience of staying in that particular hotel. For most professional service firms (PSFs) the accountant, or consultant, or lawyer interacts directly with the client to discuss the service required and how it will meet that client's needs.

Consider personal services such as hairdressers. Clients make appointments with the hairdressing salon and then arrive to have their hair cut. They have to physically be present to participate in the delivery of the service and it is certainly an experience good, since the client will not be sure until it is over whether they like the haircut or not. This illustrates another aspect of simultaneous production and consumption of a service: risk. Since customers cannot 'test drive' many services, purchasing a service is a higher risk for the customer than purchase of a product. It is also more difficult to return a service if dissatisfied. Customers can only decide to go to a different provider next time, for example change accountant, or not stay in that hotel again. Ways of attempting to reduce the risk arising from *simultaneity of production and consumption* of a service (especially experience or credence services) include the recommendation of someone else who has used it, or to buy a respected service brand. Well-known service brands represent to the consumer some form of guarantee of standards of service delivery.

The growth of service brands has been a feature of service strategies in the last decade. It is why clients will pay extra to go to a well-known global firm of accountants such PwC (Price Waterhouse Coopers) rather than a cheaper local firm, because they have greater confidence in the reliability of the global brand. This has even been occurring in personal services such as hairdressing, where chain brands (e.g. Toni & Guy) have also been spreading internationally. However, there are risks attached to service businesses having strong global brands. Consider what happened to the much-respected brand of Andersen

Consulting when its sister firm Andersen Accounting imploded in the aftermath of the Enron accounting scandals in the US in the late 1990s. To survive, Andersen Consulting had to change its name and rebrand itself as 'Accenture' because the Andersen brand had been so tarnished by the scandals.

The final point to consider in relation to simultaneous production and consumption of services is another implication for the design of global strategies for service firms. Consider the enormous growth in delivery of global services via the internet. Internet retailers ('e-tailers') such as Amazon have gradually realized that unless their product can be delivered by pure internet transaction (e.g. downloading a software program or a piece of music), then at some point service companies like Amazon.com have to provide channels for local delivery of the service to customers. That has meant the building of enormous warehousing hubs for the warehousing and distribution of goods such as books and DVDs prior to delivery. Even global services must therefore often have a local final delivery point close to the customer for reasons of simultaneity.

Perishability

Perishability means that it is difficult to apply the concept of inventory or stock to services. A meal in a restaurant or a holiday or an hour of billed time with a lawyer cannot be stored. Although they are part of the total capacity of that restaurant, that holiday company or that law firm, if they are not sold (that is used) on a particular day and time, they cannot be stored and shown tomorrow to another potential customer. Therefore capacity utilization in service organizations is crucial. Optimal capacity must be sold today because if not, it is gone forever. That is why professional service firms (PSFs) focus on 'utilization' of their professional staff, that is the number of billable hours of their time they have sold in a given period. That is the PSF equivalent of productivity output, except unlike a car or a chair, you cannot attempt to sell the same hour tomorrow. If it remains unsold today it is lost. The hour sold tomorrow is a different hour, a different unit of output.

That is the perishability issue for the service organization. For the customer the problem is slightly different. Services cannot be returned or resold. They have a fragile exchange value and no second-hand value. There are no car boot sales for services, except to a very limited degree, that is there is a secondary market in insurance policies and endowment policies. However, these are credence goods (as are all financial products) so the buyer and seller must agree on a future worth of the policy well in advance of its maturity and at some risk. However, even though most services cannot be stored, some parts of a service certainly have a shelf-life and can be stored and re-used even if the service as a whole cannot e.g. software programs or some of the research or design for one advertising campaign may be re-usable for a different campaign.

The strategic issue regarding perishability is that service firms must be aware of how far it applies to their business and which, if any, of the firm's activities are re-usable and tradeable. This has massive implications for the operational systems and procedures within a service firm. They must be designed for optimal capacity utilization since for most service firms that is what both revenue and margins depend upon. That is why airlines use the measure of 'yield management' to fill seats on any flight to optimum capacity and have sophisticated software programs enabling them to release different numbers of high- and lower-priced seats on any given flight. For customers this can be frustrating when you get an internet or phone quotation for a flight on one day but by the time you decide to take it the next day, the price has changed.

THE VALUE CHAIN APPLIED TO SERVICES

We have been explaining how services differ from products. We have already said that most of the frameworks that dominate strategic management research and teaching have been derived from research into manufacturing industries. Therefore an issue of general concern for strategic

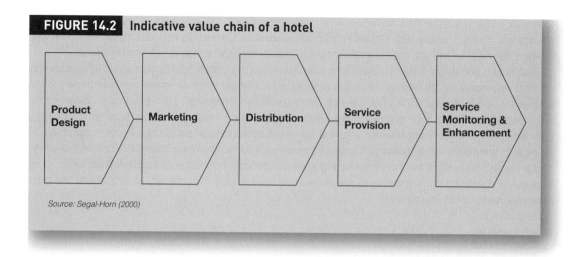

FIGURE 14.2 Indicative value chain of a hotel

Product Design → Marketing → Distribution → Service Provision → Service Monitoring & Enhancement

Source: Segal-Horn (2000)

management in service organizations is that sometimes, existing strategy frameworks have to be reconsidered when applied to services. For example, consider the well-known strategy concept of the value chain and the issue of simultaneous production and consumption in services. The point has already been made that manufacturing organizations follow one sequence of business activities: production, distribution, and then consumption; while many services follow the sequence of distribution, followed by production and consumption occurring simultaneously. Consider the implications of that sequencing of activities for the traditional construction of the value chain in strategic management. In the traditional value chain applied to manufacturing businesses, marketing, sales and service occur last. When used for a service business these activities should come *first*, since services are sold first and then produced and consumed afterwards. Consider the simplified indicative value chain for a hotel given in Figure 14.2 to illustrate this important point.

It becomes highly inappropriate to apply a value chain analysis of a service starting with inbound logistics as in the traditional model. The traditional model was designed for manufacturing businesses and needs adapting for services, as do many frequently used strategy frameworks.

SCALE AND SCOPE IN SERVICES

Much of the historic pattern of competition in services occurred within domestic market boundaries as a result of the small-scale, fragmented structure of service industries, and their culture-specific patterns of demand and consumption. Under these conditions clearly scale and volume effects were limited. Chandler (1986) showed that in sectors where few large firms appeared, it was because neither technological nor organizational innovation substantially increased minimum efficient scale. Therefore, in those industries, large plants did not offer significant cost advantages over smaller ones and 'opportunities for cost-reduction through more efficient co-ordination of high-volume throughput by managerial teams remained limited' (Chandler, 1986: 417). Managerial hierarchies (Chandler's 'visible hand' (1977)) emerged and spread 'only in those industries or sectors whose technology and markets permitted administrative co-ordination to be more profitable than market co-ordination' (p. 11).

Chandler's work (1977, 1986, 1990b) addresses the circumstances under which a firm will continue to grow to maintain a position of dominance. The economic basis of Chandler's model is 'the cost advantages that scale and scope provide in technologically advanced, capital-intensive industries' (1990b: 32). It was a model built on manufacturing industry data (e.g. oil, pharmaceuticals, agricultural machinery, steel). The structure of service industries lay outside Chandler's study. Historically, despite considerable variance across sectors, service industries had been neither as technologically advanced nor as capital-intensive as manufacturing. They had exhibited minimum efficient scale at low levels, with significant diseconomies of scale reached at modest levels of growth. The special characteristics of service businesses had dominated thinking about the design and delivery of services. Because of the different characteristics of services, the growth paths of service firms were different from manufacturing firms. However, technological and industry change may mean that the special characteristics of services have diminished in significance.

More capital-intensive asset structures and high fixed costs in services, largely IT-related, have been influential in creating extra-national economies of scale which have resulted in a prolonged process of concentration and restructuring of service industries over the past twenty years. Service industries are no longer fragmented, but increasingly concentrated. High levels of merger and acquisition activity in many service sectors have been commonplace (e.g. as already mentioned in hotel chains, accountants and management consultancy firms, airlines, telecommunications, software, information services, financial services, etc.). Many sectors now resemble oligopolies (as in international catering and contract cleaning services), although a 'tail' of small local firms coexist as local providers in most markets. Increased concentration has generated increased potential for **economies of scale** and **economies of scope**. This has great significance for the global strategies of service firms. Sources of scale economies and scope economies now commonplace in service MNCs are listed in Table 14.2.

Any asset which yields economies of scale can also be the basis for economies of scope if it provides input into two or more processes, that is when the cost of producing two outputs jointly is less than the cost of producing each output separately (Teece, 1980 and 1982). This would arise first, if two

TABLE 14.2   Potential sources of economies of scale and scope in services

Economies of scale	Economies of scope
Geographic networks	ICT and shared information networks
Physical buildings or equipment	Shared knowledge and know-how effects
Purchasing / supply	Product or process innovation
Marketing	Shared R&D
Logistics and distribution	Shared channels for multiple offerings
Technology / ICT	Shared investments and costs
Operational support	Reproduction formula for service system
	Range of services and service development
	Branding
	Training
	Goodwill and corporate identity
	Culture
	Privileged access to parent services

Source: Adapted from Segal-Horn (1993)

or more products depend on the same proprietary know-how; and second, if a specialized indivisible asset is a common input into two or more products. Both of these conditions are now routinely to be found in service firms. Often the 'proprietary know-how' and the 'specialized assets' are related to information and communication technology (ICT) related (see Table 14.2).

An example of the interaction between scale and scope benefits deriving from the same proprietary know-how and indivisible asset is the central role played by computer reservation systems (CRS) in the activities of airlines, hotel chains or car rental firms. These not only support the geographic spread of the business and the rapid processing of huge volumes of global transactions, but also provide customer databases for cross-marketing of services and the capability to design and deliver new services. American Express uses its information systems to set and monitor service standards for fast response times for card enquiries, or to provide additional services such as 'free' travel arrangement or theatre bookings for cardholders. Airlines use sophisticated software to maximize yield from higher-revenue seats on all flights, a major contribution to profitability in a service business with high fixed costs. Database management and the opportunities it provides for mining of detailed customer information and profiling provides potential for economies of scope for retail chains and financial services, for example selling travel insurance to an airline passenger booking a flight to go on holiday. It allows them to target cross-selling of additional products which is a classic economy of scope, that is using the same asset for more than one business purpose. Advertising MNCs such as Interpublic or WPP derive economies of scale from bulk purchasing of media time and space, as well as the internal transfer of market and design data in the management of global campaigns for clients. In the retailing sector, Benetton created a new retailing model by its innovative use of information systems. Twenty years ago the Italian leisure-wear retailing group became the first retailer to use real-time information from electronic point-of-sale (EPOS) systems to tailor seasonal production to current fashion trends across its international chain of boutiques. At the time this was a massive innovation which gave Benetton a genuine competitive advantage. This model is now commonplace within the retail sector. It is the basis of many economies of scope based around the use of IT systems and consumer purchasing data by retail chains.

Knowledge is often a special asset in services and a powerful source of economies of scope (Nayyar, 1990). The capability to acquire, process and analyse information is the key asset or core competence of many services (e.g. financial, software, brokerage, professional, and the agency function of ICT systems linking many service businesses). 'Know-how' here literally consists of the knowledge of how to combine human and physical resources to produce and process information. Additionally, knowledge has a shelf-life, during which time it may be repeatedly used at little or no cost (e.g. an advertisement, a software program). Many services comprise a firm-specific pool of both explicit and tacit knowledge (Nonaka and Takeuchi, 1995). Service firms (e.g. management consultancies and other PSFs, fast food chains, hotel chains) are increasingly attempting to codify this knowledge as the basis of standardization of their products, to achieve cost-reduction and increased productivity, as well as reliability of global service standards. Many large food retailers achieve scope economies by also trading in clothing, homewares and financial services such as in-house credit cards. Some of the strongest brands in services are based on perceived accumulated know-how, for example Reuters, Disney, McDonald's. Information-intensive assets are absorbing heavier investment in fixed costs which in itself exerts pressure to lower unit costs by spreading output over larger global markets (for scale economies) and a wider variety of products (for scope economies).

Individual and organizational knowledge represent a generalizable capability or core competence (Prahalad and Hamel, 1990). This implies that where diversification is based on scope economies it makes sense for service firms to manage their global expansion by means of internalization (i.e. the internal control and co-ordination of assets and activities) rather than by market transactions. Internalization (part of OLI, discussed in Chapter 2: Dunning, 1985) means that firms retain control of their internal capabilities (rather than, say, outsourcing), giving greater control over their use. Internalization is especially important in the growth of service firms in regard not just to efficiency, but to the management of the quality of their 'moments of truth'. Despite this, service outsourcing and off-shoring are now widespread and a key part of the cost structures of many global service firms.

These structural shifts in the supply of services are echoed on the demand side. Economies of scope in service firms can lower transaction costs and search costs for customers. Common examples include: internet price transparency and search availability on quality and price in comparison websites; worldwide, integrated reservation systems of hotel chains, car hire firms and airlines; cheaper products in banking and insurance; the undercutting of all brokerage services (known as 'disintermediation') such as travel agents, insurance brokers or investment analysts, as consumers do their own buyer research on the web.

These factors appear to be having some impact on the creation of global oligopolies in services. Scale and scope variables are particularly useful since they drive cost for a service firm and one of the big issues in successful global expansion is that it must involve some efficiency advantages. That is because there are additional costs of integration incurred in globalization and globalization of cross-border operations, compared to the cost of a local firm providing the same service. In strategic terms it would be hard to justify such additional costs if no actual or potential scale and scope benefits could be identified for the firm from being global.

Potential pitfalls

Despite the evidence of benefits available to both service firms and service customers from economies of scale and scope in services, a cautionary note must be sounded. Attempting to deliver multiple services through a single service delivery channel may sometimes have unintended negative consequences. For example, many people will have experienced some annoyance at booking a few days' holiday retreat for a special break at a beautiful quiet hotel only to find on arrival that most of the other guests are groups of business delegates using the hotel's 'conference' facilities. In the evenings large noisy groups of delegates wearing name badges fill the bar and the 'intimate' restaurant. Of course the hotel is only trying to obtain economies of scope by making the fullest use of its rooms and other facilities by selling them to different types of guests for different purposes. The problem arises from using the same service delivery channel for quite different types of customers who have entirely different expectations and needs. That is a potential economy of scope for the business that has negative consequences for the customer.

MANAGING 'INTANGIBLES' ACROSS BORDERS

14

Among the most widely recognized characteristics which distinguish service industries from manufacturing industries are those of the intangibility of the service offering and the simultaneous production and consumption of the service as a shared experience between the customer and the supplier of the service. Successful global strategies for service firms are about being responsible for this quality of customer experience, described earlier as 'the moment of truth' or 'the service encounter'. When the service network is extended globally, the management of the service encounter between service organization and customer is genuinely difficult to manage. There will be quality-control problems in accurately reproducing the service concept in different cultural, political and economic environments and in ensuring consistency of quality in the daily operational detail of face-to-face service delivery. Arising from the impact of these strategic issues on service firms, Carman and Langeard (1980) argued that international expansion is the most risky growth strategy for service firms in relation to the quality control problems of operating across national borders. Most global service firms have met these requirements for consistency through standardization of their offering (Campbell and Verbeke, 1994). For example, global hotel chains (such as Sheraton or Inter-Continental) undertake to make the traveller's experience of Tokyo, Cape Town, Manila or Sydney as

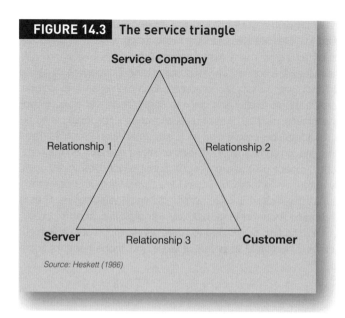

FIGURE 14.3   **The service triangle**

Service Company

Relationship 1

Relationship 2

Server

Relationship 3

Customer

Source: Heskett (1986)

similar as possible. However, issues like staff training are critical in global service firms since it is the front-line staff who are responsible for the quality of the customer's experience.

Erramilli (1990) distinguished between 'hard' and 'soft' services. Many modern service businesses contain a shifting mixture of 'hard' (tangible) and 'soft' (intangible) elements. The 'hard' elements are increasingly amenable to management by means identical to a manufacturing business. The 'soft' elements (i.e. the service encounter) retain the distinctive needs of service management and service delivery. Thus the role of management in services is particularly demanding, especially for complex services with a high intangibility content.

What Heskett (1986) called 'the service triangle' (see Figure 14.3) describes the interconnected relationship between the service company, its employees and its customers. Often the strongest relationship in a service business is between the employee (what Heskett called the 'server') and the customer. It is balance in the triangle between all three relationships that enables the company to carry out the effective management of 'intangibles' across borders.

The management task for service MNCs is to develop a mix of hard and soft resources and the internal competences to combine these into consistency of cross-border 'service encounters'. If we think back to Novotel in Chapter 8, in terms of the hotel industry, 'hardware' such as beds or televisions are relatively more straightforward to co-ordinate and deliver across borders than 'software', such as the style and atmosphere of a hotel or how staff conduct themselves in their dealings with guests (and each other). The firm infrastructure and procurement management policy and processes which support the selection and supply of beds or televisions to hotels around the world involve many levels of task and resource. However, the shared values and tacit understandings underpinning the delivery of service encounter 'software' is far more problematic in terms of management processes.

Consider (in Strategy in Action 14.2) how these issues have been addressed in a rather different international service business: contract cleaning.

If we compare Novotel with ISS, how did they each attempt to manage their service intangibles? Novotel (see Strategy in Action 8.2) first attempted to manage their cross-border 'service encounter' issues by 'industrialization of service', in other words imposing top-down rigid control processes and rulebooks (the 95 Bolts) on staff in order to ensure predictability of outcomes. After rethinking the business, they saw that their competitive advantage was much more about their concept of 'hospitality', a classic 'intangible'. They replaced the hierarchical structure with an enabling culture of front-line discretion, supported by high levels of training. By contrast, ISS is a business-to-business service. It could have designed the timing of its operations to avoid any 'service encounter' contact with customers by sending in their cleaning teams only out of office hours. Instead the company went out of its way to build it in. They wanted to utilize the service encounter both to motivate staff and to provide direct contact and feedback opportunities with customers and end users (even though these 'customers' did not themselves pay directly for the service). Both companies invested greatly in training both as a way of enhancing skill levels of staff but also as a way of ensuring a coherent and consistent worldwide knowledge base in the firm.

Strategy in Action 14.2 *Cleaning as knowledge management – ISS of Denmark*

In an industry characterized by perceptions of low status, low-skilled workers and high staff turnover, ISS invests heavily and continuously in training its staff and attempting to retain their loyalty. Although a commonplace in most other industries, it may appear unusual to emphasize knowledge, skills and staff expertise in relation to office cleaners. Yet this is a service business and customer satisfaction depends ultimately on how front-line staff (i.e. the cleaners) carry out their jobs. Commercial cleaning requires high levels of efficiency in timeliness, use of cleaning supplies, avoiding accidents and dealing with idiosyncratic customers. In many hospitals and factories, conditions are often complex and hazardous.

In the commercial cleaning business there are now several global service providers such as Rentokil (UK), ServiceMaster (US) and ISS (Denmark). These large service MNCs outbid local providers since they benefit from scale and investment in back-office systems to enable them to efficiently co-ordinate their purchasing, marketing and logistics to win national and international contracts with hospitals, offices, factories and government departments. However to retain these contracts, service delivery by staff is what counts.

ISS operates throughout Europe and Asia. It emphasizes training and has an impressive staff retention record. ISS Denmark, for example, operates a six month training programme for all employees covering things like safety and which chemicals to use on which stains. After a year with ISS, employees may become team leaders. For this they need better overall knowledge of the business. They are given prior training on the economics and finance of the business, so that they can understand where the profit in each contract is to come from and how to interpret each client contract. Team

leaders have tight performance targets, measured on both profitability and customer retention. So they also receive training on how to deal with customers and how to coach less experienced members of their team.

ISS attempts to provide its employees with technical skills but also to motivate them as front-line staff and to keep the benefit of their expensive training inside the company. To do this the company has had to think creatively about how it organizes the work. ISS Denmark has grouped its cleaners into two- or three-person 'hit squads' for its small office division. They work together travelling from site to site. This is in many ways less efficient and more costly than sending separate individuals to separate sites, but ISS believes that this system both generates higher motivation and makes possible more contact between the ISS team leaders and the client's site managers. To increase such customer contact, when crucial customer feedback may be obtained, ISS has rescheduled many of its accounts to provide overlap time between cleaning staff and office staff. As part of its focus on motivation, ISS also pays wages that are above the competitor average. So far it feels that it has not lost business as a result of its higher costs. Well-trained employees and good back-office systems have enabled it to bid for, and win, complex contracts, such as the hotel cleaning contract at Disneyland, Paris.

Partly, ISS is helped by timing, since this industry has emerged from a period of rapid concentration internationally, so that ISS faces only two or three major competitors in its market. Nevertheless profitability and productivity are major concerns, especially how ISS copes with its higher training and wage costs over the longer term. ISS is always reviewing its operations and one

14

SOURCE: ADAPTED BY AUTHORS
FROM PRESS ARTICLES

relevant recent decision concerned the delivery of its training programmes. Previously, these had been centralized and co-ordinated across regions and delivered through the ISS University. ISS University has now been sold. Instead, training is being decentralized in an attempt to tailor knowledge to local conditions.

THE NEW GLOBAL VALUE CHAIN IN SERVICES

The important difference between 'back-office' and 'front-office' activities in services is extremely significant for the globalization of services. 'Front-office' describes those activities which come into contact with the customer; 'back-office' are the operational activities which can be decoupled from the customer. The significance of this distinction in global strategy terms for service MNCs is that the larger the proportion of 'back-office' value chain activities in the service that can be decoupled from the location of the customer, the greater the potential for optimizing OLI advantages (Dunning, 1989), reconfiguring the organization's value chain (as discussed in relation to Porter's Configuration / Co-ordination matrix in Chapter 2), and securing scale and scope advantages in the same way as manufacturing MNCs. If most activities of a service organization cannot be decoupled from the customer in this way, then strategic flexibility remains low and the costs and service delivery risks for a global strategy remain high. If the international value chain for a global service company can be reconfigured to place a larger proportion of back-office activities in how the service is designed, then both risks and costs are greatly lowered.

In other words, the separation of back-office and front-office activities, combined with the standardization of many back-office processing functions, has created the opportunity for breaking out of the requirement for simultaneous consumption and production of a service. These developments, which are largely due to technological advances in ICT, have had a huge impact on potential sources of economies of scale and scope in services. They allow for the reconfiguration of service value chains which can be disaggregated (just as for manufacturers) and parts of the activity may be located geographically for optimum scale, scope or cost advantage. For example, a company like Visa International has a geographically dispersed value chain whereby all its worldwide back-office data transactions (e.g. millions of card clearances per day) are handled by just two global transaction centres in Japan and the USA. These types of global configurations for services have become technology-dependent rather than 'service encounter' dependent.

Under these changed technological and structural conditions it becomes necessary to reconsider the definition of what constitutes a service and also to consider how firms actually design and deliver their services. Figure 14.4 provides a simple illustration of some of these service design and reconfiguration possibilities. It reflects some of the differences in core assets and service delivery between 'hard' and 'soft' services. It also reflects some of the rethinking of services that has occurred. For example, the location of retail banking in the top-left box reflects the capital-intensive, volume-driven, transaction-processing part of retail banking operations. These activities are usually now centralized and regionalized (sometimes globalized). At the same time, the retail banks have been redesigning branch outlets to prioritize the face-to-face opportunities for cross-selling of other higher-margin financial services. Software houses may sometimes appear in the top-left box also if they are selling standardized rather than bespoke / customised software packages.

However, the examples in Figure 14.4 are inevitably oversimplified. It ignores the search by PSFs for methodologies to increase productivity and margins via back-office standardization or that many accounting, consulting legal and software services are standardized, for example tax audit. It is inevitable that continuous shifts such as those between standardization and customization, should result in firms continually seeking optimization of such features at the highest level of scale and cost position available to them. It is also to be expected that these positions of optimum efficiencies will be continually shifting.

FIGURE 14.4	Service standardization

Resource emphasis

	Back-office	Front-office
Standardization	Retail banking	Contract cleaning
Customization	Software	Professional service firms

Source: *adapted from Segal-Horn, 1993*

We can now usefully return to the Ghoshal (1987) framework introduced in Chapter 7 Figure 7.5. Service firms seek to benefit from the same sources of potential advantage as manufacturing firms in their global expansion. The issue is whether such benefits from global expansion are as attainable for service firms as for manufacturing firms. Ghoshal (1987) summarized three potential sources of benefit from global expansion as follows:

- National differences, for example to obtain beneficial factor costs (such as lower wages or access to a large pool of skilled engineering graduates), or to offset country-specific government policies.

- Scale economies, for example to spread cost-reduction and experience effects across national boundaries, to expand or exploit scale in purchasing, distribution, capital costs, and so on.

- Scope economies, for example sharing investments, knowledge and learning across products and markets.

A combination of structural, market, regulatory and technological changes has provided a shift in the balance of activities within service firms. Greater technological capability has led to the redesign of many services to increase the back-office proportion of activities in their value chain. For example, internet broadband connections across the world (albeit with varying degrees of reliability) have enabled 24/7 service and back-office availability. Some organizations call this a 'follow-the-sun' capability. They mean that as Paris goes to bed, Seattle wakes up and then Kolkotta, and so on, enabling 24/7 operational availability. Global law firms use this facility to get rapid document-production for corporate clients so that completed draft contracts can be e-mailed from India to the UK enabling 24-hour turnaround. Such developments have lowered considerably the levels of perceived risk, and enhanced the potential benefits attached to global expansion of service firms.

REVISITING OLI FOR SERVICES

Enderwick (1989) provides insight into firm-specific advantages (FSA) and location-specific advantages (LSA) available to the service MNC. He builds on the work of Dunning (1985, 1989), and the eclectic paradigm of international production based on ownership, location and internalization (OLI) advantages introduced in Chapter 2. Ownership incorporates competitive advantages; location incorporates configuration advantages; and internalization incorporates co-ordination advantages. (You may recognize some similarities to Porter's (1986) conceptualization of configuration and co-ordination in the allocation of international value chain activities by the firm.)

14

Enderwick includes under FSA, factors familiar from the earlier scale and scope debate in services: privileged access to assets such as goodwill and brand name, particularly important in consumer buying processes for services; scale economies obtainable from high fixed costs and low variable costs of operation; other economies of common governance available from single hierarchical management of complementary assets; and scope economies which enable incumbent firms to offer innovatory or complementary services which reinforce their competitive position. Under LSA factors, most significant is the differential between services which are location-specific because production and consumption are inseparable and therefore where wide international representation is mandatory (e.g. fast food chains), compared to those services which are tradeable and therefore choice of international location would result from considerations of comparative advantage (e.g. software houses). Lastly, the internalization issue is of exceptional importance for service MNCs, since they will wish to retain internal control over anything affecting their management of the 'service encounter'.

The continual search for optimization of OLI advantages in services, using the same models and criteria as for manufacturing firms, now makes simple distinctions between product and service obsolete.

WHAT HAS CHANGED?

Restructuring and concentration in most service sectors in recent years has meant that many service industries (such as travel, fast food, some financial services, information services) now meet Kobrin's (1991: 18) definition of a global industry, defined in terms of 'the significance of the competitive advantages of international operations' arising mainly from the structural characteristics of scale economies and technological intensity. Strong global market segments exist for many types of services. Therefore both demand for, and the efficient supply of, global services, does exist. The main changes can be simply summarized in Strategy in Action 14.3.

Nevertheless, the concepts of economies of scale and economies of scope explored in this chapter operate at the level of the firm, with international growth driven by sustained investment in the development of firm-specific asset structures. Therefore, while the issue of change in service industry structure is central to any discussion of the growth of global competition in services, it may be that the most important factors determining successful global expansion in services should be understood at the level of the firm, as in the Novotel, TutorVista, Wipro or ISS examples already given. This is particularly

14

Strategy in Action 14.3 *Changes in the nature of services*

Then: services were time-dependent and could not be inventoried.

Now: because of technology, information is the one part of a solution which can be stored, retrieved and transported.

Then: services always had to have local presence with service providers physically on the scene.

Now: many services can come from far away via remote web connections.

Then: services were culturally bound and were difficult to transplant from one country to another.

Now: technology has created many new types of services which have no prior cultural associations.

Then: services were considered to be a domestic business.

Now: many services are global, customers neither know nor care where they originate.

Then: most services were accessible only at certain times in clearly defined places.

Now: it's possible to deliver a growing proportion of services anyplace and anytime.

important with regard to the managerial and organizational capabilities of the firm. The point has been made with regard to MNC activity in general (Dunning, 1989), and service MNC activity in particular (Enderwick, 1989), that the way in which firms organize their global activities may itself be a crucial competitive advantage. This is strongly reinforced in work by Rumelt (1991), concluding that the most important sources of long-term business rents 'are not associated with industry, but with the unique endowments, positions and strategies of individual businesses' (p. 168). These points may go some way towards explaining both the successes and the failures in global expansion undertaken by individual service firms.

SUMMARY

- This chapter has discussed issues of global strategy specific to service industries and service firms. It has emphasized both the enormous growth in services and how both service industries and service firms have been changing.
- Services have special characteristics, such as intangibility, which make them different from products.
- These service characteristics create additional risks for service firms in implementing global strategies.
- The special characteristics of services mean that many strategic management frameworks must be applied differently to services.
- However, these special characteristics of services have reduced in significance due mainly to structural and technological changes. Many services now contain 'hard' tangible components which are capital-intensive, amenable to separation from the point of service delivery, and responsive to standardization.
- Core knowledge and information-based assets of service firms are codifiable and transferable across national boundaries, as is the consumer franchise from strong service brands.
- In particular there is increasing potential for service firms to utilize the economies of scale and economies of scope that Ghoshal (1987) argued are crucial in order for an organization to benefit from global expansion.
- As a result of this combination of factors, service industry dynamics are becoming more similar to those of manufacturing.
- Even the most distinctive characteristic of services, the interface with the customer at the 'moment of truth', is in many cases being managed remotely.
- The emphasis on customer service in manufacturing, and the emphasis on efficient deployment of back-office assets in services through the reconfiguration of the global service value chain, are each trying to capture the advantages the other has traditionally utilized. This once again illustrates the 'dynamics' of strategy-making.

14

DISCUSSION QUESTIONS

1 Define the four main service characteristics that are usually considered to be the factors that make services different from products.
2 Are there any particular ways in which these service characteristics make it more difficult or risky for a service business to pursue an internationalization or globalization strategy?
3 Provide some examples of economies of scale and economies of scope in service businesses.

4 Describe some of the ways in which economies of scale or economies of scope are significant in designing and implementing global strategies for service firms.

5 Have there been any recent developments that have changed the feasibility of global strategies for service firms?

6 Under what circumstances should a service firm pursue a global strategy?

7 To what extent do you agree that services are different from products and that service organizations are different from manufacturing organizations?

FURTHER READINGS

1 Pine, B.J. and Gilmore, J.H. (1998) 'Welcome to the experience economy', *Harvard Business Review*, July/August: 97–105.

Pine and Gilmore go further than discussing service industry restructuring and the impact of capital-intensive ICT investments on service firms. They describe not services but experiences as the next stage of service industry development. They see the next great transition as that of shifting from selling services to selling experiences. As more services follow products eventually into becoming commodities (as telephone calls and airline seats already have) then experiences may offer the next route to added value.

2 Lovelock, C.H. and Yip, G.S. (1996) 'Developing global strategies for service businesses', *California Management Review*, 38(2): 64–86.

Lovelock and Yip provide evidence and an analysis to demonstrate that both demand for, and efficient supply of, global services exists.

3 Segal-Horn, S. and Dean, A. (2009) 'Delivering "effortless experience" across borders: managing internal consistency in professional service firms', *Journal of World Business*, 44(1): 41–50.

When clients require consistent services delivered across borders, then firms need an organization that is sufficiently flexible to be able to support such cross-border consistency. This paper takes a detailed look at how globalization strategies are implemented in large corporate law firms. Primarily globalization takes place in terms of investments in the processes and practices that enhance internal consistency such that clients receive an 'effortless experience' of the service across multiple locations worldwide.

14

CHAPTER 15

The ethical MNC

LEARNING OBJECTIVES The objectives of this chapter are to:

■ explore the relevance and interpretation of ethics within global business

■ describe the relative nature of bribery and corruption in global business

■ explain the nature of sustainability

■ identify the three legs of sustainability, that is economic, environmental and social

■ introduce corporate social responsibility (CSR)

■ emphasize the importance of reputation to competitiveness in MNCs

■ illustrate how good CSR policies can enhance reputation

■ describe how international institutions are attempting to encourage sustainability.

INTRODUCTION

Corporate governance is defined by the OECD (Organization of Economic Co-operation and Development) as the system by which business corporations are directed and controlled. The governance structure of a firm will therefore specify the distribution of rights and responsibilities within the organization as well as the rules and procedures for decision-making. As you would expect, such governance structures and the systems of national and international ethics in which different business corporations are embedded (as discussed in Chapter 4 on the emerging economies) vary greatly in content and interpretation from country to country, region to region, and culture to culture. One of the most difficult problems facing organizations that operate across borders is to decide which standards to adopt: those of the home base country or those of the new country market. Either choice carries costs and creates problems. If the home base standards are adopted, throughout all global markets, misunderstanding or accusations of cultural imperialism may result in a general inability to operate effectively in the different context of the local market. If local market standards are adopted, this may lead in some circumstances to stake-holder criticism in the home country or even accusations of illegal and criminal behaviour. Obvious examples would include attitudes to bribery and corruption, to relative pay and working conditions in home or local markets and to copyrights, patents and intellectual property rights. For example, it has been estimated that 95 per cent of software in China is pirated and that 60 per cent of 'Honda' motorbikes or 40 per cent of 'Procter & Gamble' hair shampoos are counterfeit.

CORPORATE GOVERNANCE AND GLOBAL ETHICS

Transparency International is an independent research group based in Berlin. It has established itself as a very reliable global source of information on, and analysis of, corruption in all its forms. Each year since 1995 it has published an international Corruption Perceptions Index and an annual Global Corruption Report. In their 2008 Global Corruption Report, Switzerland and Denmark are listed as first and second, in other words the least corrupt countries to trade with. Nigeria and Sudan come at the other end of the scale. Transparency International uses thirteen indicators of international perception from a wide variety of sources, although it recognizes that these are judgements and therefore are, by definition, subject to potential dispute. By acting as an information agency, Transparency International is attempting to raise the profile of corruption as a very serious issue within international trade. In countries dependent on foreign direct investment (FDI), which includes all emerging, developing and transitional economies, if the use of bribery is expected as a normal part of the contract negotiation process, then at the very least organizations and governments will significantly raise their cost of capital. That is an entirely separate and additional cost from other calculable costs of manufacturing and trading. However, the definition of what constitutes a bribe is by no means easy to determine, as is shown in Strategy in Action 15.1.

It is clear that standards vary according to culture, and that it is very difficult to establish absolute standards universally applicable in all places and in all circumstances. The changing global financial context has had an impact on corporate governance, and has been in part held responsible for some of the corporate scandals that have occurred. Some of the best-known recent corporate scandals include: Enron (US energy trading company), Ahold (Dutch food retailer), and Parmalat (Italian food producer).

Management practices based on shareholder value became increasingly important in the US in the 1980s, from where they spread to Europe, but not so much to the Asia-Pacific region. These practices included the use of such performance measurement systems as Economic Valued Added® (EVA®).

15

Strategy in Action 15.1 *What is a bribe?*

In the US since 1977, the Foreign Corrupt Practices Act (FCPA) outlaws payment of bribes by US corporations to foreign officials or political parties or candidates. American MNCs claim this has placed them at a disadvantage in bidding for international contracts. The OECD Convention on bribery has been signed by 35 countries. It states: 'enterprises should not, directly or indirectly, offer, promise, give, or demand a bribe or other undue advantage to obtain or retain business' anywhere in the world.

However, such attempts to prevent bribery are rendered ineffective by what is known as 'facilitation payments'. These are payments made to expedite routine business needs (e.g. clearing customs, obtaining permits). There is no clear definition of a facilitation payment or how precisely it differs from a bribe. An amendment to the FCPA specifically exempts 'facilitating payments for routine governmental action' from the US definition of a bribe. Two UK MNCs admitted to a British Parliamentary committee in 2001 that they make facilitation payments while at the same time one (BP Oil) declared that: 'we will never offer, solicit or accept a bribe in any form'.

SOURCE: *THE ECONOMIST*, 2 MARCH 2002

EVA® aligns many elements of management control through the use of one common measure based on a given return due to shareholders. These developments in the late 1990s were part of a period of spreading '**financialization**' (Froud et al., 2000) involving a new form of competition which meant an orientation towards financial results as the dominant performance measure, but also involved a speeding up of management work.

> The new forces of the capital market, via investment institutions and professional fund managers, are generally much more mobile and rapidly threatening than the old forces of the product market via retailers and consumers.
>
> (Froud et al., 2000)

This has proved to be an extremely insightful comment in light of the destructive economic and financial forces unleashed a few years after that comment was published largely as a result of a type of financialization.

It is very unusual for a firm to lose product positioning, brand identity and market share overnight by consumers deserting them en masse. However, financial investors with a 'value' mentality can be altogether more volatile and desert a firm overnight if they become nervous. They evaluate management performance only on short-term financial gains and act collectively to sell when expectations are disappointed. This attitude of financial 'short-termism' puts heavy pressure on (mainly Western) management to focus almost exclusively on share price as the measure of value and strong performance, as discussed in Strategy in Action 15.2.

Strategy in Action 15.2 *Some recent corporate scandals: Enron, Ahold and Parmalat*

Enron
The global energy supply firm Enron was the fifth-largest firm in the US Fortune 500 list of companies a matter of weeks before it had to cease trading in late 2001. Enron had been using (with the apparent blessing of its accountants / auditors Arthur Andersen) 'special-purpose entities' (SPEs) which are non-consolidated off-balance-sheet financial vehicles. They were being used to hide major liabilities, so that they did not have to be entered into the consolidated balance sheet. Enron had set up partnerships with outside investors, funding the partnerships by lending partners its own shares which could be sold for cash. One such partner (Raptor) was lent $500 million of Enron shares. Raptor gave Enron an IOU for $500 million, which Enron entered on its balance sheet as an asset. Raptor had no assets or income; only Enron stock which it cashed in

to buy hi-tech shares. When these rapidly lost value, the hole in Enron's accounts could not be made good. This was repeated in other similar arrangements with other SPE partners. Their accountant Andersens made $52 million in audit and consulting fees from Enron in 2000, including signing the accounts as true and fair. One of the consequences resulting from Enron's own collapse was the rapidly following collapse of Andersen in 2002 and then the passing of the Sarbanes-Oxley Act in 2002 in the US which tightened the rules of behaviour of listed companies, their auditors and lawyers. One of the more far-reaching results has been the sale by most accounting firms (or at least the separation from audit), of their consulting businesses. It also highlighted the failure of oversight by internal audit committees and the poor performance of non-executive directors on corporate

15

boards. In 2004, senior managers of Enron, including the Chairman Kenneth Lay, were put on trial in the US on fraud charges. Kenneth Lay was later convicted of major fraud charges and imprisoned for many years.

Ahold

Ahold (Netherlands) was the world's third-biggest food retailer after Wal-Mart (US) and Carrefour (France). In February 2003, Ahold announced the resignation of its CEO and its finance director, after finding that it had overstated profits by more than $500 million (Euros 463 million – at 2003 exchange rates) in the past two years. This was immediately labelled 'Europe's Enron', although it was rapidly exceeded by an even worse financial scandal at Italy's Parmalat ten months later. Ahold's market value fell by 90 per cent to Euros 3.3 billion, having been Euros 30 billion in 2001. Similarities emerge from a comparison of Ahold and Enron. In particular, both Boards were dominated by their overpowerful CEO. Ahold's Board extended the CEO's contract for another seven years only a few months before the scandal. Its auditors (the Dutch office of accountants Deloitte Touche) had failed to act. Ahold kept billions of debt off its balance sheet, claimed acquired firms' profits as organic growth and booked capital gains from sale-and-leaseback deals as profit. Unlike Enron, there is no evidence of personal reward for the CEO being involved. Instead it seemed to be about not wanting to lose his reputation for spectacular year-on-year growth (23 successive quarter-years of double-digit profit growth for the company and its shareholders had been achieved and this was prominently advertised in company brochures). EU companies adopted new international accounting standards in 2005. The Dutch market regulator admitted it still had no powers over faulty auditing.

Parmalat

Parmalat was one of the world's biggest producers of milk and dairy products and premium quality (Parma) ham. Although a public company, its shares were still controlled by the founding Tanzi family. In 2002, it employed 36,000 people in 30 countries with a turnover of Euros 7.6 billion ($7.2 billion). The Parmalat scandal began with the disappearance of billions of euros and the emergence of complex and confusing financial engineering including many off-shore financial vehicles. Grant Thornton (UK accounting firm with many European clients) was the auditor for 17 of Parmalat's 200 subsidiaries. In December 2003, Grant Thornton was horrified at a reply it received from Bank of America concerning Euros 3.95 billion, supposedly held in the account of a Parmalat subsidiary Bonlat, based in the Cayman Islands (a well-known tax haven). Bank of America now said the Euros 3.95 billion did not exist and that a letter from them confirming its existence was a forgery. The Italian office of Grant Thornton had signed off those Bonlat accounts the previous year. One consequence of the Parmalat scandal was that Grant Thornton expelled the Italian member of its 585-office international network. One young accountant at Parmalat committed suicide in January 2004. An Italian turnaround expert, Enrico Bondi, was appointed to run Parmalat after its shares were suspended in December 2003. Grant Thornton had been Parmalat's main auditor until 1999, when Italy's rules on rotation of auditors at regular intervals forced Parmalat to switch to Deloitte Touche, one of the world's four remaining global accounting firms (after the demise of Andersen which had been the fifth). Rotation of auditors was one of the measures introduced by the Sarbanes-Oxley Act. Rotation of auditors seems to have made no difference whatsoever in Parmalat's case.

SOURCE: AUTHORS BASED ON A VARIETY OF PRESS CLIPPINGS

15

It is useful to compare the three examples of corporate fraud given in Strategy in Action 15.2. Enron's and Ahold's actions were certainly fuelled by an internal culture of rapid growth. Although there is some validity therefore in blaming financialization, and the pursuit of short-term financial targets above other objectives for these scandals, other factors are also significant. Poor corporate governance was certainly a factor, with weak, ineffective (and sometimes complicit) auditors at least as important. SPEs are legal, but not for the purpose for which Enron and Parmalat used them. Their accountants' job was to trace not just the existence of these financial vehicles, but also the uses to which they were being put. All the auditors failed in that. This ineffective oversight was, in Andersen's case, very likely to have been affected by their dual roles as auditors and consultants and the conflicts of interest to which that can give rise. Legislation has now put a stop to dual accounting / consulting roles. In Grant Thornton's case there was a lack of internal controls within their European network (an alliance or coalition of 'best friends' accounting firms across Europe) to ensure similar standards operating at all their international offices. What this shows, also, is the risk attached to managing international networks, since mistakes or wrong-doing in one national office can cause the collapse of the whole global corporation, as happened with Andersen, and cause serious reputational damage, as happened at Grant Thornton.

There were also clear shortcomings in the corporate governance of all three companies: at Enron and Ahold their boards were dominated by over-powerful, ambitious CEOs; and at Parmalat by the limitations of a dominant family ownership. These only became serious problems because they were combined with weak boards and poor oversight. It is important to note that these scandals have had a lasting impact in the subsequent shake-up of the accounting industry and increased international awareness has led to changed regulatory regimes for financial reporting and corporate responsibility in both Europe and the US.

That very large firms can make appalling strategic decisions or can collapse rapidly illustrates the flaws in the assumption that big is always successful. As companies such as Ahold become global MNCs, they encounter a whole range of national regulations and regulators. It is the weakest regimes that are likely to lead to wrong-doing. A better response is therefore for global MNCs to adopt the standards of the strongest regulatory regimes to govern their internal corporate decision-making and managerial controls. These scandals have led to MNCs giving more attention to these concerns. However, despite the genuine shock and rapid legal, governmental and regulatory responses to Enron, Parmalat, and others, similar financial scandals are still occurring regularly. See Strategy in Action 15.3 for a brief description of a scandal in 2009 in India which seems to have some very similar characteristics to those of Enron, Ahold and Parmalat.

Moral hazard
....

A concept that may be very useful in understanding the reasons for these recent financial and managerial scandals is 'moral hazard'. What is meant by **moral hazard** is where a potential conflict of interest may exist between two roles or two aspects of a situation leading the individual to decide on the riskier option, but one that gives that individual private benefit at the expense of public good. A well-researched example is the fact that drivers of cars who are wearing seat belts that will increase their protection in case of an accident, have been found to then drive faster, that is raise their level of risk-taking. It is in this sense that having insurance coverage can be argued to increase moral hazard because people with insurance are likely to behave more recklessly.

If we apply the concept of moral hazard to business managers or owners of companies, we can explain the behaviour of the owners, managers, CEOs and Board members of Enron, Ahold, Parmalat or Satyam as arising from moral hazard because they used their discretion to use assets for which they were responsible and accountable to others (such as shareholders) to control these assets for their own benefit. They could, so they did.

15

Strategy in Action 15.3 *The Satyam scandal*

Satyam Computer Services was, until very recently, India's fourth-largest software and services firm. The fraud carried out by its founder B. Ramalinga Raju and his brother is puzzling. On 7th January 2009, Mr Raju confessed to fiddling Satyam's accounts for years and admitted that a $1 billion cash pile did not exist. However, many suspect that this is only half the story. After all, Satyam's books were audited by Price Waterhouse Coopers. The auditor says that it verified Satyam's fixed deposits with the banks that held them. So – did the money exist or not? Opinion is that the money did in fact exist, but that it was subsequently spirited out of the company and hidden. Such things are not so unusual in India. It is more the $1 billion size of the fraud that makes Satyam noteworthy.

One of the main problems that makes such frauds easier in India than elsewhere is the system of 'promoters', who are mostly business families and other company 'insiders'. It tends to be these promoters that hold the bulk of shares in India's publicly quoted companies on the National Stock Exchange (NSE). In fact such 'promoters' still hold about half of all of India's NSE companies. But many such family firms are evolving into more widely held corporations. That has created an opportunity and a short-term incentive, as the proportion of shares held by insiders falls, for the existing 'promoter' insiders to cheat other shareholders by siphoning off money while they still have the chance, and before the shares become much more widely owned and more open to public scrutiny.

Some of the techniques commonly used for siphoning off cash include: managers making loans to another company owned by a close relation; overpaying greatly for a training weekend and then taking a cut from the hotel owner for the difference.

It is difficult for foreign investors, non-Indian firms with stakes in Indian firms, to have much influence on these practices while the proportion of shares held by insiders remains so high. In fact they too have a disincentive to annoy the internal owners too much.

SOURCE: ABRIDGED FROM *THE ECONOMIST*, 10 JANUARY 2009

TYPES OF CORRUPTION

Let us now try to unpack a little further the concept of corruption. Mauro (1997) identified five categories of corruption:

1 *Administrative resource allocation* – where administrative authorization replaces the market, opportunities for corruption (such as government officials expecting bribes in return for contracts or licences) increase.

2 *Lack of institutional checks and balances and information* – a weak legal and auditing system enables corruption to flourish because it is difficult to monitor transactions.

3 *Insufficient funding of public services* – where public servants are poorly paid the incentive arises to supplement their wages corruptly.

4 *Social and cultural factors* – for example division of society on religious or ethnic lines can easily lead to nepotism or other forms of unfair and restricted access to resources withheld from one group by another.

5 *Natural resources* – abundant natural resources are also an incentive for bribery, for example the impact of its valuable diamond mining industry on the Democratic Republic of Congo has not been beneficial.

At least three of these categories of corruption are the result of the kinds of 'institutional voids' that we discussed in Chapter 4.

Such conditions may lead to growth in levels of corruption which can have five major effects (Lasserre, 2003):

1 It discourages domestic investment and FDI, since the corrupt payments add to necessary costs and operate like an extra tax.

2 It distorts public expenditure, for example inefficient awarding of contracts or purchasing unnecessary new equipment in order to receive a payoff from the company with whom the order is placed.

3 It reduces the productivity of public investments by adding to costs and not to revenues.

4 It reduces work productivity by encouraging cynicism in the workforce and reduced motivation.

5 It reduces the integrity of the social fabric.

All of these outcomes are detrimental to both economic good and social good.

SUSTAINABILITY

Sustainability is a term often used specifically to refer to the relationship between organizations and the environment. In particular it implies that an organization will have a neutral effect on its environment. Over the last two decades there has been increasing public debate about what decision-making and governance systems might best implement values of sustainability in the behaviour and decisions of companies, governments and the wider society. However, sustainability is also an umbrella term that may be used to cover three separate but overlapping areas: first, *sustainable development* of the environment; second, **corporate social responsibility (CSR)** by organizations; and third, *inclusivity and social justice* for the individual. Sometimes the three areas are called environmental, economic and social sustainability.

1 *Sustainable development* of the environment has been the subject of much scientific research and is predominantly concerned with such matters as global warming, the hole in the ozone layer, excess carbon emissions (e.g. resulting in increased carbon taxes and international systems for the trading of carbon emissions between countries); and corporate and governmental activities and policies that may prevent or exacerbate the damage caused to the planet from economic activity.

2 *CSR* (economic) is concerned with the behaviour of companies, especially MNCs, since MNCs are the largest companies and their actions therefore have the greatest impact. In so far as they behave unethically, or follow policies that may be economically sound but environmentally hostile, they are perceived as having poor CSR records by the external organizations which monitor such matters. These are mainly non-governmental organizations (NGOs) such as Friends of the Earth. Negative CSR reports on MNCs by such NGOs may damage their reputations and hence their share price. They have sometimes even led to consumer boycotts, as for Monsanto (see Strategy in Action 15.4) and Royal Dutch Shell oil company (see Strategy in Action 15.6).

3 *Inclusivity* (social) is concerned with how individuals are treated, and thus involves topics like human rights, equality of opportunity, anti-racism or ageism and absence of discrimination against minority groups. It also includes agendas such as 'fair' treatment for all workers around the world,

15

by which is meant that the hiring of workers in developing or emerging economies should be on terms and conditions identical to those of workers in developed (i.e. usually richer) economies. Otherwise such MNCs are accused of exploitation of labour in poorer economies. The term 'sweatshop' is often used to describe such exploitative conditions of employment, meaning a factory or workshop where workers are employed for extremely long hours in very poor conditions.

The triple bottom line

These three areas are conceptualized separately but clearly overlap in practice. A commonly used concept has emerged from the CSR movement that captures all of these concerns and is used to assert a broader basis for evaluating corporate performance than purely financial performance. This is known as the **triple bottom line** (Elkington, 1997). It is a basic concept within CSR, used to suggest that environmental, economic and social sustainability should all be of equal importance to organizations. The further implication of the triple bottom line concept is that organizations should be held accountable for environmental and social performance indicators as well as for their financial performance. This view has certainly gained ground such that it is probably now the view that holds the moral high ground, at least in developing economies among governments, companies and the wider public. Increasingly the triple bottom line approach has led to MNCs in a wide range of industry sectors reporting annual 'social audits' of their activities, alongside the regular financial performance covered in their traditional annual report to shareholders. At an international institutional level the UN has adopted a Global Compact covering human rights, labour and the environment. However, since the UN depends upon the support of its members and exerts only indirect influence rather than actual power, its ability to enforce the terms of its Global Compact is mainly moral.

A further comment on the triple bottom line is necessary before moving on. There is a significant and noteworthy difference between the triple bottom line and what *The Economist* calls 'the good old single bottom line' (22 Jan. 2005: 12), that is measuring profits. *The Economist* argues that there is a very real problem with the triple bottom line: it is not easily or clearly measurable and therefore does not offer a clear test of business success or effective performance in the use of resources. Whereas measuring profits is very straightforward, measuring environmental protection and social justice is not. It further asks how these three objectives are to be traded off against each other? In the end, and bearing in mind the cost of CSR implementation, how can it be demonstrated that any company has actually improved its triple bottom line? This view is echoed in a comment made by the global accounting firm KPMG expressing 'concern at the asymmetric link between the resources devoted to investor relations and governance and the likely improvement in the company's performance' (quoted in *The Business*, 29–30 May 2005: 11).

Many of these arguments are therefore far more complex than we have so far implied. We shall unpack them a little further in the next section.

15

SHAREHOLDERS VERSUS STAKEHOLDERS

CSR refers to the relationship between business and its broad stakeholders, including society and the wider community at large. Beliefs and attitudes concerning what this relationship should be, and the way businesses should behave, do vary as attitudes change over time (Pinkston and Carroll, 1996). In the 1960s and 1970s the Nobel prize-winning economist Milton Friedman had famously argued that 'the business of business is business' (Friedman, 1962 and 1970; see discussion also in Kok et al., 2001), that is that the primary and most significant duty of a company is to increase profits for the benefit of shareholders. This is in direct contrast to the current views of many NGOs which have grown greatly in power, influence and public support since the 1980s. Over a twenty-year period they have shifted from minority bodies on the fringe of public policy-making, to being respected stakeholders in public and political debate. They are invited to advise, or at least make inputs to, government policies and other international institutional bodies. NGOs such as Greenpeace, Forum for the Future or Friends of the Earth, have genuine influence and public support. Elsewhere, such as at the annual Economic Forum of the world's leaders at Davos, Switzerland, leaders of NGOs are popular and respected speakers. *The Economist* has commented (22 Jan. 2005) that 'this marks a significant victory in the battle of ideas'. The accepted public definition of what constitutes 'good corporate citizenship' has shifted very much to the triple bottom line.

Two questions help us to capture the difference between the opposing positions of Milton Friedman, who espoused shareholder capitalism, and modern-day CSR, with its emphasis on stakeholder capitalism. First, 'why does our organization exist?' Second, 'who should the organization serve?' The answers of the two groups would be respectively, to serve shareholders and to serve wider stakeholders. It is therefore very important to understand this distinction between stakeholder capitalism and shareholder capitalism: their viewpoints, their potential spheres of influence over organizations, and their implications. In a shareholder perspective, profit maximization and shareholder value are the key concerns of the organization: in a stakeholder perspective, the organization considers its impact upon a wider body of stakeholders concerned with broader issues than the organization's ability to make profits. A generic diagram of the most common set of stakeholders of an MNC is given in Figure 15.1. In this broader set of generic stakeholders, shareholders are only one amongst a range of powerful and influential groups.

Monsanto (a large US biotechnology company) is one company whose fate has been strongly tied to this shift in 'the battle of ideas' from shareholders to stakeholders. It was involved in the 1990s in what was probably one of the earliest, and most-publicized, of these battles of ideas. What happened to Monsanto summarizes the point at which the shift in opinion, and the impact that wider organizational stakeholders can have, became publicly manifest. In Strategy in Action 15.4 one of the earliest significant exercises in stakeholder power is discussed.

If we try to make sense of what happened to Monsanto it is a useful exercise to distinguish the various stakeholders. The principal stakeholder groups mentioned in Strategy in Action 15.4 are:

■ Monsanto's senior managers

■ The environmental NGO Greenpeace

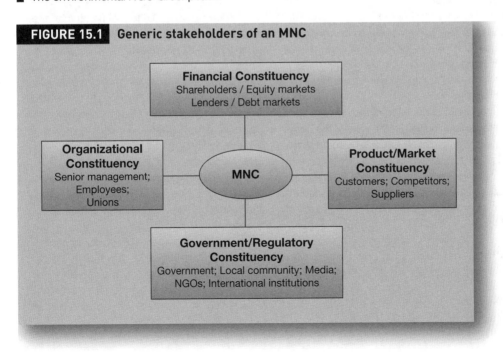

FIGURE 15.1   **Generic stakeholders of an MNC**

Financial Constituency
Shareholders / Equity markets
Lenders / Debt markets

Organizational Constituency
Senior management;
Employees;
Unions

MNC

Product/Market Constituency
Customers; Competitors;
Suppliers

Government/Regulatory Constituency
Government; Local community; Media;
NGOs; International institutions

15

Strategy in Action 15.4 *Stakeholder power: the GM crops disaster at Monsanto*

Monsanto, a US biotechnology firm, had enjoyed great success in the US with its range of genetically modified (GM) food products, for which they had won regulatory approval in the US. Monsanto argued that their genetically modified foods would lower pesticide use, increase crop yields and promote more efficient land use. These were all objectives that were highly desirable economically and environmentally and they appeared to be completely in harmony with the sustainable development agenda emerging from the European environmental lobby. However, when Monsanto entered the European markets with these GM products, disaster struck. The introduction of GM foods into Europe was a fiasco. Monsanto had assumed that European environmentalists would be enthusiastic about its products and it was therefore completely unprepared for the negative publicity and overwhelmingly hostile campaigns that greeted it in Europe.

The attacks were led by the international environmental NGO, Greenpeace. GM crop trials were sabotaged. Huge public support was obtained in a campaign to have GM foods banned and removed from supermarket shelves. European governments placed a moratorium upon the licensing of GM products for human consumption. How did this happen?

Monsanto had a wide range of interested stakeholders. Indeed, in the view of the company, it was precisely because it could demonstrate the benefits of GM seeds for a wide range of its stakeholders (e.g. farmers in poor countries) that Monsanto was confident that its products would prove as welcome in Europe as in the USA. The products certainly offered significant advantages to three key external stakeholders: first, to farmers who achieved improved yields and profitability; second, to consumers in lower prices; and third, to environmentalists in the reduction in the range and number of herbicides, leading to lower soil and crop residues and less pollution of waterways. Other groups of direct stakeholders would also benefit: the shareholders in Monsanto who could expect higher dividends; and Monsanto employees who would benefit from the growth of the organization.

However, Monsanto had not expected the resistance of European consumers to GM foods. Despite a large amount of scientific research showing no risk to consumers, European consumers totally rejected the claims made by Monsanto about the safety of GM crops and seeds. Things were made even worse by a hugely powerful media campaign with the slogan: 'Frankenstein Food'. Consumers were convinced of unspecified health and environmental dangers that far outweighed any conceivable social, environmental or economic benefits. Supermarkets, who dominated the food distribution channels, had no incentive to stock the GM foods and every incentive to publicize the fact that their shelves were clear of all GM produce.

Although many EU governments, and the European Commission itself, have argued that field trials needed to be carried out in order to establish experimental evidence, no GM crops are yet developed commercially in Europe and any field trials have to be held under conditions of absolute secrecy and tight security, otherwise masked environmental protestors will arrive to dig up the test fields.

The cost to Monsanto of their venture into Europe has been a long-term commercial and public relations disaster. Other wider economic and social costs have included the cost to European agriculture of lack of access to more cost-effective advanced crops, which has affected the competitiveness of European farmers and their ability to compete internationally. This lack of competitiveness

SOURCE: COMPILED BY AUTHORS
FROM VARIOUS PRESS CLIPPINGS

has reinforced the protectionism of the EU's Common Agricultural Policy and to delay further its necessary reform. The level of investment in scientific research in Europe has also been affected, with many innovative biotechnology companies leaving Europe for the more welcoming research and commercial environment of the US.

■ European farmers, Monsanto's customers

■ The supermarkets, the European farmers' customers

■ European consumers

■ European governments

■ Monsanto's shareholders

■ Monsanto's employees

■ The media

■ The wider public

■ Environmental campaigners.

Were the claims of all of these stakeholders equally legitimate?

Argenti (2003, see Table 15.1) provides us with a finer lens for making sense of the relative identity and power of various types of stakeholders. He suggests that stakeholders may be either *primary* or *secondary*, depending upon the nature of the resources they provide to the organization, as given in Table 15.1.

Perhaps Argenti's (2003; Table 15.1) formulation of primary and secondary stakeholders may help us conceptualize what happened to Monsanto, especially since Monsanto itself truly thought that it had the support of its major stakeholders. Table 15.1 provides an initial indication of why Monsanto's

TABLE 15.1	Organizational stakeholders
Primary	*Secondary*
Manager	Media
Employees	Suppliers
Customers	Government:
Shareholders	Local
Communities	Regional
	National
	Supra-national
	Creditors
	NGOs

Source: Adapted from Argenti (2003)

15

strategy failed. It suggests that Monsanto focused its efforts upon the primary stakeholder groups, and underestimated the ability that influential secondary stakeholders (e.g. an NGO such as Greenpeace) could have upon the attitude of some of its primary stakeholders such as its customers (the farmers) and their customers (the supermarkets) and wider communities. Although probably lacking in legitimacy, and certainly lacking in accountability, nevertheless Greenpeace managed to influence effectively other powerful secondary stakeholders such as suppliers and the media, despite the interests of governments (national and supra-national) in continuing GM research and products.

SUSTAINABILITY, CSR AND INNOVATION

Surveys have shown that (Western) advanced economy consumers will pay 10 per cent more for a product if they are assured that is has been manufactured in non-exploitative conditions (e.g. no sweat-shop working conditions or starvation-level wages), (Bhattacharya and Sen, 2004). However, the research also shows that consumers will not pay 20 per cent extra or more. We therefore have a context that is generally supportive of the concepts of sustainability and CSR, in principle and up to a point, after which a degree of consumer self-interest re-emerges. Therefore advancing the sustainability agenda is most likely to be by:

■ statutory regulation

■ 'green' taxation policies, for example the polluter pays

■ changes in MNC strategies arising from perceived linkages between CSR and firm performance.

Porter and van der Linde (1995) made this connection between CSR and improved performance some while ago. They argued for a dynamic rather than a static view of environmental regulation. In their view, properly designed environmental legislation could trigger innovations that would lower the total cost of a product or service or improve its value. They argued that legislation would create the pressure that motivates companies to innovate. We can see this occurring currently as the EU's new tough emissions standards have put pressure on the entire world car industry to redesign engines, exhausts and create fuel innovation by 2015.

Thus adopting CSR measures, despite the costs involved, may be to the firm's advantage in the longer term. Consider the case of the Dutch flower industry described in Strategy in Action 15.5.

Porter and van der Linde (1995) use this example of (enforced) innovation in the Dutch flower industry to argue that policy makers, business leaders and environmentalists have focused on the static costs of environmental regulation and have ignored the dynamic opportunities for enhanced productivity benefits from innovation.

15

CSR AND REPUTATION

Within the shareholder capitalism view it might be argued that the only incentive for adopting CSR measures which increase costs without conferring additional financial benefits, would be the avoidance of costs associated with breaching legislation (Carlisle and Faulkner, 2004). However, as sustainability and CSR ideas have become more popular, there have arisen reputation effects in regard to corporate behaviour. Reputation is a major intangible asset for organizations. It can explain the difference between the book value and market values of companies. (Shrivaster et al., 2000; Black and Carnes, 2000; Kotha et al., 2001). Therefore reputation building, and avoiding Enron or Satyam-style reputation-destruction, is in the interests of shareholders and investors.

SOURCE: ADAPTED FROM PORTER AND VAN DER LINDE (1995): 120

Strategy in Action 15.5 *Innovation in the Dutch flower industry*

The Dutch flower industry had been facing extreme environmental problems. Fresh flowers are a national passion in Holland. The cut flower industry had been engaged in the intensive cultivation of flowers in small areas, with the result that soil and groundwater were being contaminated by high levels of pesticides, herbicides and fertilizers. With increasingly strict regulations coming into effect against the release of chemicals, it became clear that the only effective way to address the problems was to develop a closed-loop system. In advanced Dutch greenhouses, flowers now grow in water and rock wool instead of in soil. This has lowered the risks of infestation, which further reduced the need for fertilizers and for pesticides. Such fertilizers and pesticides that are still used are delivered in water that re-circulates and is re-used. This closed-loop system is closely monitored and has been able to reduce variations in growing conditions, thus also improving quality. Handling costs have gone down because the flowers are cultivated on specially designed platforms. Therefore, in addressing its environmental problem, the Dutch flower industry has responded by developing innovations that have raised the productivity derived from many of the resources used in growing flowers. The net result has been dramatically lowered environmental impact plus lower costs, improved product quality and enhanced global competitiveness.

Reputation-building increasingly includes adopting socially responsible policies which maintain or enhance reputation. Handy (2002) commented upon the relationship between good CSR and financial performance and concluded that social performance was a key factor in the management of company stakeholders, including owners, customers, employees, communities, and the environment. The suggestion is that positive CSR policies constitute an investment in positive stakeholder relations. An empirical study of 500 companies in the Standard and Poor Index (Hillman and Keim, 2001) found that managing stakeholder relations leads 'to customer or supplier loyalty, reduced turnover among employees, or improved reputation' (Hillman and Keim, 2001: 126). The suggestion is that reputation helps companies to retain customers and good suppliers and to recruit or retain good employees.

There is evidence to suggest that some corporations and senior managers aspire to 'mainstream' good CSR practices into their companies (Carlisle and Faulkner, 2004). The term 'mainstreaming' is used in this context to describe a strategy in which good CSR practice becomes structurally and culturally embedded into the organization. There is much support for corporations to integrate CSR policies into their business strategies (Bhattacharya and Sen, 2004; Hutchinson, 1996; Lober, 1996; Porter and Van der Linde, 1995; Shrivastava, 1995). However, there are also potential risks and liabilities in CSR. Such potential liabilities 'have the potential to bankrupt many companies' and 'the only prudent approach for boards of directors is to set about active risk mitigation since most CSR risks are uninsurable' (Banks, 2003: 11). In the section on flexibility, risks and ethics in Chapter 1 Strategy in Action 1.3, we discussed some examples of ethical dilemmas facing MNCs in their global operations (e.g. Starbucks in Ethiopia, Shell oil company in Nigeria), or just straightforward corruption (e.g. Siemens' suitcases of cash for bribes). These are examples also of risks and liabilities attached to CSR, either if it goes badly wrong, or simply the unintended consequences of other actions. Probably one of the most (in)famous ethical disasters in corporate history must be what has become known as the 'Brent Spar' incident that happened to Royal Dutch Shell in the 1990s. In some ways it was almost single-handedly responsible for transforming the environmental movement from a specialist interest group into a mass movement. We describe it in Strategy in Action 15.6.

Strategy in Action 15.6 *The Royal Dutch Shell Company and the Brent Spar incident: a profile of a socially irresponsible action by a major multinational company*

In December 1994 Shell Oil submitted a plan to sink Brent Spar, a 14,500-ton oil platform in the north Atlantic Sea, to the ocean floor. This action was decided upon after weighing many alternatives. However, the decision to sink the massive platform was a product of overvaluing financial costs, undervaluing environmental costs, and ignoring the views of stakeholders who were not directly involved in the decision-making process. Shell rapidly learned that it could no longer afford to ignore the views of the wider community of stakeholders. The environmental organization Greenpeace inspired widespread protests against Shell's plans when, on 30 April 1995, activists occupied the Brent Spar in an effort to prevent the deep sea disposal of the oil platform. Public outrage was so extreme in Germany, that 200 Shell service stations were threatened: 50 were damaged, two fire-bombed, and one was fired at. While Shell eventually decided upon other means for the disposal of the Brent Spar, it still maintained that sinking the platform would have been the best option if it were not for misconceptions about the environmental implications of this method of disposal.

Between 1991 and 1993 Shell conducted decommissioning studies to determine the best way to dispose of the massive oil platform. Out of thirteen suggested methods, Shell chose six to explore further. These included the following: (1) horizontal dismantling and onshore disposal, (2) vertical dismantling and onshore disposal, (3) in-field disposal, (4) deep water disposal, (5) refurbishment and re-use, and (6) continued main-

tenance. Ultimately Shell chose deep sea disposal as the best practical environmental option, and sought and received approval for this action from the British government.

When Greenpeace and other environmental advocates learned of this plan, they were outraged. Greenpeace mistakenly claimed that there were more than 5,000 tons of oil remaining in the Brent Spar. Greenpeace later retracted that figure and the amount of oil remaining in the oil platform was later demonstrated to be about 100 tons. However, the principles behind their objection remained valid and have subsequently influenced future environmental debate: in particular the idea that dumping the Brent Spar could set a precedent for dumping other giant structures, and the idea that generation of wastes should be minimized.

The general public reaction to Shell's plan included the extreme reaction of the violence carried out against Shell service stations in Germany. An equally strong consumer message was sent to Shell's managers through a widespread boycott of Shell products. As a result of this boycott, Shell lost millions of dollars in sales. It was forced to change its decision and not sink Brent Spar on the ocean floor, but have it towed to a fjord in Norway.

Many years later, it is still unclear which would have been the best environmental option; but that has almost become beside the point. The Brent Spar incident permanently changed the balance of power between MNCs, their managers, their shareholders and wider stakeholders.

Consequent upon the terrible publicity and negative public attitudes towards Royal Dutch Shell, it has transformed itself into a leader of CSR and established the philanthropic Shell Foundation and it is a prominent member of the World Business Council for Sustainable Development whose membership is made up of 175 MNCs, including Shell, ABB, Ford, Dow Chemical, Time Warner and so on.

IS VIRTUE VIRTUOUS IN BUSINESS?

The principles and practices of corporate social responsibility (CSR) date back more than a century, but the current wave of interest in this topic is unprecedented. This heightened attention is global and widespread. It is reflected in the growth of social and ethical investment funds; in the dramatic increase in voluntary codes of conduct for companies and industries; and in the number of companies that issue reports on their social and environmental practices and policies. Similarly, the mobilization of NGOs to challenge a wide range of corporate environmental and human rights practices; the frequency of consumer boycotts and protests; and the number of organizations and institutions established to monitor, measure, and report on corporate social and environmental performance; these all demonstrate deep public interest and concern.

Vogel (2005a) reviews the accomplishments of the contemporary CSR movement in both the United States and Europe. He appraises the movement's accomplishments and limitations, including a critical evaluation of the business case for CSR. While acknowledging the movement's achievements, most notably in improving some labour, human rights, and environmental conditions in developing countries, he also argues that CSR's potential to bring about a significant change in corporate behaviour is exaggerated. Vogel (2005a and 2005b) considers it unlikely that future improvements in corporate conduct will occur without more extensive or effective government regulation in the United States, Europe, the Far East, and in the emerging economies. Vogel poses fascinating questions: What does it mean to be a virtuous company? Is there a market for virtue? In other words, what is the long-term potential for business self-regulation without government intervention and regulation? Vogel concludes that the amount of improvement that can be expected is far more modest than much contemporary writing on corporate responsibility has claimed. He suggests that there is a market for virtue, but it is limited by the substantial costs that are required to implement more responsible business behavior.

Vogel (2005a) debates both sides of CSR: on the one hand, that a company's business practices often go beyond what it is legally required to do; on the other hand, that CSR is seen as what companies have to do to survive in a world where more and more of their behaviour is under a microscope. In the latter case, CSR may therefore be simply disguised self-interest or what was described in *The Economist* (22 Jan. 2005: 1) as: 'CSR is the tribute that capitalism everywhere pays to virtue'.

MNCs are always in the front line with regard to potential ethical dilemmas, partly because they are so visible and their brands so well-known. Should Wal-Mart (the world's largest retailer) be considered a responsible company for providing consumers with low-priced goods, especially food, or as an irresponsible company for paying its employees low wages and driving out independent shops? Should oil companies (such as BP with its publicly stated renewable energy development policies) be praised for recognizing the problem of global climate change and investing in renewable technologies or criticized for its continued development of fossil fuels? The answer is probably – both. That is because CSR is a complex, multidimensional issue, not a single issue problem.

Strategy in Action 15.7 provides us with a classic example of this perpetual mixture in relation to the giant US internet company Google.

A further issue is raised by the issues discussed in relation to Google in Strategy in Action 15.7 and it is an issue of moral hazard. What Google proposes to do with its philanthropic division Google.org is to allocate 1 per cent of the firm's annual profits, equity and employee's time to its philanthropic projects. However, the issue of moral hazard arises when we consider whether it is up to the managers of a publicly owned company to give away the profits of that company? Corporate philanthropy may be described as: 'charity with other people's money' (*The Economist*, 22 Jan. 2005: 8). By contrast, consider what Bill Gates has done in setting up his own Bill and Melinda Gates Foundation with its initial endowment of $27 billion. This is a very different situation since the Bill and Melinda Gates Foundation is spending Bill Gates's own private money. Philanthropy that is financed from private wealth is quite different from that financed out of the profits of publicly owned companies.

15

Strategy in Action 15.7 *Both sides of Google*

Google, the US internet giant, has an informal company motto: 'Don't be evil'.

Google scenario 1

Dr Larry Brilliant heads a 40-strong team at Google.org which is Google's philanthropy division. He may have one of the best jobs in the world, although he has had previous interesting jobs, including a period as doctor to the legendary rock band Grateful Dead. Google's co-founders Larry Page and Sergei Brin decided to commit Google to serious philanthropy and created a separate division of the company (Google.org) in 2006 for that purpose. It will be funded with 1 per cent of the firm's equity, annual profits and employee's time. Google.org can pursue its philanthropic mission both by for-profit investing and by making charitable grants. After two years' deliberations and internal debate, in January 2008 Google finally announced the five philanthropic initiatives that it has selected. The decisions were made based on what Google specifically had to offer in each area. Google will pursue five 'core initiatives' in three areas: fighting climate change; economic development; and building an early warning system for pandemics and other disasters. Google has already made a $5 million grant to InSTEDD, an NGO that is building a rapid-reporting platform to connect people on the ground with those monitoring pandemics. It hopes to raise the quality of public services in poor countries by improving the flow of information both to those who run them and to those they serve. It also has big ambitions to help SMEs in developing countries. It has launched a project to develop renewable energy that is cheaper than coal. Its target is in years, not decades. All of the initiatives selected by Google are deliberately high risk / high return; but they are extremely focused and can be scaled up quickly. Google, its founders and Dr Brilliant believe that the world's companies can play a big part in solving the world's problems.

Google scenario 2

In 2006, the world's online chat forums were full of headlines asking: 'is Google sacrificing its ethics for profit?' and 'Google must stop snooping on us'. Google was in a battle with the US Department of Justice which had demanded disclosure of two months' worth of search queries from its customers. Google issued a 21-page response that it 'would undermine the trust Google users have that when they enter a search query into a Google search box, not only will they receive back the most relevant results but that Google will keep private whatever information users communicate'. However, there is a view that Google's stance in defence of liberty has as much to do with protecting their proprietary technology as with users' rights, since an analysis of Google's query data would reveal key proprietary information. Google takes extraordinary measures to protect its trade secrets. Google's stance on this issue follows shortly after the huge amount of criticism it attracted in 2006, when launching its services in China, because it had caved in to Chinese government demands for online censorship. It suffered huge criticism in the blogosphere for hypocrisy for collaborating with China's rulers in censoring its new Chinese service. The China strategy created great unease. Google's motto has been tarnished.

SOURCE: COMPILED FROM THE ECONOMIST, 19 JAN. 2008: 69 'GOOGLE'S GURU OF GIVING'; AND VARIOUS PRESS ARTICLES

GROUNDS FOR ETHICAL OPTIMISM

The CSR agenda has moved beyond what Hirschman (1970) called the 'paradigm-based gloomy vision' of humanity. As Ghoshal (2005) pointed out, humanity exhibits a taste for friendship, can be altruistic up to a point, and frequently shows concern for justice and fair play. Sen (1998) also notes:

> in acknowledging the possibility of a prudential explanation of apparently moral conduct, we should not fall into the trap of presuming that the assumption of pure self-interest is, in any sense more elementary than assuming other values. Moral or social concerns can be just as basic or elementary.

In 1999, 35 per cent of Fortune 250 companies made a Sustainability Report. By 2001 this percentage had increased to 45 per cent, broken down by sector as shown below:

Chemicals	100%
Pharmaceutical	86%
Electronics	84%
Automotive	73%
Oil and Gas	58%
Finance	24%

Despite the low percentage for the finance sector, there has been a growth of ethical investment funds which have proved very popular with investors. Innovest Strategic Value Advisors (2002) noted a strong correlation between beneficent environmental policies in companies and better than average stock market performance. Deloitte Touche (2002, SRI Survey), on a qualitative basis, found that 40 per cent of 65 fund managers interviewed believed the Innovest finding to be true, and 90 per cent of them believed that a strong CSR position in a company positively enhanced reputation, which in turn increased share price.

Perhaps more promising on a global level are the responses to the recent (2007) five-country survey carried out by McKinsey asking: 'which issues will be the most important in the next five years?' The results are reported in Table 15.2.

The responses from Brazil and China are particularly noteworthy, especially in relation to their ranking of: the environment; workplace conditions; ethically produced products; and safer products. This creates genuine optimism for the future balance of priorities. The lead on CSR could even shift from the rich world to the big emerging markets, each with its own traditions and priorities. For global companies this means that a one-size-fits-all approach to corporate responsibility may not work. What is right for Europe may not be appropriate for India. Such differences in priorities (as shown Table 15.2) are bound to grow in importance as the BRIC countries and other emerging markets continue growing.

Brazil has a lively CSR scene where about 1,300 companies are members of Instituto Ethos, a network of businesses committed to social responsibility. A few Brazilian firms – such as Natura, a cosmetics company, and Aracruz, a pulp and paper producer – are widely known for their CSR efforts. (*The Economist*, 17 Jan. 2008). India has a long tradition of paternalistic philanthropy. Big family-owned firms such as Tata are particularly active in providing basic services, such as schools and health care, for local communities. For the rich, who have prospered as the economy has boomed in recent years, generous philanthropy is also a way of heading off a backlash against business. However, a broader culture of ensuring better working conditions has been slow to spread.

Traditional MNCs are developing their own approaches to CSR. In true BOP style (see Chapter 6) the oil giant BP has been working with NGOs to distribute stoves for heating and cooking in rural India. MNCs have complex reasons for the CSR strategies they develop. Even if it does begin as a strategy for

15

TABLE 15.2	Global rankings of 'the things that matter' – 2007					
Which issues will be the most important in the next five years? Select three:						
Global rank	*Issue*	*United States*	*Britain*	*Germany*	*China*	*Brazil*
1	The environment	2	1	2	2	1
2	Safer products	5	4	6	3	2
3	Retirement benefits	4	2	1	4	7
4	Health-care benefits	1	5	8	1	8
5	Affordable products	6	3	3	5	3
6	Human-rights standards	8	8	9	9	4
7	Workplace conditions	9	10	4	7	6
8	Job losses from outsourcing	3	6	5	13	13
9	Privacy and data security	7	7	7	6	10
10	Ethically produced products	10	9	10	8	9
11	Investment in developing countries	16	11	14	12	5
12	Ethical advertising and marketing	12	12	16	11	11
13	Political influence of companies	11	14	12	14	14
14	Executive pay	15	16	11	10	15
15	Other	13	13	15	16	12
16	Opposition to freer trade	14	15	13	15	16

Source: McKinsey survey, September 2007

15

reputation management, it can rapidly provide them with surprisingly valuable market intelligence, particularly in emerging markets where trends are often freshest and so many market segments remain untapped. Certainly this does represent a mixture of business and social motivation. However, they are mutually reinforcing in many ways as Porter and Van der Linde (1995) showed with the Dutch flower market.

CSR may gradually become owned by emerging economies rather than developed economies. As investment flows to developed countries from Russia, China and the other sovereign wealth funds of the Middle East, a completely new agenda for CSR may be created.

SUMMARY

■ Approaches to ethics and to corporate governance vary greatly in different countries in different parts of the world.

■ Definitions of, and understandings about, corruption vary greatly in different parts of the world.

- Legal and regulatory practices in relation to ethics, governance and corruption are equally variable and different interpreted and enforced.

- Sustainability is a movement which attempts to ensure the planet is habitable for future generations.

- Sustainability has three related legs: economic, environmental and social. All three must operate effectively if sustainability is to be achieved.

- Corporate social responsibility is the movement that encourages MNCs to operate in ways that are sustainable and ethical. It is often evaluated using the triple bottom line.

- Both the economic and environmental aspects of sustainability are likely to increase costs for a business.

- Shareholders and wider stakeholders may have different views and priorities about the activities of MNCs.

- Having a positive CSR policy, however, can improve competitiveness by increasing reputation, and companies with good reputations survive in the long run better than those with poor reputations.

- The degree to which MNCs 'genuinely' embrace CSR is hotly debated, although most do operate some aspects of CSR in their formal functioning.

DISCUSSION QUESTIONS

1 What is sustainability?
2 To what extent are ethics relative or absolute? Is that also the case for business ethics?
3 What are the difficulties in attempting to define corruption?
4 What is corporate social responsibility?
5 What does it mean to be a virtuous company?
6 Explain the ways in which CSR might improve competitiveness.
7 Explain the differences between shareholders and stakeholders.
8 Describe the ways in which stakeholder analysis might be helpful or unhelpful to MNCs in achieving CSR.
9 Is CSR simply disguised self-interest by companies?

15

FURTHER READINGS

1 Crane, A. and Matten, D. (2004) *Business Ethics: A European Perspective*, Oxford: Oxford University Press.

As the title suggests, this approaches the area of business ethics from a specifically European as opposed to an American perspective. The book is comprehensive in its coverage and deals in detail not only with issues of business ethics but also with related matters such as the implications of globalization, sustainability and corporate citizenship in the modern world.

2 Klein, N. (2000) *No Logo*, New York: Picador.

A very easy read; this is an entertaining and slightly worrying view of the role of some multinational corporations in a globalized world. Not an academic book, but it has been very influential and attracted a wide public readership, as well as promoting much discussion about the ethical issues raised. The author makes a forceful, very polemical argument for a strong CSR movement.

3 Vogel, D. (2005) 'Is there a market for virtue? the business case for corporate social responsibility', *California Management Review*, 47(4): 19–45.

or – for a longer version, see the book instead of the journal article:

4 Vogel, D. (2005) *The Market for Virtue: The Potential and Limits of Corporate Social Responsibility*, Brookings Institution Press.

In this book, David Vogel provides a comprehensive, in-depth review of the contemporary CSR movement in both the United States and Europe. A more measured and balanced discussion than in Naomi Klein's book (see above). He presents a careful and balanced appraisal of the CSR movement's accomplishments and limitations, including a critical evaluation of the business case for CSR. He discusses the movement's achievements, most notably in improving some labour, human rights, and environmental conditions in developing countries, but also its limitations.

15

CHAPTER 16

Reflections: final thoughts

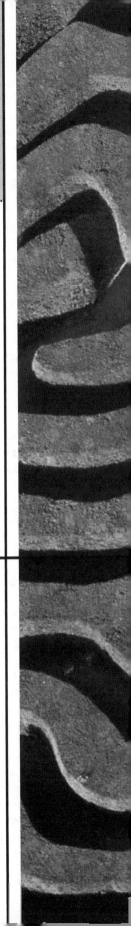

LEARNING OBJECTIVES After reading this chapter you should understand that:

- the world is complex, therefore strategies also need to be complex

- low-context frameworks are useful but do not sufficiently reflect the world's variety

- continual fine-tuning of strategies is required

- even the best global strategy will not stay that way forever

- international trade and global strategy are not only about commercial but also about human needs

- the effort to reconcile similarities and differences between products and markets to achieve the best strategic fit between them is the permanent paradox and central dilemma at the heart of global strategy for firms

- global strategy occurs within the most sensitive mix of dynamic factors in relation to which no permanent, or even stable, solution is possible

- despite complexity and uncertainty, strategic decisions need to be made and this book provides learning and guidance as to how to achieve them effectively.

INTRODUCTION

Most global strategy textbooks focus on MNCs. While the MNC is ever-present in our discussions, we have tried not to neglect the smaller firms and the bottom of the pyramid markets. There are other areas of global strategy that have grown in importance in the last decade. For example, the place of emerging economies within world trade has shifted from being marginal to being central. In many industries emerging market MNCs are beginning to dominate. The knowledge economy and the information industries operate on different principles from traditional industries and occupy the high ground for future growth. That is why we have devoted two chapters to different aspects of how they are to be understood and managed. Ethics, corporate social responsibility and sustainability have also become central, rather than marginal, matters for strategic thinking for global managers. MNCs are highly visible and high expectations are attached to their performance and legitimacy around the world. Ethical failures by MNCs are socially, politically and economically disastrous; such failures attract harsh judgements. Nevertheless, a large proportion of the world's workforce is employed by MNCs; even more rely on their products and services just as governments rely on their corporate tax revenues. The debate about the most effective combination of strategy and organizational structure for MNCs has been a major theme throughout the book: how best to organize an MNC? That is because the organizational structure debate for MNCs mirrors what we have called the central dilemma of global strategy: managing the integration–responsiveness paradox.

We have made heavy use of long-established research, concepts and frameworks. It may be surprising to find references to work from the 1960s or even the 1930s throughout this book. Yet, often, these are seminal works. Researchers like Alfred Chandler are towering figures in international business and global strategy research. So we do as Isaac Newton tells us: we stand on the shoulders of giants so that our readers understand the building-blocks underpinning the points we make.

At the time of going to press with this book, a review article was published (Peng et al., 2009) about what were the most significant current debates in global strategy. Just for interest, we cross-checked the contents of the chapters of this book against the global strategy domains and themes mentioned. What did we find? Highlighted were: global versus regional strategy; combinations of product and geographic diversification in global expansion; domestic versus overseas corporate governance standards and attitudes to corporate social responsibility; cultural and institutional context as aspects of global strategy, especially as affecting our understanding of emerging economies; and the effects of a contingency perspective on global performance. Having read this book, you should be able to explain each of these issues with reasonable confidence.

In this concluding section, rather than summarizing the topics already presented within the book, we will instead highlight some areas of critical thinking which are, in our view, those of great importance for the next generation of managers of MNCs. Having read the preceding chapters, none of these areas should surprise you: they are embedded in our earlier discussions. However, they are the thoughts that we would like to leave in your minds.

A CONTINGENCY APPROACH TO THE GLOBAL INTEGRATION / LOCAL RESPONSIVENESS DEBATE

Throughout the book we address the problems and challenges raised by the endless tensions between standardization and adaptation, between global integration and local responsiveness. This applies not only to product or service offerings – it also applies to how you organize the MNC. The pure organizational forms of the global, transnational and multidomestic offer conceptual blueprints for the structure and organizational design of MNCs. However, for organizations, just as for products and services, local adaptation is generally necessary. This emphasizes a recurring theme in the book: that of similarities versus differences. We come down on the side of more differences than similarities still remaining in the world across its nations and markets; more high-context than low-context global strategy formulation. That is why we have argued strongly for a contingency approach to global strategy by international managers. This is what we discussed at length in Chapter 8. That does not mean that managers should not seek to achieve every configuration and co-ordination benefit available from how they construct their business activities across their disaggregated global value chains. It does mean that some types of businesses in some types of markets may be able to achieve relatively few of them.

Li and Fung (Chapter 8 Strategy in Action 8.3) tell us all that we need to know to understand the symbiotic relationship between global and local and also about the impact of ICT on building businesses opportunities anywhere in the world. Global businesses depend upon Li and Fung's deep local and regional knowledge. Global and local organizations need each other and feed off each other.

16

LIVING WITH INDUSTRY DYNAMICS

As this book goes to press, in early 2009 we are in the midst of world-business, market and financial chaos. It is being called the 'credit crunch' to reflect the key to, and the continuing consequence of, the chaos. Unemployment is rising; consumption and production are both in rapid decline; asset prices, especially of domestic and commercial property, as well as of all types of investments, are tumbling; and living standards generally (but not universally) are falling. We have shifted from boom into bust on a global scale in a matter of months. It will take considerably more than a matter of months for world trade, business and financial confidence, and people's living standards to recover.

The underlying cause of this global economic and financial crisis has been the massive growth in securitization of debt, and the complexity and opacity of the sophisticated financial instruments (such as 'derivatives') used to achieve this. Equally significant has been the widespread impact of globalization, which has ensured that the problems have spread like ripples in a pond in ever-wider circles of financial indebtedness throughout the world's banking and financial systems and markets and across most parts of the world simultaneously. This crisis could therefore be regarded as even more serious than the 1930s world depression, since few countries are unaffected because of this global interconnectivity. It is now very difficult for any one country to insulate itself from the rest of the world economically, financially and politically.

Could we ask for a more telling example of the point we have continually emphasized throughout this book? As was argued in the introduction: 'Although all strategic thinking occurs in a dynamic context, developing robust strategies deliverable across international borders is the most dynamic and complex context of all'. A sense of dynamics is critical in strategy because strategies are always being developed and refined, reviewed and implemented against a set of moving targets which combine every aspect of industry conditions. Industries change, markets change, competitors change or may become partners in certain activities; sometimes the whole world changes. How changing industry dynamics and competitive dynamics affect the relevance of current and future strategies, structures, resources and capabilities has already been illustrated in many examples including the reorganizations at Citigroup (Chapter 7 Strategy in Action 7.3), or the evolution of Novotel (Chapter 8 Strategy in Action 8.2) over time, or the shifts between regional to global and back to regional again for Ford car company as described in Chapter 8 (Strategy in Action 8.1). These companies had to adjust not once, but again and again, to changes in their business context. Each time they had to review what they were doing, why they were doing it that way and how effective their strategy was relative to what their customers wanted and what their competitors were doing. Sometimes the company is always just a bit too late, as maybe Philips was (Strategy in Action 7.1), behind rather than ahead of the wave.

The top management of each of these organizations had to continually review and monitor strategic positioning, structure, resources and processes. For all businesses, what at one point had been considered excellent, gradually becomes average or even substandard as the market develops and customer expectations rise and change. Costs rise too, and competition gets ever tougher. It was not that these companies were doing anything particularly bad; more that the context was shifting all around them all the time. Structures, resources and capabilities which have been developed and work well under one set of conditions can become inappropriate or downright inadequate when those conditions change, as they always do.

THE COMPARATIVE ADVANTAGE OF NATIONS AND THE COMPETITIVE ADVANTAGE OF FIRMS

In the earlier part of this book, considerable discussion was devoted to explaining the concept of comparative advantage, both from its original roots in economic theory with Adam Smith and David Ricardo and its relevance to the design of global strategies. Most importantly we wanted to make clear two

16

things. First, that comparative advantage occurred within countries and had only an *indirect* relationship with global competitive advantage for a particular firm. In other words, comparative advantage at the level of the country did not automatically translate into competitive advantage for the firm located within that country. It was dependent upon the capabilities of the firm to utilize the potential sources of comparative and other advantages effectively. This should be clear from our lengthy discussion of the competition between Caterpillar and Komatsu in the 1970s, 1980s and 1990s, or indeed from many of the minicase discussions we have used in the book.

Secondly, many types of comparative advantage may be relatively short-lived. The example of cheap wage rates rising over time as living standards and welfare expectations rise has already been mentioned. One may add to this other examples such as the potential erosion of many infrastructure advantages like transportation or education, either because governments do not invest adequately in them (as Mexico has not) or because others have invested heavily over a period and caught up (as China is doing).

There is also a third aspect of comparative advantage that was discussed earlier in Chapter 2: the comparative advantage related to a company's 'home-base' and its national industry 'clusters'. With his introduction of the 'diamond' framework into global strategy thinking in 1990, Porter put the idea of 'country-specific advantage' (CSA) back into global strategy. Porter notes that some industries take successful root in some places, and some in others. Porter thinks that these clusters of excellence are most usefully defined by nation. Nations affect demand conditions (affected by a government's macroeconomic policy); the dynamism of competition (affected by a government's antitrust / monopoly and trade policies); the level and type of skills (affected by a government's approach to the education system); and attitudes of managers, workers and consumers (affected by each national culture).

Porter's research, covering ten countries and more than 100 industries, suggested that the conditions at a company's home-base were crucial to its competitiveness abroad. Porter calls this the 'paradox of location' in a global economy:

> What happens *inside* companies is important, but clusters reveal that the immediate business environment *outside* companies plays a vital role as well. This role of locations has long been overlooked, despite striking evidence that innovation and competitive success in so many fields are geographically concentrated – whether it's entertainment in Hollywood, or consumer electronics in Japan.
>
> (Porter 1998: 78)

We have already discussed Ohmae's (1990a) opposing view of the 'truly global' company in Chapter 8, but wanted here to extend the notion of comparative advantage to include national clusters.

INSTITUTIONAL VOIDS

A related but opposite aspect of the relevance of the home base is the existence in some contexts of 'institutional voids'. This is a most useful concept for every MNC and every MNC manager. It was discussed in Chapter 4 in relation to emerging economies. The argument was simply that doing business in most emerging economies is very different from doing business in developed economies because the broad context in which business is done is so different. It can therefore be a difficult experience for managers from developed economies because of their expectations concerning available institutional infrastructure. 'Institutional voids' (Khanna et al. 2005) means an absence of important 'soft' (e.g. political openness; the power of business groups), and also sometimes 'hard' infrastructure, such as adequate road or other transportation facilities. MNC managers have to learn to work around these infrastructure issues. As discussed in Chapter 4, these may commonly relate to legal voids making contracts hard to enforce and ownership of land or plant unreliable. Enforcement of such things as intellectual property rights or patents is very problematic. Different assumptions need to be made about the business model and the relevant level and types of resources to support business activity. Context is all, and institutional context varies considerably in various parts of the world. That is also why we argue for high-context approaches to global strategies.

Ethical convergence or divergence?

Institutional voids and widely differing expectations about business contexts can mean that the 'rules of the game' for how you do business and how firms compete are radically different from those of the home base or home region. Having to operate outside existing business groups; lack of appropriate business and governmental contacts in a context where these form the basis for doing business; differing understandings of what may or may not constitute corruption or simply be how business is done; all of these may have consequences for individuals and firms, values and the legal and social responsibilities of the firm imposed by its home market and home institutional context.

THE RISE OF KNOWLEDGE COMPETITION

The term 'Red Queen effect' has been introduced into strategic thinking (Barnett, 2008; Barnett and Hansen, 1996). It has been taken from the field of evolutionary biology where it is used to denote a self-reinforcing system of evolution in response to a continuous cycle of external pressures on the survival of a given species. In the field of strategy it has been applied to explaining competitive success or failure over time and how exposure to competition affects organizational survival. Successful organizations (in terms of survival) were found to be those facing a competitive environment in which they were required to continually search for ways of adapting and improving. Thus the consequence of an organization being exposed to competition is that it is likely to learn. This learning and the resultant adaptation by the firm is likely to make it a stronger competitor. This response by the firm, in turn, triggers a similar adaptive learning response in its competitors, and so on. Although each adjustment may be minor, over time they add up to a formidable amount of change. 'In my country you have to run forward in order to stand still' said the Red Queen in Lewis Carroll's famous book *Alice in Wonderland*.

However, competitiveness within a dynamic marketplace is a property of *organizations* rather than markets. Some organizations are better at it than others. Sometimes learning which has happened in the past teaches organizations outdated lessons.

Barnett and Hansen's (1996) work led to the conclusion that learning from recent experience is likely to increase competitiveness and likely survival; whereas learning from experience in the distant past is likely to decrease competitiveness and likelihood of survival, since the wrong things are likely to be learned. It appears, then, that organizations benefit if they have strong present competition, even though their competitors also learn and thus competition is endlessly intensified. This reinforces two of the themes discussed so far in this conclusion: the continuously dynamic nature of competition and the beneficial effect of industry clusters on the ability of organizations to compete. We will now discuss further a third area of critical thinking in global strategy which needs to be carried forward: knowledge management and organizational learning in MNCs.

'Knowledge' and 'learning' have been discussed extensively either implicitly in terms of information industries (Chapter 5) or explicitly (Chapter 13; Chapter 14 Strategy in Action 14.2). Quinn (1992) has used the term 'knowledge-based intangibles' to capture his view that the value of most modern products and services lies in how the creative and intellectual capabilities of a firm are managed (advanced factors of production), rather than on traditional factors of production such as capital or equipment (as we discussed in Chapters 1 and 2). Quinn further argued that the capacity to manage 'knowledge-based intellect' is the most important managerial skill for advanced corporations. That is the basis for

16

the view that knowledge, knowledge management and learning are the *only* truly differentiating resources for long-term advantage. We endorsed that view in Chapter 13 and there is a high degree of unanimity on the importance of this subject in the strategy literature.

Many problems associated with knowledge management and shared learning within organizations have been clearly articulated, but remain difficult to implement. We have discussed in particular knowledge 'stickiness' and knowledge protection.

Knowledge 'stickiness'

Internal 'stickiness' of knowledge refers to internal impediments to the transfer of best practice within a firm. The transfer of best practice within a firm has an unambiguous meaning defined by Szulanski (2003) as:

> the firm's replication of an internal practice that is performed in a superior way in some part of the organization and is deemed superior to internal alternate practices and known alternatives outside the company.

Internal transfers should be straightforward. Still, barriers to internal knowledge transfer are common and the transfer process highly complex. Since this is of great practical importance to organizations it would be useful to understand why that should be so.

Most assumptions concerning 'sticky knowledge' assume 'motivational' barriers such as: interdivisional jealousy; lack of incentives; lack of confidence; low priority; lack of buy-in; an inclination to reinvent the wheel; refusal by employees to do exactly as they are told; resistance to change; lack of commitment; turf protection; and NIH ('not invented here') syndrome. However, Szulanski's (2003) own findings highlight quite different factors. His research covered 122 best practice transfers in eight companies, including both technical and administrative practices. His findings suggest that it is knowledge-related barriers and not these motivation-related barriers which are the dominant causes of stickiness in internal transfers. He calls these knowledge-related barriers:

- Lack of absorptive capacity: that is inability to assimilate or apply the new knowledge.

- Causal ambiguity: that is inability to clearly separate out, and therefore replicate, the interactions between different knowledge elements.

- The arduousness of the relationship: that is lack of ease of communication between the knowledge source and the recipient.

This is important work which is useful in its wider implications for global strategy, and reflects many issues raised earlier in this book. Barriers to the transfer of skills and capabilities reduce: organizational flexibility; the chances of success of strategic alliances, technology partnerships or joint ventures; and the ability of an MNC to leverage its own current knowledge. It goes a long way to explain why organizations do not seem to know what they know. It may be less because they do not want to learn, than that they do not know *how* to learn.

Knowledge protection

If organizational knowledge is as important as we have suggested in the previous sections, then just as important as learning how to share knowledge internally, is the ability to protect it from expropriation or imitation externally. In contrast to the problem of internal stickiness, where the organization seeks to enhance openness and remove blockages to shared learning, the problem of knowledge protection is to construct appropriate protective barriers. Most MNCs will face both requirements simultaneously.

Traditional discussions about the boundaries of the firm have been largely derived from transaction-cost economics and have focused mainly on identifying the boundaries of the firm between markets and hierarchies: it has paid little attention to knowledge. For intangible assets such as knowledge, legal protection by means of copyrights and patents are narrowly defined, costly to enforce and of limited use, especially in countries with institutional voids in how the legal system operates. An obvious example is the CD industry in China, which exists largely as a counterfeiting industry; there is little MNCs can do to enforce international copyright or patent law except exert moral pressure. Global expansion has actually increased the exposure of many firms to loss of proprietary knowledge through expropriation or (unlicensed) imitation. This will undoubtedly become an area of growing sophistication in how MNCs operate to protect their knowledge-base.

WHAT WORKS OVER TIME: THE SUSTAINABILITY OF STRATEGIES

We have stressed our view of the dynamic, contingent and aggressive nature of global strategy. Competition is profoundly dynamic in character. There is no stable state: no equilibrium. Every chapter in this book, and every section in this concluding chapter, has addressed the reasons why this is so. Managers in every type of organization and context agree with the assertion that their jobs and their organizations are subject to continuous change. Uncertainty is taken for granted. Some of the causes may be industry-specific or sector-specific: most (technological change; financial shifts) are not. Sometimes, turbulence overwhelms us all, as in the global financial crises of the 1990s and mid-2000s. Yet firms still need to develop their global strategies in the midst of it all.

We know that many traditional industry boundaries are breaking down but that existing corporations still have to create viable strategies for an uncertain future within unclear industry frameworks. We assume that control of resources often depends on alliances with others outside your own organizational or geographic boundaries, so that issues of control are more about alliance-building and coalition-management. We assume that flexible learning organizations depend upon the motivation and commitment of knowledge-workers while at the same time operational efficiency may require them to be outsourced, often in different cultures in different parts of the world. Strategic innovation requires cross-functional, interdisciplinary collaboration across organizational boundaries or within virtual organizations by managers who often remain more comfortable with hierarchies or multidivisional matrix structures.

Strategy for all large organizations is about managing tensions between integration and co-ordination, centralization and decentralization, stability and innovation, to achieve the optimal configuration of resources to achieve its strategic objectives. To the extent that this is true, competition to acquire resources such as specialist knowledge and to use them most effectively, is at the heart of global strategy. Over the longer term, and sometimes in the short term, most sources of advantage fade away. This book has provided you with many frameworks to use in developing and implementing global strategies. However, let us be clear that models and frameworks do not make strategic decisions; they are made by people. Strategy is about individuals thinking, exercising their judgement, taking risks and making choices and hopefully developing 'practical wisdom'.

16

SUMMARY

Thus the global strategy agenda has changed. Figure 16.1 summarizes our view of these changes. In this book we have discussed both the causes and the nature of these changes, so that MNC managers may understand them and respond to them appropriately.

FIGURE 16.1   The changed global strategy agenda

Then	Now
firm-specific and country-specific sources of advantage	building cross-border capabilities and sharing knowledge within continuous uncertainty
Then global location and configuration issues	**Now** global flexibility and responsiveness issues
Then decisions about the boundaries of the firm and its business scope	**Now** global co-operative strategies and network organizations
Then strategic emphasis on performance management for revenue-generation	**Now** strategic emphasis on performance management for economic, financial, social and governance contributions

Perhaps we should leave the last word in this book to Lewis Carroll and the phenomenon of the Red Queen. The Red Queen is a chess piece that Alice meets in the book *Through the Looking Glass*, who perpetually runs without getting very far because as she runs, the landscape moves with her. When Alice asks the Red Queen about this phenomenon, the Red Queen replies that Alice must be from a slow world, since in a fast world we all have to run just to stand still. Given environmental uncertainty and industry dynamics, the faster you run, the more the world moves with you, so the least we can try is to ensure that we are running in the right direction.

The field of global strategy is continually evolving. It is critical that managers' mindsets and understanding continue to evolve too.

16

PART 4
CASE STUDIES

CASE STUDY 1

COMPARATIVE COST ADVANTAGE AND THE AMERICAN OUTSOURCING BACKLASH

"If a foreign country can supply us with a commodity cheaper than we ourselves can make it, better buy it of them with some part of produce of our own industry, employed in a way in which we have some advantage."[1]

–Adam Smith, Economist and Philosopher

"If a car can be made more cheaply in Mexico, it should be. If a telephone enquiry can be processed more cheaply in India, it should be.... trade is a positive-sum game."[2]

–The Economist

"The capitalist incentive to seek the lowest cost and most profit will seek to substitute cheap labor for expensive labor. India and China are gaining, and the First World is losing."[3]

–Paul Craig Roberts, Former Assistant Treasury Secretary in the Reagan Administration

INTRODUCTION

Amidst anaemic job growth and in the face of mounting protests against offshoring of jobs to low wage countries, N. Gregory Mankiw, chairman of the White House Council of Economic Advisors, declared in early February 2004, that if services could be sourced more cheaply from outside, then it was in the best interests to the US. John Snow, the US treasury secretary, echoed similar views and stated that the practice of moving jobs to low-cost countries, was part of trade and could make the economy stronger.[4] But contrary to the dictum of free trade, the public angst against the shifting of white collar jobs overseas, had been increasing and the Democrat presidential candidate, John Kerry, had been taking a strong stance against "Benedict Arnold CEOs"[5] who shifted the US' jobs overseas.

www.ibscdc.org

Copyright © IBS Case Development Centre

IBS
CDC

COMPARATIVE COST ADVANTAGE AND OUTSOURCING GAINS

Supporters of free trade, including free trade in services that resulted in outsourcing to offshore locations, derived their arguments from the theory of Comparative Advantage (Exhibit I) put forward by David Ricardo, in 1817.[6] Indeed, offshoring was driven by the significant labour cost savings, resulting from the transfer of jobs to low-wage countries. McKinsey estimated that a software developer costing as much as $60 an hour in the US, would cost one-tenth that amount in a country like India. Similarly the equivalent of a data entry agent in the US who made $20 an hour in the US, received only $2 in India. Thus, even after accounting for telecommunication costs and costs pertaining to management of the offshore facility, savings of up to 45% to 55% could be made through offshoring. In some cases where the process design had been reengineered, gains of up to 65% to 70% could be realized.[7] Costs apart, another significant rationale behind outsourcing had been the growing expertise and efficiency of labour in offshore destinations. As Craig Barrett, CEO of Intel remarked ". . . it's no longer just low cost labour that you are looking at. It's well-educated labour that can do effectively any job that can be done in the United States."[8] Rajiv Salkar, Vice President of Business Partners, Geometric Software Solutions Co. Ltd., stated, "Using cost effective centers like India ensures control of costs, quality and standards in the deliverables, while avoiding permanent overheads in terms of manpower and infrastructure. Importantly, outsourcing helps manage fluctuations in demand by moving from a fixed model to a variable model."[9]

EXHIBIT I   **Theories of absolute and comparative advantage**

Theory of Absolute Advantage
Adam Smith propounded the 'Theory of Absolute Advantage' in his book *An Inquiry into the Nature and Causes of the Wealth of Nations*. According to this theory a country is said to have absolute advantage in a product if it can produce the same quantity of the product with a lower input than what other countries can, and therefore enjoys greater productivity vis-a-vis other countries. The theory states that countries should engage in the production of only those goods in which they enjoy absolute advantage.

Theory of Comparative Advantage
In his book *The Principles of Political Economy and Taxation*, written in 1817, David Ricardo (1772–1823) said that the theory of absolute advantage was insufficient to explain the occurrence of international trade. This was because there might be a situation wherein a single country is abundantly endowed with resources, labour, capital and technology. This would imply that it would have absolute advantage in the manufacture of all goods, hence discouraging it from trading with any other country.

Ricardo put forward an alternative basis for trade known as the 'Theory of Comparative Advantage'. The theory states that countries should engage in the manufacture of those goods in which they have the least opportunity cost. Opportunity cost refers to the cost of the next best opportunity forgone. This means that countries can benefit through trade because it would entail reallocation of resources from the relatively less efficient to the relatively more efficient sectors. A country may not be efficient in the production of any good; yet it will have a comparative advantage in the industry in which it is relatively least bad. Hence it is impossible for a country to have no comparative advantage in anything. The theory assumes full employment and costless mobility of labour between the sectors.

Compiled by the author

1

ANNEXURE I	Benefits of offshoring to US	
Benefit of $1 of US offshore spending		
To India:		**$**
Offshoring Sector	Labour	0.10
	Profits retained in India	0.10
Suppliers		0.09
Taxes	Central Government	0.03
	State Government	0.01
Net Benefit to India		**0.33**
To the US:		**$**
Direct Benefits	Savings	0.58
	Imports of US goods by providers in India	0.05
	Transfer back of profits	0.04
Indirect Benefits	Value from US Labour Re-employed	0.45–0.47
Potential Benefit for US Economy		**1.12–1.14**

Source: McKinsey Global Institute

Research conducted by McKinsey Global Institute estimated that of the $1.45 to $1.47 value that was created for every $1 that was spent in offshoring, the US captured $1.12 to $1.14, while the country at the receiving end captured just 33 cents on an average (Annexure I). Another study conducted at the behest of the Information Technology Association of America, by Global Insight, a private consulting firm, stated that while outsourcing did result in some short-term US unemployment, its long-term benefits outweighed its costs. It further added that the cost savings resulting from offshore outsourcing, resulted in lower inflation and interest rates, and also higher real wages and increased productivity. This in turn, resulted in increased consumer spending and hence heightened economic activity that led to the creation of about 90,000 net new jobs by the end of 2003.[10] The study expected the creation of 317,000 net new jobs by 2008, as a consequence of outsourcing. It also said that the outsourcing added about $33.6 billion to the US Gross Domestic Product (GDP) in 2003, and might well add a total of $124.2 billion by 2008.[11]

OFFSHORING – THE RHETORIC

The roots of the controversy sprang from the disparaging job growth in the US economy (Annexures II and III). About 2.7 million jobs had been lost since recession hit, in early 2001. Even though the economy bottomed out in November 2001, jobs had been scarce and people in the US found the adjustment to the new trend of outsourcing particularly painful, during a recovery short on natural job creation.[12] A majority of them had begun to blame offshoring of manufacturing and more recently, white collar, service jobs, for the shortfall in employment (Annexure IV).[13] Adding fuel to the fire, a study conducted in 2002 by Forrester Research, predicted that about 3.3 million jobs in the US, which included about 473,000 in IT, would move abroad by 2015 (Annexure V).

Politicians had thus been under pressure to discourage the companies and private agencies from offshoring their service work. Upon winning the New Hampshire presidential primary, John

ANNEXURE II	Labour force unemployment rate											
Year	Jan	Feb	Mar	Apr	May	Jun	Jul	Aug	Sep	Oct	Nov	Dec
2000	4.0	4.1	4.0	3.8	4.0	4.0	4.0	4.1	4.0	3.9	3.9	3.9
2001	4.2	4.2	4.3	4.4	4.3	4.5	4.6	4.9	5.0	5.4	5.6	5.7
2002	5.6	5.7	5.7	5.9	5.8	5.8	5.8	5.7	5.7	5.7	5.9	6.0
2003	5.8	5.9	5.8	6.0	6.1	6.3	6.2	6.1	6.1	6.0	5.9	5.7
2004	5.6	5.6	5.7									

(Seasonally adjusted)

Source: US Department of Labor; Bureau of Labor Statistics

Kerry declared, "Together we will build a prosperity … where we create jobs here at home and where we shut down every loophole, every incentive, every reward that goes to some Benedict Arnold CEO or company that take the jobs overseas and stick Americans with the bill."[14] Refuting Mankiw's[15] view that outsourcing was a "new way to do international trade", Dennis Hastert, speaker of the US House of Representatives, issued a press statement saying, "I understand that Mr. Mankiw is a brilliant economic theorist, but his theory fails a basic test of real economics. An economy suffers when jobs disappear … Outsourcing can be a problem for American workers and for the American economy. We can't have a healthy economy unless we have more jobs here in America."[16] Calling the administration policy on outsourcing as 'Alice in Wonderland economics', Senator Tom Daschle, condemned the US government for giving priority to corporate profits ignoring the fact that millions of Americans and countless communities across the country, had been hurt due to job exports.[17]

Several states such as Colorado, Wisconsin, Indiana and Minnesota, had introduced legislation to ban offshoring. In early March 2004, the US Senate passed a bill sponsored by the Ohio Republican Senators, George Voinovich and Craig Thomas, banning private firms from outsourcing federal government contracts overseas. The Democrats too had introduced a 'Jobs for America Act' in the Senate, that required the corporations to warn employees and communities, before moving jobs overseas.[18] The loss of jobs due to offshoring, had become a central political issue in the presidential election. However, the Indian outsourcing firms were growing fast and were ready to dismiss all talks of protectionism as mere electoral noise.[19]

CHALLENGING THEORY

Proponents of the theory of Comparative Advantage and free trade, had put forward arguments to defend the loss in jobs. Forrester research showed that out the 2.7 million jobs lost since 2001, about 300,000 had been because of outsourcing.[20] There were many service sector jobs that could not be offshored due to technological and geographical constraints as it is necessary for the companies to stay close to the customers.[21] Ben S. Bernanke, a board member of the Federal Reserve, said that foreign trade may have led to the loss of 167,000 jobs a year since 2001 and that these numbers were negligible as compared with US's overall pace of job creation and destruction.[22] It had also been pointed out that foreigners, including Indians, were not only outsourcing but also insourcing into the US, thus creating jobs in the US.[23] For example, Bharti Televentures, a leading Indian telecom operator, had awarded an in-house IT services contract to US computer giant IBM, worth up to $750 million in

1

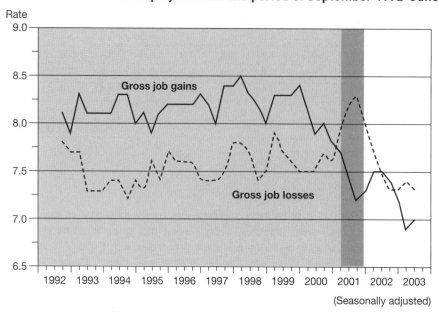

ANNEXURE III   Private sector gross job gains and gross job losses as a percentage of employment for the period of September 1992–June 2003

(Seasonally adjusted)

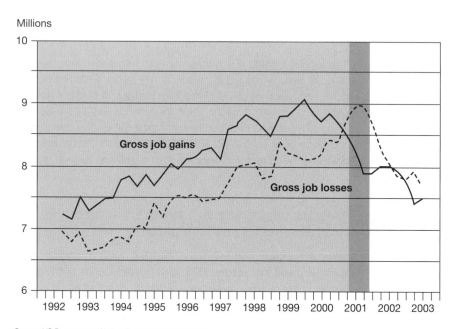

Source: US Department of Labor; Bureau of Labor Statistics

Note: Shaded area represents recession period.

1

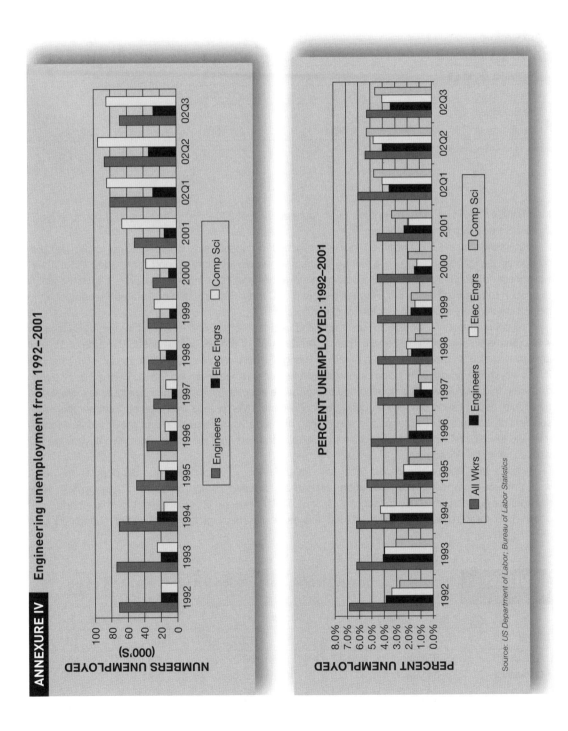

ANNEXURE V	Jobs expected to move offshore from the US by 2015		
Job Area	*Within 2005*	*Within 2010*	*Within 2015*
Architecture	32	83	184
Business Operations	61	162	348
Computer Science	109	277	473
Law	14	35	75
Life Sciences	3.7	14	37
Management	37	118	288

Source: Forrester Research Inc.

March 2004.[24] Also, Infosys Technologies announced in April 2004 that, it had set up a consulting unit in the US that employed 500 workers.[25]

Atul Vashistha, the CEO of NeoIT, a California based consultancy, while agreeing to the fact that outsourcing might turn out to be a painful process for employees in the short-term, added that if services were not outsourced, then US would lose more jobs and its companies would not have the ability to grow in the future.[26] Also, T. J. Rogers, the head of Cyprus Semiconductors, stated that outsourcing helped create more jobs for the indigenous workforce.[27]

A report by James C. Cooper in *BusinessWeek* said that, offshoring was not the primary reason for weak job market; rather, it was the increasing productivity of the US companies to the tune of 5% per annum since 2001, that had led to a dearth in hiring.[28] And even as competition forced some service jobs abroad, the productivity boom would create newer and better paying jobs in their place.[29] It was observed that people who lost jobs in one sector, were absorbed in other sunrise industries. However, this could result in short run friction, during which, redistribution of jobs would take place; but this reabsorbtion time would be less for economies having higher rates of innovation and growth of new industries like the US.[30] "In practice as well as in principle, the fusty old idea of comparative advantage still works", said *The Economist.*[31]

Besides, McKinsey also pointed at the changing demographic profile of the US population, which would reduce its working-age population (defined as between 25 and 54 years of age) from 44% of the total population in 2001, to about 39% in 2015 (Annexure VI). In the light of this shortage of about 15.6 million people, it believed that the same standard of living could be maintained only

ANNEXURE VI	Reduction in the working-age population between 25 and 54 years in the US				
		Millions		*Percentage*	
Total		277.8	312.3	100	100
Age of US population	>= 55 years	77.8	106.2	28	34
	25–54 years	122.2	121.8	44	39
	<= 24 years	77.8	84.3	28	27
		2001	2015	2001	2015
Net Shortfall by 2015 = 5% = 15.6 million workers					

Source: US Census Bureau; McKinsey Global Institute

1

through increased immigration and greater productivity gains, which can easily be achieved through offshoring.

While the economists belived that the jobs lost would be replaced by better ones due to internal mechanisms of free trade, the detractors of the theory argued that it would be difficult to identify the new jobs. Paul Craig Roberts, former treasury secretary under the Reagan administration and a columnist in *BusinessWeek* felt that the economists did not understand that cheap, skilled, foreign labour, which had attracted tradable goods and services, might also lure the 'replacement' industry and jobs to offshore locations.[32] He said that, for Comparative Advantage to work, labour, capital and technology, should not move offshore; further, such international immobility of factors was necessary to prevent a business from seeking Absolute Advantage (Exhibit I) by moving abroad. He wrote, "The internal cost ratios that determine comparative advantage reflect the quantity and quality of the country's technology and capital. If these factors move abroad to where cheap labor makes them more productive, absolute advantage takes over from comparative advantage."

Paul Davidson, editor of the *Journal of Post Keynesian Economics*, University of Tennessee, believed that the theory of Comparative Advantage had severe 'logical weaknesses' and its application could spell danger to the US economy.[33] He pointed out that, the increased supply of goods resulting from the application of the theory of Comparative Advantage, did not create its own demand.[34] According to him the theory of Comparative Advantage assumed that, neither capital nor labour are mobile across national boundaries. Hence, if capital were to be mobile, as is the case with offshoring, then gains from trade for all the nations did not logically follow. He believed that the rampant application of the Law of Comparative Advantage, might turn dangerous for the Western and even the global economy.

LOOKING AHEAD

"What we have to understand is that every dollar that China or India earns is recycled into global economy either as demand for goods and services of these countries or as capital investments abroad. It's up to developing countries and their companies to develop areas where they have a comparative advantage ..." said Sir Edward George, the former governor of the Bank of England.[35] C. Gopinath, an associate professor of the Sawyer School of Management, Suffolk University, Boston said that, "The US companies who undertake outsourcing, or offshoring, benefit from seeing a drop in operating costs and a boost to profitability. However, the economy is seeing a loss of white collar jobs, which is worrying, and is currently an election issue. No amount of trade theory and discussion of value propositions can satisfy highly educated individuals who see their jobs moving overseas.... These are the kind of jobs people expected would always remain in the U.S."[36]

According to *The Economist*, trade in services like, trade in goods, had caused agonising redistributions of employment. It pointed out to a study conducted by the Bureau of Labour Statistics for the International Institute of Economics, which said that, between 1979–1999, 69% of the people who lost jobs in the US because of the cheap imports in sectors other than manufacturing, settled themselves in new jobs. Out of this 69%, 55% of the people found out jobs at lower pay and 25% took pay cuts of 30%, or more. It suggested that, a part of the returns from free trade should be used to ease this transition.[37] An estimate by the McKinsey Global Institute, based upon an insurance proposal developed by Lori Kletzer of University of California at Santa Cruz and Robert Litan of the Brookings Institution for trade displaced workers,[38] pointed out that the companies could insure all jobs displaced from outsourcing, by using as little as 4% to 5% of the savings from outsourcing.[39]

NOTES

1 "The Wisdom of Adam Smith (1723–1790)", http://www.adamsmith.org/smith/quotes.htm

2 "The new jobs migration", http://www.economist.com/opinion/displayStory.cfm?story_id=2442 040, February 19th 2004.

3 Roberts Paul Craig, "Guest Commentary: The Harsh Truth About Outsourcing", http://www. businessweek.com/magazine/content/04_12/b3875614.htm, March 22nd 2004.

4 Andrews Edmund L., "Treasury Chief Defends Outsourcing of U.S Work", http://select.nytimes. com/gst/abstract.html?res=F40F12FB3C5D0C728FDDAA0894DC404482&n=Top%2fReference% 2fTimes%20Topics%2f Organizations%2fT%2fTreasury%20Department%20, March 31st 2004.

5 In 1780, an embittered US Major Gen. Benedict Arnold plotted to surrender to the British the critical colonial army fortress at West Point and its 3,000 soldiers, in exchange for £20,000. When his scheme was exposed, he switched sides, became a British general and then fought against the revolution.

6 "Guest Commentary: The Harsh Truth About Outsourcing", op.cit.

7 "Outsourcing: Is it a Win-Win Game?", McKinsey Global Institute.

8 Bob Herbert, "Education Is No Protection", http://www.velocityreviews.com/forums/t130758-ot-interesting-article-in-the-ny-times.html, January 26th 2004.

9 (Quoted in the article) "To B(PO) or not to B(PO)", *The Economic Times*, April 8th 2004.

10 "Outsourcing creates jobs, study says", http://money.cnn.com, March 30th 2004.

11 Ibid.

12 Sharma Ruchir, "Is the heat off on outsourcing?", *The Economic Times*, April 6th 2004.

13 Cooper James C., "The Price of Efficiency", *BusinessWeek*, March 22nd 2004.

14 Moschella David, "Political Rhetoric Has Run Amok", http://computerworld.com/management topics/outsourcing/story/0,10801,90332,00.html, February 23rd 2004.

15 "Bush Adviser Supports Outsourcing", http://www.foxnews.com/story/0,2933,111225,00.html, February 12th 2004.

16 N. Gregory Mankiw is a macroeconomist and was the chairman of President George Bush (Jr)'s Council of Economic Advisors.

17 www.foxnews.com, February 13th 2004.

18 Kumara Kranti, "India reacts with dismay to recent US legislation on outsourcing", www.wsws.org, March 16th 2004.

19 "On the other foot", *The Economist*, February 5th 2004.

20 "The Price of Efficiency", op.cit.

21 "The new jobs migration", op.cit.

22 "Treasury Chief Defends Outsourcing of U.S Work", op.cit.

23 Mohan N. Chandra, "Unknown Knowns About Outsourcing", *Financial Express*, April 1st 2004.

24 "India's Infosys sets up US consultancy, hopes to offset outsourcing anger", http://sg.news. yahoo.com, April 8th 2004.

25 Ibid.

26 Herbert Bob, "Is outsourcing a bane for the US?", *Deccan Chronicle*, January 27th 2004.

27 Venkatchaliah M.N., "BPO, A Small Step on a Long Journey?", http://fecolumnists.expressindia. com/full_column.php?content_id=55974, April 1st 2004, April 1st 2004.

28 "The Price of Efficiency", op.cit.

29 Mandel Michael J., "Productivity: Who Wins, Who Loses", *BusinessWeek*, March 22nd 2004.

30 Ray Alok, "What remains of the case for free trade", *Business Line*, April 6th 2004.

31 "The new jobs migration", op.cit.

32 "The Harsh Truth about Outsourcing", op.cit.

33 Davidson Paul, "Will Free Trade and Outsourcing of U.S Jobs Inevitably Increase the Wealth of All Nations?", http://csf.colorado.edu

34 Jean Baptiste Say (1767–1832) propounded the Say's Law. It states that "Supply creates its own demand." According to this law, any increase in output of goods and services (supply) will lead to an increase in expenditure to buy those goods and services (demand). There will not be any shortage of demand and there will always be jobs for all workers – full employment. If there were any unemployment it would be temporary as the pattern of demand shifted and the same process would soon restore equilibrium. Keynes believed that Say's Law faultily assumed that there would be no obstacle to free employment and demonstrated that Say's Law could not be applied to money-using entrepreneurial economies and that full employment was not the natural consequence of a free market economy.

35 "The Rt Hon Sir Edward George – Governor Of The Bank Of England", http://www.bankofengland. co.uk/publications/speeches/2001/speech154.pdf, December 12th 2001.

36 "To B(PO) or not to B(PO)", op.cit.

37 "Stolen Jobs?", *The Economist*, December 11th 2003.

38 Kletzer Lori G. and Litan Robert E., "A Prescription to Relieve Worker Anxiety," Policy Brief 01-2. *IIE*, March 2001.

39 "Outsourcing: Is it a Win-Win Game?", op.cit.

1

CASE STUDY 2

TOYOTA'S GLOBALIZATION STRATEGIES

"If people started living at the South Pole, we would want to open a dealership there."[1]

–Fujio Cho, President of Toyota Motor Company, in March 2002

"Toyota is a car company that challenges itself in a way that makes the world shudder. Toyota announces it is shooting for 15% of the global market and 50% cost cuts, and everyone goes 'Ooof!' It is like getting hit in the solar plexus."

–Maryann Keller, a US-based consultant (auto industry), in April 2003[2]

CASTING A GLOBAL SPELL

In January 2004, leading global automobile company and Japan's number one auto-maker, Toyota Motor Corporation (Toyota), replaced Ford Motors (Ford), as the world's second largest automobile manufacturer; Ford had been in that spot for over seven decades. In 2003, Toyota sold 6.78 million vehicles worldwide while Ford's worldwide sales amounted to 6.72 million vehicles (General Motors, the world's largest car manufacturer sold 8.60 million vehicles). According to reports, while Toyota's market share in the US increased from 10.4% in 2002 to 11.2% in 2003, Ford's declined from 21.5% to 20.8% during the same period.

Reaching the No.2 slot was a major achievement for Toyota, which had begun as a spinning and weaving company in 1918. Ford was reportedly plagued by high labor costs, quality-control problems, lack of new designs and innovations, and a weak economy during the early 21st century, which made it vulnerable to competition. Toyota, aided by its new product offerings and strong financial muscle had successfully used this scenario to surpass Ford and affect a dramatic increase in its sales figures.

This case was written by **A. Neela Radhika**, under the direction of **A. Mukund**, ICFAI Center for Management Research (ICMR). It was compiled from published sources, and is intended to be used as a basis for class discussion rather than to illustrate either effective or ineffective handling of a management situation.

© 2004, ICFAI Center for Management Research. All rights reserved. No part of this publication may be reproduced, stored in a retrieval system, used in a spreadsheet, or transmitted in any form or by any means, electronic or mechanical, without permission.

TABLE I	Major global automobile companies – key statistics	
		(in $ billion)
Company	_Market capitalization*_	_Operating profits**_
Toyota	110	12.7
Nissan	54	7.5
Honda	40	6.1
Daimler Chrysler	38	5.7
General Motors	24	3.8
Ford Motors	22	3.6

Source: BusinessWeek, November 17, 2003.
*As of November 05, 2003.
**Fiscal 2002.

In November 2003, Toyota announced its financial results for the half-year ended September 30, 2003. The company reported a 23% increase in net income (as compared to the corresponding period of the previous year) to $4.4 billion on revenues of $69.7 billion. This took Toyota way ahead of World's top three automobile makers (at that time) by sales, General Motors (GM), Ford Motors (Ford) and Daimler Chrysler. Its market capitalization of $110 billion (on November 05, 2003) was more than the combined market capitalization of these three players. (See Table I).

Given the fact that in 2003, these top three companies were struggling to maintain their sales and profitability targets, Toyota's performance was termed remarkable by industry observers (See Exhibit I for the company's financials). Toyota had emerged as a formidable player in almost all the major automobile markets in the world. Interestingly, one of its strongest markets was the US, the world's largest automobile market and the home turf of Ford and GM.

Toyota had emerged as a strong foreign player in Europe as well, with a 4.4% market share. In China, which the company had identified as a strategic market for growth in the early 21st century, it had a 1.5% market share. The other major markets in which the company was fast strengthening its presence were South America, Southwest Asia, Southeast Asia and Africa.[3] Back home in Japan, it enjoyed a market share of over 43%.

Analysts attributed Toyota's growing sales across the world to its aggressive globalization efforts that began in the mid-1990s. The company constantly strived to ensure that each of its market segments – Japan, North America, and Europe and other markets – generated one-third of the annual sales (See Exhibits II and III for revenues and revenue growth data in its core markets). This goal was at the heart of Toyota's three globalization programs – New Global Business Plan (1995–1998), Global Vision 2005 (1996–2005) and Global Vision 2010 (2002–2010).

In the light of Toyota's intensifying globalization efforts, Toyota's competitors themselves stated that Toyota could not be taken lightly. GM's Chairman, John F. Smith Jr., said, "I would not say they will not make it. Toyota is an excellent company. They are very focused on what they do and they do it well, and that is what makes them great."[4]

BACKGROUND NOTE

Toyota's history dates back to 1897, when Japan's Sakichi Toyoda (Sakichi) diversified from his traditional family business of carpentry into handloom machinery. He founded Toyoda Automatic Loom Works (TALW) in 1926 for manufacturing automatic looms. Sakichi invented a loom that stopped

EXHIBIT I	Toyota – financial highlights		
	(Yen Millions except per share data and share information)		
	2001	*2002*	*2003*
Net revenues:			
Sales of products	12,402,104	13,499,644	14,793,973
Financing operations	553,133	690,664	707,580
Total	**12,955,237**	**14,190,308**	**15,501,553**
Costs and expenses:			
Cost of products sold	10,218,599	10,874,455	11,914,245
Cost of financing operations	427,340	459,195	423,885
Selling, general and administrative	1,518,569	1,763,026	1,891,777
Total	**12,164,508**	**13,096,676**	**14,229,907**
Operating income	**790,729**	**1,093,632**	**1,271,646**
% of Net Revenues	6.1%	7.7%	8.2%
Income before Income Taxes, Minority Interest and Equity in Earnings of Affiliated Companies	1,107,289	972,101	1,226,652
Provision for Income Taxes	523,876	422,789	517,014
Net Income	**674,898**	**556,567**	**750,942**
ROE	9.6%	7.8%	10.4%
Per Share Data (¥):			
Net Income (Basic)	180.65	152.26	211.32
Cash Dividends	25.00	28.00	36.00
Shareholders' Equity	1,921.29	2,015.82	2,063.43

Source: Toyota Annual Report 2003

EXHIBIT II	Toyota – revenues by core markets (fiscal 2003)

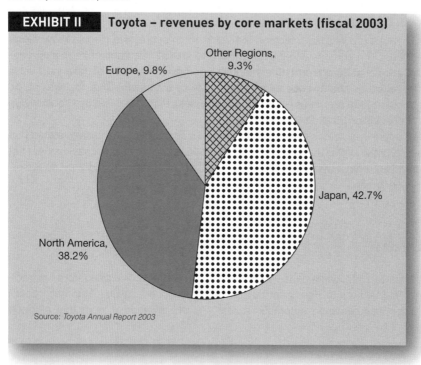

Other Regions, 9.3%

Europe, 9.8%

Japan, 42.7%

North America, 38.2%

Source: *Toyota Annual Report 2003*

2

EXHIBIT III   Toyota – revenue growth in core markets

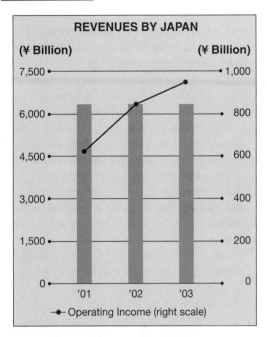

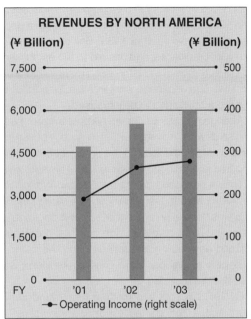

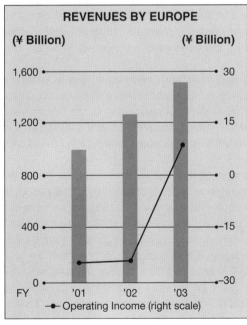

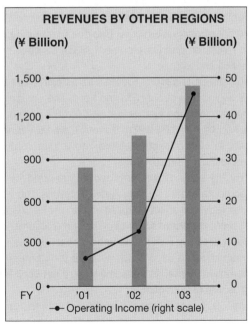

Source: Toyota Annual Report 2003

automatically when any of the threads snapped. This concept (designing equipment to stop so that defects could be fixed immediately) formed the basis of the Toyota Production System (TPS) and later became a major factor in the company's success.

In 1933, Sakichi established an automobile department within TALW and the first passenger car prototype was developed in 1935. Sakichi's son, Kiichiro Toyoda (Kiichiro), convinced him to enter the automobile business, and this led to the establishment of Toyota in 1937. During a visit to Ford to study the US automotive industry, Kiichiro saw that an average US worker's production was nine times that of an average Japanese worker. He realized that to compete globally, the Japanese automobile industry's productivity had to be increased.

After going back to Japan, he customized the Ford production system to suit the Japanese market. He also devised a system wherein each process in the assembly line produced only the number of parts needed at the next step on the production line. This made logistics management easier as material was procured according to consumption. This system was named Just-in-Time (JIT).[5]

Toyota flourished during the Second World War by selling trucks and buses to the army. The company launched its first small car (SA Model) in 1947. After the war, Toyota faced a series of financial problems. However, a financial support package from a consortium of banks (on the intervention of the Bank of Japan) helped it tide over its problems. The package consisted of a series of steps that included downsizing and restructuring the company into separate manufacturing and sales divisions. As per the revival package, The Toyota Motor Sales Company Ltd. was formed in 1950. In the same year, Kiichiro resigned.

By 1952, Toyota had made a turnaround and in 1953, it appointed distributors in El Salvador and Saudi Arabia and started exports. Meanwhile, Taiichi Ohno (Ohno) took charge of the company. In 1957, Toyota entered the US market through its subsidiary, Toyota Motor Sales, USA. In 1959, Toyota established its first overseas production unit in Brazil and over the next few years, developed a vast network of overseas plants. Besides manufacturing, the company started a global network of design and Research and Development (R&D) facilities covering the three major car markets of Japan, North America and Europe.

By the early 1970s, Toyota's sales exceeded that of Chrysler and Volkswagen, and its production was behind that of only GM and Ford. The company continued its efforts to make its production system more efficient and also developed flexible manufacturing systems. It also began to tap the markets in the Middle East. By 1974, Toyota Corolla, (launched in 1965) became the largest selling car in the world. In 1984, Toyota entered into a joint venture with GM and established the New United Motor Manufacturing Inc., (NUMMI).

By the early 1990s, as Toyota expanded its overseas operations, excessive capital expenditure affected its profit margins. Apart from this, the economic slowdown in Japan during this period also had an adverse affect on its sales and profits. As a result, the company was forced to readjust its sales and profit projections. Tatsuro Toyoda (Tatsuro), who became the President in 1992, took initiatives to control costs by eliminating unnecessary expenditure. But, even by 1995, it could not improve its performance within Japan. However, as the company recognized huge potential for growth in the global automobile market, in the same year, it set itself a target to achieve a 10% market share in that market by the turn of 20th century.

In 1995, Hiroshi Okuda (Okuda) became the president of Toyota. To improve the company's sales in the domestic market, Okuda chose to focus on the dealer network, already considered the best in the country. As part of this initiative, Toyota took initiatives to improve communication with its dealers – it offered more incentives to increase sales and encouraged them to attract more prospects for test drives.

Having identified the younger generation as the means to increase its market share in Japan, Toyota took aggressive measures to attract youngsters to its products. The company realized that the dealer outlets could play an important role in attracting young customers. However, it soon recognized some

2

functional discrepancies among its dealer outlets – dealer outlets were located too close to each other in some places; and even displayed the same models. Toyota stopped supplying similar models to such dealer outlets to avoid unnecessary price competition. It also decided to take a strict stance with those who failed to meet the targets and withdrew the monetary incentive schemes for them. Instead, it declared that the dealers who failed to meet sales targets might run the risk of losing their dealerships. Apart from this, Toyota also asked some of its dealers to restructure and rename their outlets in such a way as to attract young buyers.

In addition to the above measures, the company also invested heavily (around $200 million) on advertising in fiscal 1995. As a result of Okuda's game plan, Toyota's performance began picking up. As the financial base strengthened, Okuda decided to focus on improving the global sales performance, and took Toyota on the path of aggressive globalization.

EARLY GLOBALIZATION EFFORTS

In June 1995, Toyota announced the 'New Global Business Plan,' aimed at advancing localization (of production) and increasing imports (through collaboration with foreign automobile companies) over a three year period. A major objective of this plan was to increase Toyota's offshore production capacity to 2 million units by 1998. As part of the localization efforts, Toyota focused on increasing overseas production significantly by establishing new plants and expanding the capacity of the existing plants (See Table II for major initiatives taken under the New Global Business Plan).

Apart from this short-term global business plan, Toyota also came up with a long-term global business vision in June 1996, named the 'Global Vision 2005.' The major components of "Global Vision

TABLE II	**Major initiatives taken under the new global business plan**

- In North America, the company expanded the capacity of Toyota Motor Manufacturing Kentucky, Inc., (TMMK), from 400,000 units/annum to 500,000 units/annum and of Toyota Manufacturing Canada Inc., (TMMC) from 100,000 per year to 200,000 units per year. It established new manufacturing plants such as Toyota Motor Manufacturing, Indiana, Inc. (TMMI) and Toyota Motor Manufacturing, West Virginia Inc., (TMMWV).

- In Europe, it established Toyota Motor Manufacturing France S.A.S (TMMF) in November 1998 (to be operational in 2001) with a production target of 150,000 units/annum of the Yaris, the company's strategic vehicle for the European market. In Asia, the company established secondary plants in Thailand, Indonesia, Taiwan and Philippines.

- As part of increasing imports, the company strengthened the sales structure of its Duo stores that sold Volkswagen and Audi cars; expanded imports of completely built-up cars; and also began selling the Avalon, a passenger car built at TMMK, and Toyota Cavalier (made by GM). It established TACTI Corporation to source and sell new brands of aftermarket parts.

- Apart from this, the company also made significant progress in optimizing its global purchasing. It established the 'Toyota Global Optimum Purchasing System,' under which it took many initiatives to optimize its global procurement operations. It published the contents of its 'Supplier Guide' on the Internet to enable new suppliers to understand its procurement and sales policies and procedures. It also established a Suppliers Center (April 1998) to let suppliers exhibit their innovations.

Source: Adapted from www.autointell.com

2

2005" were, asserting a competitive edge in technology[6] and accelerating globalization, while sustaining market leadership in Japan, by reclaiming its above 40% market share.

As part of its globalization efforts, the company focused more on increasing the production of automobiles in the areas where they were sold. According to analysts, Japan's economic difficulties, which led to constant fluctuations in the value of its currency (Yen) during the 1990s, was one of the major reasons that forced the company to consider localization of production.

Toyota focused on attaining a regional balance for its global operations by focusing equally on all its three core regions. It also invested heavily on upgrading its R&D capabilities to develop a new line of products that met the diverse needs of its varied customer base across the world. Toyota replaced the engines of its Lexus range of cars with stronger models and made design changes as per customer feedback results. As a result of this, the car's sales soared in the US.

In 1997, the company launched Prius, a gasoline-electric car, the world's first ever mass-produced hybrid car. The car received good reviews for its energy conservation and environment friendly features. *Popular Science* magazine commented that Prius was "solid evidence that the ponderous development process that produces new automobiles is finally on the brink of a genuine technological breakthrough."[7] Toyota also launched new Lexus variants such as the new GS sedan (1997), and the RX 300 sports utility vehicle (SUV, in 1998). All these became instant successes in the US, helping it further consolidate its position in that market.

Toyota launched a new small car, Yaris, in April 1998 for the European market. This car was specifically designed to appeal to the Europeans' style and quality demands. Yaris was expected to improve the company's brand image in the minds of European customers and boost its growth in the region. The car received very good reviews at various European auto shows. According to Andrew Golby, deputy editor (road-tests), *Autocar* magazine, London, "Toyotas in the past have been dull to look at. This car (Yaris) looks pretty and stands out."

The company's overseas production increased from 1.22 million units per year in 1994 to 1.54 million units per year in 1998. However, this was still much below the expected 2 million mark. Moreover, while Toyota was drastically increasing its market share in the US, it was finding it difficult to perform well in Europe and Japan. Its market share was still below 3% in Europe and below 40% in Japan despite aggressive marketing efforts.

DOMESTIC PROBLEMS AND SOLUTIONS

According to industry observers, the above scenario was due to a host of reasons such as excessive capacity, choosy customers, surplus workforce and intensified competition within Japan. In 1998, Japan sales accounted for a mere 38% of the company's total sales, as compared to 52% in 1990. Also, Toyota's Japan sales contributed to a very small share of its total profits. US sales contributed to the majority share (80%) of the profits, followed by Europe.

By the late 1990s; young buyers accounted for 30% of the customer base as compared to over 45% in the late 1980s. In 1998, models from rival companies such as Honda and BMW were more popular than the ones offered by Toyota. According to reports, Japanese youngsters felt that Toyota cars 'lacked attitude.' Toyota realized that by losing its young customers to other companies, it ran the risk of losing its future market as well.

Analysts claimed that despite its efforts to cater to the young, the company had failed to give them zippy compact minivans and sports utility vehicles. They even said that if the conditions prevailing on the home front persisted, Toyota could find it difficult to finance its global ambitions and survive competition in the domestic and international markets.

Alarmed by this scenario, Toyota embarked on an aggressive restructuring exercise and started a new company, Virtual Venture Co. (VVC), to design and sell cars that appealed to the young generation.

VVC experimented with many unconventional sales strategies to improve the Toyota brand image among youngsters. For a small fee, it offered test-drives of many Toyota models to people; it built a $83 million amusement park in April 1998, where it displayed Toyota's visions for future models and also allowed people to design their own cars.

Beginning in 1999, the company rolled out many new cars specifically designed for the young Japanese buyers. These cars such as Vitz compact, FunCargo compact, and MR-S sports car, had the distinctive looks and attitude sought by these buyers. More significantly, a majority of these were entry-level. To keep the prices down, Toyota shared platforms with other models.

Apart from these new launches, the company also launched upgraded versions of its existing models such as Windom (Lexus ES 300), Verossa and Brevis. To attract the young buyers, Toyota took the risk of even de-emphasizing the Toyota brand. For instance, the new car bB, which became very popular with young buyers, had no visible signs of the 'Toyota' name, except for a Toyota symbol on the steering wheel. Similarly, WiLL VS, another car aimed at the youngsters, also had no visible signs that associated it with the Toyota brand.

As part of making the company's dealer outlets more appealing to young buyers, the company renamed one of its five dealership chains Netz, and targeted it exclusively at entry-level buyers. The Netz outlets were designed in such a way as to attract young buyers. For instance, a Netz outlet in the suburban Tokyo had an on-site pizza parlor and a playground. Toyota also undertook aggressive marketing efforts such as focused advertising of its new models besides offering high cash rebates to buyers of its flagging models.

Toyota focused on streamlining and reducing its workforce and decided to hire contract employees against its policy of lifetime employment. It planned to cut about $678 million in costs, employment mainly by designing cars with fewer and simpler parts and by sharing platforms and parts among its models. In 1999, Okuda replaced Chairman Shoichiro Toyoda and Fujio Cho (Cho) became the President. Cho's arrival marked the next phase of globalization at Toyota, beginning with the listing of the company's shares on the New York and London stock exchanges.

THE SECOND PHASE OF GLOBALIZATION

Cho decided to focus more on localization – he believed that by doing so, Toyota would be able to provide its customers with the products they needed, where they needed them. This was expected to help build mutually benefiting, long-term relationships with local suppliers and fulfill Toyota's commitments to local labor and communities.

Cho defined globalization as 'global localization.' Therefore, besides focusing on increasing the number of manufacturing centers and expanding the sales networks worldwide, Toyota also focused on localizing design, development and purchasing in every region and country. Toyota successfully propagated the TPS and its unique corporate culture, 'The Toyota Way' throughout its global manufacturing concerns.

As a result, Toyota employees everywhere practiced philosophies such as Kaizen (continuous improvement), PDCA (plan, do, check, action), Pokayoke (mistake-proofing), JIT and Construction of Cost Competitiveness (CCC21).[8] In this way, the company proved that its strategies were flexible enough to be adapted to work anywhere. As a result, overseas Toyota plants also achieved the quality levels the company had achieved at its plants in Japan. For instance, its Kentucky plant won four 'Gold Plant Quality Awards' from J.D. Power and Associates.

In 2001, to support its globalization drive, the company compiled a booklet, *The Toyota Way 2001*, aimed at transcending the diverse languages and cultures of its worldwide employees and to communicate the company's corporate philosophy and work culture to them. Toyota also decided to provide more autonomy to its regional operations. It expected that this would result in expansion of its overseas operations and increased profits.

Toyota's top management adopted a few Western management practices in addition to the traditional Japanese ones. Commenting on this, Cho said, "We are developing a management hybrid. We are trying to incorporate the best elements of the Japanese and Western traditions while avoiding some of the shortcomings of both."[9] This decision was in line with the company's decision to focus on its key global markets, North America, Europe and China.

North America

In line with its plans to open new plants (and expand the capacity of existing plants) in North America, Toyota decided to increase the engine production capacity of the West Virginia engine assembly plant (built in 1998) to 540,000 units by 2003. In 2002, the company built a manufacturing plant in Alabama (US). Production at this plant was expected to be 120,000 V8 engines per year. According to company sources, these initiatives were engineered to increase the annual production capacity in North America to 1.45 million units by fiscal 2003.

Toyota realized that the majority of its customers in the US were middle-aged, with their average age being 47 years. As against this, the average age was 44 years for Honda Motors Co., and 40 years for Volkswagen (the other two major importers in the US). To expand its customer base beyond this segment, Toyota decided to create new models targeted at budget minded young buyers, mainly in the age group of 20s–early 30s.

Starting in 1999, Toyota launched many new models (and new versions of existing models) targeting young customers in North America. Some of these included two new versions of Corolla Saloon, and Matrix, a sports wagon. The company decided to price Matrix and the new versions of Corolla low enough to compete with the low-priced Korean models that had flooded the US automobile market since 2000.

To further strengthen its position in the region, Toyota focused on new product launches in all segments of the market (viz. compacts, mid-size sedans, luxury SUVs and trucks), and also on aggressive sales and marketing efforts. The company maintained close relationships with its dealers; top executives visiting from Japan always made it a point to call on their dealers in the US. Analysts stated that such a healthy relationship with its dealer network helped Toyota identify market changes early on and take necessary action. For instance, when car sales began falling in 2000, Toyota's dealers informed it of the stock pile-up. The company immediately reduced the production of vehicles and saved significantly on the cost front. In sharp contrast, it took a lot of time for other automobile companies to identify and react to the crisis.

Europe

Commenting on Toyota's initiatives in Europe, Cho said, "Europe is a difficult market, and we are totally aware of that. We are learning and trying all kinds of things to understand the market."[10] The company had been making many aggressive moves to strengthen its position in this region since 1999. Its earlier decision to model the Yaris to cater to European tastes had paid off well as the car became an instant success. To match with that success, Toyota decided to engage European designers to design more cars that met the requirements of European customers. In line with this, the company started the French Riviera design center in May 2000 and hired European designers for its new Lexus SC430 Soarer sports car.

Another major strategic move was to increase its manufacturing capacity in Europe. According to company sources, this was expected to eliminate the external currency risk. Commenting on this, Akira Imai, President and CEO, Toyota (Europe) said, "As soon as possible, we will establish our entire organization and its systems to avoid external currency risk. That means more local procurement and more locally produced units."[11]

2

In 2001, Toyota started two new plants in Europe – the Valenciennes plant in France for manufacturing the Yaris; and the Polish plant for making manual transmissions for the Yaris, Corolla and Avensis. In 2002, the company established Toyota Motor Manufacturing Turkey, which manufactured Corolla sedans for export markets. The company also announced plans to increase the capacity of its UK engine plant to 400,000 units per year, 2003. In 2002, it also shifted the production of the Corolla 3-door Hatchback model to the UK vehicle plant. With this, the output of this plant rose by 30%, reaching its full capacity of 220,000 units per year.

In order to survive the intensifying competition in the European market, the company decided to enter into partnerships with other automobile companies in the region. Toyota partnered with PSA Peugeot Citroen to increase its manufacturing capacity in Europe. The two companies began work on jointly building a $2.7 billion manufacturing plant in the Czech Republic, with a capacity of 300,000 units per year. This plant was expected to become operational by 2005.

China

Toyota had identified China as one of the strategic markets, expected to drive growth in the future. According to company sources, China had a vast untapped market as compared to the developed countries. Though Toyota made a late entry (in 1989) into this high potential market, it lost no time in strongly establishing itself.

Since 1999, the company had entered into many joint ventures and alliance agreements in China. It manufactured the Toyota Coaster bus through a joint-venture (Sichuan Toyota Motor Co. Ltd.) with Sichuan Luxing Chechang. In 2002, the company also entered into a strategic alliance with the state-owned China FAW Group Corporation (FAW), the country's largest automaker, to manufacture automobiles for the Chinese market.

In 2000, Toyota began constructing a new plant in Tianjin. This plant became operational in early 2002 and began manufacturing compact cars based on the Yaris platform. The target volume was 30,000 units per year.

Toyota strengthened its presence in China through new model launches and expanded manufacturing capacities to meet local demand. In the passenger car market, it aimed to catch up with its rivals, Volkswagen (market leader) and GM, which controlled 35% and 10% of the passenger car market respectively. To do so, Toyota launched Vios, its first passenger car in China, in 2002. To strengthen its position in the market, the company planned to soon launch its Corolla and Crown brands in China.

THE 2010 GLOBAL VISION

In April 2002, Toyota announced another corporate strategy to boost its globalization efforts. This initiative, termed the '2010 Global Vision' was aimed at achieving a 15% market share (from the prevailing 10%) of the global automobile market by early 2010, exceeding the 14.2% market share held by the leader GM. The theme of the new vision was 'Innovation into the Future,' which focused on four key components: Recycling Based Society; Age of Information Technology; Development of Motorization on a Global Scale; and Diverse Society (See Table III).

For achieving these objectives, Toyota announced some plans – focus on accelerating technology reforms and technology development across its global operations to help it strengthen its core technologies like engines and platforms, management restructuring to clarify responsibilities and authority to provide more freedom to local entities in each region; and restructuring the profit structure so that Toyota was supported by three profit bases – Japan, North America and Europe.

2

TABLE III	**Four key components of Toyota's global vision 2010**

- **Recycling Based Society:** Be a driving force in global regeneration by implementing the most advanced environmental technologies.

- **Age of Information Technology:** Create automobiles and a motorized society in which people can live safely, securely and comfortably through the use of advanced technology.

- **Development of Motorization on a Global Scale:** Promote the appeal of cars throughout the world and realize a large increase in the number of Toyota fans.

- **Diverse Society:** Be a truly global company that is trusted and respected by all peoples around the world.

Source: www.toyota.co.jp

According to reports, '2010 Global Vision' had essentially evolved from the '2005 Global Vision.' Analysts felt that this new vision had been necessitated by the changing market dynamics across the world. They also said that if the company wanted to reach its goal of attaining a 15% share of the global car market, it needed to sell 2.7 million more vehicles per year (in addition to the six million vehicles per year figure in 2003). To do so, Toyota needed to add 18 new manufacturing plants and a workforce of 36,000.

Industry observers felt that since Toyota's home market had reached the saturation level, such a growth would only be possible by targeting market segments where it had little presence until then and the developing economies which offered high potential for growth in the early 21st century. The company began focusing more on the truck market in the US, small car market in Europe and began targeting emerging economies such as China, India, and African countries.

Toyota also planned to revamp its production and supply strategies. To cut costs, it decided to source parts from those countries where they were available cheap. The decision to manufacture vehicles or the various parts in countries such as India, Malaysia, Thailand, Philippines, Indonesia and Vietnam was due to the fact that labor was cheap in these places.

In early 2003, Toyota announced plans to evolve the Lexus brand into a truly global, premium-end brand in China and Japan. At the turn of the 20th century, the demand for diesel engines grew in Europe. So, Toyota released diesel-powered versions of the Yaris, Corolla and Avensis during 2002 and 2003. During 1998-2003, the company invested nearly $1.3 billion on global manufacturing and marketing of its vehicles. By early 2003, the company succeeded in garnering a 5% market share of the Chinese passenger car market. Toyota also planned to build a second manufacturing plant in Tianjin China (operational in 2005) to manufacture a mid-luxury car (called Crown in Japan).

Toyota targeted sales of about 400,000 units per year (10% market share) in China by 2010. As part of achieving this goal, the company decided to manufacture three types of vehicles (in collaboration with FAW) that included mini vehicles (to be sold under the Daihatsu brand), large/medium class luxury sedans and large/medium class luxury SUVs.

In North America, Toyota focused its new launches in the SUV, minivan, truck, environmental and youth segments. It launched new models in the Tundra (truck) Series, Sienna (minivan) Series, Lexus Lx 470 and different models of Prius by early-2003. By April 2003, Toyota had a 10.4% market share in North America, and it aimed to increase this to 12.4% by 2005.

By mid-2003, the company controlled more than 12% of the high margin SUV segment in North America with eight models. It succeeded in appealing to the youth through its focus on this segment since 1999. Another model, Scion xB compact, unveiled in June 2003, was received well by young buyers. The company also established an exclusive Scion marketing group, aimed at developing a range of vehicles that appealed to young car buyers.

In September 2003, Toyota unveiled the new hybrid gasoline Prius sedan, one of the world's first vehicles that could park itself. It had an electronically operated steering wheel that guided the car when reversing into parking spaces. The new Prius was reportedly more fuel-efficient, driver-friendly and cheaper than its predecessors.

The company expected to sell 76,000 new Prius cars worldwide in 2004, in the light of the growing popularity for environment-friendly cars. The target of 76,000 was reportedly more than double the company's target for Prius cars for the previous two years (28,000 units per year). At the same time, the company announced plans to launch a hybrid Lexus RX 330 SUV by mid-2004. Toyota revealed that it was building a $800 million manufacturing plant in San Antonio, Texas, which would manufacture 250,000 Tundra trucks per year by 2006.

THE GLOBALIZATION PAY-OFF

By mid-2003, Toyota was present in almost all the major segments of the automobile market that included small cars, luxury sedans, full-sized pickup trucks, SUVs, small trucks and crossover vehicles. According to reports, while global vehicle production increased by 3.3 times since the early 1960s, Toyota's production had increased by 38 times. As a result of its localization initiatives, Toyota had 45 manufacturing plants in 26 countries and regions by this time, and sold vehicles in 160 countries (See Exhibit IV and V for Toyota's worldwide manufacturing operations and production details). The company's overseas sales accounted for more than 50% of its annual vehicle sales and Toyota expected this figure to rise in the future (See Exhibit VI for Toyota's overseas sales highlights).

In fiscal 2003, the company achieved record sales of 730,000 units in Europe. For the fiscal 2004, Toyota decided to focus mainly on these areas – developing core models (by launching remodeled versions of models such as the Yaris, Corolla, Avensis, Lexus and other hybrid, diesel and SUV models); rebuilding its sales network by making its distributors into subsidiaries; giving more autonomy to its European headquarters; strengthening its sales network; and expanding local manufacturing capacity, cutting costs and increasing production volumes.

In Japan, the company had a strong hold on many profitable market segments such as large and midsize sedans and large and mid-sized SUVs, which it decided to further strengthen in fiscal 2004. Apart from this, Toyota also aimed at expanding its lineup of compact cars and minivans, which had picked up momentum during the early 21st century. The company had launched many new models in fiscal 2003, tailored to the customer's changing lifestyles. Some of these vehicles included the Camry, Allion and Premio sedans, the Ipsum, Noah, Voxy and Sienna minivans, the Scion and 'ist' compact cars, and the Solara sports coupe.

In China, Toyota succeeded in acquiring a 1.5% market share of the total automobile market by late 2003. It aimed at manufacturing 250,000 vehicles per year by 2005 in this country. The company announced plans to sell one million vehicles annually in China by 2010. Apart from this, it aimed at acquiring more than a 20% market share in other major countries in Asia such as Thailand and Indonesia.

In the US car market, Toyota outsold all other companies. Commenting on its dominance in the US car market, Brian Lund, equity analyst, *Morningstar*, said, "In cars, Toyota owns the place. GM and Ford and Chrysler have, in many ways, given up on cars. They have retained interest in luxury vehicles and light trucks, because they are high margin. In terms of cars, they maintain what they do because of fuel efficiency requirements."[12] Paul Rubin, analyst, UBS Securities, who surveyed car dealers in the US, observed, "The Toyota brand finished at the top of the pack in almost every measure – desirability, market-share prospects, relationships with manufacturers and customers. Toyota is truly in a class of its own."[13]

Toyota's market share in the US increased from 10.4% in 2002 to 11.2% by late 2003, mainly at the expense of GM, Ford and Daimler Chrysler. Fueled by the growing sales across its core markets, the

EXHIBIT IV	Toyota – worldwide operations (manufacturing)			
Location	Name	Start of operations	Toyota related equity	Products
Argentina	Toyota Argentina S.A.	Mar. 1997	TMC 100%	Hilux
Australia	Toyota Motor Corporation Australia Ltd.	Apr. 1963	TMC 100%	Avalon, Camry, engines
Bangladesh	Aftab Automobiles Ltd.	Jul. 1982	TMC 0%	Land Cruiser, Hino trucks
Brazil	Toyota do Brasil Ltd.	May 1959	TMC 100%	Corolla
Canada	Canadian Autoparts Toyota Inc.	Feb. 1985	TMC 100%	Aluminum wheels
	Toyota Motor Manufacturing Canada Inc.	Nov. 1988	TMC 100%	Camry Solara, Corolla, Matrix, engines
China	Sichuan Toyota Motor Co., Ltd.	Dec. 2000	TMC 45%	Coaster , Land Cruiser Prado
	Tianjin Toyota Motor Engine Co., Ltd.	Jun. 1998	TMC 50%	Engines
	Tianjin Fengjin Auto Parts Co., Ltd.	May 1998	TMC 90%	Continuous velocity joints, axles, steering column
	Tianjin Toyota Forging Co., Ltd.	Dec. 1998	TMC 100%	Forging parts
	Tianjin Toyota Motor Co., Ltd.	Oct. 2002	TMC 40%TMCI 10%	Vios
	Tianjin Jinfeng Auto Parts Co., Ltd.	Jun. 1997[2]	TMC 30%	Steering parts, propeller shafts
Colombia	Sociedad de Fabricacion de Automotores S.A.	Mar. 1992	TMC 28%	Land Cruiser, Hilux, Land Cluiser Prado
Czech Republic	Toyota Peugeot Citroën Automobile Czech s.r.o.	2005 (plan)	TMC 50%	New small car
France	Toyota Motor Manufacturing France S.A.S. (TMMF)	Jan. 2001	TMEM 100%	Yaris
India	Toyota Kirloskar Motor Private Ltd. (TKM)	Dec. 1999	TMC 99%	Qualis, Corolla
	Toyota Kirloskar Auto Parts Private Ltd. (TKAP)	Apr. 2002	TMC 64%Toyota Industries 26%	Axles, Propeller shafts

2

EXHIBIT IV	(Continued)			
Location	Name	Start of operations	Toyota related equity	Products
Indonesia	P.T. Toyota-Astra Motor	May 1970	TMC 49%	Camry, Corolla, Dyna, TUV, engines
	PT. Astra Daihatsu Motor	Jan. 1992	Diahatsu 61.75%	New Small Car, Zebra[*1], Taruna[*1], Ceria[*1]
Kenya	Associated Vehicle Assemblers Ltd.	Aug. 1977	TMC 0%	Hiace, Hilux, Land Cruiser
Malaysia	Assembly Services Sdn. Bhd.	Feb. 1968	UMW Toyota 100%	Camry, Corolla, Hiace, Hilux, Vios, TUV, engines
Mexico	Toyota Motor Manufacturing de Baja California S. de R.L.de C.V.	2004 (plan)	TABC Holding 99% TMMNA 1%	Truck beds (2004), Tacoma (2005)
Pakistan	Indus Motor Company Ltd.	Mar. 1993	TMC 12.5% TTC 12.5%	Corolla, Hilux, Cuore[*1]
Philippines	Toyota Autoparts Philippines Inc.	Sep. 1992	TMC 95%	CVJ, Transmissions
	Toyota Motor Philippines Corp.	Feb. 1989	TMC 34%	Camry, Corolla, TUV, engines
Poland	Toyota Motor Manufacturing Poland SP.zo.o. (TMMP)	Apr. 2002	TMEM 100%	Transmissions
	Toyota Motor Industries Poland SP.zo.o. (TMIP)	2005 (plan)	TMEM 60% Toyota Industries 40%	Engines
Portugal	Salvador Caetano I.M.V.T., S.A.	Aug. 1968	TMC 27%	Dyna, Hiace, Optimo
South Africa	Toyota South Africa Motors (Pty) Ltd.	Jun. 1962	TMC 75.0%	Corolla, Dyna, Hiace, Hilux, TUV, engines
Taiwan	Kuozui Motors, Ltd.	Jan. 1986	TMC 51.7%	Camry, Corolla, TUV, Hiace, Dyna, Vios engines, parts for press and assembly
Thailand	Siam Toyota Manufacturing Co., Ltd.	July 1989	TMC 96%	Engines
	Toyota Auto Body Thailand Co., Ltd.	May 1979	TMT 48.9%	Stamped parts
	Toyota Motor Thailand Co., Ltd.	Dec. 1964	TMC 86.4%	Camry, Corolla, Hilux, Soluna-vios

2

EXHIBIT IV	*(Continued)*			
Location	Name	Start of operations	Toyota related equity	Products
Turkey	Toyota Motor Manufacturing Turkey Inc.	Sep. 1994	TMEM 90% Mitsui 10%	Corolla
U.K.	Toyota Motor Manufacturing (UK) Ltd.	Dec. 1992	TMEM 100%	Avensis, Corolla, engines
U.S.A.	Bodine Aluminum, Inc.	Jan. 1993	TMMNA 100%	Aluminum castings
	New United Motor Manufacturing, Inc. (NUMMI)	Dec. 1984	TMC 50% GM 50%	Corolla, Tacoma,
	TABC, Inc.	Nov. 1971	TABC Holding 100%	Truck beds, catalytic converters, stamped parts
	Toyota Motor Manufacturing, Alabama, Inc.	May 2003	TMMNA 100%	Engines
	Toyota Motor Manufacturing, Kentucky, Inc.	May 1988	TMMNA 100%	Avalon, Camry, engines
	Toyota Motor Manufacturing, Indiana, Inc.	Dec. 1998	TMMNA 100%	Tundra, Sequoia, Sienna
	Toyota Motor Manufacturing, Texas, Inc.	2006 (plan)	TMMNA 100%	Tundra
	Toyota Motor Manufacturing, West Virginia, Inc.	Dec. 1998	TMMNA 100%	Engines, transmissions
Venezuela	Toyota de Venezuela Compania Anonima	Jan. 1963	TMC 90%	Corolla, Dyna, Land Cruiser, Terios[*1] engines,
Vietnam	Toyota Motor Vietnam Co., Ltd.	Aug. 1996	TMC 70%	Camry, Corolla, Hiace, Land Cruiser, TUV, Vios

Source: www.toyota.co.jp

Notes:

1) Data as of December 2002.
2) *1 Daihatsu brand.
3) *2 Start of Toyota's equity participation.
4) TMC: Toyota Motor Corp., TMMNA: Toyota Motor Manufacturing North America Inc., TMEM: Toyota Motor Engineering & Manufacturing Europe.

2

EXHIBIT V	Toyota – production figures (by region)*					
						(1 = 1000 Vehicles)
Region	*1998*	*1999*	*2000*	*2001*	*2002*	*2003 (Jan.–Sept.)*
North America	962.8	1,061.9	1,104.0	1,088.5	1,205.3	940.3
Latin America & the Caribbean	15.3	16.8	19.6	17.8	42.9	41.5
Europe	175.7	181.5	173.3	216.9	344.6	275.6
Africa	74.1	68.4	77.5	77.5	75.5	71.9
Asia	124.8	182.1	248.4	254.3	345.7	396.8
Oceania	100.4	91.0	92.4	94.6	86.6	84.6
Middle East & Southwest Asia	14.4	9.4	36.1	31.0	65.1	49.4
Overseas total	1,467.6	1,611.0	1,751.4	1,780.3	2,150.5	1,860.0
Domestic total	3,165.8	3,118.2	3,429.2	3,354.4	3,485.2	2,604.1
Worldwide total	4,633.4	4,729.2	5,180.6	5,134.7	5,635.7	4,464.1

Source: www.toyota.co.jp

Notes:
1   Figures for 'overseas production' indicate 'local production,' i.e., the number of vehicles that were manufactured with the value of parts imported from Japan (F.O.B. price) less than 60% the total value of the parts in the vehicle. Figures for 'domestic production' include the number of CKD vehicles.
2   *Regions as defined by the company.

company raised its global sales forecast for fiscal 2004 from 6.41 million units to 6.57 million units. For North America, it raised the sales target from 2.03 million units to 2.12 million and for Europe, it expected to reach the 800,000 unit target set for 2005, in 2004 itself.

WHICH WAY TO DRIVE FROM HERE?

By the end of 2003, Toyota seemed to be well on its way to achieving its globalization goals – world-wide sales of 6.57 million units in fiscal 2004; sales of 2.12 million units in North America by 2004; a 5% market share (800,000 units sales) in Europe by 2004; a 15% market share in the global market and a 10% market share in China by 2010.

Analysts felt that the following factors were helping the company in its quest to become a truly global automobile major: strong financial condition, globally efficient production system, unique corporate culture, and the ability to develop a product range that met the unique needs and desires of customers in different regions. Now that Toyota had overtaken Ford, analysts stated that its next target would be to surpass GM and become the biggest automaker in the world. They felt that if the company succeeded in maintaining its track record of growth, achieving this goal might not be very difficult.

Some analysts were however, of the opinion that the company would not be able to sustain this growth in the future as the global automobile market was getting saturated. But Toyota sources were not ready to accept this argument. According to Cho, the world's emerging markets offered huge potential for growth. He said, "The international automobile market is anything but saturated. I think it

2

would be more accurate to say that it has just turned the corner toward an era of new growth. A wave of motorization is sweeping across China, Russia and India, to name just the largest regions. The world's emerging markets represent a huge number of people that have yet to receive the benefits of automobiles. This is a vast, uncharted territory for automobile manufacturers. I am convinced that an age of full-scale global motorization is almost upon us."[14]

Skeptics pointed out that Toyota's over-dependence on the US market could prove problematic. In 2003, the company derived 70% of its profits from this region. With Germany's BMW gaining ground in

EXHIBIT VI	Toyota – overseas sales (by region)*					
						(1=1000 Vehicles)
Region	1998	1999	2000	2001	2002	2003 (Jan.–Sept.)
North America	1,516.0	1,631.3	1,766.3	1,893.6	1,940.8	1,571.4
Latin America & the Caribbean	125.0	99.9	105.6	107.5	96.9	85.6
Europe	540.9	592.3	655.8	666.0	755.6	644.4
Africa	129.7	123.2	121.8	126.5	139.8	118.2
Asia	229.5	252.9	339.3	342.2	455.0	454.2
Oceania	176.5	171.8	176.7	162.2	182.2	158.8
Middle East & Southwest Asia	212.4	186.6	217.2	248.6	267.9	235.2
Overseas total	2,930.0	3,058.1	3,382.7	3,546.7	3,838.3	3,267.9
Domestic total	1,711.0	1,664.4	1,771.7	1,715.2	1,680.5	1,308.4
Worldwide total	4,641.0	4,722.5	5,154.3	5,261.9	5,518.8	4,576.3

Source: www.toyota.co.jp
*Regions as defined by the company.

Toyota – overseas sales (by brand)			
			(1=1000 Vehicles)
Region	Toyota brand	Lexus brand	Total
North America	1,699.4	241.3	1,940.8
Latin America & the Caribbean	96.7	0.3	96.9
Europe	734.5	21.2	755.6
Africa	139.7	0.1	139.8
Asia	444.2	10.9	455.0
Oceania	178.6	3.6	182.2
Middle East & Southwest Asia	257.6	10.3	267.9
Overseas Total	3,550.7	287.6	3,838.3

Source: www.toyota.co.jp

2

Toyota – top 10 sales in overseas market

(1=1000 Vehicles)

Location	2000	Location	2001	Location	2002
US	1,619.2	US	1,741.3	US	1,756.1
Australia	158.9	Australia	143.6	Australia	161.0
Canada	123.6	Canada	127.8	Canada	152.8
UK	98.8	UK	115.4	UK	130.1
Taiwan	91.1	Taiwan	100.2	Taiwan	122.0
Indonesia	87.8	Indonesia	96.3	Indonesia	121.4
Italy	87.8	Italy	87.6	Italy	105.0
Germany	86.8	Germany	83.5	Germany	100.1
Saudi Arabia	81.4	Saudi Arabia	82.7	Saudi Arabia	95.4
South Africa	79.3	South Africa	82.2	South Africa	82.6

Source: www.toyota.co.jp

the luxury sedan segments and the average Toyota customer age still hovering around 46, analysts felt that Toyota might not be able to sustain its growth in the US in the future.

Another potential roadblock to the company's growth target was the intensifying competition from other top players. GM was on the verge of finishing a $4.3 billion revamp of its popular Cadillac model and was also restructuring its quality initiatives to meet the quality levels of Toyota's products. At home, the company was facing high competition from both domestic and foreign players such as Nissan, Honda, Volkswagen and BMW, in its major market segments.

Despite these challenges, Toyota expressed confidence that it would meet its targets with the help of its new products, expanded manufacturing base, and production and quality control strategies. Industry observers were of the view that even if it failed to achieve its targets, it might not be a major disappointment, given its strong financial condition. By the turn of 2004, the company was reportedly confident of the success of its globalization plans.

DISCUSSION: QUESTIONS

1 Study Toyota's evolution into a market leader in the Japanese automobile market over the decades. What were the factors that helped Toyota attain (and sustain) the leadership status in Japan? What problems did the company face in this market later on? Analyze and discuss the efforts made to overcome these problems.

2 Critically examine the rationale behind Toyota's decision to spread its operations across various geographical regions and to focus on young buyers in its core markets. Elaborate upon the three different programs adopted, and analyze how localization of manufacturing was expected to help the company.

3 Considering the extremely competitive global market scenario and the nearly saturated demand in its core automobile markets (US and Japan), do you think Toyota will be able to achieve its goal of attaining a 15% market share by 2010? Justify your stand. Also suggest some measures that could help the company achieve its global targets.

2

NOTES

1 Green and Global Are the Road to Success, www.toyota.co.jp, March 18, 2002.

2 The "Oof Company," www.forbes.com, April 14, 2003.

3 Toyota sold its vehicles worldwide under its Toyota, Lexus, Diahatsu and Hino brands.

4 The "Oof Company," www.forbes.com, April 14, 2003.

5 JIT production was defined as 'producing only necessary units in a necessary quantity at a necessary time, resulting in reduction in excess inventories and excess workforce, thereby increasing productivity.'

6 Toyota's technology initiatives were aimed at developing environment friendly and user friendly vehicles. For this, the company initiated efforts to develop advanced technologies such as hybrid-electric systems that doubled the fuel efficiency and reduced harmful emissions; direct-injection system that increased the efficiency of gasoline engines; and pure electric, 'zero emission' vehicles to reduce urban pollution.

7 A Smarter Way to Get Around, www.toyota.co.jp, March 18, 2002. Prius won a lot of recognition over the years. In 2001, *The Automotive Engineering International* recognized it as the 'world's best engineered passenger car.' By 2002, it was being sold in North America, Japan, Europe, Hong Kong, Australia and Singapore. Having sold 120,000 units, Prius was the best selling hybrid car model in the world in 2003.

8 Through the CCC21 program, Toyota challenged itself to achieve world-class cost competitiveness for its 170 key components which accounted for about 90% of the total component purchase costs. The company planned to achieve this target through the combined and collaborative efforts among parts suppliers and its engineering, production, production engineering and purchasing divisions.

9 Toyota DNA: Change or Die, www.toyota.co.jp, March 25, 2002.

10 Cho driving Toyota into Europe, Business Asia, September 2000.

11 Toyota Targets European Expansion, http://news.bbc.co.uk, March 06, 2002.

12 Why Toyota is Beating Ford, www.forbes.com, November 17, 2003.

13 The Americanization of Toyota, *Fortune*, December 08, 2003.

14 Green and Global Are the Road to Success, www.toyota.co.jp, March 18, 2002.

FURTHER READINGS

1 **Exclusive Interview: Toyota's Okuda,** http://waw.wardsauto.com, December 01, 1995.

2 **Toyota's Midlife Crisis,** www.businessweek.com, December 21, 1998.

3 **Lexus: All Revved up with Somewhere to Go,** www.businessweek.com, December 21, 1998.

4 **Feels Roomy, Looks Small: Will The Yaris Play in Paris?** www.businessweek.com, December 21, 1998.

5 **Toyota's Okuda May Leave behind Big Problems,** www.businessweek.com, February 01, 1999.

6 **Toyota: Final Report on New Global Business Plan,** www.autointell.com, March 30, 1999.

7 **Young, Funky, Hip ... Toyota?** www.businessweek.com, April 23, 2001.

8 **Sickly Yen Steers Toyota towards Record Profit,** www.guardian.co.uk, May 10, 2001.

9 **Toyota: Taking on BMW,** www.businessweek.com, July 30, 2001.

10 **Toyota Boosts Profits as Yen Slides,** http://news.bbc.co.uk, November 08, 2001.

11 **Toyota to Present New Car Model to Chinese Customers,** http://fpeng.peopledaily.com.cn, January 07, 2002.

12 **Toyota Targets Youth with New Cars,** http://news.bbc.co.uk, January 08, 2002.

13 **Toyota Targets European Expansion,** http://news.bbc.co.uk, March 06, 2002.

14 **Toyota Announces 2010 Global Vision,** www.wintoy.com.au.

15 **2010 – Global Vision for a Decade,** www.fastlane.com.au, April 18, 2002.

16 **Your Father's Toyota?** www.businessweek.com, May 27, 2002.

17 **Fall in Demand: Toyota to Revamp Home Operations,** http://finance.indiainfo.com, July 29, 2002.

18 **Japanese Car Makers in America,** www.economist.com, September 12, 2002.

19 **Cho Driving Toyota into Europe,** Business Asia, September 2002.

20 Keller Maryann, **Toyota: Can it be Stopped,** Automotive Industries, October 2002.

21 **Putting Theory to Work,** www.kybiz.com, November 2002.

22 **Lexus Brand to Be Introduced in Japan,** PR Newswire, February 24, 2003.

23 Armstrong Larry, **Toyota's Scion: A Siren to Young Buyers?** www.businessweek.com, March 04, 2003.

24 **Toyota Roars into China,** www.businessweek.com, April 07, 2003.

25 Meredith Robyn and Fulford Benjamin with Fahey Jonathan, **The "Oof" Company,** www.forbes.com, April 14, 2003.

26 Bremmer Brian, **Toyota's Doubled-Edged Triumph,** www.businessweek.com, September 08, 2003.

27 Peter John, **Hybrid Driven: Toyota Aims the 2004 Prius at a Mass-Market Audience and Gives us a Glimpse of Things to Come,** Automotive Industries, October, 2003.

28 Kageyama Yuri, **Riding on U.S. Success, Toyota's Lexus Luxury Cars Coming Home to Japan,** www.miami.com, October 30, 2003.

29 **Toyota Posts Surprise Profit Jump,** http://edition.cnn.com, November 05, 2003.

30 Kim Chang-Ram, **Toyota Profit Stuns All,** http://in.news.yahoo.com, November 06, 2003.

31 **Why Toyota Is Beating Ford,** www.forbes.com, November 17, 2003.

32 **Can Anything Stop Toyota?** BusinessWeek, November 17, 2003.

33 **The Americanization of Toyota,** Fortune, December 08, 2003.

34 **The Year of the Car,** www.economist.com, December 30, 2003.

35 www.toyota.co.jp

36 www.autointell.com

2

CASE STUDY 3

LG ELECTRONICS: GLOBAL STRATEGY IN EMERGING MARKETS

KANAN RAMASWAMY

Mr. Nam Woo, President of LG Electronics (LG), was collecting his thoughts after the press conference in Beijing. He had been appointed as the President of LG Electronics in China in 2006 and was unveiling an ambitious agenda to accelerate LG's presence in the country. He reflected on the emergence of South Korea as a major hub in the consumer electronics business and the role that LG had played in the rapid transformation. Having spearheaded a significant part of LG's forays into emerging markets such as Brazil, Russia, China, and India, Mr. Woo had synthesized some crucial lessons that he would have to bring to bear as China moved up the scale in economic importance. He had told the press that LG would target local Chinese managers to fill at least 80% of its managerial ranks shortly. "We want to make China a strategic base for our business, so we must be a leader not only in sales, but also in research and development and in localization."[1] It was a classic summary of the essence of LG's success in emerging economies.

LG had bet an important part of its future on success in emerging markets. It had entered countries such as Brazil, China, and India fairly early in its evolution, and those investments were providing healthy returns. In many of these markets, LGE had emerged as the market leader and was setting the trend for other competitors to follow. Many believed that the company was defining the broad contours of successful global strategy for a multinational from the developing world. However, LG realized that it had to demonstrate success in developed markets to rightfully claim its position among the leading global consumer electronics and appliance manufacturers. Having conquered the major emerging markets, what would LG have to do in order to breach established markets such as the U.S. and Western Europe where the global giants were active? Would the lessons it had learned in the BRIC countries (Brazil, Russia, India, China) be helpful in making the transition from emerging to developed markets? What were the implications for its global strategic positioning? These were the key questions that Mr. Woo had to ponder.

Copyright © 2007 Thunderbird School of Global Management. All rights reserved. This case was prepared by Professor Kannan Ramaswamy for the purpose of classroom discussion only, and not to indicate either effective or ineffective management.

The active support of Mr. Nam Woo, President, LG Electronics, is gratefully acknowledged. Mr. Jin Kang, LG Electronics, provided research assistance.

THUNDERBIRD
SCHOOL OF GLOBAL MANAGEMENT

THE KOREAN ELECTRONICS INDUSTRY

By 2007, Korea had become synonymous with high quality, innovative consumer electronics products. Within the short span of a few decades, Korean manufacturers had managed to shake off the stigma of upstarts in an industry dominated by established Japanese and European players. Gone were the days when products carrying labels such as Goldstar, Samsung, and Zenith were relegated to the back rooms of electronics retailers. When the titans of the digital age such as Bill Gates of Microsoft and Craig Barrett of Intel headlined the Consumer Electronics Show (CES) in 2005, they demonstrated digital convergence using equipment from Korea. In 2007, LG showcased the world's first dual-system DVD player that was compatible with both Blue Ray and HD-DVD standards. The Korean manufacturers had indeed climbed into the spotlight. In the last two decades alone, the market value of LG Electronics had grown at a compound growth rate of 22% from $200 million in the mid-1980s to $1 billion by the mid-1990s and almost $11 billion by early 2005. Samsung had twice the market capitalization of archrival Sony. This success story was a product of foresight, careful strategic thinking, and leveraging an array of advantages that Korea was building at home.

THE HISTORY OF LG

LG was born as the Lak Hui Chemical Industrial Co. in 1947. It was founded by Mr. In-hwoi Koo for the manufacture of cosmetic creams. Finding that there were no independent manufacturers capable of supplying bottle caps needed for packaging the cream, Lak Hui Chemical set up its own facilities and utilized the excess capacity of its injection-molding machines to manufacture small consumer products based in plastic. This led to an entry into the manufacture of plastics components for telecommunication and electrical companies presaging LG's entry into the telecommunications business. In fortifying

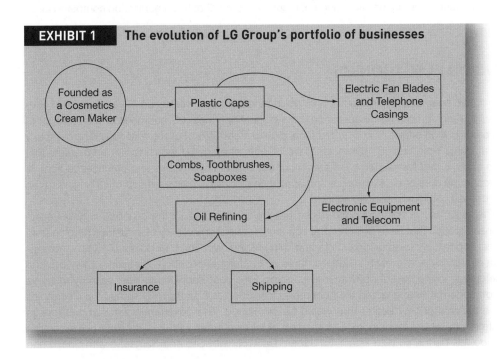

EXHIBIT 1   **The evolution of LG Group's portfolio of businesses**

3

its access to feedstock for plastics manufacture, the company moved into oil refining and later into shipping to transport crude oil. It was in 1958 that the Goldstar Co. (currently LG Electronics) was first established to consolidate expansion in the fast-growing area of plastics.

LG Electronics soon pioneered the growth of the Korean electronics and appliances industry, becoming the first Korean company to build a vacuum tube radio, electric fan, black and white television, washing machine, and an automated telephone switching system. By the mid-1960s, the company had moved into a range of industries including oil refining, cables, heavy manufacturing, and energy. Much of the meteoric growth of the group started in the 1970s. Spurred by a country that wanted to boost its exports and consolidate economic growth at home, the electronics, refining, and chemicals businesses set records in terms of revenues that they contributed to the group. This era also saw the move into financial services through the acquisition of an insurance company and a securities trading firm. The 1980s were a period of dedicated internationalization. Starting with intensive exports to developing countries, LG soon moved to capture markets in the developed world. It launched a range of joint ventures with established players from the West such as Caltex and EDS, and started testing the U.S. markets for electronics products. By then, the ground had already been laid for growth in developing markets such as China, India, and Vietnam, where the company had established a significant presence in a variety of industry sectors.

In 2007, the company was well under way with its rebalancing and restructuring program that sought to rationalize its business holdings into core and non-core groups. It had identified three focused business areas as the key domains for its activities—electronics, chemicals, and telecommunications. The group adopted a holding company structure that promoted more transparency and autonomy for subsidiary operations. It had already made its presence felt in the most developed consumer market in the world, the United States, where its CDMA phones outsold all competitors two years in a row. It had also established a strong beachhead position in flat screen televisions through its joint venture with Philips, the Dutch electronics company. LG-Philips was the largest manufacturer of flat screens in the world by a wide margin. By 2006, sales revenues at the group level were roughly $23 billion, generating profits of $500 million. The group had to consolidate these successes in developed-country markets to evolve into a global competitor across the wide range of industry sectors that the organization competed in.

BETTING ON ELECTRONICS

LG Electronics had been quite instrumental in launching the LG brand worldwide. Given its suite of consumer products, ranging from home appliances to mobile telephones, LG had been at the forefront of the group's globalization efforts. It accounted for approximately 47% of group revenues. The company exemplified a "come from behind" approach to defining its strategy by focusing first on markets that few dared to enter. It had formulated a unique mix of management principles and practices to fight its way to the top in the consumer electronics and appliances industry. It owed much of its origins to the competitive context within which it had evolved.

Much of Korea's rise in the economic sense has been attributed to the *chaebol*, largely family-owned business groups that have powered the economy forward in a variety of industries ranging from petrochemical and textiles to semiconductors and shipbuilding. Working hand in hand with the government's industrial policy and growth initiatives, three of the largest *chaebol*—Samsung, Daewoo, and LG—led the charge in the field of consumer electronics. President Park Chung Hee, seen by many as the creator of modern Korea, enacted the Economic Development Plan that highlighted the electronics industry as a national priority sector that would be developed. The government encouraged foreign direct investment to secure technology and creation of joint ventures with leading electronics companies worldwide. LG partnered with Hitachi of Japan, Daewoo with GE, and Samsung with Sanyo and

NEC. Soon thereafter, foreign companies through their joint ventures in Korea were exporting close to 70% of all electronics products from the country. This formative period focused on labor-intensive, low value-added products that did not have any significant technology dimension with foreign companies assuming leadership roles in much of the technologically sophisticated products.

It was only in the 1980s that the industry accelerated its drive to prominence by emphasizing technology and indigenous research. Firms were encouraged to invest in local R&D, and the government created a research infrastructure to help this initiative. Resulting from these efforts, Korea had 120 private research institutes and 18 research consortia in operation by the mid-1980s.[2] Industry promotion councils and co-operative institutions were formed to ensure technology access across all Korean firms. A national education policy that emphasized science and technology education went into effect. Vocational schools attracted more students for technical education, while the universities were encouraged to build an elite group of experts in science and technology. As a result of these initiatives, the number of people engaged in R&D jobs in consumer electronics multiplied roughly five-fold in a 20-year period from 1975 to 1995.

Encouraged by the technology investments, many of the companies started to explore export markets under their own labels and tried to break out of the OEM mode. Many of these firms, like Samsung and LG, were quite surprised to find that their products were not well received in the developed markets. Retailers relegated their wares to the back rooms of their stores where they only collected dust. This proved to be an important lesson in understanding the value of differentiated products, innovative design, and superior product quality. Chastened by the experience, these companies invested much more effort into developing a world-class range of products.

Since the home market was relatively small, Korean companies had to establish a firm foothold in overseas markets. Building on this early exposure to demanding foreign markets, Korean companies were forced to differentiate their previous-generation products from those of past global leaders. Years of aggressively exploiting technological innovations while simultaneously improving internal value-chain arrangements and organizational structures to reduce their costs had pushed Korean firms harder than their global competitors, whom they had now surpassed. This called for audacious investments in R&D, anticipatory internationalization, a focus on process innovation, and careful cost control.

If you are not hungry, you cannot find food
....

The big three Korean electronics manufacturers leveraged their relationships with the leading consumer electronics companies to understand the markets that their main buyers served. The OEM relationship offered a fairly comprehensive view of the markets where the established veterans from Japan were fighting their competitive battles. Squeezed by the very small and economically poor home market on the one hand, and constrained by the OEM relationship on the other, LG and others could not visualize a future that was not global. Although the OEM relationships had helped LG and others in numerous ways, it was clear that this would not lead to global competitiveness.

Having studied the developed-country markets secondhand through their joint venture partners, LG and others felt emboldened to launch their own branded lines in these challenging markets. LG used the *Goldstar* brand to sell a range of home appliances such as microwave ovens and toaster ovens in the U.S. It found the battle for shelf space in retail outlets a very difficult challenge to overcome. Dogged by poor brand recognition, and questions about product reliability and quality, it found that its products were not showcased to sell. The prime spots on the shop floor were always set aside for the more elegant Japanese and European product lines. *Goldstar* appliances were relegated to the corners of the store or hidden away in back rooms gathering dust. LG realized that it would have a lot of work to do in order to give its products the appeal that developed-country buyers often sought. Faced with the difficulties in establishing a foothold in developed-country markets, LG started to craft an alternative approach.

3

Anticipatory globalization through bold and audacious investments in emerging markets became a centerpiece of the LG strategy. Mr. Kwang-Ro Kim (currently President of LG Southeast Asia), who led LG's meteoric rise in India, for example, observed, "We have seen many Japanese and Chinese companies arriving in India, but like other foreign-owned businesses, they typically put one foot in the water to see if it is warm or cold. They have doubts. They lack determination."[3] The ability to visualize markets in the long term was a critical ingredient in LG's success recipe. While some of its competitors were concerned about making sustainable profits in the short term, LG was willing to enter a market if it believed in its long-term potential. For example, LG entered India in the early 1990s, but it took more than a decade for the company to navigate local regulations and market structures to establish a position of significance. Although the company had set its sights early on Europe and North America, much of its success came from the emerging markets, specifically Brazil, Russia, India, and China.

BRAZIL: A BOLD MOVE FORWARD

LG established its Brazilian operations in the mid-1990s and started manufacturing televisions and VCRs at its factory in Manaus. The government of Brazil was promoting investment in the underdeveloped rainforest region around the headwaters of the Amazon, and offered tax incentives and subsidized land for investors setting up operations. In parallel, the company also established a factory in Taubate, located between the major Brazilian cities of Sao Paulo and Rio de Janeiro. While the factory in Manaus produced audio/video products and related equipment, the other plant focused on communications products such as cellular telephones and monitors.

The Brazilian market of the late 1990s was characterized by very high import tariffs, significant competition from the gray goods market, and very low brand awareness. The major consumer electronics players such as Sony and Philips were operating in Brazil with mixed fortunes. Things started to turn sour in 1999 when the local currency became unstable, leaving managers scrambling to manage operations. The exchange rates started to plummet with increasing levels of uncertainty. This made planning nearly impossible. Many of the global players decided to either scale down their operations as a consequence or to temporarily exit the market. This proved to be a turning point in LG's Brazil strategy. Despite the precipitous exchange losses, LG decided to not only stay in Brazil but also expand its presence there and conceived a strategy that would leverage Brazil as a regional manufacturing hub serving South America and the U.S. markets. Thus, with the dropping value of the local currency, the real, LG was able to shore up some of the low-cost advantages that made exporting increasingly advantageous. It could balance its accounts receivables and payables accordingly, and thus build a viable hedge against exchange rate fluctuations. In due course, LG became one of the largest electronics exporters from Brazil, vaulting the company into the ranks of organizations that the local government saw as a preferred partner in national growth.

LG augmented its Brazil strategy through a series of well-orchestrated moves. First, upon entry, it focused on maximizing the benefits that the government was providing by way of preferential land access, and lower tax rates for locating in underdeveloped areas. Given the rampant smuggling of gray-market goods, LG made it a priority to join with the government in combating this problem. Since imported gray goods were sold at cheaper prices, it had made it difficult for manufacturers to build a strong revenue base when their prices were relatively higher given the incidence of local taxes, something that the smugglers did not have to contend with. Perhaps the biggest challenges were in the areas of marketing and financial management.

The LG brand was hardly known in Brazil when the company first entered, and much needed to be done to build consumer awareness. Taking a cue from the immense popularity of soccer in the country, LG piggybacked its branding campaign on sports events sponsorship. It even sponsored a football club in Sao Paulo, one that was ranked among the top clubs in the country. This sponsorship activity gave the company the instant brand recognition it sought. Leveraging this brand recognition into tangible revenues required careful customization of its product offerings. It started by adopting a premium positioning strategy in the market for displays, televisions, and home appliances. Its approach to product quality was refreshingly new for the Brazilian market, although it demanded a price premium for it. It backed most of its products with a three-year warranty coupled with a guarantee of almost instantaneous service in case of product failures and breakdowns. It employed a fleet of service vehicles that could be dispatched to a customer's location within a very short period of time. This ensured that the consumers could expect a level of reliability that was unknown in the market at the time.

It signed agreements with local distribution chains to gain quick access to the market. The development of its own preferred/authorized dealership network complemented third party distribution arrangements. It placed an enormous focus on relationship development in nurturing its networks of dealers by scheduling periodic product events, social gatherings, and educational opportunities. The portfolio of products that it sold was also customized to address local market realities. Its approach to customization was, however, unique. Where others had sought to downscale their offerings to suit the thinner wallets of the impoverished customers in emerging markets, LG sought to expand its offerings to encompass a wider range. It typically complemented its global product line with customized offerings at appropriate price points, chiefly at the lower end. The customization effort focused on the unique cultural and social dimensions of their consumers' lives.

The local market clearly saw that LG had come to stay in Brazil and was not about to leave in the face of difficult economic crises. This endeared the company's brand to the consumers and helped it fill the void that had been left in the wake of exits by other players. LG capitalized on this sentiment in its dealings with the Brazilian government as well and built on it. It expanded its manufacturing facilities in both Manaus and Taubate. As of 2007, the Manaus plant produced air conditioners, PDP televisions, and audio equipment in addition to the original line of televisions and VCRs it started out with. The Taubate plant also expanded to produce GSM phones and CDMA phones in addition to monitors. The company reported sales of roughly $1.8 billion in 2006, a 35% increase over the previous year.

THE PASSAGE TO INDIA

LG made a start in India in 1993 and entered a joint venture with a consumer products company named Bestavision. The intent was to first distribute its *Goldstar* line of products in India while building a manufacturing operation to serve the market. Unfortunately, this proved to be a false start when the partner could not bring in additional funds to bankroll the manufacturing operation. LG had learned an important lesson about the challenges of managing joint ventures in emerging markets. Since the Indian government at the time insisted that all foreign firms would have to enter India only through a local partnership, LG had begun negotiations with one of India's leading business groups for a possible joint venture arrangement. During this negotiation phase, the Indian government announced significant market reforms and allowed foreign companies to set up their own wholly owned subsidiaries in India. LG decided to shelve the partnership negotiations and launch LGEIL (LGE India Ltd.), a fully owned subsidiary. LGEIL was launched in 1997, and for a year imported its entire line of products as it built its own manufacturing facilities locally.

Its manufacturing operations in Greater Noida, close to India's capital, New Delhi, were set up to manufacture televisions, washing machines, air conditioners, and refrigerators. Right from the start, LGEIL focused on customizing parts of its product lines to address local needs. While the fundamental product platforms remained invariant across country markets, local R&D teams were involved in coming up with product variations that would reflect the unique demands of the local marketplace. For

3

example, it launched a cricket television set with a built-in cricket video game to cater to the teeming millions who are cricket fanatics in the country. Its "golden eye" technology used in television sets was designed to automatically sense the levels of ambient lighting and adjust picture brightness and contrast accordingly. This proved to be an important feature in the local market, especially given the periodic variation in lighting intensity resulting from power supply imbalances. Similarly, it designed a unique air filtration system for its range of air conditioners to filter the fairly high levels of particulate pollution in metropolitan cities in India. All its home appliances were equipped with circuits that could weather dramatic voltage fluctuations that were very common in the country. These customized products were flanked by LG's typical product range that included high-end appliances that it sold in developed markets as well. LGEIL believed that this blended approach to product portfolio development was a crucial ingredient to succeed in India. Mr. Kwang-Ro Kim, LGEIL's Managing Director at the time, observed, "We knew it was important, for example, not to downgrade the Indian market and instead to treat it just as seriously as we would any developed market. This meant preparing a full strategy and emphasizing good-quality products, the best technology, the best network, and access to the best people."[4]

LGEIL recognized very early on that there was enormous potential to be tapped at the lower rungs of the economic pyramid in India, and set about formulating a strategy to address the rural markets. In an important departure from common practice, it was decided not to drop prices on existing lines as they were moved to rural markets. Instead, the company built new versions of its products with a more compact set of features and cost-efficient materials so that they could be manufactured at lower cost. The company did not cut corners with the engineered quality of the appliances, focusing instead on value engineering and design as the source of cost reductions. Thus, LGEIL introduced a television set with a smaller screen size and a scaled-down sound system, resulting in a price reduction of roughly 40% in entry-level models. Similar efforts produced rural versions of washing machines and air conditioners, placing these traditional luxury products within the reach of India's rural majority. These customization approaches were indeed thoughtful and reflected a deep understanding of India's cultural and linguistic diversity. For example, the television sets sold in rural markets offered menus in local languages—a feature that most of the local manufacturers had themselves not offered. In due course, the company was generating over a third of its sales revenues from this rural segment and close to 60% from non-urban areas.

India's geographic diversity combined with its inadequacy of infrastructure made distribution a very challenging proposition. Most of the large players were content to establish beachheads in large metropolitan centers, but LG attempted a different approach. Realizing that a well-penetrated distribution system was crucial to success in smaller towns and villages where much of India's population lived, the company deployed a tiered approach. Although it originally depended on four national distributors to begin with, it soon moved toward a regional distribution system that was anchored by Regional Distributors who supported smaller channel partners in tier 2 and tier 3 cities. It built remote area offices in the small towns that could not support a larger channel. The company soon blanketed the country with a distribution network encompassing close to 4,000 access points reaching all areas where customers could be found. This bricks-and-mortar distribution strategy was complemented by an online channel called lgezbuy.com. The online channel offered extensive product information along with comparative pricing across geographic regions, combined with the ability to accept online orders from individual buyers. Since this was the first such attempt by any major consumer durables manufacturer in the country, it immediately created a differentiated position for LG.

Customer service was another important feature that set LG apart from its competitors. Taking a page from its Brazilian operations, the company launched a fleet of repair vans that could reach remote areas at short notice. These vans were outfitted with power generators to make sure that the equipment could be serviced in a timely manner in a country that was prone to blackouts. This proved to be an important determinant in favor of LG when customers, especially in remote areas, were shopping for appliances. These services were bolstered by a "walking-after sales service" concept under which traveling crews covered remote areas that were inaccessible.[5] The cities were well served through a chain of customer care centers that co-ordinated product service in metropolitan areas.

Brand awareness and reputation for LG products had to be carefully tended in the early years during a period when the market was not aware of the company. Local players had built dominant positions by taking advantage of local laws that prohibited foreign firms from competing on an equal footing. Building on its sports marketing efforts in Brazil that had catapulted brand awareness, LGEIL began sponsoring cricket in India. Its cricket television set was launched with much fanfare and coincided with the World Cup, an international championship contested by all cricket-playing nations. In due course, LG became the largest single sponsor of cricket in the world—no mean feat for a company that hailed from a country where cricket was not played. This was a coup for LGEIL and immediately endeared the company to millions of cricket fans. Soon, the company's dedicated cricket-game television sets, televisions with a built-in cricket video game, became a huge hit, and success followed in other product lines as well. By 2007, the company had reached the $2 billion mark in revenues and had declared its intent of increasing that five-fold to $10 billion by 2010. Having entrenched itself in the cricketing realm, LGEIL had signed on India's leading film stars to endorse its products, a brilliant move to capitalize on India's fascination with films.

LGEIL operations also reflected the company's historical beginnings in an economically disadvantaged South Korean market. It had always tried to emphasize compassion and social welfare in its initiatives, and India was no different. LGEIL realized that it had to address the health care needs of its employees on its own since India lacked a reliable public health care system. Medical clinics were set up at its manufacturing facilities to provide care to employees. These facilities were subsequently enhanced to cover vaccinations and medical screenings for families of the employees as well as the local community. Although the level of care was quite basic, it demonstrated that the company's concerns transcended mere profit motives. It also offered subsidized primary school education and books for children, and even built a village school close to its manufacturing facilities.

Local employees staffed most of the top management positions within LGEIL. There were only a handful of South Koreans at the top, and most of them were in research functions. The company believed in developing core designs centrally at its facilities in Korea, but once they were transferred to local operations, ongoing R&D and customization became a local responsibility. In time, this local R&D focus helped the company tap into the abundant engineering and design skills locally. When LG sought

EXHIBIT 2	LG market shares by volume (%) in India		
LG Electronics		*Top 2 competitors*	
Color Televisions			
Analog	26.4	Onida 10.8	Samsung 10.5
Digital	26.5	Samsung 14.3	Onida 10.5
Flat screen	26.7	Samsung 20.6	Sony 14.3
Refrigerators			
Basic	29.4	Whirlpool 23.6	Godrej 16.0
Direct cool	27.0	Whirlpool 24.7	Godrej 16.6
Frost-free	36.5	Whirlpool 20.1	Godrej 14.3
Washing Machines			
Non-automatic	35.0	Whirlpool 14.1	Samsung 13.4
Semiautomatic	36.2	Videocon 16.5	Samsung 14.5
Fully automatic	34.1	IFB 17.0	Whirlpool 14.3
Microwave Ovens	38.0	Samsung 16.8	Electrolux 9.2

Source: ORG-GfK. Cited in P. R. Sinha. 2005. Premium marketing to the masses: An interview with LG Electronics India's Managing Director. *McKinsey Quarterly*, Special Edition.

3

engineers to manage parts of its niche analog television business that had run out its lifespan in most developed countries, it was able to find qualified personnel in India who were up to the task.

The localization philosophy encompassed administrative and managerial functions as well. All branch offices in the country were staffed with locals, and even at the country headquarters expatriate managers were a rarity. Only major investment decisions and annual targets had to be approved by the head office in Korea. Investments in ongoing projects were within the domain of the country office. Mr. Kwang-Ro Kim observed that on one occasion when the company was looking to buy a very expensive piece of capital equipment for its Indian operations, Indian engineers favored a supplier in Italy over alternatives from the home country of South Korea. This purchase was approved without any further inquiry or involvement from Korean expatriate managers. This signaled trust and was reciprocated in full measure by the engineers who worked night and day installing the equipment. The level of autonomy afforded the local managers was significant and allowed them to gain confidence in their own managerial abilities. The company had begun rotating some of these managers into positions in third countries in the Middle East and Africa.

By early 2006, LG had established a leadership position in a variety of product lines ranging from refrigerators and washing machines to VCRs and televisions. However, there were signs of intense competition on the horizon. Global rivals such as Philips and Samsung were also focusing on some of the same pieces of the success recipe—culture marketing, rural distribution, and customized products. Local players such as Videocon had launched ambitious moves to fight their way back to the head of the pack in home appliances. Global rivals like Motorola that preceded LG in the mobile phone market seemed to have the experience edge in some product categories. Undoubtedly, the intensity of competition was set to increase. In a further twist to the competitive scene, Videocon announced that it was pursuing talks to take over the consumer electronics business of Daewoo, a South Korean conglomerate that had fallen on bad times.

RUSSIA: AN EARLY FORAY

When South Korea established diplomatic relations with Russia in 1990, LG was at the forefront of Korean companies leading the charge to capture Russian markets for some of its products. However, the market was fraught with unique risks given the communist heritage, state-sponsored business enterprises, and the challenging economic environment. LG commenced operations in Russia with a bonded warehouse business through which it imported goods manufactured at its plants elsewhere for sale in Russia. This business largely focused on the *Goldstar* brand and was limited to operations in and around the city of Moscow.

Gaining momentum in the early years was a very slow process since Russian consumers were not yet familiar with the brand. Drawing on its successes in other similar markets, LG launched a charm offensive that included opening LG brand shops, dedicated retail channels that carried the LG brand portfolio, culture marketing events such as the LG Festivals and cooking events. It also set up a regional office in St. Petersburg to oversee its operations in the CIS countries. By this time, the company had also made a determined effort to source local talent to support its global R&D mission. It set up an R&D center in St. Petersburg dedicated to software development for a range of products. Russia soon became an important location within the LG R&D network.

In 1998, soon after LG had introduced the LG brand in the country, Russia faced a debt moratorium and was in the throes of a severe economic crisis. Many of LG's competitors immediately scaled back their Russia plans, while others retreated from the market entirely. LG on the other hand began investing heavily in the market by supporting its channels, focusing even more on local customization of its product range and by enhancing its visibility through event sponsorships. This paid off rich dividends in that it helped establish a foundation upon which the company built its premium strategy. By 2004, the company had introduced several localized offerings ranging from a hot and cold air-conditioning unit that could be used year-round, to a karaoke machine that came with a library of popular Russian folk songs, and a microwave oven designed to match the specific needs of the Russian kitchen.

In 2005, the company received permission from the Government allowing it to use the *Narodnaya Marka* logo on its products, implying that the products were considered to be national brands.[6] This honor is bestowed on the most popular branded products sold in Russia and is displayed prominently in all company advertising and promotional materials, often considered among global players as the ultimate tribute to a successful localization strategy.

All was not rosy, however. LG had leased land close to Moscow to build an assembly plant for the manufacture of refrigerators, washing machines, and video equipment. The plant was supposed to commence operations in 2006, and an investment of $150 million had been earmarked for the purpose.[7] However, the local authorities claimed that the company did not have proper approvals for the structures it was building and threatened to halt construction.[8] It was widely believed that factions who did not want LG to succeed in the region were purposely raising these legal obstacles. It remained to be seen if this was a routine occurrence in an emerging market or a sign of more setbacks to come.

ACROSS THE SEA TO CHINA

China had proved to be a beacon of opportunity for some time, given its geographic proximity to Korea. LG had sought to tap this market through the establishment of a sales subsidiary in Hong Kong as early as 1988. This scouting mission was followed up with a joint venture established in Huizhiou on the mainland in 1991. Much of the initial period was spent in understanding local market conditions and assessing the feasibility for ramping up LG's exposure in China. By 2006, LG had built 16 corporate entities in the country, many of which were focused on sizable product lines such as manufacture of plasma televisions, white goods, and significant research and development as well.

LG's approach to China had been built on the very same foundations that it had used in entering markets such as Brazil and India. However, given the unique nature of governmental regulations and geographic proximity to the home market, it had used some variations in overall strategy. Perhaps the most important variation had to do with local consumption v. exports. Lured initially by the significant labor cost advantages that China offered, LG moved to build a strong manufacturing presence there using it as a hub for exports to other markets. It soon built up enough plants all across the country to be able to leverage an entire manufacturing network to serve countries such as Russia and the United States. Its location choices reflected a very carefully orchestrated emphasis on ensuring that China's developmental needs ideally would be matched with the aspirations of LG. The first wave of substantial investment occurred through a joint venture in Tianjin for the manufacture of refrigerators and air conditioners. By 2002, ten years after it had entered China, the company had 12 production subsidiaries and sales centers spanning cities such as Guangzhou, Shenyang, Wuhan, and Nanjing. It had established a central China office in Beijing to orchestrate the implementation of its China strategy. In the process of expansion, LG had managed to capture the hearts of the local public, evidenced by the fact that the city of Huizhou declared an LG Day to be celebrated each year on the 31st of January, and a downtown street that bears the name of LG—the very first time a major thoroughfare had been named after a foreign company in China.

The company expended significant effort to be seen as a local player because it believed that integrating itself into the local environment was a viable defense against the onslaught of rivals both Chinese and foreign that was already challenging LG. A significant amount of local initiative was left in the hands of the local workers. About 98% of all LG personnel in China were local Chinese. This move allowed the company to signal trust with local employees who then started taking an ownership role in carrying out company-wide welfare projects and promoting LG as a company that embraced Chinese cultural practices. Although much of the production effort in China was launched on the basis of product designs originating in Seoul, LG quickly realized that it had to win the war for talent locally. Having already leveraged its Korean R&D base to achieve the first or second positions in almost its entire product portfolio in

China, LG set up a modern R&D facility in Beijing in 2002. It had trained several of its employees at its training facilities in Beidaihe and Beijing in anticipation of the R&D investment. It had already established a Chinese Product Design team to oversee localization of design. In conjunction with the emphasis on local R&D, the company launched an LG Village, where it had transformed a rundown village in an agricultural location into one where it would showcase state-of-the-art technologies for local buyers.

At the height of the SARS crisis in China, LG initiated an "I love China" campaign and passed out free sanitary masks to local citizens. Unlike many other foreign plants that decided to scale down operations, LG persisted, often exhorting its dealers to stay open. It donated much-needed equipment to hospitals during the crisis. This approach left an indelible imprint in the minds of the local consumers. Such efforts demonstrated its strong sense of corporate responsibility and complemented its tried-and-tested approaches to establish itself locally through event sponsorships. In China, these activities encompassed launching schools, offering scholarships to economically disadvantaged students, sponsoring a touring cultural festival that would bring traditional Chinese cultural experiences to small towns and villages, and founding a hospital program to provide surgical treatment to children with cleft palates. These good citizenship activities bolstered LG's commercial objectives in the country. By 2005, the company had achieved a commanding position in China across all its product lines. It was the largest exporter of televisions from the country, dominant in white goods, leading in computer memory chips and displays with strong potential for even higher levels of revenues within China.

CLOUDS ON THE HORIZON

The company seemed to have written a playbook that contained repeatable plays guaranteed to succeed in emerging markets. The competitive landscape had, however, started to shift in two fundamental ways. Competition within the emerging markets was increasing rapidly, and many new entrants, along with revitalized oldtimers, had begun to capture market share. This was quite visible in two of LG's most salient emerging markets—India and China.

In India, Samsung, LG's hometown rival, was in second place in many of the product categories dominated by LG. It was widely believed that Samsung was gearing up to make a run for the top spot. Others such as Videocon, Onida, and Whirlpool were nipping at LG's heels as well. In China, there were many more local players in addition to the usual global giants such as Samsung and Sony. Local firms such as Konka and Kelon had traveled the well-worn path of using low labor costs combined with relatively small investments in product R&D to compete on price.[9] They had deftly copied global technology advances and used their low-cost manufacturing resources to underprice multinational rivals and steal market share. This was really beginning to erode LG's entry-level range of products across most categories.

While LG was busy capturing the emerging markets, its Japanese rivals along with European and U.S. companies had continued to dominate the developed-country markets. The U.S., for example, was seeing an influx of European design in the white goods sector. Sony, Matsushita, and Toshiba were still dominant powers to reckon with in consumer electronics. By early 2005, in a return to the lime-light, U.S. companies such as Apple, palmOne, and Treo were at the forefront of a new wave of portable electronic devices to share and store music, manage e-mails, and surf the Internet. The advantage in many of these segments had shifted to software, and the skills in manufacturing and engineering were proving to be insufficient bases on which global strategies could be built.[10] Although LG had made a splash in the American market with a conspicuous presence at the largest U.S. trade fair, CES in Las Vegas, and had launched a very sizable branding campaign, it remained to be seen whether it had made substantial inroads. The company had successfully shed its *Goldstar* heritage in the U.S., a brand name that was viewed more as a commodity. In 2005, the company had introduced a range of high-end televisions in the U.S., a launch that was widely believed to have been successful. At the Consumer Electronics Show in Las Vegas, a bell-weather event showcasing new product innovation, LG won as many as 14 awards for excellence in design and creativity in 2006.

APPENDIX 1	Operational and financial performance of LG Electronics

INCOME STATEMENT

	2003	2004	2005	2006
	KRW bn	*KRW bn*	*KRW bn*	*KRW bn*
Sales	20,177	24,659	23,774	23,171
Domestic	4,794	5,086	5,509	
Exports	15,383	19,573	18,265	
Cost of Sales	15,351	18,736	17,664	17,726
Gross Profit	4,826	5,923	6,111	5,445
SG&A	3,764	4,674	5,196	4,910
Operating Profit (EBIT)	1,062	1,250	915	535
Income Before Income Taxes	837	1,860	741	261
Tax	174	314	39	49
Net Profit	663	1,546	703	212

BALANCE SHEET

	2003	2004	2005	2006
	KRW bn	*KRW bn*	*KRW bn*	*KRW bn*
Current Assets	3,773	4,111	3,985	2,974
Quick Assets	2,269	2,436	2,577	1,439
Inventories	1,504	1,675	1,408	1,535
Fixed Assets	7,505	9,124	10,051	10,128
Investment Assets	3,546	4,859	5,481	5,417
Tangible Assets	3,123	3,630	4,150	4,423
Intangible Assets	836	636	420	288
Total Assets	11,277	13,234	14,036	13,102
Current Liabilities	5,091	4,959	5,208	5,020
Fixed Liabilities	2,682	3,259	2,666	1,898
Total Liabilities	7,773	8,218	7,874	6,918
Total Shareholders' Equity	3,505	5,016	8,163	6,184
Total Liabilities and Shareholders' Equity	11,277	13,234	14,036	13,102

The challenges that lay ahead were quite clear. Having conquered the emerging markets, LG would have to successfully hold off local competition that was getting feisty. Simultaneously, it would have to come up with new dimensions to its emerging market prowess in order to stake a claim in the developed markets as well. Analysts were divided on whether the lessons were indeed transferable from emerging markets and whether LG would be better off playing second fiddle to Samsung, allowing its hometown rival to plunge ahead into developed markets while it continued its onslaught into emerging markets. After all, the population growth in emerging markets and less-developed countries was quite promising. Large areas of Africa and the Middle East along with Latin America remained to be exploited fully by the LG machine. The board of LG had asked Mr. Nam Woo to take charge in China. He would be overseeing the entire spectrum of LG operations in the country and helping the company through the challenges it faced there. The time had come for him to apply some of his emerging market prowess in what was the world's largest emerging market.

3

NOTES

1 Liu Baijia. 2006. LG wants local managers to aid growth. *China Daily.* April 20, 2006.

2 W. R. Shin, and A. Ho. 1997. Industrial transformation: Interactive decision-making process in creating a global industry. *Public Administration Quarterly.* Summer.

3 P. R. Sinha. 2005. Premium marketing to the masses: An interview with LG Electronics India's Managing Director. *The McKinsey Quarterly Special Edition: Fulfilling India's Promise.*

4 Ibid.

5 Duk-Woo Lee. 2005. LG The No. 1 company in India. *LG News.* February, Vol. 24.

6 Korean businesses ride Russian economy: High-end marketing strategy. www.gateway2russia. com/st/art_243266.php.

7 LG Electronics to build plant in Russia. *RIAN.* May 11, 2005.

8 Mitvol threatens to kick LG out of Moscow region. *Novecon Press Digest.* October 26, 2005.

9 Kathy Wilhelm. 2002. Innovation—Electronics—Global ambition: China's electronic makers are rapidly upgrading their skills to challenge the multinationals. *Far Eastern Economic Review.* June 15.

10 Gary McWilliams. 2005. Power switch in electronics: U.S. companies seize momentum from Japan. *Wall Street Journal.* March 10.

CASE STUDY 4

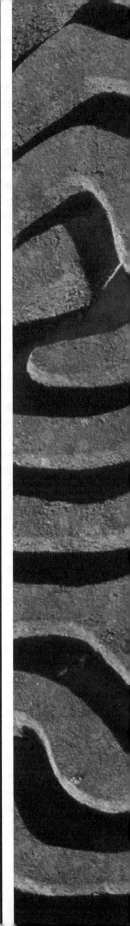

INFORMATION ECONOMY STRATEGIES IN THE MOBILE TELECOMMUNICATIONS INDUSTRY

The mobile telecommunications industry is a highly interconnected industry, interconnected with the competitors and with its customers on a long-term basis. Industry players in the mobile communications market moderate their strategic behaviour and opt for strategies that imply a form of complex adaptive behaviour. The common goal becomes the collective survival of the firms in order to eliminate the probability that one firm will prevail and the rest will fail. A set of copy-cat strategies generally emerges at the level of technical standards, network platforms and the consumer platform. As a result market shares of competing firms become almost equal and network externalities are reconfigured to act for the benefit of the whole industry.

INDUSTRY LANDSCAPE AND STRUCTURE

The industry can be divided into five interacting levels. Each of the levels has its own economic dynamics and each contributes to the overall network, with technology and regulation in the background.

Regulatory background

In the UK, mobile communications companies fall under the UK Wireless Telegraphy Acts 1948–1967 and the UK Telecommunications Act 1984. The Radio Communications Agency has the authority to grant licences under the Wireless Telegraphy Act. The Office of Communications (Ofcom) is responsible for the enforcement of the licences issues. The regulatory institutions' main concern was to encourage and preserve competition. In order to stimulate the growth of a new supply chain, Cellnet and Vodafone were not allowed to market their services directly to the consumer from 1985 to the mid 1990s. The direct sales restriction was lifted when the third and fourth licences

---

Abridged from a case by Tanya Sammut-Bonnici, written jointly with John McGee and Robin Wensley, Warwich Business School.

came into operation. Orange and One 2 One were not subject to such restrictions, as they were viewed to be at a disadvantage compared to earlier entrants.

The regulation of the UK mobile network operators (MNOs) has a balancing effect on how the networks develop and on competition. Regulation is starting to match the demands of complex dynamic markets. It is creating new forms of control that fall under the definition of self-organising systems. In this case the regulatory objective is to create self-correcting mechanisms that preserve competition. Although the original objective is maintained, the way of doing it is novel as the outcomes are not entirely predictable.

A classical example would be the 3G spectrum auctions in the UK and across the globe. The auctions were designed to match the industry's predicted profitability of the introduction of a new generation of technology. The idea was that firms would bid to the maximum of the technology's feasibility. Thus governments found a way of introducing a licensing system that generated a self-correcting form of revenue, which gauged future profitability. However, as with all complex systems, the outcome was unpredictable and other factors took hold of the system. The auctions were essentially a taxation procedure on an infant industry, and a key factor to allow MNOs to continue operating. Prospective MNOs faced the situation of having to bid for their future existence, or give up their operation once and for all. Thus the bidding did not stop at the profitability limits, but moved into the limits of what the companies could borrow from their banks. The mobile spectrum in Europe generated £200 billion with Britain and Germany raising £22.5 and £60 billion respectively. The result was the depletion of cash flow, a delay in third generation launches and uncertainty in the stock markets.

Another form of self-correcting regulation is the concept of 'market influence' inbuilt into the licence agreements of the MNOs. The definition set in the Telecommunications Act licences implies that MNOs should not exploit price inelasticity that may arise for the demand-side of the market. Market influence behaves as a self-regulatory measure whereby MNOs keep their market strength in check, in order to preserve their licence agreements. As competition in the industry grew, the need for market influence mechanisms diminished and this form of regulatory control was reduced substantially throughout Europe.

Technology standards

The telecommunications standards we have today are a product of protracted market strife. Mobile technology has become widespread and practical only after going through a period of struggle between competing standards. The process is reminiscent of VHS vs. Betamax, and Microsoft vs. everyone else. As the wireless industry moves into 3G, it is going through the same arduous process. The industry has also experienced hybrid standard setting. This type of standardisation emerges as private firms adopt strategies to undercut collaborative decisions taken in negotiated standardisation. They introduce new products, which initiate unprecedented developments, but also create incompatibilities, lock-in effects, and pockets of market power. Mobile Internet is a typical example, where companies, standards organizations, and governments create a hybrid standard setting environment.[1]

Standards organizations are playing an increasingly important role in the strategy for establishing standards. The GSM Association is guiding the evolution of the mobile industry through a family of wireless technology standards from today's standard through to GPRS (General Packet Radio Service), EDGE (Enhanced Data Rated of GSM Evolution) and 3GSM. Each subsequent standard offers a higher level of service. GPRS provides open Internet. EDGE facilitates faster data streaming, and 3GSM provides video streaming.

Switching costs are minimised when standards are designed to evolve from one another. The introduction of revolutionary standards would be costly. The pay-off is superior performance against the high cost of switching standards. The example is the price paid by mobile telephone operators to switch to third generation licences.

4

Physical platforms
······························

Physical platforms in mobile communications are the technical networks connecting mobile phones, base stations, mobile exchanges and land line exchanges. The system extends from a national to an international level. Telecommunications platforms have had to cope with the complexity of interoperability among different systems, and to master the agility required to shift rapidly to newer standards.

Interoperability: Companies divided their platform structure into separate modules, each with some degree of autonomy.[2] Each module is designed with the flexibility for rapid change,. The complexity feature is retained because each module is interoperable with other modules to form a web-like complex system. The modules are therefore interdependent through the nodes, or joints between the modules. Interoperability between modules creates value for the user, as we observe in the ability to call overseas on a mobile telephone. Roaming of mobile telephones from country to country is another example. Interoperability exists between platforms of different MNOs[1] in the same country, or different platforms in different countries. Physical platforms have evolved from the simple structures such as the older regional railway system, to a complex structure of interconnected sub-platforms.

For this reason, the joints between the sub-networks become the strength of the whole structure, or conversely it could be its Achilles heel. It is therefore vital to define standards for joints. The standards that govern how a system and its modules interact are called the network's architecture (Morris and Ferguson, 1993). Henderson and Clark (1990) review two kinds of dynamic processes in modular systems: modular innovation and architectural innovation.

The former type retains the architecture of the network including its joints, but modifies the modules. By preserving the basic architecture of a system, MNOs offer users enough compatibility to shift from one product generation to the next. The changes occur in the innovations and improvements of the modular components. They are fitted into the system when required, and will be removed when obsolete. The result is a hybrid dynamic of change that preserved the platform's architecture, whilst creating innovations within the module structure. A series of minor incremental modular changes can lead to an overall network platform that is radically new.

Capacity: A further aspect of network platforms concerns communication capacity and its expansion over time. The Government can decide to release significant amounts of additional radio spectrum for the mobile communications sectors as and when it decides to do so. Telecommunications networks fall under an 'integrative class' of complex networks, because of their tendency to integrate information from a large number of sources. Other networks that form part of this class are air traffic control and management systems, military command and control systems and electricity network sharing. The integrative class is characterised by: a large number of diverse information sources; the need to interoperate and integrate both equipment and information; to detect events in a complex network of connections; to operate across techno-socio barriers; and to operate as an open system, which includes interoperability, portability, scalability; and the need to evolve.

The interconnectivity in mobile communications hinges on two important factors: the interconnections in the networks and the sharing of call revenue. The original objective of operating an open platform determined the survival of all the competing mobile platforms, which could evolve from one generation of transmission standards to the next in a concerted effort. Call revenue sharing ensured that the interconnectivity was kept at a high level of reliability across all the networks, in order to preserve revenue streams.

Interconnectivity in the information economy leads to the concept of 'co-evolution'. Evolving to meet the needs of other members in the value chain, is becoming a more effective strategy than satisfying the company's own needs. Adapting to meet other companies' need leads to more business. Riding the new wave of co-evolution, companies are avoiding costly races against each other, in favour of a

4

strategy of joining forces to gain more customers. We are observing this effect in NEC and Siemens who have joined forces to supply the networks for Hutchison 3G, which will be a key network provider for third generation telecommunications in Europe.

Co-evolution and collaboration are even more relevant in industries where network externalities are a vital part of corporate success. The more customers join a network, such as a telecommunications service, the higher is the incentive for other customers to join. This effect is causing companies to collaborate on issues of compatibility. With 3G mobile phones in Europe and the US, the standards war for a mobile Internet operating system has begun. Microsoft, Linux, Symbian and Openwave are in the race to establish a widely accepted standard. This is an example of old style competition, but it has caused a wave of co-evolution in another layer of competitors.

The issue of standards has motivated Nokia and Siemens, Europe's largest manufacturers of mobile phones, to collaborate. They have teamed up to accelerate the introduction of third generation mobile services. The collaboration of the companies will guarantee that Nokia and Siemens handsets can communicate with each other seamlessly. In this way the two companies, which have a combined global market share of 45%, will benefit from network externalities and the positive feedback generated from a larger compatible technology platform. Nokia and Siemens anticipate that other equipment vendors will link up with them to minimise industry fragmentation.[3]

Image phones gave the Japanese market a boost similar to when DoCoMo introduced I-Mode wireless web service. DoCoMo, which had planned to concentrate on the introduction of 3G system with video capabilities, still bolstered its line of second generation phones with a camera phone called the I-shot. DoCoMo President Keiji Tachikawa said: "we recognise there is strong demand for cellular phones with cameras, so we will increase the number of current-generation camera models." Companies saw their revenue from basic voice phone services decline, while sales of those equipped with cameras and related services were bringing in more money. The new models were reinvigorating a market that was becoming sluggish.

Japan was one of the first countries in the world to introduce the 3G standard, almost two years before it appeared in Europe. DoCoMo led the world in starting 3G services in October 2001, followed by KDDI in April 2002, and J-Phone in December 2002, so all three have a 3G presence. The European market gradually saw 3G services coming online in 2003 and 2004.

Supply chain

The structure of the industry is built on layers of communication network companies, hardware and software manufacturers, Internet service providers, e-commerce transaction companies, and media and content companies, and the myriad of service companies The network infrastructure suppliers are companies such as Alcatel, Nortel Networks, Motorola, and Ericsson that provide communications networking equipment. Intel and 3Com form a sub set of companies in this category, which supply interfacing hardware and software.

The network operators provide the basis of the exchange of information between companies and their customers. The medium they operate could be based on satellite, telephone, mobile, television or area networks. British Telecom, AT&T, Vodafone, T-Mobile offer landline and mobile telecommunications networks. The operation of these companies is interconnected with other companies. For example, Vodafone uses BT's network. Credit card companies use Vodafone's mobile network for offsite credit verification. Vodafone has sold fixed line telephone services from Energis and Racal Telecom networks. The interoperability of different telecom networks has become a complex business operation.

The 3G telephone, which will become the new customer interface, would dictate a change in Internet transmission management and the nature of media content, all the way down the supply chain. The supply chain in the information economy takes the form of a web-like network where each member may have to collaborate with all the other members. Inter-collaboration is necessary partly because of software and hardware compatibility. An example of this web-like structure is the relationship between e-transaction companies, ISPs, media content providers, and the companies that own the web pages.

The nature of the supply chain of the UK mobile communications industry changed dramatically as the network operators became more powerful. In spite of the regulators' intention to equalise power in the supply chain the network operators grew more and more powerful. They progressed to the top of a hierarchical distribution pyramid in just a few years, through a deliberate strategy of controlling the supply chain. This was achieved through the three stages described below.

1 *Buyouts and Mergers of Distributors and Service Providers*: By reducing or freezing prices Vodafone and Cellnet eroded the margins of hardware retailers. Survival of distributors and service providers became a direct function of market share. The larger companies were able to stay in business whilst the smaller ones were forced to merge or to sell-out. In the late 1980's we see the takeovers of National Radiophone, Advanced Car Telephone, and the sale of a 40% in Air Call. Takeovers continued through the 1990's. The service provider arm of Robert Bosch, Hi-Time, MCP, and Excell were the next companies to be bought out of the supply chain, by competitors in their own tier.

2 *Acquisition of Suppliers by Vodafone and Cellnet*: In the mid 1990's, acquisitions changed in nature. This time the MNOs started to buy into the supplier tier, further strengthening their power in the supply chain. Vodafone bought Hawthorn Leslie and Peoples Phones. It acquired shares in Astec Communications, Martin Dawes, and Talkland. By the end of 1996, Vodafone had direct control of the 70% of the customers connected to its network. Cellnet joined the acquisitions game in the late 1990's. In 1997, it bought shares in The Link and acquired Martin Dawes, and DX Communications in 1999. It bought The Mobile Phone Store in 2000.

3 *Supply Chain Control Strategies*: In the history of mobile communications, we see repeated evidence of the mobile operators determining the prices of phones and tariffs, even though the regulator intended that service providers would have some market power.

In 1992, the Federation of Communications Services (FCS), the mobile communications industry criticised Vodafone for quoting prices in its advertising. At the time, Vodafone was not allowed to sell its service direct to the customer. Oftel issued a report on unfair practices by Vodafone and Cellnet against independent providers. The companies were cross-subsidised by BT Mobile Communications, Securicor Cellular Services and Vodac, which were daughter companies. The regulator concluded that cross-subsidies were in contravention of the Cellnet and Vodafone licences. Independent cellular service suppliers continued to diminish. By 1996, the network operators owned 10 service providers that captured 77.5% of the market. A determining factor of the power of the network operators was that they controlled the bottleneck of the supply chain. The number of network operators that could enter the market was determined by government licences and limited to four firms.

Consumer networks

The consumer network is the final level of interacting dynamics in the industry. The behaviour of consumers is affected by regulation (choice and pricing), technology standards (service offering), physical platforms (reliability) and the supply chain (retail access). Nonetheless, the consumer network exhibits strong characteristics of its own, such as network externalities.[2] Consumers affect each other's buying behaviour in a positive feedback loop, resulting in critical mass effects and exponential growth.

Network externalities are a powerful force in the UK industry. They affect the individual firms from the industry's total installed base and not the individual network platforms. This is the main difference between competing platforms that are independent and communications platforms that are typically interconnected (telecommunications). This effect shows us how and why market shares converge in the presence of strong network externalities and how market shares become similar for the four companies over the long run.

The increase in subscribers is interdependent with the utility of the whole network as well as with the utility of competing networks. The utility of other networks has a similar stronger effect on new subscribers to a company's own utility. Thus we can start to understand why market shares converge even in the presence of strong network externalities.

EMERGENCE OF THE MOBILE NETWORKS

The UK subscriber base increased to 50 million users from 1985 to 2004. Most of the industry's growth occurred from 1999 to 2000 when 30 million subscribers joined the four networks. This represents an increase of 66% of the subscriber base in just two years, out of a total industry life span of 17 years. The industry's history has been through a period of duopoly and a period of increased competition. Up to 1993 there were only two operators, Cellnet[3] and Vodafone. One 2 One[4] and Orange entered the market in 1993 and 1994, respectively.

The UK Government granted licences to Vodafone and Cellnet for the operation of mobile communications networks in 1983. Vodafone was initially owned by Racal Electronics and was later floated on the stock exchange as a separate company. Cellnet was 60% owned by British Telecom, and 40% by Securicor. The two companies launched their networks concurrently in 1985. One 2 One, was originally owned by Mercury Personal Communications. Orange was created by the Microtel consortium led by British Aerospace, which was subsequently purchased by Hutchison Telecommunications. The industry started with analogue networks in 1985 and moved on to digital network in the 1990s. Vodafone and Cellnet switched on digital networks in 1992 and 1994. One 2 One and Orange entered the market with digital networks from their launch date.

INDUSTRY LEADERSHIP

Three out of the four MNOs held the position of the largest networks at different periods. Only One 2 One failed to attain the largest subscriber base at any point in its history. Cellnet, Vodafone, and Orange became industry leaders in 1985, 1986 and in 2001 respectively. Cellnet was the industry leader up to the third quarter of 1985. The company never regained the lead position but came close to having the same market share as Vodafone in 1996 and in 2001. The Cellnet story defeats the idea of 'first mover advantage', and the concept of a seed value[5] from the innovations diffusion literature.

Cellnet started to relinquish market share to Racal-Vodafone[6] in mid 1986. At that point, it had 32,000 subscribers, representing 54% of the UK mobile market. In just nine months, Cellnet made three price changes in fixed and variable rates. Its pricing structure was cheaper in the London areas, but more expensive in what were called the provincial areas. Growth in connections and traffic in the provincial areas was increasing in significance. Cellnet suffered because of real and perceived price differentials, and its miscalculation of growth potential of non-London territories.

In an effort to protect margins, Cellnet attempted to increase its connection and standing charges in April 1986. It withdrew them only four days after they had been introduced. The move followed the decision by the rival operator, Racal-Vodafone, to hold its prices steady and to increase the usage charge. Racal-Vodafone's increase was confined to the London area. Cellnet increased all its call charges at the beginning of this month. Racal, which had 27,000 customers at the time, said that its move was not designed to put pressure on Cellnet. Its mix of charges was intended to meet its target of another 35,000 customers over the next year, and that it decided to hold down connection and standing charges. These types of charges were viewed as the 'most emotive issues' for customers. Vodafone intended to act according to the psychological response of the consumer.

The fact that Cellnet cancelled its plans to increase prices meant that it would not meet its planned target to reach break-even point by 1987. The company, which was 60% owned by British Telecom,

4

thought that the proposed increases would be reasonable, and that they would have been acceptable to the market. The results showed otherwise, and new customers drifted slowly towards Racal-Vodafone. In spite of the freeze in prices, Cellnet continued to lose market share. It claimed that the average customer would pay 6% less than under Racal, but it believed that customers perceive the Vodafone offering to be better. As a result, Cellnet was losing out in provincial areas where Racal's charges were cheaper. At that point in the industry's timeline, Vodafone was getting about 60% of its traffic from outside London, while Cellnet got 40-50%.

By January 1987, the pressure from customers increased and Cellnet was forced to introduce a new price structure. The move marked an attempt by Cellnet to win back market share from Racal, which had gained 53% of the UK's 114,000 subscribers. Cellnet announced a decrease in price of its basic cell phone by £450 to £899. However, the company lost its opportunity to gain a price differential in the eyes of its customers because Racal-Vodac followed suit the next day. Cellnet had started another price war. When sales were slow in August 1986, Cellnet brought the price of its cheapest unit below £1,000 for the first time. This move was the subject of a complaint to Oftel, but it did not lead to an investigation since Cellnet put its prices up again after six weeks. In May 1987, Cellnet instigated another price war against Vodafone with the announcement that new subscribers to its network would only pay half the subscription price for the first six months.

The competition battles were played through pricing strategies as well as advertising strategies. In May 1987, Cellnet unveiled a £5 million promotional drive, including a £1 million TV campaign. Vodafone rapidly took up battle in its fight with Cellnet for dominance in the UK mobile telephone market. It launched a £2 million TV campaign through Saatchi and Saatchi just two weeks after Cellnet's release. Interestingly Vodafone used its new campaign to push the other services it offered, besides the mobile telephone network. The move may have enhanced the image of Racal-Vodafone in terms of its size, reliability, experience in communications and its overall capability to build and sustain a mobile network. This drive to promote Racal-Vodafone's overall product offering was set to balance Cellnet's strong corporate image as a subsidiary of British Telecom.

Once Vodafone gained the position of the largest network in 1986, Cellnet slipped into second place and remained there for the next twelve years. Orange challenged both Cellnet and Vodafone's positions in the year 2001 when it rapidly gained market share and became the largest mobile communications network. In July 2001 Vodafone's market share was seen to trail that of Cellnet and Orange. Vodafone slipped behind the two companies to become Britain's third largest mobile phone operator.

Orange was the last operator to enter the industry yet it grew rapidly to become the largest network to date. Its strategy to overtake competitors started prior to the date it switched on its network. Its main strategies were: to set off with a network which had a larger coverage than its closest competitor; to offer better handsets; to offer simplified pricing structures.

When Mercury launched One 2 One in September 1993, Hutchinson was close to launching Orange. However, research had showed 50% coverage of the UK population to be the minimum level acceptable to customers. Whilst Mercury had a strong proposition, with new phones and cheaper calls, their 30% coverage of the UK market was not enough to challenge large operators. After the launch of One 2 One both Vodafone and Cellnet initially resisted calls to cut their prices. One 2 One felt the pressure to reduce its tariffs because it did not offer national coverage like its competitors. In view of the price cuts, Orange's launch was delayed further.

Hutchinson felt that it was important to have a minimum of 50% coverage on entry into the UK Market and to rapidly achieve over 90% coverage. An investment of £450 million was allocated for 1994 when the service was to reach 70% of the population. This commitment required considerable capital outlay by Hutchinson, the owner of Orange. Commitment of capital outlay on this scale made the challenge of Orange to Vodafone and Cellnet of a different order to that of Mercury. It allowed Orange to take the process of change in the mobile telephone market forward, benefiting from the effect One 2 One had as an earlier catalyst of change.

4

The Orange network was attractive to consumers from the outset. Since it covered the main UK metropolitan areas and the connection motorways at launch, it immediately had a significant advantage over its closest rival One 2 One. From its launch period, Orange offered more benefits than One 2 One. Its Nokia handsets doubled as radio pagers, and had screens that could display voicemail and caller identification. Business customers were initially the principal target, predominantly middle managers and small business owners. The new target was predominantly younger age groups attracted by the possibilities of digital technology. Orange was to benefit from the larger population of the new target segment.

In July 2001, Orange's network grew to 3.4 million subscribers, which challenged Vodafone's position as industry leader. Orange was attracting more customers on both the subscription and the pre-paid tariffs. At the beginning of 2002, Orange and Vodafone were in dispute over market leadership claims. The debate saw the rise in popularity of a most important acronym in the mobile industry: average revenue per user (ARPU). Operators in developed mobile markets were struggling to push up ARPU, even at the expense of growth in terms of subscriber numbers. Vodafone said it was still the UK's biggest mobile phone operator in terms of both revenue and profits and noted that the industry was now more focused on ARPU. Vodafone, which had 99.9 million customers worldwide in 2002, reported an ARPU of £274 in 2001. Orange, on the other hand, was reporting revenues alongside customer data. The company reported 2001 revenue up 25% at £8.3 billion. It added 8.8 million customers in that year, to take the total to 39.3 million, a 29% increase.

In the period under analysis there is no overall industry leader in the mobile communications industry. Vodafone is seen to have held the longest lead, from 1986 to 2001, yet Orange's meteoric rise is equally significant. The industry shows evidence of shifting patterns of leadership. This implies that the growth of MNOs is not a result of positive feedback from previous subscribers, but a result of other factors such as network externalities.

MARKET SHARE CONVERGENCE

Cellnet started out with a high market share, relinquishing it to Vodafone over a period of 2 years. Vodafone and Cellnet held their positions at a stable level, until the entry of One 2 One and Orange in 1993 and 1994. At that point the market share of the older companies diminished as the new companies rapidly increased their hold on the market.

Cellnet held the highest market share from the start of the industry up to August 1985. Vodafone held the longest lead, from 1985 to 2001. Orange's dramatic growth moved it to the top position in 2001. The change in industry leadership clearly shows that winner-takes-all strategies, were not, or could not be exploited in this industry.

At the time when Orange overtook Vodafone, Cellnet's subscriber base dropped for the first time ever. Cellnet's subscriber base fell by 268,000 in accounting terms over the quarter to settle at 10.9 million in July 1 2001. The operator also saw a decline of 20,000 in its post-paid base. This decline was due to a move towards a three-month accounting standard similar to Vodafone. At this point Cellnet started to count only those customers who had used the phone at any point in the last three months. The new accounting measure reduced the bias on over inflation of subscriber figures. Orange had the fastest growth rate in the industry. Orange saw its contract base increase by 222,000 net new customers to 3.4 million in the three months to the end of June, compared with 89,000 in the first quarter and with Vodafone's overall growth of 269,000. Orange, which allowed for 1 million inactive prepaid customers in its accounting, was outperforming Vodafone, even in the battle for more valuable post-paid customers.

BRAND CONSISTENCY

Orange underwent three ownership changes over the period and grew into the largest network. Vodafone had one change in ownership, when it separated from Racal and floated its stocks in 1991. Cellnet and One 2 One changed ownership twice. Orange was originally owned by Hutchison Whompoa and BAE, which shed its ownership in 1998. Mannesmann bought Orange in 1999. Orange was bought out again by France Telecom it in 2000, when Vodafone took over Mannesmann. Vodafone was the only network operator that was not bought out by third parties. Cellnet was originally owned by British Telecom and Securicor. It became wholly owned by British Telecom in 1999. Cellnet was demerged from British Telecom in the same year and floated on the stock exchange in 2001. One 2 One was originally owned by Cable and Wireless and US West Media Group. It was partly floated in 1997, and bought out by Deutsche Telekom in 1999.

From the four companies there is some indication that consistent branding can be linked to performance. Brand name consistency is the common characteristic of Orange and Vodafone, which have the highest brand equity in our research sample. They kept their brand name unchanged for the duration of their life span in mobile communications. Orange and Vodafone are almost equally successful. On the other hand, One 2 One was rebranded twice from Mercury One 2 One to One 2 One to T-Mobile. Cellnet was rebranded from BT Cellnet to Cellnet to O2.

CRITICAL MASS AND MARKET GROWTH

In the early days of the mobile communications industry, the achievement of a critical mass was a clearly stated goal. Vodafone and Cellnet, the pioneers in the industry, invested substantially to set the 'watershed' of subscribers in motion. The industry was striving to gain enough subscribers to move into an area of the demand function where it would be easier to attain more subscribers. In its objectives, the industry was showing the characteristics of a positive feedback system.

Critical mass acts on the adoption of the MNO platforms in a similar manner for all companies. The deviations in the occurrences of critical mass are limited to a maximum of eighteen months, notwithstanding that the second set of MNOs entered the market a decade after the first set. The individual MNO network size has a small effect on the date of attainment of critical mass. The exponential rise in demand was combined with a rapid reduction in cost in sales effort per subscriber. In 1999, both Vodafone and Cellnet changed their sales strategy significantly. Post critical mass, the sales forces were transformed to support high street and supermarket distributors, where most of the sales were occurring on a cash and carry basis.

Furthermore, by the end of 1999, when the first signs of decline were noticeable, the industry was anticipating major upheaval with the impending government auctions of 3G licences and the announcement of Vodafone Airtouch's takeover of Mannesmann. The 3G auctions were to determine the future survival or lack thereof of Cellnet, Vodafone, One 2 One and Orange. The takeover was to affect two out of these network operators, as Mannesmann owned Orange at the time. There was no reference to the small decrease in growth in a sample of 400 articles from industry publications and the general business media from November 1999 to October 2000. Even up to October 2000, just a few months prior to the slow down, the industry was still reporting signs of a growing market and record sales.

End 2000 marked the start of the decline in growth of the UK mobile communications industry. The demise was not apparent for over two years later, when clear signs of saturation started to emerge. The decline in sales growth was picked up by the stock market. In May 2002, Vodafone shares closed below 100p, the lowest since February 1988. The weakness in mobile stocks spread across the sector.

4

Analysts said investors were concerned about the short-term outlook for revenue growth, and the delays in bringing out commercial products and services related to GPRS and 3G.[4]

PRODUCT LIFE CYCLE EXTENSION

Other forces that affect demand will come into play in the future of the UK mobile communications industry. Firstly, mobile phone users may own more than one telephone. The mathematical calculation of the demand curve would thus have to be adjusted, as the figure for the total population is no longer the upper limit of the demand curve. The upper limit would shift above the population threshold. Secondly, the mobile phone industry will expand its product life cycle by promoting subscriptions on automated equipment, which will relay consumption information through a mobile connection. The industry would thus push out of the population threshold even further, and extend its full potential to encompass individuals, as well as machinery.

As the statistical total population for the industry is pushed beyond the national population, the total potential population becomes less finite and more extendible. For example, a household with two adults has the potential to provide the mobile industry with a minimum of two subscriptions. The same household could also provide a number of additional mobile subscriptions for energy and water meters, feedback channels for satellite television channels, and remote operation of domestic appliances. M-commerce, which is commerce conducted via mobile telephony, has the potential to boost the sales figures even further. Wireless shopping, travel information, ticketing, mapping, banking, and trading are some of the applications that will see m-commerce revenues rise.

COPY CAT STRATEGIES

Copy cat strategies between among Cellnet, Vodafone, One 2 One and Orange are common. Strategic isomorphism has strong appeal because of its risk reduction properties, which ensures the survival of more firms in the industry. However there are some serious caveats. Industry profit margins are likely to decline as shown in Natterman's study (2000) of the German mobile market.[5] Deutsche Telekom's D1 and Mannesmann's D2 joined the incumbent C-Tel in 1992. Herding effectively removed divergence among the MNOs services, tariffs, and customer niches. When another MNO, E-Plus, emerged in 1994, it differentiated itself with pricing packages for low-volume private users, including students, families, and senior citizens. Within a few months, the other networks copied E-Plus's strategy, destroying its brave effort to increase differentiation in the industry. Nattermann's (2000) analysis of the impact of such crowding shows that a 10% decline in the wireless industry's SDI[7] resulted in an 11.2% decline in profit margins. Between 1992 and 1998 the SDI fell by 83%, reducing margins down 50% from their maximum point. The reduction in strategic differentiation created by the incumbent operators was responsible for the lost earnings, which amounted to more than £495 million in 1998 alone. As strategic differentiation and margins decline, companies anxiously endeavour to reintroduce differentiation from competitors, typically by expensive brand enhancement campaigns and higher marketing spending.

A study by the Federal Reserve Bank in 1998 shows that the US personal-computer industry is another field which suffered a lowering in margins due to isomorphism.[8] From 1976 to 1988 the PC industry's SDI went down by over 37% as companies copied the now dominant IBM-clone model. As a result of the decline, margins fell by 56%, representing £1.8 billion in destroyed margins by 1988. The increased herding effect in product design diminished "brand" effects, which would have been developed over time from the firms' distinguishing characteristics. Brand effects, including such intangibles as reputation and image, are the drivers of price differentiation, which creates premium pricing margins.

4

If isomorphism erodes distinctive brand characteristic, it will also erode the opportunity to charge for intangible factors.

THE FUTURE OF THE MOBILE COMMUNICATIONS INDUSTRY

The future of mobile telephony will depend on the development of technical capability that generates a personal transaction environment that supports identity and payment. Digital money transacted through electronic cash payments and billing will have a revolutionary impact on the industry. The industry is moving towards multi-application SIM cards integrated with network services. The technology opens up opportunities for non-telecom applications whereby a mobile phone would act as a bank payment card. New technologies will sustain electronic identity through public key infrastructure (PKI) and biometrics. Identification of users will be integral to ordering, and paying through a mobile phone. Data transmission of wireless will increase dramatically and information exchange protocols such as XML are expected to evolve accordingly.

Voice recognition and synthesis technologies are expected to create the next wave of usage in mobile communications. The lack of space for a keyboard on a mobile handset has limited its range of use. Voice recognition would open up new possibilities for the mobile industry as the capability of a mobile phone moves closer to that of a personal computer. The impact of voice technologies is expected to increase mobile usage dramatically, as it opens the channels for people to speak directly to machines, without a keyboard interface. Mobile network operators, such as Vodafone, T-Mobile, O2 and Orange will need to adapt their business models as they progressively move from a model that is based on the economics of utilities to a business model that is rooted in the wireless economy.

STRATEGIC CHALLENGES

The challenge for future mobile phone products and services lies in the significance of interdependence between consumers and networks. Network externalities need to be addressed directly rather than tacitly as the evolution from one technological generation to another will follow in rapid succession. New products face the challenge of having to replace older platforms. Each new product faces the gradual climb towards critical mass, a period of exponential growth and the limitation of market size. The strategies to be adopted are wide and varied. Should the strategy of open platforms be retained? When is the best time for a network operator to introduce a new service? What is the role of innovation and process efficiency in the quest for new subscribers? Would the current copy-cat strategies lead to a reduction in innovation, or would the equipment providers balance out this factor?

NOTES

I Vodafone, Cellnet, Orange and One 2 One are Mobile Network Operators (MNOs).

II Network externalities are observed in products where the possession of a product by one consumer, affects the value of product for some other consumer. Telecommunications is a classic example where the value of the telephone for any individual depends on the number of colleagues, friends, and relatives in possession of a telephone.

III Cellnet later became O2 in November 2001.

IV One 2 One became T-Mobile in April 2002.

4

V The seed value, which is the initial size of a network, is thought to provide enough impetus for network to grow at an increasing rate, outstripping competitors.

VI Racal and Vodafone demerged in September 1991.

VII Strategic Differentiation Index. See Nattermann (1999).

VIII The findings are summarised by Nattermann in McKinsey Quarterly (2000) Number 2, pp. 22–31.

REFERENCES

1. Vercoulen, F., Wegberg, M. (1998) Standard Selection Modes in Dynamic, Complex Industries: Creating Hybrids Between Market Selection and Negotiated Selection of Standards. Maastricht: Nibor Working Paper, Nib98006.
2. Langlois, R.N., Robertson, P.L. (1992) Networks and Innovation in A Modular System: Lessons from the Microcomputer and Stereo Component Industries. Research Policy, 21(4) 297–313.
3. Sammut-Bonnici, T., Wensley, R. (2002) Darwinism, Probability and Complexity – Transformation and Change Explained through the Theories of Evolution, International Journal of Management Reviews, 4, pp. 291–315.
4. Financial Times, May 4, 2002
5. Nattermann, P.M. (1999). The German cellular market: A case of involuntary competition?, McKinsey Quarterly Info, Volume 1, Number 4, August.
6. Nattermann, P.M. (2000). Best practice does not equal best strategy, McKinsey Quarterly Info, Number 2, May.
7. Morris, C. R. and Ferguson, C. H., How architecture wins technology wars, *Harvard Business Review*, March-April 1993.
8. Henderson, R., & Clark, K.B. (1990). Architectural innovation: The reconfiguration of existing product technologies and the failure of established firms, *Administrative Science Quarterly*, 35(1), 9–30.

CASE STUDY 5

MANAGING A DUTCH–CHINESE JOINT VENTURE: WHERE TO START?

When Jan van der Werde, director of Marketing for the Asia-Pacific region of Global Beverage, boarded the plane in Shanghai to fly to Qingdao in the Chinese Shandong Province he felt a bit uneasy.

It was the first meeting of the board of Dhangtu Beer, a regionally dominant brewery, in which Global Beverage had bought a 45.8% stake as part of its expansion strategy in China. Dhangtu Beer – Global Beverage's biggest investment in China so far – had formerly been a state-owned company; the majority was still in Chinese hands, mostly through the existing management and employees, and the local government, which still had a 10% stake.

Jan could not help thinking that Global Beverage had paid too much for its stake in Dhangtu Beer. However, what was preoccupying him more than reaping the economic benefits of the joint venture was to make an essential pre-condition work: To manage the complex corporate governance issues. During the due diligence of Dhangtu Beer, when Jan had had a first glimpse of the company and its board members, he had told his boss:

> As one would expect in that remote area, Dhangtu Beer has serious transparency problems due to its very arcane accounting structures.

What made the collaboration even more difficult was that all the board meetings had to be translated, as did the dinner conversations. Furthermore, Jan was worried by the holding structure of the group, since it would probably not provide fast decision making. Rather there were possible conflicts of interest on the horizon, since the former state bureaucracy had no tradition of behaving like a company in a competitive environment – neither on the board level nor further down in the organization. This became especially clear to Jan during the due diligence: Despite Dhangtu Beer's dominant position in the region being threatened by its competitors, Jan did not feel any sense of urgency in the company to react, especially not on the board.

Research Associate Christoph Nedopil prepared this disguised case under the supervision of Professor Ulrich Steger as a basis for class discussion rather than to illustrate either effective or ineffective handling of a business situation.

Copyright © 2007 by **IMD** – International Institute for Management Development, Lausanne, Switzerland. Not to be used or reproduced without written permission directly from **IMD**.

COMPANY BACKGROUND

Dhangtu Beer had a long tradition of brewing beer. Established by Germans in the city of Qingdao in Shandong Province in 1899, the brewery became famous across the province borders. It was one of the oldest breweries in China and had a production volume of around 10 million hectoliters in 2006 (the total beer volume in China was almost 212 million hectoliters in 2006 and the biggest beer producer, Tsingtao, had a market share of approximately 12%).

Dhangtu Beer had been state owned for almost 60 years and was only officially privatized in 2005 when the government sold 10% of the shares as an experiment to the Hong Kong-based One National Bank. Only after this trade was successful did the government go on to find more shareholders.

At this point, 10% of its stocks were still owned by the local government through the Jiao'ao Group Co. Ltd (Jiao'ao Group). The Jiao'ao Group itself was also a former state-owned holding company and was now partly privatized with different shareholder groups such as the local government (80%) and various employee groups (20%).

The remaining shares of Dhangtu Beer were held by several institutions: 20% of the shares were held by the existing management and the employees through a private holding company – the Pilsnyu Group – and 14.2% of the shares were floated on the Shenzhen Stock Exchange. The relative majority owner with 45.8% though was Global Beverage, a Dutch-based brewing company with holdings in breweries around the world (*refer to **Exhibit 1** for the ownership structure of Dhangtu Beer*).

Global Beverage knew that this was a unique opportunity to acquire a share in one of the oldest and best-known breweries in China. But of course other investors were also aware of this, and with all of them vying to get their tenders accepted, the bidding went through the roof.

| EXHIBIT 1 | Ownership structure of Dhangtu Beer |

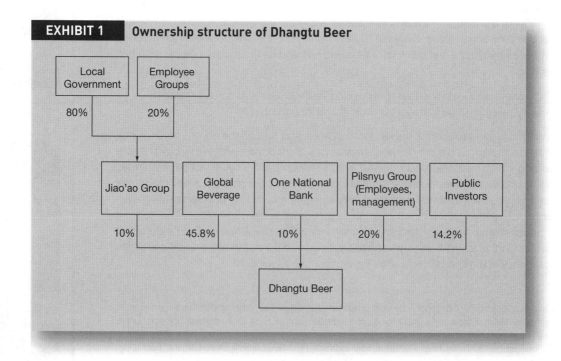

Finally, on June 21, 2005 Global Beverage signed an Equity Sales and Purchase Agreement with the Jiao'ao Group to acquire a 45.8% stake in Dhangtu Beer. However, this acquisition did not come without demanding conditions. For example, Global Beverage had to agree to a five-year lockup period, as the shares were classified as "Legal Person Shares". By contrast, despite being the relative majority shareholder, Global Beverage was granted very few concessions by the Chinese, many of which had not yet been established, either formally or informally.

JAN VAN DER WERDE

Jan van der Werde, 43, was of Dutch origin and had worked for Global Beverage for over 15 years. He had quickly made a career for himself thanks to a dynamic and focused management style and, of course, his flexibility: In the last few years, he had not only held top management positions in Europe, South America and the Middle East but also had served on several boards of the companies Global Beverage had invested in. During the last 18 months he had been working in Asia as marketing director for the Asia-Pacific region for Global Beverage.

Jan van der Werde had already got to know Dhangtu Beer through his work in the due diligence team, which had been analyzing the company before Global Beverage took its final decision to buy the stake. Jan had also played a major role in the negotiations between the Chinese and Global Beverage.

Sitting in the plane and thinking about his past experience with Dhangtu Beer, Jan remembered the performance and governance issues that the due diligence team had revealed – and he knew that they had only scratched the surface.

GLOBAL BEVERAGE'S BIG PLANS FOR DHANGTU BEER

Dhangtu Beer had been a fairly successful company, considering its state ownership. However, since other breweries had been privatized earlier they had had a head start in streamlining their operations and had become much more competitive than Dhangtu Beer. When, during the due diligence, Jan asked a senior manager why Dhangtu was losing ground to its competitors, he replied:

> Jan, sorry to tell you that, but we currently have a rather weak position considering our production efficiency and our marketing capabilities compared to our competition.

In fact, when the due diligence team compared Dhangtu Beer with one of Global Beverage's other investments – a smaller brewery in Shanghai – it found out that Dhangtu Beer's sales force productivity was only 40% of the other investment's productivity. This came as a big shock to Global Beverage, since they were not only looking for a great brand, but also they were urgently looking for a strategic distribution platform for other Global Beverage products in China.

Jan's boss was outraged when he received the information. Jan remembered the call he received shortly after he had sent the due diligence report:

> How the hell are we supposed to sell our products? How have things been working there for all this time? Jan, you've got to get things done over there! Dhangtu Beer is a real jewel and we really must make this work!

But things were unfortunately not that easy and further investigations revealed that Dhangtu Beer was in fact operating below its RWA cost of capital.

THE GOVERNANCE STRUCTURE OF DHANGTU BEER

Directors
....

The board of directors of Dhangtu Beer had recently been extended from five to nine board members. According to the Shenzen Stock Market regulations, at least one-third of the board members of publicly listed companies had to be independent, non-executive directors.

Jan van der Werde himself was considered to be an outside director, but due to his engagement with Global Beverage, not independent. For that reason, Jan was afraid that he might be cemented in an *outsider* position without any influence.

Investors from the Shenzen Stock Exchange, the Jiao'ao Group and the Pilsnyu Group nominated the three independent, non-executive directors of Dhangtu Beer:

■ Mr Jiang Flyu – Dean of the Business School of the local University, also consultant to the local government

■ Mr Wang Zingzo – Director of a local accounting firm

■ Mr Jungo Zhou – Director of the Chinese Beer Association

Whether these three directors would be considered as truly independent according to international standards remained unclear. For their work at Dhangtu they were compensated with RMB 30,000 (around €3,000) per year without any stock options, which was in line with similar listed enterprises.

The remaining five members of the board were: one director from the Jiao'ao Group (government official), one director from One National Bank, two directors from the management through the Pilsnyu Group and Mr Liao Dxingdhu, the chief of operations for Global Beverage, China (*refer to* **Exhibit 2** *for the composition of the board*).

Mr Dxingdhu and Jan had worked together before, but things had not always been easy between them. Mr Dxingdhu was a Chinese local and it was only 10 months since he had taken over the job as chief of operations from another Dutch expatriate. In fact, this had happened more as a sign of goodwill on the part of Global Beverage to accommodate Chinese employee groups than because of his qualifications.

Board committees
....

The board had an audit committee as well as a recently established remuneration committee. The audit committee was composed of three members, none of whom were board members: two members from the internal audit were appointed by two shareholders and one member was appointed as a representative of the employees – certainly not a configuration that reflected international standards, which required the composition of the audit committee of non-management directors chaired by an independent non-executive director.

As yet, no members had been appointed to the remuneration committee since mostly the inside directors wanted to be on this committee. However, due to the nature of the work of this committee, it was necessary to select only non-executive directors.

THE STRUGGLE FOR PERFORMANCE

Jan lay back in his seat, trying to collect his thoughts, but his boss's words kept coming back into his head:

Jan, you've got to get things done over there!

EXHIBIT 2	Board composition of Dhangtu Beer	
Name	Designation	Nominated by
Mr Lu Hongjing	Executive Director	Jiao'ao Group
Mr Bin Qu	Executive Director	Pilsnyu Gropu
Mr Qiang Sun	Executive Director	Pilsnyu Group
Mr Jan van der Werde	Non-Executive Director	Global Beverage (Marketing Director, Global Beverage Asia Pacific)
Mr Liao Dxingdhu	Non-Executive Director	Global Beverage (Chief of Operations, Global Beverage China)
Mr Ted Minko	Non-Executive Director	One National Bank
Mr Jiang Flyu	Independent, non-executive Director	Free-Flow Investors
Mr Wang Zingzo	Independent, non-executive Director	Pilsnyu Group
Mr Jungo Zhou	Independent, non-executive Director	Jiao'ao Group

He knew that his boss was mostly concerned about the economic performance of this joint venture. But as he looked out of the plane window onto the runway he pondered how he should push for economic performance with so many governance issues to resolve.

One of these issues was the remuneration of senior management – an important performance incentive in Western companies. Dhangtu Beer had recently engaged an HR consultant to revamp the compensation structure for senior management after Jan had pointed out that the structure and level of compensation were totally obscure.

Senior management remuneration was in fact a difficult topic in China, since the general level of compensation for senior managers was not yet high enough to provide sufficient incentive for managers to really care about the company performance. The HR consultant had explained to Jan:

> You've got to understand, Jan: China is traditionally a consensus-driven culture. Individual accountability is consequently difficult to institutionalize.

Nevertheless, managers at Dhangtu Beer had the feeling that they were being compensated above average compared to other listed companies. The exact level and details of the compensation though were yet to be disclosed and then to be fairly determined by the remuneration committee.

Another issue Jan was musing about was the relationship with the Jiao'ao Group. Jan figured – also from past experience – that since the Jiao'ao Group was mostly a state owned holding group with employee interests, its goals for Dhangtu Beer might be very different from those pursued by Global Beverage. Some difficulties had already surfaced during the negotiations, when one of the government officials said:

> Even if you find one or two divisions which don't fulfil your expectations considering efficiency during your due diligence, please consider: There is no way that you will close any of them in the next 24 months. Remember, employment is our major concern and we expect shareholders to respect that obligation.

The fact that the Jiao'ao Group only had one executive director on the board of Dhangtu Beer did little to appease Jan either, since he was afraid that the government might be able to influence decisions

5

through the independent non-executive director they appointed as well as through party members on all management levels. As Jan was aware, through his work in the negotiations, the directors from the Jiao'ao Group had also established close ties with the three directors from the Pilsnyu Group, leaving him even less leverage in board negotiations.

Jan's best hope of getting more leverage on the board was through the director from One National Bank, although he had not yet met him. But since he was working for a bank in Hong Kong, Jan dared to hope that this director might pursue more economic interests than the others did.

HOW TO TACKLE THE DILEMMA

Jan van der Werde knew what it took to make a joint venture successful: shared and aligned goals, a trusting attitude, shared knowledge and, certainly in China, the involvement of people who had the right amount of influence to change things (*refer to Exhibit 3 for a more comprehensive list of success factors of joint ventures*). But would the current structure really allow this joint venture between Dhangtu and Global Beverage to flourish? How could it be changed in order to influence the performance? What would be needed to initiate the change and more importantly, what could Jan do?

Yet Jan saw another dilemma for himself: Where should he start his battle – push for rationalization to make Dhangtu Beer more competitive again or make the board and the governance work? What were his leverages? Who could he trust?

As the plane took off, he brushed aside his negative thoughts and remembered what his boss in headquarters had told him:

In China the signing of the contract is the beginning of the negotiations!

When he started reading the board book, his mind was focused on the questions: Where should he start with the negotiations? What priorities did he really need to set in this "must-win battle"?

EXHIBIT 3	Success factors in a joint venture	
Success factors	*Failure factors*
1 Trusting attitude/behavior	1 Absence of shared and aligned goals, objectives
2 Shared and aligned goals, objectives	2 Absence of clear/consistent goals, objectives
3 Open behavior	3 Absence of trusting attitude/behavior
4 Shared knowledge/information	4 Absence of open and unhindered communication
5 Clear roles	5 Presence of culture differences
6 Commitment	6 Absence of strong/proactive leadership
7 Co-operative/supportive behavior	7 Presence of adversarial, non-co-operation and/ or conflict
8 Openness, honesty, integrity etc.	8 Absence of fair allocation of risks, rewards and profits
9 Integrated team, without inter-company boundaries	9 Absence of open behavior and willingness to change
10 Involvement of people who can influence outcome	10 Absence of commitment of members to relationship

Source: Hacque et al. (2004): Survey conducted 1999 – representative sample of 99 managers from UK oil and gas industry

CASE STUDY 6

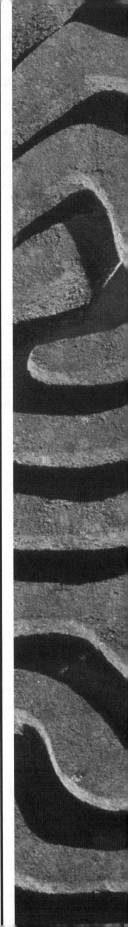

IKEA: CULTURE AS COMPETITIVE ADVANTAGE

I IKEA THE WORLDWIDE STANDARD SETTER

After firmly attaining leadership within Sweden, where it holds more than 20% of the overall market, IKEA has succeeded over the last twenty five years to do what no furniture distributor has ever attempted: to become a global player in an industry considered by nature to be local.

Today IKEA delivers low priced quality furniture to key markets throughout the world. It is the only distributor in its field to have successfully established itself in all parts of Europe, including Southern and Eastern Europe, and more notably in North America, including the USA. It has stores today in the Middle East, Singapore and Hong Kong and is preparing to enter the Chinese market sometimes in the early part of the next century. Recently Ingvar Kamprad has secured his position in Europe with the acquisition of British based Habitat, IKEA's chief rival in the UK and France.

To provide some idea of its worldwide presence, IKEA receives annually over 120 million visitors in its 125 stores, and distributes 35 million catalogues. Its sales revenues increased steadily over the last 10 years by an average of 12% annually, in spite of the flattening out of its business in Western Europe which still represents nearly 80% of its annual volume. **(See Exhibit 1.)**

Founder Ingvar Kamprad's stubborn insistence that people will buy more furniture if the price is low enough, the furniture of decent quality and no delays in delivery has gradually revolutionized the conservative national furniture markets in Europe and beyond. Kamprad intuitively anticipated the rise of consumerism in the 1950s and 60s, and virtually invented the practices of cash and carry, self-service, and volume buying in Europe.

This case was written by **Paul Grol** and **Christopher Schoch** under the direction of **Michel Roger** CPA, Paris Chamber of Commerce, Paris. It is intended to be used as the basis for class discussion rather than to illustrate the effective or ineffective handling of an administrative situation.

This case was made possible by the co-operation of IKEA.

© 1998 CPA, Paris Chamber of Commerce and Industry, Paris, France.

Printed with permission from ecch.com Ref: 398-173-1.

IKEA was to invent many other concepts and new ways of dealing with logistics, sourcing, and retailing, many of these innovations have become industry standards: knock-down furniture that can be stored and shipped in flat boxes; involving customers in the value adding process by handling the transportation and doing easy home-assembly themselves; and turning shopping into a family event by creating attractive open store environments that contain IKEA trademarks like the children's areas with brightly colored plastic balls, and the buffet style restaurants where you can eat Swedish meatballs.

IKEA has affected the way furniture is sold and distributed in every country where it is doing business, inspiring imitation and drawing respect, sometimes begrudgingly, from traditional furniture dealers.

One aspect of IKEA's success has been the development of unique product design capabilities, based on an almost religious dedication to the simple, yet graceful design of contemporary Swedish furniture. In so doing it has introduced millions of households around the world to the Swedish style that it more than others have come to typify. **(See Exhibit 2.)**

IKEA's strength today comes from their mastery of three key aspects of the value chain: **unique design capabilities, unique sourcing, and tightly controlled logistics**. This means that they are able to produce products that are distinctive enough to provide market recognition, secure sourcing for long runs at profitable levels, and reduce inventory costs through regional warehouses which work very closely with stores. In this way they have been able to buck industry trends and steadily increase their share of slow growing, sometimes shrinking markets.

IKEA has become a household reference as much in Warsaw, as in Los Angeles, attracting customers who just want to come to a store, look around and have some fun. Something universally irresistible about IKEA makes it very difficult for people to come away from one of its stores without making a purchase and instills unprecedented loyalty among its customers and employees.

IKEA's successful development, particular organizational capacities, and the bold and inspired leadership of its entrepreneur-founder have all been largely written up and commented. Its organization, communication, marketing, product range, and store layouts all tell the same story – the story of the "IKEA-Way". A way strongly rooted in the personality of founder Ingvar Kamprad and the Swedish (regional) culture that he grew up in.

II THE "IKEA-WAY": DOING THINGS DIFFERENTLY

What is it that makes IKEA so different? Is it just "low priced quality goods at affordable prices"? Or is there a deeper explanation? When asked these questions, IKEA managers and personnel become mystical and somewhat vague. "It is really a winning combination of price and a merry feeling, a feeling of delight" a Dutch marketing manager answers. This feeling and a conscious awareness that, in addition to the competitive advantage there is something strong and intangible at IKEA that drives and motivates its success, is shared by Ikeans throughout the organization. Could it be that the IKEA-Way's combination of vision, charismatic leadership, sound business principles is subtly reinforced by the influence of Swedish culture? Could it be that Swedish, or Scandinavian culture contains elements that facilitates international expansion?

Can a company's national culture in this case be a competitive advantage? Throughout our investigation of IKEA we have kept these questions in the back of our minds, and we invite you to consider them as we explore the IKEA-Way more closely.

2.1 How it all started

IKEA's name is derived from the initials of the company's founder, architect, and driving force **I**ngvar **K**amprad, those of the farm where he was raised, **E**lmtaryd, and those of his native village **A**gunnaryd, located in Smaland a poor farming region in the south-east of Sweden. Coming from a modest background, Kamprad began as a trader in everything from matches to Christmas cards, he almost accidentally got into the furniture business after buying out a failed furniture plant in the early 1950s. He demonstrated from the very beginning a combination of strong salesmanship, practical business acumen, thrift, an identity with ordinary people, and an unconventional perseverance in the face of adversity. Always modest he was none the less a true entrepreneur, and more significantly a non-conformist who was not the least bit restrained by the conventions and traditions of the Swedish furniture trade of his day.

His habit of staying close to his customers and his reluctance to own manufacturing furniture plants gave him freedom to focus and innovate on all the facets of distribution. With nearby furniture producers he co-designed furniture to meet very specific requirements for quality products that average customers could afford, and then printed them up in catalogues, which he had discovered as an economical and effective way of marketing to a growing customer base in his early days as a trader.

In 1953 he opened his first showroom at the furniture plant he had bought earlier in Almhult which has become the heart of his furniture empire. The only transportation link to the factory was by road at a time when more and more working class Swedes were purchasing their first automobiles, so what was originally a problem would become a solution.

Kamprad was obsessed with low prices, and the only way to offer them was to keep costs as low as possible: this conviction became a driving force of his business development. He would constantly seek new ways to lower prices. For example he bought fabrics for his furniture directly from textile mills, placing large orders and then supplying the material himself to his network of small furniture manufacturers. In this way at the same time he was able to cut costs a bit more, and ensure that his customers would have a wider selection of upholstery to choose from in the catalogue. Unwittingly he had introduced the notion of vertical integration, which provided IKEA even then with a strong competitive advantage compared to traditional distributors who only displayed and sold furniture.

Such practices enabled him to have close contact with his suppliers, and eventually to learn intimately the parameters of furniture production. The relationship between him and his suppliers were so good that to obtain their commitment he needed only to draw rough sketches of the furniture he wanted and discuss with them how to adapt production to their capabilities. In so doing, he established over the years another cornerstone of his business philosophy: marrying the customer's need for low prices with the suppliers' need for profit through efficiency and long production runs. This was a strong departure from the kind of relationship that distributors traditionally maintained with their suppliers, buying furniture as it was ordered piece by piece at high prices with long waiting periods for delivery.

Balancing customer's requirements and producers' needs, which enabled him to sell furniture at prices 30 to 50% below traditional distributors, is now the foundation of the IKEA-Way. This notion is so basic and even imperative that a store manager in Germany told me, when walking through the accessories department where some Chinese gadgets were displayed, that this balancing of optimal product design with the supplier with the needs of the customer is the "Yin and Yang" of the IKEA strategy. It was already present in the way Ingvar Kamprad developed his business through the fifties when his innovative ways provoked stubborn counter attacks from his more established Swedish competitors.

A legendary showdown took place at the Sankt Erik's Fair in Stockholm where, for the first time, IKEA introduced its products. Feeling threatened by Kamprad's unexpected success and many new customers, the Swedish furniture cartel tried to block IKEA's entry at the fair. They failed, but soon thereafter managed a successful boycott of IKEA by Swedish furniture manufacturers accusing Kamprad of unfair practices. Undaunted by this seemingly insurmountable obstacle, Kamprad looked for and found new suppliers in Poland at the height of the Cold War.

Although Polish manufacturers were willing to sell at prices well below their counterparts in Sweden, the cost of transportation offset this advantage. This new obstacle was at the origin of yet another IKEA invention, as Kamprad discovered that by "knocking down" furniture into disassembled parts it could be packed and shipped in flat cardboard reducing by more than 80% the cost of transportation. To

6

further save on costs, the furniture could be sold directly to customers in these same flat boxes. To help customers participate in the distribution cycle IKEA offered to rent roof racks and invented the simple assembly tool which had become another of its trademarks.

To reach the largest possible market and benefit fully from volume sales, in 1964 IKEA opened Europe's first large "warehouse scale" store in Stockholm. Unexpectedly large crowds of people attended the grand opening causing yet another problem. Seemingly endless queues formed at the check-out stands as employees scurried to the storage areas to fetch the purchased furniture. Instead of hiring more employees, Kamprad simply opened the storage area to customers and invited them to fetch the furniture themselves. Such practices were unheard of then, but understanding that this would lead to lower prices, customers willingly complied. In just a few years IKEA had invented the concept of "prosumers" whereby customers actively participate in the distribution cycle.

Suddenly the whole system was in place: customers were able to purchase attractive quality furniture at low prices; furniture suppliers benefited from long production runs, and IKEA, through volume sales, was able to make a considerable profit from small margins.

IKEA's business strategy did not evolve from "strategic planning" which is still scorned today in the company as "too sophisticated". It evolved from creative responses to difficult problems, turning them into solutions pragmatically and often with considerable risk. Not going by the book, or adopting conventional solutions. Learning by doing appears to be a distinguishing trait of Ingvar Kamprad's and IKEA's intuitive way of doing business.

2.2 The IKEA mission

As IKEA grew Ingvar Kamprad found ways to explain his unique way of doing business always using simple language and metaphors. He has consistently maintained that IKEA's mission is **to offer "a wide range of home furnishing items of good design and function, at prices so low that the majority of people can afford to buy them"**. This statement is at the heart of the IKEA's philosophy and has shaped all of the phases of its business, particularly product range. The concept is protected through numerous guidelines and special legal entities. Changes in the criteria for product range can only be made by joint decisions of INGKA Holding BV and Inter IKEA Systems BV both of which are outside the sphere of management.

The essential guidelines appear in a 1976 publication "Testament of a Furniture Dealer" in which Kamprad emphasizes the company's ambition to cover furnishing and decorative needs of the total home area with a distinctive style that reflect "our thoughts and be as simple and straightforward as ourselves". The guidelines also express such modern ideals as furniture that is durable and easy to live with, reflects a natural and free life style, and appeals to youthfulness with color and joy. Most of IKEA's products are designed by Swedes in Almhult who consciously reproduce the designs that reflect these values which are very consistent with Swedish culture. At the same time there is something universally appealing in that specific design in markets throughout the world.

2.3 Business principles

IKEA has developed unique competencies and ability to deliver products which are distinctly Swedish, attractively presented in warm value adding environments, and at consistently lower prices than competition.

What has made IKEA so different from other distributors is the balanced focus it has maintained on product range, sourcing, vertical integration, mass marketing, cost leadership, and a distinctive image. As such they are not market driven, and tend to react rather slowly to new consumer trends, studying them to see how they can fit into their operating systems and what value IKEA can add within their proven framework, before adopting them into their range. The issue of range is vital for them as, when they introduce new products they must ensure that the volumes they produce are leveraged from within-sourcing-logistics-store layouts.

The Yin/Yang metaphor mentioned earlier illustrates the imperative balance of strategic sourcing and marketing mix.

The balance and complementariness of

Strategic sourcing and the marketing mix

In the area of **strategic sourcing,** IKEA has established a long-standing competitive advantage. The durable partnerships that it has developed with furniture producers and other suppliers is based on the producers' capacity to provides long runs of parts, and their willingness to comply with IKEA's quality standards and IKEA's guaranteed purchase of all parts produced. IKEA considers their producers as key stakeholders and provides them with technical assistance to increase their productivity sometimes underwriting investments of new technology. Together they actively contribute to both cost reduction and quality enhancement, that optimize the marketing mix.

Through such partnerships IKEA has virtually integrated production into its value-added chain without the heavy investments of actually owning and running its own furniture plants.

2.4 Management style and practices

IKEA management style is described by non-Swedish members as informal, open, and caring. Hierarchy is not emphasized and in a typical store there are only three levels of responsibility between the store manager and co-workers (which is what employees are called). A pragmatic approach to problem solving and consensus-based decision-making are also strongly embedded in IKEA management practice.

Co-workers at all levels are encouraged to take initiatives, and making mistakes is considered a necessary part of "learning by doing". Managers are expected not only to share information with co-workers but also their knowledge and skills. IKEA wants their co-workers to feel important, they can express their ideas, and should feel responsible for improving the way things are done.

An entrepreneurial zeal for getting the job done in the most direct way and a distaste for bureaucratic procedures are basic managerial attitudes that have long been promoted within IKEA. Managers are expected to be close to their co-workers with few if any status barriers, and not to take themselves seriously. This egalitarian approach to management has also made it easy for motivated employees to work their way up the organization with little formal training. It is significant that Swedish managers' titles do not appear on their business cards, and that company cars are the same economy models for all of those who need them for work or business regardless of their position.

6

Rather than establish extensive training programs and detailed rules and procedures to propagate its unique culture, IKEA prefers a softer approach through discussion and explanation. The IKEA-Way has been spelled out through wide distribution of Kamprad's "**Testament**", which has been translated into a dozen languages. Kamprad himself explains that IKEA has "**a strong and living culture**" based on doing things differently. "**It has grown step by step**", and together with its business principles is the "**cornerstone of our operations. . . . which helps us retain the spirit and vitality of the early years . . . and create a feeling of belonging in a large international organization. Our corporate culture binds us together**". To ensure that the IKEA-Way is understood, the organization relies heavily on managers to act as "**missionaries**" carrying all that it embodies through their example and willingness to explain to new and older employees why things are done the way they are. This, as much as anything else, provides the reason for the extensive presence of Swedish managers in IKEA's international units, as their knowledge stems from their direct exposure to Ingvar Kamprad and IKEA's subtle way of doing business and managing people. For those managers who do not have that exposure, weeklong IKEA-Way seminars are organized periodically in Almhult, the IKEA equivalent of Mecca and the heart of its culture.

III IKEA'S STRATEGY OF INTERNATIONAL EXPANSION: FLEXIBILITY WITHIN ESTABLISHED PARAMETERS

3.1 Patterns of international expansion

IKEA's international expansion has taken place progressively over the last twenty-five years with an eye towards markets in countries with growth potential. Expansion outside of Scandinavia was driven by Ingvar Kamprad's intuitive quest for new opportunities, and his previous successful search for suppliers outside of Sweden more than by any formal development strategy. Some insights are provided by one of IKEA's Swedish executives, an early companion of Ingvar Kamprad. "When we opened our first store outside Scandinavia in Switzerland, people asked why there? It was a difficult market. Ingvar said that if we could succeed there, we should succeed anywhere. He had intuitions, he spoke to people on the streets to learn what they were looking for". Such an empirical experiential approach goes against the orthodox rules of international retailing which are preaching extensive market studies before entering a new market, catering to local tastes, and gaining expertise through acquisitions and joint ventures.

When IKEA expanded into Germany, competition was strong and German distributors didn't take them seriously. "They called us those crazy Swedes, but we didn't mind, we even used this label in our advertising. It took them five years to really react, but by then we had eight stores and were setting the standards."

Charting its own course, IKEA has developed internationally, finding cheap land for stores, availability of sourcing, proximity to central warehouses, or lowering marketing costs. When in the late 70s they decided to go into Belgium because it was cost effective to service the country from their central warehouse in Germany they ran into problems with building permits and so decided to develop in France instead. The preference has been for leveraging market costs by concentrating several stores in the same area. This explains why they opened four stores in the Philadelphia/Washington DC/New Jersey area sometimes in locations that were rather isolated. They also preferred concentrating four stores in the Paris area even if this could dilute individual store sales and creates potential competition between stores.

Typically development has been done on a store by store basis. IKEA opens a beachhead in a given country with a group of trusted and experienced Swedish "Missionaries". Together they form a tight-knit group who can solve problems and make decisions quickly. They supervise the building, lead operational

6

teams who open the store, and run the store until local management has learned how the system works. After a short while store management is turned over to local managers, while most of the key national positions remain in the hands of Swedes until the operation and market has reached maturity.

3.2 Adapting to national markets

Adapting to new markets in Western Europe throughout the 70s and early 80s was fairly simple. Catalogue offerings were virtually the same. However concessions had to be made, particularly in bedroom furnishings since bedding could be substantially different from country to country.

"When we entered a new country we did things our way. The idea was to be IKEA everywhere, after all, our furniture is a cultural statement. But as the years went by we learned to be more flexible, particularly when demand in Sweden declined and we became more dependent on our non-Scandinavian markets".

Adapting to the US market was a real learning experience for IKEA, since many standards were different. Few product managers from IKEA of Sweden had traveled to North America since the price of air travel was prohibitive to IKEA's cost-conscience policies. They expected their European range to sell just as easily in the US, which did not turn out to be the case. As a former U.S. country manager explains: "IKEA ran into problems in the US so we had to ask ourselves what can we offer to Americans. Should we become an American company, or merely adapt our merchandising to American customers? We finally decided on a solution: Merchandising to the American customer by speaking English with a Swedish accent. Capitalizing on our strengths as an outsider".

Development of the range is now closely monitored by IKEA of Sweden (IOS) and the Board of Directors of INGKA Holding. The issue of range is vital for them as, when they introduce new products they must ensure that the volumes they produce are balanced from within (sourcing-logistics-store layouts). It took IKEA of Sweden several years to introduce "futons" in Europe, and American store managers had to work hard to convince them that a "Home Entertainment" line was feasible in North America.

As a former French country manager described, obtaining concessions from product managers to take into account specific national preferences was a consensual process that required many negotiation skills. "Some room is allowed for national considerations in our catalogue range. But since changes mean that it will be more expensive for the country manager, only a limited number is requested. Still 90% of our range is the same all over, only 5 to 10% is country specific. The product manager has the final word, but he usually listens to the country manager. There is a healthy tension between the two and this enables us to adapt but not to over-adapt and weaken our cost effectiveness."

Although IKEA's stated mission is to provide home furnishing for the "greatest number" and its business is conducted on a volume basis, outside of Scandinavia it is in reality a niche player, appealing to the educated population with mid to upper level incomes. This segment is looking for non-traditional lines of furniture, and finds the Swedish style of IKEA suitable to its modern taste.

"In spite of our image as the "common man's store" the majority of our customers have a university degree" admits a French store manager. This may appear paradoxical considering IKEA's avowed mission statement, but the paradox has proven successful as it keeps IKEA at the same time close to its roots and still makes it highly distinctive in foreign market places. It also plays neatly into its strengths of sourcing, volume, long runs, and cost-efficient distribution.

3.3 Human resource management

Management of international operations has largely followed the IKEA-Way and its strong Swedish flavor. The belief in IKEA is that their way of managing people has universal appeal. "People like to participate in making decisions. They like to feel respected, and that they can take responsibility", one Swedish expatriate states.

6

For recruitment, IKEA looks for people who have good communication skills, open minds, positive work attitudes and have good potential without necessarily having diplomas. It attracts people with its pleasant working environment, job security, and the **care that shows** towards the individual. IKEA employees regardless of nationality are more than likely to have strong preferences for co-operative informal relations, being independent and have a tolerant approach to others. "We look for people who know how to listen, and who are able to transmit their knowledge to others. They should not feel they are better than others and be curious about what is going on around them".

Being an IKEA manager overseas isn't just running the stores and distribution systems smoothly. They must be able to explain to employees and managers why things are done that way, and win peoples hearts and minds to the "IKEA-Way". They are expected to be ambassadors and must educate their non-Swedish co-workers through patience, common understanding, and example. It is not always easy to transmit IKEA's egalitarian management style. While it goes down easily in the Netherlands, it is less easy for Germany or for France. But for different reasons. In the United States long term employees generally feel more comfortable with Scandinavian managers than with Americans, younger American managers don't seem to know how to show "**equalness**".

The challenge IKEA may be facing is that, with its extended international network, it is becoming more difficult to find enough Swedish IKEA managers who are willing to work overseas for long periods. IKEA had to hire Swedes from outside the company. In the past the company has not systematically searched out and developed its international "high potentials" early enough, although it does send its most loyal and successful foreign managers to week-long seminars in Sweden and encourages its co-workers to learn something about the culture.

It is still very difficult for non-Scandinavians to work their way up the corporate ladder. To do so they need to learn all of IKEA's key trades: retailing, logistics, product design, and purchasing. Non Swedes can work their way up in retailing through the national organizations and sometimes in the logistical organizations which are run regionally, but very few have gone into product management because this function is part of IKEA of Sweden in Almhult, where IKEA's product managers and furniture school are located. It is a very remote area and only Swedish is spoken. So, speaking the language as well and knowing the culture becomes a pre-requisite that very few managers from the foreign branch have been able to fill.

There are no formal career paths for advancement as a long term Swedish expatriate executive admits. "To get ahead in IKEA you first have to know the range intimately, then you have to know and use the informal internal network, and then you have to understand the subtleties of the IKEA-Way, its cultural roots. It is really difficult for an outsider to know his way around. In reality it is a difficult company to understand. Humbleness is not a sign of weakness. It comes from Ingvar. People are expected to learn from their experience, and this takes time and patience, you can't be in a hurry to move up the ladder".

3.4 Dealing with the Europeans – Germany

Germany is the largest national organization of the IKEA group accounting for ±30% of the total group sales with more than 20 stores, including the newly opened stores in former East Germany.

Although IKEA has been established in Germany for more than two decades, (its first store was opened in Munich in 1974), Swedish management is still perceived by German IKEA members as peculiar. As described by Thomas Larson, the store manager of Cologne: "Some older co-workers still have problems addressing me by my first name or use the German "Du" (the informal equivalent for you, "tu" in French)". "Dutzen", using the informal you, is often felt as undermining the respect and prestige of the boss. As Heike Oestreich, the personnel manager said: "There are two different "Du's", the IKEA Du and the Du which is used between friends".

The Germans are very disciplined and precise. They do exactly what the boss asks them to do and what is agreed is put down in writing. A problem is that the Swedish notion and cornerstone of our work policy "to take your own responsibility" is not perceived in the same way by the Germans. There is a tendency to adhere very closely to precisely defined rules and instructions. When IKEA translated the corporate brochure "the IKEA-Way" into German, a need was felt to sharpen and make more explicit the original Swedish text, which presented key IKEA concepts in sometimes vague terms in order to give freedom to people to adapt them and take personal responsibility for carrying them out. Once Anders Moberg, I. Kamprad's successor, suggested in a letter that certain merchandising displays could be used in a variety of places. In Germany department managers interpreted this as an order, and systematically set up the displays in every part of their stores.

In general German employees feel that the Swedes are more result oriented and treat every problem as a challenge that should be met. However they believe that Swedish management does not sufficiently assess risks before taking action. According to Heike Oestreich, Human Resource Manager in Cologne: "The Swedes", to reduce bureaucracy, "would like to dump all our office desks in the back yard". The lack of formality is also dismaying to Germans. To implement a decision "notes on the back of a cigarette package are often sufficient" for the Swedes. In contrast, Germans are more comfortable adhering to formal procedures; "We need procedures and forms. Germans love administration because it provides them with security".

3.5 Dealing with the Europeans – France

Development in France, which has fewer than half the number of stores in Germany, was always considered problematic because of multiple administrative regulations on the retail trade and a hostile attitude towards discounters that prevailed in the late 70s and early 80s. By carefully avoiding too much public attention and with only a limited number of store openings it managed to secure a safe place for itself on the Market and develop an 8% share of market.

The main challenge for IKEA management in France is the French tendency to judge informality as a sign of weakness, or indecision. People here are accustomed to formal rules and strong hierarchy. In the words of a former Swedish country manager when IKEA first started in France: "Some French managers felt that with Swedish informality they could do whatever they wanted. When we told them that they should inform their subordinates they did not take us seriously". Some aspects of the informality can be irritating to the French at such as the lack of formal job descriptions and written procedures. Whereas Swedish managers will justify this by saying that they don't like to limit responsibility, and that they get more out of people with an informal approach, the French tend to be suspicious of informality for the same reasons.

In the view of IKEA's French Human Resource manager: "Working here isn't for everyone. It is very difficult for someone over 35, because this place is different from all of the others in France. When you join IKEA, you enter another world: we do not behave like a normal French company. Status is not recognized which can cause an identity problem: everyone is put on the same level – no one stands out, and you can get lost in the crowd. It is hard to explain what IKEA is, everyone will give a different answer, one shouldn't freeze the system, it is flexible, it should stay that way".

Two of the main reasons given for IKEA's appeal to French candidates are:

■ The aesthetics of our stores – they look nice and are pleasant to work in.

■ Also the intelligent way in which we work – it makes sense!

However, to make things clearer to employees, a formal communication platform has been developed in France to spell out in facts and figures which compare IKEA's benefits to those of competitors. Also more formal training programs are being developed because in France "learning by doing" is not

6

perceived as credible way of developing competency. You typically would not trust your boss to develop your skills in France, and more faith is placed in "off-site programs". In France tolerance has its limits and when IKEA hired "too many" people of non-French origins, they received complaints from their customers, so now they make a point of keeping "non-French" workers to a minimum.

Four years ago relations with unions were hostile. There was a nasty strike and widespread discontent. French labor unions did not trust or understand IKEA's Swedish management style with its tendency to seek consensus. More recently IKEA's management has taken a more affirmative attitude, and relations have improved notably. They may continue to improve now that IKEA France is run by a Frenchman, Jean Louis Baillot whose wife is Swedish and who has worked in Almhult.

3.6 Doing things differently in the United States

Expanding into the US market in the 80s was certainly the boldest developmental decision that IKEA had made up to that time. From an historical perspective the venture seemed unlikely to succeed. First the culturally specific requirements for home furnishing in the United States are considerably different from those of the European markets, particularly concerning the size and functions of furniture. Secondly the American market had come to be known as the "graveyard" of European retailers with a long list of unfortunate ventures by such successful firms as Casino, Carrefour, and Marks and Spencers. But somehow IKEA seemed confident that going about it in their own way would prove an exception to the laws of failure that seemed to doom European entrants to the US market.

Initially development in the US was quite consistent with IKEA's pattern in Europe: Identifying prime markets with volume potential; purchasing cheap land in the periphery of big cities; relying on mass advertising and a unique message emphasizing its Swedishness; focusing on range and price through the catalogue, establishing a beachhead from which to launch and develop its organization. Also its approach was empirical and pragmatic, and it did not set out to take the US by storm, but merely to test its tried and true formula and learn through experience how they could succeed. In fact from the mid seventies to the early 80s IKEA opened a series of franchised stores in Canada, developing during this time its logistic capabilities and demonstrating that its European range could sell in America's back yard, before it finally entered the US market in 1985.

Its first stage of development in the US began on the East Coast with the opening of Plymouth Meeting in Philadelphia's northwest suburbs, followed by a cluster of four other stores. "Development was initially based on the potato field approach. Find someplace where there is cheap land, build and the people will follow". This approach ignored the rule of American retailing based on fine tuned segmentation and targeting. Their choice of locations, driven by cost-consciousness, led them to establish their stores in shopping centers that had no upscale "anchors stores" to draw the high income customers that IKEA appeals to. This should have been a relative disadvantage, since competitors like Home Depot locate their stores in prime centers with "anchors" like Nordstrom's and Macy's. But by maintaining the profile of a "different kind of store", very Swedish, with a wide range of products, it apparently has overcome this obstacle. Here the catalogue has served them well, as people can plan their purchases before they come and thus optimize their time investment.

Up until the early 90s IKEA enjoyed a honeymoon of sorts. The American public was attracted by the novelty of Scandinavian style, and IKEA's unique merchandising, which resembles a European village market place. Its advertising was a success. People drove six to eight hours to come to the stores and they initially came in large numbers. Riding on a high dollar, IKEA had appeared to have gotten off to a fast start as they had in Germany and other European markets. The honeymoon ended abruptly in the late eighties when the dollar went down, revealing multiple weaknesses.

First and foremost even if Americans were initially attracted by IKEA's advertising and novelty, their range of furniture was unsuited to American standards and sold poorly. One often told anecdote illustrates just how far from those standards they really were. Customers would purchase flower vases thinking they were American size drinking glasses. Americans furnish their master bedrooms with king-size beds, whereas IKEA's largest beds were 5 inches narrower. Also Americans are harder on sitting room furniture, and IKEA's sofa and armchair offerings proved too lightly dimensioned. Additionally IKEA did not offer furniture suitable to the "Home Entertainment Centers" that blossomed through the 80s and into the 90s in American households with proliferation of widescreen television, VCR, and hi-fi equipment. With declining sales revenue and shrinking profits, by 1989 the "graveyard effect" seemed to have caught up with IKEA.

A courageous decision was then made by Anders Moberg and a new management team was brought in to head the US organization. Faced with the alternatives of: holding on and waiting for better times, withdrawing humbly, or fighting back, the latter course was chosen. In 1990 the American retail management group, under the leadership of Göran Carstedt, recently hired from Volvo, convinced the product managers at IKEA of Sweden that the IKEA European range had to be adapted and American based sourcing stepped up while reassuring them that IKEA would not lose its soul. In the words of Carstedt:

> "The IKEA strategy in North America will still be blue and yellow, but we will put more stars and stripes and more maple leaves in it".

It was not easy but they succeeded in changing the design of many household products. To make the point one US manager brought a plastic American-sized turkey with him to Almhult and before a surprised group of product managers placed it on one of the best selling dining tables in the European range. Given the size of the bird there was only room for two table settings instead of the normal six. He had made his point.

However there was a condition attached to adapting the range, and that condition was volume. Lines of furniture specifically designed for the American market would have to be produced in long enough lines to meet IKEA's commitment to suppliers and be priced at the lowest levels possible.

A combination of luck and bold counter attacking led to an unexpected expansion on the West Coast that was to ease pressure on its pricing and provide needed growth to its retail business. An imitator "Stor" inspired by IKEA's success had illicitly acquired knowledge of IKEA's floor plan and merchandising schemes and successfully opened four stores primarily around Los Angeles, far from IKEA's base on the East Coast. Responding as much to the threat to their image as to the opportunity to capitalize on Stor's advertising of Swedish style furniture, IKEA decided to counter attack. It opened a store in Los Angeles and eventually, through its price and sourcing advantage, drove Stor to the brink of bankruptcy. It then bought out its imitator at a bargain price and established a solid base in a prime market on the West Coast. If IKEA's low profile stance stressed its humble origins and culture, it definitely did not mean that the company was a weakling. IKEA showed that it could be tough and decisive in that toughest of tough markets. The current US country manager Jan Kjellman in comparing the US market to his previous European experience used the following words: "The biggest difference is competition. Competitors are everywhere, and they are strong. The market is crowded, but still there always seem to be new competitors. Even with a million and a half customers, we are small. It is a total struggle for us, and it is tough to survive". Could IKEA adapt to such competition and still remain faithful to the "IKEA-Way"?

Swedish managers are impressed with the professionalism of American salesmanship. "Over here retailing is a profession. Sales persons are subjected to a lot of pressure for short term results because large retailers are publicly owned and shareholders measure quarterly results. So they are very time-efficient and masters of the hard sell", relates Kjellman. IKEA has always maintained a soft approach believing that people know what they want, so that sales personnel are there to help them find it. Moreover the strategy is that most of the selling is done by the catalogue so that people arrive with specific purchases in mind. Impulse buying takes place for smaller items like candleholders, or accessories that

6

are sought for as bargains. On this point IKEA has stood firm, and sales personnel from competitors such as Macy's or Bloomingdale have to unlearn the hard sell approach.

Americans are always looking for convenience, which means more space, more information, anything that reduces effort and saves time. To respond to these demands IKEA had to redesign its store layouts providing more directions and short cuts for people who don't want to just wander through the store. "Customers were screaming: let us out, before we remodeled our layout" reports a store manager, "They couldn't find their way out of our maze of displays, there were no windows or signs they felt lost and panicky". While making these adjustments in store layout, which have been criticized by IKEA International headquarters, IKEA has maintained its policy of minimal service. Customers who want home delivery or someone to assemble their furniture must pay the full add-on cost. In fact IKEA stores carefully outsource these services to local providers and they never promote such services in their advertising, they rather encourage their customers to do it the IKEA-Way, which means renting a roof rack and assembling it yourself.

Adapting IKEA's floor plans and furniture to American dimensions paid off, and sales has increased 25 to 30% compared to the late 80s. By 1994 IKEA had turned around the situation in the USA. Through its acquisition of Stor and by adapting its range to US requirements sales have increased steadily by about 10% annually providing them with the volume base necessary to sustain long production lines and keep prices low. Whereas only 15% of the furniture in American stores was produced locally, the figure is now at about 50%.

In the view of several IKEA senior US managers, the key to this successful turn around was the granting of more autonomy to the American country management than their European counterparts had enjoyed. "You can't steer America from Europe", admitted Anders Moberg in 1994. "When we went in we hadn't planned a clear strategy of how to supply the American market at a low cost". Learning how to succeed in the United States through its own painful expense took more than five years. Although its US operation has shown a profit over the last three years it still has not recovered its initial investment. With flat growth in Europe, heavy investment in longer term expansion into Eastern Europe and China putting pressure on IKEA's capital reserves, focus in the U.S. is now on developing sales and profit from its existing stores before expanding into new regions. Following its bold actions in the early 90s, IKEA has entered into a more conservative phase of consolidation, perhaps it has also learned that the price of being different means that you also have to be more careful about where you invest.

3.7 Unresolved issues: management and human resource development

From an American perspective Swedish managers don't show emotion in the work place, "praise is given for looking calm in all situations. They do not feel comfortable in conflictual situations. Also they tend not to set themselves apart, and self-promotion is frowned upon. They don't like drum beating, or cheer leading in a culture where both are common ways of motivating workers".

"The biggest conflicts stem from the Americans who need to know who's in charge. People expect their managers to tell them what to do here". However, at IKEA the manager's role is more subtle and they tend to have a long-term approach to management. "It takes longer but we want to train people to know how to do things the IKEA-Way". Since there are few written procedures, the golden rule for managers is helping people understand why things are done in a particular way. This can be taken for indecision by American employees new to IKEA who are more used to rules and procedures spelled out clearly and managers who take responsibility for quick decision making.

American employees perceive IKEA as being more employee oriented than average American employers. IKEA attracts and selects people who value security, job enrichment, and benefits, which are more generous than American typical employers (like five weeks of paid holiday) more than career advancement. However, with full employment in the U.S. it is becoming more difficult to find

6

candidates, particularly for management positions, who have the necessary job qualifications and whose values match IKEA's.

Although IKEA has recently initiated an American style performance review procedure, which requires documenting employee's individual performance strengths and weaknesses, Swedish managers feel uncomfortable with the formality of the system and the need to provide negative feedback. Since they hold the more senior positions their ambivalence has resulted in little real discrimination in pay increases which are directly linked to the reviews. Although turnover at IKEA is lower than the industry average, and co-workers generally appreciate IKEA's caring environment, there is some latent discontent with the way pay increases are distributed even among long term employees who feel that their individual achievements are not always rewarded.

In the opinion of one American manager "A lot of people have left IKEA because they can't move up fast enough here. Some left the store to go to the Service Center (IKEA's national headquarters) then left because it was too hard for them to adjust, there was no clear frame of reference-policies, procedures. We have lost some key American managers because they didn't have a clear idea of their role or future in the organization".

Acknowledging that there are not enough American managers in senior positions, IKEA is trying to attract management trainees through presentations at Business Schools. However its low keyed image and lack of structured career pathing is not easy to sell to "high potentials" more attuned to the packages offered by retailers such as Home Depot which forcefully promote rapid promotion and individualized pay incentives. There is a general consensus that IKEA needs to develop young American managers who can play a bigger role in the organization than at present. However there is no agreement yet on how critical the need is, nor on how to solve the problem.

Two differing views that could be overheard in a fictitious debate between two long term Ikeans illustrate the unresolved issues facing IKEA USA at the end of 1996:

The view of a young American manager:

"There is a glass ceiling here. I am at a level at which my growth will stop because I'm not Swedish. IKEA should be made less complicated for Americans, easier for us to adapt to, and develop in. Our management needs to be much more professional in managing human resources. We need to bring new people into the organization and reward individual accountability for results. This would lead to a better balance between the IKEA-Way and American management. Becoming a successful manager at IKEA requires a lot of time and effort to understand how everything fits together. Yet not everyone can go to Sweden or learn Swedish and today too many talented Americans choose to go to competition. Competition is catching up on us in terms of benefits, and with full employment we should be much more competitive than we are on the American job market".

The Swedish view:

"Being the underdog, not doing things the traditional way over here is vital to IKEA's success in the United States. We must keep a unique image and work better at getting our message across to employees and customers so that they understand why we are successful. Pride in being a part of IKEA must be built locally and since our system is unique this takes time. The real danger is assimilation. We are becoming too American. Giving people bonuses and pay incentives doesn't make them more intelligent; people are motivated by learning and improving in an organization that provides them room to grow. Rewards should be more on a give and take basis, when the company makes more it can give more, but we must remain flexible. Although we must seek balance between adapting and sticking to our proven ways we must protect our unique concepts and way of doing. This means that we will always need a strong Swedish presence in the US, they are our 'on site missionaries' who can develop loyalty to and understanding of our uniqueness".

6

IV CLOUDS ON THE HORIZON

By the mid 90s, in spite of its undisputed international success and expansion over the past 25 years, signs appeared that the pattern of growth and steady profit were slowing down. Costs were rising, complaints on quality were more frequent, and unaccustomed delays appeared in product delivery. External factors had changed from the early times in Europe. Economic growth slowed as baby boomers moved into middle age with new tastes and demands, and fewer new homes being sold. Competition had also learned from IKEA's pioneering distribution and were offering better furniture at lower prices, seeking low cost furniture suppliers in eastern Europe which put pressure on IKEA's unique sourcing.

IKEA had become a rather large international organization and in an effort to adapt to the requirements of its many domestic markets its product range had grown from 10,000 to 14,000 items thus weakening returns from long product runs and overburdening logistic supply lines, increasingly greater attention had to be given to bringing costs down, often through productivity gains which put unprecedented pressure on retail staffs to improve sales to staff ratios. During the years of rapid growth many recruits were bought in from outside the company, who were not steeped in IKEA culture. The company's extended network made it difficult to provide employees and mid-level managers with a clear perception of how their local business impacted on the corporation as a whole. Local initiatives were taken without regard to their impact on the whole system. Was this the price of diversity or was IKEA in many ways suffering from too much decentralization.

In 1993 to cope with this situation, Anders Moberg and IKEA's senior management launched a company wide operation "Nytt Läge" (New Situation) with task forces and project teams to suggest ways of improving communication and eliminating snags in distribution. Many suggestions were implemented, including creation of new regional divisions in Europe for closer co-ordination of country operations, and the hiring of more professionals at headquarters to provide guidelines and more efficient corporate control systems Although the "Nytt Läge" program met with a lot of enthusiasm and did achieve improvement in some areas, it soon became clear to Ingvar Kamprad that a more radical change in the organization was needed.

In early 1996 a major organizational change was introduced to "shorten the value chain" between customers and suppliers. Regional organizations were eliminated to bring stores in more direct contact with IKEA of Sweden. New emphasis was given to the importance of a living corporate culture based on the IKEA values of simplicity and self-discipline, rather than relying on formal policies and procedures. At the same time IKEA's expansion plans in Europe and the United States were delayed. The fear at corporate headquarters was that IKEA had drifted too far from the basic principles that were behind its legendary success.

4.1 Back to the roots
....

In May Ingvar Kamprad gathered IKEA's 250 worldwide store managers and senior managers at an important meeting in Poland to explain IKEA's need to re-focus and re-direct its efforts. He actually used the word "rejuvenate".

"Our product range and purchasing people often have an unequal battle with retailers and their far too many interests. Many of our suppliers got stuck in the middle. Our IKEA idea as one of the world's few production oriented companies is under threat.

Perhaps we were blinded by the boom years of the 80s, which increased geographical spread of our operations to new markets, both on retail and the trading side. Internal communication also became difficult, our administration expanded and our overheads became increasingly heavy. Our costs rose, and our customers and suppliers felt lost, many of them got in touch with me directly.

Decision-making took longer and longer, and endless discussions took place. It became more difficult to see the company as a whole. Far too much of our product development had too little to do with the tastes and wallets of the majority of people. Our product range expanded in every direction and could not be handled in a reasonable way on our sales floors. Our price advantage compared to competitors began to shrink.

Even IKEA's soul, our fine corporate culture, was in danger. Have we forgotten to explain to our new workers about the IKEA-Way? Have our desks removed us too far from reality? Have we lost our way?"

The managers who attended that meeting felt galvanized by their founder's strong message, and their confidence and belief in the IKEA-Way had been doubtlessly reinforced. In an increasingly complex world environment, simplicity indeed appeared to be a true virtue that had guided the company in the past. Several wondered as they left how Kamprad's intuitive ability to see through the complexity of a worldwide organization and re-ignite the dynamics of IKEA's success could be transmitted throughout the organization? Others wondered if they would have as much autonomy as they had previously enjoyed in adapting to very different markets? Some wondered if the company could regain its developmental thrust through the late 90s.

6

EXHIBIT 1

FACTS AND FIGURES
95/96
IKEA

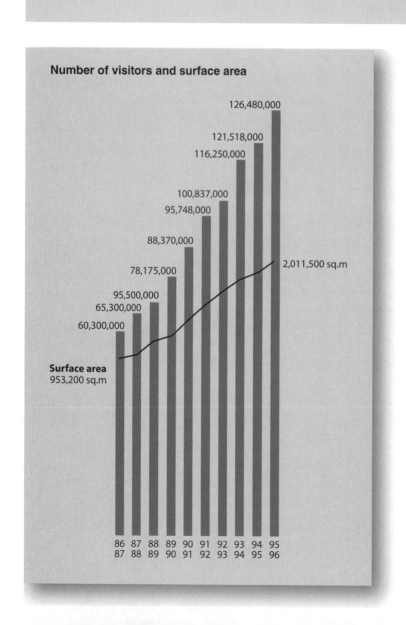

Number of visitors and surface area

126,480,000

121,518,000

116,250,000

100,837,000

95,748,000

88,370,000

78,175,000

95,500,000

65,300,000

60,300,000

2,011,500 sq.m

Surface area
953,200 sq.m

| 86 | 87 | 88 | 89 | 90 | 91 | 92 | 93 | 94 | 95 |
| 87 | 88 | 89 | 90 | 91 | 92 | 93 | 94 | 95 | 96 |

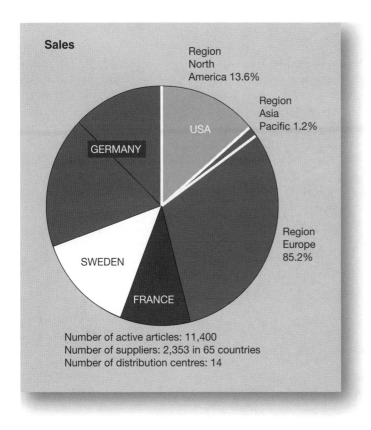

Sales

Region North America 13.6%

Region Asia Pacific 1.2%

USA

GERMANY

Region Europe 85.2%

SWEDEN

FRANCE

Number of active articles: 11,400
Number of suppliers: 2,353 in 65 countries
Number of distribution centres: 14

TABLE 1	The IKEA Expansion			
	Outlets	*Countries*	*Co-Workers*	*Turnover in NLG*****
1954	1	1	15	2,200,000
1964	2	2	250	55,500,000
1974	10	5	1,500	372,900,000
1984	66	17	8,300	2,678,700,000
1994	120 (125*)	25 (26*)	26,600**	8,350,000,000
1996	129 (136*)	27 (28*)	33,400**	9,626,000,000***

*Including stores opening after 1 September 1996 1 NLG=USD 0.603,SEK 3.99
**33,400 co-workers are equivalent to 26,400 full-time
***Corresponding to new sales of the IKEA Group of companies
****The holding company is in the Netherlands which explains the use of NLG

6

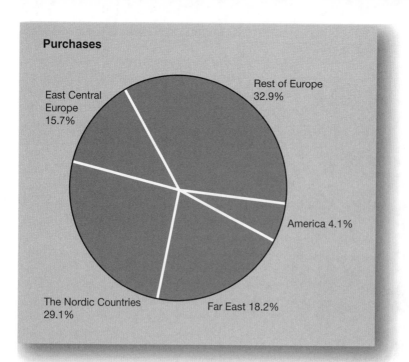

Purchases

Rest of Europe
32.9%

East Central
Europe
15.7%

America 4.1%

The Nordic Countries
29.1%

Far East 18.2%

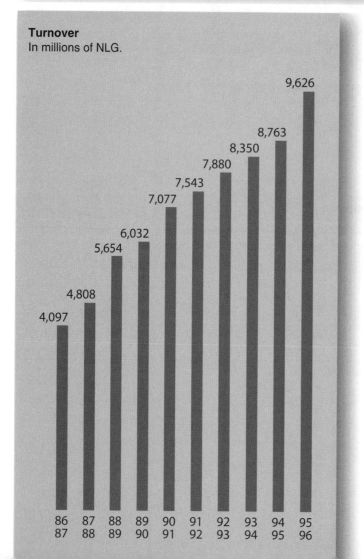

Turnover
In millions of NLG.

9,626

8,763

8,350

7,880

7,543

7,077

6,032

5,654

4,808

4,097

| 86 87 | 87 88 | 88 89 | 89 90 | 90 91 | 91 92 | 92 93 | 93 94 | 94 95 | 95 96 |

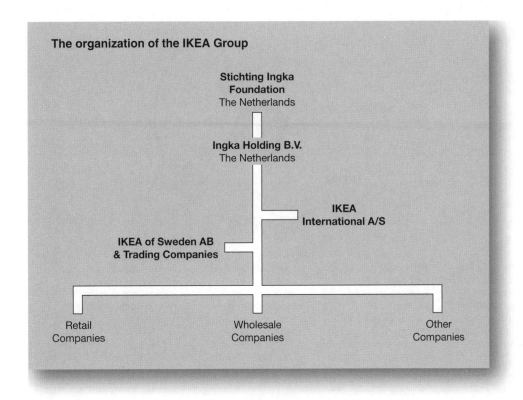

The organization of the IKEA Group

The operations of the IKEA Group are based on four basic functions; Product range, Trading, Wholesale and Retail. These functions develop, purchase, distribute and sell IKEA products via IKEA stores. The Management Services to the IKEA Group are provided by IKEA International A/S in Humlebaek, Denmark, managed by the President of the IKEA Group, Anders Moberg.

The functions Retail and Wholesale are regionally divided into three regions; Region North America, Region Europe and Region Asia Pacific.

The IKEA Group belongs to Stichiting Ingka Foundation in the Netherlands and its retail operations are based on the IKEA Concept, which is owned by Inter IKEA Systems B.V.

Inter IKEA Systems B.V. makes the IKEA Concept available to users within – as well as outside – the IKEA Group.

The IKEA functions

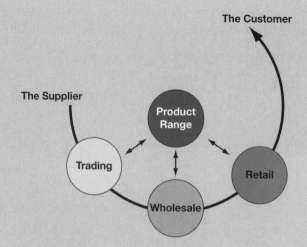

The Supplier → **Trading** ↔ **Product Range** ↔ **Retail** → **The Customer**

(Product Range ↕ Wholesale)

Trading has the overall responsibility for purchasing activities including product quality, service levels and delivery information.

Wholesale with its Commercial and Supply Support function (CSS) has the overall responsibility for all warehousing activities, the phasing in and out of products, delivery information and the transportation of goods.

The **Product Range** company IKEA of Sweden has the overall responsibility for the entire IKEA range and for its effectiveness and competitive strength on all IKEA markets. It also has the overall responsibility to ensure goods availability in the stores and warehouses.

Retail companies are responsible for marketing and sales on each local market.

Co-workers

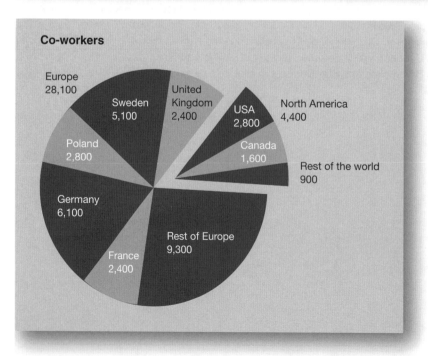

Europe 28,100

Sweden 5,100

United Kingdom 2,400

USA 2,800

North America 4,400

Poland 2,800

Canada 1,600

Rest of the world 900

Germany 6,100

Rest of Europe 9,300

France 2,400

TABLE 2	Outlets		

Year of first location and of major rebuild or relocation.

Gross area in sq.m. including adjacent warehouses.

Australia			
Sydney (Gordon)	1975	(78)	2,100
Sydney (Blacktown)	1981	(92)	5,700
Melbourne (Moorabbin)	1986		7,000
Perth**	1986		5,200
Brisbane (Springwood)	1987		7,800
Melbourne (Nunawading)	1989		5,800
Sydney (Moore Park)	1991		4,100
Austria			
Vienna	1977	(81)	26,200
Graz	1989		15,200
Linz (Haid)	1991		15,500
Belgium			
Brussels (Ternat)	1984		15,100
Brussels (Zaventem)	1984		12,100
Antwerp (Wilrijk)	1985		14,600
Liège (Hognoul)	1985		13,000
Canada			
Vancouver	1976	(93)	21,100
Toronto	1977	(95)	28,900
Edmonton	1978	(95)	12,400
Calgary	1979	(96)	9,300
Ottawa	1979	(94)	9,200
Montreal	1982	(86)	16,400
Toronto (Burlington)	1991		17,000
The Czech Republic			
Prague (Zlicin)	1991	(96)	21,800
Denmark			
Copenhagen (Tåstrup)	1969	(75)	37,000
Århus	1980		10,500
Odense	1985		1,400
Copenhagen (Gentofte)	1995		18,100
Finland			
Helsinki*(Esbo)	1996		17,800
Lyon	1982		18,800
France			
Paris (Evry)	1983	(94)	28,300
Marseille (Vitrolles)	1985		15,800
Paris-Nord	1986		24,900
Lille (Lomme)	1988		16,200

TABLE 2	*(continued)*		
Bordeaux	1990		14,200
Paris (Plaisir)	1992		20,600
Toulouse	1995		19,000
Paris (Villiers s. Mar)	1996		22,300
Germany			
Munich (Eching)	1974	(86)	25,300
Cologne (Godorf)	1975	(91)	23,000
Dorsten	1975	(93)	7,600
Hannover (Gossburgwedel)	1976		15,200
Bremen (Stuhr)	1976		13,200
Frankfurt (Wallau)	1977	(85)	25,900
Dortmund (Kamen)	1978		17,900
Stuttgart	1978		5,500
Berlin (Spandau)	1979	(81)	22,000
Düsseldorf (Kaarst)	1979	(93)	19,900
Kassel	1980	(94)	19,400
Fürth	1981	(91)	20,400
Saarbrücken (Schwalbach-Bous)	1981	(92)	10,400
Freiburg	1981		7,400
Heidelberg (Walldorf)	1981		20,300
Hamburg (Schnelsen)	1989		24,000
Leipzig	1992	(94)	20,500
Chemnitz	1992	(94)	20,500
Essen	1993		23,500
Berlin (Waltersdorf)	1993		26,000
Braunschweig	1993		19,400
Bielefeld	1996		19,400
Frankfurt* (Hanau)	1997		22,000
Hong Kong			
Shatin**	1987		2,800
Tsuen Wan**	1992		1,500
Causeway Bay**	1993		3,700
Kowloon**	1995		5,800
Hungary			
Budapest	1990		12,600
Iceland			
Reykjavik**	1981	(94)	9,200
Italy			
Milan (Cinisello Balsamo)	1989		11,900
Turin	1990		14,600
Milan (Corsico)	1992		21,300
Brescia	1992		12,700

6

TABLE 2	*(continued)*		
Bologna* (Casalecchio)	1997		18,300
Kuwait			
Kuwait City**	1984	(95)	10,000
Malaysia			
Kuala Lumpur**	1996		12,400
The Netherlands			
Rotterdam (Sliedrecht)	1979		14,600
Amsterdam	1982	(85)	23,300
Duiven	1983		10,900
Eindhoven	1992		13,200
Delft**	1992		19,500
Heerlen	1994		9,300
Utrecht	1996		17,300
Norway			
Oslo (Slependen)	1963	(95)	20,200
Bergen	1984		10,700
Stavanger (Forus)	1988		14,200
Poland			
Warsaw	1990		3,200
Poznan	(92)		6,600
Gdansk	1991		3,700
Warsaw (Janki)	(94)		13,600
Wroclaw*	1993		11,700
Saudi-Arabia			
Jeddah**	1983	(85)	17,300
Riyadh**	1993		16,600
Singapore			
Singapore**	1978	(95)	21,900
Slovakia			
Bratislava	1992	(95)	9,100
Spain			
Las Palmas (Gran Canaria)**	1980	(92)	6,900
Santa Cruz (Tenerife)**	1983	(91)	6,600
Palma (Mallorca)**	1992		7,500
Barcelona	1996		22,100
Madrid* (Alcocorn)	1996		20,500
Sweden			
Älmhult	1958		23,400
Stockholm (Skärholmen)	1965		45,800
Sundsvall	1966		13,000
Malmö	1967	(77)	22,600
Gothenburg (Kallered)	1972		26,600

TABLE 2	*(continued)*		
Linköping	1977		18,200
Jönköping	1981	(90)	7,500
Gävle	1981	(92)	12,600
Helsingborg	1982	(92)	13,500
Orebro	1982	(91)	13,100
Uppsala	1982	(86)	13,500
Västeras	1984		12,600
Stockholm (Järfälla)	1993		27,100
Switzerland			
Zürich (Spreitenbach)	1973	(90)	28,300
Lausanne (Aubonne)	1979	(93)	19,300
Lugano	1991		10,400
Zürich (Dietlikon)	1992		7,500
Bern* (Kirchberg)	1996		17,400
Taiwan			
Taiper*	1994		3,000
United Arab Emirates			
Dubai**	1991	(95)	11,300
United Kingdom			
Manchester (Warrington)	1987		19,100
London (Brent Park)	1988		23,500
Birmingham	1991		17,600
Newcastle	1992		15,800
London (Croydon)	1992		22,000
Leads	1995		16,600
London III* (Thurrock)	1996		19,300
USA			
Philadelphia	1985	(90)	15,500
Washington (Woodbridge)	1986		14,800
Baltimore	1988		19,400
Pittsburg	1989	(94)	15,600
New Jersey (Elizabeth)	1990		24,900
Los Angeles (Burbank)	1990		22,100
New York (Long Island)	1991		21,000
Los Angeles (Fontana)	1992		14,200
Los Angeles (Tustin)	1992		13,500
Los Angeles (City of Industry)	1992		13,200
Houston	1992		14,400
Los Angeles (Carson)	1992		19,600
Seattle**	1994		13,800

*Has been or will be inaugurated after 01.09.96 and is not included in total figures
**Outlets outside the IKEA Group
© Inter IKEA Systems B.V. 1996

EXHIBIT 2

Design for everyone

Swedish and Scandinavian design have been world-famous since the start of this century. The Swedish model has also become synonymous with a high usage value, fine function and quality together with large-scale availability.

IKEA PS is a supplement to the standard IKEA range which seeks to underline this. A reminder of the quality of present-day modern Swedish furniture design and the fact that high-quality furniture with the correct shape and function need not necessarily be equated with high prices.

In the 1990s, we have new standards and requirements. A greater need for lasting quality and function. A resource efficient and discriminating design. Concern for the environment and for people and, not least, availability. All these are criteria which people in Sweden and the Nordic area carry with them by tradition.

IKEA PS is based on the ethos of simplicity which was defined back in the middle of the 19th century and was known for many years as Swedish Modern.

The PS collection encompasses the best of contemporary Swedish design, produced exclusively for IKEA. It includes everything from shelving and sofas to lamps and porcelain. Modern basic products for a modern home.

The products included in IKEA PS have been selected, and will continue to be, on the basis of the way we live at present. Which new needs and habits do we have? Which needs will we have in the future?

IKEA PS offers rational solutions. The first PS collections with a total of some 40 products, is the result of a collective partnership between 19 different Swedish designers working in the spirit of Swedish modernism.

Everyday furniture that functions. Resource-efficient products. Good living.

The forest – the backbone of Nordic design

The Nordic countryside is characterised by forest. Half Europe's coniferous forests (excepting the European part of Russia) grow in Sweden, Finland and Norway.

The Nordic belt of coniferous forest, which circles the globe on a line of latitude about 50 degrees north, is also the world's most valuable forest resource.

The timber from pine trees, which is usually known as softwood, is straight, strong and light in weight. It is therefore ideal as building timber

By taking good care of their forests. Nordic forest owners have doubled their stocks of timber during this century. Of an estimated annual growth of some 100 million cubic metres of forest, around 70 million are cut.

The Nordic forests are not simply of great financial significance – they are also important for outdoor life.

This close contact with nature – and respect for it – typifies Nordic culture. Nordic designers work in a resource-efficient manner, in harmony with nature.

"It's a question of life – life in our homes"

History of Nordic Design: From the Late 1800s to the Late 1900s

The first issue of Home was published in Sweden in 1859. Several women with ideas of their own had taken the initiative. The magazine's orientation and contents were in keeping with the times. During the latter part of the 19th century, a large number of energetic middle-class women began to take an interest in home furnishing and design.

EXHIBIT 2 *(Continued)*

One of the female debaters expressed herself as follows, "You should be on your guard against magnificent wallpaper. It puts the furniture in the room to shame and, if it is not especially tasteful, it gives the entire room a vulgar appearance." Nor was she overly taken with what was known at that time as illusionist painting. "Imitations of oak, birch, walnut and so on should be rejected out of hand. Nothing benefits from being seen to be something it is not" ... "Imitations of every type are an example of false taste." She advocated sober, refined and discriminating furniture. In her opinion children should have the largest, sunniest room in the house for "children, like flowers, do not thrive without the sun". So, at this early stage, the ethos of purity and simplicity was formulated.

The women who were involved in the Friends of Textile Art Association were the driving force in the debate on taste which took place at that time. Similar initiatives were taken in other Nordic countries. One of the tasks was to save the popular textile riches of the countryside by using the techniques and patterns to suit the needs of townsfolk. The stripes on ticking were transferred to striped woolen curtains and Flemish tapestry to the covers of cushions and pillows. The long-pile covers, which previously provided protection from cold nights both outdoors and in fishing boats, were now laid as rugs on the floor. The runic characters from Viking times inspired patterns on damask or embroidered tablecloths and serviettes. It was a question of rescuing old techniques, dyeing methods, materials and patterns from obscurity.

Beauty for everyone

Interest in the aesthetic aspects of the home became what could almost be described as a popular movement in Sweden, closely associated with the local handicraft associations which developed around the turn of the century. Young architects gave advice on interior design and produced drawings of buildings and furniture. Even the working class should be able to purchase furniture which was light, beautiful, comfortable, hygienic and easy to care for. Unlike the rest of Europe, the aesthetic debate in the Nordic countries was part of the democratisation process.

The home environment and beauty was supposed to help people, according to the writer, lecturer and debater Ellen Key in her book Beauty for Everyone. The principal role model was Carl and Karin Larsson's home in Sundborn – a vibrant environment which was ideal for children, with rooms in bright colours, a charming mixture of furniture old and new and Karin's own textiles. Aesthetics which were in no way connected with the "dusty" drawing-rooms of the 19th century. Young artists and architects made the new living ideal a reality. It was naturally influenced by the English Arts and Crafts movement, but transformed to suit Swedish conditions. A little lighter, more colourful, more popular, more childish in appeal, more simple and more rustic in inspiration than in England. Many painters chose to design furniture, dinner services, glass, metal objects, patterns and fabrics – and not simply paint and sculpt.

The approach to the homes, developed by the artistically talented designers and architects around the turn of the century, has since influenced Swedish interior design.

Life at the turn of the century was just as aesthetically vital in Finland. In 1893, a furniture and ceramic factory, the Iris Factory, opened in Borga. Its furniture and pottery made an important contribution to Finland's international success. As did innovative long-pile rugs and the interior design and architecture of Eliel Saarinen, Armas Lindgren and Herman Gesellius. Pictorial art, handicrafts and architecture entered into a new form of symbiosis. In these families' joint home and studio, the large Karelian magnificent and weighty living-room had been partially recreated. Tarred logs and grey granite on the outside, benches attached to the walls and a gigantic fireplace inside.

EXHIBIT 2 *(Continued)*

The aesthetic characters of the Nordic countries were already clearly defined. Sweden's love of air, sunlight and a light, airy, preferably classicistic – but soft – language of design. Finland's weight, power and gloomily ardent colourfulness. In Sweden and Finland, people researched, introspectively, their own history to find a genuine domestic style. The seafaring country Denmark was more extrovert and was inspired by both classical Greek and English furniture culture. A feeling for proportion and precision could already be seen in Danish middle-class interior design at the start of the 19th century, in the peaceful, refined, neo-classical rooms of the so-called golden age.

Artists and architects to industry

In 1914, the Swedish Society for Industrial Design opened an agency with the aim of encouraging as many furniture and household goods industries as possible to co-operate with artists/designers. The next stage was the permanent employment of artists in Sweden industry, at glassworks and porcelain factories. Typification, standardisation and efficient industrial production would make these goods less expensive and thus accessible to more people.

The Home Exhibition at Liljevalchs in 1917 was an attempt to produce better furniture and household goods and more effective heating in working-class homes. The architects Gunnar Asplund and Uno Ahren and the furniture designer Carl Malmsten presented their work for the first time at this exhibition.

Internationally, the group – and first and foremost the glass designers – made a breakthrough at the Paris Exhibition. Exposition des Arts Décoratifs Modernes, in 1925. Italian classicism with its austere decoration, pillars, symmetry and clear-cut spatiality had been merged to produce something which visitors interpreted as typically Swedish. The English architect Philip Morton Shand called the exhibition "Swedish Grace" and he thereby coined a slogan with real impact. Sweden was invited to the Metropolitan Museum in New York and this started a number of successful exhibitions in the USA and England.

However, for the Swedish Society for Industrial Design, responsible for the Swedish pavilion, the Paris Exhibition led to a period of soul-searching. The young Swedish architects and participants had been more impressed by Le Corbusier's house. L'Esprit Nouveau. Design should be freed from decoration and should appear in all its simplicity. Air, light and greenery were the order of the day. At the Stockholm Exhibition in 1930, they were given the chance to realise their ideal. The lightweight structures and light interiors were a perfect match for Swedish aesthetics.

Danish furniture makers

Paris in 1925 also saw the introduction of the Danish architect Kaj Fisher's tightly sealed cubic pavilion, illuminated on the inside by Poul Henningsen's flowerbell-like glass lighting. With an impressive feeling for and understanding of the properties of light, Poul Henningsen had succeeded in creating non-dazzle lighting. He used the same principle over the following decades to create a wide range of lighting, which was adapted to match new sources of light. The famous PH lamp, with its coloured, reflecting shades, produces a non-dazzle, warm and pleasant light.

The 1920s and 1930s represented a renaissance for Danish interior design. Kaare Klint encouraged his students at the Academy of Art to study the proportions of furniture in great depth. Ole Wanscher studied the furniture design of past epochs. His research produced findings which other furniture designers could utilize. In one of his books, Hans J Wegner found the Chinese chair which inspired him to create a number of variations, the first of which was the China Chair from 1944. The model from 1949, the Round Chair, was known as The Chair – the archetypal chair – the purest representation of a chair.

EXHIBIT 2   *(Continued)*

The reason for the upswing experienced by Danish furniture was the Copenhagen Furniture Makers, who held the first of their annual furniture shows in 1927. The idea was that architects and furniture makers should work together. Genius, new concepts and creativity would be combined with craftsmanlike skills and material expertise.

The combination would stimulate development.

Functionalism becomes softer

At the end of the 1920s, the Finnish architect Alvar Aalto, together with factory-owner Otto Korhonen at Abo Joinery, had started to experiment with compression-moulded cross laid veneer in chair seats. From 1932, Aalto also designed furniture for the sanatorium in Pemar which was light, hygienic and inexpensive. This was followed by some of his best known models in layer-glued veneer with bentwood underframes, including the famous Pemar chair.

In 1935, Artek was set up to help Abo Joinery with exports. Until then, language problems had delayed the international launch. However, success was soon a fact. In New York in 1939, Alvar Aalto's exhibit, a 7-metre high and 40-metre long, gently flowing wall of wood, was greatly admired. Aalto also achieved success as a glass designer during the 1930s. In 1932, he designed the "Riihimaki's flower" set of glass, followed by the "Eskimos' leather trousers" in 1936, which was later re-worked to become the successful Savoy vase. Using the wood-bending technique and compression moulding, Alvar Aalto created a gently flowing language of design in both wood and glass.

Sweden during the 1930s witnessed a battle between the orthodox functionalists, devoted to the international, industrial and innovative language of design, and the more traditional architects and furniture designers. Carl Malmsten belonged to the latter group, popularly known as the traditionalists. Back in the 1910s, he had become famous for his rustic-inspired and handicraft-oriented interpretations of Swedish tradition.

Malmsten was unable to accept the functionalists' view of things "as silent servants". He felt furniture should have a character, express feelings, be masculine or feminine (just like the approach during the 19th century). The universal, standardized and typified went against the laws of nature.

Bruno Mathsson, on the other hand, was a modernist and, in 1934, he produced his first working chair in laminated, compression-moulded wood. Although it was influenced by German tubular steel furniture, it felt far softer and inviting as a result of the natural material. From just a few parts and a minimum of wood. Bruno Mathsson succeeded in creating a stable furniture skeleton, which was combined with woven saddle-girth upholstery.

The violent debate soon resulted in a modification of the strictly innovative functionalism. The language of design became rounder and more inviting. The rectangular innovativeness of the Bauhaus school with its underframe of chrome-plated tubular steel was regarded by many people as cold and technocratic. The gently flowing wooden furniture which Alvar Aalto and Bruno Mathsson designed created warmer and "more human" interiors.

The virtually textile-free interiors of the Stockholm Exhibition could not be said to be deeply-rooted in Swedish living traditions and, during the 1930s and 1940s, a wide range of new, patterned – often flowery – home furnishing fabrics was introduced. At the textile department at the NK department store, a young talent, the textile designer Astrid Sampe, had taken over the rudder. Swedish interior design was a success at the World Exhibition in Paris in 1937, followed by New York in 1939. The new style became known as Swedish Modern. However, the objective was the same as before, to make the everyday lives and homes of ordinary people more beautiful.

6

| **EXHIBIT 2** | *(Continued)* |

A time of crisis – necessity is the mother of invention

Sweden's neighbours were hard hit by the Second World War. The shortage of wool and cotton led people in Finland to start experimenting with paper textiles. Wallpaper was made from birch bark and greaseproof paper. Carpets were woven from materials like straw and paper-twine. Roots, birch bark and other fibres were used for drapery. Iron-rich, domestic sand produced green melted glass. The Danish silver company Georg Jensen went over to stainless steel when it no longer had access to silver. The shortage was not just a disadvantage, it was a spur to creativity.

Despite, or as a result of, the war, people in Sweden continued to take an interest in accommodation; how minimal apartment space could best be utilised using functional furniture, duplicate usage and ingenious solutions. More and more young people were getting married and, at the beginning of the 1940s, more children than ever were born. In Finland, the accommodation situation was even worse. The population of Karelia had been forced to flee. Young families needed apartments and furniture.

Towards the end of the war, in 1944, the Danes also began to study the way well-planned furniture could make things easier in cramped living conditions. The challenge of using a minimum of resources to achieve the optimum solution became a model which a number of Nordic designers continued to use after the war.

Scandinavian Design became an accepted term

In 1945, Arabia employed the furniture designer Kaj Franck. His task was to produce services. Even though he had never sat at a potter's wheel, the choice was a successful one. His Kilta service was introduced in 1953 and became a success. In design terms, it was inspired by the bowls and basins Franck had seen as a child and by the geometrical language of design of functionalism. However, Kaj Franck was not a formalist for the sake of form. He thought in a practical space-saving manner and therefore chose to focus on the ability to stack and combine. It was a question of facilitating everyday life for ordinary people.

After the war, there was an almost irrepressible urge in Denmark, Finland and Norway to manifest their individual creative power. As a result, the art industry and furniture design thrived. Design was going to serve democracy. Home comfort became a symbol of a healthy, happy society. In Stockholm, Elias Svedberg, with his colleagues Erik Wørtz and Lena Larsson, had created a new furniture series called Triva in 1944. It was the first which had consciously been made for quick assembly. The idea was to facilitate freight and reduce transport and storage costs.

The major Triennial Exhibitions in Milan, at which the post-war aim of creating a better and more beautiful world was expressed, played an important part in the international success of Nordic design. These manifestations gave a large group of Nordic designers, architects and artists the opportunity to develop their professionalism and versatility. Many of them expressed an "exotic scent" of Nordic nature and a modern, organically flowing or unadorned and simple language of design.

This group of designers comprised a large number of Swedish glass artists, textile and porcelain designers, as well as several Nordic furniture designers, like Carl-Axel Acking, Elias Svedberg, Nisse Strinning, Hans Wegner, Finn Juhl, Verner Panton, Poul Kjaerholm and Arne Jacobsen. Jacobsen's Myran chair from 1952, with its compression-moulded, double-bent seat of cross-laid veneer, became one of the world's most successful designs ever. The versatile artistic giants included Tapio Wirkkala and Timo Sarpaneva, while Erik Herlow's, Åke H Huldt's and Antti Nurmesniemi's exhibition architecture created an elegant and witty setting for what eventually became known as Scandinavian Design.

6

EXHIBIT 2   *(Continued)*

In the US, the Lunning Award, only given to young Nordic designers, helped to spread an awareness of Scandinavian design. The Danish furniture manufacturers were most skilful at taking advantage of the fine publicity and ran joint export operations. Danish teak furniture became well-known. Swedish glassworks launched themselves successfully in the US under the name "Swedish Crystal".

The H55 Exhibition in Helsingborg represented the culmination of Scandinavian Design and the minimalistically elegant style with its vital contours and functionally well planned form was associated with this slogan. H55 was an international but first and foremost Nordic manifestation of the art of interior design and housing architecture, new techniques and new materials, new products and new concepts like self-service restaurants, tray lunches, school canteens and driving schools for children.

Patterned and dyed fabrics for the linen cupboard were on display. New household goods materials like plastic, new ceramics, stainless steel and combined furniture and ingenious storage systems, of which Nisse Strinning's string shelves became the most famous. In Sweden, the Swedish Society for industrial Design's systematic studies of furniture functions, dimensions, area and design had led to a wide range of practical and functional furniture. New building methods involving the use of lightweight concrete. Siporex®, enamelled metal, iron and new housing concepts were presented. In the family room, the entire family got together to play, eat and pursue their hobbies. There was a tremendous belief in the future. Technology was man's ally and a means of making "good" design less expensive and thereby available to more people.

Freedom of choice

The economy developed rapidly during the post-war years. The need for mini-areas, the minimization of material consumption, the optimisation of functions and economising on resources, which had characterised people's lives until now, was less pressing. Desire was instead aroused.

Instead of meticulously planned rooms, interior design should now express flexibility and change. Television brought world events into the home and the TV set made the sitting room the place where the family gathered and not, as before, the best room from which the children were normally banned. The furniture was also affected. Washable upholstery for seating was needed. Coffee tables which could withstand coffee stains and soft drinks. People wanted to sit, perhaps even recline, in comfort in front of the TV set. Tables and chairs were given wheels to make them easy to move. And a number of young Swedish furniture designers put a loose cover and upholstery on their Multomanen sofa. Two of them, Johan Huldt and Jan Dranger, started the company known as Innovator, which specialised in furniture for young people made of shaped steel tubing, particleboard and loose cushions, covered in canvas or corduroy. Other furniture designers experimented with collapsible corrugated cardboard furniture, inexpensive, simple particleboard systems and lamps that could be raised and lowered, modified and extended.

The "grey" 1940s and somewhat more colourful yet still sober 1950s had aroused a longing for colour. The textile designers were inspired by pop and spontanesous art. Playful, large-scale, colourful patterns were produced by Finnish Marimekko and Swedish Boras Wafveri with Sven Fristedt and Inez Svensson as the designers.

The tactile properties of material

After the turbulent 1960s and early 1970s, the Nordic design world ran out of steam. The "undesigned" pine furniture and basic furniture launched may have been morally unimpeachable, but aesthetically uninteresting.

EXHIBIT 2   *(Continued)*

However, something happened at the beginning of the 1980s. A number of furniture designers in Finland, whose work was unadorned, minimalistic and bright, emerged. It was as though functionalism had returned, but in a more comfortable and undisciplined form.

The new furniture designers who now stuck their necks out were certainly undisciplined. The balance chairs for more ergonomic seating which were designed in Norway looked like nothing that had ever been seen before. The same applied to the geometrically designed chairs interior designer Jonas Bohlin presented as his degree project in 1981. A cut off triangle, an extended rectangle were joined together using a bent steel tube; a mathematical equation had been given a form – and in concrete and rusty iron. Bohlin demonstrated that design is also a language – a language of design. His pieces of furniture were concepts which were transformed into figures. Jonas Bohlin's highly original approach to things inspired others with courage.

In recent years, a new, young generation of designers has appeared. Many of them consciously continue to work in true Scandinavian spirit using light materials and bright colours, often in limited space and multifunctional in character. Sometimes their work has been cheeky and insistently post modernistic, sometimes unobtrusive and sensual.

Nature – forest, sky, water, countryside – is a constant source of inspiration when it comes to both the choice of materials and the colour scheme. What distinguishes Nordic design from that of other countries perhaps most markedly is the tactile properties of materials and the way they are experienced in rooms. The way something feels is just as important as the way it looks. It is a question of life – life in our homes.

Kerstin Wickman

CASE STUDY 7

KNOWLEDGE MANAGEMENT AT CAP GEMINI ERNST & YOUNG

> "When Cap Gemini purchased Ernst & Young, knowledge management was strategic. Not only for the business but also for the merger's success"
>
> Alberto Almansa,
> Chief Knowledge Officer – Southern Europe

It was coming up to Cap Gemini Ernst & Young's (CGEY) second 'wedding anniversary'. Since May 23, 2000, when Cap Gemini (CG) purchased Ernst & Young's (E&Y) consulting unit, events had followed at considerable speed and intensity. The birth of CGE&Y was the result of the merger of the Cap Gemini Group of companies (Cap Gemini and Gemini Consulting) with E&Y Consulting. Alberto Almansa, CGE&Y's Chief Knowledge Officer (CKO) for Southern Europe, recalled how CGE&Y had become a global operator, and the challenges and hard work the merger had entailed.

Mr. Almansa was going to the CGE&Y headquarters in Paris. He was to head an important meeting at which the KM & IT Chief would be asking for his advice regarding the path knowledge management (KM) should follow at CGE&Y. While waiting for the plane in Barcelona airport, he remembered how experts were sceptical about the merger at the very beginning. Their arguments were based on geographical and therefore cultural differences. He also remembered how experts had changed their minds about the merger, after the 2000 results were presented, to decide that they were the perfect match. However difficult the merger had seemed

This case was prepared by Emma Lara, Research Assistant and Professors Rafael Andreu and Sandra Sieber, as the basis for class discussion rather than to illustrate either effective or ineffective handling of an administrative situation. June 2004.

Copyright © 2004, IESE. To order copies or request permission to reproduce materials, call IESE PUBLISHING 34 932 534 200, send a fax to 34 932 534 343, or write Juan de Alós, 43 – 08034 Barcelona, Spain, or iesep@iesep.com

No part of this publication may be reproduced, stored in a retrieval system, used in a spreadsheet, or transmitted in any form or by any means – electronic, mechanical, photocopying, recording, or otherwise – without the permission of IESE.

To use this case in class, please get your copies at www.IESEP.com.

at the beginning, the financial data supported all the adjustments that had been made up to the year 2001. However, there was no room for complacency in the recent economic slowdown that had seriously affected the technology industries. News of changes in other consultancy firms included restructuring plans to cut costs (with layoffs and other initiatives) to compensate for lost business. CGE&Y had to face up to the tough environment while it was still immersed in the process of integration.

Pondering the year ahead and the still-to-be-completed integration, Mr. Almansa was considering how the adjustments already made would fit with the company and its environment. He was specifically concerned about the services provided by the Center for Business Knowledge (CBK), owned by Ernst & Young LLP (what remained of E&Y after the merger), under a contract that expired in March 2002. They would have to decide whether to renew it or whether they could do without it. There was a decision to be made and a date to be fixed. Mr. Almansa's thoughts were interrupted by the announcement that his plane was delayed. He took a seat, opened his laptop and considered, for the last time, all the arguments that would lead to a final resolution.

THE BACKGROUND OF THE COMPANIES

Cap Gemini
··················

With an economics degree, tired of a series of jobs he had been working through, and frustrated with Groupe Bull, a French computer company, Serge Kampf thought 1967 was the right moment, and Grenoble, his hometown, the right place to found Sogeti, a software company orientated towards information technology (IT) support. Three years later, success led to a branch being opened in Paris. In 1973 the company's focus was redefined, encompassing consultancy, software and technical assistance as well as the original data processing services.

In 1975 Sogeti merged with C.A.P. (Computerized Applications Programming) and Gemini, both French companies that provided software services. The resulting company was Cap Gemini Sogeti. At first it operated as a freelance programming organization offering help to computer users. In 1978, it created a team of consultants in the US. That triggered a series of acquisitions that ended with the formation of Cap Gemini America in 1981. Meanwhile, in France, the parent company was a leading firm in information technology services.

During the 1980s and 90s, a series of basically European and American acquisitions and partnerships were undertaken in response to the new strategy: to become a global operator. In 1991 Kampf, the company's founder, sold 34 per cent of Cap Gemini Sogeti to Daimler-Benz to fulfil its international expansion plans. Rapid expansion was followed by decentralization, causing imbalances in the sharing of business and expertise. Facing its first losses in 1993, the company initiated a restructuring program that put both business areas and product lines in order. The program experienced its first positive results in 1995, when profitability returned. Completion of the reorganization process came later, in 1996, when the holding company Cap Gemini (CG) was created and its corporate headquarters were moved to Paris.

By the time of the merger, CG offered IT services through its 39,626 employees in 20 countries. These services were organized in the following three core business areas:

- Management and strategy consulting, through Gemini Consulting

- IT consulting and systems integration

- Application management, infrastructure management and business process outsourcing (BPO).

7

EXHIBIT 1   Operating revenues by geographical area

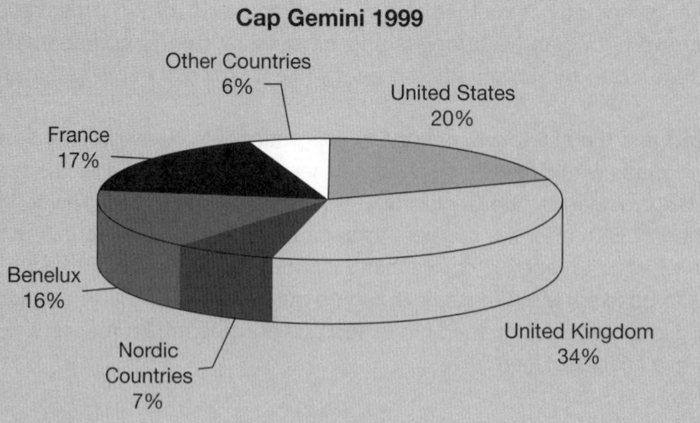

Cap Gemini 1999

Other Countries 6%
United States 20%
France 17%
Benelux 16%
Nordic Countries 7%
United Kingdom 34%

Source: *Cap Gemini 1999 Financial Report.*

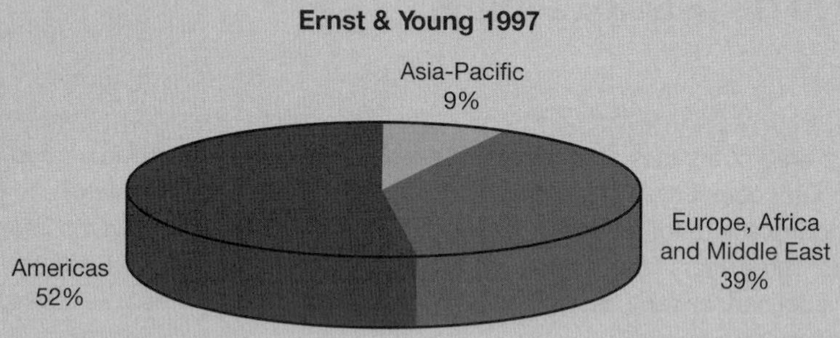

Ernst & Young 1997

Asia-Pacific 9%
Europe, Africa and Middle East 39%
Americas 52%

Source: *Cap Gemini Ernst & Young.*

The company closed the 1999 fiscal year with €7.674 billion of revenue distributed across six regions, of which Europe was traditionally its strongest area (**Exhibit 1**) generating more than 80 per cent of total business. Cap Gemini was publicly traded on the Paris Bourse.

Ernst & Young

The origins of E&Y go back to 1989, with the merger of Ernst & Whinney and Arthur Young. However, the real roots of the company can be found in the nineteenth century. In 1849 Frederick Whinney started working at Harding & Pullein, a British company constituted after the hat-making company R. P. Harding ceased trading. His books were so clear it was recommended that he remain in the accountancy business, a growing industry at that time.

In 1859 he became a partner, and by 1894 his sons took on part of the business, which was then named Whinney, Smith & Whinney (WS&W). At about the same time, in 1903, but on the other side of the Atlantic, in Cleveland, the brothers Alwin and Theodore Ernst founded Ernst & Ernst. After the Second World War the companies formed an alliance agreement, each working in their own countries but representing the alliance. In 1965 Whinney merged with Brown, Fleming & Murray becoming Whinney & Murray. In 1979, two British companies, Whinney & Murray and Turquands Barton Mayhew merged with the American company Ernst & Ernst, to become Ernst & Whinney.

Ernst & Whinney finally became Ernst & Young (E&Y) in 1989 after merging with Arthur Young, founded in Kansas City in 1895 by a Scot. These two consultancy firms merged in accordance with the integration movements that were taking place at the time between the main companies in the auditing, consultancy and accountancy industries as a result of increasing competition.

E&Y was one of the 'Big 5' consulting firms. Like the others, it was owned by a partnership. It had an international presence in 130 countries, 77,000 workers and revenue for 1999 had been $12.3 billion. Prior to the merger it worked in Auditing, Legal and Tax Advice, Consulting and Corporate Finance. Although most of its revenues came from the Tax and Audit divisions, the Consulting branch was interesting for the geographical composition of its revenue sources, as 65 per cent came from North America and 7 per cent from Germany, Switzerland and Austria (**Exhibit 1**).

Cap Gemini Ernst & Young

On May 23, 2000, CG acquired the E&Y consulting unit, to become a global IT and management consultancy player (**Exhibit 2**). The E&Y Consulting business had had 1999 revenues of around €3.5 billion. CG issued 42.7 million new shares to E&Y partners and paid €375 million in cash. The resulting company was renamed Cap Gemini Ernst & Young (CGE&Y) and also included Gemini Consulting, a Cap Gemini Group Company (**Exhibit 3a**). The E&Y acquisition not only helped CG to consolidate geographically (**Exhibit 4**), operating in 31 countries now organized in eight geographical regions, but it also provided access to complementary industries, sectors and clients. After the purchase, CGE&Y employed 57,000 people (18,000 from E&Y). In 2000, CGE&Y revenues were €8.4 billion.

CGE&Y helped its clients find their way through the whole value chain, from strategy design to implementation. Its range of service lines was organized in the following three core business areas:

■ Strategy Consulting

■ Business Solutions and Systems Transformation

■ Information Systems Management – via outsourcing contracts

The first area was focused on business strategy, operations, and information management and people, helping companies make the best decisions on how to build strategies and allocate resources. The Business Solutions and Systems Transformation area concentrated on business process consulting and the development of customized software and hardware and system-integration projects. The last area included information systems management to supervise the clients' day-to-day operations.

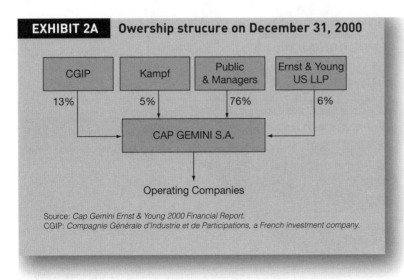

EXHIBIT 2A   **Owership strucure on December 31, 2000**

Source: *Cap Gemini Ernst & Young 2000 Financial Report.*
CGIP: *Compagnie Générale d'Industrie et de Participations, a French investment company.*

7

EXHIBIT 2B   **Stock performance**

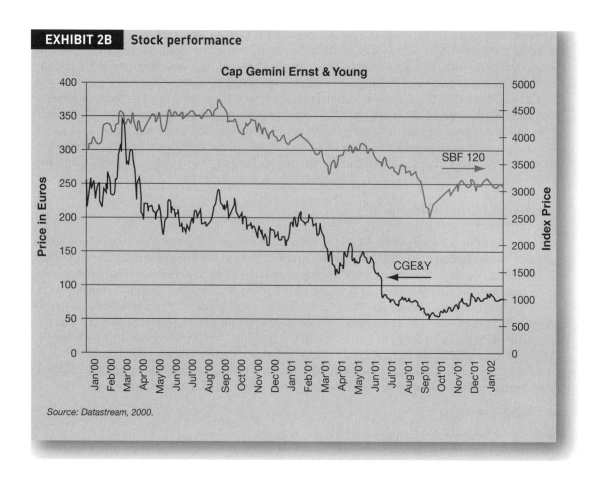

Cap Gemini Ernst & Young

Source: Datastream, 2000.

EXHIBIT 3A   **Cap Gemini Ernst & Young, merger**

23 May 2000. The birth of CGE&Y

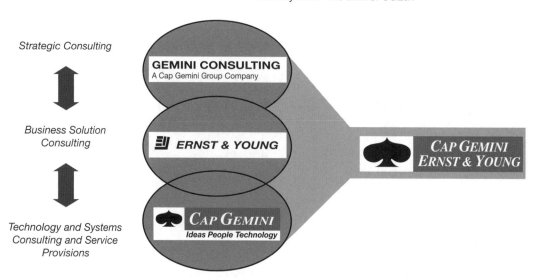

Strategic Consulting

Business Solution Consulting

Technology and Systems Consulting and Service Provisions

Source: Cap Gemini Ernst & Young.

7

EXHIBIT 3B **Cap Gemini Ernst & Young: vertical industries and services**

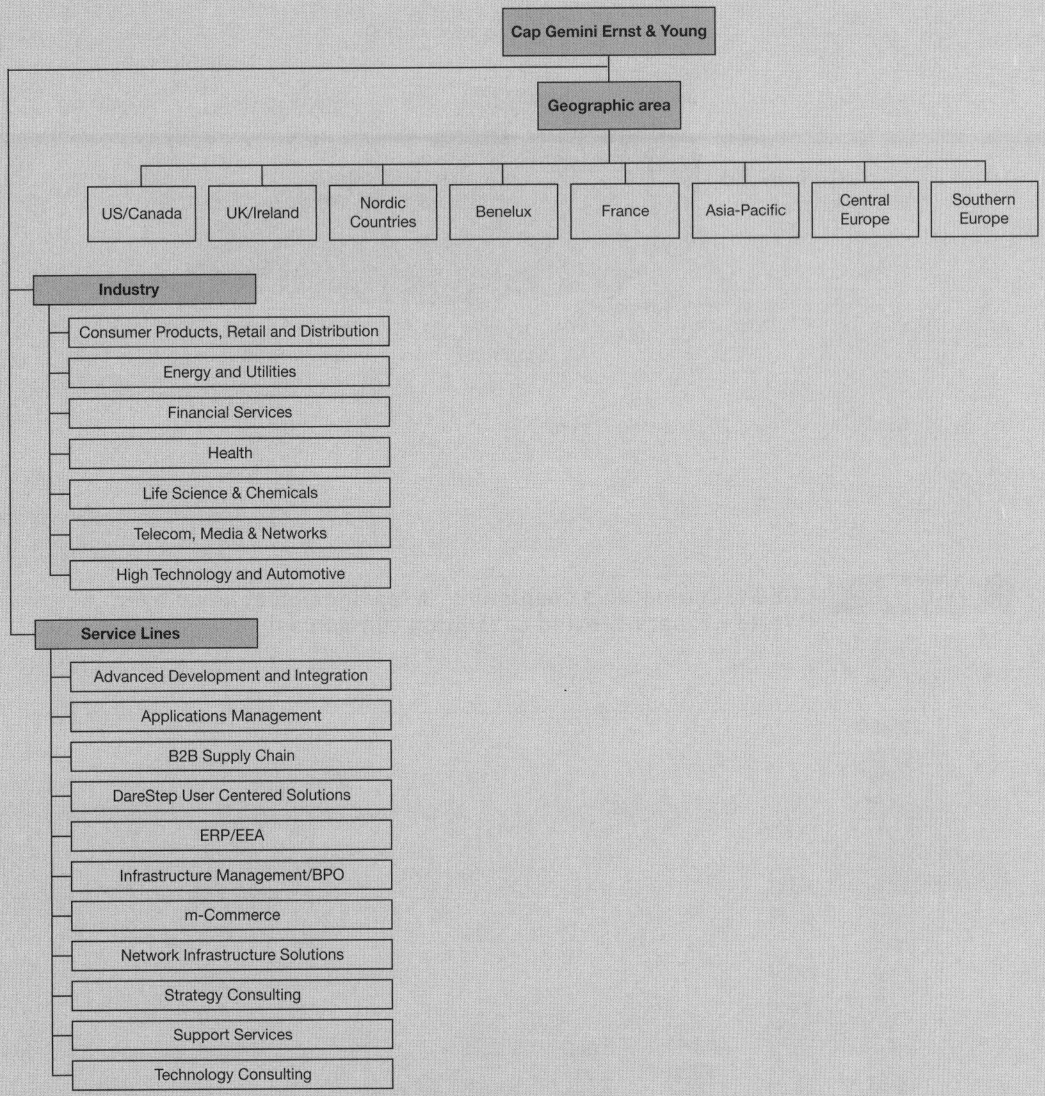

```
                              Cap Gemini Ernst & Young

                                   Geographic area

   US/Canada  UK/Ireland  Nordic    Benelux  France  Asia-Pacific  Central   Southern
                          Countries                                Europe    Europe

   Industry

     Consumer Products, Retail and Distribution
     Energy and Utilities
     Financial Services
     Health
     Life Science & Chemicals
     Telecom, Media & Networks
     High Technology and Automotive

   Service Lines

     Advanced Development and Integration
     Applications Management
     B2B Supply Chain
     DareStep User Centered Solutions
     ERP/EEA
     Infrastructure Management/BPO
     m-Commerce
     Network Infrastructure Solutions
     Strategy Consulting
     Support Services
     Technology Consulting
```

Source: IESE.

CGE&Y had a 'glocal' approach: a global company offering global solutions but adapted and implemented according to the local markets' needs. For this purpose, CGE&Y was organized geographically in eight regions and included two types of global entities: global industry sectors and three lines of business that grouped thirteen offerings (**Exhibit 3b**).

To provide the best possible service levels in the deployment of the global solutions they were offering, CGE&Y created an 'alliances ecosystem' with business partners such as Microsoft, Sun, Siebel, Oracle, Nokia, Meta4 and SAP among others, continuing a trend that CG had started a few years previously. CGE&Y was ready to face up to Accenture, its number-one rival. Other competitors were IBM, EDS and CSC, to name a few (**Exhibit 5**).

7

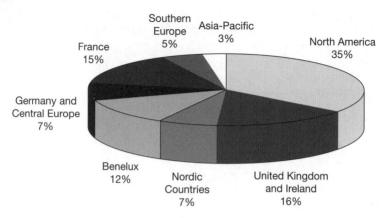

EXHIBIT 4 Cap Gemini Ernst & Young. 2000 revenues by geographical area

Source: Cap Gemini Ernst & Young. 2000 Financial Report.

EXHIBIT 5 CGE&Y. Competitive positioning. A leading global key player (World I.T. services and consulting companies)

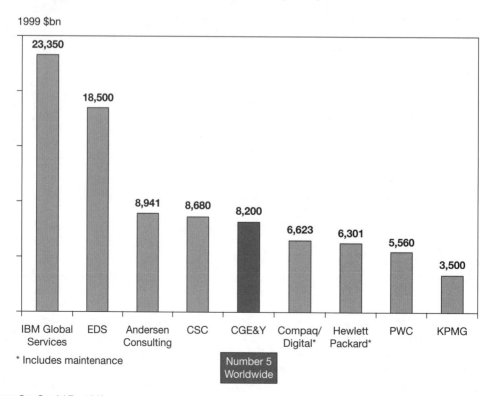

Source: Cap Gemini Ernst & Young.

The American company Beechwood also joined the Cap Gemini Group in April 1999. Beechwood was one of the leading American companies in IT services for the telecom operator market. After the purchase of Beechwood, the CG Group formed a unit to strengthen the Telecom & Media Global Market. In March 2000, Cap Gemini and Cisco Systems joined efforts in a strategic alliance to enhance the Internet economy. They formed Telecom Media Networks, a new company at which Cap Gemini held 95.1 per cent of the stake, while Cisco held the rest.

On January 15, 2002, CGE&Y officially launched Sogeti, a localized IT service firm which had been operating since January 1, 2002. Sogeti was actually a fully-owned subsidiary that would operate on a local basis, concentrating on France, Germany, Benelux, Switzerland and the United States – countries where the merger between CG and E&Y had had little effect on its local services structure.

THE CONSULTANCY INDUSTRY: MERGERS AND KNOWLEDGE MANAGEMENT

Up until the mid-1980s, the consultancy industry had been calm and even, to a certain extent, comradely. From that time onwards, the industry really took off and the peaceful environment was exchanged for one of increasing competition.

Companies that had started as accountancy firms moved into other services such as management consulting, to satisfy existing clients and increasing demand. In order to expand their businesses, the main accountancy firms negotiated a number of mergers after 1986: Peat, Marwick & Co. with KMG in 1987, Ernst Whinney with Arthur Young in 1989 and Deloitte, Haskins & Sells with Touche Ross in the same year. The 'Big 8' accountancy firms prior to 1986 were reduced to the 'Big 6' in 1989, and the 'Big 5' by 1998 (Andersen Consulting, Ernst & Young, KPMG, Deloitte Touche Tohmatsu and PricewaterhouseCoopers). However, the spectacular growth in the consulting industry in the 1990s resulted in consulting units outgrowing their parents. The umbrella organization for consulting and accountancy companies worried the Securities and Exchange Commission, which saw conflicts of interest when providing what should be an 'independent' and quality auditing service. The pressures to separate consulting from auditing could have been one of the reasons behind the separation of the consulting arm from the corporate body of KPMG in January 2000, E&Y in May 2000 and Andersen Consulting, which officially became Accenture in 2001. PricewaterhouseCoopers also considered selling its consulting unit to Hewlett-Packard Co. The new trend the consulting business had adopted in 2000 had another characteristic: the transformation of partnerships into public companies. The first to make its market debut was Ernst & Young (by joining Cap Gemini) followed by KPMG Consulting in February 2001 and Accenture in July 2001.

The panorama was further complicated as the IT firms looked for more services to deliver as their market matured. The traditional areas covered by IT companies, such as computer science and software, came to represent a smaller part of the business, while the scope of new areas such as networking expanded. The role of IT had evolved and companies also demanded technology solutions that solved business problems.

Like other industries, consultancy was also affected by new competitive circumstances such as globalization. Technological advances and the opening up of frontiers had not only intensified competition but had also transformed the way business was carried out. Companies were confronting these challenges by paying more attention to those aspects that could become a source of competitive advantage, and information (and in particular knowledge) was one of them. Information technology development had provided companies with a large amount of information. But the simple accumulation of information did not have any special advantage, since all companies had access to it. "Putting value into this information" was often mentioned as a key issue in gaining competitive advantage. It was especially critical in the service industry, and in the consultancy industry in particular, where knowledge and information management was seen as a matter of survival.

Clients turned to consultancy firms for advice about their businesses, while consulting firms relied on their strong workforces to provide the best service. Thus, consultancy firms were characterized by possessing a remarkably large amount of knowledge, and the fact this knowledge was highly dispersed across the whole organization created a need for teamwork. Working in teams allowed companies to accumulate and combine specific industry or sector knowledge that each team member owned and that was required for a given project or consultancy engagement. At the same time, relying on a complete and abundant knowledge base allowed the consultancy firm to offer better solutions to its clients. As such, and in Alberto Almansa's words "knowledge is critical for this business since it contributes to the professional's value and sales levels, as in the last resort consultants sell knowledge". When it became a question of integrating the knowledge of two companies that had just merged, this whole issue became crucial.

The nature of the business required distributing the knowledge across the whole organization. In addition, knowledge tended to be specific to an industry, a client and a geographical area. However, clients turned to consultancy firms because their knowledge, although dispersed, was greater and more complete than they could acquire themselves, including previous experiences and best practices. Clients therefore expected all relevant knowledge to be brought into play in their projects. This meant that experiences and knowledge generated in one part of the organization could later be useful for other engagements. Not only did this imply accumulating information and knowledge from different parts of the organization, but also making them available to consultants for further use. Consultants, the owners of specific knowledge, helped to put knowledge together when assigned to the same team under a given engagement. However, consultants did not belong to a specific team on a permanent basis, since teams were formed according to project needs, and for a given length of time. All this made it difficult to share and transfer knowledge through interpersonal relationships, and for this reason alternatives were being considered to exploit knowledge more effectively, in an attempt to avoid "reinventing the wheel" time and again on a global scale.

In the past, organizations used to file away all sorts of papers and documents so they could be consulted later. However, technological advances had allowed improvements in the access to information. The suppression of time and space barriers had a direct benefit on communication and an indirect impact on knowledge. All this partly justified the significant investments in technological systems that had been taking place in recent years, especially in the 1990s, to support knowledge management.

Immersed in a highly competitive environment and in an industry where knowledge is a precious asset, the consultancy firms had emphasized their knowledge management skills.

THE IMPORTANCE OF KNOWLEDGE MANAGEMENT

Both CG and E&Y had followed their own knowledge management (KM) initiatives in the past. Their merger early in 2000 made clear the need for an integrated system. The aim of the transition was to focus on technological and cultural elements.

Knowledge management at Ernst & Young

When he was asked about a knowledge management company, Hugh McKellar, executive editor of *KMWorld*, cited the example of E&Y, saying that "E&Y stands out as one of the drivers of the knowledge economy." E&Y was a knowledge management pioneer, and had become a well-known leader in the field. To prove it, there were the numerous prizes it had been awarded and its outstanding position in several KM rankings. For instance, the 2000 MAKE award (Most Admired Knowledge Enterprise) listed E&Y as one of the top ten knowledge management companies in the world, for the third year in a row. E&Y also received recognition for its strategic and innovative programs in knowledge management and learning, which embraced the whole business process and business spectrum.

Organizational structure

Although KM initiatives existed before, it wasn't until 1993 that E&Y explicitly recognized KM as an outstanding part of its strategy. From that moment onwards, E&Y made clear efforts to focus on knowledge. In the organizational field for instance, it created four centres to support KM: the Center for Business Innovation, the Center for Business Transformation, the Center for Business Knowledge and the Center for Technology Enablement (**Exhibit 6**).

Based in Boston, the Innovation Center was in charge of generating new knowledge, which usually came from multi-client research, co-ordinating theory and applications, identifying and investigating new business concepts and collaborating with other organizations including universities. This centre led the research and development of new innovative solutions related to business process, strategies, people and technology. The centre's profound knowledge of market trends and businesses provided a valuable future vision that made designing and implementing clients' strategies easier. Consultants proposed or initiated research sheets following internal interest, hot topics, etc. Contributions were both internal and external, and the results were published and diffused to all E&Y professionals, E&Y clients and other audiences, through articles, books and conferences.

Located in Dallas, the Transformation Unit's role was to structure knowledge into methodologies, techniques and automated tools that improved the speed and value of the services that consultants provided. About one hundred people from different parts of the world were working at it as a virtual

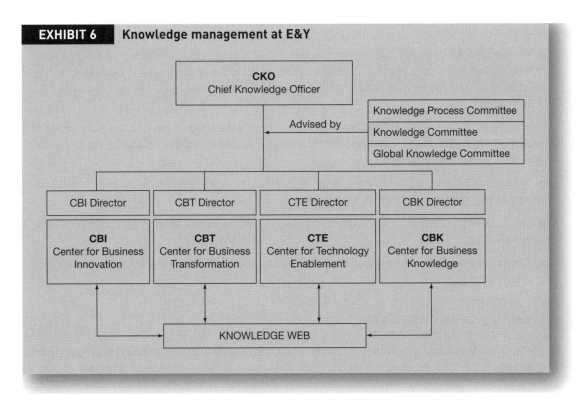

EXHIBIT 6 **Knowledge management at E&Y**

7

organization. Their work concentrated on reengineering processes, knowledge management, information technologies, organizational changes, etc.

In Virginia the Technological Division backed up and complemented the consultancy practice. This division was devoted to the research and development of high technology, so that companies could benefit from the centre's experience, especially when clients were improving or transforming their business processes. The technology division comprised a wide variety of services ranging from technology architecture to networking and technology management.

The Center for Business Knowledge (CBK) was a resource with approximately 650 workers worldwide in 2000, whose purpose was to serve the consultancy and corporate finance units. E&Y, being such a geographically widespread organization, had a centralized CBK in Cleveland, USA, complemented by local CBK's (KM teams of 'Knowledge Managers'). The number of knowledge managers in these local CBK teams varied from one country to another, and they were in charge of all KM in one region, not only for consultancy, but for all E&Y divisions. The knowledge managers were the people who actually managed, revised and maintained knowledge to satisfy the consultants' local needs. Each region worked as a deployment team, although they reported to the CBK, which was responsible for filtering documents and making them available for everyone in the organization.

The CBK was the key centre giving central support to all KM practices for all E&Y's geographic areas. The CBK was an internal resource with a clear mission: to gather, select, filter, store and distribute both internal and external knowledge and information to the entire organization. The CBK offered a wide range of services to ensure that professionals had access to relevant information from any source, at any time and for any given situation:

■ Knowledge Navigation, acting as a call centre was in charge of dealing with consultants' requests. When this centre wasn't able to give an answer within thirty minutes from the moment an inquiry was made, the matter was passed on to Business Research.

■ Business Research & Analysis carried out research and detailed reports that were client or sector specific.

■ KM Systems Adaptation & Deployment, under the CBK's responsibility, included the Engagement Team Database, a Lotus Notes Database specially designed for global teams to connect and share knowledge, and Powerpacks Customization, a highly filtered knowledge database (also a Lotus Notes database).

On the organizational side, new positions and committees were created. Each of the four centres that supported KM had a director who reported to the Chief Knowledge Officer (CKO). Three committees advised all the centres (**Exhibit 6**):

■ The Knowledge Process Committee, which recommended topics on which knowledge was necessary as well as means to integrate knowledge,

■ The Knowledge Committee, which directed knowledge management to other E&Y units such as audit and tax,

■ The Global Knowledge Committee, whose role was to address matters relevant to the whole E&Y organization.

Technological infrastructure

The EY/KnowledgeWeb, also known as KWeb, was the link between consultants and the organization's knowledge base. The KWeb was actually Ernst & Young's intranet, providing immediate access to the collective knowledge of its 77,000 employees distributed across the 130 countries where E&Y

operated. Internal access to collective knowledge was attained through thousands of high quality knowledge bases that included a variety of sections such as press articles, sector information, best practices, experiences, etc. Updated information, direct access to specialized data, and good and reliable advice were some of the advantages this system offered under the supervision of the CBK. In addition, EYInfoLink provided access to over 1,000 sources of external information.

The technological platform for knowledge management at E&Y was based on Lotus Notes, which allowed capture and dissemination of internal knowledge. A major investment in technology infrastructure was made in 1995, when E&Y abandoned Apple Macintosh computers and went over to PC-standards instead. It also implemented a common operating system, and spreadsheet, word processing and e-mail software that made document exchange within the organization easier.

To accomplish its mission, the CBK had to promote infrastructure as well as methodologies. This meant it was responsible for developing a knowledge architecture and taxonomy that simplified and focused knowledge acquisition and data retrieval. In this context, the Powerpacks were at first a collection of multi-volume files whose content (proposal templates, sales presentations, competitive information, models and other kinds of information) was copied and recovered as needed. The knowledge they contained responded to specific issues, and was previously structured and filtered by the CBK team to ensure its quality. The 200 existing Powerpacks evolved until they became sophisticated electronic containers of information, internal and external, that were easy to use and continually revised and updated in order to ensure usefulness. The consultants in the field appreciated being able to download the selected Powerpacks to their laptops and therefore to be able to work off-line at the client site.

This architecture was completed with a Large Document Repository (a huge, low-filtered-content, global database) and its local versions, called Small Document Repositories.

In terms of socialization and virtual collaboration, 22 knowledge networks where consultants could have online discussions were also formed. Consultants joined a given network (or virtual team) if they shared the same specialized expertise in a given business activity. In fact, consultants ended up specializing in an area and in an industry, and were also known as Subject Matter Experts or Specialists (SMEs/SMSs). Each network was responsible for detecting new subjects that had to be investigated, for designing and keeping the basic databases updated as well as capturing the network knowledge and learning. The network co-ordinators were the people from the CBK in charge of assisting and co-ordinating the different networks.

However much technology was a knowledge enabler, it was E&Y's belief that the focus should be on people, as they were the true repositories of knowledge. E&Y made an effort to foster contribution and teamwork. This was precisely one of the CBK's goals: to achieve a culture of co-operation through the KWeb. In fact, E&Y was recognized for its organizational culture, for being the "king of teamwork" and for its high contribution rates. Nevertheless, contribution rates and database numbers differed a lot from country to country.

The KWeb simplified consultants' work by enabling them to find documents easily. Not only did it possess a wide range of databases, but it was also strengthened by a strategic content architecture and global taxonomies (ways of naming and organizing knowledge). On the other hand, this meant consultants had to follow the whole process and methodology to embed and structure their knowledge, as they were partly evaluated on this basis. This contribution procedure was so long, highly structured and centralized that some found it daunting.

Knowledge management at Cap Gemini

Knowledge management at CG was more decentralized than at E&Y. Top level managers in Paris had recognized the importance of KM and had taken the first steps in the KM direction by designing learning programs throughout the company, and designing a technological platform, although they had not drawn up a specific programme with the roles and processes necessary to materialize KM activities related to content management and research and analysis.

Cap Gemini's university on the outskirts of Paris had been created in 1989 to train CG's professionals, as well as to give them the chance to share experiences. The next and most important step at the corporate level was the Galaxy, created in 1995; a web-based intranet that was cheap to use and easy to connect to other systems. It was an internal tool designed to publish, share and manage knowledge.

Knowledge Galaxy was the CG knowledge intranet, featuring "planets" or different knowledge areas. All of the company's consultants could access the Knowledge Galaxy through 'My Galaxy', an Internet portal personalized by every employee according to his/her preferences and areas of interest. My Galaxy also provided a personal space with private areas accessible via the Internet, allowing virtual collaboration.

The 'planets' or knowledge areas included the following sections:

■ Specific Knowledge Areas; for specific products, packages, technology, businesses.

■ Service Offerings; including reference model documents.

■ Human Resources; including internal job opportunities, "Who knows what" pages, social benefits and company rules.

■ Virtual Collaboration or Communication; either by e-mail or video-conference, with forums or news groups.

■ Markets; referring to sales, clients, market segments, partners and competitors.

■ Corporate; with all the elements related to marketing, communication, a group manual (how to work and live within CG) and the Cap Gemini University learning programs.

■ Methods and Standard Processes; with its corresponding models, quality systems, guides and patterns of the CG global methodology called PERFORM.

■ Engagement Profiles Databases; with Project Experiences and qualitative data about them.

■ Local Intranet Access; organized according to the needs of the geographical area. (See **Exhibit 7** for further details.)

The Knowledge Galaxy was not just an investment to improve internal processes at CG. Initially, it was a knowledge management project with the aim of achieving easy access to all information, experience and knowledge acquired and accumulated in consultancy engagements that had taken place in CG.

Excluding the official content related to the Knowledge Areas, Service Lines, Corporate and Methodology 'planets', that was revised and filtered at the corporate level, employees in CG could, at will, publish information in the different "planets" of the Galaxy in a very democratic way. Documents referring to client engagements were published on a database called Engagement Profiles International Collection and were supervised by a knowledge manager, who ensured the quality of the document and that it had a reference indicating whether or not it could be reused. The knowledge managers were also in charge of promoting the KM processes and encouraging employees to contribute. In general, there were no common or generally applied mechanisms to ensure the quality or the updating of the published information.

In terms of socialization and virtual collaboration, a huge number of forums were created within each "planet" to allow sharing and collaboration between international or related teams.

Contribution rates differed, as in Ernst & Young, depending on the area and the location.

| EXHIBIT 7 | Knowledge management at Cap Gemini |

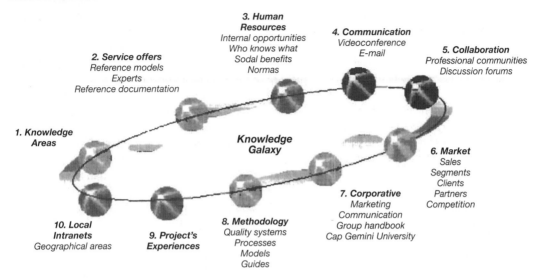

Source: Cap Gemini Ernst & Young.

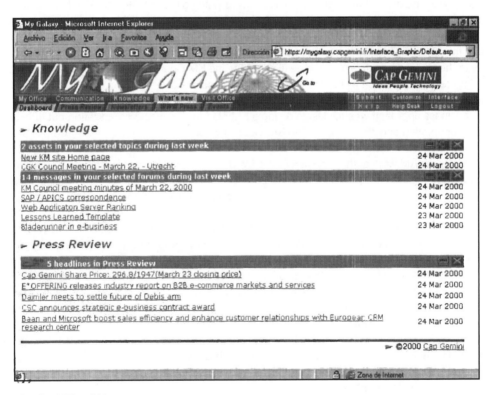

Source: Cap Gemini Ernst & Young.

Knowledge management at Cap Gemini Ernst & Young

Starting in March 2000, and as a result of their merger (formally an acquisition, but referred to as a 'merger' among the employees, in line with the friendly spirit of the purchase), each company's KM strengths were to be extended to the other and vice versa. Furthermore, as stated by Mr. Almansa, KM was perceived as strategic for the merger's success, and therefore it was to be developed in a coherent and purposeful fashion. Hence, from that moment onwards initiatives were unified.

At the time of the merger, Cap Gemini purchased the E&Y Consulting Unit, the Center for Innovation and all the CBK's contents related to the consultancy practice. The companies had reached a service-level agreement regarding the CBK's service (which belonged to E&Y LLP) that expired in March 2002. For CGE&Y, the outsourcing of this service for KM maintenance was costly as well as critical for the business.

Although both CG and E&Y had similar matrix structures, only differing in naming conventions or the industries in which each of them operated and which in some cases coincided, they had organized their KM approaches so differently that deciding how to arrange KM within the combined CGE&Y was a major challenge. Each industry area had its own KM budget and its own knowledge that employees needed in that area, on a common basis. However, the common basis was decided centrally at E&Y and minimally at CG.

Organizational structure was one of the first 'visible' elements to consider. KM had to be represented in every domain of the company (by industry or market, by service offering, by location). It was agreed that each of these areas would have a KM team lead by a Chief Knowledge Officer (CKO) and all of them would report to Bruno Nigrelli, the recently appointed CGE&Y Group CKO. KM would be run by these people, in the KM Council. The KM Council was to be responsible for overall KM strategy, while local KM teams were to be in charge of strategy execution. The KM Council reported to François Carrière, the KM and IT Chief (a newly-created position that embraced both KM and IT) who reported directly to the Global Executive Committee (**Exhibit 8**). The KM Council would take geographical distribution into account, as each of its members would represent a given geographical area, but it would define a minimal centralized policy on KM for the whole company. The system thought to best suit the 'glocal' business approach was to design a single KM plan for the whole organization but able to provide local adaptation and deployment. The KM Council would also help co-ordinate KM plans across countries.

To simplify the KM work at the local level, CGE&Y identified two role profiles for knowledge workers. The knowledge managers would be responsible for the internal knowledge content management and KM systems customization, whereas the information specialists would focus on external information and research services. The knowledge managers would support sales, projects and KM solutions on a day-to-day basis. They would work to satisfy the knowledge needs or requirements that service lines and sectors reported. They would also be aware of what was happening in all sectors, service lines, etc. and therefore would have a global vision. Their role was not only to provide information to consultants, but also to teach them where they could find the relevant information or knowledgeable person, by showing them how the knowledge bases worked and preparing them, in future, to help themselves. The information specialists would be more of a 'back office' service, offering information services and documentation. They would capture, store and prepare information packs.

The Innovation Center was included in the merger, as it had no equivalent in CG and its role in creating knowledge, doing research and having a long-term vision was valuable in the consultancy industry. CG believed it could easily replicate the Center for Transformation and the Technological Center because of its strong IT expertise.

The CBK case was more complex. The CBK supplied content through its thousands of databases and it also provided the necessary services to maintain them (**Exhibits 9a** and **9b**). The content was a pillar of E&Y's day-to-day work, and a cornerstone of its strategy; in fact it was one of the reasons

7

EXHIBIT 8   Knowledge management organization in CGE&Y

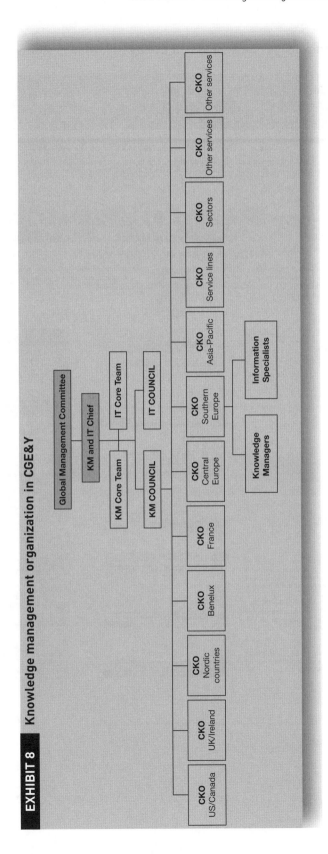

EXHIBIT 9A Knowledge management at CGE&Y: knowledge storing

KNOWLEDGE MANAGEMENT
FINDING the KNOWLEDGE YOU NEED   User Guide

This guide is designed to help you find the knowledge you need.

Our knowledge is stored in a variety of containers or tools within MyGalaxy.

This guide gives you an overview of each container and where to go to access the knowledge you need.

http://mygalaxy.capgemini.fr

MyGalaxy is the entry point for all your knowledge needs. MyGalaxy is CGE&Y's intranet portal that can be customised to meet your own interests and needs.

MyGalaxy comes with a pre-determined basic structure however you are free to modify this to suit your needs.

The Daily Planet is daily news of what's happening at CGE&Y worldwide

Daily Planet
Daily News from the CGEY Group

The Search Engine performs fast, full-text searches for documents across multiple Knowledgebases. Use it to search across: Repositories, PowerPacks and other knowledgebases.

EPiC - Engagement Profile International Collection contains details of all CGE&Y credentials

The Global Catalogue is a comprehensive listing of all the Groups local and international databases. You can access knowledge databases in Lotus Notes even if you don't have Lotus Notes on your computer.

K-Web contains access to the Search Engine, the Global Catalogue, Community Home Spaces, a variety of External Sources and Internal Web Sites.

Community Homespaces (CHS's) are a one-stop service centre designed to provide you with a wealth of market, solution, and administrative information. The CHS acts as a portal to collective knowledge by providing highly filtered information in one easily accessible location.

My Connections contains your skills profile and links to other consultants contact details and skills profile

The Virtual Room tool has been designed to enable CGE&Y and clients to work together on a project, sharing and exchanging information (files, notes, events, actions, forums) across the Web

External Sources

Through External Sources you can access Gartner Group DataQuest Research, aForrester Research, Standard & Poors Market Insight, IDC, Net, META...

My Directory is your access to CGE&Y Group-wide online business cards. Find details such as office locations, telephone numbers etc.

connect!now →KLM

Electric Library™ provides CGE&Y consultants easy access to a vast collection of high-quality information through one single-source

Internal Sites has a selection of specialised knowledge and information sites including: KLM - integrated Knowledge, Learning and Methods and LEAP - Desktop learning

For assistance please contact your Knowledge Manager in your location

6   CAP GEMINI ERNST & YOUNG

Source: Cap Gemini Ernst Young.

EXHIBIT 9B   **Knowledge management at CGE&Y**

KNOWLEDGE MANAGEMENT
FINDING the KNOWLEDGE YOU NEED

What Knowledge Do I Need?	Where Do I find it?
Market & Account Planning	
• Account Work in Progress Knowledge	• Account Team Virtual Room
• Sector or Service Line Work in Progress Knowledge	• Sector or Service Line Virtual Room
• Company & Competitor Information	• KWeb External Sources, Contact CBK
• Industry Information & Analysis	• KWeb External Sources, Contact CBK
• News Articles	• Electronic Library, Contact CBK
• Market Share Information	• Contact CBK
• Technology Trends	• KWeb External Sources ie. IDC, GartnerGroup etc.
• Sales & Marketing Material	• CHS's, Search Engine, PowerPacks via Global Catalogue
• Share Prices & Exchange Rates	• Internet, Contact CBK
• Annual Reports	• External Sources, Internet, Contact CBK
• Sales & Marketing Information	• CHS's, Search Engine, PowerPacks via Global Catalogue
Opportunity Assessment & Relationship Building	
• Credentials	• EPIC - Engagement Profiles International Collection, PowerPacks
• Account Work in Progress Knowledge	• Account Virtual Rooms
• Sector or Service Line Work in Progress Knowledge	• Sector or Service Line Virtual Rooms
• Industry Information & Analysis	• External Sources, Contact CBK
• Company & Competitor Information	• External Sources, Contact CBK
• News Articles	• Electronic Library, Contact CBK
• Market Share Information	• Contact CBK
• Sales Presentations	• CHS's, Search Engine, PowerPacks via Global Catalogue
• Sales & Marketing Materials	• CHS's, Search Engine, PowerPacks via Global Catalogue
• Technology Trends	• External Sources ie. IDC, GartnerGroup, eForrester etc.
• Vendor Information & Product Specifications	• External Sources ie. GartnerGroup DataQuest
Finalising Solution & Proposing	
• Benchmarking, Best Practice & Leading Practices	• CHS's, Search Engine, Contact CBK
• Process Models	• CHS's, Search Engine, PowerPacks via Global Catalogue
• Proposals	• CHS's, Search Engine, PowerPacks via Global Catalogue
• Vendor Information & Product Specifications	• External Sources ie. GartnerGroup, IDC etc.
• Technology Trends	• External Sources ie. GartnerGroup, IDC etc.
• Sales Presentations	• CHS's, Search Engine, PowerPacks via Global Catalogue
• Credentials	• EPIC - Engagement Profiles International Collection
Engagement Delivery	
• Engagement Deliverable's	• CHS's, Search Engine, PowerPacks via Global Catalogue
• Solution Components	• CHS's, Search Engine, PowerPacks via Global Catalogue
• Benchmarks, Best Practices & Leading Practices	• CHS's Search Engine, Contact CBK
• Process Models	• KLM Internal Web Site, CHS's, Search Engine
• News Articles	• Electronic Library, Contact CBK
• Methodology Information	• KLM Internal Web Site, CHS's
• Learning Resources	• KLM Internal Web Site, LEAP Internal Web Site
• Knowledge Sharing Tool	• Virtual Room via Sector or Service Line Knowledge Manager

For assistance please contact your Knowledge Manager in your location

7   **CAP GEMINI ERNST & YOUNG**

Source: Cap Gemini Ernst & Young.

7

EXHIBIT 10	KM figures 2001
KM COSTS	
Central Team	10%
Regional Teams	38%
Applications	
Galaxy	7%
CBK/Kweb	35%
Central External Sources	8%
Other	3%
Total	100%

Source: Cap Gemini Ernst & Young.

behind E&Y's high performance level in the consultancy business and this could not be replicated easily. On the face of it, this justified its purchase. But from another perspective, this was a centre that provided services fitted to a different organization and context, with a specific culture and a given architecture, through different processes and under a different strategy. Summing up, the CBK was useful and it seemed necessary, although it was somewhat costly. The CBK and KWeb took around 35 per cent of the KM budget while Galaxy cost around 7 per cent (**Exhibit 10**). These arguments had led CG to buy its content and buy some time by reaching a service level agreement until March 2002. CGE&Y would then have the right to renew the service level agreement or do without it. Meanwhile E&Y LLP owned the CBK and used it for its other business units that had not been included in the merger. As for employees, CGE&Y kept all CG's KM teams while 90 of E&Y's local KM workers were transferred to CGE&Y. 250 KM employees remained in the E&Y-owned CBK. The number of knowledge workers in CGE&Y increased after the merger to a total of approximately 260 by the end of 2001.

With regard to the general workforce, CGE&Y focused on employee retention after the merger, achieving a rate that was close to the industry average. Furthermore, the Human Resources Department reorganized the workforce, allocating the staff into six professions according to the consultancy discipline employees belonged to, in order to unify and clarify career paths. The evaluation system was linked to each profession, and included a number of factors relating to KM.

Adjusting the knowledge infrastructure was another of the big issues CGE&Y was concerned about. Their wish was to completely integrate people, resources and capabilities, and, to the greatest extent possible, to do it in a friendly manner involving everyone. However, choosing one technological system meant excluding the other, and this went against the peaceful merger spirit. It was therefore decided, at least in a first stage, to focus on a front-end integrated access to the knowledge infrastructure, through accessing E&Y's KWeb and CG's Knowledge Galaxy. The outcome was the Knowledge Portal (KPortal), based on CG's architecture, which in fact was a newer version of My Galaxy, including specific links to the K-Web (**Exhibit 11**). Employees still used the system they were most familiar with, although access to each system had been generalized for everyone in the organization (**Exhibit 9a**). The same applied to the contribution processes. Each employee followed and used the one they had before the merger; that is, My Galaxy for ex-CG employees and the KWeb for ex-E&Y employees (see Figure 1). After the merger, there was a larger amount of information available. However, as each professional followed a different process according to the departure point, information was not standardized for the whole organization. The first consequence was a drop in the contribution rates, especially noticeable in the E&Y part of the merged business.

7

EXHIBIT 11	The K-Portal

My Galaxy, the personal portal for accessing the Galaxy

Access

- **Latest news and events at CGEY**

- **Knowledge areas and intranet links**
  - Corporate Area, Kweb (E&Y), G. Consulting
  - Human Resources (E&Y), G.
  - Local Intranets
  - Discussion forums

- **Applications in the corporate intranet**
  - Project reference search (EPIC)
  - Contact data from companions at CGE&Y
  - Knowledge search in the intranet or search (My Directory)

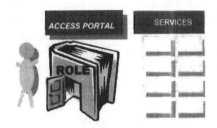

- **Latest news and knowledge in**
  - The projects I have taken part in
  - The knowledge area I am interested in
  - The discussion forums I am subscribed to
  - Internet press

- **My e-mail inbox**

- **Chat and videoconference**

- **My personal area**
  - My folders
  - My notes
  - My bookmarks

Source: Cap Gemini Ernst & Young.

FIGURE 1   Evolution of the knowledge management infrastructure

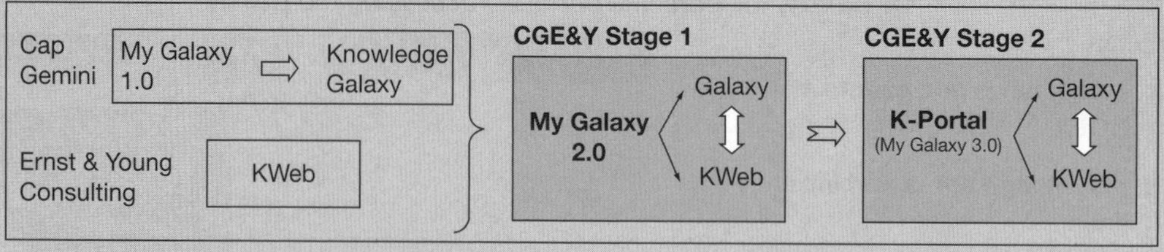

Merging the two cultures into one was not a goal that could be achieved rapidly, especially when considering that CG was a publicly traded European firm with a solid technological base while E&Y was an American partnership.

Despite all this, the implicitly held view, voiced for example by José Luis Guerra, a former E&Y employee, now Knowledge Manager in Spain, was that the complementarities between the two firms would ensure that integration would be "an easy landing". Beyond their KM differences, their entrepreneurial cultures were similar and their values were alike. It was perceived that this made the merger an easier operation than when E&Y had tried in October 1997 to merge with KPMG, only to discover that their cultural differences could not be overcome. To reinforce a common culture, CGE&Y came up with a list of seven values to provide people with a behavioural guideline: honesty, boldness, trust, freedom, team spirit, modesty and fun were to be the explicit values for the merged organization (**Exhibit 12**).

Work at CGEY, as in many consultancy firms, was in most cases based on teams. Communication, therefore, played an outstanding role as it fostered knowledge sharing. The medieval castle in Behoust, Paris, where CG had its university, was now CGE&Y's university and was opened to all the organization's professionals, clients and partners in order to attain a stronger global cohesion. The focus of the university was to establish 'on-campus' communication and a collaborative atmosphere that would help, together with the coursework, to build networks and foster and maintain communities of interest and of practice. The university also provided a wide range of traditional classroom courses as well as experiential learning and distance-learning or 'virtual' programmes focused on real business issues.

FUTURE CHALLENGES

Integration had been carried out as an extension of what both companies had been doing so far, without discontinuities. However, there was also a desire to develop CGE&Y as a business that was more than simply the sum of what the two previous ones had been. This did not exclude taking the best of each company, like adopting E&Y's KM philosophy or building a new technical infrastructure based on CG's architecture. Mr. Almansa considered the CGE&Y KM experience in 2000 and 2001 to be a serene transition, and was now concerned about future events, especially how to continuously adapt the KM approach to serve the business needs of CGE&Y.

The most significant issue that continued to worry him was the expiry date of the agreement for the CBK's services. The CBK was critical for the consultancy practice but it carried a high price tag, not only in strict financial terms, but also in terms of homogenization, or the lack of it, in CGE&Y KM practices. The co-existence of two systems seemed to have worked so far, but was it reasonable to keep a temporary solution in the long run? Behind this issue was a more fundamental one: what was the right KM approach for the new organization?

7

EXHIBIT 12	CGE&Y Seven core values

Honesty, that is at the same time integrity, sincerity, a sense of honour, respect for a person's word and for commitments made, and also a refusal of any dishonest methods used to facilitate gaining a contract or a particular advantage.

Boldness, that is, a taste for undertaking things, to like taking risks and to enjoy competing, constant questioning of directions taken and of the circumstances in which we find ourselves. A boldness which should go hand in hand with a certain wisdom, without which the audacious manager would in fact be just a dangerous daredevil.

Trust, that is, the wish to give people and teams responsibility and to make sure that decisions are made at as close a level as possible to those who are to implement them. Trust also consists of ensuring total openness amongst people within the company and as free a flow of information and ideas as possible.

Freedom, that is, independence of mind, of judgement, of action, the spirit of initiative and creativity, as well as tolerance and respect for others, of their culture, of their habits. This independence of judgement provides our clients with an essential guarantee of the quality of the advice we give.

Team Spirit, that is, solidarity, friendship, loyalty, transparency. This solidarity, necessary if we are to work efficiently with our clients, also implies generosity and the sharing of the fruits of a collective labour.

Modesty, that is, the opposite of affectedness, pretentiousness, arrogance and boastfulness. Modesty means discretion, spontaneity, listening to others and frank relations.

Fun, that is, the feeling one gets when one is happy to work, feels good in the team to which one belongs, is proud of what one does and achieves one's objective in the never-ending search for top quality and the greatest possible effectiveness.

Source: http://www.cgey.com

To answer this question, CGE&Y had asked its strategic consultancy division to write a sheet of recommendations, called the Roadmap. Mr. Almansa still had not seen the sheet but he could imagine some of the suggestions it would contain.

Asking the best consultants for advice was natural given the scope of this decision, since the KM base was common for all Cap Gemini Group companies (also for Telecom Media Networks and Sogeti) and given that KM was of critical importance for the whole CGE&Y business. It was especially serious given the present economic environment, because CGE&Y, being an IT and consultancy service provider, was susceptible to the volatility of market trends, and these had not been very positive in 2001. Consultancy companies had suffered from the economic slowdown and generalized uncertainty, and had had to cut costs and jobs. CGE&Y was no exception and had started staff cutbacks.

Further measures were expected to be taken in 2002, after the new Chief Executive Officer (CEO) Paul Hermelin took the helm. Paul Hermelin, a 49-year-old Frenchman, officially took over on January 1, 2002 from Geoff Unwin, a 59-year-old Briton, who had long planned to retire at the age of 60. Mr. Hermelin had been the Chief Operating Officer, focusing on operations and costs, which made him seem the perfect successor in a restructuring environment.

7

Concurrently, CGE&Y was immersed in its internal KM restructuring plan. In the first place, the merger had taken place to improve KM performance and since KM strongly supported the consultancy business, it would help them compete better. However, at this precise time, in January 2002, the coexistence of the two systems with their corresponding procedures, roles, etc. created unnecessary complexity. And complexity could interfere with business performance.

The loudspeaker interrupted Mr. Almansa's deliberations. The Paris fight was ready for passengers to board. Mr. Almansa closed his laptop, stood up and walked to the boarding gate. He knew what he was going to say.

CASE STUDY 8

COMPETING BY THE BOOK: DESTINATION CHINA

As he leaned back in his chair on a gloomy April evening in the late 2005, Michael Kraft looked at the financial report on his desk. Overcoming daunting obstacles was nothing new to the entrepreneur and chief executive of Toronto-based Lingo Media Inc. (formerly called Alpha Communications Corp.), but his company's efforts to crack the tightly controlled Chinese publishing market were proving more challenging than he ever thought possible.

Kraft had invested a considerable amount of energy and personal money into pursuing his vision of doing business in China, and by many standards, Lingo Media had achieved great levels of success. It had established a quality brand in China, delivering more than 90 million textbooks and supplemental teaching aids to students across the country's classrooms. While, these were prodigious numbers for any publishing company, Lingo Media was barely turning its strengths into a steady stream of profits, with royalties based on the government-controlled low list price of textbooks in China.

As new opportunities started to emerge as a result of China's accession to the World Trade Organization (see Exhibit 1), Kraft wondered what set of initiatives should capture his attention next. It was high time he started to put a solid grip on the Chinese market.

William Hawkins and John Jarrett Wegener prepared this case under the supervision of Assistant Professor Cyril Bouquet solely to provide material for class discussion. The authors do not intend to illustrate either effective or ineffective handling of a managerial situation. The authors may have disguised certain names and other identifying information to protect confidentiality.

Ivey Management Services prohibits any form of reproduction, storage or transmittal without its written permission. This material is not covered under authorization from CanCopy or any reproduction rights organization. To order copies or request permission to reproduce materials, contact Ivey Publishing, Ivey Management Services, c/o Richard Ivey School of Business, The University of Western Ontario, London, Ontario, Canada, N6A 3K7; phone (519) 661-3208; fax (519) 661-3882; e-mail cases@ivey.uwo.ca.

Copyright © 2005, Ivey Management Services Version: (A) 2005-10-28
One-time permission to reproduce granted by Ivey Management Services on 1 December 2009.

Richard Ivey School of Business
The University of Western Ontario

EXHIBIT 1	Lingo Media Reports 2004 year end results

Toronto, Canada, May 2, 2005 — Lingo Media Inc. (LMD: TSX V; LNGMF: OTC BB) (the "company" or "Lingo Media"), announces its financial results for the year ended December 31, 2004. The 2004 year-end results compared with 2003, reported in Canadian dollars, are as follows:

	2004	2003
Revenue	$ 589,654.00	$1,017,817.00
Net loss	$(795,377.00)	$ (257,082.00)
Loss per share	$ (0.04)	$ (0.01)

The net loss included amortization expense of $488,776. The complete annual financial statements and management discussion and analysis for the year ended December 31, 2004 are available at www.sedar.com.

During 2004, the Chinese State Ministry of Education ("MOE") mandated People's Education Press ("PEP") to increase its market share by shifting from Finished Product Sales to Licensing Sales. As a result of this new MOE stance, PEP had significantly reduced the size of its print runs for Finished Product Sales in 2004 and is now focusing on Licensing Sales. The impact of this new policy resulted in significantly lower revenues from Finished Product Sales and only a marginal increase in Licensing Sales revenues in 2004.

"This past year has been a year of significant events for Lingo Media. More changes lie ahead as we execute our business plan to transform Lingo Media from a royalty-based company into a significant educational print media distribution company in China" said Lingo Media President & CEO Michael Kraft.

"This transformation began back in February 2004 when we announced our China Expansion Plans to establish a joint venture with a Chinese publishing and distribution company. Under World Trade Organization (WTO) market reforms, the Chinese government has opened up its print media wholesale distribution sector, effective in December 2004," he continued.

Foreign companies are now allowed to own up to 100% of businesses engaged in wholesale distribution and the retail sale of books, newspapers and magazines, according to The Press and Publication Administration and the Ministry of Foreign Trade and Economic Co-operation who jointly issued the Measures for the Administration of Book, Newspaper and Periodical Distribution Enterprises with Foreign Investment.

"We are aggressively pursuing acquisition opportunities that fit our model of acquiring majority interests in educational distribution companies. In order to meet our human resources needs, we have enhanced our management team and have added media-industry veterans to our board of directors," Mr. Kraft said.

Source: www.lingomedia.com

CHINA FOCUS

Lingo Media started in 1994 as a Canadian-based specialty publisher of "promotional" books and complementary products. The business consisted of publishing popular subjects that would be branded with corporate logos (such as *Corning Cookbooks*) and distributed at supermarkets, mass-market retailers, departmental stores, etc. While this business generated good steady profits for Lingo Media, Kraft was getting increasingly tired of the lengthy delays and procedures involved in getting approvals from these corporations on their review of the content.

It didn't take long for Kraft to turn his attention to China in 1997, especially after he heard that steps were being taken by the Chinese Central Government to mandate that all of the country's schools would start teaching English in Grade 3. In the past, Chinese students did not have to take English classes until Grade 7. This proposed policy change would create a huge market for textbooks and other teaching materials, one that Lingo Media could not easily ignore. Of the approximately 1.1 billion people globally who were learning or improving their English language skills, an estimated 200 million were located in China.

Kraft knew the challenges were commensurate to the size of the market opportunity. While Lingo Media had never before published a textbook, it would face huge competition from major multinational publishing houses, such as Pearson Education, Oxford University Press, Cambridge University Press and Macmillan Publishing. As well, the amount of state regulation in China was enormous: all media content, including the educational sector, was subject to censorship restrictions and pre-approval from central and provincial authorities; foreign investment in publishing, and distribution was largely prohibited. The threat of piracy was another source of complexity. And there was a shortage of English teachers, especially in central and western China where 65 per cent of China's 1.3 billion people lived.

Yet, an opportunity arose to develop the company's presence in China with a Canadian insurance company, Manulife, as Kraft offered to develop and publish a customer-oriented book on the basics of insurance as an investment under the Manulife brand. The Canadian insurer had entered China as a new growth imperative, and now realized the importance of educating Chinese customers on how insurance works, while promoting the company's brand in the process. Realizing it would be difficult for Lingo Media to import books without some form of local support, Kraft signed a contract with China International Publishing Group (CIPG), a leading state-owned publisher of trade books. Through this venture, Kraft also saw an extremely valuable possibility to further investigate and negotiate the possibility of investing into the English-language textbook market. CIPG indeed had a subsidiary called Foreign Languages Press, which published and distributed books to retail bookstores across China.

A CO-OPERATIVE APPROACH

In June 1998, CIPG convinced Lingo Media to enter into a co-publishing agreement to develop English as a Foreign Language (EFL) materials that would be sold throughout China, within the school system itself. The agreement involved a series of textbooks targeted at the municipal educational authority in Beijing, supplemental readings on technology and science, and an interactive learning portal on the Internet.

Part of the value proposition that Lingo Media offered to CIPG, Kraft believed, was a true bilateral approach to co-publishing original materials. In contrast to other multinational publishers who would roll out existing EFL products on a worldwide basis, without paying attention to idiosyncratic differences across country markets, Lingo Media and CIPG would work together as a team in creating an entirely new and original series of culturally relevant EFL products. This approach was facilitated by the fact that Lingo Media was a true newcomer in the world of educational publishing, and thus did not have an existing library of EFL materials that could be leveraged in foreign markets, specifically China.

To implement this approach, Lingo Media sent well-known Canadian authors and editors of children's education materials overseas to ensure they would observe Chinese students in the classroom and develop greater sensitivity to the local culture; Chinese educational experts were also brought to Canada for a period of six months to facilitate their understanding and appreciation of Canadian educational publishing practices. The end result of these valuable exchanges was the development of innovative teaching EFL materials that relied heavily on colors, music and even poetry to address the specific needs of Chinese students, while also being adapted to the teaching infrastructures available locally.

8

This effort naturally exerted a significant drain on Lingo Media's limited resources. With only eight people on staff, the company quickly realized how difficult it was to master a 12-hour time-zone difference, a different language and a different business mindset all at once. Further, strong personal relationships were so important to gaining the confidence of the Chinese that Kraft now had to include numerous 17-hour flights on his already busy agenda. To gain further credibility with CIPG, Lingo Media also recognized the importance of demonstrating that the Canadian government officially endorsed the partnership, while also acting as a constant source of support. This objective was time-consuming as it involved the organization of regular meetings and social receptions between Kraft and Lingo Media management, CIPG representatives and Canadian government officials.

As a result of this added complexity, and to more effectively focus the company's efforts, the decision was made to abandon Lingo Media's specialty publishing business so that more time and resources could be devoted to the Chinese venture. As a symbolic gesture, Kraft also committed to loaning up to $500,000[1] of his own money to finance the firm's working capital requirements throughout this realignment period.

DISAPPOINTING RESULTS

While there was much expectation from the Chinese venture, initial results turned out to be abysmal failures. The first objective consisted of selling English textbooks for Grade 3 to Grade 12 students in Beijing. But after spending $300,000 in direct expenses on this project—expert authors in EFL textbook development and Chinese culture had to be located, contracted and co-ordinated throughout a total period of 18 months—the project failed when CIPG (a national state-owned trade publisher) lost the bid to Beijing Educational Press (a Beijing municipally owned educational publisher), so that the income generated would flow back to the Beijing municipal government. Kraft nevertheless remained enthusiastic, his mood buoyed by CIPG's offer to co-publish another textbook project, *Let's Learn English,* which this time would be targeted to kindergarten to Grade 2 students and was not part of the controlled curriculum. This time, Lingo Media spent around $200,000 developing this project, which was successfully piloted in Beijing's classrooms. But then it discovered that CIPG was not aware of a required special tax license necessary to sell educational products to schools.

Lingo Media's financial position was quickly deteriorating. At current spending levels, the firm would exhaust its financial reserves within a period of two months. One possible exit strategy existed with Cinar Corporation (Cinar), the Canadian animation company, which had expressed interest in investing or buying into Kraft's business. It was now believed Lingo Media would be awarded a large co-publishing contract for the primary school market across China. By putting its cartoon characters in Lingo Media's books, Cinar felt it could achieve great levels of success in China, and urged Kraft to quickly enter into a round of negotiations. Although the board was becoming increasingly skeptical, many felt this was an offer that could not be turned down. Yet Kraft couldn't envision the possibility of walking away at this critical juncture of the company's history.

A NEW STRATEGIC DEPARTURE

Kraft took several initiatives to restore confidence at the board level. First, he exploited the interest expressed by Cinar to sell the idea that if he wasn't the only one to see the potential associated with selling educational textbooks in China, the idea must have a future and great potential. Second, he took it upon himself to troll Toronto's financial district in search of new strategic investment partners, and was able to raise about $2 million through a private placement of common shares on the Canadian

Venture Exchange (now the TSX Venture Exchange). Third, he was also able to convince the board that the company's initial forays in China had not gone to waste by adapting some of the Lingo Media English as a Foreign Language (EFL) content for use in the Canadian primary school system through a new series of books called *The Out Loud Program.* Together, these initiatives provided the support and financial relief needed to restore confidence and credibility at the board level.

A defining moment in the company's history came in 1999, shortly after Kraft joined the Canada China Business Council in Toronto, a private-sector, non-profit membership organization designed to facilitate and promote trade, investment and the exchange of ideas between Canada and China. It was at one of the events that Kraft met Chen Geng (a.k.a Geoff Chen), who was then the vice-consul for China. Chen suggested the need to rethink the company's strategy along three specific angles.

Stay focused

Chen believed Lingo Media needed to be more focused in terms of the markets it intended to pursue. Recent initiatives suggested the company was keen to pursue market opportunities in the hugely attractive Chinese market as they arose, without careful strategic planning. If reaching schools was the ultimate objective, it didn't necessarily make a lot of sense to pursue unrelated projects in the trade-book business. For example, selling insurance books and EFL products required different strategic mindsets, and a unique set of contacts, approaches and capabilities. As well, the returns in the trade-book business were quite small considering that a bestseller in China typically generated 5,000 copies at the average price of $1 to $2 per copy.

Create value

The company's value proposition also needed to be refined. Chen agreed with Kraft that textbooks had to be differentiated in China as there was a kind of national obsession with the idea of superior education. Certainly the one-child family had created a perception in every household that the future of the entire nation resided in the success of that one child. This perception in turn required products to be highly adapted to local needs, ideologies and culture. Competing on low cost was also extremely important, as many parents could not afford expensive learning materials.

Forge relationships

Finally, Chen suggested CIPG probably didn't offer the best strategic fit, compared to People's Education Press (PEP), another national state-owned publisher that supplied textbooks to about 65 per cent of all Chinese kindergarten to Grade 12 classrooms. By chance, Gong Yafu, the director of the English Department at PEP, was spending the year in Toronto taking courses at York University. This lucky circumstance created an opportunity to engage in a fruitful dialogue.

Kraft was enthused by Chen, who decided to leave his diplomatic career to pursue a business career and act as Lingo Media's chief representative in China. Lingo Media was chosen as the new name in June 2000, replacing Alpha Communications Corp., to more effectively convey its focus on EFL educational publishing. Lingo Media was derived from the French Provincial term for "tongue," and was often used to refer to a strange or incomprehensible language or speech. Lingo Media conveyed the idea that the company was pursuing the goal of making the difficult-to-comprehend English language accessible to Chinese students through state-of-the-art language learning applications.

Kraft's willingness to design original material specifically targeted for Chinese students put Lingo Media ahead in its negotiations with PEP. All major multinational publishing houses were simply engaged in the business of utilizing their existing libraries of products for China. In August 2000, Lingo

8

Media had reached a 12-year agreement with PEP to co-develop two core series and one supplemental series of English language training materials:

- *PEP Primary English*: textbooks, audio tapes and supplemental components (Grades 3 to 6)

- *Starting Line*: textbooks, audio tapes and supplemental components (Grades 1 to 6), and

- *Reading Practice*: supplemental books and audio tapes (Grades 7 to 9).

The materials were expected to reach about three million Grade 1 students in September 2001, and increase proportionally each year as new students began the next grade level. Lingo Media was able to secure a royalty of four per cent to eight per cent on every book sold, for a total contract estimated to be worth up to $18 million. PEP, however, would not guarantee any level of income, and Lingo Media was required to invest significant time, resources and effort to co-ordinate the development of all materials.

MILESTONES

During 2004, Lingo Media achieved significant results in China. It had become the market leader of English-language learning programs in primary schools across the country, commanding more than a 60 per cent market share. Since the PEP program was initiated in September 2001, more than 90 million components had been published and sold from more than 250 program components. These components included 60 million student textbooks and 30 million supplemental teaching aids, such as activity books, audio cassettes, teacher resource books, flash cards, DVDs and other teaching materials.

These were prodigious numbers for any publishing company. By way of comparison, the Harry Potter series of books had sold 200 million units worldwide in the 2001 to 2004 time period. The strategy consisting of co-managing an international team of respected educational authors and editors was obviously working. And the sheer number of students using Lingo Media materials was clearly a strong boost to the brand.

Another milestone consisted of securing the help of Bailing Xia, a prominent Chinese businessman based in Toronto who was also the son of a former executive vice-chairman for the State Education Commission in China. Bailing later accepted a seat on the board of directors, thus providing further guidance, credibility and contacts to help master the intricacies of doing business in China.

Yet, the company was barely turning these strengths into a steady stream of profits since the royalties were based on the government-controlled low list price of textbooks in China. As new opportunities were emerging as a result of China's accession to the World Trade Organization, Kraft wondered what to do next.

A NEED FOR EXPANSION

In April 2005, Lingo Media was at a critical juncture point. It had just opened a new office in Beijing, as a permanent base from which to pursue its Chinese expansion plan. The office was staffed by company vice-presidents, Nicolas Chapman and Jessica Zhang, two young ambitious business executives with extensive experience in China. Several attractive options for profits and growth existed, and priorities now had to be established.

Mergers and acquisitions

Merger and acquisition opportunities in publishing had started to be more abundant across China as a result of newly implemented reforms in the print media industry. Lingo Media was now considering possibilities to acquire majority stakes in Chinese-based print media distribution companies. To that end, it hired Daniel Wiseman, a corporate finance and mergers and acquisitions (M&A) specialist to help with its acquisition strategy. This strategy could also provide good access to the direct-to-consumer channel by featuring Lingo Media's English-language learning publications inside educational newspapers, as well as increased opportunities to leverage the company's brand awareness among Chinese households. This option created some amount of risk as Lingo Media's financial resources were limited, and much of its experience was in managing co-publishing programs.

International markets

Lingo Media directed its initial efforts toward China because, with some 200 million students and adults currently learning English, it was the largest English as a Foreign Language (EFL) market in the world. However, English was an official language in more than 75 countries. According to a recent study published by the British Council, an estimated 1.5 billion people worldwide were actively studying English. Kraft felt the strengths developed in the Chinese market could potentially propel the company into other international markets as well, from Southeast Asia to the Americas and beyond. Khurram Qureshi, the company's chief financial officer (CFO), was a strong advocate of international expansion. Business, after all, was based on successful relationships, one domain where Lingo Media truly excelled.

Lingo Media had recently approached the second largest Mexican-owned publisher, based in Mexico City, which claimed to have established contacts with all key decision-makers within the Mexican educational community. Mexico was the world's 11th most populous country, home to more than 100 million inhabitants. Education in Mexico was highly centralized, with funding and curriculum decisions taking place mostly at the federal level through the Secretaría de Educación Pública or SEP (Secretariat of Public Education). The student population in the country was also extremely young: in 2004, 75 per cent of all Mexicans were below the age of 35, and 32 per cent were under 14.

Out-of-the-box solutions

Several MBA students at the Schulich School of Business of York University were asked to dissect Lingo Media's business, as part of a competition aimed at developing new product ideas and growth strategies for the company in China. All students recognized the necessity to leverage new products and ideas. One possibility consisted of developing and offering supplemental "school supply kit" aimed at Chinese students from kindergarten to Grade 6, with easy-to-comprehend Chinese-to-English phrases. The kits would include pencils, paper, pens, crayons, pencil sharpeners, notebooks, glue, scissors, rulers, a basic calculator and other items typically used by Chinese school children. Cartoon characters could also be developed and licensed to further promote the Lingo Media brand and encourage Chinese to learn English fundamentals. It was even suggested that Lingo Media focus its limited resources on developing English-language training programs that could be delivered through web-based learning portals and/or mobile phones.

As Michael Kraft was sitting at his desk, he started to ponder which actions would provide the greatest value to the company.

NOTE

1 All amounts in Cdn$ unless otherwise specified.

8

CASE STUDY 9

LENOVO'S BRAND BUILDING STRATEGIES: TAKING THE COMPETITION TO COMPETITORS WITH "TRANSACTIONAL MODEL"

"We have the best locations in the malls. It sends the signal to customers that ours is the most important brand."[1]

–Yang Yuanqing Lenovo Chairman

"The key advantages of Lenovo are twofold. First, we are well positioned in high-growth areas, such as emerging and SMB markets. Second, we have a very clear strategic focus on our PC business. With this strategy, we continue to sustain our strong momentum in China while enhancing our relationship business outside of China. At the same time, we are expanding our transaction business outside of China. Going forward, we will continue to implement our strategy with decisive and persistent execution to keep the growth momentum."[2]

–Yang Yuanqing, Lenovo Chairman

"Around the world, the Lenovo and Think brands stand for the highest standards of innovation, performance, and service. Excellent progress in recognizing the potential of this company has been made, but our path going forward is very clear. We must first keep a laser sharp focus on our cost and expense structure to continue to drive operating efficiency. Second, we must drive product competitiveness with innovative, high quality, appropriately priced products that address key growth areas. Third, we must leverage our success in China and the success of the dual transaction/relationship model in support of our products. I'm looking forward to building on the strong momentum Lenovo has delivered to date."[3]

–William Amelio President and CEO Lenovo

www.ibscdc.org

Copyright © IBS Case Development Centre

IBS
CDC

EXHIBIT 1	Market share of top ten global PC brands for 2006
Company	*% Share*
Dell	15.9
Hewlett Packard	15.9
Lenovo	7.0
Acer	5.9
Toshiba	3.8
Fujitsu Siemens	3.5
Apple	2.4
NEC	2.1
Gateway	2.1
Sony	1.6
Total (Top 10)	60.1
Total (Others)	39.9

Source: Gartner, http://global.acer.com/about/investor/pdf/2006.pdf

Lenovo Group Ltd., the Chinese PC-maker – after establishing a strong foothold in its domestic market – is striving hard to expand across the globe. It enjoys a whopping 37% market share in China's PC industry. It wishes to adopt its domestically successful transactional and relationship business model in global markets. In 2005, Lenovo acquired IBM's PC division for $1.75 billion. Because of which Lenovo became the world's third biggest PC-maker. But it faces numerous challenges, among which competition from major players such as Dell, HP and Acer (Exhibit 1) is the toughest to address.

GLOBAL PC INDUSTRY: THE LANDSCAPE

The PC industry has been the most dynamic electronic industry sector, since early 1980s. The industry has been extremely prosperous, both in terms of growth and number of new firms. The PC industry continued to develop new management practices and organizational structures – with new means of production, logistics, distribution and marketing in an ever-changing highly competitive market. A number of PC innovations are taken up by other sectors in electronics industry and also by other industries. The PC industry is a convergence of diverse networks of companies engaged in various sectors – ranging from microprocessors to operating systems and applications software.

Asia offers most of hardware manufacturing, Europe has become self-sufficient in production of hardware, software and services for its domestic markets and the US has expertise in design and delivery of sophisticated components including microprocessors, software and services. With all this, the global PC industry reached a considerably mature level by mid-1990s. However, the industry began changing with the emergence of novel competitive forces such as shorter PC production process, which improved the magnitude of depreciation and logistics considerations in deciding end-user location. According to a Taiwanese PC executive "Even if you manufacture a machine at very low cost in Asia and save 5% on the production cost, by the time it gets shipped to the US the price erosion is 10%."

PC-makers including Dell and Gateway, following build-to-order strategies, developed a new segment – on-demand customised PC configurations. This resulted in making the total supply chain respond swiftly to changes in demand for particular components, peripherals and software, rather than general product lines. Outsourcing of manufacturing and other product assembly-related activities to

9

contract manufacturers (CMs) has also widened the gap of final product delivery to the end users. Advent of e-commerce. (online sales) has further hastened the PC industry's clock speed, thereby decreasing the gap between PC vendor and end user. Additionally, customers can now easily configure products and compare prices online – resulting in increased demand for customisation. To address these competitive forces, many PC-makers have established one or more assembly plants in every major nation they are operating. The phenomena compelled few suppliers and contract manufacturers, to build their factories nearer to PC-vendor's build-to-order assembly sites.

In 1990, of the total PC industry, PC-makers enjoyed 49% of profits, whereas suppliers including Intel and Microsoft cornered the remaining 51%. However, by 1995 PC-maker's profits percentage declined to 27.5% and in 2000, it was just 13%.[4] PC component makers – engaged in production of flat-panel displays, hard disk drives and DRAM[5] among others – were the most affected with zero profits in the industry. In early 2000, the PC industry experienced an extreme downfall. With most PC companies upset about declining revenues and zero margins, it was expected that the situation would further deteriorate. How the industry is transforming can be assessed by the 2002 acquisition of the world's second biggest PC-producer, Compaq by the world's fourth biggest PC-seller, Hewlett-Packard.

In 2004, vendor consolidation was the last option left for companies, facing slower growth rates and reduced profit margins. Although the market was enjoying double-digit PC shipment growth over the last few years it was believed that the industry would foresee a tough time. Leslie Fiering, research vice president for Gartner's Client Platforms group, predicted, "Local PC vendors in emerging markets should consider acquiring local rivals as a means to consolidate home market position and develop the scale economies required to springboard into a global presence,"[6]

Leslie Fiering also added "Global vendors will be forced to continue maximizing supply chain efficiencies and, finally, abandon any efforts to differentiate other than on price and service levels. Vendors that have yet to do so may attempt to diversify into related markets pursuits, such as consumer electronics, to bolster margins. Others may attempt mergers with rivals to improve margins through economies of scale."[7]

George Shiffler, research director at Client Platforms Markets Group of Gartner Dataquest, commented, "Emerging markets and mobile PCs will continue to provide growth. However, falling average selling prices (ASPs), slowing replacement activity and further declines in mature market desk-based PC shipments will keep PC vendors under pressure to rationalize their operations or exit the market."[8]

Global PC industry is currently affected by two major trends: commoditisation and the absence of 'mid-market'. Commoditisation is generally visible in all industries; however, it particularly affects the mass-produced electronics industry. As electronics products are quickly produced, the market gets overstocked easily and therefore prices drop swiftly. Though the trend turns out to be beneficial to the end user, it becomes a bottleneck to the industry players who find it tough to earn margins. By 2007, in all markets, a basic desktop PC is available for $400 or less that was around $2000 in the 1990s. Another global phenomenon is 'mid-market' challenge. A market faces challenge from two types of customers: one who demand cheapest products and the other who were always in search of exclusiveness – most expensive, feature-rich products. For instance, in the mobile telecommunication market, there are customers who keep looking for cheap affordable voice-only cell phones (or get it free from the service provider). And there are also some customers who keep switching to latest phone models.

Moreover PC industry is expected to experience challenges, including proliferation of technologies with the potential to be interconnected in future digital homes. Consumers don't want to buy PCs, TVs cameras or audio systems as separate items with distinct functions; instead they want all in one. As of now, they can store digital photos on PCs, play movies on portable DVDs, save their favorite TV shows on PCs and download music from PCs to iPods. Moreover, they are enjoying games and music on cell phones. Tech companies are finding it hard to combine all these functions in one product.

LENOVO: FROM EMERGING TO SURGING?

Lenovo is China's biggest IT enterprise and PC-maker. Established as Legend Group in 1984 in Beijing, the company has global presence with production and distribution facilities in the US, UK, Mexico, Malaysia, Hungary, China and Brazil. The company's growth, as it maintains, is based on innovation, operational efficiency and customer satisfaction. In April 2003, it changed its brand name from Legend to Lenovo. With the acquisition of IBM's PC division, Lenovo strengthened its foothold in the global IT sector. It also helped Lenovo become the world's third biggest PC-maker. Liu Jun, chief operating officer of Lenovo China, says, "Backed by the merger with IBM's PC business, the combination of IBM's technologies and our low costs in China will greatly strengthen our competitiveness in the global arena."[9] Neeraj Sharma, managing director of Lenovo South Asia, points, "The acquisition of IBM's PC division was the fastest and most cost-efficient way for Lenovo to achieve a global presence and become an international company."[10]

Jiang, associate professor at the University of Alberta in Canada, adds, "This is a new Chinese business model emerging. It shows there is an integrated strategy that in order to break into the world markets, you have to be brand conscious, build up domestic production and dare to buy and expand."[11] However, buying out the loss-making PC division of IBM was a tough task for Lenovo's chairman Yang Yuanqing. This decision was strongly opposed by all board members, as they felt, "A $3 billion company based in China would be taking over a $10 billion global behemoth. IBM had practically invented the PC industry; if Big Blue couldn't make money selling these machines worldwide, how could little Lenovo hope to do any better?"[12] Yang Yuanqing explained that in order to become a global PC conglomerate, the company needs to grasp the opportunity of pocketing IBM's PC division.

After the acquisition, Lenovo's profits increased significantly – in fact, HK$357 million ($46 million) from January 2005-June 2005. Yang Yuanqing says, "The board of directors are satisfied with the business results, IBM's PC business has started to yield profits from business integration in only two months, which indicates the acquisition was a right step for Lenovo's global expansion."[13] Yang Qing-feng, IT research director at Analysys International, held, "This is a good beginning for Lenovo."[14]

Similarly, in the first quarter of 2006, the company's consolidated revenue increased by 38% to $3.5 billion. William J. Amelio, Lenovo's president and CEO, says, "We are encouraged with the progress we are making in transforming the company while at the same time growing market share and maintaining our overall profit margin in a highly competitive market. That said, we still have much to do; and we are moving swiftly and aggressively to take the necessary steps needed to make Lenovo a truly world-class global competitor. This will not be easy and it will take time, but I am confident in our ability to execute our action plan to transform this company."[15]

After cementing its roots in China, Lenovo started implementing a worldwide expansion plan – wanting to become a household name across the globe. In July 2007, it announced that it would invest $11 million to construct a second manufacturing unit in Baddi, Himachal Pradesh, India. The plant would be capable of producing two million units annually and will produce both desktop and notebook PCs. Jeff Gallinat, Lenovo's vice president – global manufacturing, points out, "India is an integral part of Lenovo's global manufacturing strategy. With our second plant in India, we expect to improve our supply chain efficiency and better serve our growing base of customers in this region."[16]

The company also intends to solidify its presence in the US, the world's biggest PC market, where it relies mostly on the sales of ThinkPad (a brand of IBM) laptops to business customers. Lenovo wants to be among the US' top-five PC companies, thereby selling Lenovo-branded products to the US consumers through retail stores. Similarly, to tap the European market in August 2007, the company announced its plans to pocket Packard Bell BV, the fifth biggest PC-maker in Western Europe.

9

Moreover, the company plans to invest $260 million on brand building. In mid-2007, to target China's low-income consumers, Lenovo decided to offer a new PC at a retail price of 1,499 renminbi (£100). Besides, it also plans to cut prices on its servers. Yang Yuanqing says, "The company has the ability to grow faster and tap the growth potential of the PC industry."[17] All through its expansion plans, the company faces competition from HP, Dell and Acer. In 2005, of the total worldwide PC market, Dell enjoyed 16.8%, HP trailed with 15.2% and Acer sliced 4.4% market share.

LENOVO'S GLOBAL BRAND BUILDING STRATEGIES: "TRANSACTIONAL MODEL"

"The most important thing is to make sure that Lenovo continues to grow in China", opined Ravi Marwaha, senior vice-president of Lenovo Group in charge of global sales. Ravi also added that "the Chinese market is the company's primary concern and will act as a growth engine driving Lenovo's expansion in global markets."[18] Sanjit Sinha, senior manager, Hardware Research Group, IDC India[19] thinks, "The scenario ahead for Lenovo will depend to a large extent on how the company carries forward with the IBM legacy products. It can pose a challenge for HP in some time, provided it brings in a comprehensive product portfolio for both the enterprise and consumer space like its rival."[20]

In China, Lenovo follows two business models: relationship model and transactional model. To target and establish long-term business relationships with big enterprises, Lenovo follows a relationship business model – under which it receives bulk orders for pre-configured PCs from big enterprises. On the other hand, to target small- to mid-size companies and individual customers, the company follows a transactional business model – serving customers with common requirements and who need lesser customisation. Lenovo believes that its transactional model helped in gaining market coverage in small cities also. Lenovo credits its success in China to both these business models and wants to do the same in global markets.

The acquired IBM PC division is helping Lenovo boost its sales to big corporations in the West. However, to tap the small- and mid-size businesses, it plans to adapt its successful home market business model. Yang Yuanqing said, "We want to extend the business model that was so successful in China out across the world."[21] Besides, the company's long-term goal is to make Lenovo a prestigious global brand. In this context, in 2004, the company entered into an agreement with International Olympic Committee – to become the tech-sponsor for the Turin and Beijing Olympic Games. Furthermore, the company inked a marketing and partnership deal with the National Basketball Association in US, to promote its Lenovo brand. After acquiring IBM's PC division, the company started detaching customers from the IBM brand. By late 2006, Lenovo ceased using IBM in ad campaigns and the company also started removing IBM brand name – replacing Lenovo on ThinkPad laptop computers.

In order to gain market share globally, Lenovo – along with its own branded product line – is continuing to market IBM's Notebook PCs, available in ThinkPad X, T and R models, desktop PCs available in ThinkCentre A, M and S series; and also Think Accessories, which includes projectors and the ThinkVision range of TFT monitors. Neeraj Sharma feels, "We believe that the new combined brands, products and competitive strengths make us an extremely strong competitor in worldwide markets, with potential for growth that neither organization could completely realise on its own."[22]

After the IBM acquisition, Lenovo continued offering the same legacy product brands, ThinkPad and ThinkCentre – instead of upsetting their image in customer minds. Sharma adds "During the transition, we will leverage the Think brand appropriately to communicate that the same quality, innovation and service. Subsequently, the introduction of Lenovo products will complement the brand that has already been built so that there is no segment for which we don't have an offering. Thus, we will be the one-stop-shop in the industry with products that are unmatched in terms of innovation and cutting-edge technology—qualities that are common to both the Think line as well as Lenovo's other products."[23]

In China, Lenovo holds a very efficient supply chain network. With around 12 distribution centres, it fulfills every order on time. Small orders are even delivered by bicycles. To be successful in other markets globally, Lenovo plans to implement its China-based supply chain model everywhere. William Amelio, president and CEO of Lenovo quips, "The way to get a world-class supply chain is to have a rich mix between transaction business and relationship business. A dual model is inherently more complex, but with SAP we can do it because we have a better IT system that can better support our business."[24] The company believes that an efficient supply chain system helps the product to be delivered to the end-user faster. Computers tend to depreciate and become outdated easily, owing to continuous drumbeat of cheaper and faster technology once they move out of the factory as finished products. As such, long duration in making the product reach the end-user will curb profits. For Lenovo, shipping PCs from China to the US took 30 days – hampering its sales and market share. Therefore Lenovo started building manufacturing units in every geographic region it operated, to save shipping time and costs.

THE CHALLENGES

Building a global brand in a highly commoditised PC industry is Lenovo's biggest challenge. There are hurdles in popularising its brand in the US, where customers think Lenovo as a state-owned Chinese company whose products may endanger national security. American Department of State's decision not to use Lenovo's computers prevented it from having a strong foothold there. Improving the supply chain network internationally is the other major obstacle to Lenovo's growth. Chinese counterfeits of computer components also alarmed Lenovo. According to Timothy Trainer, a representative of multinational companies and entities from Global Intellectual Property Strategy Center, a consulting firm in Washington DC, "Despite a few shipments being stopped at China's ports, the flood of massive amounts of counterfeit and pirated goods from China continues to reach the shores of countries around the world, demonstrating that China is not doing enough to police its borders. Chinese counterfeiters continue to trade off of the success of US companies, big and small."[25] Lenovo is also threatened by more local PC companies establishing strong distribution networks to offer PCs at lower prices.

Growing competition from international players is squeezing Lenovo to expand its business globally. Dell is giving it tough competition, both in China and other international markets. Unlike Lenovo, which follows a dual business model, Dell uses a direct-selling business model that helps it remain in touch with its customer's requirements. It is reported that this gives Dell a 6% cost advantage over others and also rewards it with detailed customer knowledge. Dell could provide customised solutions to its bigger clients and forge long-term relationships with them.

Acer, world's fourth biggest branded PC vendor, is striving hard to go one up and beat Lenovo. Acer adopts 'three-ones and three-many's' management strategy – 'one company, one brand, one global team', and operating through 'many vendors, many product lines and many business partners'. The strategy enabled Acer to come up with a unique channel business model, which helps it hold full control of brand name, marketing, technology and products, service capacity and worldwide logistics. Similarly all other big players, mainly HP and Fujitsu Siemens, are striving hard to increase their market share in an environment where margins are directly correlated to units sold, and cost-cutting has become a profit mantra. In the highly matured global PC market, observers opined that it will not be as easy an outing as was the Chinese home market.

9

NOTES

1 Hamm Steve, "Lenovo Still the Mainland's Main etc. Choice", http://www.businessweek.com/bwdaily/dnflash/content/dec2006/db20061204_310058.htm?chan=search, December 4th, 2006.

2 "Lenovo Reports First Quarter 2006/07 Results", http://www.lenovo.com/news/us//en/2006/08/1Q06-07.html, August 3rd, 2006.

3 "Lenovo Reports Third Quarter FY2005/06 Results", http://www.lenovo.com/news/us/en/2006/01/3q_earnings.html January 26th, 2006.

4 Kraemer L. Kennet and Dedrick Jason, "Globalization of the Personal Computer Industry: Trends and Implications", http://repositories.cdlib.org/cgi/viewcontent.cgi?article=1026&context=crito, 2002.

5 Dynamic random access memory (DRAM) is the most common kind of random access memory (RAM) for personal computers and workstations.

6 "Gartner Says Three of Top 10 PC Vendors Will Exit the Market by 2007", http://www.gartner.com/press_releases/asset_115083_11.html, November 29th, 2004.

7 Ibid.

8 "Indian PC Market to show Double Growth than the World", http://www.investinginwireless.com/News/r041307a.asp.

9 "China still key for Lenovo PC sales", http://english.people.com.cn/200505/20/eng20050520_186033.html.

10 Makhija Kusum, "How is IBM's PC business doing five months after it was sold to Lenovo?", http://www.expresscomputeronline.com/20051024/market01.shtml.

11 "Global Cachet Comes With Chinese Deal for IBM Unit (12/10)", http://www.appliancedesign.com/CDA/Archives/beb63a6c89a38010VgnVCM100000f932a8c0, December 10th 2004.

12 "China's First Global Capitalist", http://www.businessweek.com/magazine/content/06_50/b4013062.htm?chan=globalbiz_asia_today's+top+story, December 11th 2006.

13 "Lenovo records profit rise", http://kuching2.mofcom.gov.cn/aarticle/chinanews/200508/20050800251819.html, August 11th 2005.

14 Ibid.

15 "Lenovo Reports First Quarter 2006/07 Results", op.cit.

16 "Lenovo to invest 11m USD in HP factory", http://economictimes.indiatimes.com/Infotech/Hardware/Lenovo_to_invest_11m_in_HP_factory/articleshow/2237593.cms, July 27th 2007.

17 Ong Janet, "Lenovo's Profit Jumps 13-Fold on Job Cuts, Orders (Update3)", http://www.bloomberg.com/apps/news?pid=newsarchive&sid=a5WpFAYaLi10, August 2nd 2007.

18 "China still key for Lenovo PC sales", op.cit.

19 IDC (India) Limited, the Indian affiliate of IDC the world's leading provider of technology intelligence, industry analysis and market data to builders, providers and users of IT forecasts IT markets and technology trends and analyses IT products and vendors, using a combination of rigorous primary research and in-depth competitive analysis.

20 "How is IBM's PC business doing five months after it was sold to Lenovo?", op.cit.

21 Roberts Dexter and Hamm Steve, "China's First Global Capitalist", http://www.businessweek.com/magazine/content/06_50/b4013062.htm?chan=globalbiz_asia_today's+top+story, December 11th 2006.

22 "How is IBM's PC business doing five months after it was sold to Lenovo?", op.cit.

23 Ibid.

24 http://www.sap.com/germany/company/investor/reports/gb2006/en/success-stories/lenovo-2.html.

25 Trainer Timothy, "Global Intellectual Property Strategy Center, P.C.: China's Counterfeiters Assault On Consumers, Not Just The Brands", http://www.eworldwire.com/pdf/14703.pdf, June 7th 2006.

9

CASE STUDY 10

MEXICO, MITSUBISHI, AND THE GRAY WHALE: A CASE STUDY OF LAW, ETHICS, AND ENVIRONMENTAL ISSUES IN INTERNATIONAL BUSINESS[1]

BACKGROUND

In 1997, Laguna San Ignacio, located in Baja California, was the last pristine gray whale nursery along the Pacific migratory corridor. This corridor extended from Baja California to the Bering Sea in Alaska. The 6.2 million acre Vizcaino Desert Biosphere Reserve ("Vizcaino Reserve") included Laguna San Ignacio.

Created in 1988 by Mexican presidential decree to protect the gray whale and other resident species, the Vizcaino Reserve provided habitat to 308 terrestrial and marine vertebrates, including bighorn sheep, pronghorn antelope, bobcats, coyotes, dolphins, sea turtles, and many species of birds.[2] In 1993, the United Nations Educational, Scientific and Cultural Organization ("UNESCO") designated the Vizcaino Reserve as a World Heritage Site[3] pursuant to The Convention Concerning the Protection of the World Cultural and National Heritage[4] ("World Heritage Convention"). This treaty provided a "legal framework for the protection of important and significant cultural and natural heritage sites in member countries."[5] Mexico ratified the World Heritage Convention in 1984.[6]

Despite Laguna San Ignacio's protected status, Exportadora de Sal, S.A. de C.V. (ESSA), a joint venture between the Mitsubishi Corporation (Mitsubishi) and the Mexican federal government, chose it as the future site for what would be the world's largest salt mining operation.

The Vizcaino Reserve contained two regions designated as the nuclear zone and the buffer zone. Mexican law allowed for limited development within the buffer zone, but prohibited development activities within the nuclear zone. Laguna San Ignacio existed wholly within the buffer zone. In order to receive development approval, projects within the buffer zone were required to conform to Mexico's General Law of

Copyright © 2005 by Lisa Johnson. Printed with permission from ecch.com Ref: 706-015-1.

Ecological Balance and Environmental Protection (Environmental Protection Law)[7]. In accordance with this law, a comprehensive environmental impact statement (EIS) was required to aide the Mexican government in its evaluation of the proposed project.[8]

Objectives within the diverse set of stakeholders varied. Many environmental groups worldwide demanded cancellation of the project on the basis that industrial development would damage critical gray whale habitat. They also maintained that the project was incompatible with the protected status of the Vizcaino Reserve. Mitsubishi, on behalf of ESSA, asserted that the proposed salt mining operation was environmentally benign and that it was required to forestall a shortage of salt. Mexico played a double role in this case. Julia Carabias, the Mexican Secretary of the Environment, Natural Resources, and Fisheries, promised that the Mexican government, as the majority partner in ESSA, would not move forward with the project if it jeopardized the conservation of the Vizcaino Reserve's natural resources.[9] The Mexican government, as a regulatory agency, was obligated to make a decision on whether to approve or deny ESSA's industrial salt mining proposal based upon the contents of the EIS. The state government of Baja California Sur (BCS) welcomed the proposed project as consistent with its mission to increase the economic stability of the region. However, the local population predominately opposed the project based upon its fears that agricultural land and potable water would become scarce, and fishing rights would be forfeited.

ESSA had made an earlier bid to develop a salt mining operation at Laguna San Ignacio. The Mexican government rejected that proposal because the required EIS insufficiently addressed the impact of the project on the gray whale. ESSA first appealed the rejection, and then dropped the appeal in favor of submitting a new EIS. The project at Laguna San Ignacio had to be re-evaluated based upon the second EIS.

THE GRAY WHALE

Whales exhibit certain characteristics that humans value and find appealing. Whales engage in recreation, and conspicuously exhibit playfulness and humor. Not only do they have a highly developed language of their own, but also they have developed inter-species communication with dolphins.[10] They are curious, friendly, and their intelligence might rival that of humans.[11] They swim near the coastline when migrating, and navigate by the sounds of the surf. Whales are social animals that have their own communities. In short, many believe whales are sentient beings.

In 1997, twenty thousand gray whales existed in the eastern Pacific Ocean. Once almost hunted to extinction, the population of the gray whale was slowly recovering. Females did not breed annually, but when they did breed, the gestation period was 12 to 13 months. Gray whales migrated to the lagoons of Baja California to deliver and nurse their young. This migration took two to three months from their summer feeding waters of the Arctic. Led by the pregnant females, the whales swam night and day, averaging 20 to 100 miles per day during the duration of their 5,000-mile journey.[12]

The lagoons of Baja California offered safety from predators, warmth to help the newborn calves retain body heat, and higher salinity that increased the calves' floating abilities. Except for southern Baja California, suitable nursery sites have been eliminated by development. At least half of the time, expectant mother whales were not able to wait for the safety of the lagoons and gave birth in the open sea. Newborn whales in that situation often fell prey to orcas or sharks, or died from the cold water or lack of swimming experience.

ESSA: THE MEXICAN GOVERNMENT AND MITSUBISHI

The Mexican government owned 51 percent of ESSA, and Mitsubishi owned 49 percent. According to Mexican law in the late 1990's, a foreign interest could own a maximum of 49 percent in an industry of this nature.[13] Although it was the minority partner, Mitsubishi had greater practical control of ESSA than Mexico because, unlike Mexico, Mitsubishi had the funding for operations and expansion.

In the late 1990's, Mitsubishi identified Laguna San Ignacio as an ideal site for its salt mine. It maintained that suitable sites were rare. ESSA already owned two other salt mining operations in the Mexican state of Baja California Sur – one at Ojo de Liebre and the other at Guerrero Negro. ESSA produced seven million tons of salt annually at these other salt production facilities. According to ESSA, the existing facilities provided no more room for growth, and without additional sources, the demand for salt was projected to exceed supply by 2007.[14]

Projected annual revenue from the new salt works was $100 million.[15] The Mexican federal government would receive direct revenues from taxes paid by ESSA; as co-owner of ESSA, Mexico would also receive revenue from profits received from the sale of salt. Furthermore, the new salt works would create 208 jobs, half of which would be available to Mexican nationals.

Mitsubishi anticipated direct profits too, but there were also other financial incentives for Mitsubishi. The existing salt works in Baja California Sur supplied fifty percent of Mitsubishi Chemical's demand for salt. Mitsubishi Chemical was one of Mitsubishi's main subsidiaries. The estimated seven million annual tons that the Laguna San Ignacio salt works would produce translated into a three- to four-percent increase in the world supply of salt. According to accepted economic theory, this increase would have a significant downward effect on the price of salt. Mitsubishi itself stood to be one of the main beneficiaries of this project because it would lower the cost of salt for Mitsubishi Chemical. For these reasons, ESSA sought to open the salt works at Laguna San Ignacio.[16]

ENVIRONMENTAL GROUPS

El Grupo de los Cien, a prominent Mexican environmental organization largely responsible for bringing this case to the world's attention, solidly opposed this development as incompatible with critical whale habitat. Their deep concern for the future of the gray whale mirrored that of many other environmental groups that opposed ESSA's efforts to expand, including The Natural Resources Defense Council (NRDC), the International Fund for Animal Welfare, and the World Wildlife Fund.[17]

These environmental groups also criticized the multi-layered potentials for conflict of interest. For example, the Mexican federal government had dual roles. The majority partner of ESSA, the Mexican government had to decide whether the project would proceed. Furthermore, Mexico's Secretary of Commerce also chaired the ESSA Board of Directors. Julia Carabias, the Secretary for Environment, Natural Resources, and Fisheries (SEMARNAP), headed the department in the Mexican government responsible for reviewing – and approving or rejecting – the proposed project. Moreover, the Secretary of Commerce oversaw SEMARNAP's review and, presumably, their recommendation to approve or reject projects.[18]

In 1995 el Grupo de los Cien successfully campaigned against ESSA's first bid for a salt works permit on the grounds that the required EIS did not adequately address the project's impact on the gray whale. This group had been vocal in their opposition to this project, because they believed that the environmental degradation would cause irreparable harm to the gray whale and critical gray whale habitat.

Similarly, international environmental NGOs believed this project to be incompatible with critical gray whale habitat. The NRDC had raised objections based upon its interpretation of the Mexican Environmental Protection Law. NRDC asserted that the law prohibited major industry in the buffer zone of the reserve, and that the only activities allowed were subsistence farming, fishing, research, and eco-tourism.[19]

BAJA CALIFORNIA SUR

The State of Baja California Sur ("BCS") fully supported the ESSA's proposed project. In 1997, the state's main sources of revenue for the largely rural BCS were fishing, tourism, mining, and subsistence farming. The governor of BCS hoped that the industrial investment of $120 million to develop the salt works would boost the state's flagging economy and he had publicly declared his support for the project.[20] BCS's economic development lagged behind that of the other Mexican states' due to its pre-transpeninsular highway isolation from the rest of the country.[21] If the Laguna San Ignacio salt works were allowed to proceed, 208 jobs would have been created, and half of those jobs would have been available to Mexican nationals.

Though the state supported the project, the local population did not. They feared that if approval were given to ESSA, they would lose fishing access, potable water would become scarcer, waste disposal facilities would be inadequate, groundwater would become unfit for agricultural irrigation, and urbanization would occur.[22] Their fears originated from observed conditions at the ESSA's existing salt works, Ojo de Liebre and Guerrero Negro, where those problems were already manifest.

The Vizcaino Reserve was the largest biosphere reserve in Latin America, and Mexico lacked funds to properly manage it. Though the small government budget was supplemented by trust funds,[23] it was not enough. In the late 1990s, ESSA funded much of the Vizcaino Reserve's work, and sometimes completely underwrote entire projects.[24] Furthermore, ESSA maintained that if the Laguna San Ignacio project was permitted to go forward, ESSA would provide piped fresh water, water treatment facilities, sewage systems, and support for local schools and hospitals. Baja California Sur lacked funds for those improvements. Some speculated that if travel infrastructure and available services were improved, tourism revenues would increase.[25]

Eco-tourism had already proven to be a sustainable industry in BCS, without ESSA's infrastructure improvements. Whale watching and land based eco-tourism had grown into an organized industry whose operators were licensed, multilingual, and trained in biological information. This industry was profitable and growing.[26]

THE PROPOSED LAGUNA SAN IGNACIO SALT MINE

If approved, Laguna San Ignacio would be the largest salt mining operation in the world, encompassing in excess of 100 square miles of lagoon shores. The planned facility would pump 6,000 gallons of water per second from the lagoon. This water would move through a series of man-made earth pits, or concentration ponds, where sunlight and wind would evaporate the ocean water to raise the salt content.[27] The salt water would then be moved to shallow crystallization ponds until the salt becomes crystallized. It would be harvested by earth-movers, washed, and transferred to cargo ships via a mile-long concrete pier[28] that would be located directly in the migratory path of the gray whale.[29] The entire salt making process takes two years.

Proponents of solar salt mining claimed that the process is natural and environmentally benign. Two other salt mining operations already existed in Baja California. These 43-year-old salt works, Ojo de Liebre and Guerrero Negro, produced seven million tons of salt annually. Coincidentally, these areas were also gray whale nurseries. Though el Grupo de los Cien asserted that repeated mining related dredging had rendered the lagoons incompatible with the whales' needs,[30] Mitsubishi, on behalf of ESSA, disagreed. It maintained that the number of whales sighted at the existing salt works in 1997 exceeded the numbers sighted in previous years.[31]

Opponents countered that salt mining of any kind increases the risk of diesel fuel spills from tankers, and increases the likelihood of salt brine toxicity. Furthermore, they argued that noisy saltwater pumps

10

have serious negative implications for whales. Whales rely upon hearing to navigate and communicate. Severe hearing loss in whales has been documented as a result of man-made noise.[32] Moreover, salt mining is an established source of environmental degradation. Salt mining operations have caused groundwater to become unfit for agricultural irrigation,[33] and the majority of inhabitants of Laguna San Ignacio were subsistence farmers. Opponents also feared that incessant pumping of large quantities of seawater from the lagoon would affect the salinity and temperature of the water, which would negatively affect the whale calves' heat retention and floating abilities.

ESSA described Laguna San Ignacio as "virtually lifeless" and ideal for salt production.[34] Further, it argued that such ideal conditions as those found at Laguna San Ignacio were rare, though this was another disputed point.[35] Finally, ESSA described its proposal as a model sustainable development project that would attract new wildlife through the creation of wetlands.

MEXICAN ENVIRONMENTAL LAW

In 1988, then President Salinas enacted Mexico's national Environmental Protection Law, ushering in a new spirit of environmental protection. A major component of this law was the requirement for businesses to produce an environmental impact statement (EIS) to address the environmental impact for many proposed development activities, including mining.[36] Unlike the United States' National Environmental Policy Act (NEPA), the Mexican EIS requirement had teeth.[37] The EIS formed the basis on which a project could be rejected or approved.[38] In 1995, Mexico rejected ESSA's first bid for a salt mining permit for Laguna San Ignacio under this procedure based upon an insufficient EIS. That EIS did not properly address the project's impact on the gray whale.

The enactment of the Environmental Protection Law marked a pivotal point when Mexico's focus shifted from issuing fines for environmental degradation to initiating prevention. It was modeled after environmental laws of the United States.[39] This shift towards environmental preservation illustrated Mexico's desire to achieve free trade with the United States through the North American Free Trade Agreement (NAFTA).[40, 41]

Mexico had made substantial efforts towards the improvement of its environmental laws. After ESSA's first bid for a salt mining permit was rejected based upon the EIS, the SEMARNAP commissioned an international group of whale experts to advise ESSA in the development of an appropriate EIS, and to assist SEMARNAP in its interpretation once completed. This scientific committee was also scheduled to advise SEMARNAP regarding the ecological feasibility of the proposed project.[42] This step exceeded the EIS requirement as set forth by the Environmental Protection Law. Mexico's commitment to raise its environmental standards, and its willingness to adjust its policies to bring those standards in concordance with those of the United States, had been established.

INTERNATIONAL ENVIRONMENTAL LAW

The World Heritage Convention

Mexico ratified the World Heritage Convention in 1984.[43] It nominated the Vizcaino Reserve to be designated a World Heritage Site, in part because it was the last pristine gray whale nursery. The request was granted in 1993. Article IV requires a party to "do all it can" to protect and conserve the natural heritage of World Heritage Sites situated on its own territory.[44] To do otherwise would violate the international treaty. Laguna San Ignacio's location in a World Heritage Site obligated Mexico by international treaty to preserve it from development inconsistent with the protection and conservation of that area.

The benefits of ratification of the World Heritage Convention – beyond increasing public awareness of the site and international recognition – included access to the World Heritage Fund. This fund distributes more than $3 million annually to member states to finance technical assistance, training projects, and development of conservation projects. Funds can also be used to obtain assistance in preparing site nomination proposals. Most funds are made available to low income or lesser developed countries.

NAFTA

NAFTA came into force in 1993, and Mexico fell under its environmental provisions. Therefore, it no longer tried to raise its environmental standards to United States' levels to satisfy pre-NAFTA expectations. NAFTA was the first trade agreement in history to explicitly address environmental concerns. These provisions were reminiscent of Principle 21 of the Declaration of the United Nations Conference on the Human Environment ("Stockholm Agreement"),[45] which recognized the sovereignty of states while prohibiting the causation of "damage to the environment of other States or of areas beyond the limits of national jurisdiction."[46] NAFTA set forth important environmental obligations.[47]

Pursuant to NAFTA, Mexico had an obligation not to cause environmental damage to areas beyond national jurisdiction. Gray whales were a trans-boundary, highly migratory species that spends less time overall in Mexico's jurisdiction than elsewhere. Gray whales could not be considered a permanent part of Mexican jurisdiction even when the whales were located exclusively within Mexican waters.

If degradation of the last pristine gray whale nursery in the eastern Pacific – critical gray whale habitat – occurred as a result of ESSA's industrial activities in the BCS and caused the population of gray whales to decline, then Mexico would have caused environmental damage to areas beyond Mexico's jurisdiction. If extraterritorial environmental damage occurred, measurable in loss of gray whale related tourism and associated economic activity,[48] NAFTA's environmental provisions would have been violated.

NAFTA also set forth obligations to protect endangered species,[49] just as the Stockholm Agreement emphasized humankind's responsibility to safeguard the heritage of wildlife.[50] Though the United States down-listed the gray whale in 1994 from endangered to threatened status, the International Whaling Commission (IWC), the organization responsible for setting whaling quotas and rules, maintained its whaling moratorium. Similarly, other international treaties, such as the Convention on International Trade in Endangered Species (CITES),[51] still reflected the gray whales' precarious status.

Customary International Law

Remedies for violation of international law, particularly international environmental law, were relatively mild. International treaties typically did not infringe on the rights of the sovereignty of the signatory state. However, the treaty could attempt to alter the behavior of signatory states – indeed, that was the fundamental purpose underlying most treaties. But the fact remained that international treaties required voluntary participation, and if penalties were too harsh, states had less incentive to participate. Resolutions may be passed by other member countries that condemn the actions of a country in violation of an international treaty, economic sanctions may be imposed, or certain rights or privileges granted to the signatory state by the treaty may be revoked. But the fact remained that international law relies on voluntary participation of its various member states. While there are incentives to co-operate, the penalties for violation of international law were not as harsh as violations of domestic law. In short, when a country violated an international environmental law, imprisonment or heavy fines were usually not imposed, and in many cases, could not have been imposed.

Customary international law served as an important indicator regarding acceptable behavior, and deviations from this behavior could draw negative worldwide attention. Customary international law indicated a strong propensity to protect whales.

Specific customary international law regarding whales had developed through the twentieth century from simple whaling quota regulation, to conservation, to protection, to the presently recognized custom of whale preservation.[52] The IWC generally followed this route throughout its history, and endorsed a global moratorium on whaling. Nations such as Japan and Norway, which refused to abide by this moratorium and proceeded with their whaling activities, drew worldwide criticism for their actions from other countries, non-governmental organizations, and consumers. Mexico publicly supported a global moratorium on whaling well before one was established.[53]

The gray whale was listed on CITES Appendix I,[54] which was further evidence that the international community had chosen to protect it. This status indicated that the gray whale was considered to be threatened with extinction, and trade in specimens of Appendix I species was severely restricted.

Moreover, the United Nations Convention on the Law of the Sea provided that cetaceans, including whales, must be conserved.[55] This provision had a direct impact on customary international law.[56] While the proposed salt works at Laguna San Ignacio was clearly not a whaling pursuit, the end result could be tantamount to such a pursuit vis-à-vis the gray whale. Customary international law regarding whales indicated that human-caused whale mortality was unacceptable.

The international community expressed misgivings about the proposed Laguna San Ignacio salt works development because it appeared to violate international treaty provisions and customary international law. The international community was interested in this case because gray whales were considered to be a trans-boundary resource, and not simply a Mexican resource. However, this stakeholder was willing to listen to evidence that the salt works would not be harmful to the gray whale.

MEXICAN CULTURE AND THE GRAY WHALE

Mexico had a long history of marine mammal protection dating from the early 1930s. It had always been a non-whaling nation. Julia Carabias, Secretary of SEMARNAP, asserted that killing marine mammals to further Mexico's economy is an idea "alien to [Mexico's] national culture and tradition."[57] Despite the Mexican government's status as the majority partner of ESSA, in 1997 it had thus far remained true to its environmental commitment to the Vizcaino Reserve. One of the Mexican government's expressed purposes for establishing the Vizcaino Reserve was to protect the gray whale and the 2.5 million hectares of calving grounds. Mexico's efforts to protect the gray whale have been credited for the comeback of the species.

DECISION FOCUS

Decision makers at Mitsubishi, ESSA, and the Mexican federal government had to wrestle with the many issues presented in this case to reach a decision that best represented its interests. Remember that the Mexican federal government was not only acting in the capacity of government, but also was the majority shareholder of ESSA. Decisions might have been influenced by potential affects on other stakeholders, competing objectives, and the conflicting evidence presented. If you had been an advisor to a decision maker at Mitsubishi, ESSA, or the Mexican federal government, what factors would have influenced your advice? What course of action would you have recommended?

10

NOTES

1 This case was written by Lisa Johnson, Assistant Professor at the University of Puget Sound School of Business and Leadership, as a basis for classroom discussion. It is part of the CIBER Case Collection, sponsored by Indiana University CIBER and distributed by the ECCH @ Babson.

2 *El Vizcaino: Reserva de la Biosfera,* (visited Jan. 19, 2004) <http://www.vizcaino.gob.mx/ifaun.html>.

3 *Report on the Convention Concerning the Protection of the World Cultural and National Heritage,* World Heritage Committee of the United Nations Educational, Scientific and Cultural Organization, 17th session (December 6–11, 1993), Cartagena, Colombia.

4 The Convention Concerning the Protection of the World Cultural and National Heritage, *opened for signature* November 23, 1972, 15511 U.N.T.S. 1972.

5 http://gomexico.miningco.com.

6 *The Convention Concerning the Protection of the World Cultural and National Heritage: Ratification Status* (visited Jan. 11, 2004) <http://whc.unesco.org/nwhc/pages/doc/main.htm>.

7 "Ley General del Equilibrio Ecológico y la Protección al Ambiente," Diario Oficial de la Federacion ("D.O."), at 1 (Jan. 28, 1988) (Mex.).

8 Id. at Art. 28 and 29. See also, Reglamento de la Ley General del Equilibrio Ecologico y la Proteccion al Ambiente, D.O., at 86 (June 7, 1988) (Mex.).

9 Carabias, Julia, *Baja: Open Letters to NRDC Members*, 19 The Amicus Journal 3 (1997).

10 D'Amato, Anthony and Sudhir K. Chopra. *Whales: Their Emerging Right to Life*, 85 Am. J. Int'l L. 21 (1991)

11 *Id.* Finding from D. Day, *The Whale War.* Though the whale's body is very large in relation to its brain size, only a minor percent of its cerebral cortex is concerned with control of the body. The majority is devoted to memory and conceptual thought, and is much larger than humans'.

12 Five thousand miles was one way. Gray whales annually migrated both south to Baja California and north to the Arctic Sea for an annual round trip of ten thousand miles.

13 *A Guide for Foreign Investors* (visited Nov. 14, 1997) <http://mexicool.com/investor/legal.html#limit>.

14 *San Ignacio Solar Evaporation Facility: Key Characteristics – Physical Features* (visited Oct. 26, 1997) <http://www.bajasalt.com/SIG/sigkey-1main.html>.

15 Rembert, Tracey C. *Mitsubishi Mayhem*, 8 E 5 p 18 (1997).

16 *The Gray Whale Nursery at Laguna San Ignacio: An Introductory Briefing*, The Amicus Journal (1997).

17 *Id.* Other groups opposed to ESSA's expansion included RARE Center for Tropical Conservation, Pro Natura, Pro Esteros, CIRIO, Grupo Sierra de la Laguna, Amigos de la Laguna, and Kuyima Servicios Ecoturisticos.

18 *Supra,* note 16.

19 Holing, Dwight. *Controversy*, The Amicus Journal 1997.

20 *Supra,* note 16.

21 *Supra,* note 16, *citing,* Schulte-Peevers, Andrea. Baja California. Lonely Planet P. 1994.

22 *Supra,* note 16.

23 *Id.* Mexico had received funds from the Global Environmental Facility, private sector support generated through ECONAP, and the Fideicomiso Nacional para las Areas Naturales Protegidas.

24 *Id.*

10

25 *San Ignacio Solar Evaporation Facility: Key Characteristics – Local Socioeconomic Effects,* (visited Oct. 26, 1997) <http://www.bajasalt.com/SIG/sigkey-8main.html>.

26 *Supra,* note 16.

27 The water pumped from the lagoon would have a salt content up to 4.1% and by the time it is moved to the crystallization ponds it would have a salt content of 27%. Average ocean water salinity is 3.5%.

28 Holing, Dwight. *Close Encounters: The Gray Whales of Laguna San Ignacio*, e-Amicus 1997 (visited Oct. 26, 1997) <http://www.igc.org/nrdc/eamicus/97sum/wh1.htlm>.

29 ESSA's position was that the pier would be well clear of the majority of gray whale traffic. However, whales use the sound of the surf to navigate and, therefore, they swim close to the coastline. ESSA stated that marine life would have adequate room to pass through, because the pier would have 34 meters of space between its trestles.

30 *Supra,* note 16.

31 Brumm, James E. *Baja: Open Letters to NRDC Members,* 19 n. 3 The Amicus Journal 9 (1997). When considering this fact, it is useful to bear in mind that whale population itself has increased from previous years. That fact might serve as a more plausible explanation to an increased whale presence at the salt mining operations, rather than the explanation that salt mining attracts whales.

32 Alker, Susan C. *The Marine Mammal Protection Act: Refocusing the Approach to Conservation*, 44 U.C.L.A.L. Rev. 527 (1996).

33 Malone, Linda A. *The Necessary Interrelationship Between Land Use and Preservation of Groundwater Resources*, U.C. L. A. J. Env't L & Pol'y, (1990), *citing* Miller v. Cudahy Co., 858 F. 2d 1449 (10th Cir. 1988).

34 *Mexican Biosphere Reserve Threatened by Saltworks*, (Nov. 21, 1999), <http://forests.org/archive/samerica/mexbiore.htm>.

35 *Controversy*, e-Amicus (1997).

36 *Supra,* note 7.

37 NEPA requires the preparation of an EIS for the purpose of producing the information for decision makers, but does not require decision makers to reject a project based upon negative environmental consequences.

38 Kublicki, Nicolas. *The Greening of Free Trade: NAFTA, Mexican Environment Law, and Debt Exchanges for Mexican Environmental Infrastructure Development*, 1994 19 Colum. J. Envtl. L. 59 (1994).

39 Steinberg, Richard H. *Trade-Environmental Negotiations in the EU, NAFTA, and WTO: Regional Trajectories of Rule Development*, Am J. Int'l L. (1997). The U.S. Environmental Protection Agency trained Mexican environmental enforcement inspectors.

40 *Id.* For a similar discussion, see Schoenbaum, Thomas J. *International Trade and Protection of the Environment: The Continuing Search for Reconciliation*, 91 Am. J. Int'l L. 268 (1997), concerning Mexico's decision to defer action on the General Agreement on Tariffs and Trade (GATT) panel's favorable decision concerning the U.S. tuna embargo. GATT ruled that the United States could place restrictions on the product standards relating to health and safety, but not on the process of producing the product.

41 North American Free Trade Agreement, Dec. 17, 1992. Can-Mex.-U.S., 32 I.L.M. 296 and 32 I.L.M. 605.

42 *Environmental Safeguards – Scientific Committee*, <http://www.bajasalt.com/SIG/sigsafe-4-1.html>.

43 *Supra,* note 6.

44 *Supra,* note 4, at Art. IV.

45 Declaration of the United Nations Conference on the Human Environment. UN Doc. A/CONF.48/14/ Rev.1, 11 I.L.M 1416 (1972). The Stockholm Agreement on the Human Environment, Principle 21, appeals to states to be responsible by not causing damage to the environment of other states or of areas beyond the limits of their national jurisdiction.

46 *Id*, at Principle 21. See also, Bustani, Alberto A. and Patrick W. Mackay. *NAFTA: Reflections on Environmental Issues During the First Year*, 12 Ariz. J. Int'l & Comp. Law 543 (1995), *citing* North American Agreement on Environmental Co-operation, Sept. 14, 1993, Can.–Mex.–U.S., art. 3., 32 I.L.M. 1482 (1993).

47 *Supra,* note 41. *See generally* Art. 104 and Annex 104.1.

48 Another economic loss can be measured in loss of existence value.

49 *Supra,* note 41.

50 *Supra,* note 45 at Principle 4. Other principles of importance to whale conservation are Principle 13, Principle 21, and Principle 25.

51 Convention on International Trade in Endangered Species of Wild Flora and Fauna, *entered in force* July 1, 1975, 12 I.L.M. 1085.

52 *Supra,* note 10. Conservation refers to sustaining the whaling industry, while protection and preservation refer to sustaining the whale.

53 *Supra,* note 10.

54 *Supra,* note 51, at Appendix I. Appendix I includes species threatened with extinction. Trade in specimens of these species is permitted only in exceptional circumstances.

55 United Nations Convention on the Law of the Sea, Art 65, December 10, 1982, 21 I.L.M. 1261.

56 *Supra,* note 10.

57 *Supra,* note 9.

CASE STUDY 11

MICRO CREDIT: CASE OF BANK RAKYAT INDONESIA

INTRODUCTION

Since ages past, the global banking industry was biased against the loans extended to poor individuals living in rural areas. Most commercial banks and other financial institutions considered lending to the poor as 'unbankable' and 'uncreditworthy'.[1] They shied away from microlending, which they deemed as costly and labour-intensive exercise with little profit. The organized financial markets thus neglected this segment. The poor were left with limited alternatives such as moneylenders, who charged high interest rates or they were simply denied access to investment.[2] Thus, Grameen Banks and other similar Micro Financing Institutions (MFIs) were set up to bridge the gap and provide resources to the poor for revenue generating purposes.

The Bank Rakyat Indonesia (BRI) was recognized as one of the best micro-finance institutions in the world.[3] BRI was a government commercial bank that offered various services including micro finance products. Within six-years (1984-1990) from incorporation, it became a model bank in Asia for transforming the ailing government owned agricultural bank, into a viable and self-sufficient financial intermediary with increasing financial resources and customers (Exhibit 1). Its success revealed to the world how micro credit could help maintain a bank's long-term stability even in times of crisis. Even at the height of the Asian crisis, in 1998, BRI's micro lending unit recorded a pre-tax profit of $89 million, while its corporate and retail banking units posted losses of $3.4 billion. As of September 2003, it was the country's largest micro bank. Its total outstanding loans amounted to Rupiah 45.6 trillion of which 86.25% were channelled to small and medium-sized enterprises. During this period, the bank recorded an ROE of 45.23%, almost twice the average return booked by any other bank in Indonesia.[4]

www.ibscdc.org

Copyright © IBS Case Development Centre

EXHIBIT 1

Micro Credit: BRI's microlending unit

- Contributes a consistent share of BRI's total profits

- Provides liquidity to BRI's other units

- Made profits even during the Asian financial crisis

- Helps maintain BRI's long-term stability

BRI

Bank Rakyat Indonesia was set up on December 16th, 1895 at Purwokerto, Central Java, Indonesia. It was formed with the merger of Bank Prekreditan Rakyat and the Algemeene Volkscredietbank. BRI was formed with the motive to provide rural banking services with an emphasis on the promotion of agriculture development. In 1946, it was declared as the first Government owned bank of the Republic of Indonesia.

In mid and late 1960s, BRI played a major role in nation building. It was the channel for subsidized credit distributed by the Government of Indonesia. BRI was one of the major providers of agricultural credit to rural farmers. During the seventies, the government of Indonesia declared self-sufficiency in rice production which was one of the national agendas. In the mid 1970s, the government introduced Bimbingan Massal (BIMAS) or 'Mass Guidance Program', an agricultural credit program. Under this scheme, the government channeled its loans through BRI's 3,300 village banks (Unit Desas) spread all over the country at interest rates of around 12% per annum which were much below the market rates that ranged from 36% to 300% per annum. However, in the absence of incentives for small farmers to repay, and lack of incentives for BRI staff (of 14,300) to monitor and enforce the collections, the repayments were around 40% of total loans disbursed. This resulted in huge losses, which led to the financial unsustainability of the program. There were several other factors that contributed to the failure of BIMAS program. In the BIMAS programme, officials of Ministry of Agriculture were in charge of loan disbursements. Unit Desa staff that were in charge of payments and collections had no authority over selection of borrowers, which resulted in allocation of work without proper authority. This had severe negative-impact on the working of the bank.

By 1983, the bank was in heavy losses. As part of a restructuring exercise the government decided to commercialize its operations by transforming the Unit Desas into self–sustaining profit centers. They were redesigned to provide a range of financial services to borrowers at market rates. Many of the units were moved to rural places and an accounting system was installed in each unit to ensure accountability and performance. With the technical assistance from Harvard Institute of International Development, in the year 1984 the bank designed two commercial products SIMPEDES (Simpanan Pedesaan, rural savings) and KUPEDES (Kredit Umum Pedesaan, General Rural Credit). SIMPEDES was a popular rural saving scheme, which provided rural people with savings deposit facilities. KUPEDES was a market-based rural finance program to support the growth of rural sector. Its features included simple procedures for loan disbursement, short maturities and regular monthly installments made from non-agricultural income. It was set up with the motive to transform village banks into self-sustaining full-service financial units.

With the launch of the new programme, by 1986 the financial position of the bank revived and all of BRI village units turned into profit centres. KUPEDES, which evolved with the failure of the BIMAS programme, took a major challenge of making market based interest rates approach an acceptable option.

11

By 1994, KUPEDES became one of the popular credit programs of Indonesia and between 1984 and 1994 the loans disbursed under this programme grew six times.

In mid-1997, Indonesia was severely affected with the East Asian monetary crisis. Between January 1998 and March 1999, the bank registered a decline of 3.5% in the total outstanding micro credit. Inflation rose to roughly 80%, the highest ever inflation recorded in Indonesia since the 1960's.[5]

In 1998, BRI was reorganized into a Corporate Banking Division to extend loans above Rp 3 billion, a Retail Banking Division with 323 branches which offer savings deposit services, provide loans on commercial terms from Rp 25 million to Rp 3 billion ($2,500-300,000), and handle the remaining subsidized targeted credit programmes. A Micro banking Division was set up, with 4,185 outlets (2,566 village units, 1,220 semi-urban units, and 379 village posts).

Since 1999, the bank recorded a consistent growth in the loan disbursements. The average loan outstanding increased from $ 341 million in 1999 to $ 440 million in 2002. As of 2003, the bank had the highest return on equity at 45.23%, almost twice the average return booked by other banks. Rudjito, the chairman of the bank said that by the third quarter ending September 2003, the bank's pre-tax profit had increased by 104 % to Rp 2.70 trillion, from Rp 1.31 trillion for the same period ended September 2002.[6]

REASONS FOR BRI's SUCCESS

Rural Financing: KUPEDES

In the year 1983, the BIMAS program was discontinued. During this period the Government scrapped 32 out of the 36 subsidized credit programmes. This raised doubts whether the Government completely shifted its focus from priority sector agricultural lending to the commercial, market oriented rural finance. Under the subsidized BIMAS credit program, Rp 2.55 trillion were lent over a 14-year period, averaging Rp 182 billion per year (approx. $100 million) an unknown portion of which flowed into non-agricultural activities.

In line with the financial liberalization reforms introduced in mid-1983, KUPEDES programme was launched in 1984. The government provided a loan of about Rp 210 billion ($ 20 million) as seed capital. KUPEDES made credit available to small borrowers in villages across the country. It made available reliable credit cheaper than informal channels. The majority of borrowers were landless farmers who used their house plot or house to guarantee their loans. The minimum loan extended was equivalent to Rp 0.25 million and the maximum to Rp 9.8 million. Under this scheme, banks followed rural lending patterns prevalent at those times and interests were charged on a monthly rather than on yearly basis. The bank charged a monthly interest rate of 1.5%. This method translated into a yearly interest rate of 33% as opposed to 12% under BIMAS programme. During this period, the informal lenders demanded a rate ranging from 6% to 30% per month whereas private banks offered credit at 3 % per month. The higher interest rates on KUPEDES loans kept wealthier farmers who could obtain cheaper loans for their purpose far from the scheme. Borrowers had flexibility to use loans for their own purposes as long as they could prove their ability to repay the loan. Unlike subsidized credit, KUPEDES loans have continued to increase rapidly year after year, reaching disbursements of Rp. 4.57 trillion in 1996. Under KUPEDES scheme, small loans were extended to poor farmers and Rp. 5.28 trillion were lent over the seven-year period, 1984-1990, averaging Rp 753.9 billion per year. It was established that about 20-30% of KUPEDES loans were directly invested in agriculture, i.e. between Rp. 151 and 226 billion. The shift in the focus of the company from agricultural to rural financing led to a considerable growth of the company. Apart from this, the deposit mobilisation policy of the bank was considered to be one of the key factors of success for the bank.[7]

11

Deposit mobilisation mechanism: 'Savings as a source of funds'

Since 1984, BRI vigorously mobilized savings at village levels. In 1986 it launched SIMPEDES, a voluntary savings product that helped in mobilizing huge deposits (Exhibit 2). SIMPEDES offered a safe, convenient and liquid savings instrument that paid depositors market-based interest rates. It allowed savers anytime withdrawal of their deposited money. The savings plan evolved from market surveys of villagers and its design was refined through pilot studies. Its purpose was to meet the needs of rural organizations and households who demanded high liquidity. To mobilize deposits, banks used creative approaches. They identified potential savers and advertised their services, visited customers and established links with village chiefs and community leaders. There was a wide response ranging from village treasuries and government offices to religious institutions.

As the unit network expanded into urban areas, in 1989, SIMASKOT (savings of the urban community) an urban counterpart to SIMPEDES was created. SIMASKOT had same features as SIMPEDES, except the interest rate structure. It took into consideration the larger savings capacity of urban customers and the stronger competition from other banks into account. Interest rates were generally higher than those for SIMPEDES and ranged from 11% to 14.5% p.a.

According to a study conducted by BRI in 1993, at any point of time, for every borrower there were five savers and their savings provided capital for all BRI loans. BRI offered three savings facilities. The 'Liquid' savings scheme permitted unlimited number of withdrawals. The semiliquid with specific

EXHIBIT 2	Savings and loans outstanding in BRI village units, 1984–2000				
	Savings deposits		Loans outstanding		
Year	No. of accounts	Amount in billion Rp.	No. of accounts	Amount in billion Rp.	Total savings to loan ratio
1984	2655	42.2	640746	111.1	38%
1985	36563	84.9	1034532	229.0	37%
1986	418945	175.8	1231723	334.3	53%
1987	4183983	287.5	1314780	429.6	67%
1988	4998038	493.0	1386035	542.3	91%
1989	6261988	959.1	1643980	846.5	113%
1990	7262509	1694.8	1893138	1381.8	122%
1991	8587872	2540.5	1837549	1455.7	174%
1992	9953294	3399.1	1831732	1648.5	206%
1993	11431078	4325.2	1895965	1957.4	220%
1994	13066854	5231.9	2053919	2458.1	213%
1995	14482763	6015.7	2263767	3191.2	189%
1996	16147260	7091.7	2488135	4076.2	174%
1997	18143316	8836.5	2615679	4685.4	188%
1998	21698594	16146.0	2457652	4696.8	344%
1999	24235889	17061.4	2473923	5956.5	286%
July	25098169	18472.1	2577180	6869.3	269%

Source: Hans Dieter Seibel & Petra Schmidt, 'How an Agricultural Development Bank revolutionized Rural Finance. The case of bank Rakyat Indonesia', www.microfinancegateway.org

11

number of withdrawals per month and the fixed deposit scheme. Another major merit was that it was a Government owned bank. People had enough faith in the bank and even in the hardest times, for instance during the 'East Asian Crisis' they believed in the bank and increased their deposits.[8]

Loan disbursement mechanism

The key position in the BRI loan lending mechanism was the Accounts Officers (AOs). The AOs were responsible for the entire loan cycle of the customer, from selection to recovery. The AOs served up to 400 borrowers and spent most of their time out in the field. This enabled AOs to gain intimate knowledge of the borrowers enterprise and character. This left little room for problems like poor selection of borrowers and bad debts. The unit chief usually rechecked larger loans with a size above $ 4,200. For the borrowers who repeatedly borrowed from BRI, the client's loan repayment record was used to set the borrower's personal loan limit. The rating system outlined below served as a guideline for loan disbursements.

TABLE 1	Record-based borrower classification system	
Rating	Criteria	Subsequent loan ceiling
A	All payments made on time	Increase of 100%
B	Final payment on time, one or two late payments	Increase of 50%
C	Final payment on time, two or more late installments	Same amount
D	Final payment late, but paid within month of due date	Reduction by 50%
E	Final payment more than two months late	No new loan

Design of demand-oriented savings products

Market studies and research, conducted in 1982, indicated that there was an extensive demand for financial savings facilities in rural areas. They revealed that the financial assets, usually kept in the house, and savings from income flows could be safely deposited. In addition, it became evident that many villagers would convert some non-financial savings into institutional deposits if appropriate facilities were available. BRI found that the key to market research was to learn from the clients what they wanted. They conducted surveys and the information collected was used in the design of products. Studies on savings motives and preferences of rural people throughout Indonesia identified four major characteristics a savings facility must combine: safety/security, convenience, liquidity and positive return.

As far as the security was concerned, the depositor was concerned mostly about the reputation of the bank. BRI was well known among the villagers because it was the only major bank in rural areas for decades. Further, BRI had a comparative advantage of being a government bank, which gave a feeling of safety and security to the rural people.

One of the key concerns of BRI was to provide better convenience to its depositors. BRI observed that for the customer, convenience was measurable in terms of cost per transaction. Easy access to the unit branches, little waiting time and fast services were some elements that reduced the cost and time needed for making deposits and withdrawals. BRI, unit network was the most extensive of all the banks in Indonesia. BRI units were found in more than 80% of all sub-districts in the country and thus were within easy reach of the majority of the rural population. Further, physical reallocation of units from far away places to the places accessible to customers was done to better service its clients.[9]

11

The third element identified, was the liquidity of deposits or ease of withdrawals, an aspect particularly important for the design of savings products. BRI decided to offer a product mix of liquid, semi-liquid and fixed deposits to cater to different liquidity preferences of different customers. The national savings product TABANAS had been offered by the units since 1976. Studies showed that the limitation of withdrawals (two per month) was an important psychological barrier to the people in rural areas, though few customers actually make two withdrawals a month. The findings resulted in the design of SIMPEDES, where savers were permitted unlimited withdrawals, a feature that has proved most important for the success of the programme. In addition, TABANAS was continued as a semi-liquid product and fixed deposits previously available from BRI only through its branches were introduced at the units as well.

Furthermore, research findings showed that lucky games and gambling were popular among rural people. Drawing the lot in an *Arisan*, the Indonesian version of Rotating Savings and Credit Associations (ROSCA) (Exhibit 3), which was highly popular, was always a notable social event. This observation induced policy makers to equip the SIMPEDES savings product with a lottery. Further market research was carried out on such specific matters as what kind of lottery prizes were popular, what kind of bankbook was wanted, and what kind of publicity was effective.[10]

New Unit Desas

The transformation of unit desa took place within the context of overall financial sector deregulation. In June 1983, the government of Indonesia suspended ceilings on loans, removed controls on interest rates for both deposits and loans and prioritized savings mobilization. These changes provided an opportunity for BRI's management to explore new services and products.[11] As of December 1996, the unit desa comprised of 16.1 million deposit accounts with a deposit volume of Rp 6 trillion ($ 2.7 billion) and 2.5 million borrowers with loans outstanding in the amount of Rp 4.1 trillion ($1.7 billion). Since the introduction of KUPEDES, 18.5 million loans at a value of more than $ Rp 23.64 trillion ($ 10 billion) had been disbursed. Most of the loans were repaid on time. In 1996, loans in arrears accounted for less than 4 % of the loan portfolio and the long-term loss ratio was just 2.1% of the total loan outstanding. The outreach of the savings programme was even more impressive. It was estimated that more than 30% of all households in Indonesia had a SIMPEDES account. In December 1996, the average savings balance stood at Rp 0.39 million ($ 163) and the average outstanding loan size at Rp 1.6 million($ 689). Data collected in 1995 on a survey basis indicated that 71% of the savers held a balance of less than

---

EXHIBIT 3

Rotating Savings and Credit Associations (ROSCAs) are essentially a group of individuals who come together and make regular cyclical contributions to a common fund, which is then given as a lump sum to one member in each cycle. For example, a group of 12 persons may contribute Rs. 100 (US$33) per month for 12 months. The Rs. 1,200 collected each month is given to one member. Thus, a member will lend' money to other members through his regular monthly contributions. After having received the lump sum amount when it is his turn (i.e. borrow' from the group), he then pays back the amount in regular/further monthly contributions. This explains the name rotating savings and credit associations' for such groups [Bouman, 1979: 253]. Depending on the cycle in which a member receives his/her lump sum, members alternate between being lenders and borrowers. That is, there is a mutual give-and-take involved in ROSCAs.

Source: "The Mutuality of Credit: Rotating Savings and Credit Associations", www.gdrc.org

$ 87. The small sizes of account balances demonstrated a significant degree of outreach to small and micro customers. As of 1998, the unit system accounted for 25% of total BRI assets and 15% of the loan portfolio, but it contributed 70% of the bank's total savings deposits. The unit system has developed into a major fund provider for BRI.

As part of reorganization, unit desas were separated from the district-level branch offices into autonomous financial entities. A unit was a small bank office with four to eleven staff. The units also maintained 319 cash posts, which remained open three to five days a week to receive and pay out savings and to receive loan repayments. Each unit is a separate profit/loss centre with its own balance sheet and profit and loss statement. The units made advances of Rp 25 thousand to Rp 25 million. The units also provided savings and time deposits accounts. As of 2003, BRI's Unit Desa system had more than three million active borrowers and over 27 million active savings accounts.[12]

Organizationally the position of the President-Director solely responsible for the 'unit desa' banking system was created at BRI's head office. This appointment increased the importance given to the unit desa system at the head office level. It also depoliticized the decision-making and placed the responsibility for the reform and subsequent performance of the unit desas in the hands of BRI's management.[13]

In the new unit desa system, there was an increased emphasis on staff accountability. Employees were made responsible for the performance of unit desas. Direct responsibility for the loan approvals and repayments rested with unit desa staff, particularly loan officers. The units performance guided the staff recruitment and incentives. An incentive bonus that distributed 10% of unit desa's annual profits among its staff was introduced.

Lower transaction costs

BRI demonstrated that in a de-regulated policy environment, a government owned agricultural development bank was capable of serving vast numbers of micro-savers and micro-borrowers at competitive interest rates. BRI proved that institutional viability, sustainability and out-reach to low-income people were compatible. In case of BRI, the transaction costs amounted to 26% of loans below Rp 5,00,000, 10% of loans between Rp 500 thousands and Rp 5 million and 3% of loans between Rp 5 million and Rp 25 million.[14] With the low cost advantage as of 1998, BRI held 78% of all saving deposit accounts and 52.2% of all loan accounts of the country. In terms of volume BRI accounted for 85.7% of all saving deposits and 68.7% of all loans outstanding compared to second largest rural bank BPR that accounted for around 30% of loans outstanding of entire country. BRI and BPR together held about 24 million individual accounts an outreach to about half of the population.[15]

Staff recruitment and training

The transformation of units from government-type loan disbursement agencies to full-service rural banks operating in an increasingly competitive environment had to be accompanied by a major effort in the development of human resource. After the breakdown of the BIMAS program, the unit system employed more than 14,000 staff that had to be re-oriented. BRI faced a major challenge in transforming administrators and bureaucrats into bankers. This required not only massive training for the transfer of knowledge and the development of new skills, but necessitated a fundamental change in attitude. The transition from old to new culture was supported by the recruitment of new, young and well-educated staff.[16]

The recruitment policy emphasized the hiring of professional staff, and preferably were from the area where the unit was located, who mastered the local language, were familiar with local culture and customs. One of the success factors of BRI was the staff-training programme. The bank offered three types of standard training programme. The first being the training for the newly recruited staff, which lasted for nearly two months. BRI offered 'promotional training' for staff selected for promotion to new positions and 'refresher training' for introducing new regulations or procedures. The bank offered the 'application' or 'refresher training' for all the staff at unit level at least twice a year.

Incentive system

BRI considered 'incentives' as a powerful device to guide the performance of people in the right direction. It developed a number of positive incentives to motivate unit managers, staff and customers.

For depositors, BRI offered differentiated interest rates. It offered higher interest rates on larger balances and encouraged savers to increase their deposit balances to be entitled for higher interest payments. It offered coupons on the deposits made by the customers. Participation in a lottery with attractive prizes turned out to be a popular incentive for maintaining and increasing deposit balances.

For borrowers, the most important incentive was the knowledge that a subsequent loan would be quickly available for an increased amount, provided the payments were made on time. Borrowers were made fully aware that the prompt repayment would help in procuring larger loans. Under 'Incentive for Prompt Payment ' scheme, BRI offered incentives for the borrowers who were prompt at repayment of loans. Initially, BRI charged an interest rate of 2% (0.5% in addition to the real interest charge) on the borrowers who took working capital loans under KUPEDES scheme. If all payments in the last six-months period were made on time, the prepaid incentive of 0.5%, which was collected as an interest charge, was returned to the customer. If payments were late, the unit, as a penalty charge retained the prepaid incentive. KUPEDES borrowers were required to open a savings account before the loan disbursement and the incentives were credited to their respective accounts.

For unit managers/staff, a principal incentive for unit-staff was a profit linked bonus, based on the individual units performance. 10% of unit's annual profits were distributed to the staff in proportion to their salaries. The bonus was paid twice a year based on the semi-annual performance evaluation. On average, individual staff received upto one and a half month's salary.

For Institutions, BRI offered unique incentive programme for the best performing units. To promote competition among units, the central office devised a system to recognize the top 20 performers of each region, who then competed at the national level. Finally the top 20 performers were selected and the winners of the competition received prizes and recognition from top management for their performance. The competition was based purely on performance and there was little room for politics. [17]

Liquidity management

BRI liabilities were highly diversified. The majority of the unit's funds (87% as of 1998) originated from 16 million small savings deposit accounts. In spite of changes in the short-term economic conditions, the savings of the units have not fluctuated widely. Rural savings have proven to be much more stable than time deposits and other saving instruments of larger businesses in the urban areas, including deposits of government corporations. Overall, liquidity risks of the bank were well diversified and kept at a minimum.

A major advantage and a crucial success factor for BRI's saving mobilization programme was the access to an almost unlimited pool of liquidity from the BRI branch network. In case of need, a unit could borrow from the branch at the prevailing transfer price or could deposit excess funds at the same rate in the BRI branch office.[18]

CONCLUSION

The case of BRI demonstrated that demand-driven approaches to rural finance and banking, offered dramatic opportunities for success to any financial institution. Money could be safely and profitably lent in small amounts in rural areas if the products offered met the borrowers' needs and if the pricing, incentives and enforcement agreements were appropriate. The success in small savings mobilization was rooted in BRI's ability to provide a well-conceived combination of what small savers needed: safety, convenience, liquidity and positive yield. Directing the system with all the features and details towards these essential elements of demand was a major key to success. With some of the popular schemes like KUPEDES and SIMPEDES, the BRI unit system was considered as one of the most successful rural financial institutions in the world. Some of the features were certainly unique and were related to the specific context of rural Indonesia, but there were many others that could be generalized and applied to other countries. The BRI experience has become a learning ground for policy makers and practitioners from institutions and countries around the world (Exhibit 4).[19]

EXHIBIT 4

Lessons that can be drawn from BRI's experience:

- Financial sector policies work and are conducive to financial innovations

- With attractive savings and credit products, appropriate staff incentives, and an effective system of internal regulation and supervision, rural micro finance can be profitable

- The poor can save; rural financial institutions can mobilize their savings cost-effectively

- If financial services are offered without a credit bias, demand for savings deposit services exceeds the demand for credit by a wide margin

- Incentives for timely repayment work

- Outreach of a financial institution to vast number of low-income people and financial self-sufficiency (including viability and self-reliance) are compatible

- Average transaction costs can be lowered, and both profitability of a financial institution and the volume of loanable funds can be increased by catering for both the poor and the non-poor with their demands for widely differing deposit and loan sizes

Source: Hans Dieter Seibel & Petra Schmidt, 'How an Agricultural Development Bank revolutionized Rural Finance. The case of bank Rakyat Indonesia', www.microfinancegateway.org

NOTES

1 'Thoughts on Micro-Credit Financial Viability', *SOAS Economic Digest*, March 1998.

2 ibid.

3 Sundarii, Mrs Nasution Siti, 'The East Asian Crisis and Micro finance', July 2000.

4 'BRI sees profit growing by 18-20%", www.thejakartapost.com, November 20th, 2003.

5 Nasution, Mrs. Siti Sundari, 'The East Asian Crisis and Micro Finance', the Experience of Bank Rakyat Indonesia, September 11th, 2000.

6 'BRI sees profit growing by 18-20%', www.thejakartapost.com, November 20th, 2003.

7 'KUPEDES: Indonesia's Model Small Credit Program', www.worldbank.org, January 1st, 1996.

8 Klaus, Maurer, 'Bank Rakyat Indonesia (BRI); Indonesia CASE STUDY', www.gtz.de.

9 Klaus, Maurer, 'Bank Rakyat Indonesia (BRI); Indonesia CASE STUDY', www.gtz.de.

10 Klaus, Maurer, 'Bank Rakyat Indonesia (BRI); Indonesia (CASE STUDY), www.gtz.de.

11 Meyer, Richard L., 'Performance of rural financial markets, Comparative Observations from Asia, Latin America and the U.S., www.agecon.ag.ohio-state.edu, July 28th–31st, 2002.

12 David J. Green, 'Commercialization of Micro Finance: Indonesia Country Workshop', www.adb.org.

13 Siebel Hans Dieter & Schmidt, Petra, 'How an Agricultural Development Bank revolutionized Rural Finance.- The case of bank Rakyat Indonesia', www.microfinancegateway.org.

14 Richard L. Meyer, 'Performance of rural financial markets, Comparative Observations from Asia, Latin America and the U.S., www.agecon.ag.ohio-state.edu, July 28-31,2002.

15 Hans Dieter Seibel & Petra Schmidt, 'How an Agricultural Development Bank revolutionized Rural Finance.- The case of bank Rakyat Indonesia', www.microfinancegateway.org.

16 Klaus, Maurer, 'Bank Rakyat Indonesia (BRI); Indonesia (CASE STUDY), www.gtz.de.

17 ibid.

18 Klaus Maurer, Bank Rakyat Indonesia (Case Study), www.cgap.org/assets/images/bri.PDF, 1999.

19 ibid.

GLOSSARY

Arbitrage The simultaneous buying and selling of assets in different markets, taking advantage of the differing prices.

Aspirational An 'aspirational' lifestyle is one that has a hope or an ambition to copy as much of the desired target as possible before having actually reached it. Consumer behaviour involving global brands is usually part of this. Another popular term for this phenomenon is 'wannabee', meaning someone who 'wants to be' as similar as possible to their role model or to a particular group of people.

BOP The 'bottom of the pyramid', sometimes referred to as the 'base of the pyramid'. The pyramid in question is the economic pyramid of earnings and purchasing power of the different percentages of population around the world. The BOP population level is the one often regarded as earning less than $1 per day.

Born global The important characteristic of a *born global* firm is that it globalizes very soon after being set up and does most of its business in overseas markets with very little business in its domestic market. It is closely associated with internet-based businesses.

BRIC The four biggest emerging economies – Brazil, Russia, India and China – are now referred to jointly as the BRIC economies.

Business groups Confederations of legally independent firms that are nevertheless united in many financial, economic, social and business ties of mutual support.

Cloud computing The centralization of data storage and information management by computer systems and servers but not within the organization. Instead it is outsourced to massive specialist server farms.

Collaboration Form of alliance that does not involve the creation of a joint venture company but is based normally on discrete co-operative projects.

Comparative advantage The (opportunity) costs of goods made in one country compared to the same goods made in another country.

Competitive advantage The superior performance of one company over another company in the creation of similar products or services.

Configuration The geographic distribution of where an MNC carries out the various business activities of its value chain.

Contingency theory That set of theories developed in the 1950s that held that there is no uniquely optimal way to organize a corporation and that the best way to do so depends on the 'contingent' circumstances.

Co-ordination How the MNC manages the appropriate organizational structure, systems and linkages between the configuration of the different parts of its business to ensure effectiveness.

Corporate governance The system by which business corporations are directed and controlled. The governance structure of a firm will specify the distribution of rights and responsibilities within the organization as well as the rules and procedures for decision-making.

Corporate social responsibility (CSR) That form of company policy that takes into account not only financial requirements for profitability from the business activities of firms, but also wider social, human and environmental considerations.

Creative destruction The famous term invented by the economist Joseph Schumpeter to describe how industries with their existing industry structure contain the seeds of their own destruction because new firms will always use new strategies and innovatory products to displace dominant firms. This will result in a new industry structure. Industries are thus dynamic, not static, and will be continually challenged and restructured as a result of forces such as innovation and entrepreneurship.

Disintermediation A reduction in the use of intermediaries between producers and consumers. One of the important consequences of the internet is that it makes direct contact between buyers and sellers much easier.

Dominated network A network in which a 'flagship firm' dominates and generally provides the brand name.

Economy of scale An economy of scale rises if fixed costs remain constant as output increases, thus lowering cost per unit of output. The concept is usually used to explain the benefits of size in an organization. It can arise in relation to all types of costs such as cost of capital, purchasing costs, advertising costs, and so on. All are capable of generating benefits to scale.

Economy of scope An economy of scope is available when a resource or asset acquired for one purpose can be used for additional purposes at little or no extra cost in a multi-product firm. It arises from intensity of usage of a resource or asset by the organization.

Emerging economy An emerging economy is one that has an average annual per capita income of less than $9,000 and is experiencing rapid growth and economic transformation.

Equal partner network A network of companies that are accustomed to work together and provide each other with information and support. It has no hierarchy and partners take varying roles in varying projects.

Federal structure An organization in which the top level has only limited powers in relation to the institutions or bodies underneath it, yet it provides an identifying or unifying umbrella function.

Financialization A 'new form of competition which involves a change in orientation towards financial results … also a kind of speed up in management work' (Froud et al., 2000: 104).

Flagship firm A firm that provides direction and leadership to a network of partners with whom a deep collaborative relationship is developed over time.

Global corporation An organizational form that maximizes scale economies by standardizing and thus minimizing variations in offerings in different markets.

Global industry An industry can be defined as global 'if there is some competitive advantage to integrating activities on a worldwide basis' (Porter, 1986: 19).

Global market A *market* can be defined as global if consumers worldwide can be treated as *homogeneous* within them. It is much more common for *market segments* to be global than entire markets.

Glocalization The process of combining the advantages of both global and local operations.

Heterarchies A system of organization with many overlaps, multiplicity of processes, and networks. Heterarchies are networks of elements in which each element shares the same 'horizontal' position of power and authority, each playing a theoretically equal role.

Hierarchies Normally described as integrated companies or corporations.

High context The argument that external context remains very important in designing and implementing strategies.

Industrialization of service Applying manufacturing-style methods of operations to services to improve service efficiency. It most often means substituting technology for people.

Industry 'clusters' Defined by Porter (1998: 78) as 'critical masses – in one place – of unusual competitive success in particular fields'.

Information economy Advanced economies characterized by a high proportion of their economic activity being dependent upon technology, information and knowledge management. Many industries within such economies are dominated by knowledge intensity, network effects and increasing returns to scale.

Installed capacity The total volume of take-up by customers of a particular technology that is already in use and installed with customers. It is the amount of this installed capacity which will determine the success or failure of a given technology or product. If not enough installed capacity exists then customers (and suppliers, e.g. of related software) will gravitate to a rival technology or product that has a bigger take-up by customers (installed base).

Integrated company A traditional company in which the majority of the functions and processes are provided by one corporation under unitary ownership, either privately or publicly through a stock exchange listing.

International exporter A company based in a domestic economy but exporting its surplus product capacity abroad.

Isomorphism A process that creates great pressure for one unit in a population to resemble other units that face the same set of environmental conditions. It explains why companies in the same industry or sector are becoming more similar to each other.

Low context The suggestion that context, that is the external environment in which an organization is placed, is gradually becoming less and less relevant to business strategy and structure.

Microfinance A formalized banking system that makes available very small amounts of money as loans to borrowers whom other banks or financial institutions would regard as not creditworthy. Although interest is always charged on these loans, it is at a far better rate than any other available to such poor borrowers.

Monopolistic competition A brand-name-dominated market with too many companies for collusion to take place, characterized by much advertising, considerable price discretion and above normal profits for the successful brands.

Moral hazard A situation where an individual experiences a conflict of interest between two or more roles or factors resulting in an increase in reckless behaviour, for example wearing a seat belt makes car drivers feel safer so they actually drive faster (i.e. less responsibly) than before.

'Most-favoured-nation' (MFN) This principle means that any tariff cuts or agreements offered to one country must be offered to them all.

Multidomestic An MNC composed of a portfolio of separate national companies with a financially co-ordinating centre. Common brand names are used but with varying product offerings around the world. A declining organization form in the world of converging tastes and scale economies.

National responsiveness The degree to which it is necessary to adapt products or services to the specific preferences of a national market in order to be successful within that market.

Offshoring Outsourcing that takes place in another country.

Oligopoly Competition in a market that has come to be dominated by a few (usually large) competitor organizations. A potential opportunity for collusion, and interdependency of strategies between a few firms. A game theory situation where the success of one competitor depends in part on the behaviour of the others.

Organizational structure Structure needs to be an appropriate match to the international strategy of the organization and to reflect strategy. Since MNCs operate in a multiplicity of national, regional and global markets, their organization structure must reconcile the need for cross-border operational *integration* to achieve scale efficiencies, without losing the ability to be *responsive* to local / national market differences that best meet customer needs. This is the central strategy / structure dilemma for MNCs.

Outsourcing This means that an organization places some of its activities with other external companies to provide, rather than carrying them out in-house. These are most often support activities such as payroll, cleaning, catering, insurance, accounting, travel and so on. This is seen as a way of reducing the cost of non-core business processes to the core business. The outsourcing provider is also likely to be more efficient at providing the service since that is its core business.

Perfect competition A market where the price is developed from the interaction of many buyers and sellers, characterized by little or no pricing discretion and no more than 'normal' profits in equilibrium, no brand names and no differentiation. Most common in commodity markets.

Platform A standard for the hardware of a computer system that determines which kinds of software it can run.

Public goods Goods that are consumed collectively and are of benefit to society as a whole, for example railways or roads or state schools.

Purchasing-power parity (PPP) This is used as an essential benchmark for judging the level of exchange rates. Exchange rates are routinely calculated and reported by governments, international organizations and financial institutions to show a country's exchange-rate-adjusted prices relative to its trading partners. PPP is empirically useful as it gives the price of a common basket of goods in two or more countries, when measured in a common currency, e.g. US dollars.

Regionalization The grouping of countries into regional clusters based on geographic proximity, usually for trading purposes.

Resource-based view The currently dominant theory of competitive strategy that attributes the achievement of competitive advantage to the particular qualities, resources and capabilities of the firm, rather than to market positioning.

Scale economies Economies derived from decreased cost per unit of output as a result of producing larger absolute volumes.

Scope economies Economies derived from using a resource that was acquired for one business in additional businesses at little or no additional cost. The scope economy is achieved by utilizing the same component over again.

Strategic Alliance A particular mode of inter-organizational relationship in which partners make substantial investments in delevoping a long-term collaborative effort and common orientation.

Strategic market A market is determined by the pattern of sales of a product. With the development of the internet, the sales pattern is not necessarily any longer selected geographically or on traditional market characteristics lines. Previously a lot of effort was required to determine strategic markets where most sales and marketing effort would be devoted. The internet allows such market entry to become unplanned and frequently accidental.

Subsidiary Any operational unit controlled by the MNC and situated outside the home country.

Sustainability The aim for an organization to have a neutral effect on its environment.

Sweatshop Derogatory term for exploitative conditions of employment, meaning a factory or workshop where workers are employed for extremely long hours in very poor conditions.

Tipping-point An act or a factor that exerts a disproportionate influence on a given situation so that it unlocks change or movement into a new (usually preferred) scenario.

Transaction cost analysis (TCA) The theory that organizations take the form that minimizes their transaction costs.

Transnational An MNC with an organizational form that maximizes both scale economies and local responsiveness by being extremely flexible and building on centres of excellence rather than hierarchy.

The 'triad' The three major regional trading blocs in the world's most economically developed regions of Europe, Asia and North America.

Triple bottom line A basic concept within CSR used to suggest that environmental, economic and social sustainability should all be of equal importance to organizations. The further implication of the triple bottom line concept is that organizations should be held accountable for environmental and social performance indicators as well as for their financial performance.

Value Chain The linkages in the totality of the business activities carried out by an organization.

Virtual corporation A company in which different functions are provided by different legal entities under different ownership linked together for specific projects by an electronic controlling body, often providing the brand name.

Zero-sum game An interaction which involves one actor winning at the expense of the other. Both cannot gain in such circumstances.

REFERENCES

Afuah, A. (2000) 'How much do your co-opetitors' capabilities matter in the face of technological change?', *Strategic Management Journal*, 21(3): 387–404.

Amit, R. and Schoemaker, P.J.H. (1993) 'Strategic assets and organisational rent', *Strategic Management Journal*, 14: 33–46.

Andersson, T. and Fredriksson, T. (1996) 'International organization of production and variation in exports from affiliates', *Journal of International Business Studies*, 27(2).

Andreu, R. and Ciborra, C. (1996) 'Core capabilities and information technology: an organizational learning approach', in B. Moingeon and A. Edmondson (eds) *Organizational Learning and Competitive Advantage,* London: Sage.

Angwin, D. (2000) *Implementing Successful Post-Acquisition Management*, London: Financial Times–Prentice Hall.

Argenti, P.A. (2003) *Corporate Communication*, 3rd edn, Boston: MGraw-Hill.

Argyris, C. and Schon, D. (1978) *Organizational Learning: A Theory of Action Perspective*, Reading, MA: Addison-Wesley.

Arthur, W.B. (1990) 'Positive feedback in the economy', *Scientific American*, 262: 92–99.

Arthur, W.B. (1996) 'Increasing returns and the new world of business', *Harvard Business Review,* July–Aug.: 100–109.

Axelrod, R. (1984) *The Evolution of Cooperation*, New York: HarperCollins.

Banks, A. (2003) 'Taking responsibility', *Strategic Risk*, February: 10–12.

Barnett, W.P. (2008) *The Red Queen Among Organizations: how competitiveness evolves*, Princeton, NJ: Princeton University Press.

Barnett, W.P. and Hansen, M.T. (1996) 'The Red Queen in organizational evolution', *Strategic Management Journal*, 17 (Special Issue) (Summer): 139–157.

Bartlett, C.A. and Ghoshal, S. (1989) *Managing across Borders*, London: Hutchinson.

Bartlett, C.A. and Ghoshal, S. (1990) 'Matrix management: not a structure, a frame of mind', *Harvard Business Review*, July–August: 138–145.

Bartlett, C.A. and Ghoshal, S. (1993) 'Beyond the M-Form: toward a managerial theory of the firm', *Strategic Management Journal*, 14, Special Issue, Winter: 23–46.

Bartlett, C. and Ghoshal, S. (1998) *Managing Across Borders: the transnational solution*, 2nd edn, Boston, Harvard Business School Press.

Bartlett, C.A., Ghoshal, S. and Birkinshaw, J. (2004) *Transnational Management: text, cases and readings*, 4th edn, New York: McGraw-Hill.

Barwise, P. and Robertson, T. (1992) 'Brand portfolios', *European Management Journal*, 10(3): 277–285.

Baum, J.A.C., Calabrese, T. and Silverman, B.S. (2000) 'Don't go it alone: alliance network composition and startups' performance in Canadian biotechnology', *Strategic Management Journal*, 21(3): 267–294.

Begg, D., Fischer, S. and Dornbush, R. (1994) *Economics*, London: McGraw Hill.

Bhagwati, J. (2004) *In Defense of Globalization*, Oxford: Oxford University Press.

Bhattacharya, C.B. and Sen, S. (2004) 'Doing better at doing good: when, why and how consumers respond to corporate social intiatives', *California Management Review*, 47(1): 9–24.

Birkinshaw, J. (1997) 'Entrepreneurship in multinational corporations: the characteristics of subsidiary initiatives', *Strategic Management Journal*, 18(3): 207–229.

Birkinshaw, J. (2000) *Entrepreneurship in the Global Firm*, London: Sage.

Birkinshaw, J. (2001) 'Strategy and management in MNE subsidiaries', in A. Rugman and T. Brewer (eds) *The Oxford Handbook of International Business*, Oxford: Oxford University Press.

Birkinshaw, J. and DiStefano, J.J. (2004) 'Global account management: new structures, new tasks', in H.W. Lane, M.L. Maznevski, M.E. Mendenhall and J. McNett (eds) *The Blackwell Handbook of Global Management: a guide to managing complexity*, Oxford: Blackwell Publishing.

Birkinshaw, J., Morrison, A. and Hulland, J. (1995) 'Structural and competitive determinants of a global integration strategy', *Strategic Management Journal*, 16: 637–655.

Bjorkman, I. (1990) 'Foreign direct investment: an organisational learning perspective', *Finnish Journal of Business Economics*, 14: 271–294.

Black, E.L. and Carnes, T.A. (2000) 'The market valuation of corporate reputation', *Corporate Reputation Review*, 3: 31–42.

Black, J.S. and Mendenhall, M. (1990) 'Cross-cultural training effectiveness: a review and a theoretical framework for future research', *Academy of Management Review*, 15: 113–136.

Bleeke, J. and Ernst, D. (1993) *Collaborating to Compete: Using Strategic Alliances and Acquisitions in the Global Marketplace*, New York: J. Wiley & Sons.

Bleeke, J. and Ernst, D. (1995) 'Is your strategic alliance really a sale?', *Harvard Business Review*, January–February: 97–105.

Blili, S. and Raymond, L. (1993) 'Information technology: threats and opportunities for SMEs', *International Journal of Information Management*, 13(6): 439–448.

Boisot, M.H. (1986) 'Markets and hierarchies in a cultural perspective', *Organization Studies*, 7: 135–158.

Bowen, D.E., Chase, R.B. and Cummings, T.G. (1990) *Service Management Effectiveness*, San Francisco: Jossey-Bass.

Bowman, C. and Faulkner, D. (1997) *Competitive and Corporate Strategy*, London: Irwin Books.

Brandenburger, A. and Nalebuff, B. (1995) 'The right game: use game theory to shape strategy', *Harvard Business Review*, July–August: 63–64.

Brandenburger, A.M. and Nalebuff, B.J. (1998) *Co-opetition: A Revolutionary Mindset that Combines Competition and Cooperation*, New York: Doubleday.

Braxton Associates (1988) *Consultancy Report.*

Brown, A. (1995) *Organizational Culture*, London: Pitman.

Buckley, P.J. and Casson, M.C. (1998) 'Models of the multinational entreprise', *Journal of International Business Studies*, 29(1): 21–44.

Burns, T. and Stalker, G.M. (1961) *The Management of Innovation*, London: Tavistock.

Campbell, A. and Verbeke, A. (1994) 'The globalisation of service multinationals', *Long Range Planning*, 27(2): 95–102.

Campbell, J.L. (2007) 'Why would corporations behave in socially responsible ways? An institutional theory of corporate social responsibility', *Academy of Management Review*, 32: 946–967.

Cannella, A. and Hambrick, D. (1993) 'Effects of executive departures on the performance of acquired firms', *Strategic Management Journal*, 14(S): 137–152.

Carlisle, Y.M. and Faulkner D.O. (2004) 'Corporate social responsibility: a stages theory', *European Business Journal*, 16(4): 143–152.

Carlzon, J. (1987) *Moments of Truth*, Cambridge, MA: Ballinger.

Carman, J. and Langeard, E. (1980) 'Growth strategies for service firms', *Strategic Management Journal*, 1: 7–22.

Carr, N. (2008) *The Big Switch: rewiring the world from Edison to Google*, New York: Norton.

Cartwright, S. and Cooper, C.L. (1992) *Mergers and Acquisitions: The Human Factor*, Oxford: Butterworth Heinemann.

Cartwright, S. and Schoenberg, R (2006) 'Thirty years of M&A; recent advances and future opportunities' *British Journal of Management*, 17 (Special Issue) (March): S1–S5.

Casson, M. (1995) *The Organization of International Business: Studies in the Economics of Trust*, Aldershot: Edward Elgar.

Castells, M. (2000) *The Rise of the Network Society*, 2nd edn, Oxford: Blackwell.

Casti, J.L. (1991) *Paradigms Lost*, London: Abacus Books.

Caves, R.E. (1982) *Multinational Enterprise and Economic Analysis*, Cambridge: Cambridge University Press.

Caves, R.E. (1998) 'Research on international business: problems and prospects', *Journal of International Business Studies*, 29(1).

Cavusgil, T.S., Ghauri, P.N. and Agarwal, M.R. (2002) *Doing Business in Emerging Markets: entry and negotiation strategies*, Thousands Oaks, CA: Sage.

Chamberlain, E. (1939) *The Theory of Monopolistic Competition*, Cambridge, MA: Harvard University Press.

Chandler, A.D. (1962) *Strategy and Structure*, Cambridge, MA: MIT Press.

Chandler, A.D. (1977) *The Visible Hand*, Cambridge, MA: Harvard University Press.

Chandler, A.D. (1986) 'The evolution of modern global competition', in M. Porter (ed.) *Competition in Global Industries*, Boston, MA: Harvard Business School Press.

Chandler, A.D. (1990a) *Scale and Scope: The Dynamics of Industrial Capitalism*, Cambridge, MA: Harvard University Press.

Chandler, A.D. (1990b) 'The enduring logic of industrial success', *Harvard Business Review*, March–April: 130–140.

Chesbrough, H. and Teece, D.J. (2002) 'Organizing for innovation: when is virtual virtuous?', *Harvard Business Review*, August.

Chesbrough, H., Ahern, S., Finn, M. and Guerraz, S. (2006) 'Business models for technology in the developing world: the role of NGOs', *California Management Review*, 48(3): 48–61.

Child, J. (1972) 'Organization structure, environment and performance: the role of strategic choice', *Sociology*, 6: 1–22.

Child, J. (1987) 'Information technology, organization and the response to strategic challenges', *California Management Review*, 30: 33–50.

Child, J. (2000) 'Theorizing about organizations cross-nationally', in J.L.C. Cheng and R.B. Peterson (eds) *Advances in International Comparative Management*, Vol. 13: 27–75, Stanford, CN: JAI Press.

Child, J. and David, P. (1987) *Technology and the Organization of Work*, London: National Economic Development Office.

Child, J. and Markoczy, L. (1993) 'Host-country managerial behaviour and learning in Chinese and Hungarian joint ventures', *Journal of Management Studies*, 30: 611–631.

Child, J. and Rodrigues, S. (1996) 'The role of social identity in the international transfer of knowledge through joint ventures', in S.R. Clegg and G. Palmer (eds) *The Politics of Management Knowledge*, London: Sage.

Child, J., Faulkner, D. and Pitkethly, R. (2000) 'Foreign direct investment in the UK 1985–1994: the impact on domestic management practice', *Journal of Management Studies*, 37: 141–166.

Child, J., Faulkner, D.O. and Tallman, S. (2005) *Cooperative Strategies*, Oxford: Oxford University Press.

Child, J., Pitkethly, R. and Faulkner, D. (1999) 'Changes in management practice and the post-acquisition performance achieved by direct investors in the UK', *British Journal of Management*, 10(3): 185–198.

Chrysostome, E. and Rosson, P. (2004) 'The internet and SME internationalization: promises and illusions', *Conference of ASAC*, Quebec, Canada Oxford University Press.

Cohen, W.M. and Levinthal, D.A. (1990) 'Absorptive capacity: a new perspective on learning and innovation', *Administrative Science Quarterly*, 35: 128–152.

Coyne, K.P. (1986) 'Sustainable competitive advantage: what it is, what it isn't', *Business Horizons*, 29(1).

Corviello, N. and Munro, H. (1997) 'Network relationships and the internationalization process of small software firms', *International Business Review*, 6(4): 361–386.

D'Aveni, R.A. and Gunther, R. (1994) *Hypercompetition: Managing the Dynamics of Strategic Maneuvering*, New York: Free Press.

Davis, G.F., Diekmann, K.A. and Tinsley, C.H. (1994) 'The decline and fall of the conglomerate firm in the 1980s: the deinstitutionalization of an organizational form', *American Sociological Review*, 59: 547–570.

Defillippi, R. and Reed, R. (1991) 'Three perspectives on appropriation hazards in cooperative agreements', paper presented at the Strategic Management Society Conference, Toronto Free Press, October.

De Geus, A. (1988) 'Planning as learning', *Harvard Business Review*, 66(2): 70–74.

De la Torre, J. and Neckar, D.H. (1988) 'Forecasting political risks for international operations', *International Journal of Forecasting*, 4: 221–241.

Desai, M., Foley, F. and Hines, J. (2004) 'Venture out alone', *Harvard Business Review*, 82(3) (March): 22.

DiMaggio, P.J. and Powell, W.W. (1983) 'The iron cage revisited: institutional isomorphism and collective rationality in organizational fields', *American Sociological Review*, 48 (April): 147–160.

Douglas, S.P. and Wind, Y. (1987) 'The myth of globalization', *Columbia Journal of World Business*, Winter: 19–29.

Dunning, J.H. (1974) *Economic Analysis and the Multinational Enterprise*, London: Allen and Unwin.

Dunning, J.H. (ed.) (1985) *Multinational Enterprises, Economic Structure and International Competitiveness*, Chichester: Wiley/IRM.

Dunning, J.H. (1989) 'Multinational enterprises and the growth of services: some conceptual and theoretical issues', *Service Industries Journal*, 9(1): 5–39.

Dunning, J.H. (1998) 'Location and the MNE: a neglected factor?', *Journal of International Business Studies*, 29(1).

Dunning, J.H. (2000) 'Regions, globalization and the knowledge economy: the issues stated', in J.H. Dunning (ed.) *Regions, Globalization and the Knowledge-Based Economy*, Oxford: Oxford University Press.

Dyer, J.H. and Nobeoka, K. (2000) 'Creating and managing a high performance knowledge-sharing network: the Toyota case', *Strategic Management Journal*, 21(3): 345–368.

The Economist (2005, 22 Jan.) 'The good company', A Survey of Corporate Social Responsibility.

The Economist (2007, 14 April) Special report on Brazil.

The Economist (2008, 31 May) Special report on EU Enlargement.

The Economist (2008, 28 Aug.) 'The bottom 1.4 billion'.

The Economist (2008, 25 Oct.) Special report on Corporate IT.

The Economist (2008, 29 Nov.) Special report on Russia.

The Economist (2008, 13 Dec.) Special report on India.

Eisenmann, T., Parker, G. and van Alstyne, M.W. (2006) 'Strategies for two-sided markets', *Harvard Business Review*, 84: 1010.

Elkington, J. (1997) *Cannibals with Forks: the triple bottom line of 21st century business*, New York: Wiley.

Elkington, J. (1998) *Cannibals With Forks*, Gabriola Island, BC: New Society Publishing.

Enderwick, P. (1989) *Multinational Service Firms*, London: Routledge.

Enderwick, P. (2007) *Understanding Emerging Markets: China and India*, New York: Routledge.

Erramilli, M.K. (1990) 'Entry mode choice in service industries', *International Marketing Review*, 7(5): 50–62.

Evans, P. and Wuster, T.S. (2000) *Blown to Bits*, Cambridge, MA: HBS Press.

Farrell, D. (2006) 'Smarter offshoring', *Harvard Business Review*, June: 85–92.

Faulkner, D. (1995a) *International Strategic Alliances*, Maidenhead: McGraw-Hill.

Faulkner, D. (1995b) 'Strategic alliance evolution through learning: the Rover/Honda alliance', in H. Thomas, D. O'Neal and J. Kelly (eds) *Strategic Renaissance and Business Transformation*, Chichester: Wiley.

Fjeldstad, Ø., Gao, J. and Burkay, U. (2008) 'Relation relevance and competitive advantage: implication for international strategy in a network economy', presented at the Strategic Management Society, Cologne, Germany Wiley, October.

Forsgren, M., Holm, U. and Johanson, J. (1995) 'Division headquarters go abroad – a step in the internationalization of the multinational corporation', *Journal of Management Studies*, 32(4): 475–491.

Friedman, M. (1962) *Capitalism and Freedom*, Chicago: University of Chicago Press.

Friedman, M. (1970) 'The social responsibility of business is to increase its profits', *New York Times Magazine*, 13 September: 32–33.

Friedman, T. (2005) *The World is Flat: a brief history of the globalized world in the 21st century*, London: Penguin, Allen Lane.

Froud, J., Haslam, C., Johal, S. and Williams, K. (2000), 'Shareholder value and financialization: consultancy promises, management moves', *Economy and Society*, 29(1): 80–110.

Fu, P.P., Kennedy, J., Tata, J., Yuki, G., Bond, M.H., Peng, T.-K., Srinivas, E.S., Howell, J.P., Prieto, L., Koopman, P., Boonstra, J.J., Pasa, S., Lacassagne, M.-F., Higashide, H. and Cheosakul, A. (2004) 'The impact of societal cultural values and individual social beliefs on the perceived effectiveness of managerial influence strategies: a meso approach', *Journal of International Business Studies*, 35(4): 284–305.

Gabel, M. and Bruner, H. (2007) *Globalink: An Atlas of the Multinational Corporation*, New York: Free Press.

Galbraith, J.R. and Nathanson, D.A. (1978) *Strategy Implementation: the role of structure and process*, St. Paul: West Publishing Co.

Garrette, B. and Dussauge, P. (1995) 'Patterns of strategic alliances between rival firms', *Group Decision and Negotiation*, 4: 429–452.

Gauri, P. (1992) 'New structures in MNCs based in small countries: a network approach', *European Management Journal*, 10(3): 357–364.

Geppert, M., Matten, D. and Williams, K. (2002) 'How global convergence interacts with national diversities'. *Academy of Management Conference 2002 Proceedings*.

Gerlach, M.L. (1992) *Alliance Capitalism*, Berkeley and Los Angeles: University of California Press.

Ghemawat, P. (2001) 'Distance still matters', *Harvard Business Review*, September: 137–147.

Ghemawat, P. (2003) 'Semiglobalization and international business strategy', *Journal of International Business Studies*, 34: 138–152.

Ghemawat, P. (2007a) *Redefining Global Strategy*, Boston: Harvard Business School Press.

Ghemawat, P. (2007b) 'Managing differences: the central challenge of global strategy', *Harvard Business Review*, 85 (March): 59–68.

Ghoshal, S. (1987) 'Global strategy: an organising framework', *Strategic Management Journal*, 8: 425–440.

Ghoshal, S. (2005) 'Bad management theories are destroying good management practices', *Academy of Management Learning and Education*, 4(1): 75–91.

Ghoshal, S. and Nohria, N. (1993) 'Horses for courses: organizational forms for multinational corporations', *Sloan Management Review*, Winter: 23–35.

Giddens, A. (2000) *Runaway World: how globalization is reshaping our lives*, London: Routledge.

Gladwell, M. (2000) *The Tipping Point: How little things make can make a big difference*, New York: Little Brown.

Grant, R. (1991a) 'The resource-based theory of competitive advantage: implications for strategy formulation', *California Management Review*, Spring: 114–135.

Grant, R.M. (1991b) *Contempoary Strategy Analysis: Concepts, Techniques, Applications*, Oxford: Blackwell Business.

Grindley, P. (1995) 'Regulation and standards policy: setting standards by committees and markets', in M. Bishop, J. Kay and C. Mayer (eds) *The Regulatory Challenge*, Oxford: Oxford University Press.

Gulati, R. and Zajac, E. (2000) 'Reflections of the study of strategic alliances', chapter 17 in D. Faulkner and M. De Rond (eds) *Cooperative Strategy*, Oxford: Oxford University Press.

Gulati, R., Nohria, N. and Zaheer, A (2000) 'Strategic networks', *Strategic Management Journal*, 21(3): 203–215.

Gupta, A.K. and Govinderajan, V. (1994) 'Knowledge flows and the structure of control within multinational corporations', *Academy of Management Review*, 16(4): 768–792.

Hamel, G. (1991) 'Competition for competence and interpartner learning within international strategic alliances', *Strategic Management Journal*, 12 (Special Issue) (Summer): 83–103.

Hamel, G. and Prahalad, C.K. (1985) 'Do you really have a global strategy?', *Harvard Business Review*, July/August: 139–148.

Hamel, G. and Prahalad, C.K. (1989) 'Strategic intent', *Harvard Business Review*, May–June: 63–76.

Hamel, G., Doz, Y.L. and Prahalad, C.K. (1989) 'Collaborate with your competitors and win', *Harvard Business Review*, January–February: 133–139.

Hamil, J. (1997) 'The internet and international marketing', *International Marketing Review*, 14(5): 300–311.

Hamil, J. and Gregory, K. (1997) 'Internet marketing in internationalization of UK SMEs', *Journal of Marketing Management*, 13(1): 9–28.

Hampden-Turner, C. (1990) *Corporate Culture: From Vicious to Virtuous Circles*, London: The Economist Books.

Hampden-Turner, C. and Trompenaars, F. (1993) *The Seven Cultures of Capitalism*, New York: Doubleday.

Handy, C. (1989) *The Age of Unreason*, London: Hutchinson.

Handy, C. (1992) 'Balancing corporate power: a New Federalist paper', *Harvard Business Review*, November–December: 59–72.

Handy, C. (2002) 'What's a business for?', *Harvard Business Review*, November–December.

Harrington, J. (1991) 'Virtual organization', in *Organization Structure and Information Technology*, Hemel Hempstead: Prentice Hall, pp. 207–238.

Hart, S.L. (1997) 'Beyond greening: strategies for a sustainable world', *Harvard Business Review*, Jan.–Feb.: 66–76.

Hart, S.L. (2007) *Capitalism at the Crossroads: aligning business, earth and humanity*, 2nd edn, Upper Saddle River, NJ: Pearson Education Inc., Wharton School Publishing.

Hart, S.L. and Christensen, C.M. (2002) 'The great leap: driving innovation from the base of the pyramid', *Sloan Management Review*, 44(1): 51–56.

Haspeslagh, P. and Jemison, D. (1991) *Managing Acquisitions: Creating Value Through Corporate Renewal*, New York: Free Press.

Hayward, M.L.A. and Hambrick, D. (1997) 'Explaining the premiums paid for large acquisitions: evidence of CEO hubris', *Administrative Science Quarterly*, 42(4): 422–436.

Hedberg, B. (1981) 'How organizations learn and unlearn', in P. Nystrom and W. Starbuck (eds) *Handbook of Organizational Design*, Vol. 1: 3–27, New York: Oxford University Press.

Hedlund, G. (1986) 'The hypermodern MNC – a heterarchy?', *Human Resource Management*, 25: 9–25.

Hedlund, G. (1994) 'A model of knowledge management and the N-form corporation', *Strategic Management Journal*, Special Issue, Summer: 73–90.

Henderson, B. (1989) 'The origins of strategy', *Harvard Business Review*, 67: 139–143.

Heskett, J.L. (1986) *Managing in the Service Economy*, Boston: Harvard Business School Press.

Hewitt, D. (2008) *Getting Rich First: Life in a Changing China*, London: Vintage.

Hill, C.W.L. and Jones, G.R. (1998) *Strategic Management: an integrated approach*, New York: McGraw Hill.

Hillman, A.J. and Keim, G.D. (2001) 'Shareholder value, stakeholder management and social issues: What's the bottom line?', *Strategic Management Journal*, 22(2): 125–139.

Hirschman, A.O. (1970) 'The search for paradigms as a hindrance to understanding', *World Politics*, March.

Hofstede, G. (1980) *Culture's Consequences: International Differences in Work-Related Values*, Beverly Hills, CA: Sage.

Hofstede, G. (1991) *Cultures and Organizations: Software of the Mind*, Maidenhead: McGraw-Hill.

Hofstede, G. (1996) 'Riding the waves of commerce: a test of Trompenaars' "model" of national culture differences', *International Journal of Intercultural Relations*, 20: 189–198.

Hofstede, G. and Bond, M.H. (1988) 'The Confucious connection: from cultural roots to economic growth', *Organizational Dynamics*, 16: 4–21.

Hopper, T., Wickramasinghe, D., Tsamenyi, M. and Uddin, S. (2003) 'The state they're in', *Financial Management*, 16–19.

Hosmer, L.T. (1994) 'Strategic planning as if ethics mattered', *Strategic Management Journal* , 15: 17–34.

House, R.J., Hanges, P.J., Javidan, M., Dorfman, P.W. and Gupta, V. (eds) (2004) *Culture, Leadership and Organizations: the GLOBE study of 62 societies*, Thousand Oaks, CA: Sage.

Huang, Y. (2008) *Capitalism with Chinese Characteristics: entrepreneurship and the state*, Cambridge: Cambridge University Press.

Hutchinson, C. (1996) 'Integrating environment policy with business strategy', *Long Range Planning*, 29(1): 11–23.

Hyder, A.S. and Abrada, D. (2006) 'Strategic alliances in the Baltic states: a case of a Swedish firm', *Competitiveness Review*, 16(3): 173–196.

Inkpen, A. (1995) *The Management of International Joint Ventures: An Organizational Learning Perspective*, London: Routledge.

Inkpen, A. and Crossan, M.M. (1995) 'Believing is seeing: joint ventures and organizational learning', *Journal of Management Studies*, 32: 595–618.

Inkpen, A. and Ramaswamy, K. (2006) *Global Strategy: creating and sustaining advantage across borders*, New York: Oxford University Press.

Innovest Strategic Value Advisors (2002) *CSR Social Responsibility News*, Internet Advice Paper.

International Monetary Fund (1993) *Balance of Payments Manual*, fifth edition.

Jarillo, J.C. (1988) 'On strategic networks', *Strategic Management Journal*, 9: 31–41.

Jarillo, J.C. (1993) *Strategic Networks: Creating the Borderless Organization*, Oxford: Butterworth Heinemann.

Jashapara, A. (2004) *Knowledge Management*, London: Financial Times Prentice Hall.

Javidan, M., House, R.J., Dorfman, P.W., Hanges, P.J. and Sully de Luque, M. (2006) 'Conceptualizing and measuring cultures and their consequences: a comparative review of GLOBE's and Hofstede's approaches', *Journal of International Business Studies*, 37(6): 897–914.

Johnson, G. (1990) 'Managing strategic change: the role of symbolic action', *British Journal of Management*, 1: 183–200.

Johanson, J. and Mattsson, L.-G. (1991) 'Interorganisational relations in industrial systems: a network approach compared with the transaction-cost approach', in G. Thompson, J. Frances, R. Levacic and J. Mitchell (eds) *Markets, Hierarchies and Networks*, London: Sage, pp. 256–264.

Johanson, J. and Vahlne, J. (1977) 'The internationalisation process of the firm: a model of knowledge development on increasing foreign commitments', *Journal of International Business Studies*, Spring-Summer: 23–32.

Jones, C., Hesterly, W.S. and Borgatti, S.P. (1997) 'A general theory of network governance: exchange conditions and social mechanisms', *Academy of Management Review*, 22: 911–945.

Jonsson, S.A. and Lundin, R.A. (1977) 'Myths and wishful thinking as management tools', in P.C. Nystrom and W.H. Starbuck (eds) *Prescriptive Models of Organizations*, Amsterdam: North-Holland Sage.

Julien, P.A., Raymond, L., Jacob, R. and Ramangalahy, C. (1996) 'An empirical investigation of manufacturing SMEs', in P.D. Reynolds et al. (eds) *Frontiers of Entrepreneurship Research*, Babson Park, MA Sage, pp. 584–598.

Kaplan, S. and Weisbach, M. (1992) 'The success of acquisitions: evidence from divestitures', *Journal of Finance*, 57(1): 107–138.

Kale, P. and Anand, J. (2006) 'The decline of emerging economy joint ventures: the case of India', *California Management Review*, 48(3): 62–76.

Katz, M. and Shapiro, C. (1985) 'Network externalities, competition and compatibility', *American Economic Review*, 75(3): 424–440.

Keesing, R.M. (1974) 'Theories of culture', *Annual Review of Anthropology*, 3: 73–97.

Khanna, T. and Rivkin, J.W. (2001) 'Estimating the performance effects of business groups in emerging markets', *Strategic Management Journal*, 22(1): 45–74.

Khanna, T., Palepu, K.G. and Sinha, J. (2005) 'Strategies that fit emerging markets', *Harvard Business Review*, June: 63–76.

Knight, G., Madsen, T.G. and Servais, P. (2004) 'An inquiry into born-global firms in Europe and the USA', *International Marketing Review*, 21(6): 645–665.

Kobrin, S.J. (1991) 'An empirical investigation of the determinants of global integration', *Strategic Management Journal*, 12 (Special Issue) (Summer): 17–31.

Kogut, B. (1985a) 'Designing global strategies: profiting from operational flexibility', *Sloan Management Review*, Fall: 27–38.

Kogut, B. (1985b) 'Designing global strategies: comparative and competitive value added chains', *Sloan Management Review*, 26(4): 15–28.

Kogut, B. (1989) 'A note on global strategies', *Strategic Management Journal*, 10(4): 383–389.

Kogut, B. (2000) 'The network as knowledge: generative rules and the emergence of structure', *Strategic Management Journal*, 21(3): 405–425.

Kogut, B. (2008) *Knowledge, Options and Institutions*, Oxford: Oxford University Press

Kok, P., Weile, T.V.D., McKenna, R. and Brown, A. (2001) 'A corporate social responsibility audit within a auality management framework', *Journal of Business Ethics*, 31(4): 285–297.

Kotha, S., Rajgopal, S. and Rindoa, S. (2001) 'Reputation building and performance: an empirical analysis of the top-50 pure internet firms', *European Management Journal*, 19: 571–586.

Krugman, P. (1995) *Development, Geography, and Economic Theory*, Cambridge, MA: MIT Press.

Krugman, P. (2008) *The Return of Depression Economics and the Crisis of 2008*, Harmondsworth: Penguin Books.

Lane, P.J. and Lubatkin, M.H. (1998) 'Relative absorptive capacity and interorganizational learning', *Strategic Management Journal*, 19(5): 461–477.

Larsson, R. and Finkelstein, S. (1999) 'Integrating strategic, organisational, and human resource perspectives on mergers and acquisitions: a case survey of synergy realization', *Organization Science*, 10(1): 1–26.

Lasserre, P (2003) *Global Strategic Management*, Basingstoke: Macmillan.

Lawrence, P. and Lorsch, J. (1967) *Organization and Environment*, Boston, MA: Harvard Business School Press.

Levinthal, D.A. and March, J.G. (1993) The myopia of learning', *Strategic Management Journal*, 14 (Special Issue) (Winter): 95–112.

Levitt, T. (1960) 'Marketing myopia', *Harvard Business Review*, July–August.

Levitt, T. (1983) 'The globalization of markets', *Harvard Business Review*, May–June: 92–102.

Levitt, T. (1986) *The Marketing Imagination*, New York: The Free Press.

Lituchy, T. and Rail, A. (2000) 'Bed and breakfast, small inns and internet: the impact of technology on the globalization of small businesses', *Journal of International Marketing*, 8(2): 86–98.

Lober, D. (1996) 'Evaluating the environmental performance of corporations', *Journal of Management Issues*, 8(2): 184–205.

London, T. and Hart, S.L. (2004) 'Reinventing strategies for emerging markets: beyond the transnational model', *Journal of International Business Studies*, 35: 350–370.

Lorenzoni, G. (1982) 'From vertical integration to vertical disintegration', paper presented at the Strategic Management Society Conference, Montreal The Free Press, September.

Lorenzoni, G. and Ornati, O.A. (1988) 'Constellations of firms and new ventures', *Journal of Business Venturing*, 3: 41–57.

Makhija, M.V., Kim, K. and Williamson, S.D. (1997) 'Measuring globalisation of industries using a national industry approach: empirical evidence across 5 countries over time', *Journal of International Business Studies*, 28(4).

Malnight, T. (1996) 'The transition from decentralized to network-based MNC structures: an evolutionary perspective', *Journal of International Business Studies*, 27(1): 43–65.

Markoczy, L. and Child, J. (1995) 'International mixed management organizations and economic liberalization in Hungary: from state bureaucracy to new paternalism', in H. Thomas, D. O'Neal and J. Kelly (eds) *Strategic Renaissance and Business Transformation*, Chichester: Wiley.

Mattsson, L.G. (1988) 'Interaction strategies: a network approach', Working Paper.

Mauro, P. (1997) 'Why worry about corruption', *Economic Issues*, 6; Washington DC: IMF Wiley.

McGee, J. and Sammut-Bonnicci, T.A. (2002) 'Network industries in the new economy', *European Business Journal*, 14(3): 116–132.

McKinsey and Co. (1993) *Emerging Exporters*, Report to Australian Manufacturing Council.

Melin, L. (1992) 'Internationalization as a strategy process', *Strategic Management Journal*, 13, Special Issue (Winter): 99–118.

Meyer, K. and Peng, M.W. (2005) 'Probing theoretically into Central and Eastern Europe: transactions, resources and institutions', *Journal of International Business Studies*, 36(6): 600–621.

Micklethwait, J. and Wooldridge, A. (2000) *A Future Perfect: the challenge and hidden promise of globalization*, London: William Heinemann.

Mosakowski, E. (1994) 'Managerial prescriptions under the resource-based view of strategy: the example of motivational techniques', *Strategic Management Journal*, 19(1)2: 1169–1182.

Mowshowitz, A. (1994) 'Virtual organization: a vision of management in the information age', *The Information Society*, 10: 267–294.

Nagel, P. and Dove, M. (1991) 'The virtual corporation', working paper, Illinois Le High University.

Narayanan, V.K. and Fahey, L. (2005) 'The relevance of the institutional underpinnings of Porter's Five Forces framework in emerging economies: an epistemological analysis', *Journal of Management Studies*, 42(1): 207–223.

Nayyar, P.R. (1990) 'Information asymmetries: a source of competitive advantage for diversified service firms', *Strategic Management Journal*, 11: 513–519.

Newman, W.H. (1992a) *Birth of a Successful Joint Venture*, Lanham, MD: University Press of America.

Newman, W.H. (1992b) 'Launching a viable joint venture', *California Management Review*, 35: 68–80.

Nohria, N. and Eccles, R.G. (eds) (1992) *Networks and Organizations*, Boston, MA: Harvard Business School Press.

Nonaka, I. and Takeuchi, H. (1995) *The Knowledge-Creating Company*, Oxford: Oxford University Press.

Nonaka, I. and Toyama, R. (2007) 'Strategic management as distributed practical wisdom (phronesis)', *Industrial and Corporate Change*, 16(3): 371–394.

Normann, R. (1991) *Service Management: Strategy and Leadership in Service Businesses*, 2nd edn, Chichester: Wiley.

North, D. (1990) *Institutions, Institutional Change and Economic Performance*, Cambridge, MA: Cambridge University Press.

North, D.C. (1996) 'Reflections on economics and cognitive science', public lecture, Judge Institute of Management Studies, May.

Ohmae, K. (1985) *Triad Power: the coming shape of global competition*, New York: Free Press.

Ohmae, K. (1989a) 'Managing in a borderless world', *Harvard Business Review*, May–June: 152–161.

Ohmae, K. (1989b) 'The global logic of strategic alliances', *Harvard Business Review*, March–April: 143–154.

Ohmae, K. (1990a) *The Borderless World: power and strategy in the international economy*, New York: Harper Business.

Ohmae, K. (1990b) 'Managing in a borderless world', *Harvard Business Review*, May–June: 152–161.

Pauly, L.W. and Reich, S. (1997) 'National structures and multinational corporate behaviour: ending differences in the age of globalization', *International Organization*, 51: 1–30.

Peng, M.W. (2003) 'Institutional transitions and strategic choices', *Academy of Management Review*, 28(2): 275–296.

Peng, M. and Delios, A. (2006) 'What determines the scope of the firm over time and around the world? An Asia Pacific perspective', *Asia Pacific Journal of Management*, 23: 385–405.

Peng, M.W. and Pleggenkuhle-Miles, E.G. (2009) 'Current debates in global strategy', *International Journal of Management Review*, 11(1): 51–68.

Peng, M.W., Wang, D.Y.L. and Jiang, Y. (2008) 'An institution-based view of international business strategy: a focus on emerging economies', *Journal of International Business Studies*, 39(5): 920–936.

Perlmutter, H.V. (1969) 'The tortuous evolution of the MNC', *Columbia Journal of World Business*, 4: 9–18.

Pfeffer, J. and Salancik, G. (1978) *The External Control of Organizations: A Resource Dependence Perspective*, New York: Harper & Row.

Pinkston, T. and Carroll, A. (1996) 'A retrospective examination of CSR orientations: Have they changed?', *Journal of Business Ethics*, 15(2): 199–207.

Polanyi, K. (1966) *The Tacit Dimension*, London: Routledge & Kegan Paul.

Poon, S. and Jevons, C. (1997) 'Internet enabled international marketing', *Journal of Marketing Management*, 13(1): 29–41.

Porter, M.E. (1980) *Competitive Strategies: Techniques for Analyzing Industries and Competitors*, New York: Free Press.

Porter, M.E. (1985) *Competitive Advantage: Creating and Sustaining Superior Performance*, New York: Free Press.

Porter, M.E. (1986) *Competition in Global Industries*, Boston, MA: Harvard Business School Press.

Porter, M.E. (1987) 'From competitive advantage to corporate strategy', *Harvard Business Review*, May–June.

Porter, M.E. (1990) *The Competitive Advantage of Nations*, Basingstoke: Macmillan.

Porter, M.E. (1998) 'Clusters and the new economics of competition', *Harvard Business Review*, November–December: 77–90.

Porter, M.E. and Fuller, M.B. (1986) 'Coalitions and global strategy', in M.E. Porter (ed.), *Competition in Global Industries*, Cambridge, MA: Harvard University Press.

Porter, M. and Van der Linde, C. (1995) 'Green and competitive: ending the stalemate', *Harvard Business Review*, September–October: 120–134.

Powell, W.W. (1987) 'Hybrid organizational arrangements: new form or transitional development', *California Management Review*, 30: 67–87.

Powell, W.W. (1990) 'Neither market nor hierarchy: network forms of organization', *Research in Organizational Behavior*, 12: 295–336.

Prahalad, C.K. (2005) *The Fortune at the Bottom of the Pyramid: eradicating poverty through profits*, Upper Saddle River, NJ: Pearson Education Inc., Wharton School Publishing.

Prahalad, C.K. and Doz, Y. (1987) *The Multinational Mission*, New York: Free Press.

Prahalad, C.K. and Hamel, G. (1990) 'The core competence of the corporation', *Harvard Business Review*, 90: 79–91.

Prahalad, C.K. and Hamel, G. (1994) 'Strategy as a field of study: Why search for a new paradigm?', *Strategic Management Journal*, 15 (Special Issues): 5–116.

Prahalad, C.K. and Hart, S.L. (2002) 'The fortune at the bottom of the pyramid', *Strategy+Business*, 26: 54–67.

Price Waterhouse Coopers (1998) *Pursuing Profitability: Variations on a Theme*.

Quelch, J.A. and Hoff, E.J. (1986) 'Customizing global marketing', *Harvard Business Review*, May–June: 59–68.

Quinn, J.B. (1992) *Intelligent Enterprise*, New York: The Free Press.

Quinn, J.B. (2001) *Services and Technology, Revolutionizing Economics, Business and Education*, Dartmouth College.

Radebaugh, L.H. and Gray, S.J. (1997) *International Accounting and Multinational Enterprises*, 4th edn, Chichester: Wiley.

Rasmussen, E.S. and Madsen, T.K. (2002) 'The born global concept', EIBA Conference.

Raymond, L. (2003) 'Globalization, the knowledge economy, and competitiveness: a business intelligence framework for the development of SMEs', *Journal of American Academy of Business*, 3(1–2): 260–269.

Rayport, J. and Sviokla, J. (1996) 'Exploiting the virtual value chain', *McKinsey Quarterly*, 1996(1): 20–38.

Richardson, G.B. (1972) 'The organisation of industry', *Economic Journal*, 82: 883–896.

Ricardo, D. (1817) *On the Principles of Political Economy and Taxation*, London University of South Denmark, reprint, Harmondsworth: Penguin, 1971.

Riddle, D.L. (1986) *Service-Led Growth*, New York: Praeger.

Roberts, J. (2004) *The Modern Firm*, Oxford: Oxford University Press.

Rugman, A. (1980) 'A new theory of the multinational enterprise; internationalization versus internalization', *Columbia Journal of World Business*, 15: 23–29.

Rugman, A. (1996) *The Theory of Multinational Enterprises*, Cheltenham: Edward Elgar.

Rugman, A.M. (2003) 'Regional strategies for service sector multinationals', *European Business Journal*, 15(1): 1–9.

Rugman, A. (2005) *The Regional Multinationals*, Cambridge: Cambridge University Press.

Rugman, A. and D'Cruz, J.R. (1993) 'The double diamond model of international competitiveness: the Canadian experience', *Management International Review*, 2: 17–39.

Rugman, A. and D'Cruz, J.R. (1997) 'The theory of the flagship firm', *European Management Journal*, 15(4): 403–412.

Rugman, A. and D'Cruz, J.R. (2000) *Multinationals as Flagship Firms*, New York: Oxford University Press.

Rugman, A.M. and Hodgetts, R. (2001) 'The end of global strategy', *European Management Journal*, 19(4): 333–343.

Rugman, A. and Verbeke, A. (2001) 'Location, competitiveness and the multinational enterprise', in A. Rugman and T. Brewer (eds), *The Oxford Handbook of International Business*, Oxford: Oxford University Press, pp. 150–180.

Rugman, A.M., Lecraw, D.J. and Booth, L.D. (1985) *International Business, Firm and Environment*, New York: McGraw-Hill.

Rumelt, R.P. (1991) 'How much does industry matter?', *Strategic Management Journal*, 12: 167–185.

Rumelt, R., Schendel, D. and Teece, D. (1991) 'Strategic management and economics', *Strategic Management Journal*, 12 (Special Issue) (Winter): 5–29.

Saloner, G., Shepherd, A. and Podalny, J. (2001) *Strategic Management*, New York: Wiley.

Sammut-Bonnicci, T.A. and McGee, J. (2002) 'Network strategies for the new economy', *European Business Journal*, 14(4): 174–185.

Sanchez, R. (1996) 'Strategic product creation: managing new interactions of technology, markets and organizations', *European Management Journal*, 14(2): 121–138.

Schein, E.H. (1985) *Organizational Culture and Leadership*, San Francisco, CA.: Jossey-Bass.

Schoenberg, R. (1999) 'Deconstructing knowledge transfer and resource sharing in international acquisitions', Paper presented to 19th Annual International Conference of the Strategic Management Society, Berlin. (Imperial College Management School Working Paper SWP9911/BSM.)

Schoenberg, R. (2003) 'The influence of cultural compatibility within cross-border acquisitions: a review', *Advances in Mergers and Acquisitions*.

Schoenberg, R. and Reeves, R. (1999) 'What determines acquisition activity within an industry?', *European Management Journal*, 17(1): 93–98.

Schumpeter, J.A. (1934) *The Theory of Economic Development*, Cambridge, MA: Harvard University Press.

Segal-Horn, S. (1993) 'The internationalisation of service firms', *Advances in Strategic Management*, 9: 31–61.

Segal-Horn, S. (2000) 'The search for core competencies in a service multinational: a case study of the French hotel Novotel', in Y. Aharoni and L. Nachum, *Globalisation of Services: some implications for theory and practice*, London: Routledge.

Segal-Horn, S. (2003) 'Strategy in service organisations', in D. Faulkner and A. Campbell (eds) *The Oxford Handbook of Strategy*, Vol. 1, Oxford: Oxford University Press.

Segal-Horn, S.L. and Dean, A. (2007) 'The globalization of law firms: managerial issues', *International Journal of Service Industry Management*, 18(2): 206–219.

Sen, A. (1998) 'Foreword', in A. Ben-Ner and L. Putterman (eds) *Economic Values and Organization*, Cambridge: Cambridge University Press.

Senge, P.M. (1992) *The Fifth Discipline*, London: Century Business.

Shapiro, C. and Varian, H.R. (1999) *Information Rules: a strategic guide to the network economy*, Cambridge, MA: HBS Press.

Shrivastava, P. (1995) 'The role of corporations in achieving ecological sustainability', *Academy of Management Review*, 20(4) (October): 936–960.

Shrivaster, R.K., Crosby, J.R., McInsh, T.H., Wood, R.A. and Capraro, A.J. (2000) 'The value of corporate reputation: evidence from the equity markets', *Corporate Reputation Review*, Part IV, Summer special issue: 'How do reputations affect corporate performance?', pp. 62–68.

Sirkin, H., Hemerling, J. and Bhattacharya, A. (2008a), "Globality: challenger companies are radically redefining the competitive landscape", *Strategy and Leadership*, (2008) Vol. 36 No. 6: 36–41.

Sirkin, H., Hemerling, J. and Bhattacharya, A. (2008b), *Globality: competing with everyone from everywhere for everything*.

Skinner, W. (1978) *Manufacturing in the Corporate Strategy*, London: Wiley.

Smith, A. (1776) *An Enquiry into the Nature and Causes of the Wealth of Nations*, London Wiley (reprinted in E. Cannon (ed.), New York: The Modern Library, 1937).

Smith, K., Grimm, C. and Wally, S. (1997) 'Strategic groups and rivalrous firm behaviour: towards a reconciliation', *Strategic Management Journal*, 18: 149–157.

Snow, C.S. and Thomas, J.B. (1993) 'Building networks: broker roles and behaviours', in P. Lorange (ed.), *Implementing Strategic Processes*, Oxford: Blackwell.

Snow, C.S., Miles, R.E. and Coleman, H.J. (1992) 'Managing 21st century network organizations', *Organizational Dynamics*, 20: 5–20.

Stiglitz, J. (2002) *Globalization and its Discontents*, London: Allan Lane, The Penguin Press.

Stopford J. and Strange, S. (1991) *Rival States Rival Firms*, Cambridge: Cambridge University Press.

Stopford, J.M. and Wells, L. (1972) *Managing the Multinational Enterprise*, London: Longman.

Szabo, A. (2002) 'Internationalisation of SMEs', UNECE Paper.

Szulanski, G. (2003) *Sticky Knowledge*, London: Sage.

Tajfel, H. (ed.) (1982) *Social Identity and Intergroup Relations*, Cambridge: Cambridge University Press.

Teece, D. (1980) 'Economies of scope and the scope of the enterprise', *Journal of Economic Behaviour and Organisation*, 1(3): 223–247.

Teece, D. (1982) 'Towards an economic theory of the multiproduct firm', *Journal of Economic Behaviour and Organisation*, 3: 39–63.

Teece, D. (2006) 'Reflections on profiting from innovation', *Research Policy*, 35(8): 1131–1146.

Teece, D. (2007) 'Explicating dynamic capabilities: the nature and microfoundations of (sustainable) enterprise performance', *Strategic Management Journal*, 28: 1319–1350.

Teece, D., Pisano, G. and Shuen, A. (1997) 'Dynamic capabilities and strategic management', *Strategic Management Journal*, 18(7): 509–533.

Thorelli, H.B. (1986) 'Networks: between markets and hierarchies', *Strategic Management Journal*, 7: 37–51.

Trompenaars, F. (1993) *Riding the Waves of Culture: Understanding Cultural Diversity in Business*, London: The Economist Books.

Tung, R.L. (1993) 'Managing cross-national and intra-national diversity', *Human Resource Management*, 32: 461–477.

Tushman, M.L. and Anderson, P. (1986) 'Technological discontinuities and organisational environments', *Administrative Science Quarterly*, 31: 439–465.

Uzzi, B. (1996) 'The sources and consequences of embeddedness for the economic performance of organizations: The network effect', *American Sociological Review*, 61: 674–698.

Vercoulen, F. and Wegberg, M. (1998) 'Standard selection modes in dynamic complex industries', NIBOR Conference, WP 98006.

Vernon, R. (1966) 'International investment and international trade in the product cycle', *Quarterly Journal of Economics*, May: 190–207.

Vogel, D. (2005a) 'Is there a market for virtue? the business case for corporate social responsibility', *California Management Review*, 47(4): 19–45.

Vogel, D. (2005b) *The Market for Virtue: The Potential and Limits of Corporate Social Responsibility,* Brookings Institution Press.

Waldman, D.A., Sully de Luque, M., Washburn, N., House, R.J. et al. (2006) 'Cultural and leadership predictors of corporate social responsibility values of top management: a GLOBE study of 15 countries', *Journal of International Business Studies*, 37 (6): 823–837.

Walsham, G. (1994) 'Virtual organization: an alternative view', *The Information Society*, 10: 289–292.

Wernerfelt, B. (1984) 'A resource-based view of the firm', *Strategic Management Journal*, 5: 171–180.

White, E. and Campos, J. (1986) *Alternative Technology Sources for Developing Countries; the role of small and medium sized enterprises from industrialised countries*, Buenos Aires: Cederi Estudios.

Whittington, R. (2001) *What is Strategy – and does it matter?*, 2nd edn, London: Thomson Learning.

Williamson, O.E. (1975) *Markets and Hierarchies*, New York: Free Press.

Wolf, M. (2004) *Why Globalization Works*, New Haven: Yale University Press.

Woolsey Biggart, N. and Hamilton, G.G. (1992) 'On the limits of a firm-based theory', in N. Nohria and R.G. Eccles (eds) *Networks and Organization: Structure, Form and Action*, Boston, MA: Harvard Business School Press.

Yip, G. (1992) *Total Global Strategy*, Englewood Cliffs, NJ: Prentice-Hall.

Yip, G. (1996) *Total Global Strategy*, 2nd edn, Englewood Cliffs, NJ: Prentice-Hall.

Yip, G.S. (2002) *Total Global Strategy II*, Englewood-Cliffs, NJ: Prentice-Hall.

Yip, G.S. and Bink, A.J.M. (2008) *Managing Global Customers*, Oxford: Oxford University Press.

Yip, G.S. and Madsen, T. (1996) 'Global account management: the new frontier in relationship marketing', *International Marketing Review*, 13(3): 24–42.

Young, M.N., Peng, M.W., Ahlstrom, D., Bruton, G.D. and Jiang, Y. (2008) 'Corporate governance in emerging economies: a review of the principal–principal perspective', *Journal of Management Studies*, 45(1): 196–220.

Zeithaml, V.A. and Bitner, M.J. (1996) *Services Marketing*, New York: McGraw-Hill International.

Zeng, M. and Williamson, P.J. (2007) *Dragons At Your Door: how Chinese cost innovation is disrupting global competition*, Boston, MA: Harvard Business School Press.

Zukin, S. and DiMaggio, P. (eds) (1990) 'Introduction', in *Structures of Capital: The Social Organization of the Economy*, Cambridge: Cambridge University Press.

Zyglidopoulos Stelios, C. (2002) The social and environmental responsibilities of multinationals: evidence from the Brent Spar case, *Journal of Business Ethics*, 36: 141–151.

INDEX